SHELLY CASHMAN SERIES®

ADVANCED

T0198224

Microsoft® Office 365® &
OFFICE 2019

**SANDRA E. CABLE | ELLEN F. MONK | SUSAN L. SEBOK
JOY L. STARKS | MISTY E. VERMAAT**

Cengage

SHELLY CASHMAN SERIES®

Australia • Brazil • Canada • Mexico • Singapore • United Kingdom • United States

Shelly Cashman Series® Microsoft® Office 365® & Office 2019 Advanced
Sandra Cable, Ellen Monk, Susan Sebok, Joy Starks, Misty Vermaat

SVP, GM Skills & Global Product Management: Jonathan Lau

Product Director: Lauren Murphy

Product Assistant: Veronica Moreno-Nestojko

Executive Director, Content Design: Marah Bellegarde

Director, Learning Design: Leigh Hefferon

Learning Designer: Courtney Cozzy

Vice President, Marketing - Science, Technology, and Math: Jason R. Sakos

Senior Marketing Director: Michele McTighe

Marketing Manager: Timothy J. Cali

Director, Content Delivery: Patty Stephan

Senior Content Manager: Anne Orgren

Digital Delivery Lead: Laura Ruschman

Designer: Lizz Anderson

Cover image(s): Sergey Kelin/ShutterStock.com (Ocean), nikkytok/ShutterStock.com (Crystal), PARINKI/ShutterStock.com (Marble), Erika Kirkpatrick/ShutterStock.com (Driftwood), Vladitto/ShutterStock.com (Skyscraper), Roman Sigaev/ShutterStock.com (Clouds)

Mac Users: If you're working through this product using a Mac, some of the steps may vary. Additional information for Mac users is included with the Data files for this product.

Disclaimer: This text is intended for instructional purposes only; data is fictional and does not belong to any real persons or companies.

Disclaimer: The material in this text was written using Microsoft Windows 10 and Office 365 Professional Plus and was Quality Assurance tested before the publication date. As Microsoft continually updates the Windows 10 operating system and Office 365, your software experience may vary slightly from what is presented in the printed text.

Windows, Access, Excel, and PowerPoint are registered trademarks of Microsoft Corporation. Microsoft and the Office logo are either registered trademarks or trademarks of Microsoft Corporation in the United States and/or other countries. This product is an independent publication and is neither affiliated with, nor authorized, sponsored, or approved by, Microsoft Corporation.

Some of the product names and company names used in this book have been used for identification purposes only and may be trademarks or registered trademarks of Microsoft Corporation in the United States and/or other countries.

Unless otherwise noted, all non-Microsoft clip art is courtesy of openclipart.org.

For product information and technology assistance, contact us at
Cengage Customer & Sales Support, 1-800-354-9706 or support.cengage.com.

For permission to use material from this text or product, submit all requests online at **www.copyright.com.**

Library of Congress Control Number: 2019941606

Student Edition ISBN: 978-0-357-35999-0
Looseleaf available as part of a digital bundle

Cengage
200 Pier 4 Boulevard
Boston, MA 02210
USA

Cengage is a leading provider of customized learning solutions with employees residing in nearly 40 different countries and sales in more than 125 countries around the world. Find your local representative at: **www.cengage.com.**

To learn more about Cengage platforms and services, register or access your online learning solution, or purchase materials for your course, visit **www.cengage.com.**

Notice to the Reader
Publisher does not warrant or guarantee any of the products described herein or perform any independent analysis in connection with any of the product information contained herein. Publisher does not assume, and expressly disclaims, any obligation to obtain and include information other than that provided to it by the manufacturer. The reader is expressly warned to consider and adopt all safety precautions that might be indicated by the activities described herein and to avoid all potential hazards. By following the instructions contained herein, the reader willingly assumes all risks in connection with such instructions. The publisher makes no representations or warranties of any kind, including but not limited to, the warranties of fitness for particular purpose or merchantability, nor are any such representations implied with respect to the material set forth herein, and the publisher takes no responsibility with respect to such material. The publisher shall not be liable for any special, consequential, or exemplary damages resulting, in whole or part, from the readers' use of, or reliance upon, this material.

Printed in Mexico
Print Number: 3   Print Year: 2022

Microsoft® Office 365® & OFFICE 2019

ADVANCED

Brief Contents

Microsoft® Office 365® & OFFICE 2019

ADVANCED

Contents

Microsoft **PowerPoint 2019**

MODULE EIGHT

Creating Photo Albums and Delivering Presentations

Microsoft Excel 2019

MODULE EIGHT
Working with Trendlines, PivotTables, PivotCharts, and Slicers

Microsoft Access 2019

Microsoft® Office 365® &
OFFICE 2019

ADVANCED

Getting to Know Microsoft Office Versions

Cengage is proud to bring you the next edition of Microsoft Office. This edition was designed to provide a robust learning experience that is not dependent upon a specific version of Office.

Microsoft supports several versions of Office:

- **Office 365:** A cloud-based subscription service that delivers Microsoft's most up-to-date, feature-rich, modern productivity tools direct to your device. There are variations of Office 365 for business, educational, and personal use. Office 365 offers extra online storage and cloud-connected features, as well as updates with the latest features, fixes, and security updates.

- **Office 2019:** Microsoft's "on-premises" version of the Office apps, available for both PCs and Macs, offered as a static, one-time purchase and outside of the subscription model.

- **Office Online:** A free, simplified version of Office web applications (Word, Excel, PowerPoint, and OneNote) that facilitates creating and editing files collaboratively.

Office 365 (the subscription model) and Office 2019 (the one-time purchase model) had only slight differences between them at the time this content was developed. Over time, Office 365's cloud interface will continuously update, offering new application features and functions, while Office 2019 will remain static. Therefore, your onscreen experience may differ from what you see in this product. For example, the more advanced features and functionalities covered in this product may not be available in Office Online or may have updated from what you see in Office 2019.

For more information on the differences between Office 365, Office 2019, and Office Online, please visit the Microsoft Support site.

Cengage is committed to providing high-quality learning solutions for you to gain the knowledge and skills that will empower you throughout your educational and professional careers.

Thank you for using our product, and we look forward to exploring the future of Microsoft Office with you!

Using SAM Projects and Textbook Projects

SAM and *MindTap* are interactive online platforms designed to transform students into Microsoft Office and Computer Concepts masters. Practice with simulated SAM Trainings and MindTap activities and actively apply the skills you learned live in Microsoft Word, Excel, PowerPoint, or Access. Become a more productive student and use these skills throughout your career.

If your instructor assigns SAM Projects:

1. Launch your SAM Project assignment from SAM or MindTap.
2. Click the links to download your **Instructions file**, **Start file**, and **Support files** (when available).
3. Open the Instructions file and follow the step-by-step instructions.
4. When you complete the project, upload your file to SAM or MindTap for immediate feedback.

To use SAM Textbook Projects:

1. Launch your SAM Project assignment from SAM or MindTap.
2. Click the links to download your **Start file** and **Support files** (when available).
3. Locate the module indicated in your book or eBook.
4. Read the module and complete the project.

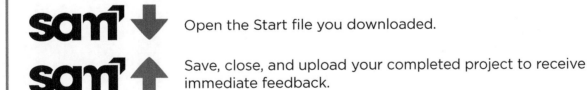

Open the Start file you downloaded.

Save, close, and upload your completed project to receive immediate feedback.

IMPORTANT: To receive full credit for your Textbook Project, you must complete the activity using the Start file you downloaded from SAM or MindTap.

8 | Using Collaboration, Integration, and Charts

Objectives

After completing this module, you will be able to:

- Track changes
- Review tracked changes
- Compare documents
- Combine documents
- Link an Excel worksheet to a Word document
- Break a link

- Create a chart in Word
- Format a Word chart
- View and scroll through side-by-side documents
- Create a new document for a blog post
- Insert a quick table
- Publish a blog post

Introduction

Word provides the capability for users to work with other users, or **collaborate**, on a document. For example, you can show edits made to a document so that others can review the edits. You also can merge edits from multiple users or compare two documents to determine the differences between them.

From Word, you can interact with other programs and incorporate the data and objects from those programs in a Word document. For example, you can link an Excel worksheet in a Word document or publish a blog post from Word. You also can use the charting features of Microsoft Office 2019 in Word.

Project: Memo with Chart

A memo is an informal document that businesses use to correspond with others. Memos often are internal to an organization, for example, to employees or coworkers.

The project in this module uses Word to produce the memo shown in Figure 8–1. First, you open an existing document that contains the memo and the Word table. Next, you edit the document, showing the changes so that other users can review the changes. The changes appear on the screen with options that allow the author of the document to accept or reject the changes. Then, you chart the Word table using charting features available in several Microsoft Office applications. In this module, you also learn how to link an Excel worksheet to a Word document and create a document for a blog post.

memo

Landmark Designs

To: Customer Service Associates

From: Shannon Popovich

Date: August 11, 2021

Subject: Available Home Designs

We have increased the number of home plans in our database by 30 percent! The table and chart below show the number of plans now available in several architectural styles, with the last column identifying the number of plans exclusive to Landmark Designs. Please familiarize yourself with all our new plans and let me know if you have any questions.

Home Plan Breakdown   Word table

Home Plan Style	Total Plans	Exclusive Plans
Colonial	1,229	98
Contemporary	3,270	214
European	3,118	323
Ranch	4,003	537
Tudor	4,326	509
Victorian	2,575	135

chart created from Word table

TOTAL AND EXCLUSIVE PLAN COMPARISON

■ Total Plans   ■ Exclusive Plans

Figure 8–1

You will perform the following general tasks as you progress through this module:

1. Track changes in the memo with the table.
2. Review the tracked changes.
3. Link an Excel worksheet to a Word document.
4. Chart a Word table using Word's Chart Tools tab.
5. Create and publish a blog post.

To Start Word and Specify Settings

If you are using a computer to step through the project in this module and you want your screens to match the figures in this book, you should change your screen's resolution to 1366 × 768. The following steps start Word, display formatting marks, change the zoom to 100%, and verify ruler and Mouse mode settings.

1 Start Word and create a blank document in the Word window. If necessary, maximize the Word window.

2 If the Print Layout button on the status bar is not selected, click it so that your screen is in Print Layout view.

3 If the 'Show/Hide ¶' button (Home tab | Paragraph group) is not selected already, click it to display formatting marks on the screen (shown in Figure 8–2).

4 To display the page the same width as the document window, if necessary, click the Page Width button (View tab | Zoom group).

5 Verify that the Ruler check box (View tab | Show group) is not selected. (If it is selected, click it to remove the check mark because you do not want the rulers to appear on the screen.)

6 If you are using a mouse and you want your screens to match the figures in the book, verify that you are using Mouse mode by clicking the Touch/Mouse Mode button on the Quick Access Toolbar and then, if necessary, clicking Mouse on the menu. (If your Quick Access Toolbar does not display the Touch/Mouse Mode button, click the 'Customize Quick Access Toolbar' button on the Quick Access Toolbar and then click Touch/Mouse Mode on the menu to add the button to the Quick Access Toolbar.)

Reviewing a Document

Word provides many tools that allow users to collaborate on a document. One set of collaboration tools within Word allows you to track changes in a document and review the changes. That is, one computer user can create a document and another user(s) can make changes in the same document. Those changes then appear on the screen with options that allow the originator (author) to accept or reject the changes. With another collaboration tool, you can compare and/or merge two or more documents to determine the differences between them.

To illustrate Word's collaboration tools, this section follows these general steps:

1. Open a document to be reviewed.
2. Track changes in the document.
3. Accept and reject the tracked changes. For illustration purposes, you assume the role of originator (author) of the document in this step.
4. Compare the reviewed document to the original to view the differences.
5. Combine the original document with the reviewed document and with another reviewer's suggestions.

BTW

The Ribbon and Screen Resolution
Word may change how the groups and buttons within the groups appear on the ribbon, depending on the screen resolution of your computer. Thus, your ribbon may look different from the ones in this book if you are using a screen resolution other than 1366 × 768.

To Open a Document and Save It with a New File Name

Assume your coworker has created a draft of a memo and is sending it to you for review. The file, called SC_WD_8-1.docx, is located in the Data Files. Please contact your instructor for information about accessing the Data Files. To preserve the original memo, you save the open document with a new file name. The following steps save an open document with a new file name.

If your instructor wants you to submit your work as a SAM Project for automatic grading, you must download the Data Files from the assignment launch page.

1 Navigate to the location of the Data Files on your hard drive, OneDrive, or other storage location.

2 sam↓ Open the file SC_WD_8-1.docx.

3 Navigate to the desired save location on your hard drive, OneDrive, or other storage location.

4 Save the file just opened on your hard drive, OneDrive, or other storage location using SC_WD_8_LandmarkDesignsMemo_withTrackedChanges as the file name (Figure 8–2).

5 To display the page the same width as the document window, click the Page Width button (View tab | Zoom group).

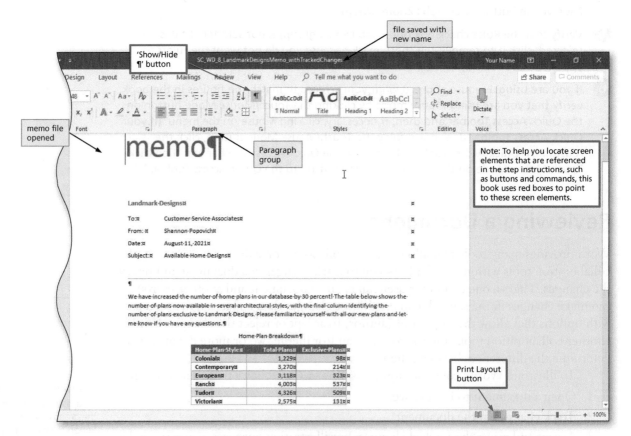

Figure 8–2

To Customize the Status Bar

You can customize the items that appear on the status bar. The status bar presents information about a document, the progress of current tasks, the status of certain commands and keys, and controls for viewing. Some indicators and buttons appear and disappear as you type text or perform certain commands. Others remain on the status bar at all times.

The following steps customize the status bar to show the Track Changes indicator. *Why? The Track Changes indicator does not appear by default on the status bar.*

- If the status bar does not show a desired item (in this case, the Track Changes indicator), right-click anywhere on the status bar to display the Customize Status Bar menu.

- Click the item on the Customize Status Bar menu that you want to show (in this case, Track Changes) to place a check mark beside the item, which also immediately may show as an indicator on the status bar (Figure 8–3).

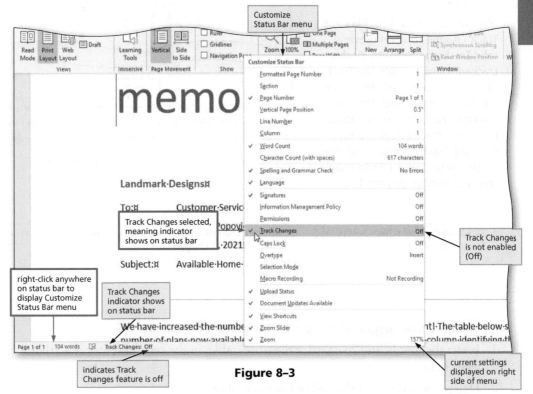

Figure 8–3

Q&A Can I show or hide any of the items listed on the Customize Status Bar menu?
Yes, click the item to display or remove its check mark.

- Click anywhere outside of the Customize Status Bar menu or press ESC to remove the menu from the screen.

To Enable Tracked Changes

When you edit a document that has the track changes feature enabled, Word uses annotations to mark all text or graphics that you insert, delete, or modify and refers to the revisions as **markups** or **revision marks**. An author can identify the changes a reviewer (user) has made by looking at the markups in a document. The author also has the ability to accept or reject any change that a reviewer has made to a document.

The following step enables tracked changes. *Why? To track changes in a document, you must enable (turn on) the track changes feature.*

- If the Track Changes indicator on the status bar shows that the track changes feature is off, click the Track Changes indicator on the status bar to enable the track changes feature.

Experiment

- Display the Review tab. Click the Track Changes button (Review tab | Tracking group) to disable tracked changes. Click the Track Changes button again to enable tracked changes. Click the Track Changes indicator on the status bar to disable tracked changes. Click the Track Changes indicator on the status bar again to enable tracked changes (Figure 8–4).

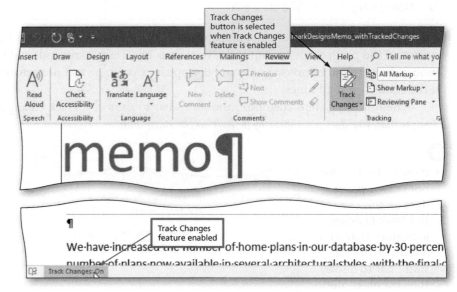

Figure 8–4

Other Ways

1. Click Track Changes button (Review tab | Tracking group)
2. Click Track Changes arrow (Review tab | Tracking group), click Track Changes
3. Press CTRL+SHIFT+E

To Track Changes

You have four suggested changes for the current document:

1. Insert the words, and chart, after the word, table, in the second sentence so that it reads: The table and chart below …
2. Delete the letter, s, at the end of the word, shows.
3. Insert the word, unique, before the word, plans, in the second sentence so that it reads: … the number of unique plans exclusive to Landmark Designs.
4. Change the word, final, to the word, last, in the second sentence so that it reads: … with the last column identifying....

The following steps track these changes as you enter them in the document. *Why? You want edits you make to the document to show so that others can review the edits.*

- Position the insertion point immediately to the left of the word, below, in the second sentence of the memo to position the insertion point at the location for the tracked change (Figure 8–5).

Figure 8–5

2

- Type **and chart** and then press SPACEBAR to insert the typed text as a tracked change (Figure 8–6).

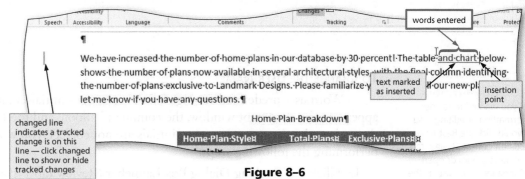

Figure 8–6

Q&A

Why is the inserted text in color and underlined?

When the track changes feature is enabled, Word marks (signals) all text inserts by underlining them and changing their color, and marks all deletions by striking through them and changing their color.

What is the vertical bar in the margin?

The bar is called a changed line, which indicates a tracked change is on the line to the right of the bar.

3

- In the same sentence, delete the s at the end of the word, shows (so that it reads, show), to mark the letter for deletion (Figure 8–7).

Figure 8–7

4

- In the same sentence on the next line, position the insertion point immediately to the left of the word, plans. Type **unique** and then press SPACEBAR to insert the typed text as a tracked change (Figure 8–8).

Figure 8–8

5

- In the same sentence, double-click the word, final, to select it.
- Type **last** as the replacement text, which tracks a deletion and an insertion change (Figure 8–9).

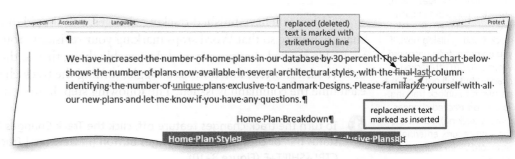

Figure 8–9

Q&A | Can I see the name of the person who tracked a change?
You can point to a tracked change in the document window; Word then will display a ScreenTip that identifies the reviewer's name and the type of change made by that reviewer.

BTW

Limiting Authors

If you wanted to restrict formatting or editing, you would click the Restrict Editing button (Review tab | Protect group) or open Backstage view, display the Info screen, click the Protect Document button, and then click Restrict Editing to open the Restrict Editing pane. To restrict formatting, select the 'Limit formatting to a selection of styles' check box, click the Settings link, select the styles to allow and disallow (Formatting Restrictions dialog box), and then click OK. To restrict editing, select the 'Allow only this type of editing in the document' check box, click the box arrow, and then select the desired editing restriction. To restrict formatting or editing to certain authors, select part of the document and select the users who are allowed to edit the selected areas and then click the 'Yes, Start Enforcing Protection' button. To block authors from making changes to selected text, click the Block Authors button (Review tab | Protect group) and then select the authors to block in the list.

TO CHANGE THE USER NAME

Word uses predefined settings for the reviewer's initials and/or name that appears in the document window, the comment balloon, and the Reviewing pane. If the reviewer's name (user name) or initials are not correct, you would change them by performing the following steps.

1a. Click the Tracking Dialog Box Launcher (Review tab | Tracking group) to display the Track Changes Options dialog box. Click the 'Change User Name' button (Track Changes Options dialog box) to display the Word Options dialog box.

or

1b. Open Backstage view and then click Options to display the Word Options dialog box. If necessary, click General in the left pane.

2. Enter the correct name in the User name text box (Word Options dialog box), and enter the correct initials in the Initials text box.

3. Click OK to change the reviewer information. If necessary, click OK in the Track Changes Options dialog box.

TO CHANGE HOW MARKUPS AND COMMENTS ARE DISPLAYED

The tracked changes entered in the previous steps appeared inline, which means that the inserts are underlined and the deletions are shown as strikethroughs. The default Word setting displays comments and formatting changes in balloons in a markup area to the right of the document and all other changes inline. If you wanted to change how markups (and comments) are displayed, you would perform the following steps.

1. Click the Show Markup button (Review tab | Tracking group) to display the Show Markup menu and then point to Balloons on the Show Markup menu.

2. If you want all revisions to appear in balloons, click 'Show Revisions in Balloons' on the Balloons submenu. If you want all revisions to appear inline, click 'Show All Revisions Inline' on the Balloons submenu. If you want to use the default Word setting, click 'Show Only Comments and Formatting in Balloons' on the Balloons submenu.

BTW

Lock Tracking

If you wanted to require a password to turn off tracked changes (lock tracking), you would click the Track Changes arrow (Review tab | Tracking group), click Lock Tracking on the Track Changes menu, enter the password in each text box, and then click OK (Lock Tracking dialog box). If you do not enter a password, Word will turn off tracked changes but will not require a password to unlock tracking. To turn off tracked changes (unlock tracking), follow the same procedure, entering the password when prompted, if necessary.

To Disable Tracked Changes

When you have finished tracking changes, you should disable (turn off) the track changes feature so that Word stops marking your revisions. You follow the same steps to disable tracked changes as you did to enable them; that is, the indicator or button or keyboard shortcut functions as a toggle, turning the track changes feature on or off each time the command is issued. The following step disables tracked changes.

1 To turn the track changes feature off, click the Track Changes indicator on the status bar, or click the Track Changes button (Review tab | Tracking group), or press CTRL+SHIFT+E (Figure 8–10).

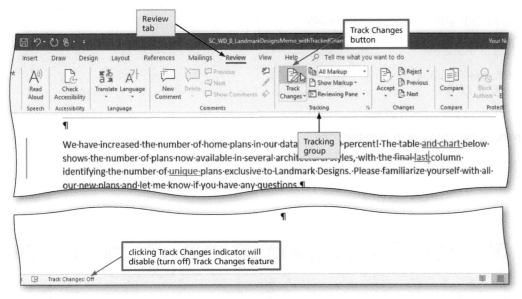

Figure 8–10

To Use the Reviewing Pane or the Markup Area

Word provides a Reviewing pane that can be opened and then displayed either at the left edge (vertically) or the bottom (horizontally) of the screen. ***Why?*** *As an alternative to reading through tracked changes in the document window or in balloons in the markup area, some users prefer to view tracked changes in the Reviewing pane.* The following steps open the Reviewing pane.

1

• Click the Reviewing Pane arrow (Review tab | Tracking group) to display the Reviewing Pane menu (Figure 8–11).

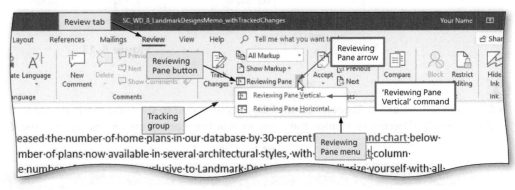

Figure 8–11

2

• Click 'Reviewing Pane Vertical' on the Reviewing Pane menu to open the Reviewing pane on the left side of the Word window (Figure 8–12).

Figure 8–12

Q&A What if I click the Reviewing Pane button instead of the arrow?
Word opens the Reviewing pane in its most recent location, that is, either vertically on the left side of the screen or horizontally on the bottom of the screen.

Can I edit revisions in the Reviewing pane?
Yes. Simply click in the Reviewing pane and edit the text the same way you edit in the document window.

3

- Click the Close button in the Reviewing pane to close the pane.

Q&A Can I also click the Reviewing Pane button on the ribbon to close the pane?
Yes.

4

- Click the Show Markup button (Review tab | Tracking group) to display the Show Markup menu.

- Point to Balloons on the Show Markup menu to display the Balloons submenu (Figure 8–13).

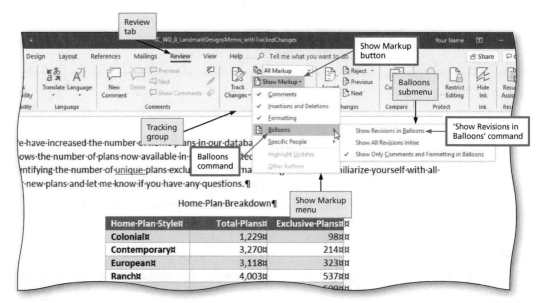

Figure 8–13

5

- Click 'Show Revisions in Balloons' on the Balloons submenu to show the markup area in the Word window (Figure 8–14). If necessary, change the zoom so that the markup area is displayed in the Word window.

Figure 8–14

- Click the Show Markup button (Review tab | Tracking group) to display the Show Markup menu.

- Point to Balloons on the Show Markup menu to display the Balloons submenu and then click 'Show All Revisions Inline' on the Balloons submenu to remove the markup area from the Word window and place all markups inline.

- If necessary, change the zoom to page width.

To Display Tracked Changes as Simple Markup

Word provides a Simple Markup option instead of the All Markup option for viewing tracked changes and comments. *Why? Some users feel the All Markup option clutters the screen and prefer the cleaner look of the Simple Markup option.* The following steps display tracked changes using the Simple Markup option.

- Click the 'Display for Review' arrow (Review tab | Tracking group) to display the Display for Review menu (Figure 8–15).

Figure 8–15

- Click Simple Markup on the Display for Review menu to show a simple markup instead of all markups in the document window (Figure 8–16).

Experiment

- Click the changed line to display the tracked changes and switch back to displaying All Markup. Click the changed line again to hide the tracked changes and switch to Simple Markup.

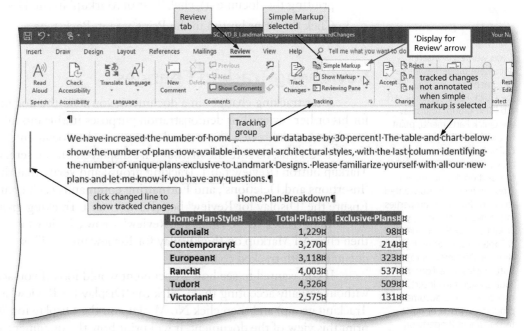

Figure 8–16

To Show All Markup

You prefer to show all markup where tracked changes are annotated in the document window. The following steps show all markup.

1 Click the 'Display for Review' arrow (Review tab | Tracking group) (shown in Figure 8–16) and then click All Markup on the Display for Review menu to instruct Word to display the document with all proposed edits shown as markup (shown in Figure 8–17).

Q&A | What are the other Display for Review options?
If you click the 'Display for Review' arrow, several options appear. Simple Markup means Word incorporates proposed changes in the document and places a changed line near the margin of the line containing the proposed change. All Markup means that all proposed changes are highlighted. No Markup shows the proposed edits as part of the final document, instead of as markup. Original shows the document before changes.

2 Save the memo again on the same storage location with the same file name.

To Print Markups

When you print a document with tracked changes, Word chooses the zoom percentage and page orientation that will best show the comments on the printed document. You can print the document with its markups, which looks similar to how the Word window shows the markups on the screen, or you can print just the list of the markups. If you wanted to print markups, you would perform the following steps.

1. Open Backstage view and then click Print in Backstage view to display the Print screen.
2. Click the first button in the Settings area to display a list of options specifying what you can print. To print the document with the markups, if necessary, place a check mark to the left of Print Markup. To print just the markups (without printing the document), click 'List of Markup' in the Document Info area.
3. Click the Print button in the Print area in Backstage view.

Reviewing Tracked Changes

After tracking changes in a document, you send the document to the originator for his or her review. For demonstration purposes in this module, you assume the role of originator and review the tracked changes in the document.

To do this, be sure the markups are displayed on the screen. Click the Show Markup button (Review tab | Tracking group) and verify that the Comments, 'Insertions and Deletions', and Formatting commands each contain a check mark. Ensure the 'Display for Review' box (Review tab | Tracking group) shows All Markup; if it does not, click the 'Display for Review' arrow (Review tab | Tracking group) and then click All Markup on the Display for Review menu. This option shows the final document with tracked changes.

If you wanted to see how a document would look if you accepted all the changes, without actually accepting them, click the 'Display for Review' arrow (Review tab | Tracking group) and then click No Markup on the Display for Review menu. If you print this view of the document, it will print how the document will look if you accept all the changes. If you wanted to see how the document looked before any changes were made, click the 'Display for Review' arrow (Review tab | Tracking group) and then click Original on the Display for Review menu. When you have finished reviewing the various options, if necessary, click the 'Display for Review' arrow (Review tab | Tracking group) and then click All Markup on the Display for Review menu.

To Review Tracked Changes

The next step is to review the tracked changes in the marked-up document using the Review tab. *Why? You could scroll through the document and point to each markup to read it, but you might overlook one or more changes using this technique. A more efficient method is to use the Review tab to review the changes one at a time, deciding whether to accept, modify, or delete each change.* The following steps review the changes in the document.

1

- Position the insertion point at the beginning of the document, so that Word begins the review of tracked changes from the top of the document.

- Click the Next button (Review tab | Changes group), which causes Word to locate and select the first markup in the document (in this case, the inserted words, and chart) (Figure 8–17).

Q&A What if my document also had contained comments?
When you click the Next button (Review tab | Changes group), Word locates the next tracked change or comment, whichever appears first.

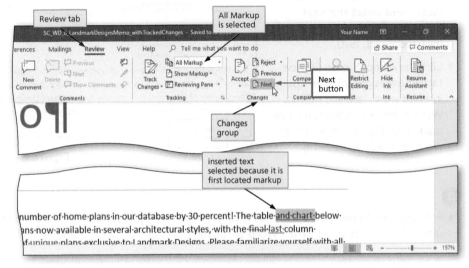

Figure 8–17

2

- Because you agree with this change, click the Accept button (Review tab | Changes group) to accept the insertion of the words, and chart, and instruct Word to locate and select the next markup (in this case, the deleted letter, s) (Figure 8–18).

Q&A What if I accidentally click the Accept arrow (Review tab | Changes group)?
Click 'Accept and Move to Next' on the Accept menu.

What if I wanted to accept the change but not search for the next tracked change?
You would click the Accept arrow and then click 'Accept This Change' on the Accept menu.

Figure 8–18

• Click the Accept button (Review tab | Changes group) to accept the deleted letter, s and instruct Word to locate and select the next markup (in this case, the deleted word, final).

• Click the Accept button (Review tab | Changes group) to accept the deleted word, final, and instruct Word to locate and select the next markup (in this case, the inserted word, last).

• Click the Accept button (Review tab | Changes group) to accept the inserted word, last, and instruct Word to locate and select the next markup (in this case, the inserted word, unique) (Figure 8–19).

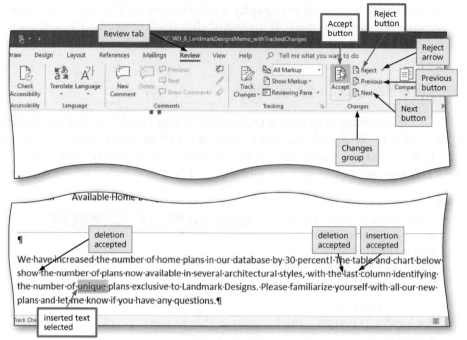

Figure 8–19

4

• Because you do not agree with this change, click the Reject button (Review tab | Changes group) to reject the marked insertion, and instruct Word to locate and select the next markup if one exists.

Q&A

What if I accidentally click the Reject arrow (Review tab | Changes group)?
Click 'Reject and Move to Next' on the Reject menu.

What if I wanted to reject the change but not search for the next tracked change?
You would click the Reject arrow (Review tab | Changes group) and then click Reject Change on the Reject menu.

What if I did not want to accept or reject a change but wanted to locate the next tracked change?
You would click the Next button (Review tab | Changes group) to locate the next tracked change or comment. Likewise, to locate the previous tracked change or comment, you would click the Previous button (Review tab | Changes group).

5

• Click OK in the dialog box that appears, which indicates the document contains no more comments or tracked changes.

• **sam**⬆ Save the reviewed file on your hard drive, OneDrive, or other storage location using SC_WD_8_LandmarkDesignsMemo_Reviewed as the file name.

Other Ways

1. Right-click comment or tracked change (or, if using touch, tap 'Show Context Menu' button on Mini toolbar), click desired command on shortcut menu

TO ACCEPT OR REJECT ALL TRACKED CHANGES

If you wanted to accept or reject all tracked changes in a document at once, you would perform the following step.

1. To accept all tracked changes, click the Accept arrow (Review tab | Changes group) to display the Accept menu and then click 'Accept All Changes' on the menu to accept all changes in the document and continue tracking changes or click 'Accept All Changes and Stop Tracking' to accept all changes in the document and stop tracking changes.

or

1. To reject all tracked changes, click the Reject arrow (Review tab | Changes group) to display the Reject menu and then click 'Reject All Changes' on the menu to reject all changes in the document and continue tracking changes or click 'Reject All Changes and Stop Tracking' to reject all changes in the document and stop tracking changes.

Changing Tracking Options

If you wanted to change the color and markings reviewers use for tracked changes and comments or change how balloons are displayed, use the Advanced Track Changes Options dialog box (Figure 8–20). To display the Advanced Track Changes Options dialog box, click the Tracking Dialog Box Launcher (Review tab | Tracking group) and then click the Advanced Options button (Track Changes Options dialog box).

Figure 8–20

BTW
Compare and Merge
If you wanted to compare two documents and merge the changes into an existing document instead of into a new document, you would click the Original document option button (Compare Documents dialog box) to merge into the original document or click the Revised document option button (Compare Documents dialog box) to merge into the revised document (shown in Figure 8–22), and then click OK.

To Compare Documents

With Word, you can compare two documents to each other. *Why? Comparing documents allows you easily to identify any differences between two files because Word displays the differences between the documents as tracked changes for your review. By comparing files, you can verify that two separate files have the same or different content. If no tracked changes are found, then the two documents are identical.*

Assume you want to compare the original SC_WD_8-1.docx document with the SC_WD_8_LandmarkDesignsMemo_Reviewed.docx document so that you can identify the changes made to the document. The following steps compare two documents.

- If necessary, display the Review tab.
- Click the Compare button (Review tab | Compare group) to display the Compare menu (Figure 8–21).

Figure 8–21

- Click Compare on the Compare menu to display the Compare Documents dialog box.
- Click the Original document arrow (Compare Documents dialog box) and then click the file, SC_WD_8-1.docx, in the Original document list to select the first file to compare and place the file name in the Original document box.

Q&A What if the file is not in the Original document list?

Click the Open button to the right of the Original document arrow, locate the file, and then click the Open button (Open dialog box).

- Click the Revised document arrow (Compare Documents dialog box) and then click the file, SC_WD_8_LandmarkDesignsMemo_Reviewed.docx, in the Revised document list to select the second file to compare and place the file name in the Revised document box. If necessary, change the name in the 'Label changes with' box to your name.

Q&A What if the file is not in the Revised document list?

Click the Open button to the right of the Revised document arrow, locate the file, and then click the Open button (Open dialog box).

- If a More button appears in the dialog box, click it to expand the dialog box, which changes the More button to a Less button.
- If necessary, in the Show changes in area, click New document so that tracked changes are marked in a new document. Ensure that all your settings in the expanded dialog box (below the Less button) match those in Figure 8–22.

Figure 8–22

3

• Click OK to open a new document window and display the differences between the two documents as tracked changes in a new document window; if the Reviewing task opens on the screen, click its Close button. Note that, depending on settings, your compare results may differ from Figure 8–23; for example, your screen already may show source documents, which is covered in Step 4.

4

• Click the Compare button (Review tab | Compare group) to display the Compare menu and then point to 'Show Source Documents' on the Compare menu (Figure 8–23).

Figure 8–23

5

• Click Show Both on the Show Source Documents submenu so that the original and source documents appear on the screen with the compared document; if the Reviewing pane opens on the screen, click its Close button (Figure 8–24). Note that, depending on settings, your compare results may differ from Figure 8–24.

Figure 8–24

Experiment

- Click the Next button (Review tab | Changes group) to display the first tracked change in the compared document. Continue clicking the Next or Previous buttons. You can accept or reject changes in the compared document using the same steps described earlier in the module.

- Scroll through the windows and watch them scroll synchronously.

6

- When you have finished comparing the documents, click the Close button in the document window (shown in Figure 8–24) and then click the Don't Save button when Word asks if you want to save the compare results.

To Combine Revisions from Multiple Authors

Often, multiple reviewers will send you their markups (tracked changes) for the same original document. Using Word, you can combine the tracked changes from multiple reviewers' documents into a single document, two documents at a time, until all documents are combined. *Why? Combining documents allows you to review all markups from a single document, from which you can accept and reject changes and read comments. Each reviewer's markups are shaded in a different color to help you visually differentiate among multiple reviewers' markups.*

Assume you want to combine the original SC_WD_8-1.docx document with the SC_WD_8_LandmarkDesignsMemo_withTrackedChanges.docx document and also with a document called Support_WD_8_LandmarkDesignsMemo_ReviewedByJPerez.docx. The following steps combine these three documents, two at a time.

1

- Click the Compare button (Review tab | Compare group) to display the Compare menu (Figure 8–25).

Figure 8–25

2

- Click Combine on the Compare menu to display the Combine Documents dialog box.

- Click the Original document arrow (Combine Documents dialog box) and then click the file, SC_WD_8-1.docx, in the Original document list to select the first file to combine and place the file name in the Original document box.

 What if the file is not in the Original document list?

Click the Open button to the right of the Original document arrow, locate the file, and then click the Open button (Open dialog box).

- Click the Revised document arrow (Combine Documents dialog box) and then click the file, SC_WD_8_LandmarkDesignsMemo_withTrackedChanges.docx, in the Revised document list to select the second file to combine and place the file name in the Revised document box.

Q&A What if the file is not in the Revised document list?

Click the Open button to the right of the Revised document arrow, locate the file, and then click the Open button (Open dialog box).

- If a More button appears in the dialog box, click it to expand the dialog box, which changes the More button to a Less button.

- In the Show changes in area, if necessary, click Original document so that tracked changes are marked in the original document (SC_WD_8-1.docx). Ensure that all your settings in the expanded dialog box (below the Less button) match those in Figure 8–26.

Figure 8–26

3

- Click OK to combine SC_WD_8-1.docx with SC_WD_8_LandmarkDesignsMemo_withTrackedChanges.docx and display the differences between the two documents as tracked changes in the original document (Figure 8–27).

Figure 8–27

- Click the Compare button again (Review tab | Compare group) and then click Combine on the Compare menu to display the Combine Documents dialog box.

- Locate and display the file name, SC_WD_8-1.docx, in the Original document text box (Combine Documents dialog box) to select the first file and place the file name in the Original document box.

- Click the Open button to the right of the Revised document box arrow (Combine Documents dialog box) to display the Open dialog box.

- Locate the file name, Support_WD_8_LandmarkDesignsMemo_ReviewedByJPerez.docx, in the Data Files and then click the Open button (Open dialog box) to display the selected file name in the Revised document box (Combine Documents dialog box).

- If a More button appears in the Combine Documents dialog box, click it to expand the dialog box.

- If necessary, in the 'Show changes in' area, click Original document so that tracked changes are marked in the original document (SC_WD_8-1.docx). Ensure that all your settings in the expanded dialog box (below the Less button) match those in Figure 8–28.

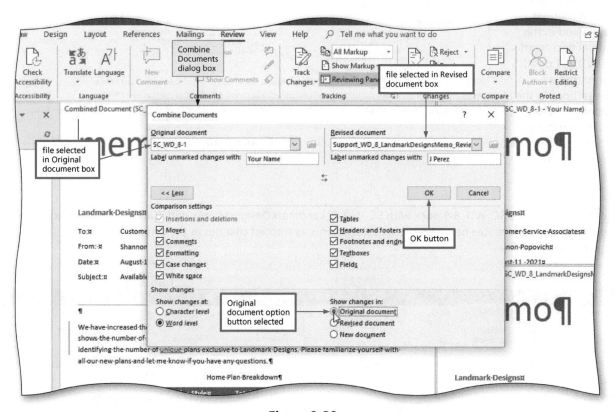

Figure 8–28

4

- Click OK to combine the Support_WD_8_LandmarkDesignsMemo_ReviewedByJPerez.docx document with the currently combined document and display the differences among the three documents as tracked changes in the original document (Figure 8–29). If necessary, scroll to see the table in the memo.

Q&A What if my screen does not display the original and source documents?

Click the Compare button (Review tab | Compare group) to display the Compare menu, point to 'Show Source Documents' on the Compare menu, and then click Show Both on the Show Source Documents submenu.

Experiment

- Click the Next button (Review tab | Changes group) to display the first tracked change in the combined document. Continue clicking the Next or Previous buttons. You can accept or reject changes in the combined document using the same steps described earlier in the module.

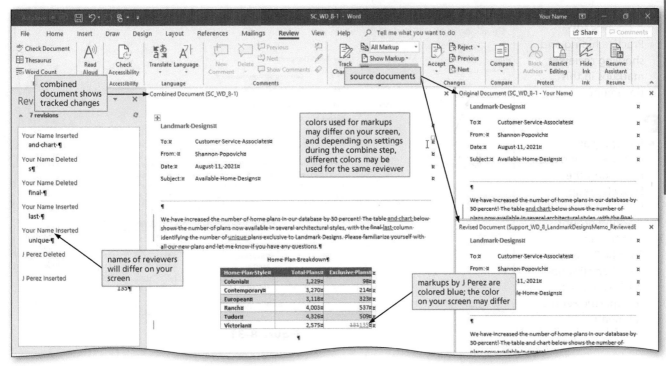

Figure 8–29

To Show Tracked Changes and Comments by a Single Reviewer

Why? *Instead of looking through a document for a particular reviewer's markups, you can show markups by reviewer.* The following steps show the markups by the reviewer named J Perez.

1

- Click the Show Markup button (Review tab | Tracking group) to display the Show Markup menu and then point to Specific People on the Show Markup menu to display the Specific People submenu (Figure 8–30).

Q&A What if my Specific People submenu differs?
Your submenu may have additional, different, or duplicate reviewer names or colors, depending on your Word settings.

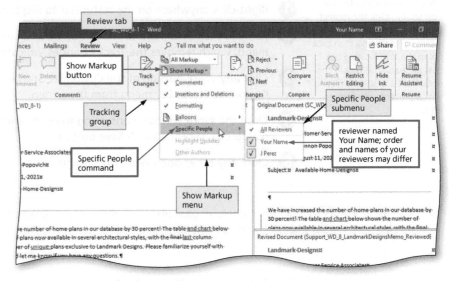

Figure 8–30

2

- Click Your Name on the Specific People submenu to hide the selected reviewer's markups and leave other markups on the screen (Figure 8–31).

Q&A Are the Your Name reviewer markups deleted?
No. They are hidden from view.

Experiment

- Practice hiding and showing reviewer markups in this document.

3

- Redisplay all reviewer comments by clicking the Show Markup button (Review tab | Tracking group), pointing to Specific People, and then clicking All Reviewers on the Specific People submenu.

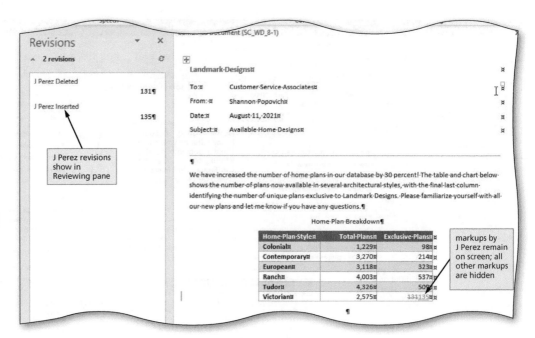

Figure 8–31

BTW

Mark as Final

If you wanted to mark a document as final so that users could not make further edits to it, you would perform these steps. Open Backstage view, display the Info screen, click the Protect Document button, click 'Mark as Final', and then click OK in the Word dialog box that appears. This makes the document a read-only file, which prevents any further edits.

To Customize the Status Bar and Close the Document

You are finished working with tracked changes in this module. The following steps remove the Track Changes indicator from the status bar and close the combined document without saving it.

1 Right-click anywhere on the status bar to display the Customize Status Bar menu.

2 Remove the check mark to the left of Track Changes on the Customize Status Bar menu, which removes the Track Changes indicator from the status bar.

3 Click anywhere outside of the Customize Status Bar menu, or press ESC, to remove the Customize Status Bar menu from the screen.

4 Close the Word window containing the combined document. When Word displays the dialog box, click the Don't Save button.

5 Close any other open Word documents.

Break Point: If you want to take a break, this is a good place to do so. You can exit Word now. To resume later, start Word and continue following the steps from this location forward.

BTW

Linking to External Content

If you wanted to link to external document content, you would click the Object button (Insert tab | Text group), click the Create from File tab (Object dialog box), locate the external file, place a check mark in the 'Link to file' check box, and then click OK.

Linking an Excel Worksheet to a Word Document

With Microsoft Office, you can copy part or all of a document created in one Office program to a document created in another Office program. The item being copied, or exchanged between another document or program, is called the **object**. For example, you could copy an Excel worksheet (the object) that is located in an Excel workbook (the source file) to a Word document (the destination file). That is, an object is copied from a source to a destination.

You can use one of three techniques to exchange objects from one program to another: copy and paste, embed, or link.

- **Copy and paste:** When you copy an object and then paste it, the object becomes part of the destination document. You edit a pasted object using editing features of the destination program. For example, when you select an Excel worksheet in an Excel workbook, click the Copy button (Home tab | Clipboard group) in Excel, and then click the Paste button (Home tab | Clipboard group) in Word, the Excel worksheet becomes a Word table.

- **Embed:** When you embed an object, like a pasted object, it becomes part of the destination document. The difference between an embedded object and a pasted object is that you edit the contents of an embedded object using the editing features of the source program. The embedded object, however, contains static data; that is, any changes made to the object in the source program are not reflected in the destination document. If you embed an Excel worksheet in a Word document, the Excel worksheet remains as an Excel worksheet in the Word document. When you edit the Excel worksheet from within the Word document, you will use Excel editing features.

- **Link:** A linked object, by contrast, does not become a part of the destination document even though it appears to be a part of it. Rather, a connection is established between the source and destination documents so that when you open the destination document, the linked object appears as part of it. When you edit a linked object, the source program runs and opens the source document that contains the linked object. For example, when you edit a linked worksheet, Excel runs and displays the Excel workbook that contains the worksheet; you then edit the worksheet in Excel. Unlike an embedded object, if you open the Excel workbook that contains the Excel worksheet and then edit the Excel worksheet, the linked object will be updated in the Word document, too.

BTW
Linked Objects
When you open a document that contains linked objects, Word displays a dialog box asking if you want to update the Word document with data from the linked file. Click Yes only if you are certain the linked file is from a trusted source; that is, you should be confident that the source file does not contain a virus or other potentially harmful program before you instruct Word to link the source file to the destination document.

How do you determine which method to use: copy/paste, embed, or link?

- If you simply want to use the object's data and have no desire to use the object in the source program, then copy and paste the object.

- If you want to use the object in the source program but you want the object's data to remain static if it changes in the source file, then embed the object.

- If you want to ensure that the most current version of the object appears in the destination file, then link the object. If the source file is large, such as a video clip or a sound clip, link the object to keep the size of the destination file smaller.

CONSIDER THIS

The steps in this section show how to link an Excel worksheet (the object), which is located in an Excel workbook (the source file), to a Word document (the destination file). The Word document is similar to the same memo used in the previous section, except that it does not contain the table. To link the worksheet to the memo, you will follow these general steps:

1. Start Excel and open the Excel workbook that contains the object (worksheet) you want to link to the Word document.

2. Select the object (worksheet) in Excel and then copy the selected object to the Clipboard.

3. Switch to Word and then link the copied object to the Word document.

Note: The steps in this section assume you have Microsoft Excel 2019 installed on your computer. If you do not have Excel 2019, read the steps in this section without performing them.

To Open a Word Document, Start Excel, and Open an Excel Workbook

The first step in this section is to open the memo that is to contain the link to the Excel worksheet object. The memo file, named SC_WD_8-2.docx, is located in the Data Files. The Excel worksheet to be linked to the memo is in an Excel workbook called Support_WD_8_HomePlanBreakdown_inExcel.xlsx, which also is located in the Data Files. Please contact your instructor for information about accessing the Data Files. The following steps open a Word document, start Excel, and open an Excel workbook. (Do not exit Word or close the open Word document during these steps.)

1 In Word, open the file called SC_WD_8-2.docx located in the Data Files (Figure 8–32).

2 Start Excel and open a blank workbook.

3 In Excel, open the file called Support_WD_8_HomePlanBreakdown_inExcel.xlsx in the Data Files.

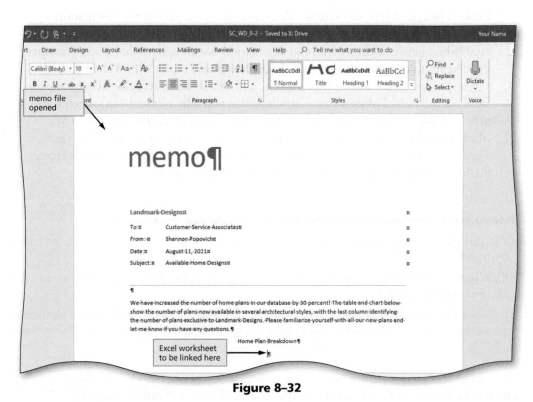

Figure 8–32

BTW
Opening Word Documents with Links
When you open a document that contains a linked object, Word attempts to locate the source file associated with the link. If Word cannot find the source file, open Backstage view, display the Info screen, then click 'Edit Links to Files' in the Related Documents area at the bottom of the right pane to display the Links dialog box. Next, select the appropriate source file in the list (Links dialog box), click the Change Source button, locate the source file, and then click OK.

Excel Basics

The Excel window contains a rectangular grid that consists of columns and rows. A column letter above the grid identifies each column. A row number on the left side of the grid identifies each row. The intersection of each column and row is a cell. A cell is referred to by its unique address, which is the coordinates of the intersection of a column and a row. To identify a cell, specify the column letter first, followed by the row number. For example, cell reference A1 refers to the cell located at the intersection of column A and row 1 (Figure 8–33).

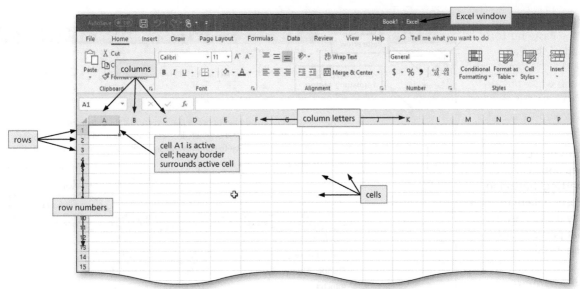

Figure 8–33

To Link an Excel Worksheet to a Word Document

The following steps link an Excel worksheet to a Word document. *Why? You want to copy the Excel worksheet to the Clipboard and then link the Excel worksheet to the Word document.*

1

• In the Excel window, drag through the cells in the range A1 through C7 to select them.

• In the Excel window, click the Copy button (Home tab | Clipboard group) to copy the selected cells to the Clipboard (Figure 8–34).

Q&A What if I click the Copy arrow by mistake?
Click Copy on the Copy menu.

What is the dotted line around the selected cells?
Excel surrounds copied cells with a moving marquee to help you visually identify the copied cells.

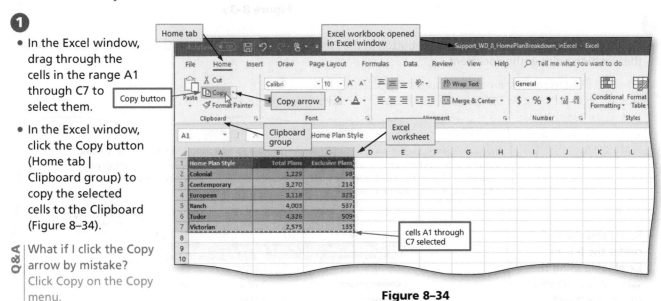

Figure 8–34

2

• Click the Word app button on the taskbar to switch to Word and display the open document in the Word window.

• Position the insertion point on the paragraph mark below the table title.

• In Word, click the Paste arrow (Home tab | Clipboard group) to display the Paste gallery.

Q&A What if I accidentally click the Paste button instead of the Paste arrow?
Click the Undo button on the Quick Access Toolbar and then click the Paste arrow.

- Point to the 'Link & Keep Source Formatting' button in the Paste gallery to display a Live Preview of that paste option (Figure 8–35).

Experiment

- Point to the various buttons in the Paste gallery to display a Live Preview of each paste option.

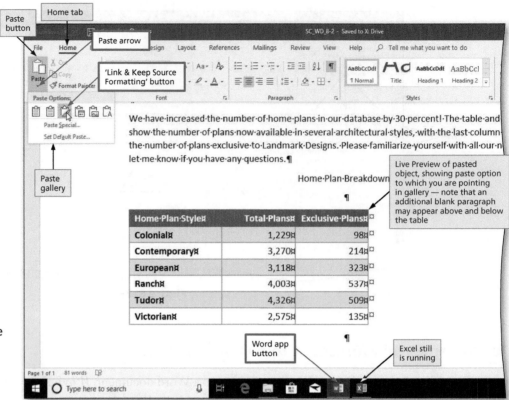

Figure 8–35

3

- Click the 'Link & Keep Source Formatting' button in the Paste gallery to paste and link the object at the location of the insertion point in the document.

Q&A What if I wanted to copy an object instead of link it?
To copy an object, you would click the 'Keep Source Formatting' button in the Paste gallery. To convert the object to a picture so that you can use tools on Word's Picture Tools Format tab to format it, you would click the Picture button in the Paste gallery.

- Select and then center the linked Excel table using the same technique you use to select and center a Word table.

- Click outside the table to deselect it (Figure 8–36).

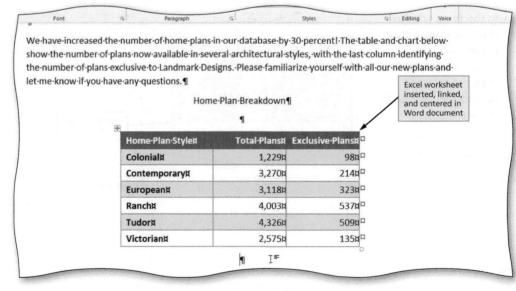

Figure 8–36

Q&A What if I wanted to delete the linked worksheet?
You would select the linked worksheet and then press DELETE.

Other Ways

1. Click Paste arrow (Home tab | Clipboard group), click Paste Special, click Paste link (Paste Special dialog box), click 'Microsoft Excel Worksheet Object' in As list, click OK

2. To link an entire source file, click Object button (Insert tab | Text group), click Create from File tab (Object dialog box), locate file, click 'Link to file' check box, click OK

TO EMBED AN EXCEL WORKSHEET IN A WORD DOCUMENT

If you wanted to embed an Excel worksheet in a Word document, instead of link it, you would perform the following steps.

1. Start Excel.

2. In Excel, select the worksheet cells to embed. Click the Copy button (Home tab | Clipboard group) to copy the selected cells to the Clipboard.

3. Switch to Word. In Word, click the Paste arrow (Home tab | Clipboard group) to display the Paste gallery and then click Paste Special in the Paste gallery to display the Paste Special dialog box.

4. Select the Paste option button (Paste Special dialog box), which indicates the object will be embedded.

5. Select 'Microsoft Excel Worksheet Object' as the type of object to embed.

6. Click OK to embed the contents of the Clipboard in the Word document at the location of the insertion point.

TO EDIT A LINKED OBJECT

At a later time, you may find it necessary to change the data in the Excel worksheet. Any changes you make to the Excel worksheet while in Excel will be reflected in the Excel worksheet in the Word document because the objects are linked to the Word document. If you wanted to edit a linked object, such as an Excel worksheet, you would perform these steps.

1. In the Word document, right-click the linked Excel worksheet, point to 'Linked Worksheet Object' on the shortcut menu, and then click Edit Link on the Linked Worksheet Object submenu to start Excel and open the source file that contains the linked worksheet.

2. In Excel, make changes to the Excel worksheet.

3. Click the Save button on the Quick Access Toolbar to save the changes.

4. Exit Excel.

5. If necessary, redisplay the Word window.

6. If necessary, to update the worksheet with the edited Excel data, click the Excel worksheet in the Word document and then press F9, or right-click the linked object and then click Update Link on the shortcut menu to update the linked object with the revisions made to the source file.

To Break a Link

Why? *You can convert a linked or embedded object to a Word object by breaking the link. That is, you break the connection between the source file and the destination file.* When you break a linked object, such as an Excel worksheet, the linked object becomes a Word object, a Word table in this case. The following steps break the link to the Excel worksheet.

- Right-click the linked object (the linked Excel worksheet, in this case) to display a shortcut menu.

- Point to 'Linked Worksheet Object' on the shortcut menu to display the Linked Worksheet Object submenu (Figure 8–37).

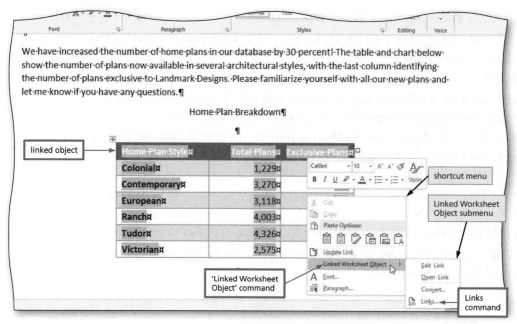

Figure 8–37

2

- Click Links on the Linked Worksheet Object submenu to display the Links dialog box.

- If necessary, click the source file listed in the dialog box to select it (Links dialog box).

- Click the Break Link button, which displays a dialog box asking if you are sure you want to break the selected links (Figure 8–38).

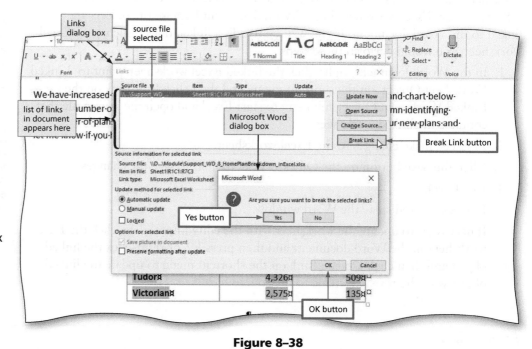

Figure 8–38

3

- Click Yes in the dialog box to remove the source file from the list (break the link).

Q&A How can I verify the link is broken?

Right-click the table in the Word document to display a shortcut menu. If the shortcut menu does not contain a 'Linked Worksheet Object' command, a link does not exist for the object. Or, when you double-click the table, Excel should not open an associated workbook.

- Close the Word document without saving it.

- Exit Excel without saving changes to the workbook.

Other Ways

1. Select link, press CTRL+SHIFT+F9

Charting a Word Table

Several Office applications, including Word, enable you to create charts from data. In the following pages, you will insert and format a chart of the Home Plan Breakdown Word table using the Chart Tools tab in Word. You will follow these general steps to insert and then format the chart:

1. Create a chart of the table.
2. Remove a data series from the chart.
3. Apply a chart style to the chart.
4. Change the colors of the chart.
5. Add a chart element.
6. Edit a chart element.
7. Format chart elements.
8. Add an outline to the chart.

To Open and Save a Document

The next step is to open the Home Plan Breakdown Memo file that contains the final wording so that you can create a chart of its Word table. This file, called SC_WD_8-3.docx, is located in the Data Files. Please contact your instructor for information about accessing the Data Files. The following steps open a document and then save it with a new file name.

1 Navigate to the Data Files and then open the file called SC_WD_8-3.docx.

2 Save the memo on your hard drive, OneDrive, or other storage location using SC_WD_8_LandmarkDesignsMemo_withTableandClusteredChart as the file name.

To Insert a Chart

The following steps insert a default chart and then copy the data to be charted from the Word table in the Word document to a chart spreadsheet. *Why? To chart a table, you fill in or copy the data into a chart spreadsheet that automatically opens after you insert the chart.*

1

- Position the insertion point on the centered paragraph mark below the table because the chart will be inserted at the location of the insertion point.
- Display the Insert tab.
- Click the Chart button (Insert tab | Illustrations group) to display the Insert Chart dialog box.
- Click Bar in the left pane (Insert Chart dialog box) to display the available types of bar charts in the right pane.

Experiment

- Click the various types of charts in the left pane and watch the subtypes appear in the right pane. When finished experimenting, click Bar in the left pane.

- If necessary, click Clustered Bar in the right pane to select the chart type (Figure 8–39).

Experiment

- Click the various types of bar charts in the right pane and watch the graphic change in the right pane. When finished experimenting, click Clustered Bar in the right pane.

Figure 8–39

2

- Click OK so that Word creates a default clustered bar chart in the Word document at the location of the insertion point (Figure 8–40).

Q&A

What are the requirements for the format of a table that can be charted?
The chart spreadsheet window shows the layout for the selected chart type. In this case, the categories are in the rows and the series are in the columns. Notice the categories appear in the chart in reverse order.

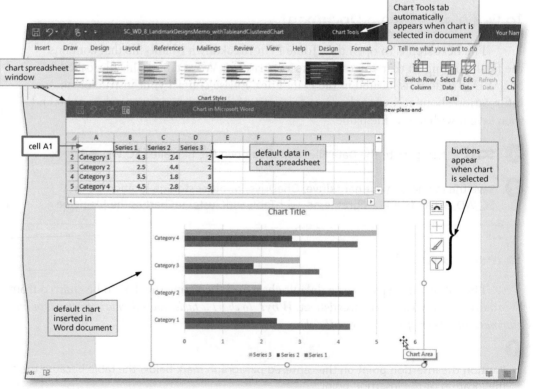

Figure 8–40

3

- In the Word document, if necessary, select the table to be charted. (If necessary, drag the chart spreadsheet window or scroll in the document window so that the table is visible.)

- Click the Copy button (Home tab | Clipboard group) to copy the selected table to the Clipboard (Figure 8–41).

Figure 8–41

 Q&A

Instead of copying table data to the chart spreadsheet, could I type the data directly into the spreadsheet?

Yes. If the chart spreadsheet window does not appear, click the Edit Data arrow (Chart Tools Design tab | Data group) and then click Edit Data on the menu. You also can click the 'Edit Data in Microsoft Excel' button to use Excel to enter the data (if Excel is installed on your computer), or click the Edit Data arrow (Chart Tools Design tab | Data group) and then click 'Edit Data in Excel' on the Edit Data menu. You edit (modify) existing data and add new data in rows and columns the same way you would in an Excel worksheet.

4

- In the chart spreadsheet window, click the Select All button (upper-left corner of worksheet) to select the entire worksheet.

- Right-click the selected worksheet to display a Mini toolbar or shortcut menu (Figure 8–42).

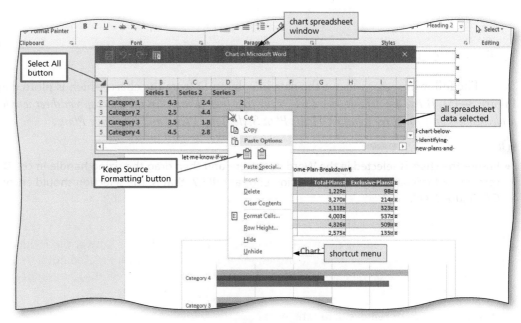

Figure 8–42

5

- Click the 'Keep Source Formatting' button on the shortcut menu to paste the contents of the Clipboard starting in the upper-left corner of the worksheet.

- When Word displays a dialog box indicating that the pasted contents are a different size from the selection, click OK.

Q&A Why did Word display this dialog box?

The source table contains three columns, and the target worksheet has four columns. In the next section, you will delete the fourth column from the chart spreadsheet.

- Resize the chart worksheet window by dragging its window edges and move it by dragging its title bar so the worksheet window appears as shown in Figure 8–43. Notice that the chart in the Word window automatically changes to reflect the new data in the chart worksheet (Figure 8–43).

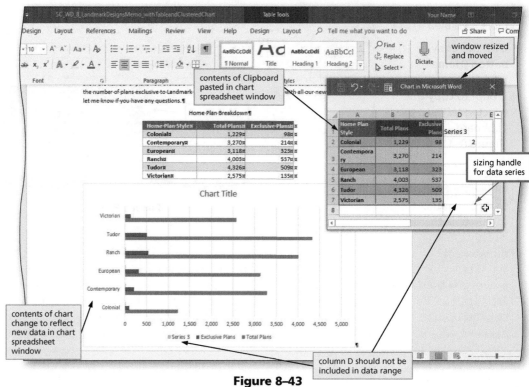

Figure 8–43

To Remove a Data Series from the Chart

The following steps remove the data in column D from the chart, which is plotted as Series 3 (shown in Figure 8–43). *Why? By default, Word selects the first four columns in the chart spreadsheet window. The chart in this project covers only the three columns: Home Plan Style, Total Plans, and Exclusive Plans.*

1

- Ensure the chart is selected in the Word document and then drag the sizing handle in cell D7 of the chart spreadsheet leftward so that the selection ends at cell C7; that is, the selection should encompass cells A1 through C7 (Figure 8–44).

Q&A How would I add a data series?

Add a column of data to the chart spreadsheet. Drag the sizing handle outward to include the series, or you could click the Select Data button (Chart Tools Design tab | Data group), click the Add button (Select Data Source dialog box), click the Select Range button (Edit Series dialog box), drag through the data range in the worksheet, and then click OK.

How would I add or remove data categories?

Follow the same steps to add or remove data series, except work with spreadsheet rows instead of columns.

Figure 8–44

- Close the chart spreadsheet window by clicking its Close button.

Q&A How would I copy an existing chart and paste it with source formatting?

To copy the chart, you would select it and then click the Copy button (Home tab | Clipboard group), or right-click the chart and then click Copy on the shortcut menu, or press CTRL+C. To paste the chart with source formatting, you would position the insertion point at the desired paste location, click the Paste arrow (Home tab | Clipboard group) or right-click the chart, and click the 'Keep Source Formatting' button on the Paste menu or shortcut menu.

Other Ways

1. Click Select Data button (Chart Tools Design tab | Data group), click series to remove (Select Data Source dialog box), click Remove button, click OK

To Apply a Chart Style

The next step is to apply a chart style to the chart. *Why? Word provides a Chart Styles gallery, allowing you to change the chart's format to a more visually appealing style.* The following steps apply a chart style to a chart.

- If necessary, click the chart to select it.

- Display the Chart Tools Design tab.

- Point to Style 8 in the Chart Styles gallery (Chart Tools Design tab | Chart Styles group) to display a Live Preview of that style applied to the graphic in the document (Figure 8–45).

Experiment

- Point to various styles in the Chart Styles gallery and watch the style of the chart change in the document window.

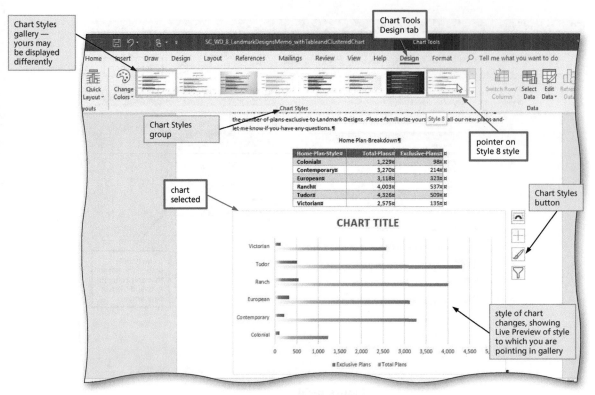

Figure 8–45

2
- Click Style 8 in the Chart Styles gallery (Chart Tools Design tab | Chart Styles group) to apply the selected style to the chart.

Other Ways

1. Click Chart Styles button attached to chart, click Style tab, click desired style

To Change Colors of a Chart

The following steps change the colors of the chart. *Why? Word provides a predefined variety of colors for charts. You select one that best matches the colors already used in the letter.*

1
- With the chart selected, click the Change Colors button (Chart Tools Design tab | Chart Styles group) to display the Change Colors gallery.

Q&A What if the chart is not selected? Click the chart to select it.

- Point to 'Colorful Palette 3' in the Change Colors gallery to display a Live Preview of the selected color applied to the chart in the document (Figure 8–46).

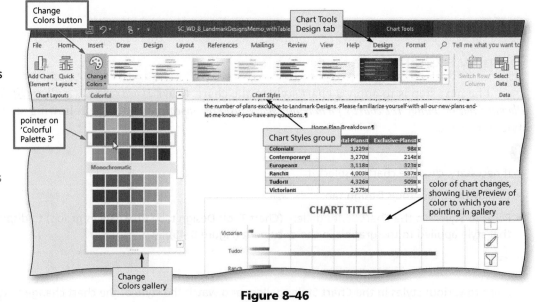

Figure 8–46

Experiment

- Point to various colors in the Change Colors gallery and watch the colors of the chart change in the document window.

2

- Click Colorful Palette 3 in the Change Colors gallery to apply the selected color to the chart.

Other Ways
1. Click Chart Styles button attached to chart, click Color tab, click desired style

To Add a Chart Element

The following steps add minor vertical gridlines to the chart. *Why? You want to add more vertical lines to the chart so that it is easier to see the dollar values associated with each bar length.*

1

- With the chart selected, click the 'Add Chart Element' button (Chart Tools Design tab | Chart Layouts group) to display the Add Chart Element gallery and then point to Gridlines to display the Gridlines submenu (Figure 8–47).

Experiment

- Point to various elements in the Add Chart Element gallery so that you can see the other types of elements you can add to a chart. When finished, point to Gridlines.

Figure 8–47

2

- Click 'Primary Minor Vertical' on the Gridline submenu to add vertical minor gridlines to the chart (Figure 8–48).

Q&A

How would I add data labels to a chart?
Click the 'Add Chart Element' button (Chart Tools Design tab | Chart Layouts group), point to Data Labels, and then click the desired location for the data labels.

How would I remove a chart element?
Select the chart element and then press DELETE.

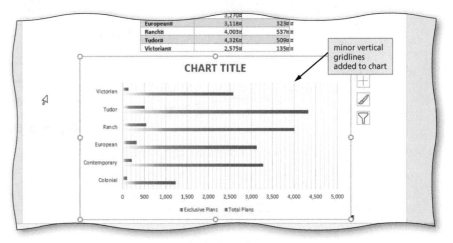

Figure 8–48

To Select a Chart Element and Edit It

The following steps change the chart title. *Why? You want to change the title from the default to a more meaningful name.*

- Display the Chart Tools Format tab.

- With the chart selected, click the Chart Elements arrow (Chart Tools Format tab | Current Selection group) to display the Chart Elements list (Figure 8–49).

Figure 8–49

- Click Chart Title in the Chart Elements list to select the chart's title.

- Type **Total and Exclusive Plan Comparison** as the new title (Figure 8–50).

Q&A

How would I add an axis title to the chart?
Click the 'Add Chart Element' button (Chart Tools Design tab | Chart Layouts group), point to Axis Titles, and then click the desired axis to be titled (Primary Horizontal or Primary Vertical). Click the default axis title added to the chart and then edit it as desired.

How would I add an axis to a chart?
If a chart did not already contain an axis when you created it, you could add one by clicking the 'Add Chart Element' button (Chart Tools Design tab | Chart Layouts group), point to Axis, and then click the desired axis.

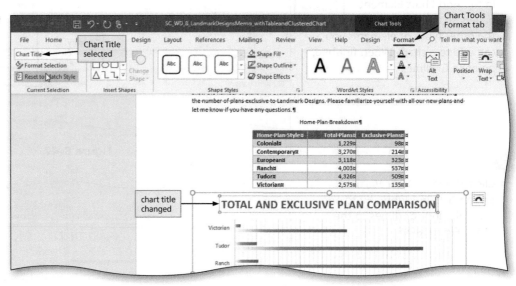

Figure 8–50

Other Ways

1. Click chart element in chart to select element

To Format Chart Elements

Currently, the category names on the vertical axis are in reverse order of the row labels in the table; that is, category names are in alphabetical order from bottom to top and the row labels in the table are in alphabetical order from top to bottom. The following steps format axis elements. *Why? You want the categories to display in the same order as the table, the maximum value on the horizontal axis to be 4,500 instead of 5,000, and the legend to appear at the top of the chart.*

- If necessary, select the chart by clicking it.

- With the chart selected, click the Chart Elements arrow (Chart Tools Format tab | Current Selection group) to display the Chart Elements list and then click 'Vertical (Category) Axis'.

- Click the Chart Elements button attached to the right of the chart to display the Chart Elements gallery.

- Point to and then click the Axes arrow in the Chart Elements gallery to display the Axes fly-out menu (Figure 8–51).

Figure 8–51

- Click More Options on the Axes fly-out menu to open the Format Axis pane.

- If necessary, click the Chart Elements arrow (Chart Tools Format tab | Current Selection group) to display the Chart Elements list and then click 'Vertical (Category) Axis' to select the vertical axis.

- If necessary, click Axis Options in the Format Axis pane to expand the section.

- Place a check mark in the 'Categories in reverse order' check box in the Format Axis pane so that the order of the categories in the chart matches the order of the categories in the table (Figure 8–52).

Q&A | Why did the horizontal axis move from the bottom of the chart to the top?
When you reverse the categories, the horizontal axis automatically moves from the bottom of the chart to the top of the chart. Notice that the series names below the chart also are reversed.

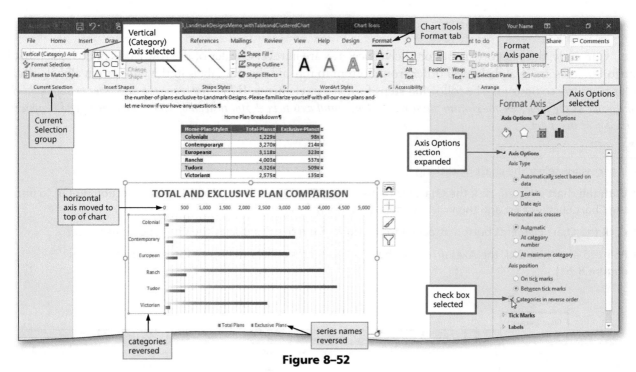

Figure 8–52

3

- With the chart selected, click the Chart Elements arrow (Chart Tools Format tab | Current Selection group) to display the Chart Elements list and then click 'Horizontal (Value) Axis' to select the horizontal axis.

- Change the value in the Maximum box in the Axis Options section from 5000 to 4500 so that the right edge of the chart ends at 4,500.

- If necessary, click Labels at the bottom of the Format Axis pane to expand this section in the pane.

- If necessary, scroll the pane to display the entire Labels section.

- In the Labels section, click the Label Position arrow and then click High to move the axis to the bottom of the chart (Figure 8–53).

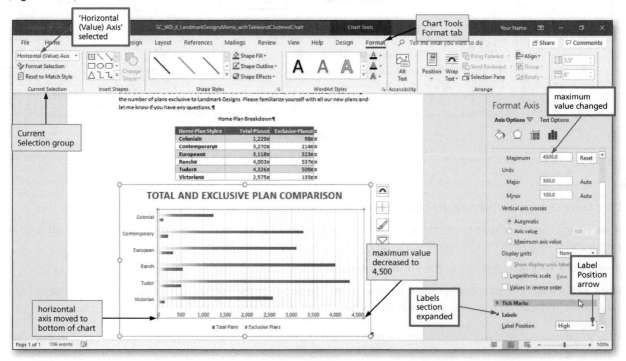

Figure 8–53

Experiment

- Click Number at the bottom of the Format Axis pane to expand this section and review the various number formats you can apply.

4

- With the chart selected, click the Chart Elements arrow (Chart Tools Format tab | Current Selection group) to display the Chart Elements list and then click Legend.

Q&A | What happened to the Format Axis pane?
It now is the Format Legend pane. The pane title and options change, depending on the element you are using or formatting.

- If necessary, click Legend Options to expand the section in the Format Legend pane.

- Click Top to select the option button and move the legend to the top of the chart (Figure 8–54).

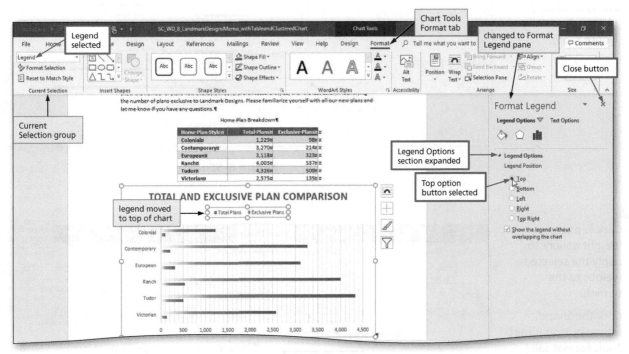

Figure 8–54

5

- Close the Format Legend pane by clicking its Close button.

Q&A | How would I add a legend to a chart?
Click the 'Add Chart Element' button (Chart Tools Design tab | Chart Layouts group), point to Legend, and then click the desired location for the legend.

To Add an Outline to a Chart

The following steps add an outline to the chart with a shadow. *Why? You want a border surrounding the chart.*

1

- With the chart selected, click the Chart Elements arrow (Chart Tools Format tab | Current Selection group) to display the Chart Elements list and then, if necessary, click Chart Area to select the chart area.

- Click the Shape Outline arrow (Chart Tools Format tab | Shape Styles group) to display the Shape Outline gallery.

● Click 'Purple, Accent 4' (eighth color, first row) in the Shape Outline gallery to change the outline color.

● Click the Shape Outline arrow (Chart Tools Format tab | Shape Styles group) again and then point to Weight in the Shape Outline gallery to display the Weight gallery (Figure 8–55).

Figure 8–55

● Click ½ pt in the Weight gallery to apply the selected weight to the outline.

● Click the Shape Effects button (Chart Tools Format tab | Shape Styles group) and then point to Shadow in the Shape Effects gallery to display the Shadow gallery (Figure 8–56).

● Click 'Offset: Bottom Right' in the Shadow gallery to apply the selected shadow to the outline.

● Save the modified memo in the same storage location using the same file name.

Figure 8–56

To Change a Chart Type

The following steps change the chart type. *Why? After reviewing the document, you would like to see how the chart looks as a 3-D clustered bar chart.*

- Display the Chart Tools Design tab.

- Click the 'Change Chart Type' button (Chart Tools Design tab | Type group) to display the Change Chart Type dialog box.

- Click Column in the left pane to change the chart to a column chart.

- Click '3-D Clustered Column' in the right pane (Change Chart Type dialog box) in the right pane to change the chart type (Figure 8–57).

Figure 8–57

Experiment

- Point to the chart preview in the dialog box to see in more detail how the chart will look in the document.

❷

- Click OK to change the chart type (Figure 8–58).

- Click outside the chart to deselect it.

- **sam**⬆ Save the revised memo on your hard drive, OneDrive, or other storage location using the file name, SC_WD_8_LandmarkDesignsMemo_withTableand3-DColumnChart.

Figure 8–58

TO CHART A WORD TABLE USING MICROSOFT GRAPH

BTW

Conserving Ink and Toner

If you want to conserve ink or toner, you can instruct Word to print draft quality documents by clicking File on the ribbon to open Backstage view, clicking Options in Backstage view to display the Word Options dialog box, clicking Advanced in the left pane (Word Options dialog box), scrolling to the Print area in the right pane, placing a check mark in the 'Use draft quality' check box, and then clicking OK. Then, use Backstage view to print the document as usual.

In previous versions of Word, you charted Word tables using an embedded program called Microsoft Graph, or simply Graph. When working with the chart, Graph has its own menus and commands because it is a program embedded in Word. Using Graph commands, you can modify the appearance of the chart after you create it. If you wanted to create a chart using the legacy Graph program, you would perform these steps.

1. Select the rows and columns or table to be charted.

2. Display the Insert tab.

3. Click the Object button (Insert tab | Text group) to display the Object dialog box.

4. If necessary, click the Create New tab (Object dialog box).

5. Scroll to and then select 'Microsoft Graph Chart' in the Object type list to specify the object being inserted.

6. Click OK to run the Microsoft Graph program, which creates a chart of the selected table or selected rows and columns.

To View and Scroll through Documents Side by Side

Word provides a way to display two documents side by side, each in a separate window. By default, the two documents scroll synchronously, that is, together. If necessary, you can turn off synchronous scrolling so that you can scroll through each document individually. The following steps display documents side by side. *Why? You would like to see the how the document with the clustered chart looks alongside the document with the 3-D clustered column chart.*

- Position the insertion point at the top of the document because you want to begin viewing side by side from the top of the documents.

- Open the file called SC_WD_8_LandmarkDesignsMemo_withTableandClusteredChart.docx so that both documents are open in Word.

- Display the View tab (Figure 8–59).

Figure 8–59

2

- Click the 'View Side by Side' button (View tab | Window group) to display each open window side by side (Figure 8–60).

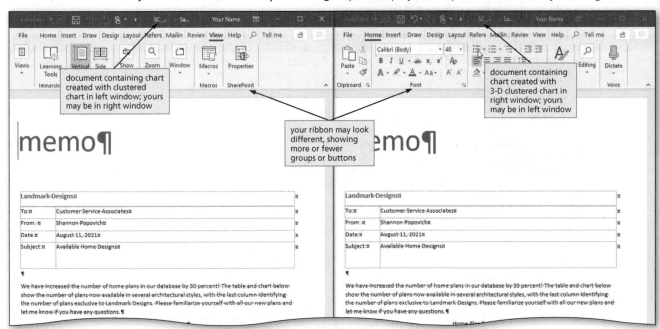

Figure 8–60

3

- If necessary, adjust the zoom to fit the memo contents in each window.
- Scroll to the bottom of one of the windows and notice how both windows (documents) scroll together (Figure 8–61).

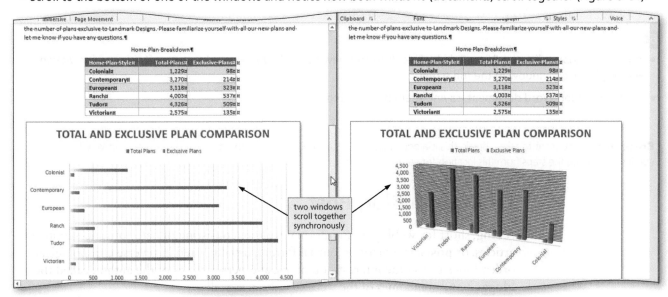

Figure 8–61

Q&A Can I scroll through one window separately from the other?
By default, synchronous scrolling is active when you display windows side by side. If you want to scroll separately through the windows, simply turn off synchronous scrolling.

- If necessary, display the View tab (in either window). (Note that because the ribbons are smaller you may need to click the Window group button first so that the Synchronous Scrolling button is visible.)
- Click the Synchronous Scrolling button (View tab | Window group) to turn off synchronous scrolling.

5

- Scroll to the top of the window on the right and notice that the window on the left does not scroll because you turned off synchronous scrolling (Figure 8–62).

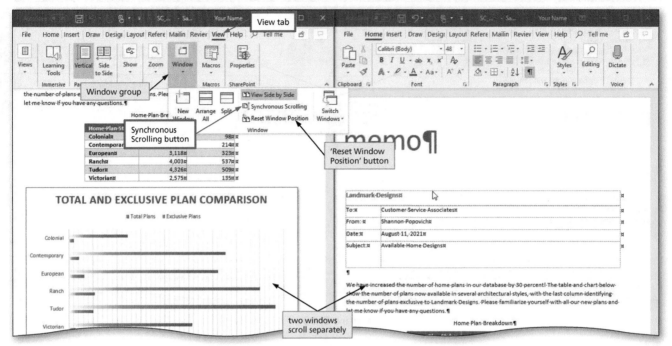

Figure 8–62

What is the purpose of the 'Reset Window Position' button?
It repositions the side-by-side windows so that each consumes the same amount of screen space.

6

- In either window, click the 'View Side by Side' button (View tab | Window group) to turn off side-by-side viewing and display each window in the full screen.

- Close each open Word document, saving them if prompted.

Break Point: If you want to take a break, this is a good place to do so. You can exit Word now. To resume later, start Word and continue following the steps from this location forward.

Creating a Blog Post

A **blog**, short for **weblog**, is an informal website consisting of date- or time-stamped articles, or **posts**, in a diary or journal format, usually listed in reverse chronological order. Blogs reflect the interests, opinions, and personalities of the author, called the **blogger**, and sometimes of the website visitors as well.

Blogs have become an important means of worldwide communications. Businesses create blogs to communicate with employees, customers, and vendors. Teachers create blogs to collaborate with other teachers and students, and home users create blogs to share aspects of their personal life with family, friends, and others.

This section of the module creates a blog post and then publishes it to a registered blog account at WordPress, which is a blogging service on the web. The blog relays current events for the employees of Landmark Designs. This specific blog post is a communication about the upcoming events.

What should you consider when creating and posting on a blog?

When creating a blog post, you should follow these general guidelines:

1. **Create a blog account on the web.** Many websites exist that allow users to set up a blog free or for a fee. Blogging services that work with Word 2019 include SharePoint blog, Telligent Community, TypePad, and WordPress. For illustration purposes in this module, a free blog account was created at WordPress.com.

2. **Register your blog account in Word.** Before you can use Word to publish a blog post, you must register your blog account in Word. This step establishes a connection between Word and your blog account. The first time you create a new blog post, Word will ask if you want to register a blog account. You can click the Register Later button if you want to learn how to create a blog post without registering a blog account.

3. **Create a blog post.** Use Word to enter the text and any graphics in your blog post. Some blogging services accept graphics directly from a Word blog post. Others require that you use a picture hosting service to store pictures you use in a blog post.

4. **Publish a blog post.** When you publish a blog post, the blog post in the Word document is copied to your account at the blogging service. Once the post is published, it appears at the top of the blog webpage. You may need to click the Refresh button in the browser window to display the new post.

TO REGISTER A BLOG ACCOUNT

Once you set up a blog account with a blog provider, you must register it in Word so that you can publish your Word post on the blog account. If you wanted to register a blog account, with WordPress for example, you would perform the following steps.

1. Click the Manage Accounts button (Blog Post tab | Blog group) to display the Blog Accounts dialog box.

2. Click the New button (Blog Accounts dialog box) to display the New Blog Account dialog box.

3. Click the Blog arrow (New Blog Account dialog box) to display a list of blog providers and then select your provider in the list.

4. Click the Next button to display the New [Provider] Account dialog box (i.e., a New WordPress Account dialog box would appear if you selected WordPress as the provider).

5. In the Blog Post URL text box, replace the <Enter your blog URL here> text with the web address for your blog account. (Note that your dialog box may differ, depending on the provider you select.)

Q&A | **What is a URL?**
A URL (Uniform Resource Locator), often called a web address, is the unique address for a webpage. For example, the web address for a WordPress blog account might be smith.wordpress.com; in that case, the complete blog post URL would read as http://smith.wordpress.com/xhlrpc.php in the text box.

6. In the Enter account information area, enter the user name and password you use to access your blog account.

Q&A | **Should I click the Remember Password check box?**
If you do not select this check box, Word will prompt you for a password each time you publish to the blog account.

7. If your blog provider does not allow pictures to be stored, click the Picture Options button, select the correct option for storing your posted pictures, and then click OK (Picture Options dialog box).

8. Click OK to register the blog account.

9. When Word displays a dialog box indicating the account registration was successful, click OK.

To Create a Blank Document for a Blog Post

The following steps create a new blank Word document for a blog post. **Why?** *Word provides a blog post template you can use to create a blank blog post document.*

1

- Open Backstage view.

- Click New in Backstage view to display the New screen.

- Click the Blog post thumbnail to select the template and display it in a preview window (Figure 8–63).

Figure 8–63

2

- Click the Create button in the preview window to create a new document based on the selected template (Figure 8–64). If necessary, adjust the zoom so that the text is readable on the screen.

Figure 8–64

Q&A What if a Register a Blog Account dialog box appears?

Click the Register Later button to skip the registration process at this time. Or, if you have a blog account, you can click the Register Now button and follow the instructions to register your account.

Why did the ribbon change?

When creating a blog post, the ribbon in Word changes to display only the tabs required to create and publish a blog post.

To Enter Text

The next step is to enter the blog post title and text in the blog post. The following steps enter text in the blog post.

1 Click the 'Enter Post Title Here' content control and then type **Appreciation Events** as the blog title.

2 Position the insertion point below the horizontal line and then type these two lines of text, pressing ENTER at end of each sentence (Figure 8–65):

Thank you to everyone for helping our organization realize an increase in revenue during the second quarter!

See the following calendar for key dates, including appreciation events!

Figure 8–65

Q&A

Can I format text in the blog post?

Yes, you can use the Basic Text and other groups on the ribbon to format the post. You also can check spelling using the Proofing group.

To Insert a Quick Table

Word provides several quick tables, which are preformatted table styles that you can customize. Calendar formats are one type of quick table. The following steps insert a calendar in the blog. **Why?** *You will post the upcoming key dates in the calendar.*

1

- Display the Insert tab.

- With the insertion point positioned as shown in Figure 8–65, click the Table button (Insert tab | Tables group) to display the Table gallery.

- Point to Quick Tables in the Table gallery to display the Quick Tables gallery (Figure 8–66).

Figure 8–66

2
- Click Calendar 2 in the Quick Tables gallery to insert the selected Quick Table in the document at the location of the insertion point (Figure 8–67).

Figure 8–67

To Edit and Format a Table

The calendar in the blog post should show the month of September with a first day of the month starting on Wednesday. The following steps edit the table and apply a quick style.

1 Change the month in the first cell of the table from May to September.

2 Edit the contents of the cells in the table so that the first day of the month starts on a Wednesday and the 30 (the last day of the month) is on a Thursday.

3 Enter the text in the appropriate cells for September 1, 7, 16, and 22, as shown in Figure 8–68.

4 If necessary, display the Table Tools Design tab.

5 Remove the check mark from the First Column check box (Table Tools Design tab | Table Style Options group) because you do not want the first column in the table formatted differently.

6 Apply the 'Grid Table 1 Light - Accent 6' table style to the table.

7 If necessary, left-align the heading and resize the table column widths to 1".

8 Make any other necessary adjustments so that the table appears as shown in Figure 8–68.

9 Save the blog on your hard drive, OneDrive, or other storage location using SC_WD_8_LandmarkDesignsBlog as the file name.

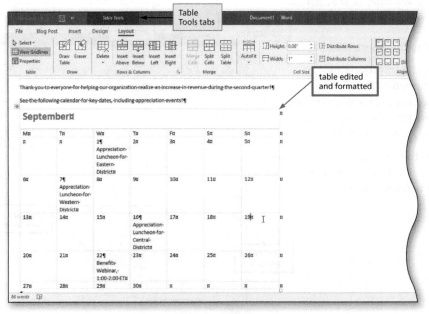

Figure 8–68

Note: If you have not registered a blog account, read the next series of steps without performing them.

To Publish a Blog Post

The following step publishes the blog post. *Why? Publishing the blog post places the post at the top of the webpage associated with this blog account.*

- Display the Blog Post tab.

- Click the Publish button (Blog Post tab | Blog group), which causes Word to display a brief message that it is contacting the blog provider and then display a message on the screen that the post was published (Figure 8–69).

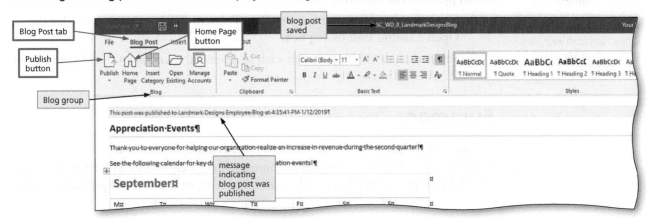

Figure 8–69

To Display a Blog Webpage in a Browser Window

The following steps display the current blog account's webpage in a browser window. *Why? You can view a blog account associated with Word if you want to verify a post was successful.*

- Click the Home Page button (Blog Post tab | Blog group) (shown in Figure 8–69), which starts the default browser (Microsoft Edge, in this case) and displays the webpage associated with the registered blog account in the browser window. You may need to click the Refresh button in your browser window to display the most current webpage contents (Figure 8–70).

Figure 8–70

What if the wrong webpage is displayed?
You may have multiple blog accounts registered with Word. To select a different blog account registered with Word, switch back to Word, click the Manage Accounts button (Blog Post tab | Blog group), click the desired account (Blog Accounts dialog box), and then click the Close button. Then, repeat Step 1.

2

- Exit both the browser and Word.

BTW

Deleting Blog Posts
If you want to delete a blog post from your blog account, sign in to your blog account and then follow the instructions from your blog provider to delete a post from your blog.

To Open an Existing Blog Post

If you wanted to open an existing blog post to modify or view it in Word, you would perform the following steps.

1. Click the Open Existing button (Blog Post tab | Blog group) to display the Open Existing Post dialog box.
2. Select the title of the post you wish to open and then click OK (Open Existing Post dialog box).

Summary

In this module, you have learned how to track changes, review tracked changes, compare documents and combine documents, link or embed an Excel worksheet to a Word document, chart a table and format the chart, and create and publish a blog post.

CONSIDER THIS: PLAN AHEAD

What decisions will you need to make when creating documents to share or publish?
Use these guidelines as you complete the assignments in this module and create your own shared documents outside of this class.

1. If sharing documents, be certain received files and copied objects are virus free.

   a) Do not open files created by others until you are certain they do not contain a virus or other malicious program (malware).

   b) Use an antivirus program to verify that any files you use are free of viruses and other potentially harmful programs.

2. If necessary, determine how to copy an object.

   a) Your intended use of the Word document will help determine the best method for copying the object: copy and paste, embed, or link.

3. Enhance a document with appropriate visuals.

   a) Use visuals to add interest, clarify ideas, and illustrate points. Visuals include tables, charts, and graphical images (i.e., pictures).

4. If desired, post communications on a blog.

BTW

Distributing a Document
Instead of printing and distributing a hard copy of a document, you can distribute the document electronically. Options include sending the document via email; posting it on cloud storage (such as OneDrive) and sharing the file with others; posting it on social media, a blog, or other website; and sharing a link associated with an online location of the document. You also can create and share a PDF or XPS image of the document, so that users can view the file in Adobe Reader or XPS Viewer instead of in Word.

Apply Your Knowledge

Reinforce the skills and apply the concepts you learned in this module.

Collaborating with Tracked Changes and Other Tools

Note: To complete this assignment, you will be required to use the Data Files. Please contact your instructor for information about accessing the Data Files.

Instructions: Start Word. Open the document, SC_WD_8-4.docx, which is located in the Data Files. Written by the public relations coordinator at Galewood Financial, the document contains tips to prevent identity theft. You are to review the document before it is finalized for customers.

Perform the following tasks:

1. Click File on the ribbon and then click Save As and save the document using the new file name, SC_WD_8_IdentityTheft_Reviewed.

2. If necessary, customize the status bar so that it displays the Track Changes indicator.

3. Enable (turn on) tracked changes.

4. If requested by your instructor, change the user name and initials so that your name and initials are displayed in the tracked changes.

5. Open the Reviewing pane. How many tracked changes are in the document? Close the Reviewing pane.

6. Change the 'Display for Review' box (Review tab | Tracking group) to Simple Markup and then notice how the screen appears. Change it to No Markup and then Original and notice the how the screen appears. Change it to All Markup for the remainder of this exercise.

7. Click the Show Markup button (Review tab | Tracking group) and be sure these types of markup are selected so that they show when tracking changes: Insertions and Deletions, and Formatting.

8. Show revisions in balloons. (*Hint*: Use the Show Markup button (Review tab | Tracking group).) Show only comments and formatting in balloons. Finally, show all revisions inline.

9. With the insertion point at the top of the document, use the Next button (Review tab | Changes group) to go to the first tracked change in the document. Use the same button to go to the next tracked change. Use the Previous button (Review tab | Changes group) to go to the previous tracked change.

10. Keep the tracked changes currently in the document. Track the changes shown in Figure 8–71 as additional tracked changes in the document. What color are the two markups that were in the original document? What color are the additional markups that you tracked in this step?

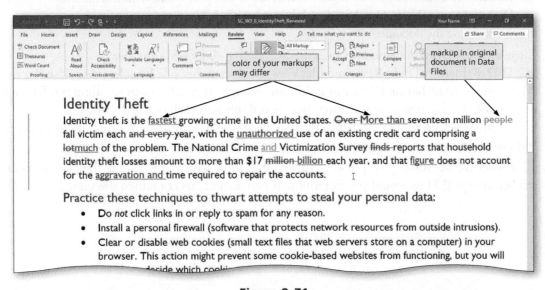

Figure 8–71

Continued >

11. Save the reviewed document with the tracked changes again with the same name and then submit it in the format specified by your instructor.

12. Lock tracked changes in the document — do not enter a password in the dialog box. (*Hint*: Use the Track Changes button (Review tab | Tracking group).) What happens to the Track Changes button when you lock tracked changes? Unlock tracked changes.

13. Print the document with tracked changes.

14. Click File on the ribbon and then click Save As and save the document using the new file name, SC_WD_8_IdentityTheft_Final.

15. Show only your tracked changes in the document. Show all users' tracked changes in the document.

16. Hide tracked insertions and deletions. (*Hint*: Click the Show Markup button (Review tab | Tracking group).) Show tracked insertions and deletions.

17. Reject the tracked change in the document that deleted the word, people.

18. Reject the tracked change in the document that inserted the word, and.

19. Accept the tracked change in the document that inserted the word, fastest.

20. Accept the tracked change in the document that deleted the word, finds.

21. Accept all the remaining tracked changes in the document.

22. Disable (turn off) tracked changes. Remove the Track Changes indicator from the status bar.

23. If requested by your instructor, add your name in the header of the document as a document property. (*Hint*: Use the Document Info button (Header & Footer Tools Design tab | Insert group).)

24. Save the final document again with the same name and then submit it in the format specified by your instructor. Close the document.

25. Compare the SC_WD_8-4.docx file (original document) with the SC_WD_8_IdentityTheft_Final file (revised document) into a new document. In the Compare Result window, hide source documents. (*Hint*: Click the Compare button (Review tab | Compare group).) In the Compare Result window, show both source documents. Save the compare result with the file name SC_WD_8_IdentityTheft_Compared and then submit it in the format specified by your instructor. Close the document.

26. Combine the SC_WD_8-4.docx file (original document) with the SC_WD_8_IdentityTheft_Final file (revised document) into a new document. Save the compare result with the file name SC_WD_8_IdentityTheft_Combined and then submit it in the format specified by your instructor. Close the document.

27. Close all open Word documents. Open the SC_WD_8-4.docx file and the SC_WD_8_IdentityTheft_Reviewed file. View the documents side by side. (*Hint*: Use the 'View Side by Side' button (View tab | Window group).) If synchronous scrolling is off, turn it on to scroll the documents at the same time. Scroll through each of the documents. Turn synchronous scrolling off. Scroll through each of the documents. Close both documents and exit Word.

28. ✸ Answer the questions posed in #5, #10, and #12. How would you change the color of your tracked changes? How would you determine if two documents contained the same content?

Extend Your Knowledge

Extend the skills you learned in this module and experiment with new skills. You may need to use Help to complete the assignment.

Working with Charts

Note: To complete this assignment, you will be required to use the Data Files. Please contact your instructor for information about accessing the Data Files.

Instructions: Start Word. Open the document, SC_WD_8-5.docx, which is located in the Data Files. The document is a memo draft, written to the district superintendent at Cherry Hill Schools from the office manager about elementary school enrollment. You are to chart the Word table in the memo using Word's charting tools. You also create another similar memo using an Excel table.

Perform the following tasks:

1. Use Help to learn more about charts in Word, linking objects, and embedding objects.

2. Click File on the ribbon and then click Save As and save the document using the new file name, SC_WD_8_SchoolEnrollmentsMemo.

3. Insert a Line with Markers chart on the centered paragraph below the table. In the document window, select the bottom five rows in the table (do not copy the table title row) and then copy the selected rows. In the chart spreadsheet window, select the entire worksheet and then paste the contents with source formatting.

4. Resize the chart spreadsheet window to display all its data. Remove the Series 3 data series from the chart spreadsheet window by dragging the sizing handle.

5. Resize the column headings in the chart spreadsheet window by dragging their borders. Close the chart spreadsheet window.

6. Remove the primary horizontal axis chart element from the chart by using the 'Add Chart Element' button (Chart Tools Design tab | Chart Layouts group). Use the same procedure to add the horizontal axis back to the chart.

7. Remove the legend chart element from the chart by using the 'Add Chart Element' button (Chart Tools Design tab | Chart Layouts group). Use the same procedure to add the legend back to bottom of the chart.

8. Select the vertical (value) axis chart element. (*Hint*: Use the Current Selection group in the Chart Tools Format tab.) Click the Format Selection button to open the Format Axis pane. Change the value in the Minimum box in the Axis Options section to 250 and the value in the Maximum box to 550.

9. Add data labels to the chart so they appear above each point (Figure 8–72). (*Hint*: Use the 'Add Chart Element' button (Chart Tools Design tab | Chart Layouts group).)

10. Change the value of the Elwood Elementary current enrollment from 443 to 453 using the Edit Data button (Chart Tools Design tab | Data group). (Note that the change may not occur immediately in the chart.) Change the value in the table in the Word document also.

11. Change the chart style to a style of your choice. (*Hint*: Use the Chart Tools Design tab.)

12. Change the colors of the chart to colors of your choice.

13. Change the position of the chart legend to a location of your choice. (*Hint*: Use the 'Add Chart Element' button (Chart Tools Design tab | Chart Layouts group).)

14. Remove the chart title from the chart by using the 'Add Chart Element' button (Chart Tools Design tab | Chart Layouts group). Use the same procedure to add the chart title back to the chart. Select the chart title and enter appropriate text as the chart title.

Continued >

Extend Your Knowledge *continued*

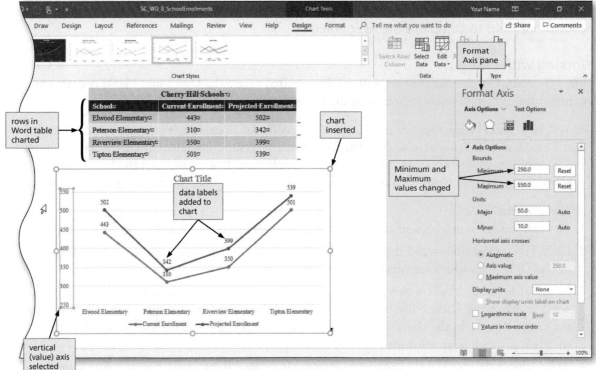

Figure 8–72

15. Add a vertical axis title with the text, Number of Students. (*Hint*: Use the 'Add Chart Element' button (Chart Tools Design tab | Chart Layouts group).) Remove the outline from around the vertical axis title using the Shape Outline button (Chart Tools Format tab | Shape Styles group).

16. Add an outline of your choice to border the chart.

17. Save the document again with the same name and then submit it in the format specified by your instructor.

18. Copy the chart. Create a new document window and then paste the chart using source formatting (and embed the workbook).

19. Change the chart type to a bar chart.

20. Use the chart spreadsheet window to add this row of data to the chart: Westside Elementary, 401 for current enrollment, and 439 for projected enrollment. Be sure to drag the sizing handle to include the newly added row of data.

21. Select the vertical axis and then open the Format Axis pane. Select the 'Categories in reverse order' check box.

22. Remove the horizontal axis title. Remove the horizontal axis chart element.

23. Make any additional changes you feel appropriate for the chart.

24. Save the revised chart document using the file name, SC_WD_8_SchoolEnrollmentsBarChart. Submit the document in the format specified by your instructor.

25. If you have Excel and your instructor requests, perform the following steps:

    a. Open the document, SC_WD_8-6.docx, which is located in the Data Files. Click File on the ribbon and then click Save As and save the document using the new file name, SC_WD_8_SchoolEnrollmentsMemo_with ExcelTable.

    b. Start Excel and open the workbook, SC_WD_8-7.xlsx, which is located in the Data Files. In Excel, copy the table (the cells in the range A1 through C5). Click File on the ribbon and then click Save As and save the workbook using the new file name, SC_WD_8_SchoolEnrollmentsTable.

c. In Word, on the blank line below the paragraph, insert the copied object (Excel table) by using the 'Keep Source Formatting' button on the Paste menu. Change one of the enrollment values and notice that you edit the inserted object as you edit any other Word element. Delete the copied table.

d. In Word, on the blank line below the paragraph, embed the copied object (Excel table) by clicking Paste Special on the Paste menu, clicking 'Microsoft Excel Worksheet Object' (Paste Special dialog box), and then clicking OK. Try changing one of the enrollment values. Notice that you cannot because the Excel table is embedded. Double-click the embedded table to open an Excel window in the Word window. Change one of the enrollment values in the embedded Excel window. Click outside the embedded Excel window to close it and notice the value changes in the embedded table. Delete the embedded table.

e. In Excel, copy the table (the cells in the range A1 through C5) again. In Word, on the blank line below the paragraph, link the copied object (Excel table) by using the 'Link & Keep Source Formatting' button on the Paste menu.

   i. In Excel, change the Elwood Elementary current enrollment from 443 to 453. Save the modified workbook in Excel. In Word, right-click the linked Excel table and then click Update Link on the shortcut menu to update the linked Excel object in Word.

   ii. Center the linked table. Copy the linked table.

   iii. Insert a chart of your choice of the linked table. Format the chart appropriately.

   iv. In Excel, change the Tipton Elementary projected enrollment from 539 to 545. Save the modified workbook in Excel. In Word, right-click the linked Excel table and then click Update Link on the shortcut menu to update the linked Excel object in Word.

   v. Edit the chart data using the Edit Data button (Chart Tools Design tab | Data group) and then change the Tipton Elementary projected enrollment from 539 to 545 in the chart spreadsheet window.

   vi. Break the link between the Excel table in the Word document and the Excel worksheet in the Excel workbook. If necessary, center the table in the Word document.

   vii. Save the document again with the same name and then submit it in the format specified by your instructor. Exit Word and Excel, closing any open documents.

26. ✳ Which chart color and styles did you use in this assignment? Why?

Expand Your World

Create a solution that uses cloud or web technologies by learning and investigating on your own from general guidance.

Creating a Blog Account Using a Blogger Service

Instructions: As a data analyst at Bradford Communications, you have been asked to create a blog account so that blog posts can be used to communicate with managers and staff. You research a variety of blogging services and select one for use.

Note: You will use a blog account, many of which you can create at no cost, to complete this assignment. If you do not want to create a blog account, perform the first step and then read the remaining steps in this assignment without performing them.

Perform the following tasks:

1. In Word, create the blog post shown in Figure 8–73. Insert a Quick Table using the tabular list option. Delete two rows from the table. Edit the data and format the table as shown in the figure. Save the blog file using the file name, SC_WD_8_InternetSubscriberBlog.

Continued >

Expand Your World *continued*

2. Start a browser. Research these blogging services: SharePoint blog, Telligent Community, TypePad, and WordPress.

3. Navigate to the blogger service with which you want to set up an account and then follow the instructions to set up an account.

4. Set up your blog in the blogger service.

5. In Word, register your blog account (refer to the section in this module titled To Register a Blog Account).

Figure 8–73

6. In Word, publish your blog post to your account.

7. ☀ Which blogger service did you select and why? Would you recommend this blogger service? Why or why not?

In the Lab

Design and implement a solution using creative thinking and problem-solving skills.

Create a Sales Summary Memo with a Table and Chart for an Office Supply Retailer
Problem: As an accounting associate director of Sunlight Office Supplies, you have been asked to create a memo to sales managers showing the second quarter sales figures by category. The memo should contain a table and chart.

Part 1: You are to create a memo to sales managers with a subject of Second Quarter Sales. Use today's date.

The wording for the text in the memo is as follows: Second quarter sales figures have been compiled. The table and chart below show sales by category for the second quarter.

The data for the table is as follows:
- technology: April $125,217, May $113,268, June $114,839
- paper: April $23,546, May $14,687, June $19,983
- office supplies: April $22,658, May $23,821, June $22,034
- breakroom supplies: April $9,302, May $8,843, June $8,001

Create a chart of all table data.

Use the concepts and techniques presented in this module to create and format the memo and its text, table, and chart. Be sure to check the spelling and grammar of the finished memo. When you are finished with the memo, save it with the file name, SC_WD_8_SalesMemo. Submit your assignment and answers to the Part 2 critical thinking questions in the format specified by your instructor.

Part 2: ☀ You made several decisions while creating the memo in this assignment: whether to use a memo template or create a memo from scratch, and how to organize and format the memo, table, and chart (fonts, font sizes, colors, shading, styles, etc.). What was the rationale behind each of these decisions? When you proofread the document, what further revisions did you make and why?

9 | Creating a Reference Document

Objectives

After completing this module, you will be able to:

- Insert a screenshot
- Add and modify a caption
- Insert a cross-reference
- Insert and link text boxes
- Compress pictures
- Work in Outline view
- Work with a master document and subdocuments

- Insert a symbol
- Insert and modify a table of contents
- Use the Navigation Pane
- Insert and update a table of figures
- Insert, modify, and update an index
- Specify different odd and even page footers
- Insert bookmarks

Introduction

During the course of your academic studies and professional activities, you may find it necessary to compose a document that is many pages or even hundreds of pages in length. When composing a long document, you must ensure that the document is organized so that a reader easily can locate material in that document. Sometimes a document of this nature is called a reference document.

Project: Reference Document

A **reference document** is any multipage document organized so that users easily can locate material and navigate through the document. Examples of reference documents include user guides, term papers, pamphlets, manuals, proposals, and plans.

The project in this module uses Word to produce the reference document shown in Figure 9–1. This reference document, titled *Using Word 2019*, is a multipage guide that is distributed by the Information Resource Center at Wilmington College to students and staff. Notice that the inner margin between facing pages has extra space to allow duplicated copies of the document to be bound (i.e., stapled or fastened in some manner) — without the binding covering the words.

The *Using Word 2019* reference document begins with a cover page designed to entice the target audience to open the document and read it. Next is the copyright page, followed by the table of contents. The document then describes how to insert four types of images in a Word document: online image, picture from a file, shape, and screenshot. The end of this reference document has a table of figures and an index to assist readers in locating information contained within the document. A miniature version of the *Using Word 2019* reference document is shown in Figure 9–1.

The section of the *Using Word 2019* reference document that is titled Inserting Images in Word Documents is a document that you create from a draft. The draft of this document is located in the Data Files. Please contact your instructor for information about accessing the Data Files. After editing content in the draft document, you will incorporate a final version in the reference document.

You will perform the following general tasks as you progress through this module:

1. Modify a draft of a document.
2. Create a master document with a subdocument for the reference document.
3. Organize the reference document.

To Start Word and Specify Settings

If you are using a computer to step through the project in this module and you want your screens to match the figures in this book, you should change your screen's resolution to 1366 × 768. The following steps start Word and verify ruler and Mouse mode settings.

1 Start Word and create a blank document in the Word window. If necessary, maximize the Word window.

2 If the Print Layout button on the status bar is not selected, click it so that your screen is in Print Layout view.

3 Verify that the Ruler check box (View tab | Show group) is not selected. (If it is selected, click it to remove the check mark because you do not want the rulers to appear on the screen.)

4 If you are using a mouse and you want your screens to match the figures in the book, verify that you are using Mouse mode by clicking the Touch/Mouse Mode button on the Quick Access Toolbar and then, if necessary, clicking Mouse on the menu. (If your Quick Access Toolbar does not display the Touch/Mouse Mode button, click the 'Customize Quick Access Toolbar' button on the Quick Access Toolbar and then click Touch/Mouse Mode on the menu to add the button to the Quick Access Toolbar.)

BTW
Touch Mode
Differences
The Office and Windows interfaces may vary if you are using Touch mode. For this reason, you might notice that the function or appearance of your touch screen differs slightly from this module's presentation.

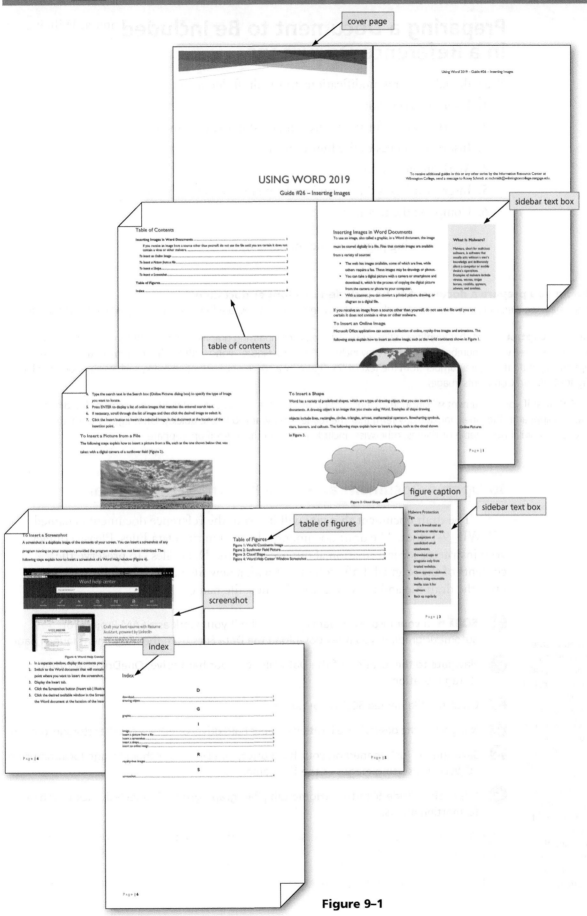

Figure 9–1

Preparing a Document to Be Included in a Reference Document

You will make several modifications to the draft document:

1. Insert a screenshot.
2. Insert captions for the figures (images) in the document.
3. Insert references to the figures in the text.
4. Mark an index entry.
5. Insert text boxes that contain information about malware.
6. Compress the pictures.

The following pages outline these changes.

How should you prepare a document to be included in a longer document?

Ensure that reference elements in a document, such as captions and index entries, are formatted properly and entered consistently.

- **Captions:** A **caption** is text that identifies, titles, or explains an accompanying graphic, figure, or photo. If the figure, for example, is identified with a number, the caption may include the word, Figure, along with the figure number (i.e., Figure 1). In the caption, separate the figure number from the text of the figure by a space or punctuation mark, such as a period or colon (i.e., Figure 1: World Continents Image).

- **Index Entries:** If your document will include an index, read through the document and mark any terms or headings that you want to appear in the index. Include any term that the reader may want to locate quickly. Omit figures from index entries if the document will have a table of figures; otherwise, include figures in the index if appropriate.

To Open a Document and Save It with a New File Name

The draft document that you will insert in the reference document is named SC_WD_9-1.docx. The draft document is located in the Data Files. Please contact your instructor for information about accessing the Data Files. To preserve the contents of the original draft, you save it with a new file name. The following steps open the draft file and then save it with a new file name.

BTW
Protected View
To keep your computer safe from potentially dangerous files, Word may automatically open certain files in Protected view, which is a restricted mode. To see the Protected view settings, click File on the ribbon to open Backstage view, click Options to display the Word Options dialog box, click Trust Center in the left pane (Word Options dialog box), click the 'Trust Center Settings' button in the right pane to display the Trust Center dialog box, and then click Protected View in the left pane to show the current Protected view settings.

1 **sam** ↓ If your instructor wants you to submit your work as a SAM Project for automatic grading, you must download the Data Files from the assignment launch page.

2 Navigate to the location of the Data Files on your hard drive, OneDrive, or other storage location.

3 Open the file named SC_WD_9-1.docx.

4 Navigate to the desired save location on your hard drive, OneDrive, or other storage location.

5 Save the file just opened on your hard drive, OneDrive, or other storage location using SC_WD_9_InsertingImages as the file name.

6 If the 'Show/Hide ¶' button (Home tab | Paragraph group) is selected, click it to hide formatting marks.

Q&A What if some formatting marks still appear after I click the 'Show/Hide ¶' button? Open Backstage view, click Options to display the Word Options dialog box, click Display in the left pane (Word Options dialog box), remove the check mark from the Hidden text check box, and then click OK.

7 Display the View tab and then click the Multiple Pages button (View tab | Zoom group) to display multiple pages in the document window; if necessary, use the Zoom slider to adjust the zoom so that all four pages are visible in the document window at once (Figure 9–2).

Note: To help you locate screen elements that are referenced in the step instructions, such as buttons and commands, this book uses red boxes to point to these screen elements.

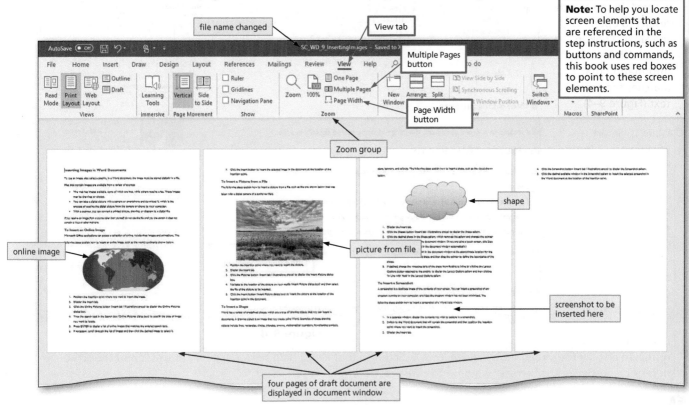

Figure 9–2

8 When you have finished viewing the document, click the Page Width button (View tab | Zoom group) to display the document as wide as possible in the document window.

To Insert a Screenshot

A **screenshot** is a duplicate image of the contents of your computer or mobile device's screen or active window. The current document is missing a screenshot of a Word help center window. To insert a screenshot, you first must display the screen for which you want a screenshot in a window on your computer or mobile device. **Why?** *From within Word, you can insert a screenshot of any app running on your computer, provided the app has not been minimized.* You then can resize or position the inserted screenshot as you do any other Word object. The following steps insert a screenshot in a document.

1

• Type **Word help center** in the Tell Me box to display search results (Figure 9–3).

Figure 9–3

* Click 'Smart Lookup on "Word help center"' in the search results to open the Smart Lookup pane with links to information that matches the search text (Figure 9–4).

Q&A What if 'Smart Lookup on "Word help center"' does not appear in my search results?
Press ESC to close the search results. Open a browser window, search for the text, office support word help center, and then click the appropriate link in the search results to display the screen shown in Figure 9–5. Scroll so that Word help center appears at the top of the screen; if necessary, maximize the browser window. Skip the rest of these steps.

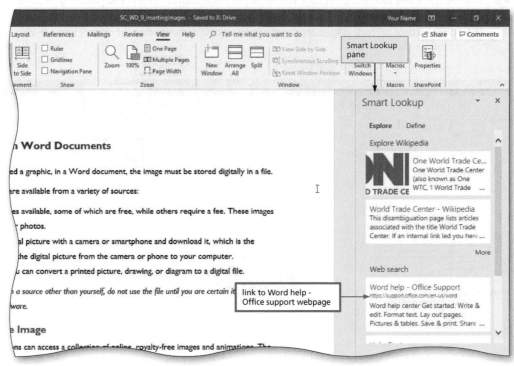

Figure 9–4

3

* Click the link to 'Word help - Office Support' in the Smart Lookup pane to open a browser window with the associated webpage displayed and then scroll so that Word help center appears at the top of the screen; if necessary, maximize the browser window (Figure 9–5).

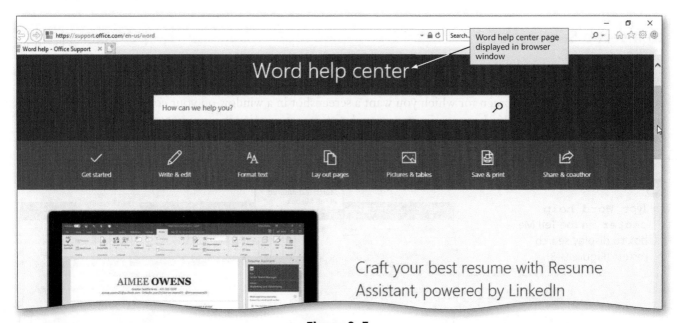

Figure 9–5

Q&A What if I do not have access to the Internet or the correct webpage does not appear?
The screenshot is located in the Data Files. You can click the Pictures button (Insert tab | Illustrations group), navigate to the file called Support_WD_9_WordHelpCenterWindow.tif in the Data Files, and then click the Insert button (Insert Picture dialog box). Close the Smart Lookup pane and then skip the rest of these steps.

- Leave the browser window open, switch to the Word window, close the Smart Lookup pane, and position the insertion point in the document where the screenshot should be inserted (in this case, on the centered blank line above the numbered list in the To Insert a Screenshot section at the bottom of the document).

- Display the Insert tab.

- Click the Screenshot button (Insert tab | Illustrations group) to display the Screenshot gallery (Figure 9–6).

Q&A

What is a screen clipping?

A screen clipping is a section of a window. When you select Screen Clipping in the Screenshot gallery, the window turns opaque so that you can drag through the part of the window to be included in the document.

Figure 9–6

Why does my Screenshot gallery show more windows?

You have additional programs running on your desktop, and their windows are not minimized.

- Click the Word help center window screenshot in the Screenshot gallery to insert the selected screenshot in the Word document at the location of the insertion point. (If a dialog box appears about hyperlinking the screenshot, click No.)

- Verify that the values in the Shape Height and Shape Width boxes (Picture Tools Format tab | Size group) are approximately 3.5" tall by 6.5" wide (Figure 9–7).

Q&A

Why can I not set the exact measurements shown above?

You may need to click the Size Dialog Box Launcher (Picture Tools Format tab | Size group) to display the Size sheet in the Layout dialog box and then remove the checkmark from the 'Lock aspect ratio' check box.

Figure 9–7

Why did the screenshot appear on a new page?

The screenshot is too tall to fit at the bottom of page 3.

To Insert a Caption

In Word, you can insert a caption for an equation, a figure, and a table. If you move, delete, or insert captions in a document, Word renumbers remaining captions in the document automatically. In this reference document, the captions contain the word, Figure, followed by the figure number, a colon, and a figure description. The following steps insert a caption for an image, specifically, the screenshot. *Why? The current document contains four images: an image from an online source, a picture from a file, a shape, and a screenshot. All of these images should have captions.*

1

- If the screenshot is not selected already, click it to select the image on which you want a caption.

- Display the References tab.

- Click the Insert Caption button (References tab | Captions group) to display the Caption dialog box with a figure number automatically assigned to the selected image (Figure 9–8).

Q&A Why is the figure number a 1?
No other captions have been assigned in this document yet. When you insert a new caption, or move or delete items containing captions, Word automatically updates caption numbers throughout the document.

What if the Caption text box has the label Table or Equation instead of Figure?
Click the Label arrow (Caption dialog box) and then click Figure in the Label list.

Figure 9–8

2

- Press the COLON key (:) and then press SPACEBAR in the Caption text box (Caption dialog box) to place separating characters between the figure number and description.

- Type **Help Center Window Screenshot** as the figure description (Figure 9–9).

Q&A Can I change the format of the caption number?
Yes, click the Numbering button (Caption dialog box), adjust the format as desired, and then click OK.

Figure 9–9

- Click OK to insert the caption below the selected image.

- If necessary, scroll to display the caption in the document window (Figure 9–10).

Q&A How do I change the position of a caption?
Click the Position arrow (Caption dialog box) and then select the desired position of the caption.

caption inserted below image

Figure 1: Help Center Window Screenshot

Figure 9–10

Caption Numbers

Each caption number contains a field. A **field** is code that serves as a placeholder for data that can change in a document. Examples of fields include page numbers, merge fields, IF fields, the current date, and caption numbers. You update caption numbers using the same technique used to update any other field. That is, to update all caption numbers, select the entire document and then press F9, or right-click the field and then click Update Field on the shortcut menu. When you print a document, Word updates the caption numbers automatically, regardless of whether the document window displays the updated caption numbers.

To Hide White Space

White space is the space displayed in the margins at the top and bottom of pages (including any headers and footers) and also space between pages. To make it easier to see the text in this document as you scroll through it, the following step hides white space.

 Position the pointer in the document window in the space between the pages or below the last page in the document and then double-click when the pointer changes to a 'Hide White Space' button to hide white space.

To Insert a Cross-Reference

The next step in this project is to insert a reference to the new figure. *Why? In reference documents, the text should reference each figure specifically and, if appropriate, explain the contents of the figure.*

Because figures may be inserted, deleted, or moved, you may not know the actual figure number in the final document. For this reason, Word provides a method of inserting a **cross-reference**, which is text that electronically refers the reader to another part of the document, such as a heading, caption, or footnote. You can click a cross-reference to move directly to that specific location in the document. By inserting a cross-reference to the caption, the text that mentions the figure will be updated whenever the caption to the figure is updated. The following steps insert a cross-reference.

BTW

Captions
If a caption appears with extra characters inside curly braces ({}), Word is displaying field codes instead of field results. Press ALT+F9 to display captions correctly as field results. If Word prints fields codes for captions, click File on the ribbon to open Backstage view, click Options in Backstage view to display the Word Options dialog box, click Advanced in the left pane (Word Options dialog box), scroll to the Print section in the right pane, remove the check mark from the 'Print field codes instead of their values' check box, click OK, and then print the document again.

1

- At the end of the last sentence below the To Insert a Screenshot heading, position the insertion point to the left of the period, press SPACEBAR, and then press the LEFT PARENTHESIS [( ] key.

- Display the References tab.

- Click the Cross-reference button (References tab | Captions group) to display the Cross-reference dialog box (Figure 9–11).

Figure 9–11

2

- Click the Reference type arrow (Cross-reference dialog box) to display the Reference type list; scroll to and then click Figure, which displays a list of figures from the document in the For which caption list (which, at this point, is only one figure).

- If necessary, click 'Figure 1: Help Center Window Screenshot' in the For which caption list to select the caption to reference.

- Click the 'Insert reference to' arrow and then click 'Only label and number' to instruct Word that the cross-reference in the document should list just the label, Figure, followed by the figure number (Figure 9–12).

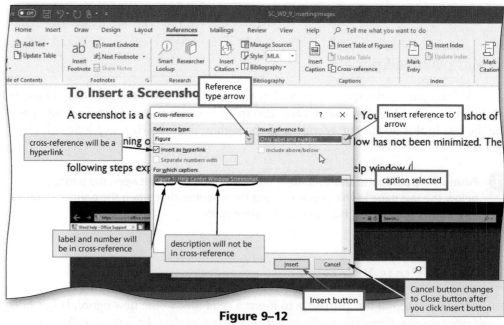

Figure 9–12

3

- Click the Insert button to insert the cross-reference in the document at the location of the insertion point.

 What if my cross-reference is shaded in gray?

The cross-reference is a field. Depending on your Word settings, fields may appear shaded in gray to help you identify them on the screen.

- Click the Close button (Cross-reference dialog box).

- Press the RIGHT PARENTHESIS [ )] key to close off the cross-reference (Figure 9–13).

Q&A How do I update a cross-reference if a caption is added, deleted, or moved?

In many cases, Word automatically updates a cross-reference in a document if the item to which it refers changes. To update a cross-reference manually, select the cross-reference and then press F9, or right-click the cross-reference and then click Update Field on the shortcut menu.

Figure 9–13

Other Ways

1. Click Cross-reference button (Insert tab | Links group)

To Go to an Object

Often, you would like to bring a certain page, image, or other part of a document into view in the document window. Although you could scroll through the document to find a desired page, image, or part of the document, Word enables you to go to a specific location via the Go To sheet in the Find and Replace dialog box.

The following steps go to an image. **Why?** *The next step in this module is to add a caption to another image, which is a type of graphic, in the document, so you want to display the image in the document window.*

- Display the Home tab.

- Click the Find arrow (Home tab | Editing group) to display the Find menu (Figure 9–14).

- Click Go To on the Find menu to display the Go To sheet in the Find and Replace dialog box.

- Scroll through the Go to what list and then click Graphic to select it.

Figure 9–14

- Click the Previous button to display the previous graphic in the document window (which is the cloud shape, in this case) (Figure 9–15).

- Click Close button to close the dialog box.

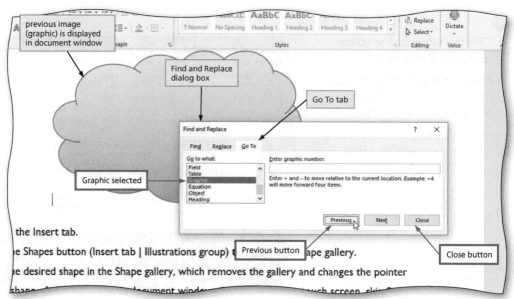

Figure 9–15

Q&A

What if I wanted go to the next section or other location in a document?

You can go to any location listed in the Go to what list, including a page, section, line, bookmark, comment, footnote, endnote, field, table, graphic, equation, object, or heading. To go to a section, for example, you would select section in the Go to what list and then click the Next button in the Go To sheet (Find and Replace dialog box). You also can go to the next section header or footer using the Next button (Header & Footer Design Tools tab | Header & Footer group).

Other Ways

1. Press CTRL+G

BTW

The Ribbon and Screen Resolution

Word may change how the groups and buttons within the groups appear on the ribbon, depending on the screen resolution of your computer. Thus, your ribbon may look different from the ones in this book if you are using a screen resolution other than 1366 × 768.

To Insert Captions and Cross-References

The previous steps inserted a caption for the screenshot image and then inserted a cross-reference to that caption. The following steps insert captions for the remaining three images in the document (that is, the cloud shape, the picture, and the online image).

1. Click the cloud shape to select the image for which you want to insert a caption.

2. Display the References tab. Click the Insert Caption button (References tab | Captions group) to display the Caption dialog box with a figure number automatically assigned to the selected image.

3. Press the COLON (:) key and then press SPACEBAR in the Caption text box (Caption dialog box) to place separating characters between the figure number and description.

4. Type **Cloud Shape** as the figure description and then click OK to insert the caption below the selected image.

5. At the end of the last sentence above the cloud image, change the word, below, to the word, in, and then press SPACEBAR.

6. Click the Cross-reference button (Insert or References tab | Links or Captions group) to display the Cross-reference dialog box, if necessary, click 'Figure 1: Cloud Shape' in the For which caption list to select the caption to reference, click the Insert button (Cross-reference dialog box) to insert the cross-reference at the location of the insertion point, and then click the Close button in the Cross-reference dialog box.

Q&A Why did I not need to change the settings for the reference type and reference to in the dialog box?
Word retains the previous settings in the dialog box.

7 Display the Home tab. Click the Find arrow (Home tab | Editing group) to display the Find menu and then click Go To on the Find menu or press CTRL+G to display the Go To sheet in the Find and Replace dialog box. With Graphic selected in the Go to what list, click the Previous button to display the previous image in the document window (which is the sunflower field picture in this case). Click the Close button to close the dialog box.

8 Repeat Steps 1 through 7 to insert the caption, Sunflower Field Picture, for the picture of the sunflower field and the caption, World Continents Image, for the image of the world continents. Also add a cross-reference at the end of the sentences above each image, with the sunflower field picture cross-reference in parentheses (similar to the cross-reference shown in Figure 9–13 for the Word Help window) and the world continents image cross-reference following the word, in, as shown in Figure 9–16.

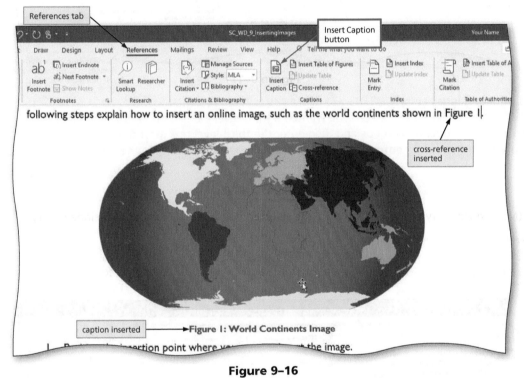

Figure 9–16

BTW

Link to Graphic
If you wanted to link a graphic in a document to a webpage, you would click the Link button (Insert tab | Links group), click 'Existing File or Web Page' in the Link to bar, enter the web address in the Address box (Insert Hyperlink dialog box), and then click OK. To display the webpage associated with the graphic, CTRL+click the graphic.

To Mark an Index Entry

The last page of the reference document in this project is an index, which lists important terms discussed in the document along with each term's corresponding page number. For Word to generate the index, you first must mark any text you wish to appear in the index. **Why?** *When you mark an index entry, Word creates a field that it uses to build the index.* Index entry fields are hidden and are displayed on the screen only when you show formatting marks, that is, when the 'Show/Hide ¶' button (Home tab | Paragraph group) is selected.

In this document, you want the words, drawing object, in the second sentence below the To Insert a Shape heading to be marked as an index entry. The following steps mark an index entry.

- Select the text you wish to appear in the index (the words, drawing object, in the To Insert a Shape section of the document in this case).

- Click the Mark Entry button (References tab | Index group) to display the Mark Index Entry dialog box with the selected text entered in the Main entry text box (Figure 9–17).

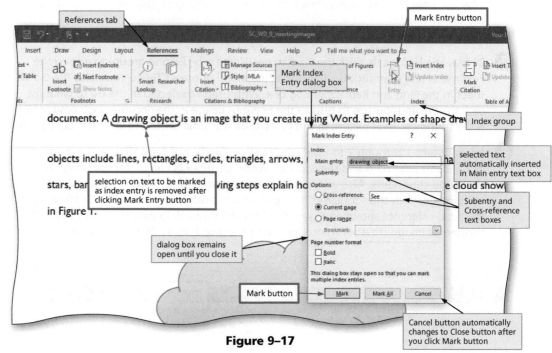

Figure 9–17

How would I enter a second-level index entry?

Enter the second-level text in the Subentry text box. If you wanted a third-level index entry, you would place a colon after the second-level in the Subentry text box and then enter the third-level text after the colon. You also can enter a cross-reference to another index entry by entering the text for the other entry in the Cross-reference text box after the text, *See*.

- Click the Mark button (Mark Index Entry dialog box) to mark the selected text in the document as an index entry.

Why do formatting marks now appear on the screen?

When you mark an index entry, Word automatically shows formatting marks (if they are not showing already) so that you can see the index entry field. Notice that the marked index entry begins with the letters, XE.

- Click the Close button in the Mark Index Entry dialog box to close the dialog box; scroll up, if necessary, to display the To Insert a Shape heading (Figure 9–18).

How could I see all index entries marked in a document?

With formatting marks displaying, you could scroll through the

Figure 9–18

document, scanning for all occurrences of XE, or you could use the Navigation Pane (that is, place a check mark in the Navigation Pane check box (View tab | Show group)) to find all occurrences of XE.

Other Ways

1. Select text, press ALT+SHIFT+X

To Mark Multiple Index Entries

Word leaves the Mark Index Entry dialog box open until you close it, which allows you to mark multiple index entries without having to reopen the dialog box repeatedly. To mark multiple index entries, you would perform the following steps.

1. With the Mark Index Entry dialog box displayed, click in the document window; scroll to and then select the next index entry.
2. If necessary, click the Main entry text box (Mark Index Entry dialog box) to display the selected text in the Main entry text box.
3. Click the Mark button.
4. Repeat Steps 1 through 3 for all entries. When finished, click the Close button in the Mark Index Entry dialog box.

To Hide Formatting Marks

To remove the clutter of index entry fields from the document, you should hide formatting marks. The following step hides formatting marks.

1 Display the Home tab. If the 'Show/Hide ¶' button (Home tab | Paragraph group) is selected, click it to hide formatting marks.

Q&A What if the index entries still appear after clicking the 'Show/Hide ¶' button?
Open Backstage view, click Options to display the Word Options dialog box, click Display in the left pane (Word Options dialog box), remove the check mark from the Hidden text check box, and then click OK.

To Show White Space

For the remainder of creating this project, you would like to see headers, footers, and margins. Thus, you should show white space. The following step shows white space.

1 Position the pointer in the document window on a page break notation and then double-click when the pointer changes to a 'Show White Space' button to show white space.

To Insert a Sidebar Text Box

A **sidebar text box** is a text box that is positioned adjacent to the body of a document, running across the top or bottom of a page or along the right or left edge of a page, and contains auxiliary information. The following steps insert a built-in sidebar text box. *Why? Sidebar text boxes take up less space on the page than text boxes positioned in the middle of the page.*

1
• Be sure the insertion point is near the top of page 1 of the document, as shown in Figure 9–19.

Q&A Does the insertion point need to be at the top of the page?
The insertion point should be close to where you want to insert the text box.

• Display the Insert tab.
• Click the Text Box button (Insert tab | Text group) to display the Text Box gallery.

BTW

Index Entries
Index entries may include a switch, which is a backslash followed by a letter inserted after the field text. Switches include \b to apply bold formatting to the entry's page number, \f to define an entry type, \i to make the entry's page number italic, \r to insert a range of page numbers, \t to insert specified text in place of a page number, and \y to specify that the subsequent text defines the pronunciation for the index entry. A colon in an index entry precedes a subentry keyword in the index.

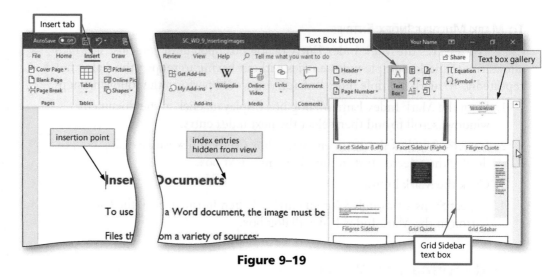

Experiment

- Scroll through the Text Box gallery to see the variety of available text box styles.

- Scroll to display Grid Sidebar in the Text Box gallery (Figure 9–19).

Figure 9–19

2

- Click Grid Sidebar in the Text Box gallery to insert that text box style in the document (Figure 9–20).

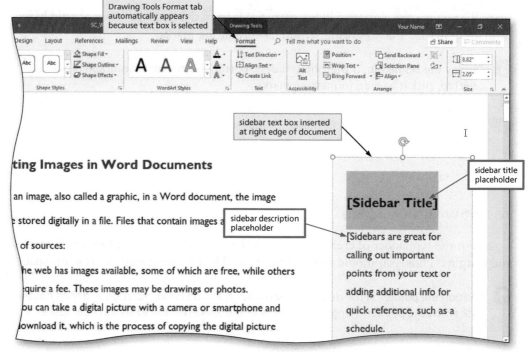

Figure 9–20

Other Ways

1. Click 'Explore Quick Parts' button (Insert tab | Text group), click 'Building Blocks Organizer' on Explore Quick Parts menu, select desired text box name in Building blocks list, click Insert button

To Enter and Format Text in the Sidebar Text Box

The next step is to enter the text in the sidebar text box. The following steps enter text in the text box.

1 If necessary, click the sidebar title placeholder in the text box to select it.

2 Type **What Is Malware?** and then change the font size of the entered text to 12 point.

3 Click the sidebar description placeholder and then type the following paragraph: **Malware, short for malicious software, is software that usually acts without a user's knowledge and deliberately alters a computer or mobile device's operations. Examples of malware**

include viruses, worms, trojan horses, rootkits, spyware, adware, and zombies. Change the font size of the entered text to 10 point.

④ Press ENTER. Change the font size to 12 point. Type **Malware Protection Tips** and then press ENTER.

⑤ Change the font size to 10 point. Click the Bullets button (Home tab | Paragraph group) to bullet the list. Click the Decrease Indent button (Home tab | Paragraph group) to move the bullet symbol left one-half inch. Type **Use a firewall and an antivirus or similar app.** and then press ENTER.

⑥ Type **Be suspicious of unsolicited email attachments.** and then press ENTER.

⑦ Type **Download apps or programs only from trusted websites.** and then press ENTER.

⑧ Type **Close spyware windows.** and then press ENTER.

⑨ Type **Before using removable media, scan it for malware.** and then press ENTER.

⑩ Type **Back up regularly.** to enter the last line.

⑪ Change the line spacing of the paragraphs entered in Steps 3 and 4 to 1.15 using the Line and Paragraph Spacing button (Home tab | Paragraph group).

⑫ Select the text box by clicking its edge and then change its fill color to Blue-Gray, Accent 6, Lighter 40% by using the Shape Fill arrow (Drawing Tools Format tab | Shape Styles group).

⑬ Click the One Page button (View tab | Zoom group) so that you can see all of the entered text at once (Figure 9–21).

⑭ Change the zoom to page width.

BTW
Building Blocks
Many of the objects that you can insert through the Building Blocks gallery are available as built-in objects in galleries on the ribbon. Some examples are cover pages in the Cover Page gallery (Insert tab | Pages group), equations in the Equation gallery (Insert tab | Symbols group), footers in the Footer gallery (Insert tab | Header & Footer group), headers in the Header gallery (Insert tab | Header & Footer group), page numbers in the Page Number gallery (Insert tab | Header & Footer group), text boxes in the Text Box gallery (Insert tab | Text group), and watermarks in the Watermark gallery (Design tab | Page Background group).

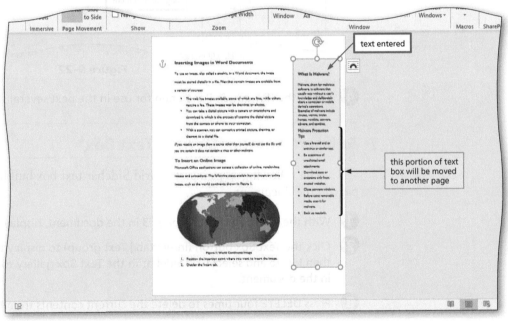

Figure 9–21

To Use the Navigation Pane to Go to a Page

Instead of one long text box, this project splits the text box across the edge of two pages, specifically, the first and third pages of this document. The following steps use the Navigation Pane to display page 3 in the document window so that you can insert another text box on that page.

① If necessary, display the View tab. Place a check mark in the Navigation Pane check box (View tab | Show group) to open the Navigation Pane at the left edge of the Word window. If desired, drag the edge of the Navigation Pane to widen or narrow the pane so that it looks like Figure 9–22.

BTW
Deleting Building Blocks
To delete an existing building block, click the 'Explore Quick Parts' button (Insert tab | Text group) to display the Explore Quick Parts menu, click 'Building Blocks Organizer' on the Explore Quick Parts menu to display the Building Blocks Organizer dialog box, select the building block to delete (Building Blocks Organizer dialog box), click the Delete button, click Yes in the dialog box that appears, and then close the Building Blocks Organizer dialog box.

2 Click the Pages tab in the Navigation Pane to display thumbnail images of the pages in the document.

3 Scroll to and then click the thumbnail of the third page in the Navigation Pane to display the top of the selected page in the top of the document window (Figure 9–22).

Figure 9–22

4 Leave the Navigation Pane open for use in the next several steps.

To Insert Another Sidebar Text Box

The following steps insert a Grid Sidebar text box building block on the third page in the document.

1 With the insertion point on page 3 in the document, display the Insert tab.

2 Click the Text Box button (Insert tab | Text group) to display the Text Box gallery and then locate and select Grid Sidebar in the Text Box gallery to insert that text box style in the document.

3 Press DELETE four times to delete the current contents from the text box (Figure 9–23).

Figure 9–23

To Link Text Boxes

Word allows you to link two separate text boxes. ***Why?*** *You can flow text from one text box into the other.* To link text boxes, the second text box must be empty, which is why you deleted the contents of the text box in the previous steps. The following steps link text boxes.

- Click the thumbnail of the first page in the Navigation Pane to display the top of the selected page in the document window.

- Click an edge of the text box on the first page to select it.

- If necessary, display the Drawing Tools Format tab.

- Click the Create Link button (Drawing Tools Format tab | Text group), which changes the pointer to the shape of a pitcher.

- Move the pointer in the document window to see its new shape (Figure 9–24).

Figure 9–24

- Scroll through the document to display the second text box, which is located on the third page, in the document window.

Q&A Can I use the Navigation Pane to go to the second text box?
No. If you click in the Navigation Pane, the link process will stop and the pointer will return to its default shape.

- Position the pointer in the empty text box, so that the pointer shape changes to a pouring pitcher (Figure 9–25).

Figure 9–25

- Click the empty text box to link it to the first text box (or, if using a touch screen, you will need to use a stylus to tap the empty text box).

- Scroll to display the first text box in the document window and then, if necessary, select the text box.

- Resize (shorten) the text box by dragging its bottom-middle sizing handle upward until the amount of text that is displayed in the text box is similar to Figure 9–26.

 How would I remove a link?
Select the text box in which you created the link and then click the Break Link button (Drawing Tools Format tab | Text group).

Figure 9–26

4

- Use the Navigation Pane to display the third page in the document window.

- If necessary, scroll to display the second text box in the document window and then select the text box.

- Resize (shorten) the text box by dragging its bottom-middle sizing handle upward until the amount of text that is displayed in the text box is similar to Figure 9–27.

- Drag the entire text box downward to position it as shown in Figure 9–27.

- Verify that all of Step #5 in the document fits on the third page. If it does not, adjust the size or location of the text box or the line and paragraph spacing on the page so that all of the To Insert a Shape text fits on the third page.

Figure 9–27

- Select the text box by clicking its edge and then change its fill color to Blue-Gray, Accent 6, Lighter 40% by using the Shape Fill arrow (Drawing Tools Format tab | Shape Styles group) so that the final text box appears as shown in Figure 9–27.

- If necessary, insert a page break to the left of the To Insert a Shape heading so that the heading begins at the top of the third page.

To Compress Pictures

If you plan to use email to send a Word document that contains pictures or other images or post it for downloading, you may want to reduce its file size to speed up file transmission time. *Why? Pictures and other images in Word documents can increase the size of these files.* In Word, you can compress pictures, which reduces the size of the Word document. Compressing the pictures in Word does not cause any loss in their original quality. The following steps compress pictures in a document.

- Click a picture in the document to select it, such as the sunflower field, and then display the Picture Tools Format tab.

- Click the Compress Pictures button (Picture Tools Format tab | Adjust group) to display the Compress Pictures dialog box.

- If the 'Apply only to this picture' check box (Compress Pictures dialog box) contains a check mark, remove the check mark so that all pictures in the document are compressed.

- If necessary, click 'Print (220 ppi): excellent quality on most printers and screens' in the Resolution area to specify how images should be compressed (Figure 9–28).

- Click OK to compress all pictures in the document.

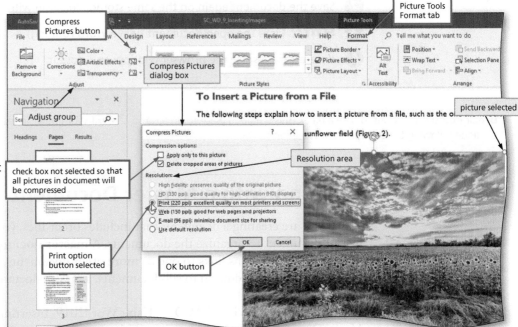

Figure 9–28

Q&A | Can I compress a single picture?
Yes. Select the picture and then place a check mark in the 'Apply only to this picture' check box (Compress Pictures dialog box).

Other Ways

1. Click the Tools button in Save As dialog box, click Compress Pictures on Tools menu, select options (Compress Pictures dialog box), click OK

TO SAVE PICTURES IN OTHER FORMATS

You can save any image in a document as a picture file for use in other documents or apps. If you wanted to save an image in a Word document, you would perform the following steps.

1. Right-click the image to display a shortcut menu.

2. Click 'Save as Picture' on the shortcut menu to display the File Save dialog box.

3. Navigate to the location you want to save the image.

BTW
Compressing Pictures
Selecting a lower ppi (pixels per inch) in the Resolution area (Compress Picture dialog box) creates a smaller document file but also lowers the quality of the images.

4. Click the 'Save as type' arrow (File Save dialog box) and then select the image type for the saved image.

5. Click the Save button (File Save dialog box) to save the image in the specified location using the specified image type.

To Close Open Panes, Documents, and Windows

The following steps close the open Word document and the browser window.

1 Close the Navigation Pane.

2 Save the document again on the same storage location with the same file name.

3 **sam**⬆ Close the open document (leave Word running).

4 If necessary, display the browser window and close it.

Break Point: If you want to take a break, this is a good place to do so. You can exit Word now. To resume later, start Word and continue following the steps from this location forward.

Working with a Master Document

BTW
Master Documents
Master documents can be used when multiple people prepare different sections of a document or when a document contains separate elements, such as the modules in a book. If multiple people in a network need to work on the same document simultaneously, each person can work on a section (subdocument); all subdocuments can be stored together collectively in a master document on the network server.

When you are creating a document that includes other files, you may want to create a master document to organize the documents. A **master document** is simply a document that contains links to one or more other documents, each of which is called a **subdocument**. In addition to subdocuments, a master document can contain its own text and images.

The master file is SC_WD_9_UsingWord2019_InsertingImages_ MasterDocument.docx in this project. This master document file contains a link to one subdocument: SC_WD_9_InsertingImages.docx. The master document also contains other items: a cover page, a copyright page, a table of contents, a table of figures, and an index. The following sections create this master document and insert the necessary elements in the document to create the finished SC_WD_9_UsingWord2019_InsertingImages_MasterDocument.docx.

To Change the Document Theme

The first step in creating this master document is to change its document theme to Gallery. The following steps change the document theme.

1 **sam**⬇ If necessary, start Word and create a new blank document.

2 Click Design on the ribbon to display the Design tab.

3 Click the Themes button (Design tab | Document Formatting group) to display the Themes gallery.

4 Click Gallery in the Themes gallery to change the document theme to the selected theme.

Outlines

To create a master document, Word must be in Outline view. You then enter the headings of the document as an outline using Word's built-in heading styles. In an outline, the major heading is displayed at the left margin with each subordinate, or lower-level, heading indented. In Word, the built-in Heading 1 style is displayed at the left margin in Outline view. Heading 2 style is indented below Heading 1 style, Heading 3 style is indented further, and so on. (Outline view works similarly to multilevel lists.)

You do not want to use a built-in heading style for the paragraphs of text within the document, because when you create a table of contents, Word places all lines formatted using the built-in heading styles in the table of contents. Thus, the text below each heading is formatted using the Body Text style.

Each heading should print at the top of a new page. Because you might want to format the pages within a heading differently from those pages in other headings, you insert next page section breaks between each heading.

To Switch to Outline View

The following steps switch to Outline view. **Why?** *To create a master document, Word must be in Outline view.*

1
- Display the View tab (Figure 9–29).

2
- Click the Outline button (View tab | Views group), which displays the Outlining tab on the ribbon and switches to Outline view.

- Be sure the 'Show Text Formatting' check box is selected and the 'Show First Line Only' check box is not selected (Outlining tab | Outline Tools group) (Figure 9–30).

Q&A Can I specify the number of levels (headings) that will be displayed in the outline?
Yes, click the Show Level box (Outlining tab | Outline Tools group) and then select the desired level. The selected level and all higher levels will appear in the outline. To show all levels, select All Levels.

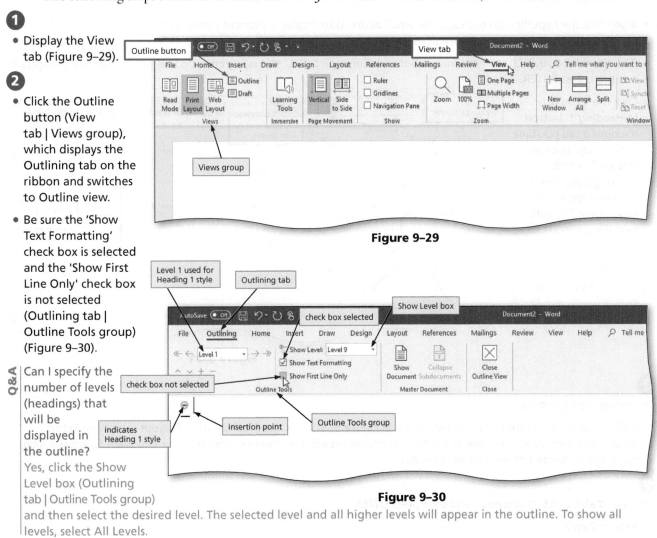

Figure 9–29

Figure 9–30

To Enter Text in Outline View

The SC_WD_9_UsingWord2019_InsertingImages_MasterDocument.docx document contains these three major headings: Inserting Images in Word Documents, Table of Figures, and Index. The heading, Inserting Images in Word Documents, is not entered in the outline. *Why not? It is part of the subdocument inserted in the master document.*

The first page of the outline (the copyright page) does not contain a heading; instead it contains three paragraphs of body text, which you enter directly in the outline. The Inserting Images in Word Documents content is inserted from the subdocument. You will instruct Word to create the content for the Table of Figures and Index later in this module. The following steps create an outline that contains headings and body text to be used in the master document.

- Click the 'Demote to Body Text' button (Outlining tab | Outline Tools group), so that you can enter the paragraphs of text for the copyright page.

- Type **Using Word 2019 – Guide #26 – Inserting Images** as the first paragraph in the outline and then press ENTER.

- Type **To receive additional guides in this or any other series by the Information Resource Center at Wilmington College, send a message to Rosey Schmidt at rschmidt@wilmingtoncollege.cengage.edu.** as the second paragraph in the outline and then press ENTER.

- Right-click the hyperlink (in this case, the email address) to display a shortcut menu and then click Remove Hyperlink on the shortcut menu.

- Click the third Body Text style outline symbol and then type **2021 Wilmington College** as the third paragraph and then press ENTER.

- Click the 'Promote to Heading 1' button (Outlining tab | Outline Tools group) because you are finished entering body text and will enter the remaining headings in the outline next (Figure 9–31).

Figure 9–31

- Display the Layout tab.

- With the insertion point positioned as shown in Figure 9–31, click the Breaks button (Layout tab | Page Setup group) and then click Next Page in the Section Breaks area in the Breaks gallery because you want to enter a next page section break before the next heading.

- Type **Table of Figures** and then press ENTER.

- Repeat Step 2.

- Type **Index** as the last entry (Figure 9–32).

Figure 9–32

To Show Only the First Line of Each Paragraph in Outline View

Users often instruct Word to display just the first line of each paragraph of body text. *Why? When only the first line of each paragraph is displayed, the outline often is more readable.* The following step displays only the first line of body text paragraphs.

1

- Display the Outlining tab.

- Place a check mark in the 'Show First Line Only' check box (Outlining tab | Outline Tools group), so that Word displays only the first line of each paragraph (Figure 9–33).

Q&A

How would I redisplay all lines of the paragraphs of body text?
Remove the check mark from the 'Show First Line Only' check box (Outlining tab | Outline Tools group).

Figure 9–33

Why do the outline symbols contain a minus sign?
The minus sign means the outline level does not have any subordinate levels. If an outline symbol contains a plus sign, it means the outline level has subordinate levels. If you double-click an outline symbol that contains a plus sign, the section under the heading will expand (show) if it is collapsed (hidden) and will collapse if it is expanded. Or with the insertion point in the heading, you can click the Expand and Collapse buttons (Outlining tab | Outline Tools group).

How do I move headings in Outline view?
You can drag the outline symbols up or down to rearrange headings. You also can position the insertion point in a heading and then click the Move Up or Move Down button (Outlining tab | Outline Tools group) to move a heading up or down, respectively.

- Save this master document on your hard drive, OneDrive, or other storage location using the file name, SC_WD_9_UsingWord2019_InsertingImages_MasterDocument.

Other Ways

1. Press CTRL+SHIFT+L

To Insert a Subdocument in a Master Document

The next step is to insert a subdocument in the master document. The subdocument to be inserted is the SC_WD_9_InsertingImages.docx file, which you created earlier in the module. Word places the first line of text in the subdocument at the first heading level in the master document. *Why?* *The first line in the subdocument was defined using the Heading 1 style.* The following steps insert a subdocument in a master document.

● Display the Home tab. If formatting marks do not appear, click the 'Show/Hide ¶' button (Home tab | Paragraph group) to display formatting marks.

● Position the insertion point where you want to insert the subdocument (on the section break above the Table of Figures heading).

● Display the Outlining tab. Click the Show Document button (Outlining tab | Master Document group) so that all commands in the Master Document group appear.

● Click the Insert button (Outlining tab | Master Document group) to display the Insert Subdocument dialog box.

● Locate and select the SC_WD_9_ InsertingImages. docx file (Insert Subdocument dialog box) (Figure 9–34). (Depending on settings, the file extension of .docx may or may not appear in the dialog box.)

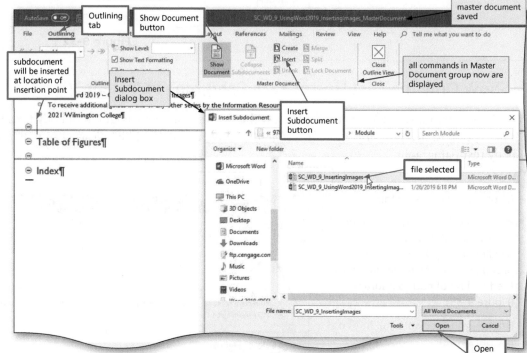

Figure 9–34

● Click the Open button (Insert Subdocument dialog box) to insert the selected file as a subdocument.

● If Word displays a dialog box about styles, click the 'No to All' button.

● Press CTRL+HOME to position the insertion point at the top of the document (Figure 9–35).

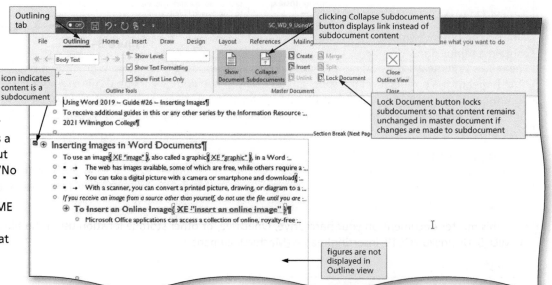

Figure 9–35

Master Documents and Subdocuments

When you open the master document, the subdocuments initially are collapsed; that is, they are displayed as hyperlinks (Figure 9–36). To work with the contents of a master document after you open it, switch to Outline view and then expand the subdocuments by clicking the Expand Subdocuments button (Outlining tab | Master Document group).

You can open a subdocument in a separate document window and modify it. To open a collapsed subdocument, click the hyperlink. To open an expanded subdocument, double-click the subdocument icon to the left of the document heading (shown in Figure 9–36).

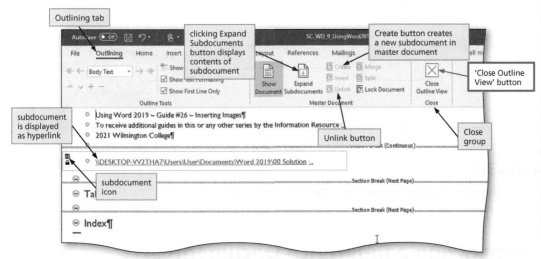

Figure 9–36

If, for some reason, you wanted to remove a subdocument from a master document, you would expand the subdocuments, click the subdocument icon to the left of the subdocument's first heading, and then press DELETE. Although Word removes the subdocument from the master document, the subdocument file remains on the storage media.

Occasionally, you may want to convert a subdocument to part of the master document — breaking the connection between the text in the master document and the subdocument. To do this, expand the subdocuments, click the subdocument icon, and then click the Unlink button (Outlining tab | Master Document group).

To Hide Formatting Marks

To remove the clutter of index entry fields from the document, you should hide formatting marks. The following step hides formatting marks.

 Display the Home tab. If the 'Show/Hide ¶' button (Home tab | Paragraph group) is selected, click it to hide formatting marks.

To Close Outline View

The following step closes Outline view. ***Why?*** *You are finished organizing the master document.*

- Display the Outlining tab.

- Click the 'Close Outline View' button (shown in Figure 9–36) (Outlining tab | Close group) to redisplay the document in Print Layout view, which selects the Print Layout button on the status bar.

- If necessary, press CTRL+HOME to display the top of the document (Figure 9–37).

 Experiment

- Scroll through the document to familiarize yourself with the sections. When finished, display the top of the document in the document window.

- Note that the document should contain seven pages. If it contains any extra blank pages, delete the blank pages.

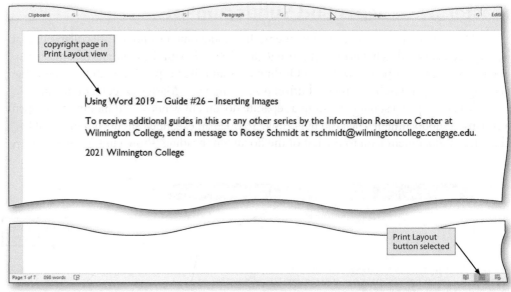

Figure 9–37

- Save the document again on the same storage location with the same file name.

Organizing a Reference Document

Reference documents are organized and formatted so that users easily can navigate through and read the document. The reference document in this module includes the following elements: a copyright page, a cover page, a table of contents, a table of figures, an index, odd and even page footers, and a gutter margin. This section illustrates the tasks required to include these elements.

CONSIDER THIS

What elements are common to reference documents?

Reference documents often include a cover page, a table of contents, a table of figures or list of tables (if one exists), and an index.

- **Cover Page.** A cover page (sometimes called a title page) should contain, at a minimum, the title of the document. Some also contain the author, a subtitle, an edition or volume number, and the date written.

- **Table of Contents.** The table of contents should list the title (heading) of each chapter or section and the starting page number of the chapter or section. You may use a leader character, such as a dot or hyphen, to fill the space between the heading and the page number. Sections preceding the table of contents are not listed in it — list only material that follows the table of contents.

- **Table of Figures or List of Tables.** If you have multiple figures or tables in a document, consider identifying all of them in a table of figures or a list of tables. The format of the table of figures or list of tables should match the table of contents.

- **Index.** The index usually is set in two columns or one column. The index can contain any item a reader might want to look up, such as a heading or a key term. If the document does not have a table of figures or list of tables, also include figures and tables in the index.

To Insert a Cover Page

Word has many predefined cover page formats that you can use for the cover page in a document. The following steps insert a cover page.

1 Display the Insert tab.

2 Click the Cover Page button (Insert tab | Pages group) to display the Cover Page gallery.

Q&A Does it matter where I position the insertion point before inserting a cover page?
No. By default, Word inserts the cover page as the first page in a document.

3 Click Facet in the Cover Page gallery to insert the selected cover page as the first page in the current document.

4 Display the View tab. Click the One Page button (View tab | Zoom group) to display the entire cover page in the document window (Figure 9–38).

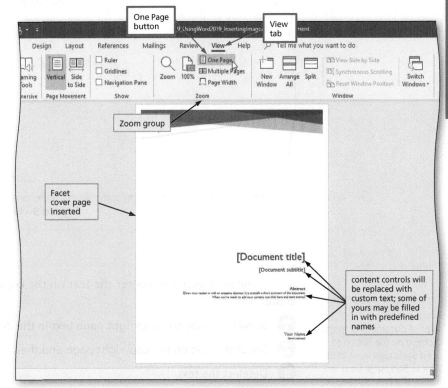

Figure 9–38

To Enter Text in Content Controls

The next step is to select content controls on the cover page and replace their instructions or text with the cover page information. Keep in mind that the content controls present suggested text. Depending on settings on your computer or mobile device, some content controls already may contain customized text, which you will change. You can enter any appropriate text in any content control. The following steps enter cover page text on the cover page.

1 Change the zoom back to page width.

2 Click the [Document title] content control and then type **Using Word 2019** as the title.

3 Click the [Document subtitle] content control and then type **Guide #26 - Inserting Images** as the subtitle.

4 Click the content control that begins with the instruction, [Draw your reader in with an engaging abstract...] and then type **A series of guides designed to strengthen your Word 2019 skills** to complete the abstract text.

5 Select the text in the author content control and then type **Information Resources Center** as the name (Figure 9–39).

Q&A Why is my author content control filled in?
Depending on settings, your content control already may display an author name.

6 Delete the [Email address] content control.

BTW
Advanced Paragraph Options
A widow occurs when the last line of a paragraph appears by itself at the top of a page, and an orphan occurs when the first line of a paragraph appears by itself at the bottom of a page. To prevent widows and orphans, click the Paragraph Dialog Box Launcher (Home tab | Paragraph group), click the Line and Page Breaks tab (Paragraph dialog box), place a check mark in the 'Widow/ Orphan control' check box, and then click OK. Similarly, you can select the 'Keep with next' check box to keep selected paragraphs together, the 'Keep lines together' check box to keep selected lines together, and the 'Page break before' check box to insert a page break before the selected paragraph.

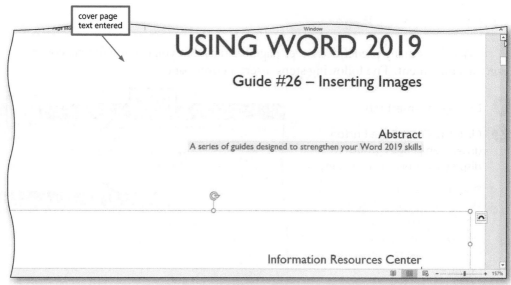

Figure 9–39

To Center Text

BTW
Printing Document Properties
To print document properties, click File on the ribbon to open Backstage view, click Print in Backstage view to display the Print screen, click the first button in the Settings area to display a list of options specifying what you can print, click Document Info in the list to specify you want to print the document properties instead of the actual document, and then click the Print button in the Print screen to print the document properties on the currently selected printer.

The next step is to center the text on the copyright page. The following steps center text.

1 Scroll to display the copyright page text in the document window.

2 Select the text on the copyright page and then center it.

3 Deselect the text.

To Insert a Continuous Section Break and Change the Margins in the Section

The margins on the copyright page are wider than the rest of the document. To change margins for a page, the page must be in a separate section. The next steps insert a continuous section break and then change the margins.

1 Position the insertion point at the location for the section break, in this case, to the left U in Using on the copyright page.

2 Display the Layout tab. Click the Breaks button (Layout tab | Page Setup group) to display the Breaks gallery.

3 Click Continuous in the Breaks gallery to insert a continuous section break to the left of the insertion point.

4 Click the Margins button (Layout tab | Page Setup group) to display the Margins gallery and then click Wide in the Margins gallery to change the margins on the copyright page to the selected settings (Figure 9–40).

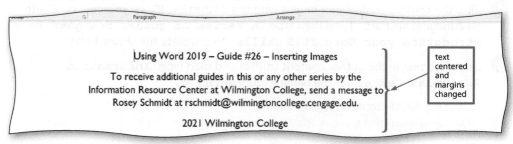

Figure 9–40

To Insert a Symbol from the Symbol Dialog Box

Word provides a method of inserting dots and other symbols, such as letters in the Greek alphabet and mathematical characters, that are not on the keyboard or in the Symbol gallery. The following steps insert a copyright symbol in the document. *Why? You want the copyright symbol to the left of the copyright year.*

1

- If necessary, position the insertion point at the location where the symbol should be inserted (in this case, to the left of the copyright year).
- Display the Insert tab.
- Click the Symbol button (Insert tab | Symbols group) to display the Symbol gallery (Figure 9–41).

Q&A What if the symbol I want to insert already appears in the Symbol gallery?
You can click any symbol shown in the Symbol gallery to insert it in the document.

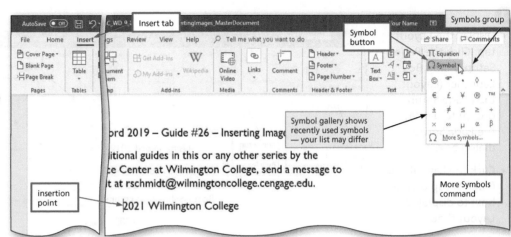

Figure 9–41

2

- Click More Symbols in the Symbol gallery to display the Symbol dialog box.
- If the font in the Font box is not (normal text), click the Font arrow (Symbol dialog box) and then scroll to and click (normal text) to select this font.
- If the subset in the Subset box is not Latin-1 Supplement, click the Subset arrow and then scroll and click Latin-1 Supplement to select this subset.
- In the list of symbols, if necessary, scroll to the copyright symbol shown in Figure 9–42 and then click the symbol to select it.
- Click the Insert button (Symbol dialog box) to place the selected symbol in the document to the left of the insertion point (Figure 9–42).

Q&A Why is the Symbol dialog box still open?
The Symbol dialog box remains open because often you will need to insert the same or additional symbols elsewhere in the document.

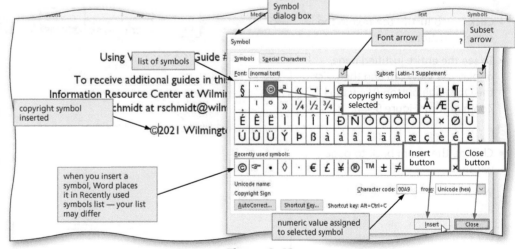

Figure 9–42

3

- Click the Close button (Symbol dialog box) to close the dialog box.
- Press SPACEBAR to insert a space between the copyright symbol and the year.

To Adjust Vertical Alignment on a Page

You can instruct Word to center the contents of a page vertically using one of two options: place an equal amount of space above and below the text on the page, or evenly space each paragraph between the top and bottom margins. The following steps vertically center text on a page. *Why? The copyright page in this project evenly spaces each paragraph on a page between the top and bottom margins, which is called justified vertical alignment.*

1

- Display the Layout tab. Click the Page Setup Dialog Box Launcher (Layout tab | Page Setup group) to display the Page Setup dialog box.

- Click the Layout tab (Page Setup dialog box) to display the Layout sheet.

- Click the Vertical alignment arrow and then click Justified (Figure 9–43).

Figure 9–43

2

- Click OK to justify the text in the current section.

- To see the entire justified page, display the View tab and then click the One Page button (View tab | Zoom group) (Figure 9–44).

3

- Change the zoom back to page width.

Q&A
What are the other vertical alignments?
Top, the default, aligns contents starting at the top margin on the page. Center places all contents centered vertically on the page, and Bottom places contents at the bottom of the page.

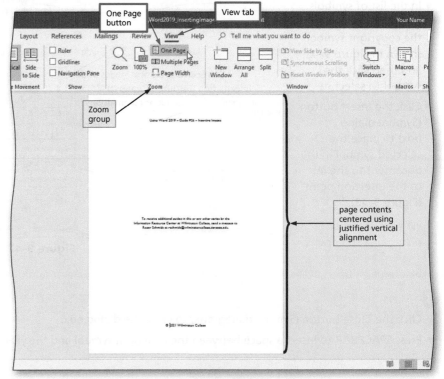

Figure 9–44

To Insert a Blank Page

The following step inserts a blank page. ***Why?*** *In the reference document in this module, the table of contents is on a page after the copyright page.*

1

- Position the insertion point to the left of the word, Inserting, on the first page of the subdocument (as shown in Figure 9–45). (Note that with the insertion point in this location, this blank page that will contain the table of contents may be housed in the subdocument instead of the master document.)

- Display the Insert tab.

Q&A Why are several of the buttons, including the Blank Page button, dimmed on the ribbon?
Your subdocument either is open in another window or is locked. If the subdocument is open in another window, close it. If it is locked, switch to Outline view and then click the Lock Document button (Outlining tab | Master Document group) to unlock it.

- Click the Blank Page button (Insert tab | Pages group) to insert a blank page at the location of the insertion point.

- If necessary, scroll to display the blank page in the document window (Figure 9–45).

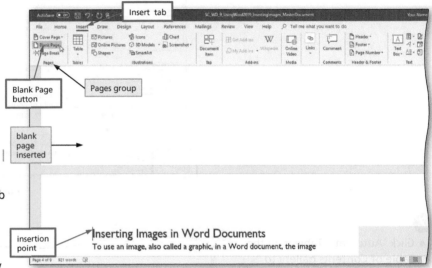

Figure 9–45

To Insert a Table of Contents

A table of contents lists all headings in a document and their associated page numbers. When you use Word's built-in heading styles (for example, Heading 1, Heading 2, and so on), you can instruct Word to insert a table of contents using these headings. In the reference document in this module, the heading of each section uses the Heading 1 style, and subheadings use the Heading 2 style.

The following steps use a predefined building block to insert a table of contents. ***Why?*** *Using Word's predefined table of contents formats can be more efficient than creating a table of contents from scratch.*

1

- Position the insertion point at the top of the blank page 3, which is the location for the table of contents. (If necessary, show formatting marks so that you easily can see the paragraph mark at the top of the page.)

- Ensure that formatting marks do not show.

Q&A Why should I hide formatting marks?
Formatting marks, especially those for index entries, sometimes can cause wrapping to occur on the screen that will be different from how the printed document will wrap. These differences could cause a heading to move to the next page. To ensure that the page references in the table of contents reflect the printed pages, be sure that formatting marks are hidden when you insert a table of contents.

- Display the References tab.

- Click the 'Table of Contents' button (References tab | Table of Contents group) to display the Table of Contents gallery (Figure 9–46).

Figure 9–46

- Click 'Automatic Table 2' in the Table of Contents gallery to insert the table of contents at the location of the insertion point (Figure 9–47). If necessary, scroll to see the table of contents.

How would I delete a table of contents?
You would click the 'Table of Contents' button (References tab | Table of Contents group) and then click 'Remove Table of Contents' in the Table of Contents gallery (shown in Figure 9-46).

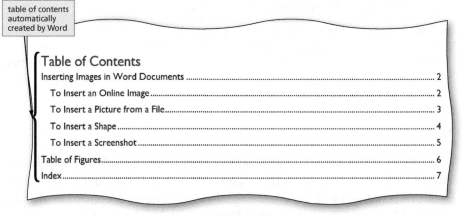

Table of Contents

Figure 9–47

Other Ways

1. Click 'Table of Contents' button (References tab | Table of Contents group), click 'Custom Table of Contents', select table of contents options (Table of Contents dialog box), click OK

2. Click 'Explore Quick Parts' button (Insert tab | Text group), click 'Building Blocks Organizer', select desired table of contents building block (Building Blocks Organizer dialog box), click Insert button, click Close

To Insert a Continuous Section Break and Change the Starting Page Number in a Section

The table of contents should not be the starting page number; instead, the subdocument should be the starting page number in the document. To change the starting page number, the page must be in a separate section. The following steps insert a continuous section break and then change the starting page number for the table of contents.

1 Position the insertion point at the location for the section break, in this case, to the left of I in Inserting Images in Word Documents on page 4 of the document.

2 Display the Layout tab. Click the Breaks button (Layout tab | Page Setup group) to display the Breaks gallery.

3 Click Continuous in the Breaks gallery to insert a continuous section break to the left of the insertion point.

4 Position the insertion point in the table of contents.

5 Display the Insert tab. Click the Page Number button (Insert tab | Header & Footer group) to display the Page Number menu and then click 'Format Page Numbers' on the Page Number menu to display the Page Number Format dialog box.

6 Click the Start at down arrow (Page Number Format dialog box) until 0 is displayed in the Start at box (Figure 9–48).

7 Click OK to change the starting page for the current section.

Figure 9–48

To Update Page Numbers in a Table of Contents

When you change a document, you should update the associated table of contents. The following steps update the page numbers in the table of contents. ***Why?*** *The starting page number change will affect the page numbers in the table of contents.*

1
- If necessary, click the table of contents to select it.

Q&A Why does the ScreenTip say 'CTRL+Click to follow link'?
Each entry in the table of contents is a link. If you hold down CTRL while clicking an entry in the table of contents, Word will display the associated heading in the document window.

2
- Click the Update Table button that is attached to the table of contents to display the Update Table of Contents dialog box.

- Ensure the 'Update page numbers only' option button is selected because you want to update only the page numbers in the table of contents (Figure 9–49).

Figure 9–49

- Click OK (Update Table of Contents dialog box) to update the page numbers in the table of contents.

- Click outside the table of contents to remove the selection from the table (Figure 9–50).

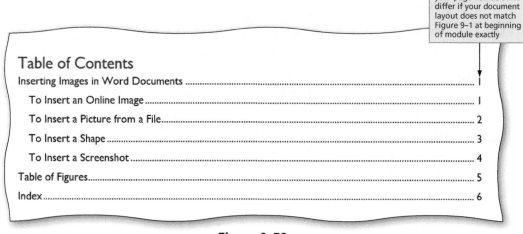

Figure 9–50

Other Ways

1. Select table, click Update Table button (References tab | Table of Contents group)

2. Select table, press F9

To Find a Format

The subdocument contains a sentence of text formatted as italic. To find this text in the document, you could scroll through the document until it is displayed on the screen. A more efficient way is to find the italic format using the Find and Replace dialog box. The following steps find a format. *Why? You want to add the text to the table of contents.*

- If necessary, display the Home tab.

- Click the Find arrow (Home tab | Editing group) to display the Find menu (Figure 9–51).

Figure 9–51

2

- Click Advanced Find on the Find menu to display the Find and Replace dialog box.

- If Word displays a More button in the Find and Replace dialog box, click it so that it changes to a Less button and expands the dialog box.

- Click the Format button (Find and Replace dialog box) to display the Format menu (Figure 9–52).

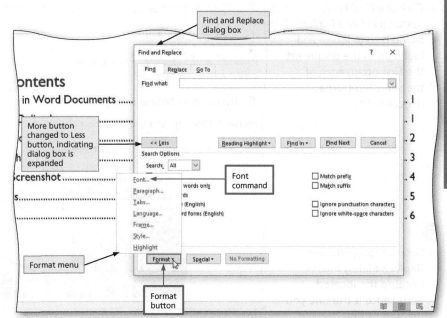

Figure 9–52

3

- Click Font on the Format menu to display the Find Font dialog box. If necessary, click the Font tab (Find Font dialog box) to display the Font sheet.

- Click Italic in the Font style list because that is the format you want to find (Figure 9–53).

Figure 9–53

4

- Click OK to close the Find Font dialog box.

- Be sure no text is in the Find what text box (or click the Find what arrow and then click [Formatting Only]).

- Be sure all check boxes in the Search Options area are cleared.

- Click the Find Next button (Find and Replace dialog box) to locate and highlight in the document the first occurrence of the specified format (Figure 9–54).

Q&A

How do I remove a find format?
You would click the No Formatting button in the Find and Replace dialog box.

5

- Click Cancel (Find and Replace dialog box) because the located occurrence is the one you wanted to find.

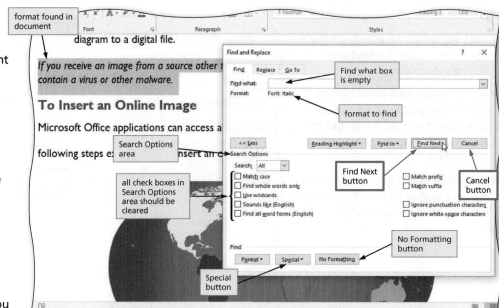

Figure 9–54

Q&A

Can I search for (find) special characters, such as page breaks?
Yes. To find special characters, you would click the Special button in the Find and Replace dialog box.

Other Ways
1. Press CTRL+F

BTW

Find and Replace
The expanded Find and Replace dialog box allows you to specify how Word locates search text. For example, selecting the Match case check box instructs Word to find the text exactly as you typed it, and selecting the 'Find whole words only' check box instructs Word to ignore text that contains the search text (i.e., the word, then, contains the word, the). If you select the Use wildcards check box, you can use wildcard characters in a search. For example, with this check box selected, the search text of *ing would search for all words that end with the characters, ing.

To Format Text as a Heading

The following steps format a paragraph of text as a Heading 3 style. Occasionally, you may want to add a paragraph of text, which normally is not formatted using a heading style, to a table of contents. One way to add the text to the table of contents is to format it as a heading style.

1 With the formatted paragraph still selected (shown in Figure 9–54), if necessary, display the Home tab.

2 Click Heading 3 in the Styles gallery (Home tab | Styles group) to apply the selected style to the current paragraph in the document. Click outside the paragraph to deselect it (Figure 9–55).

Figure 9–55

To Retain Formatting when Adding Text to the Table of Contents

If you wanted to retain formatting of text when adding it to the table of contents, you would perform the following steps.

1. Position the insertion point in the paragraph of text that you want to add to the table of contents.
2. Click the Add Text button (References tab | Table of Contents group) to display the Add Text menu.
3. Click the desired level on the Add Text menu, which adds the format of the selected style to the selected paragraph and adds the paragraph of text to the table of contents.

BTW

Table of Contents Styles
If you wanted to change the level associated with each style used in a table of contents, click the Options button in the Table of Contents dialog box (shown in Figure 9–59), enter the desired level number in the text box beside the appropriate heading or other styled item, and then click OK. To change the formatting associated with a style, click the Modify button in the Table of Contents dialog box.

To Update the Entire Table of Contents

The following steps update the entire table of contents. *Why? The text changed to the Heading 3 style should appear in the table of contents.*

- Display the table of contents in the document window.
- Click the table of contents to select it.
- Click the Update Table button that is attached to the table of contents to display the Update Table of Contents dialog box.
- Click the 'Update entire table' option button (Update Table of Contents dialog box) because you want to update the entire table of contents (Figure 9–56).

Figure 9–56

- Click OK (Update Table of Contents dialog box) to update the entire table of contents (Figure 9–57).

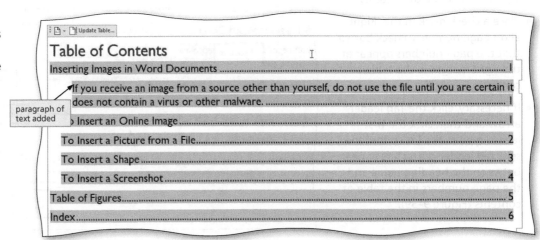

Figure 9–57

Other Ways

1. Select table, click Update Table button (References tab | Table of Contents group)
2. Select table, press F9

To Change the Format of a Table of Contents

You can change the format of the table of contents to any of the predefined table of contents styles or to custom settings. The following steps change the table of contents format. *Why? In this table of contents, you specify the format, page number alignment, and tab leader character.*

- Display the References tab.
- Click the 'Table of Contents' button (References tab | Table of Contents group) to display the Table of Contents gallery (Figure 9–58).

Figure 9–58

- Click 'Custom Table of Contents' in the Table of Contents gallery to display the Table of Contents dialog box.
- Click the Formats arrow (Table of Contents dialog box) and then click Simple to change the format style for the table of contents.
- Place a check mark in the 'Right align page numbers' check box so that the page numbers appear at the right margin in the table of contents.
- If necessary, click the Tab leader arrow and then click the first leader type in the list so that the selected leader characters appear between the heading name and the page numbers in the table of contents (Figure 9–59).

Figure 9–59

• Click OK to modify the table of contents according to the specified settings. When Word displays a dialog box asking if you want to replace the selected table of contents, click OK (Figure 9–60).

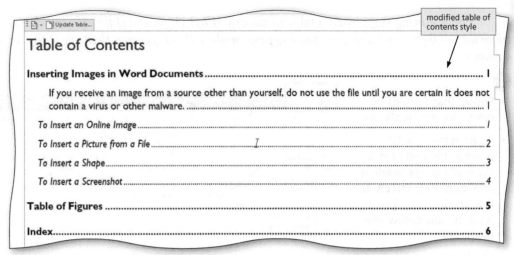

Figure 9–60

To Use the Navigation Pane to Go to a Heading in a Document

When you use Word's built-in heading styles in a document, you can use the Navigation Pane to go to headings in a document quickly. *Why? When you click a heading in the Navigation Pane, Word displays the page associated with that heading in the document window.* The following step uses the Navigation Pane to display an associated heading in the document window.

1

• Display the View tab. Place a check mark in the Navigation Pane check box (View tab | Show group) to open the Navigation Pane at the left edge of the Word window.

• If necessary, click the Headings tab in the Navigation Pane to display the text that is formatted using Heading styles.

• Click the 'Table of Figures' heading in the Navigation Pane to display the top of the selected page in the top of the document window (Figure 9–61).

Q&A

What if all of the headings are not displayed?

Right-click a heading in the Navigation Pane and then click Expand All on the shortcut menu to ensure that all headings are displayed. (Note that you can click Collapse All on the shortcut menu to collapse all headings in the Navigation Pane.) If a heading still is not displayed, verify that the heading is formatted with a heading style. To display or hide subheadings below a heading in the Navigation Pane, click the triangle to the left of the heading. If a heading is too wide for the Navigation Pane, you can point to the heading to display a ScreenTip that shows the complete title.

Figure 9–61

To Insert a Table of Figures

The following steps insert a table of figures. *Why? At the end of the reference document is a table of figures, which lists all figures and their corresponding page numbers. Word generates this table of figures from the captions in the document.*

- Ensure that formatting marks are not displayed.

- Position the insertion point at the end of the Table of Figures heading and then press ENTER, so that the insertion point is on the line below the heading.

- Display the References tab.

- Click the 'Insert Table of Figures' button (References tab | Captions group) to display the Table of Figures dialog box.

- Be sure that all settings in your dialog box match those in Figure 9–62.

Figure 9–62

- Click OK (Table of Figures dialog box) to insert a table of figures at the location of the insertion point (Figure 9–63).

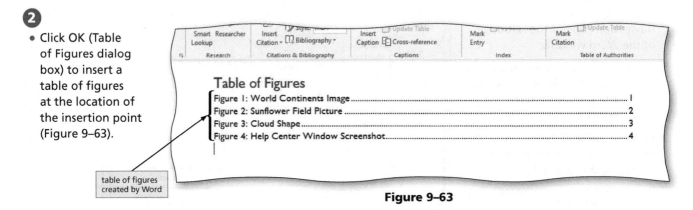

Figure 9–63

BTW
Replace Formats
You can click the Replace tab (Find and Replace dialog box) to find and replace formats. Enter the format to find in the Find what text box and then follow the same steps to enter the format to replace or the format to remove (i.e., Not Bold in the Font style list) in the Replace with text box. Next, click the Replace or Replace All button to replace the next occurrence of the format or all occurrences of the format in the document.

TO CHANGE THE FORMAT OF THE TABLE OF FIGURES

If you wanted to change the format of the table of figures, you would perform the following steps.

1. Click the table of figures to select it.

2. Click the 'Insert Table of Figures' button (References tab | Captions group) to display the Table of Figures dialog box.

3. Change settings in the dialog box as desired.

4. Click OK (Table of Figures dialog box) to apply the changed settings.

5. Click OK when Word asks if you want to replace the selected table of figures.

To Edit a Caption and Update the Table of Figures

The following steps change the Figure 4 caption and then update the table of figures. *Why? When you modify captions in a document or move illustrations to a different location in the document, you will have to update the table of figures.*

1

• Click the heading, To Insert a Screenshot, in the Navigation Pane to display the selected heading in the document window. (If this heading is not at the top of page 7, insert a page break to position the heading at the top of a new page.)

• Insert the text, Word, in the Figure 4 caption so that it reads: Word Help Center Window Screenshot (Figure 9–64).

Figure 9–64

2

• Click the heading, Table of Figures, in the Navigation Pane to display the Table of Figures heading in the document window.

• Click the table of figures to select it.

• Click the Update Table button (References tab | Captions group) to display the Update Table of Figures dialog box.

• Click 'Update entire table' (Update Table of Figures dialog box), so that Word updates the contents of the entire table of figures instead of updating only the page numbers (Figure 9–65).

Figure 9–65

3

- Click OK to update the table of figures and then click outside the table to deselect it (Figure 9–66).

Q&A

Are the entries in the table of figures links? Yes. As with the table of contents, you can CTRL+click any entry in the table of figures and Word will display the associated figure in the document window.

Research | Citations & Bibliography | Captions | Index | Table of Authorities

Table of Figures

Figure 1: World Continents Image 1
Figure 2: Sunflower Field Picture 2
Figure 3: Cloud Shape 3
Figure 4: Word Help Center Window Screenshot 4

caption updated in table of figures

Figure 9–66

Other Ways

1. Select table of figures, press F9

To Insert an Index

The reference document in this module ends with an index. Earlier, this module showed how to mark index entries. ***Why?*** *For Word to generate the index, you first must mark any text you wish to appear in the index.*

Once all index entries are marked, Word can insert the index from the index entry fields in the document. Recall that index entry fields begin with XE, which appears on the screen when formatting marks are displayed. When index entry fields show on the screen, the document's pagination probably will be altered because of the extra text in the index entries. Thus, be sure to hide formatting marks before inserting an index. The following steps insert an index.

1

- Click the heading, Index, in the Navigation Pane to display the Index heading in the document window.

- Click to the right of the Index heading and then press ENTER, so that the insertion point is on the line below the heading.

- Ensure that formatting marks are not displayed.

- Click the Insert Index button (References tab | Index group) to display the Index dialog box.

- If necessary, click the Formats arrow in the dialog box and then click Classic in the Formats list to change the index format.

- Place a check mark in the 'Right align page numbers' check box.

- Click the Tab leader arrow and then click the first leader character in the list to specify the leader character to be displayed between the index entry and the page number.

- Click the Columns down arrow until the number of columns is 1 to change the number of columns in the index (Figure 9–67).

Figure 9–67

2

- Click OK (Index dialog box) to insert an index at the location of the insertion point (Figure 9–68).

Q&A
How would I change the language used in the index?
If multiple languages are installed, click the Language arrow (shown in Figure 9–67) (Index dialog box) and then click the desired language.

Figure 9–68

To Mark Another Index Entry

Notice in Figure 9–68 that the 'insert a screenshot' index entry is missing. The following steps mark an index entry in the Insert a Screenshot section.

1 Click the heading, To Insert a Screenshot, in the Navigation Pane to display the selected heading in the document window.

2 Select the words, Insert a Screenshot, in the heading.

3 Click the Mark Entry button (References tab | Index group) to display the Mark Index Entry dialog box.

4 Type **insert a screenshot** in the Main entry text box (Mark Index Entry dialog box) so that the entry is all lowercase (Figure 9–69).

5 Click the Mark button to mark the entry.

6 Close the dialog box.

7 Hide formatting marks.

BTW
Index Files
Instead of marking index entries in a document, you can create a concordance file that contains all index entries you wish to mark. A concordance file contains two columns: the first column identifies the text in the document you want Word to mark as an index entry, and the second column lists the index entries to be generated from the text in the first column. To mark entries in the concordance file, click the AutoMark button in the Index dialog box.

Figure 9–69

BTW
Navigation Pane
You can drag any heading in the Navigation Pane to reorganize document content. For example, you could drag the To Insert a Screenshot heading upward in the Navigation Pane so that its content appears earlier in the document. You also can promote a heading by right-clicking the heading and then clicking Promote on the shortcut menu. Likewise, you can demote a heading by right-clicking the heading and then clicking Demote on the shortcut menu. To delete a heading and all its contents, right-click the heading and then click Delete on the shortcut menu. If you wanted to print all content in a heading, you would right-click the heading and then click 'Print Heading and Content' on the shortcut menu.

TO EDIT AN INDEX ENTRY

At some time, you may want to change an index entry after you have marked it. For example, you may forget to lowercase the entry for the headings. If you wanted to change an index entry, you would perform the following steps.

1. Display formatting marks.
2. Locate the XE field for the index entry you wish to change (i.e., { XE "Insert a Screenshot" }).
3. Change the text inside the quotation marks (i.e., { XE "insert a screenshot" }).
4. Update the index as described in the steps in the upcoming steps titled To Update an Index.

TO DELETE AN INDEX ENTRY

If you wanted to delete an index entry, you would perform the following steps.

1. Display formatting marks.
2. Select the XE field for the index entry you wish to delete (i.e., { XE "insert a screenshot" }).
3. Press DELETE.
4. Update the index as described in the steps in the next set of steps.

To Update an Index

The following step updates an index. *Why? After marking a new index entry, you must update the index.*

1

- Click the heading, Index, in the Navigation Pane to display the selected heading in the document window.

- In the document window, click the index to select it.

- If necessary, display the References tab.

- Click the Update Index button (References tab | Index group) to update the index (Figure 9–70).

Figure 9–70

To Change the Format of the Index

If you wanted to change the format of the index, you would perform the following steps.

1. Click the index to select it.
2. Click the Insert Index button (References tab | Index group) to display the Index dialog box.
3. Change settings in the dialog box as desired. If you want to modify the style used for the index, click the Modify button.
4. Click OK (Index dialog box) to apply the changed settings.
5. Click OK when Word asks if you want to replace the selected index.

To Delete an Entire Index

If you wanted to delete an index, you would perform the following steps.

1. Click the index to select it.
2. Press SHIFT+F9 to display field codes.
3. Drag through the entire field code, including the braces, and then press DELETE.

Table of Authorities

In addition to inserting an index, table of figures, and table of contents, you can use Word to insert a table of authorities. Legal documents often include a **table of authorities** to list references to cases, rules, statutes, etc., along with the page number(s) on which the references appear. To create a table of authorities, you mark the citations first and then insert the table of authorities.

The procedures for marking citations, editing citations, inserting the table of authorities, changing the format of the table of authorities, and updating the table of authorities are the same as those for indexes. The only difference is that you use the buttons in the Table of Authorities group on the References tab instead of the buttons in the Index group.

To Mark a Citation

If you wanted to mark a citation, creating a citation entry, you would perform the following steps.

1. Select the long, full citation that you wish to appear in the table of authorities (for example, State v. Smith 220 J.3d 167 (UT, 1997)).
2. Click the Mark Citation button (References tab | Table of Authorities group) or press ALT+SHIFT+I to display the Mark Citation dialog box.
3. If necessary, click the Category arrow (Mark Citation dialog box) and then select a new category type.
4. If desired, enter a short version of the citation in the Short citation text box.
5. Click the Mark button to mark the selected text in the document as a citation.

Q&A Why do formatting marks now appear on the screen?
When you mark a citation, Word automatically shows formatting marks (if they are not showing already) so that you can see the citation field. The citation entry begins with the letters, TA.

BTW
Field Codes
If your index, table of contents, or table of figures displays odd characters inside curly braces ({}), then Word is displaying field codes instead of field results. Press ALT+F9 to display the index or table correctly.

BTW
Inserting Endnotes
To insert an endnote, click the Insert Endnote button (Reference tab | Footnotes group), which places a separator line and the endnote text at the end of the document. Enter desired endnote text to the right of the note reference mark below the separator line.

BTW
Advanced Layout Options
You can adjust Word's advanced layout options by clicking File on the ribbon to open Backstage view, clicking Options in Backstage view to display the Word Options dialog box, clicking Advanced in the left pane (Word Options dialog box), scrolling to the Layout options for area in the right pane, placing a check mark in the desired settings, and then clicking OK.

6. Click the Close button in the Mark Citation dialog box.

Q&A How could I see all marked citation entries in a document?

With formatting marks displaying, you could scroll through the document, scanning for all occurrences of TA, or you could use the Navigation Pane (that is, place a check mark in the Navigation Pane check box (View tab | Show group)) to find all occurrences of TA.

To Mark Multiple Citations

Word leaves the Mark Citation dialog box open until you close it, which allows you to mark multiple citations without having to redisplay the dialog box repeatedly. To mark multiple citations, you would perform the following steps.

1. With the Mark Citation dialog box displayed, click in the document window; scroll to and then select the next citation.

2. If necessary, click the Selected text text box (Mark Citation dialog box) to display the selected text in the Selected text text box.

3. Click the Mark button.

4. Repeat Steps 1 through 3 for all citations you wish to mark. When finished, click the Close button in the dialog box.

To Edit a Citation Entry

At some time, you may want to change a citation entry after you have marked it. For example, you may need to change the case of a letter. If you wanted to change a citation entry, you would perform the following steps.

1. Display formatting marks.

2. Locate the TA field for the citation entry you wish to change.

3. Change the text inside the quotation marks.

4. Update the table of authorities as described in the steps at the end of this section.

To Delete a Citation Entry

If you wanted to delete a citation entry, you would perform the following steps.

1. Display formatting marks.

2. Select the TA field for the citation entry you wish to delete.

3. Press DELETE, or click the Cut button (Home tab | Clipboard group), or right-click the field and then click Cut on the Mini toolbar or shortcut menu.

4. Update the table of authorities as described in the steps at the end of this section.

To Insert a Table of Authorities

Once all citations are marked, Word can build a table of authorities from the citation entries in the document. Recall that citation entries begin with TA, and they appear on the screen when formatting marks are displayed. When citation entries show on the screen, the document's pagination probably will be altered because of the extra text in the citation entries. Thus, be sure to hide formatting marks before inserting a table of authorities. To insert a table of authorities, you would perform the following steps.

1. Position the insertion point at the location for the table of authorities.

2. Ensure that formatting marks are not displayed.

3. Click the 'Insert Table of Authorities' button (References tab | Table of Authorities group) to display the Table of Authorities dialog box.

BTW
Line Numbers
If you wanted to insert line numbers in a document, click the Line Numbers button (Layout tab | Page Setup group) and then click the desired line number setting on the Line Numbers menu.

4. If necessary, select the category to appear in the table of authorities by clicking the desired option in the Category list, or leave the default selection of All so that all categories will be displayed in the table of authorities.

5. If necessary, click the Formats arrow (Table of Authorities dialog box) and then select the desired format for the table of authorities.

6. If necessary, click the Tab leader arrow and then select the desired leader character in the list to specify the leader character to be displayed between the marked citation and the page number.

7. If you wish to display the word, passim, instead of page numbers for citations with more than four page references, select the Use passim check box.

Q&A | What does the word, passim, mean?
Here and there.

8. Click OK (Table of Authorities dialog box) to create a table of authorities using the specified settings at the location of the insertion point.

TO UPDATE A TABLE OF AUTHORITIES

If you add, delete, or modify citation entries, you must update the table of authorities to display the new or modified citation entries. If you wanted to update a table of authorities, you would perform the following steps.

1. In the document window, click the table of authorities to select it.

2. Click the Update Table button (References tab | Table of Authorities group) or press F9 to update the table of authorities.

TO CHANGE THE FORMAT OF THE TABLE OF AUTHORITIES

If you wanted to change the format of the table of authorities, you would perform the following steps.

1. Click the table of authorities to select it.

2. Click the 'Insert Table of Authorities' button (References tab | Table of Authorities group) to display the Table of Authorities dialog box.

3. Change settings in the dialog box as desired. To change the style of headings, alignment, etc., click the Formats arrow and then click From template; next, click the Modify button to display the Style dialog box, make necessary changes, and then click OK (Style dialog box).

4. Click OK (Table of Authorities dialog box) to apply the changed settings.

5. Click OK when Word asks if you want to replace the selected category of the table of authorities.

TO DELETE A TABLE OF AUTHORITIES

If you wanted to delete a table of authorities, you would perform the following steps.

1. Click the table of authorities to select it.

2. Press SHIFT+F9 to display field codes.

3. Drag through the entire field code, including the braces, and then press DELETE, or click the Cut button (Home tab | Clipboard group), or right-click the field and then click Cut on the Mini toolbar or shortcut menu.

BTW
Different First Page Header or Footer
If you wanted only the first page of a document to have a different header or footer, you could place a check mark in the 'Different First Page' check box (Header & Footer Tools Design tab | Options group). Doing so instructs Word to create a first page header or first page footer that can contain content that differs from the rest of the headers or footers.

BTW
Inserting Equations
To insert a built-in equation in a document, click the Equation arrow (Insert tab | Symbols group) and then select the desired equation to insert the equation in an equation editor in the document. To enter your own equation, click the Equation button (Insert tab | Symbols group) or click the Equation arrow and then click 'Insert New Equation' on the Equation menu to insert the equation editor in the document. Use buttons and boxes on the Equation Tools tab to enter and format the equation in the equation editor box.

To Specify Different Odd and Even Page Footers Using a Footer Building Block

The *Using Word 2019* document is designed so that it can be duplicated back-to-back. That is, the document prints on nine separate pages. When it is duplicated, however, pages are printed on opposite sides of the same sheet of paper. *Why? Back-to-back duplicating saves resources because it enables the nine-page document to use only five sheets of paper.*

In many books and documents that have facing pages, the page number is always on the same side of the page — often on the outside edge. In Word, you accomplish this task by specifying one type of header or footer for even-numbered pages and another type of header or footer for odd-numbered pages. The following steps specify alternating footers beginning on the fourth page of the document (the beginning of the subdocument).

1
- If necessary, hide formatting marks.
- Use the Navigation Pane to display the page with the heading, Inserting Images in Word Documents.
- Display the Insert tab.
- Click the Footer button (Insert tab | Header & Footer group) and then click Edit Footer to display the footer area.
- Be sure the 'Link to Previous' button (Header & Footer Tools Design tab | Navigation group) is not selected.

Q&A | What is the purpose of the 'Link to Previous' button?
If you want to continue using the same header or footer from a previous section, you would select the 'Link to Previous' button. If you want to create a different header or footer from the previous section, you would ensure the 'Link to Previous' button is not selected.

- Place a check mark in the 'Different Odd & Even Pages' check box (Header & Footer Tools Design tab | Options group), so that you can enter a different footer for odd and even pages.
- Delete any text that appears in the section 3 footer.
- If necessary, click the Next button (Header & Footer Tools Design tab | Navigation group) to display the desired footer page (in this case, the Odd Page Footer -Section 4-).

2
- Click the 'Insert Alignment Tab' button (Header & Footer Tools Design tab | Position group) to display the Alignment Tab dialog box so that you can set the position of the footer.
- Click Right (Alignment Tab dialog box) because you want to place a right-aligned tab stop in the footer (Figure 9–71).

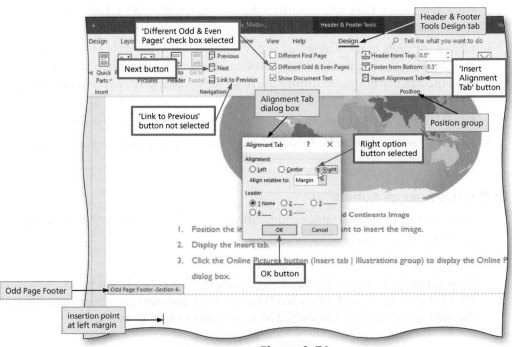

Figure 9–71

3

- Click OK to align the paragraph and insertion point in the footer at the right margin.
- Click the Page Numbers button (Header & Footer Tools Design tab | Header & Footer group) to display the Page Number gallery.
- Point to Current Position in the Page Number gallery to display the Current Position gallery (Figure 9–72).

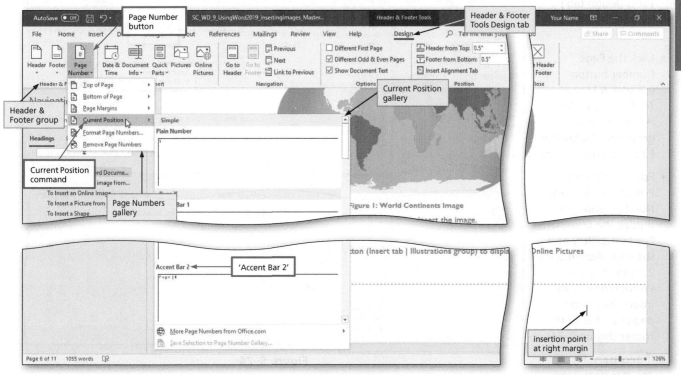

Figure 9–72

4

- Click 'Accent Bar 2' in the Current Position gallery to insert the selected page number in the footer (Figure 9–73).

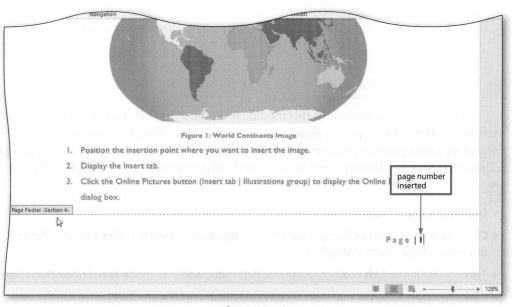

Figure 9–73

5

- Click the Next button (Header & Footer Tools Design tab | Navigation group) to display the next footer, in this case, Even Page Footer -Section 4-.

- Be sure the 'Link to Previous' button (Header & Footer Tools Design tab | Navigation group) is not selected.

- Click the Page Number button (Header & Footer Tools Design tab | Header & Footer group) to display the Page Number gallery.

- Point to Current Position in the Page Number gallery to display the Current Position gallery and the click 'Accent Bar 2' in the Current Position gallery to insert the selected page number in the footer (Figure 9–74).

Figure 9–74

- If necessary, fix any incorrect page numbers in the document by positioning the insertion point on the page, clicking the Page Number button (Insert tab | Header & Footer group), clicking the 'Format Page Numbers' command on the Format Page Numbers menu, entering the desired page number in the Start at box, and then clicking OK.

 Can I specify alternating headers?

Yes. Follow the same basic procedure, except insert a header building block or header text.

To Set a Gutter Margin

The reference document in this module is designed so that the inner margin between facing pages has extra space. *Why? Extra space on facing pages allows printed versions of the documents to be bound (such as stapled) — without the binding covering the words.* This extra space in the inner margin is called the **gutter margin**. The following steps set a three-quarter-inch left and right margin and a one-half-inch gutter margin.

1

- Display the Layout tab.

- Click the Margins button (Layout tab | Page Setup group) and then click Custom Margins in the Margins gallery to display the Page Setup dialog box.

- Type **.75** in the Left box, **.75** in the Right box, and **.5** in the Gutter box (Page Setup dialog box).

- Click the Apply to arrow and then click Whole document (Figure 9–75).

2

- Click OK (Page Setup dialog box) to set the new margins for the entire document.

Figure 9–75

To Check the Layout of the Printed Pages

To view the layout of all the pages in the document, the following steps display all the pages as they will print.

1 Open Backstage view.

2 Click Print to display all pages of the document in the right pane, as shown in Figure 9–76. (If all pages are not displayed, change the Zoom level to 10%.)

Q&A

Why do blank pages appear in the middle of the document?
When you insert even and odd headers or footers, Word may add pages to fill the gaps.

3 Close Backstage view.

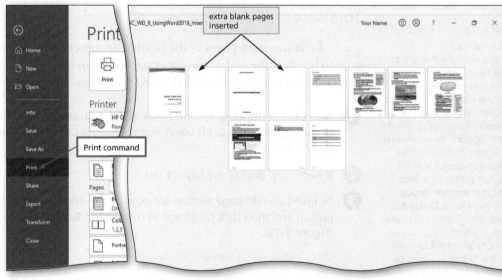

Figure 9–76

To Switch to Draft View

To adjust the blank pages automatically inserted in the printed document by Word, you change the continuous section break at the top of the document to an odd page section break. The following step switches to Draft view. **Why?** *Section breaks are easy to see in Draft view.*

1

- Display the View tab. Click the Draft button (View tab | Views group) to switch to Draft view.

- Scroll to the top of the document and notice how different the document looks in Draft view (Figure 9–77).

Q&A
What happened to the images, footers, and other items?
They do not appear in Draft view because Draft view is designed to make editing text in a document easier.

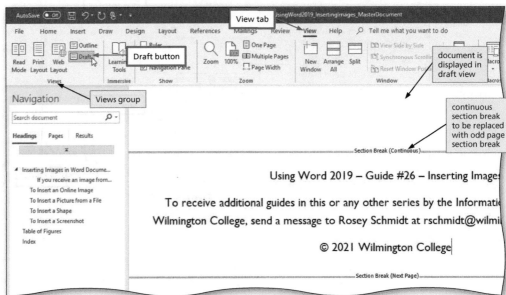

Figure 9–77

BTW
Header and Footer Margins
If you want the margins of the header or footer to be different from the default of one-half inch, you would adjust the margin in the 'Header from Top' or 'Footer from Bottom' boxes (Header & Footer Tools Design tab | Position group) or in the Layout sheet of the Page Setup dialog box through the Page Setup Dialog Box Launcher (Layout tab | Page Setup group). You also can specify alignment of items in the header or footer by clicking the 'Insert Alignment Tab' button (Header & Footer Tools Design tab | Position group) and then clicking the desired alignment in the Alignment Tab dialog box.

To Insert an Odd Page Section Break

To fix the extra pages in the printed document, you will replace the continuous section break at the end of the cover page with an odd page section break. With an odd page section break, Word starts the next section on an odd page instead of an even page.

1 Select the continuous section break at the bottom of the cover page (or top of the document in Draft view) and then press DELETE to delete the selected section break.

2 If necessary, display the Layout tab.

3 To insert an odd page section break, click the Breaks button (Layout tab | Page Setup group) and then click Odd Page in the Section Breaks area in the Breaks gallery (Figure 9–78).

Q&A Can I insert even page section breaks?
Yes. To instruct Word to start the next section on an even page, click Even Page in the Breaks gallery.

4 Click the Print Layout button on the status bar to switch to Print Layout view.

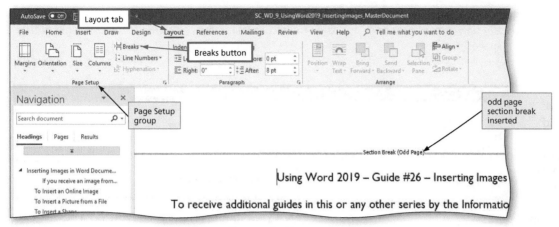

Figure 9–78

To Insert a Bookmark

A **bookmark** is a physical location in a document that you name so that you can reference it later. The following steps insert bookmarks. **Why?** *Bookmarks assist users in navigating through a document online. For example, you could bookmark the headings in the document, so that users easily could jump to these areas of the document.*

1

- Use the Navigation Pane to display the To Insert an Online Image heading in the document window and then select the heading in the document.

- Display the Insert tab and then, if necessary, display the Links group (Figure 9–79).

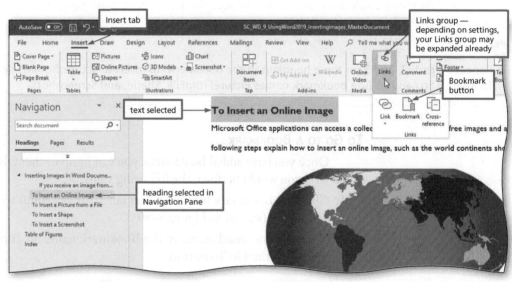

Figure 9–79

2

- Click the Bookmark button (Insert tab | Links group) to display the Bookmark dialog box.

- Type **OnlineImage** in the Bookmark name text box (Figure 9–80).

Figure 9–80

Q&A | What are the rules for bookmark names?
Bookmark names can contain only letters, numbers, and the underscore character (_). They also must begin with a letter and cannot contain spaces.

3

- Click the Add button (Bookmark dialog box) to add the bookmark name to the list of existing bookmarks in the document; click anywhere to remove the selection (Figure 9–81).

Q&A | What if my screen does not show the brackets around the bookmark?
Click File on the ribbon to open Backstage view, click Options to display the Word Options dialog box, click Advanced in the left pane (Word Options dialog box), scroll to the Show document content area in the right pane, place a check mark in the Show bookmarks check box, and then click OK

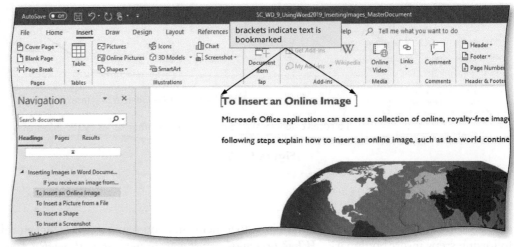

Figure 9–81

4

- Repeat Steps 1, 2, and 3 for these headings in the document: To Insert a Picture from a File, To Insert a Shape, and To Insert a Screenshot (use bookmark names PictureFromFile, Shape, and Screenshot).

TO GO TO A BOOKMARK

Once you have added bookmarks, you can jump to them. If you wanted to go to a bookmark, you would perform the following steps.

1. Click the Bookmark button (Insert tab | Links group) to display the Bookmark dialog box (shown in Figure 9–80).
2. Click the bookmark name in the Bookmark name list (Bookmark dialog box) and then click the Go To button.

or

1. Press F5 to display the Go To sheet in the Find and Replace dialog box.
2. Click Bookmark in the list (Find and Replace dialog box), click the 'Enter bookmark name' arrow, click the desired bookmark in the list, and then click the Go To button.

TO INSERT A HYPERLINK TO A LOCATION IN THE CURRENT DOCUMENT

Instead of or in addition to bookmarks in online documents, you can insert hyperlinks that link one part of a document to another. If you wanted to insert a hyperlink that links to a heading or bookmark in the document, you would follow these steps.

1. Select the text to be a hyperlink.
2. Click the Link button (Insert tab | Links group) to display the Insert Hyperlink dialog box.

BTW

Hyperlink to Bookmark
If you wanted to insert a hyperlink to a bookmark in a document, click the Cross-reference button (Insert tab | Links group), select Bookmark in the Reference type list (Cross-reference dialog box), select the desired bookmark in the For which bookmark list, be sure the 'Insert as hyperlink' check box is selected, and then click OK. To display the bookmark associated with the link, CTRL+click the link.

3. In the Link to bar (Insert Hyperlink dialog box), click 'Place in This Document', so that Word displays all the headings and bookmarks in the document.

4. Click the heading or bookmark to which you want to link.

5. Click OK.

To Save and Print a Document and Then Exit Word

The reference document for this project now is complete. The following steps save and print the document and then exit Word.

1 **sam↑** Save the document again as a Word (.docx) file on the same storage location with the same file name.

2 If requested by your instructor, print the finished document (shown in Figure 9–1 at the beginning of this module).

3 If requested by your instructor, save the document as a PDF file and submit the PDF in the format requested by your instructor.

4 If requested by your instructor, unlink the subdocument so that it is converted to be part of the master document by clicking the Outline button (View tab | Views group) to switch to Outline view, clicking the Show Document button (Outlining tab | Master Document group) to show all buttons in the Master Document group, click somewhere in the subdocument, and then click the Unlink button (Outlining tab | Master Document group) to break the connection between the text in the master document and the subdocument so that all content is in a single file. Click File on the ribbon, click Save As, save the unlinked document using SC_WD_9_UsingWord2019_InsertingImages_UnlinkedDocument as the Word file name, and then submit the unlinked Word document in the format requested by your instructor.

5 Exit Word.

Summary

In this module, you learned how to insert a screenshot, insert captions, insert cross-references, insert a sidebar text box, link text boxes, compress pictures, use Outline view, work with master documents and subdocuments, and insert a table of contents, a table of figures, and an index.

BTW

Conserving Ink and Toner

If you want to conserve ink or toner, you can instruct Word to print draft quality documents by clicking File on the ribbon to open Backstage view, clicking Options in Backstage view to display the Word Options dialog box, clicking Advanced in the left pane (Word Options dialog box), scrolling to the Print area in the right pane, placing a check mark in the 'Use draft quality' check box, and then clicking OK. Then, use Backstage view to print the document as usual.

BTW

Distributing a Document

Instead of printing and distributing a hard copy of a document, you can distribute the document electronically. Options include sending the document via email; posting it on cloud storage (such as OneDrive) and sharing the file with others; posting it on social media, a blog, or other website; and sharing a link associated with an online location of the document. You also can create and share a PDF or XPS image of the document, so that users can view the file in Adobe Reader or XPS Viewer instead of in Word.

What decisions will you need to make when creating reference documents?
Use these guidelines as you complete the assignments in this module and create your own reference documents outside of this class.

1. Prepare a document to be included in a longer document.

   a) If a document contains multiple images (figures), each figure should have a caption and be referenced from within the text.

   b) All terms in the document that should be included in the index should be marked as an index entry.

2. Include elements common to a reference document, such as a cover page, a table of contents, and an index.

   a) The cover page entices passersby to take a copy of the document.

   b) A table of contents at the beginning of the document and an index at the end helps a reader locate topics within the document.

   c) If a document contains several images, you also should include a table of figures.

3. Prepare the document for distribution, including page numbers, gutter margins for binding, bookmarks, and hyperlinks as appropriate.

CONSIDER THIS: PLAN AHEAD

Apply Your Knowledge

Reinforce the skills and apply the concepts you learned in this module.

Working with Outline View

Note: To complete this assignment, you will be required to use the Data Files. Please contact your instructor for information about accessing the Data Files.

Instructions: Start Word. Open the document, SC_WD_9-2.docx, which is located in the Data Files. Written by the school administration office manager at Washington Elementary, the document is an outline for a reference document that, when complete, will be distributed to faculty and staff. You are to modify the outline. The final outline is shown in Figure 9–82.

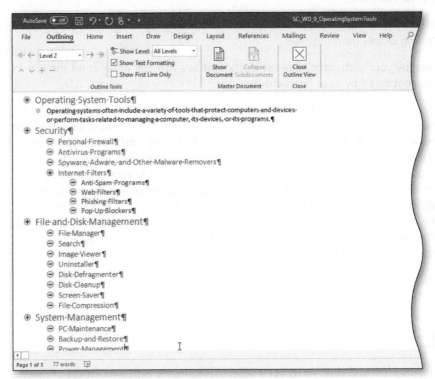

Figure 9–82

Perform the following tasks:

1. Click File on the ribbon and then click Save As and save the document using the new file name, SC_WD_9_OperatingSystemTools.

2. If necessary, switch to Outline view.

3. In the File and Disk Management section, move the Screen Saver heading down three lines so that it is immediately above the File Compression heading.

4. Promote the Security heading so that it is Level 1 instead of Level 2.

5. Demote the Power Management heading so that it is Level 2 instead of Level 1.

6. Demote the Anti-Spam Programs heading so that it is Level 3 instead of Level 2.

7. Move the File and Disk Management heading and all of its subheadings up so that they appear immediately above the System Management heading. (*Hint*: When you move a heading, all of its subheadings move with it.)

8. Practice collapsing and expanding headings in Outline view by collapsing the Security heading and then expanding the heading.

9. Change the word, Recover, in the System Management section to the word, Restore, so that heading reads: Backup and Restore.

10. Immediately below the Personal Firewall heading, insert a Level 2 heading with the text, Antivirus Programs.

11. Delete the duplicate Image Viewer heading in the File and Disk Management section.

12. Remove the check mark from the 'Show Text Formatting' check box (Outlining tab | Outline Tools group). Place the check mark in the check box again. What is the purpose of this check box?

13. Ensure that the 'Show First Line Only' check box (Outlining tab | Outline Tools group) does not contain a check mark.

14. Add a blank line below the Operating System Tools heading. Demote the heading to body text. Enter this sentence as the body text: Operating systems often include a variety of tools that protect computers and devices or perform tasks related to managing a computer, its devices, or its programs.

15. If requested by your instructor, add your name after the sentence entered in the previous step.

16. Place a check mark in the 'Show First Line Only' check box (Outlining tab | Outline Tools group). Remove the check mark from the check box again. What is the purpose of this check box?

17. Close Outline View. How does the document differ when displayed in Print Layout view?

18. Use the View tab to open the Navigation Pane.

19. Practice collapsing and expanding headings in the Navigation Pane by collapsing the Security heading and then expanding the heading.

20. Use the Navigation Pane to go to the System Management heading. Go to the Security heading. If necessary, expand the Security heading. Go to the Web Filters heading.

21. If necessary, expand the Web Filters heading. Using the Navigation Pane, promote the Phishing Filters heading so that it is the same level as the Web Filters heading.

22. Using the Navigation Pane, demote the Pop-Up Blockers heading so that it is the same level as the Web Filters heading.

23. Close the Navigation Pane.

24. Switch to Outline view.

25. Use the Show Level arrow (Outlining tab | Outline Tools group) to show only Level 1 headings. Show up to Level 2 headings. Show up to Level 3 headings. Lastly, show all levels.

26. Save the document again with the same name and then submit it in the format specified by your instructor. Close the document.

27. ✳ Answer the questions posed in #12, #16, and #17. What are two different ways to expand and collapse items in an outline, to move items up and down an outline, and to demote and promote items in an outline?

Extend Your Knowledge

Extend the skills you learned in this module and experiment with new skills. You may need to use Help to complete the assignment.

Creating a Reference Document with a Cover Page, a Table of Contents, and an Index
Note: To complete this assignment, you will be required to use the Data Files. Please contact your instructor for information about accessing the Data Files.

Continued >

Extend Your Knowledge *continued*

Instructions: Start Word. Open the draft document, SC_WD_9-3.docx, which is located in the Data Files. The draft discusses backup procedures and a disaster recovery plan, written by the information security specialist at Donner Outpatient Center. You are to insert a cover page, a table of contents, headers and footers, and an index.

Perform the following tasks:

1. Use Help to expand your knowledge about a cover page, a table of contents, headers and footers, marking index entries, and an index.

2. Click File on the ribbon and then click Save As and save the document using the new file name, SC_WD_9_DisasterRecovery.

3. Insert the Banded style cover page. Use the following information on the cover page: title – Disaster Recovery; author – Information Security Center; company name – Donner Outpatient Center; company address – 104 Whitaker Avenue, Cedar Hills, UT 84062.

4. If requested by your instructor, use your name as the author instead of Information Security Center.

5. Insert a blank page between the cover page and the Backup Procedures heading.

6. Insert a table of contents on the blank page using the Automatic Table 1 style.

7. Mark the following terms in the document as index entries: backup, backup program, full backup, differential backup, incremental backup, selective backup, continuous data protection, Cloud backup services, disaster recovery plan, hot site, failover, and cold site. Lowercase the first letter in the index entry for the words, Cloud, so that the entire entry appears in lowercase letters in the index.

8. Mark the following items in the document as index entries, that also have the subentry of the text, in a disaster recovery plan (Figure 9–83): emergency plan, backup plan, recovery plan, and test plan.

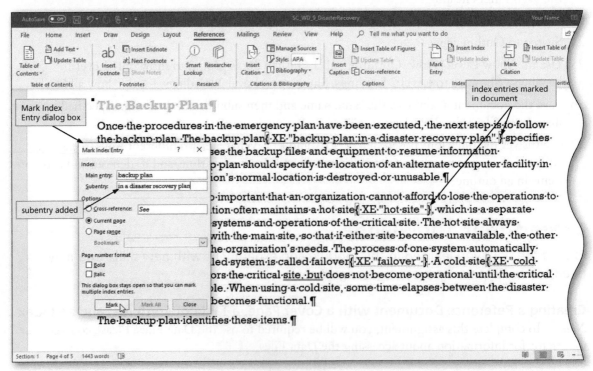

Figure 9–83

9. On a separate page at the end of the document, insert the word, Index, formatted in the Heading 1 style and then insert an index for the document. Remember to hide formatting marks prior to building the index. Use the From template format using one column, with right-aligned page numbers and leader characters of your choice.

10. Update the table of contents so that it includes the index.

11. Mark another term of your choice in the document as an index entry. Update the index so that it includes this term.

12. Change the format of the table of contents to a format of your choice. (*Hint*: Select the table of contents, click the 'Table of Contents' button (References tab | Table of Contents group), click 'Custom Table of Contents' on the menu, and then select the desired format in the dialog box.) In the Table of Contents dialog box, remove the check mark from the 'Right align page numbers' check box and then see how the table of contents looks in the document.

13. Redisplay the Table of Contents dialog box and then place a check mark in the 'Right align page numbers' check box. Select a tab leader character of your choice for the table of contents.

14. Find the bold italic format in the document and replace it with just an italic format. (*Hint*: Use the Replace dialog box and find the Bold Italic format and replace with the Not Bold format.)

15. Specify to prevent widows and orphans in the document, if necessary. (*Hint*: Use the Paragraph Dialog Box Launcher and select options in the Line and Page Breaks sheet.)

16. Select each of the numbered lists and the lead-in sentence above them, and then specify to keep with next and keep lines together so that the paragraph lines stay together. (*Hint*: Use the Paragraph Dialog Box Launcher and select options in the Line and Page Breaks sheet.)

17. Specify that the paragraph containing the Disaster Recovery Plan heading should have a page break before it. (*Hint*: Use the Paragraph Dialog Box Launcher and select options in the Line and Page Breaks sheet.)

18. Insert a continuous section break to the left of the B in the Backup Procedures heading.

19. Format the page number on page with the Backup Procedures heading to begin on page 1. (*Hint*: Use the Page Number button (Insert tab | Header & Footer group).)

20. On the page that begins with the Backup Procedures heading, insert a footer by clicking the Footer button (Insert tab | Header & Footer group) and then clicking Edit Footer. Be sure the 'Different First Page' check box (Header & Footer Tools Design tab | Options group) is not selected. Select the 'Different Odd & Even Pages' check box (Header & Footer Tools Design tab | Options group). Be sure the 'Link to Previous' button (Header & Footer Tools Design tab | Navigation group) is not selected. Use the 'Insert Alignment Tab' button (Header & Footer Tools Design tab | Position group) to set right alignment for the position of the odd page footer. Use the Page Number button (Header & Footer Tools Design tab | Header & Footer group) to insert the Accent Bar 2 page number style at the current position. If necessary, set the starting page number to 1 on the page containing the Backup Procedures heading.

21. Click the Next button (Header & Footer Tools Design tab | Navigation group) to go to the next section footer. Insert the Accent Bar 2 page number style at the left margin for the even page footer. The cover page and table of contents should not have a page number (you may need to delete the footer contents on these pages).

22. Update the page numbers in the table of contents.

23. Insert a bookmark for the Backup Procedures and Disaster Recovery Plan headings in the document.

24. Practice going to each bookmark created in the previous step.

25. If requested by your instructor, set gutter margins as follows: From the page with the Backup Procedures heading forward, set the left and right margins to .75" and set a gutter margin

Continued >

Extend Your Knowledge *continued*

of .5" (be sure to position the insertion point to the left of the B in Backup Procedures and select 'This point forward' in the dialog box). Open Backstage view and then click Print to display the Print screen so that you can see if extra pages were inserted due to the gutter margin. Close Backstage view.

26. If you performed the previous step, you may need to fix extra pages in the document by switching to Draft view, deleting the continuous section break, and then inserting an even page section break or an odd page section break using the Breaks button (Layout tab | Page Setup group). Practice inserting one, check the pages in the Print screen in Backstage view, undo the insert or delete odd or even section break and then insert the other. When finished, switch to Print Layout view. If necessary, reinsert page numbers in the even or odd footers (be sure the Link to Previous button is not selected).

27. On a blank line below the index, use the Cross-reference button (Insert tab | Links group) to insert a cross-reference to one of the bookmarks as a hyperlink. Then, practice going to the link by CTRL+clicking the link. Delete the inserted cross-reference.

28. On the same blank line, use the Link button (Insert tab | Links group) to insert a hyperlink to a place in the document of your choice. After inserting the link, practice going to the link by CTRL+clicking the link. Delete the inserted link.

29. Position the insertion point on the Backup Procedures heading. Use the Line Numbers button (Layout tab | Page Setup group) to display continuous line numbers. Scroll through the document to see how line numbers are applied. Remove the line numbers from the document.

30. Save the document again and then submit it in the format specified by your instructor.

31. If required by your instructor or if you would like to practice with citations and a table of authorities, open the draft document again, SC_WD_9-3.docx, which is located in the Data Files. Add this text to the end of the last paragraph: State v. Carstens J.3d 169 (UT, 2021). Select the text just added and then mark the citation using the Mark Citation button (References tab | Table of Authorities group). Insert a new page at the end of the document and then insert a table of authorities on the blank page. At the end of another paragraph in the document, type this text: Barnes v. Wilson 212 F.4d 228 (FL, 2021). Update the table of authorities. Close the document without saving.

32. ✸ If you wanted the index entries to appear in bold in the index but remain not bold in the document, what steps would you take to accomplish this?

Expand Your World

Create a solution that uses cloud or web technologies by learning and investigating on your own from general guidance.

Inserting Equations, Symbols, Screenshots, and Screen Clippings, and Using an Online Photo Editor

Note: To complete this assignment, you will be required to use the Data Files. Please contact your instructor for information about accessing the Data Files.

Instructions: As an assistant to the business manager at IT Training Solutions, you have been asked to insert sample mathematical symbols and equations in a Word document, take a screenshot of the screen, and then use an online photo editor to enhance the screenshot. Be creative — the screen shown in Figure 9–84 is only a sample solution. Your document should look different.

Perform the following tasks:

1. Start Word and create a blank document. Change the margins to Narrow. Enter the title, Mathematical Symbols and Equations in Word. Format the entered title appropriately at the top of the page.

2. On a line below the title, insert a mathematical symbol of your choice using the Symbol dialog box. (*Hint*: Click the Subset arrow in the Symbol dialog box and then click Mathematical Operators.) Select the entered mathematical symbol and then place it in a text box by clicking the Text Box button (Insert tab | Text group) and then clicking 'Draw Text Box'. Insert three more mathematical operators using this procedure. Position, resize, and format the text boxes as desired.

3. Insert a text box in the document. Delete any text in the text box and insert a built-in equation of your choice using the Equation arrow (Insert tab | Symbols group). Select the equation and format and position it as desired.

4. Insert another text box in the document and delete any text in the text box. So that you can type an equation in the text box, click the Equation button (Insert tab | Symbols group) or click the Equation arrow and then click 'Insert New Equation'. Use the Equation Tools tab to insert an equation of your choice in the equation editor box. Select the equation and format and position it as desired. The title and all text boxes should fit in the document window (Figure 9–84).

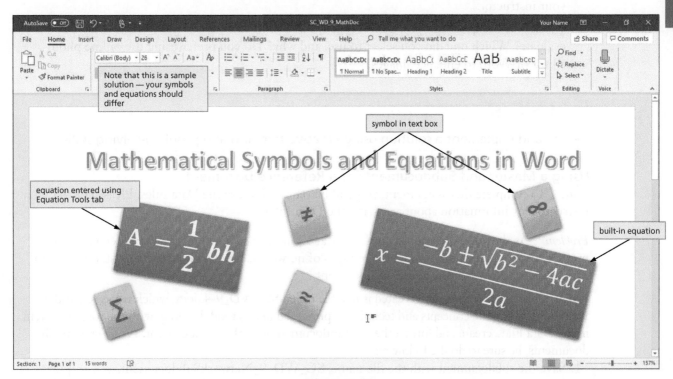

Figure 9–84

5. Save the document with the file name, SC_WD_9_MathDoc.

6. From Word, create a blank document so that you have two separate Word windows open. Enter the text, Screenshot, at the top of the blank document. Then, insert a screenshot of the window containing the SC_WD_9_MathDoc file. Center the screenshot.

7. On a blank line below the inserted screenshot, enter the text, Screen clipping. Then, insert a screen clipping of just the mathematical symbols and equations. Center the screen clipping.

Continued >

8. Save the document with the screenshot and screen clipping with the file name, SC_WD_9_MathDocScreens.

9. Save the Word screenshot as a JPEG file with the name, SC_WD_9_MathScreenshot. (*Hint*: Right-click the image and then click 'Save as Picture' on the submenu.)

10. Save the screen clipping as a JPEG file with the file name, SC_WD_9_MathScreenClipping.

11. Locate the saved JPEG files and then double-click them. In what program did they open?

12. Submit the documents in the format specified by your instructor.

13. Start a browser. Search for the text, online photo editor, using a search engine. Visit several of the online photo editors and determine which you would like to use to edit an image. Navigate to the desired online photo editor.

14. In the photo editor, open the SC_WD_9_MathScreenClipping image that you created in Step 10. Use the photo editor to enhance the image. Apply at least five enhancements. Which enhancements did you apply?

15. If requested by your instructor, add your name as a text element to the photo.

16. Save the revised image with the file name, SC_WD_9_MathScreenClippingEnhanced. In what format did the online photo editor save the file? Submit the image in the format specified by your instructor.

17. ✺ Answer the questions posed in #11, #14, and #16. Which online photo editors did you evaluate? Which one did you select to use, and why? Do you prefer using the online photo editor or Word to enhance images?

In the Lab

Design and implement a solution using creative thinking and problem-solving skills.

Using a Master and Subdocument for a Reference Document

Note: To complete this assignment, you will be required to use the Data Files. Please contact your instructor for information about accessing the Data Files.

Problem: As the public relations coordinator at Cloud Link Networks, you have been asked to prepare a guide that briefly describes the types of networks. You decide to use a master document and a subdocument for this reference document.

Part 1: The subdocument you created is in a file called SC_WD_9-4.docx, which is located in the Data Files. Using the concepts and techniques presented in this module, along with the source content in the Data Files, create and format the master document with the subdocument. While creating the documents, be sure to do the following:

1. Save the subdocument with the file name, SC_WD_9_NetworkSubdocument.

2. In the subdocument, mark at least 10 terms as index entries.

3. Insert the following six images in the Data Files in appropriate locations in the subdocument:
   - Support_WD_9_Networks.jpg
   - Support_WD_9_ClientServerNetwork.jpg
   - Support_WD_9_PeerToPeerNetwork.jpg
   - Support_WD_9_RingNetwork.jpg
   - Support_WD_9_StarNetwork.jpg
   - Support_WD_9_BusNetwork.jpg

4. Insert appropriate captions for each of the six images.

5. Insert a cross-reference to each of the captions.

6. Compress one of the images and then compress all of the images.

7. Insert a sidebar text box that contains text about networks you use at home or school. Insert another blank text box in the document. Link the two text boxes.

8. Create a master document in a new document window in Outline view. Insert appropriate headings for a Table of Figures and an Index. Insert the subdocument file that is called SC_WD_9_NetworkSubdocument in the appropriate location. Be sure to insert a next page section break between each line in the master document in Outline view. Save the master document with the file name, SC_WD_9_NetworkReferenceDocument. Switch to Print Layout view.

9. Insert an appropriate cover page.

10. Insert a table of contents, a table of figures, and an index.

11. Modify one of the figure captions and the update the table of figures.

12. Format the document with a footer that contains a page number. Practice using the 'Link to Previous' button (Header & Footer Tools Design tab | Navigation group) to continue the footer from a previous section and then create a footer that is different from the previous section.

13. Format the document with a header that is different from the first page.

14. Practice going to the next and previous sections in the document.

15. If requested by your instructor, insert an endnote that contains your name in the document.

16. Be sure to check the spelling and grammar of the finished documents.

17. When you are finished with the master document and subdocuments, save them again and then also save the file as a PDF with the file name, SC_WD_9_NetworkReferenceDocument. Submit your documents and answers to the Part 2 critical thinking questions in the format specified by your instructor.

18. Close all documents and then reopen the master document. In Outline view, expand the document. Collapse the subdocument. Show the subdocument.

19. Practice locking and unlocking a subdocument.

20. Unlink the subdocument. Close the document without saving changes.

Part 2: ✳ You made several decisions while creating the reference document in this assignment: which terms to mark as index entries, what text to use for captions, and how to organize and format the subdocument and master document (table of contents, table of figures, index, etc.). What was the rationale behind each of these decisions? When you proofread the document, what further revisions did you make and why?

10 | Creating an Online Form

Objectives

After completing this module, you will be able to:

- Save a document as a template
- Change paper size
- Add page color
- Insert and format an icon graphic
- Use a table to control layout
- Show the Developer tab
- Insert plain text, drop-down list, check box, rich text, combo box, and date picker content controls
- Edit placeholder text
- Change properties of content controls
- Insert and format a rectangle shape
- Restrict editing to filling in a form
- Open a new document based on a template
- Fill in a form

Introduction

During your personal and professional life, you undoubtedly have filled in countless forms. Whether a federal tax form, a time card, a job application, an order, a deposit slip, a request, or a survey, a form is designed to collect information. In the past, forms were printed; that is, you received the form on a piece of paper, filled it in with a pen or pencil, and then returned it manually. An **online form** contains labels and corresponding blank areas in which a user electronically enters the requested information. You use a computer or mobile device to access, fill in, and then return an online form. In Word, you easily can create an online form for electronic distribution; you also can fill in that same form using Word.

Project: Online Form

Today, businesses and individuals are concerned with using resources efficiently. To minimize paper waste, protect the environment, enhance office efficiency, and improve access to data, many businesses have moved toward a paperless office. Thus, online forms have replaced many paper forms. You access online forms on a website, on a company's intranet, or from your inbox if you receive the form via email.

The project in this module uses Word to produce the online form shown in Figure 10–1. Meal Time Express is a meal service company that provides an online form for potential customers to complete if they are interested in obtaining more

(a) Form Not Yet Filled In

(b) Partially Filled-In Form

(c) Filled-In Form

Figure 10–1

information from a company team member. Designed by the communications specialist at Meal Time Express, the form is available on the company's website, where a potential customer can download it, enter the requested information, save it, and then send it back using the email address on the form.

Figure 10–1a shows how the form is displayed on a user's screen initially, Figure 10–1b shows the form partially filled in by one user, and Figure 10–1c shows how this user filled in the entire form.

The data entry area of the form contains three text boxes (named First Name, Last Name, and Other Meal Plan Type), one drop-down list box (named Delivery Day), five check boxes (named Variety Plan, Mediterranean Plan, Gluten-Free Plan, Vegetarian Plan, and Other Meal Plan Type), a combination text box/drop-down list box (named Servings per Week), and a date picker (named Today's Date).

The form is designed so that it fits completely within a Word window that is set at a page width zoom and has the ribbon collapsed, which reduces the chance a user will have to scroll the window while filling in the form. The data entry area of the form is enclosed by a rectangle that has a shadow on its left and bottom edges.

You will perform the following general tasks as you progress through this module:

1. Save a document as a template.
2. Set form formats for the template.
3. Enter text, graphics, and content controls in the form.
4. Protect the form.
5. Use the form.

To Start Word and Specify Settings

If you are using a computer to step through the project in this module and you want your screens to match the figures in this book, you should change your screen's resolution to 1366 × 768. The following steps start Word, display formatting marks, change the zoom to page width, ensure rulers are not displayed, and verify ruler and Mouse mode settings.

1 **sam**⬇ Start Word and create a blank document in the Word window. If necessary, maximize the Word window.

2 If the Print Layout button on the status bar is not selected, click it so that your screen is in Print Layout view.

3 If the 'Show/Hide ¶' button (Home tab | Paragraph group) is not selected already, click it to display formatting marks on the screen.

4 To display the page the same width as the document window, if necessary, click the Page Width button (View tab | Zoom group).

5 If the rulers are displayed on the screen, click the View Ruler check box (View tab | Show group) to remove the rulers from the Word window.

6 If you are using a mouse and you want your screens to match the figures in the book, verify that you are using Mouse mode by clicking the Touch/Mouse Mode button on the Quick Access Toolbar and then, if necessary, clicking Mouse on the menu. (If your Quick Access Toolbar does not display the Touch/Mouse Mode button, click the 'Customize Quick Access Toolbar' button on the Quick Access Toolbar and then click Touch/Mouse Mode on the menu to add the button to the Quick Access Toolbar.)

Saving a Document as a Template

A **template** is a file with a theme applied and that may contain formatted placeholder text, headers and footers, and graphics, some of which you replace with your own information. Every Word document you create is based on a template. When you select the Blank document thumbnail on the Word start screen or in the New screen of Backstage view, Word creates a document based on the Normal template. Word also provides other templates for more specific types of documents, such as memos, letters, and resumes. Creating a document based on these templates can improve your productivity because Word has defined much of the document's appearance for you.

In this module, you create an online form. If you create and save an online form as a Word document, users will be required to open that Word document to display the form on the screen. Next, they will fill in the form. Then, to preserve the content of the original form, they will have to save the form with a new file name. If they accidentally click the Save button on the Quick Access Toolbar during the process of filling in the form, Word will replace the original blank form with a filled-in form.

If you create and save the online form as a template instead, users will open a new document window that is based on that template. This displays the form on the screen as a brand new Word document; that is, the document does not have a file name. Thus, the user fills in the form and then clicks the Save button on the Quick Access Toolbar to save his or her filled-in form. By creating a Word template for the form, instead of a Word document, the original template for the form remains intact when the user clicks the Save button.

To Save a Document as a Template

The following steps save a new blank document as a template. **Why?** *The template will be used to create the online form shown in Figure 10–1.*

- With a new blank document in the Word window, open Backstage view and then click Export in the left pane of Backstage view to display the Export screen.

- Click 'Change File Type' in the Export screen to display information in the right pane about various file types that can be opened in Word.

- Click Template in the right pane to specify the file type for the current document (Figure 10–2).

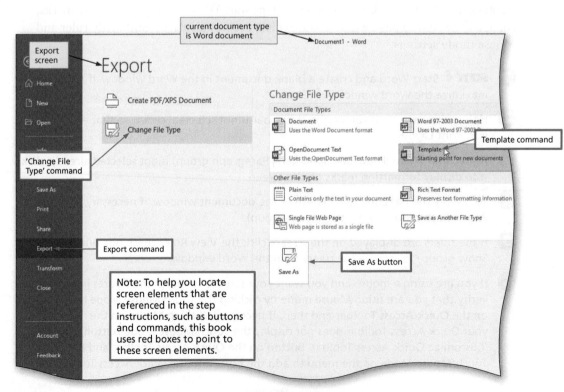

Figure 10–2

2

- Click the Save As button to display the Save As dialog box with the file type automatically changed to Word Template.

Q&A How does Word differentiate between a saved Word template and a saved Word document?
Files typically have a file name and a file extension. The file extension identifies the file type. The source program often assigns a file type to a file. A Word document has an extension of .docx, whereas a Word template has an extension of .dotx. Thus, a file named JulyReport.docx is a Word document, and a file named JulyReport.dotx is a Word template.

- In the File name box, type **SC_WD_10_MealTimeExpressForm** to change the file name and then navigate to the desired save location (Figure 10–3).

Q&A Why is my save location the Custom Office Templates folder?
The default save location for your templates may be the Custom Office Templates folder. If you are using a home computer, you can save your template in that folder. If you are using a public computer, you should change the save location to your local storage location.

3

- Click Save (Save As dialog box) to save the document as a Word template with the entered file name in the specified location.

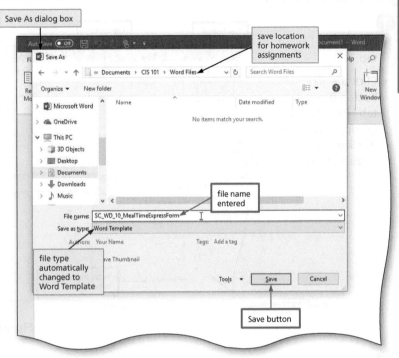

Figure 10–3

Other Ways

1. Press F12, change document type to Word Template

2. Open Backstage view, click Save As, change document type to Word Template

Changing Document Settings

To enhance the look of the form, you change several default settings in Word:

1. Display the page as wide as possible in the document window to maximize the amount of space for text and graphics on the form, called page width zoom.

2. Change the size of the paper so that it fits completely within the document window.

3. Adjust the margins so that as much text as possible will fit in the document.

4. Change the document theme to Headlines and the theme fonts to the Tw Cen MT font set.

5. Add a teal page color with a pattern.

The first item was completed earlier in the module. The following sections make the remaining changes to the document.

BTW
The Ribbon and Screen Resolution
Word may change how the groups and buttons within the groups appear on the ribbon, depending on the screen resolution of your computer. Thus, your ribbon may look different from the ones in this book if you are using a screen resolution other than 1366 × 768.

To Change Paper Size

For the online form in this module, all edges of the page appear in the document window. Currently, only the top, left, and right edges are displayed in the document window. The following steps change paper size. *Why? To display all edges of the document in the document window in the current resolution, change the height of the paper from 11 inches to 4 inches.*

- Display the Layout tab.

- Click the Size button (Layout tab | Page Setup group) to display the Size gallery (Figure 10–4).

Figure 10–4

- Click 'More Paper Sizes' in the Size gallery to display the Paper sheet in the Page Setup dialog box.

- In the Height box (Page Setup dialog box), type **4** as the new height (Figure 10–5).

- Click OK to change the paper size to the entered measurements, which, in this case, are 8.5 inches wide by 4 inches tall.

Figure 10–5

To Collapse the Ribbon

To display more of a document or other item in the Word window, you can collapse the ribbon, which hides the groups on the ribbon and displays only the main tabs. For the online form to fit entirely in the Word window, you collapse the ribbon. The following step collapses the ribbon so that you can see how the form fits in the document window.

1 Click the 'Collapse the Ribbon' button on the ribbon (shown in Figure 10–5) to collapse the ribbon (Figure 10–6).

Q&A What happened to the 'Collapse the Ribbon' button?
The 'Pin the ribbon' button replaces the 'Collapse the Ribbon' button when the ribbon is collapsed. You will see the 'Pin the ribbon' button only when you expand a ribbon by clicking a tab.

What if the height of my document does not match the figure?
You may need to show white space. To do this, position the pointer above the top of the page below the ribbon and then double-click when the pointer changes to a 'Show White Space' button (or, if using touch, double-tap below the page). Or, your screen resolution may be different; if so, you may need to adjust the page height or width values.

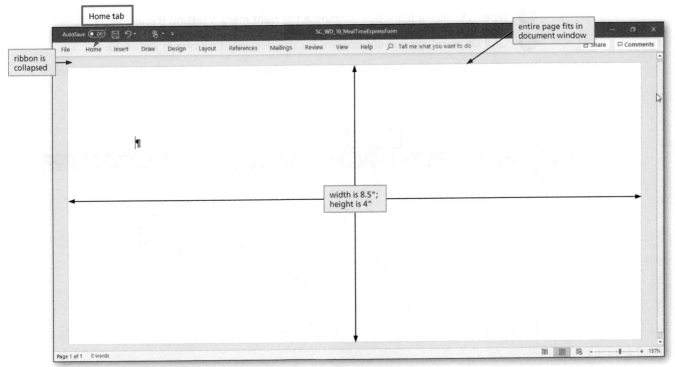

Figure 10–6

To Expand the Ribbon

After you verify that the entire form will fit in the document window, you should expand the ribbon so that you can see the groups while creating the online form. The following steps expand the ribbon.

1 Click Home on the collapsed ribbon to expand the Home tab.

2 Click the 'Pin the ribbon' button on the expanded Home tab to restore the ribbon.

Q&A Can I also double-click Home (or any other tab) on the collapsed ribbon to expand the ribbon?
Yes.

BTW
**Touch Mode
Differences**
The Office and Windows
interfaces may vary if you are
using Touch mode. For this
reason, you might notice that
the function or appearance
of your touch screen differs
slightly from this module's
presentation.

To Set Custom Margins

Recall that Word is preset to use 1-inch top, bottom, left, and right margins. To maximize the space for the contents of the form, this module sets the left and right margins to .5 inches, the top margin to .25 inches, and the bottom margin to 0 inches. The following steps set custom margins.

1 Display the Layout tab. Click the Margins button (Layout tab | Page Setup group) to display the Margins gallery.

2 Click Custom Margins in the Margins gallery to display the Margins sheet in the Page Setup dialog box.

3 Type .25 in the Top box (Page Setup dialog box) to change the top margin setting.

4 Type 0 (zero) in the Bottom box to change the bottom margin setting.

Q&A | Why set the bottom margin to zero?
This allows you to place form contents at the bottom of the page, if necessary.

5 Type .5 in the Left box to change the left margin setting.

6 Type .5 in the Right box to change the right margin setting (Figure 10–7).

7 Click OK to set the custom margins for this document (shown in Figure 10–8).

Q&A | What if Word displays a dialog box indicating margins are outside the printable area?
Click the Ignore button because this is an online form that is not intended for printing.

Figure 10–7

To Change the Document Theme and Theme Fonts

The following steps change the document theme colors to Headlines and the theme fonts to Tw Cen MT.

1 Display the Design tab. Click the Themes button (Design tab | Document Formatting group) and then click Headlines in the Themes gallery to change the document theme.

2 Click the Fonts button (Design tab | Document Formatting group) and then scroll through the Fonts gallery to display the Tw Cen MT font set (Figure 10–8).

3 Click 'Tw Cen MT' in the Fonts gallery to change the font set.

4 If necessary, change the font size to 11 point.

Figure 10–8

To Add a Page Color

The following steps add a page color. **Why?** *This online form uses a shade of teal for the page color (background color) so that the form is more visually appealing.*

1

• Display the Design tab. Click the Page Color button (Design tab | Page Background group) to display the Page Color gallery.

• Point to 'Teal, Accent 4, Lighter 40%' (eighth color in the fourth row) in the Page Color gallery to display a Live Preview of the selected background color (Figure 10–9).

🔎 **Experiment**

• Point to various colors in the Page Color gallery and watch the page color change in the document window.

Figure 10–9

● Click 'Teal, Accent 4, Lighter 40%' to change the page color to the selected color.

Do page colors print?

When you change the page color, it appears only on the screen. Changing the page color does not affect a printed document.

To Apply a Pattern Fill Effect to a Page Color

When you changed the page color in the previous steps, Word placed a solid color on the screen. The following steps add a pattern to the page color. *Why? For this online form, the solid background color is a little too bold. To soften the color, you can add a pattern to it.*

①

● Click the Page Color button (Design tab | Page Background group) to display the Page Color gallery (Figure 10–10).

Figure 10–10

②

● Click Fill Effects in the Page Color gallery to display the Fill Effects dialog box.

● Click the Pattern tab (Fill Effects dialog box) to display the Pattern sheet in the dialog box.

● Click the Stripes: Slashes pattern (fifth pattern in the second row) to select it (Figure 10–11).

Figure 10–11

- Click OK to add the selected pattern to the current page color (Figure 10–12).

selected pattern softens background color

Figure 10–12

Enter Content in the Online Form

The next step in creating the online form in this module is to enter the text, graphics, and content controls in the document. The following sections describe this process.

To Enter and Format Text

The following steps enter the text at the top of the online form.

1 Type **Meal Time Express** and then press ENTER.

2 Type **Fresh, Delicious Meals Delivered to Your Door** and then press ENTER.

3 Type **Consultation Request** and then press ENTER.

4 Type **Fill in the form below, save your form, and email it to contact@mealte.net; a team member will reply within 72 hours.** and then press ENTER.

Q&A Why did the email address change color?
In this document theme, the color for a hyperlink is a shade of teal. When you pressed ENTER, Word automatically formatted the hyperlink in this color.

5 Format the characters on the first line to 28-point Berlin Sans FB Demi font with the color of Aqua, Accent 1, Darker 25%. (Ensure that the spacing after this paragraph is 8 point.)

6 Format the characters on the second line to the color of Purple, Accent 5, Darker 50%. (Ensure that the spacing after this paragraph is 8 point.)

7 Format the characters on the third line to 16-point bold font with the color of Purple, Accent 5, Darker 25% and center the text on the line. Remove space before and after this paragraph (spacing before and after should be 0 point).

8 Center the text on the fourth line and increase the spacing after this line to 12 point.

9 Be sure that the font size of text entered on the second and fourth lines is 11 point.

10 Position the insertion point on the blank line below the text (Figure 10–13). (Ensure that the font size is 11 point at the location of the insertion point.)

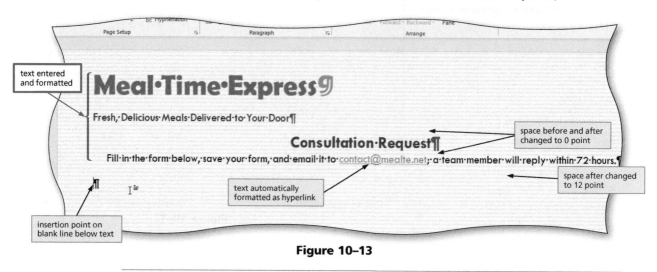

Figure 10–13

To Insert an Icon

Word includes a library of icons that you can insert in documents. The following steps insert an icon that shows an image of a fork and knife in the document. *Why? You want an image in the form to give it visual appeal.*

1
- Display the Insert tab.
- Click the Icons button (Insert tab | Illustrations group) to display the Insert Icons dialog box.
- Click the 'Food and drinks' category in the left pane and then click the fork and knife icon in the right pane to select the icon (Figure 10–14).

Figure 10–14

Q&A What if my dialog box does not contain the same category or icon?
Select any appropriate icon in the dialog box.

What if the Icons button is not available in my version of Word?
A similar image is located in the Data Files. You can click the Pictures button (Insert tab | Illustrations group), navigate to the file called Support_WD_10_Fork_and_Spoon.png in the Data Files, and then click the Insert button (Insert Picture dialog box) to insert the image. Change the height of the inserted image to 1", change the width to .73", and skip Step 2. Note that your image will look similar to, but not exactly like, the figures in this module.

Can I select multiple icons at once in the open dialog box?
Yes, all selected icons will be inserted in the document.

2

• Click the Insert button (Insert Icons dialog box) to place the selected icon in the document to the left of the insertion point (Figure 10–15).

• If necessary, use the Height and Width boxes (Graphics Tools Format tab | Size group) to change these values to 1".

Figure 10–15

Q&A What if my icon is inserted in a location different from Figure 10–15?
You will move the icon in a later step.

To Apply a Graphics Style

Word provides a variety of predefined styles you can apply to graphics. The following steps apply a graphics style to the selected icon.

① With the icon still selected, click the More button (Graphics Tools Format tab | Graphics Styles group) (shown in Figure 10–15) to display the Graphics Styles gallery.

② Point to 'Colored Fill - Accent 1, Dark 1 Outline' in the Graphics Styles gallery to display a Live Preview of the selected graphics style applied to the icon in the document window (Figure 10–16).

⊘ Experiment

- If you are using a mouse, point to various styles in the Graphics Styles gallery and watch the graphics style change in the document window.

③ Click 'Colored Fill - Accent 1, Dark 1 Outline' in the Graphics Styles gallery to apply the selected graphics style to the selected icon.

Q&A What if my version of Word did not have the Icons button and I inserted a picture from the Data Files instead?

Click the Color button (Picture Tools Format tab | Adjust group) to display the Color gallery and then click 'Aqua, Accent color 1, Light' in the Recolor area to change the color. Note that your image will look similar to, but not exactly like, the figures in this module.

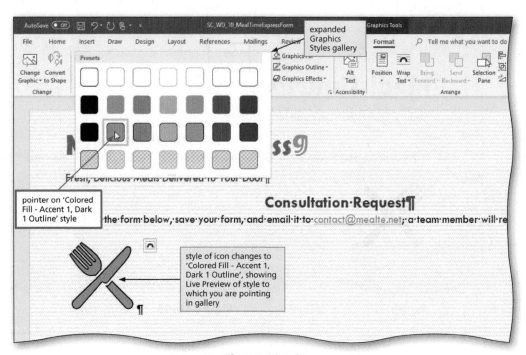

Figure 10–16

To Format a Graphic's Text Wrapping

Word inserted the fork and knife icon as an inline graphic, that is, as part of the current paragraph. In this online form, the graphic should be positioned to the right of the company name (shown in Figure 10–1 at the beginning of this module).

Thus, the graphic should be a floating graphic instead of an inline graphic. The text in the online form should not wrap around the graphic. Thus, the graphic should float in front of the text. The following steps change the graphic's text wrapping to In Front of Text.

1 With the graphic selected, click the Layout Options button attached to the graphic to display the Layout Options gallery (Figure 10–17).

2 Click 'In Front of Text' in the Layout Options gallery to change the graphic from inline to floating with the selected wrapping style.

3 Click the Close button in the Layout Options gallery to close the gallery.

Figure 10–17

BTW

Ordering Graphics
If you have multiple graphics displaying on the screen and would like them to overlap, you can change their stacking order by using the Bring Forward and Send Backward arrows (Picture Tools Format tab | Arrange group). The 'Bring to Front' command on the Bring Forward menu displays the selected object at the top of the stack, and the 'Send to Back' command on the Send Backward menu displays the selected object at the bottom of the stack. The Bring Forward and Send Backward commands each move the graphic forward or backward one layer in the stack. These commands also are available through the shortcut menu that is displayed when you right-click a graphic.

To Move a Graphic

The final step associated with the graphic is to move it so that it is positioned on the right side of the online form. The following steps move a graphic.

1 If necessary, scroll to display the top of the form in the document window.

2 Drag the graphic to the location shown in Figure 10–18.

Figure 10–18

To Use a Table to Control Layout

The first line of data entry in the form consists of the First Name content control, which begins at the left margin, and the Last Name content control, which begins at the center point of the same line. At first glance, you might decide to set a tab stop at each content control location. This, however, can be a complex task. For example, to place two content controls evenly across a row, you must calculate the location of each tab stop. If you insert a 2 × 1 table instead, Word automatically calculates the size of two evenly spaced columns. Thus, to enter multiple content controls on a single line, insert a table to control layout.

In this online form, the line containing the First Name and Last Name content controls will be a 2 × 1 table, that is, a table with two columns and one row. By inserting a 2 × 1 table, Word automatically positions the second column at the center point. The following steps insert a 2 × 1 table in the form and remove its border. *Why? When you insert a table, Word automatically surrounds it with a border. Because you are using the tables solely to control layout, you do not want the table borders visible.*

- Position the insertion point where the table should be inserted, in this case, on the blank paragraph mark below the text on the form.

- Display the Insert tab. Click the Table button (Insert tab | Tables group) to display the Table gallery (Figure 10–19).

Figure 10–19

- Click the cell in the first row and second column of the grid to insert an empty 2 × 1 table at the location of the insertion point.

- Select the table.

Q&A How do I select a table?
Point somewhere in the table and then click the table move handle that appears in the upper-left corner of the table (or, if using touch, tap the Select button (Table Tools Layout tab | Table group) and then tap Select Table on the Select menu).

- If necessary, display the Table Tools Design tab.

- Click the Borders arrow (Table Tools Design tab | Borders group) to display the Borders gallery (Figure 10–20).

Figure 10–20

- Click No Border in the Borders gallery to remove the borders from the table.

4
- Click the first cell of the table to remove the selection (Figure 10–21).

Q&A My screen does not display the end-of-cell marks. Why not?
Display formatting marks by clicking the 'Show/Hide ¶' button (Home tab | Paragraph group).

Figure 10–21

Other Ways

1. Click Table button (Insert tab | Tables group), click Insert Table in Table gallery, enter number of columns and rows (Insert Table dialog box), click OK

To Show Table Gridlines

When you remove the borders from a table, you no longer can see the individual cells in the table. To help identify the location of cells, you can display **gridlines**, which are nonprinting lines that show cell boundaries in a table. The following steps show gridlines.

1 If necessary, position the insertion point in a table cell.

2 Display the Table Tools Layout tab.

3 If gridlines do not show already, click the View Gridlines button (Table Tools Layout tab | Table group) to show table gridlines on the screen (Figure 10–22).

Q&A Do table gridlines print?

No. Gridlines are formatting marks that show only on the screen. Gridlines help users easily identify cells, rows, and columns in borderless tables.

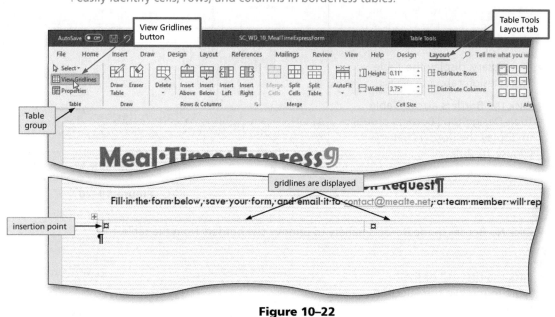

Figure 10–22

Content Controls

To add data entry fields in a Word form, you insert content controls. Word includes nine different content controls you can insert in your online forms. Table 10–1 outlines the use of each of these controls. The following sections insert content controls in the online form for the project in this module.

Table 10–1 Content Controls		
Type	**Icon**	**Use**
Building Block Gallery		User selects a built-in building block from the gallery.
Check Box		User selects or deselects a check box.
Combo Box		User types text entry or selects one item from a list of choices.
Date Picker		User interacts with a calendar to select a date or types a date in the placeholder.
Drop-Down List		User selects one item from a list of choices.
Picture		User inserts a drawing, a shape, a picture, image, or a SmartArt graphic.
Plain Text	Aa	User enters text, which may not be formatted.
Repeating Section		Users can instruct Word to create a duplicate of the content control.
Rich Text	Aa	User enters text and, if desired, may format the entered text.

How do you determine the correct content control to use for each data entry field?

For each data entry field, decide which content control best maps to the type of data the field will contain. The field specifications for the fields in this module's online form are listed below:

- The First Name, Last Name, and Other Meal Plan Types data entry fields will contain text. The first two will be plain text content controls and the last will be a rich text content control.

- The Delivery Day data entry field must contain one of these four values: Wednesday, Thursday, Friday, Saturday (additional fee). This field will be a drop-down list content control.

- The Variety Plan, Mediterranean Plan, Gluten-Free Plan, Vegetarian Plan, and Other Meal Plan Type data entry fields will be check boxes that the user can select or deselect.

- The Servings per Week data entry field can contain one of these three values: Single Plan, Double Plan, and Family Plan. In addition, users should be able to enter their own value in this data entry field if none of these three values is applicable. A combo box content control will be used for this field.

- The Today's Date data entry field should contain only a valid date value. Thus, this field will be a date picker content control.

To Show the Developer Tab

To create a form in Word, you use buttons on the Developer tab. The following steps show the Developer tab on the ribbon. *Why? Because it allows you to perform more advanced tasks not required by everyday Word users, the Developer tab does not appear on the ribbon by default.*

- Open Backstage view and, if necessary, scroll to display the Options command (Figure 10–23).

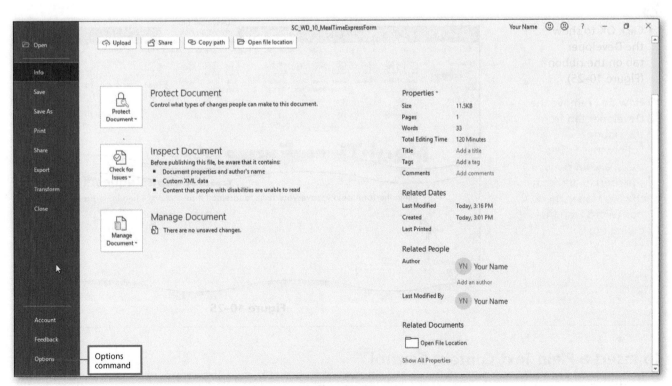

Figure 10–23

2

- Click Options in the left pane of Backstage view to display the Word Options dialog box.

- Click Customize Ribbon in the left pane (Word Options dialog box) to display associated options in the right pane.

- Place a check mark in the Developer check box in the Main Tabs list (Figure 10–24).

<table>
<tr><td>Q&A</td><td>What are the plus symbols to the left of each tab name?</td></tr>
</table>

Clicking the plus symbol expands to show the groups.

Can I show or hide any tab in this list?

Yes. Place a check mark in the check box to show the tab, or remove the check mark to hide the tab.

Figure 10–24

3

- Click OK to show the Developer tab on the ribbon (Figure 10–25).

<table>
<tr><td>Q&A</td><td>How do I remove the Developer tab from the ribbon?</td></tr>
</table>

Follow these same steps, except remove the check mark from the Developer check box (Word Options dialog box).

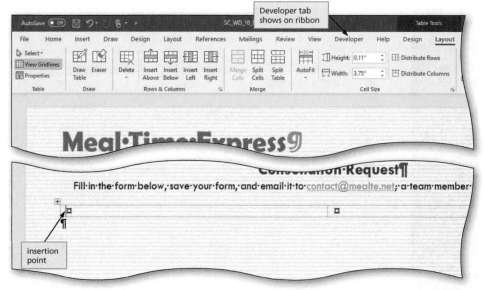

Figure 10–25

To Insert a Plain Text Content Control

The first item that a user enters in the Consultation Request is his or her first name. Because the first name entry contains text that the user should not format, this online form uses a plain text content control for the First Name data entry field. The following steps enter the label, First Name:, followed by a plain text content control. *Why? The label, First Name:, is displayed to the left of the plain text content control. To improve readability, a colon or some other character often separates a label from the content control.*

- With the insertion point in the first cell of the table as shown in Figure 10–25, type **First Name:** as the label for the content control.

- Press SPACEBAR (Figure 10–26).

Figure 10–26

- Display the Developer tab.

- Click the 'Plain Text Content Control' button (Developer tab | Controls group) to insert a plain text content control at the location of the insertion point (Figure 10–27).

Q&A Is the plain text content control similar to the content controls that I have used in templates installed with Word, such as in the letter, memo, and resume templates?
Yes. The content controls you insert through the Developer tab have the same functionality as the content controls in the templates installed with Word.

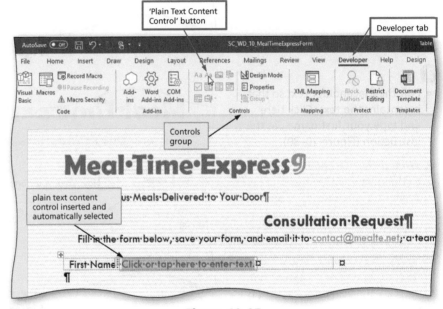

Figure 10–27

To Use Design Mode to Edit Placeholder Text

A content control displays **placeholder text**, which is default text that indicates where text can be typed in documents. The default placeholder text for a plain text content control is the instruction, Click or tap here to enter text. The following steps edit the placeholder text for the plain text content control just entered. *Why? You can change the wording in the placeholder text so that it is more instructional or applicable to the current form.*

- With the plain text content control selected (shown in Figure 10–27), click the Design Mode button (Developer tab | Controls group) to turn on Design mode, which displays tags at the beginning and ending of the placeholder text (Figure 10–28).

Figure 10–28

2

- Even if it already is selected, drag through the placeholder text, Click or tap here to enter text., because you want to edit the instruction (Figure 10–29).

Figure 10–29

3

- Edit the placeholder text so that it contains the text, Click here and type your first name., as the instruction (Figure 10–30).

Q&A What if the placeholder text wraps to the next line?
Because of the tags at each edge of the placeholder text, the entered text may wrap in the table cell. Once you turn off Design mode, the placeholder text should fit on a single line. If it does not, you can adjust the font size of the placeholder text to fit.

Figure 10–30

4

- Click the Design Mode button (Developer tab | Controls group) to turn off Design mode (Figure 10–31).

Q&A What if I notice an error in the placeholder text?
Follow these steps again to turn on Design mode, correct the error, and then turn off Design mode.

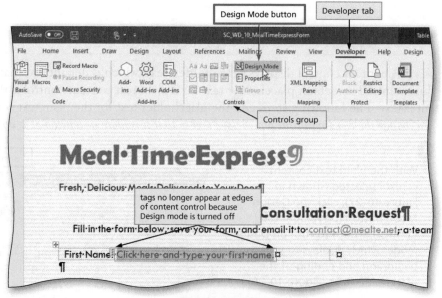

Figure 10–31

To Change the Properties of a Plain Text Content Control

You can change a variety of properties to customize content controls. The following steps change the properties of a plain text content control. *Why? In this form, you assign a tag name to a content control for later identification. You also apply a style to the content control to define how text will look as a user types data or makes selections, and you lock the content control so that a user cannot delete the content control during the data entry process.*

1

- With the content control selected, click the Properties button (Developer tab | Controls group) to display the Content Control Properties dialog box (Figure 10–32).

Q&A How do I know the content control is selected?
A selected content control is surrounded by an outline. Its placeholder text also may be shaded.

Figure 10–32

2

- Type **First Name** in the Tag text box (Content Control Properties dialog box).

- Place a check mark in the 'Use a style to format text typed into the empty control' check box so that the Style box becomes active.

- Click the Style arrow to display the Style list (Figure 10–33).

Q&A Why leave the Title text box empty?
When you click a content control in a preexisting Word template, the content control may display an identifier in its top-left corner. For templates that you create, you can instruct Word to display this identifier, called the Title, by changing the properties of the content control. In this form, you do not want the identifier to appear.

What is a bounding box?
A bounding box is a rectangle that surrounds the content control on the form. You can show content controls with a bounding box, with tags, or with no visible markings.

What if the Intense Emphasis style is not displayed in the Style list?
Close the Content Control Properties dialog box. Click the Styles Dialog Box Launcher to open the Styles pane, click the Options button in the Styles pane to display the Style Pane Options dialog box, click the 'Select styles to show' arrow and then click All Styles (Style Pane Options dialog box), click OK to close the dialog box, and then close the Styles pane. Repeat Steps 1 and 2 above.

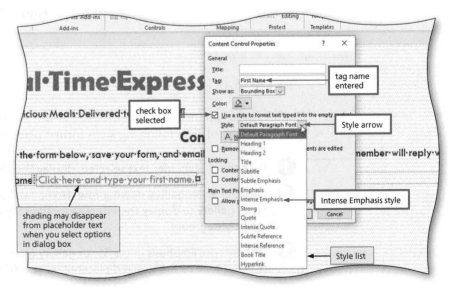

Figure 10–33

3

- Click Intense Emphasis to select the style for the content control.

- Place a check mark in the 'Content control cannot be deleted' check box so that the user cannot delete the content control (Figure 10–34).

Figure 10–34

4

- Click OK to assign the modified properties to the content control (Figure 10–35).

Q&A

Why is the placeholder text not formatted to the selected style, Intense Emphasis, in this case? When you apply a style to a content control, as described in these steps, the style is applied to the text the user types during the data entry process. To change the appearance of the placeholder text, apply a style using the Home tab as described in the next steps.

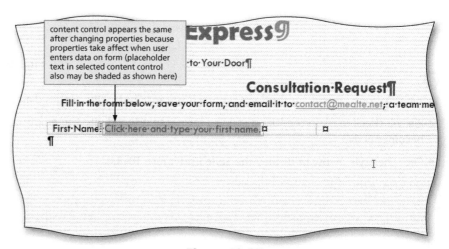

Figure 10–35

To Format Placeholder Text

In this online form, the placeholder text has the same style applied to it as the content control. The following steps format placeholder text.

1 With the placeholder text selected, display the Home tab.

2 Click the Styles gallery down arrow (Home tab | Styles group) to scroll through the Styles gallery to display the Intense Emphasis style or click the More button (Home tab | Styles group).

3 Click Intense Emphasis in the Styles gallery (even if it is selected already) to apply the selected style to the selected placeholder text (Figure 10–36).

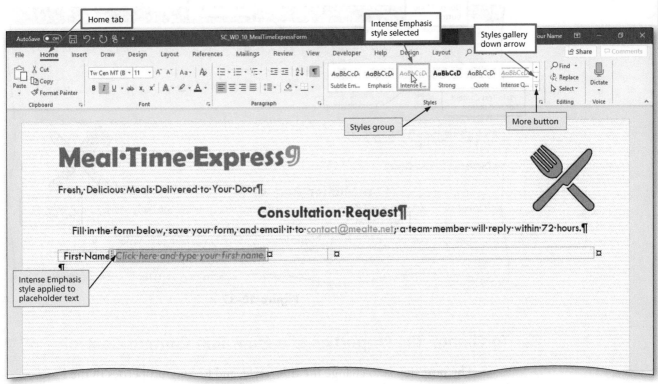

Figure 10–36

To Insert Another Plain Text Content Control and Use Design Mode to Edit Its Placeholder Text

The second item that a user enters in the Consultation Request is his or her last name. The steps for entering the last name content control are similar to those for the first name, because the last name also is a plain text content control. The following steps enter the label, Last Name:, and then insert a plain text content control and edit its placeholder text.

1 Position the insertion point in the second cell (column) in the table.

2 With the insertion point in the second cell of the table, type **Last Name:** as the label for the content control and then press SPACEBAR.

3 Display the Developer tab. Click the 'Plain Text Content Control' button (Developer tab | Controls group) to insert a plain text content control at the location of the insertion point.

4 With the plain text content control selected, click the Design Mode button (Developer tab | Controls group) to turn on Design mode (Figure 10–37).

5 Select the placeholder text to be changed.

6 Edit the placeholder text so that it contains the text, Click here and type your last name., as the instruction.

7 Click the Design Mode button (Developer tab | Controls group) to turn off Design mode.

BTW
Deleting Content Controls
To delete a content control, right-click it and then click 'Remove Content Control' on the shortcut menu.

Figure 10–37

To Change the Properties of a Plain Text Content Control

The next step is to change the title, style, and locking properties of the Last Name content control, just as you did for the First Name content control. The following steps change properties of a plain text content control.

1 With the content control selected, click the Properties button (Developer tab | Controls group) to display the Content Control Properties dialog box.

2 Type **Last Name** in the Tag text box (Content Control Properties dialog box).

3 Place a check mark in the 'Use a style to format text typed into the empty control' check box to activate the Style box.

4 Click the Style arrow and then select Intense Emphasis in the list to specify the style for the content control.

5 Place a check mark in the 'Content control cannot be deleted' check box (Figure 10–38).

6 Click OK to assign the properties to the content control.

Figure 10–38

To Format Placeholder Text

As with the placeholder text for the first name, the placeholder text for the last name should use the Intense Emphasis style. The following steps format placeholder text.

1 With the last name placeholder text selected, display the Home tab.

2 Locate and select the Intense Emphasis style in the Styles gallery (Home tab | Styles group) to apply the selected style to the selected placeholder text.

To Increase Space before a Paragraph

The next step in creating this online form is to increase space before a paragraph so that the space below the table is consistent with the space between other elements on the form. The following steps increase space before a paragraph.

1 Position the insertion point on the blank line below the table.

2 Display the Layout tab.

3 Change the value in the Spacing Before box (Layout tab | Paragraph group) to 8 pt to increase the space between the table and the paragraph (shown in Figure 10–39). (Ensure that the spacing after this paragraph also is 8 point.) (Note that you may need to type the value in the box instead of using the arrow keys.)

To Insert a Drop-Down List Content Control

In the online form in this module, the user selects from one of these four choices for the Delivery Day content control: Wednesday, Thursday, Friday, or Saturday (additional fee). The following steps insert a drop-down list content control. **Why?** *To present a set of choices to a user in the form of a drop-down list, from which the user selects one, insert a drop-down list content control. To view the set of choices, the user clicks the arrow at the right edge of the content control.*

1
- With the insertion point positioned on the blank paragraph mark below the First Name content control, using either the ruler or the Layout tab, change the left indent to 0.06" so that the entered text aligns with the text immediately above it (that is, the F in First).

- Type **On which day would you like your meals delivered every week?** and then press SPACEBAR.

2
- Display the Developer tab.

- Click the 'Drop-Down List Content Control' button (Developer tab | Controls group) to insert a drop-down list content control at the location of the insertion point (Figure 10–39).

Figure 10–39

To Use Design Mode to Edit Placeholder Text

The following steps edit the placeholder text for the drop-down list content control.

1 With the drop-down list content control selected, click the Design Mode button (Developer tab | Controls group) to turn on Design mode.

2 Edit the placeholder text so that it contains this instruction, which contains two separate sentences: Click here. Click arrow and select from list.

3 Click the Design Mode button (Developer tab | Controls group) to turn off Design mode.

To Change the Properties of a Drop-Down List Content Control

The following steps change the properties of a drop-down list content control. *Why? In addition to identifying a tag, selecting a style, and locking the drop-down list content control, you can specify the choices that will be displayed when a user clicks the arrow to the right of the content control.*

1

- With the drop-down list content control selected, click the Properties button (Developer tab | Controls group) to display the Content Control Properties dialog box.

- Type **Delivery Day** in the Tag text box (Content Control Properties dialog box).

- Place a check mark in the 'Use a style to format text typed into the empty control' check box to activate the Style box.

- Click the Style arrow and then select Intense Emphasis in the list to specify the style for the content control.

- Place a check mark in the 'Content control cannot be deleted' check box.

- In the Drop-Down List Properties area, click 'Choose an item.' to select it (Figure 10–40).

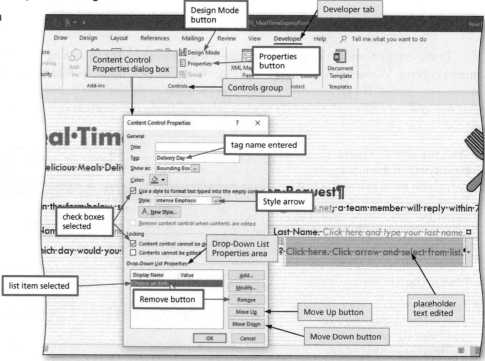

Figure 10–40

2

- Click the Remove button (Content Control Properties dialog box) to delete the 'Choose an item.' entry.

Q&A | Why delete the 'Choose an item.' entry?
If you leave it in the list, it will appear as the first item in the list when the user clicks the content control arrow. You do not want it in the list, so you delete it.

Can I delete any entry in a drop-down list using the Remove button?
Yes, select the entry in this dialog box and then click the Remove button. You also can rearrange the order of entries in a list by selecting the entry and then clicking the Move Up or Move Down buttons.

3

- Click the Add button to display the Add Choice dialog box.

- Type **Wednesday** in the Display Name text box (Add Choice dialog box), and notice that Word automatically enters the same text in the Value text box (Figure 10–41).

What is the difference between a display name and a value?

Often, they are the same, which is why when you type the display name, Word automatically enters the same text in the Value text box. Sometimes, however, you may want to store a shorter or different value. If the display name is long, entering shorter values makes it easier for separate programs to analyze and interpret entered data.

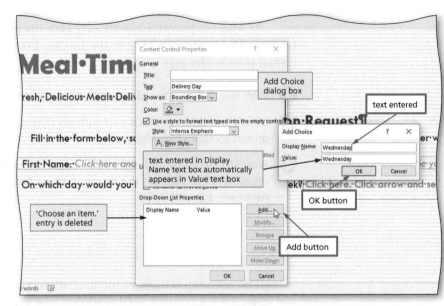

Figure 10–41

4

- Click OK (Add Choice dialog box) to add the entered display name and value to the list of choices in the Drop-Down List Properties area (Content Control Properties dialog box).

5

- Click the Add button to display the Add Choice dialog box.

- Type **Thursday** in the Display Name text box.

- Click OK to add the entry to the list.

- Click the Add button to display the Add Choice dialog box.

- Type **Friday** in the Display Name text box.

- Click OK to add the entry to the list.

- Click the Add button to display the Add Choice dialog box.

- Type **Saturday (additional fee)** in the Display Name text box.

- Click OK to add the entry to the list (Figure 10–42).

Figure 10–42

6

- Click OK (Content Control Properties dialog box) to change the content control properties.

What if I want to change an entry in the drop-down list?

You would select the drop-down list content control, click the Properties button (Developer tab | Controls group) to display the Content Control Properties dialog box, select the entry to change, click the Modify button, adjust the entry, and then click OK.

To Format Placeholder Text

As with the previous placeholder text, the placeholder text for the content Delivery Day control should use the Intense Emphasis style. The following steps format placeholder text.

1 With the Delivery Day placeholder text selected, display the Home tab.

2 Locate and select the Intense Emphasis style in the Styles gallery (Home tab | Styles group) to apply the selected style to the selected placeholder text.

3 Press END to position the insertion point at the end of the current line and then press ENTER to position the insertion point below the Delivery Day content control. If necessary, turn off italics.

To Enter Text and Use a Table to Control Layout

The next step is to enter the user instructions for the check box content controls and insert a 4 × 1 borderless table so that four evenly spaced check boxes can be displayed horizontally below the check box instructions. The following steps enter text and insert a borderless table.

1 With the insertion point positioned on the paragraph below the Delivery Day content control, click Normal in the Styles gallery (Home tab | Styles group) to format the current paragraph to the Normal style.

2 Using either the ruler or the Layout tab, change the left indent to 0.06" so that the entered text aligns with the text immediately above it (that is, the O in On).

3 Type **Which type of meal plan do you prefer?** as the instruction.

4 Click the 'Line and Paragraph Spacing' button (Home tab | Paragraph group) and then click 'Remove Space After Paragraph' so that the check boxes will appear one physical line below the instructions.

5 Press ENTER to position the insertion point on the line below the check box instructions.

6 Display the Insert tab. Click the Table button (Insert tab | Tables group) to display the Table gallery and then click the cell in the first row and fourth column of the grid to insert an empty 4 × 1 table at the location of the insertion point.

7 Select the table.

8 Click the Borders arrow (Table Tools Design tab | Borders group) to display the Borders gallery and then click No Border in the Borders gallery to remove the borders from the table.

9 Click the first cell of the table to remove the selection (shown in Figure 10–43).

BTW
Break Header or Footer Link
If you do not want the header or footer in a section to be copied to the previous section, you would deselect the 'Link to Previous' button (Header & Footer Tools Design tab | Navigation group).

To Insert a Check Box Content Control

The following step inserts the first check box content control. *Why? In the online form in this module, the user can select up to five check boxes: Variety Plan, Mediterranean Plan, Gluten-Free Plan, Vegetarian Plan, and Other.*

1
- Position the insertion point at the location for the check box content control, in this case, the leftmost cell in the 4 × 1 table.
- Display the Developer tab.
- Click the 'Check Box Content Control' button (Developer tab | Controls group) to insert a check box content control at the location of the insertion point (Figure 10–43).

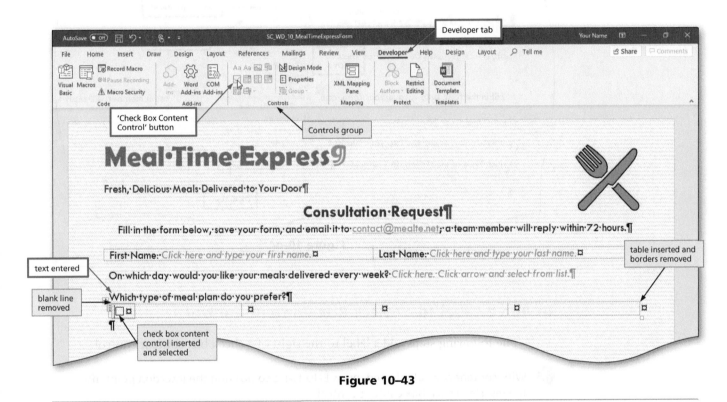

Figure 10–43

To Change the Properties of a Check Box Content Control

The next step is to change the title and locking properties of the content control. The following steps change properties of a check box content control.

1 With the content control selected, click the Properties button (Developer tab | Controls group) to display the Content Control Properties dialog box.

2 Type **Variety Plan** in the Tag text box (Content Control Properties dialog box).

3 Click the Show as arrow and then select None in the list, because you do not want a border surrounding the check box content control.

④ Place a check mark in the 'Content control cannot be deleted' check box (Figure 10–44).

⑤ Click OK to assign the properties to the selected content control.

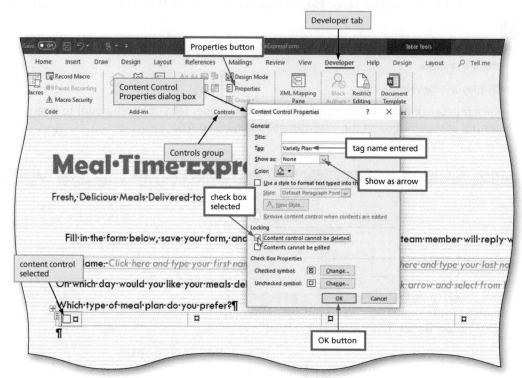

Figure 10–44

To Add a Label to a Check Box Content Control

The following steps add a label to the right of a check box content control.

① With content control selected, press END twice to position the insertion point after the inserted check box content control.

② Press SPACEBAR and then type **Variety Plan** as the check box label (Figure 10–45).

Figure 10–45

To Insert Additional Check Box Content Controls

The following steps insert the remaining check box content controls and their labels.

1 Press TAB to position the insertion point in the next cell, which is the location for the next check box content control.

2 Click the 'Check Box Content Control' button (Developer tab | Controls group) to insert a check box content control at the location of the insertion point.

3 With the content control selected, click the Properties button (Developer tab | Controls group) to display the Content Control Properties dialog box.

4 Type **Mediterranean Plan** in the Tag text box (Content Control Properties dialog box).

5 Click the Show as arrow and then select None in the list, because you do not want a border surrounding the check box content control.

6 Place a check mark in the 'Content control cannot be deleted' check box and then click OK to assign the properties to the selected content control.

7 With content control selected, press END twice to position the insertion point after the inserted check box content control.

8 Press SPACEBAR and then type **Mediterranean Plan** as the check box label.

9 Repeat Steps 1 through 8 for the Gluten-Free and Vegetarian Plan check box content controls.

10 Position the insertion point on the blank line below the 4 × 1 table and then repeat Steps 2 through 8 for the Other Meal Plan Type check box content control, which has the label, Other (please specify):, followed by SPACEBAR. If necessary, using either the ruler or the Layout tab, change the left indent so that check box above is aligned with the check box below (Figure 10–46).

Figure 10–46

To Insert a Rich Text Content Control

The next step is to insert the content control that enables users to type in any other type of meal plan they prefer. The difference between a plain text and rich text content control is that the users can format text as they enter it in the rich text content control. The following step inserts a rich text content control. *Why? Because you want to allow users to format the text they enter in the Other Meal Plan Type content control, you use the rich text content control.*

- If necessary, position the insertion point at the location for the rich text content control (shown in Figure 10–46).

- If necessary, display the Developer tab.

- Click the 'Rich Text Content Control' button (Developer tab | Controls group) to insert a rich text content control at the location of the insertion point (Figure 10–47).

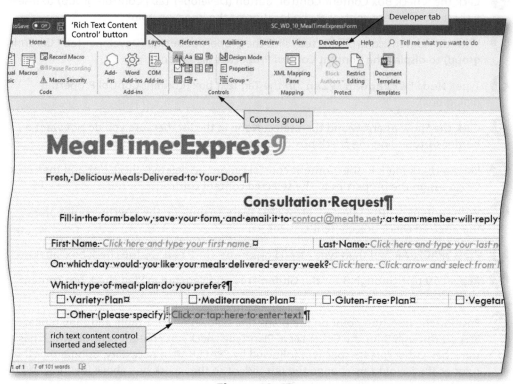

Figure 10–47

To Use Design Mode to Edit Placeholder Text

The following steps edit placeholder text for the rich text content control.

1. With the rich text content control selected, click the Design Mode button (Developer tab | Controls group) to turn on Design mode.

2. If necessary, scroll to display the content control in the document window.

3. Edit the placeholder text so that it contains the text, Click here and type another meal plan you would prefer., as the instruction.

4. Click the Design Mode button (Developer tab | Controls group) to turn off Design mode. If necessary, scroll to display the top of the form in the document window.

To Change the Properties of a Rich Text Content Control

In the online form in this module, you change the same three properties for the rich text content control as for the plain text content control. That is, you enter a tag name, specify the style, and lock the content control. The following steps change the properties of the rich text content control.

1 With the content control selected, click the Properties button (Developer tab | Controls group) to display the Content Control Properties dialog box.

2 Type **Other Meal Plan Type** in the Tag text box (Content Control Properties dialog box).

3 Place a check mark in the 'Use a style to format text typed into the empty control' check box to activate the Style box.

4 Click the Style arrow and then select Intense Emphasis in the list to specify the style for the content control.

5 Place a check mark in the 'Content control cannot be deleted' check box (Figure 10–48).

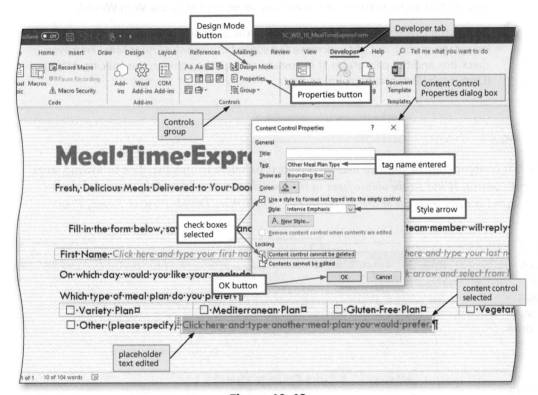

Figure 10–48

6 Click OK to assign the properties to the content control.

To Format Placeholder Text and Add Space before a Paragraph

The placeholder text for the Other Meal Plan Type text entry should use the Intense Emphasis style, and the space below the check boxes should be consistent with the space between other elements on the form. The next steps format placeholder text and increase space before a paragraph.

1 With the Other Meal Plan Type placeholder text selected, display the Home tab.

2 Locate and select the Intense Emphasis style in the Styles gallery (Home tab | Styles group) to apply the selected style to the selected placeholder text.

3 Press END to position the insertion point on the paragraph mark after the Other Meal Plan Type content control and then press ENTER to position the insertion point below the Other Meal Plan Type content control.

4 If necessary, display the Home tab. With the insertion point positioned on the paragraph below the Other Meal Plan Type content control, click Normal in the Styles gallery (Home tab | Styles group) to format the current paragraph to the Normal style.

5 Using either the ruler or the Layout tab, change the left indent to 0.06 " so that the entered text aligns with the text two lines above it (that is, the W in Which).

6 Display the Layout tab. Change the value in the Spacing Before box (Layout tab | Paragraph group) to 8 pt to increase the space between the Other Meal Plan Type check box and the paragraph. If necessary, change the value in the Spacing After box (Layout tab | Paragraph group) to 8 pt.

To Insert a Combo Box Content Control

In Word, a combo box content control allows a user to type text or select from a list. The following steps insert a combo box content control. *Why? In the online form in this module, users can type their own entry in the Servings Per Week content control or select from one of these three choices: Single Plan, Double Plan, or Family Plan.*

1
- With the insertion point positioned on the blank paragraph mark, type **How many servings per week would you prefer?** and then press SPACEBAR.

2
- Display the Developer tab.

- Click the 'Combo Box Content Control' button (Developer tab | Controls group) to insert a combo box content control at the location of the insertion point (Figure 10–49).

Figure 10–49

To Use Design Mode to Edit Placeholder Text

The following steps edit the placeholder text for the combo box content control.

1 With the combo box content control selected, click the Design Mode button (Developer tab | Controls group) to turn on Design mode.

2 If necessary, scroll to page 2 to display the combo box content control.

Q&A What if the content control moves to another page?
Because Design mode displays tags, the content controls and placeholder text are not displayed in their proper positions on the screen. When you turn off Design mode, the content controls will return to their original locations and the extra page should disappear.

3 Edit the placeholder text so that it contains this instruction, which contains two sentences (Figure 10–50): Click here. Click arrow and select from list, or type your response.

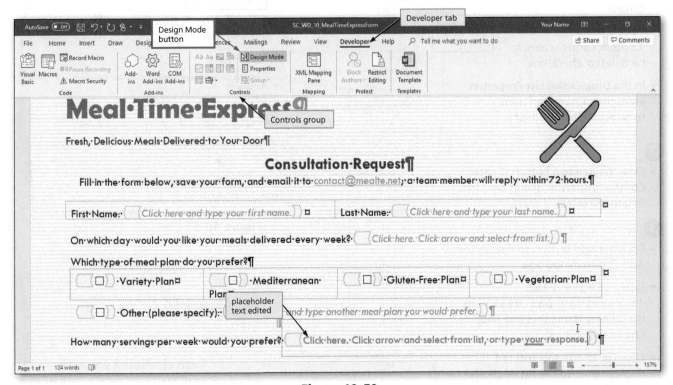

Figure 10–50

4 Click the Design Mode button (Developer tab | Controls group) to turn off Design mode.

To Change the Properties of a Combo Box Content Control

You follow similar steps to enter the list for a combo box content control as you do for the drop-down list content control. The following steps change the properties of a combo box content control. *Why? You enter the tag name, specify the style for typed text, and enter the choices for the drop-down list.*

- With the content control selected, click the Properties button (Developer tab | Controls group) to display the Content Control Properties dialog box.

- Type **Servings per Week** in the Tag text box (Content Control Properties dialog box).

- Place a check mark in the 'Use a style to format text typed into the empty control' check box to activate the Style box.

- Click the Style arrow and then select Intense Emphasis in the list to specify the style for the content control.

- Place a check mark in the 'Content control cannot be deleted' check box.

- In the Drop-Down List Properties area, click 'Choose an item.' to select it (Figure 10–51).

- Click the Remove button (Content Control Properties dialog box) to delete the selected entry.

Figure 10–51

❸

- Click the Add button to display the Add Choice dialog box.

- Type **Single Plan (4 servings per week)** in the Display Name text box (Add Choice dialog box).

- Click OK to add the entered display name to the list of choices in the Drop-Down List Properties area (Content Control Properties dialog box).

- Click the Add button and add **Double Plan (8 servings per week)** to the list.

- Click the Add button and add **Family Plan (16 servings per week)** to the list (Figure 10–52).

Figure 10–52

4

- Click OK (Content Control Properties dialog box) to change the content control properties.

Q&A | How do I make adjustments to entries in the list?
Follow the same procedures as you use to make adjustments to entries in a drop-down list content control.

To Format Placeholder Text

As with the previous placeholder text, the placeholder text for the Servings per Week should use the Intense Emphasis style. The following steps format placeholder text.

1 With the Servings per Week placeholder text selected, display the Home tab.

2 Locate and select the Intense Emphasis style in the Styles gallery (Home tab | Styles group) to apply the selected style to the selected placeholder text.

3 Press END to position the insertion point at the end of the current line and then press ENTER to position the insertion point below the Servings per Week content control.

4 Click Normal in the Styles list (Home tab | Styles group) to format the current paragraph to the Normal style.

5 Using either the ruler or the Layout tab, change the left indent to 0.06" so that the entered text aligns with the text above it (that is, the H in How).

To Insert a Date Picker Content Control

To assist users with entering dates, Word provides a date picker content control, which displays a calendar when the user clicks the arrow to the right of the content control. Users also can enter a date directly in the content control without using the calendar. The following steps enter the label, Today's Date:, and a date picker content control. *Why? The last item that users enter in the Consultation Request is today's date.*

1

- With the insertion point below the Servings per Week content control, type **Today's Date:** as the label for the content control and then press SPACEBAR.

2

- Display the Developer tab.

- Click the 'Date Picker Content Control' button (Developer tab | Controls group) to insert a date picker content control at the location of the insertion point (Figure 10–53).

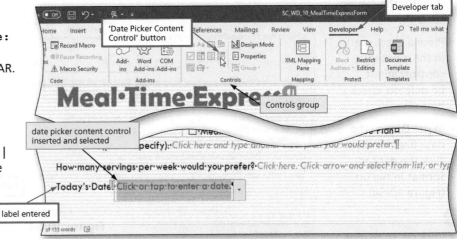

Figure 10–53

To Use Design Mode to Edit Placeholder Text

The following steps edit the placeholder text for the date picker content control.

1 With the date picker content control selected, click the Design Mode button (Developer tab | Controls group) to turn on Design mode.

2 If necessary, scroll to display the date picker content control.

3 Edit the placeholder text so that it contains this instruction, which contains two sentences: Click here. Click arrow and select today's date.

4 Click the Design Mode button (Developer tab | Controls group) to turn off Design mode.

5 If necessary, scroll to display the top of the form in the document window.

To Change the Properties of a Date Picker Content Control

The following steps change the properties of a date picker content control. *Why? In addition to identifying a tag name for a date picker content control, specifying a style, and locking the control, you will specify how the date will be displayed when the user selects it from the calendar.*

1

- With the content control selected, click the Properties button (Developer tab | Controls group) to display the Content Control Properties dialog box.

- Type **Today's Date** in the Tag text box.

- Place a check mark in the 'Use a style to format text typed into the empty control' check box to activate the Style box.

- Click the Style arrow and then select Intense Emphasis in the list to specify the style for the content control.

- Place a check mark in the 'Content control cannot be deleted' check box.

- In the Display the date like this area, click the desired format in the list (Figure 10–54).

2

- Click OK to change the content control properties.

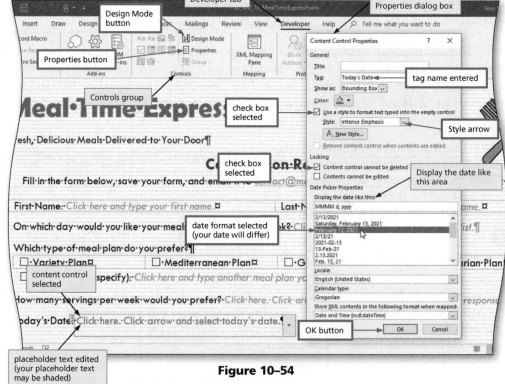

Figure 10–54

To Format Placeholder Text

As with the previous placeholder text, the placeholder text for today's date should use the Intense Emphasis style. The following steps format placeholder text.

1 With the today's date placeholder text selected, display the Home tab.

2 Locate and select the Intense Emphasis style in the Styles gallery (Home tab | Styles group) to apply the selected style to the selected placeholder text.

3 Press END to position the insertion point at the end of the current line and then press ENTER to position the insertion point below the Today's Date content control.

4 Click Normal in the Styles gallery (Home tab | Styles group) to format the current paragraph to the Normal style.

To Enter and Format Text

The following steps enter and format the line of text at the bottom of the online form.

1 Be sure the insertion point is on the line below the Today's Date content control.

2 Center the paragraph mark.

3 Format the text to be typed with the color of Purple, Accent 5, Darker 25%.

4 Type **Thank you for your interest in our service!**

5 Change the space before the paragraph to 18 point (Figure 10–55). If necessary, change the space after the paragraph to 8 point.

6 If the text flows to a second page, reduce spacing before paragraphs in the form so that all lines fit on a single page.

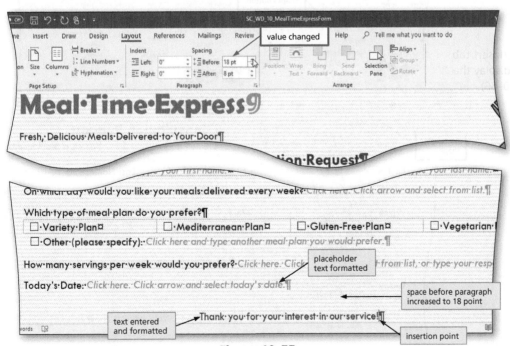

Figure 10–55

BTW
Other Content Controls
To insert a picture content control in a document or template, click the 'Picture Content Control' button (Developer tab | Controls group). When the user clicks the picture content control, the Insert Pictures dialog box is displayed, enabling the user to locate the desired picture. To insert a repeating section content control, select the table or paragraph that you want to repeat and then click the 'Repeating Section Content Control' button (Developer tab | Controls group) to create a duplicate of the selected content in the document or template. To insert a building block gallery content control, select the 'Building Block Gallery Content Control' button (Developer tab | Controls group); then click the Properties button (Developer tab | Controls group) and select the desired gallery to be displayed in the Document Building Block Properties area (Content Control Properties dialog box). When you click the 'Explore Quick Parts' button attached to the top of the building block gallery content control in the document, the selected gallery appears.

To Hide Gridlines and Formatting Marks

Because you are finished with the tables in this form and will not enter any additional tables, you will hide the gridlines. You also are finished with entering and formatting text on the screen. To make the form easier to view, you hide the formatting marks, which can clutter the screen. The following steps hide gridlines and formatting marks.

1 If necessary, position the insertion point in a table cell.

2 Display the Table Tools Layout tab. If gridlines are showing, click the View Gridlines button (Table Tools Layout tab | Table group) to hide table gridlines.

3 Display the Home tab. If the 'Show/Hide ¶' button (Home tab | Paragraph group) is selected, click it to remove formatting marks from the screen.

4 Save the template again on the same storage location with the same file name.

Break Point: If you want to take a break, this is a good place to do so. You can exit Word now. To resume later, start Word, open the file called SC_WD_10_MealTimeExpressForm.dotx, and continue following the steps from this location forward.

To Draw a Rectangle

The next step is to emphasize the data entry area of the form. The data entry area includes all the content controls in which a user enters data. The following steps draw a rectangle around the data entry area, and subsequent steps format the rectangle. *Why? To call attention to the data entry area of the form, this module places a rectangle around the data entry area, changes the style of the rectangle, and then adds a shadow to the rectangle.*

- Position the insertion point on the last line in the document (shown in Figure 10–55).

- Display the Insert tab.

- Click the Shapes button (Insert tab | Illustrations group) to display the Shapes gallery (Figure 10–56).

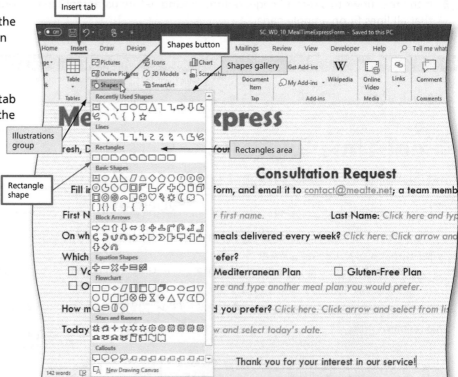

Figure 10–56

2

- Click the Rectangle shape in the Rectangles area of the Shapes gallery, which removes the gallery and changes the pointer to the shape of a crosshair in the document window.

Q&A What if I am using a touch screen?
Proceed to Step 5 because the shape is inserted in the document window after you tap the rectangle shape in the Shapes gallery.

- Position the pointer (a crosshair) in the approximate location for the upper-left corner of the desired shape (Figure 10–57).

Figure 10–57

3

- Drag the pointer downward and rightward to form a rectangle around the data entry area, as shown in Figure 10–58.

Figure 10–58

4

- Release the mouse button to draw the rectangle shape on top of the data entry area (Figure 10–59).

Q&A What happened to all the text in the data entry area?
When you draw a shape in a document, Word initially places the shape in front of, or on top of, any text in the same area. You can change the stacking order of the shape so that it is displayed behind the text. Thus, the next steps move the shape behind the text.

Figure 10–59

- If necessary, change the values in the Shape Height and Shape Width boxes (Drawing Tools Format tab | Size group) to 1.95" and 7.58" (shown in Figure 10–62).

To Send a Graphic behind Text

The following steps send a graphic behind text. **Why?** *You want the rectangle shape graphic to be positioned behind the data entry area text, so that you can see the text in the data entry area along with the shape.*

- If necessary, display the Drawing Tools Format tab.

- With the rectangle shape selected, click the Layout Options button attached to the graphic to display the Layout Options gallery (Figure 10–60).

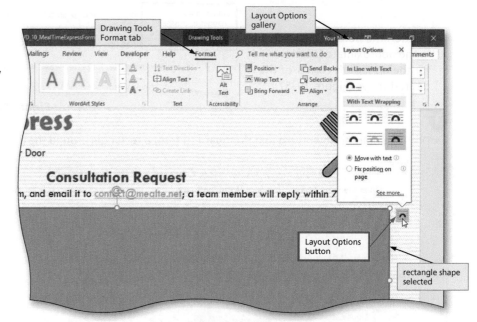

Figure 10–60

2

- Click Behind Text in the Layout Options gallery to position the rectangle shape behind the text (Figure 10–61).

Q&A What if I want a shape to cover text?
You would click 'In Front of Text' in the Layout Options gallery.

Figure 10–61

- Click the Close button in the Layout Options gallery to close the gallery.

Other Ways

1. Click Wrap Text button (Drawing Tools Format tab | Arrange group), click desired option

2. Right-click object (or, if using touch, tap 'Show Context Menu' button on Mini toolbar), point to Wrap Text on shortcut menu, click desired option

To Apply a Shape Style with an Outline

The next step is to apply a shape style to the rectangle, so that the text in the data entry area is easier to read. The following steps apply a style to the rectangle shape.

1 With the shape still selected, click the More button in the Shape Styles gallery (Drawing Tools Format tab | Shape Styles group) (shown in Figure 10–61) to expand the Shape Styles gallery.

2 Point to 'Colored Outline - Purple, Accent 5' in the Shape Styles gallery (sixth effect in first row) to display a Live Preview of that style applied to the rectangle shape in the form (Figure 10–62).

3 Click 'Colored Outline - Purple, Accent 5' in the Shape Styles gallery to apply the selected style to the selected shape.

BTW

Formatting Shapes
Like other drawing objects or pictures, shapes can be formatted or have styles applied. You can change the fill in a shape by clicking the Shape Fill arrow (Drawing Tools Format tab | Shape Styles group), add an outline or border to a shape by clicking the Shape Outline arrow (Drawing Tools Format tab | Shape Styles group), and apply an effect (such as shadow or 3-D effects) by clicking the Shape Effects arrow (Drawing Tools Format tab | Shape Styles group).

Figure 10–62

To Add a Shadow to a Shape

The following steps add a shadow to the rectangle shape. *Why? To further offset the data entry area of the form, this online form has a shadow on the outside bottom and left edges of the rectangle shape.*

- With the shape still selected, click the Shape Effects button (Drawing Tools Format tab | Shape Styles group) to display the Shape Effects menu.

- Point to Shadow on the Shape Effects menu to display the Shadow gallery.

- Point to 'Offset: Bottom Left' in the Outer area in the Shadow gallery to display a Live Preview of that shadow effect applied to the selected shape in the document (Figure 10–63).

 Experiment

- Point to various shadows in the Shadow gallery and watch the shadow on the selected shape change.

- Click 'Offset: Bottom Left' in the Shadow gallery to apply the selected shadow to the selected shape.

Figure 10–63

Can I change the color of a shadow?

Yes. Click Shadow Options (shown in Figure 10–63) in the Shadow gallery.

To Protect a Form

When you **protect a form**, you are allowing users to enter data only in designated areas — specifically, the content controls. The following steps protect the online form. *Why? To prevent unwanted changes and edits to the form, it is crucial that you protect a form before making it available to users.*

- Display the Developer tab.

- Click the Restrict Editing button (Developer tab | Protect group) to open the Restrict Editing pane (Figure 10–64).

Figure 10–64

2

- In the Editing restrictions area, place a check mark in the 'Allow only this type of editing in the document' check box and then click its arrow to display a list of the types of allowed restrictions (Figure 10–65).

Figure 10–65

3

- Click 'Filling in forms' in the list to instruct Word that the only editing allowed in this document is to the content controls.

- In the Start enforcement area, click the 'Yes, Start Enforcing Protection' button, which displays the Start Enforcing Protection dialog box (Figure 10–66).

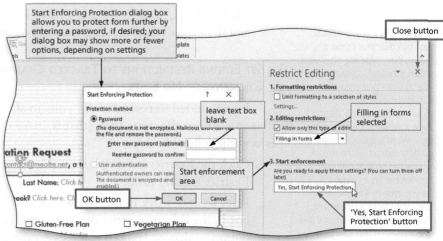

Figure 10–66

4

- Click OK (Start Enforcing Protection dialog box) to protect the document without a password.

Q&A What if I enter a password?
If you enter a password, only a user who knows the password will be able to unprotect the document.

- Close the Restrict Editing pane to show the protected form (Figure 10–67).

Figure 10–67

Other Ways

1. Open Backstage view, click Info, click Protect Document button, click Restrict Editing on Protect Document menu

BTW
Password-Protecting Documents
You can save documents with a password to keep unauthorized users from accessing files. To do this, open Backstage view, click Info, click the Protect Document button, click 'Encrypt with Password' on the Protect Document menu, type the password in the Encrypt Document dialog box, type the password again (Confirm Password dialog box), and click OK; or open Backstage view, click Save As, display the Save As dialog box, click the Tools button (Save As dialog box), click General Options on the Tools menu, type the password in the appropriate text box (General Options dialog box), type the password again (Confirm Password dialog box), and then click OK and the Save button (Save As dialog box). As you type a password in the text box, Word displays a series of dots instead of the actual characters so that others cannot see your password as you type it. To remove a password from a document, follow these steps except leave the password text box blank.

Be sure to keep the password confidential. Choose a password that is easy to remember and that no one can guess. Do not use any part of your first or last name, Social Security number, birthday, and so on. Use a password that is at least six characters long, and if possible, use a mixture of numbers and letters.

Protecting Documents

In addition to protecting a form so that it only can be filled in, Word provides several other options in the Restrict Editing pane.

TO SET FORMATTING RESTRICTIONS

If you wanted to restrict users from making certain types of formatting changes to a document, you would perform the following steps.

1. Click the Restrict Editing button (Developer tab | Protect group) to open the Restrict Editing pane.
2. Place a check mark in the 'Limit formatting to a selection of styles' check box in the Formatting restrictions area.
3. Click the Settings link and then select the types of formatting you want to allow (Formatting Restrictions dialog box).
4. Click OK.
5. Click the 'Yes, Start Enforcing Protection' button, enter a password if desired, and then click OK (Start Enforcing Protection dialog box).

TO SET EDITING RESTRICTIONS TO TRACKED CHANGES OR COMMENTS OR NO EDITS

If you wanted to restrict users' edits to allow only tracked changes, allow only comments, or not allow any edits (that is, make the document read only), you would perform the following steps.

1. Click the Restrict Editing button (Developer tab | Protect group) to open the Restrict Editing pane.
2. Place a check mark in the 'Allow only this type of editing in the document' check box in the Editing restrictions area, click the arrow, and then click the desired option — that is, Tracked changes, Comments, or No changes (Read only) — to specify the types of edits allowed in the document.
3. Click the 'Yes, Start Enforcing Protection' button, enter a password if desired, and then click OK (Start Enforcing Protection dialog box).

To Hide the Developer Tab

You are finished using the commands on the Developer tab. Thus, the following steps hide the Developer tab from the ribbon.

1. Open Backstage view and then click Options in the left pane of Backstage view to display the Word Options dialog box.

2. Click Customize Ribbon in the left pane (Word Options dialog box).

3. Remove the check mark from the Developer check box in the Main Tabs list.

4. Click OK to hide the Developer tab from the ribbon.

BTW
Setting Exceptions to Editing Restrictions
You can use the Restrict Editing pane to allow editing in just certain areas of the document, a procedure referred to as adding users excepted from restrictions. To do this, place a check mark in the 'Allow only this type of editing in the document' check box and then change the associated text box to 'No changes (Read only)', which instructs Word to prevent any editing to the document. Next, select the placeholder text for which you want to waive user restrictions and place a check mark in the Everyone check box in the Exceptions (optional) area to instruct Word that the selected item can be edited — the rest of the form will be read only.

To Hide the Ruler, Collapse the Ribbon, Save the Template, and Exit Word

If the ruler is displayed on the screen, you want to hide it. You also want to collapse the ribbon so that when you test the form in the next steps, the ribbon is collapsed. Finally, the online form template for this project now is complete, so you can save the template again and exit Word. The following steps perform these tasks.

1 If the ruler is displayed on the screen, remove the check mark from the Ruler check box (View tab | Show group).

2 Click the 'Collapse the Ribbon' button on the ribbon (shown in Figure 10–5 earlier in this module) to collapse the ribbon.

3 Save the template again on the same storage location with the same file name.

4 **sam'**↟ Exit Word.

BTW
Protected Documents
If you open an existing form that has been protected, Word will not allow you to modify the form's appearance until you unprotect it. To unprotect a form (or any protected document), open the Restrict Editing pane by clicking the Restrict Editing button (Developer tab | Protect group) or open Backstage view, display the Info screen, click the Protect Document button, and click Restrict Editing on the Protect Document menu. Then, click the Stop Protection button in the Restrict Editing pane and close the pane. If this unencrypted document has been protected with a password, you will be asked to enter the password when you attempt to unprotect the document.

Working with an Online Form

When you create a template, you use the Open command in Backstage view to open the template so that you can modify it. After you have created a template, you then can make it available to users. Users do not open templates with the Open command in Word. Instead, a user creates a new Word document that is *based* on the template, which means the title bar displays the default file name, Document1 (or a similar name) rather than the template name. When Word creates a new document that is based on a template, the document window contains any text and formatting associated with the template. If a user accesses a letter template, for example, Word displays the contents of a basic letter in a new document window.

To Use File Explorer to Create a New Document That Is Based on a Template

When you save a template on storage media, as instructed earlier in this module, a user can create a new document that is based on the template through File Explorer. *Why? This allows the user to work with a new document instead of risking the chance of altering the original template.* The following steps create a new Word document that is based on the SC_WD_10_MealTimeExpressForm.dotx template.

1

• Click the File Explorer button on the Windows taskbar to open a File Explorer window.

• Navigate to the location of the saved template (Figure 10–68).

Figure 10–68

2

- Double-click the SC_WD_10_MealTimeExpressForm.dotx file in the File Explorer window, which starts Word and creates a new document that is based on the contents of the selected template (Figure 10–69).

Q&A

Why did my background page color disappear?

If the background page color does not appear, open Backstage view, click Options to display the Word Options dialog box, click Advanced in the left pane (Word Options dialog box), scroll to the Show document content section, place a check mark in the 'Show background colors and images in Print Layout view' check box, and then click OK.

Why does my ribbon show only three tabs: File, Tools, and View?

Your screen is in Read mode. Click the View tab and then click Edit Document to switch to Print Layout view.

Figure 10–69

To Fill In a Form and Save It

The next step is to enter data in the form. To advance from one content control to the next, a user can click the content control or press TAB. To move to a previous content control, a user can click it or press SHIFT+TAB. The following steps fill in SC_WD_10_MealTimeExpressForm. *Why? You want to test the form to be sure it works as you intended.*

1

- With the First Name content control selected, type **Jordan** and then press TAB.
- Type **Wilton** in the Last Name content control.
- Press TAB to select the Delivery Day content control and then click its arrow to display the list of choices (shown in Figure 10–1b at the beginning of this module).
- Click Thursday in the list.

- Click the Gluten-Free Plan and Other Meal Plan Type check boxes to select them.
- Type **Pescatarian** in the Other Meal Plan Type content control.
- Click the Servings per Week content control and then click its arrow to display the list of choices (Figure 10–70).

Figure 10–70

- Select Single Plan (4 servings per week) in the list.
- Click the Today's Date content control and then click its arrow to display a calendar (Figure 10–71).

- Click February 13, 2021 in the calendar to complete the data entry (shown in Figure 10–1c at the beginning of this module).

Figure 10–71

- Save the file on your storage location with the file name, SC_WD_10_WiltonConsultationRequest. If Word asks if you want to also save changes to the document template, click No.

Q&A Can I print the form?

You can print the document as you print any other document. Keep in mind, however, that the colors used were designed for viewing online. Thus, different color schemes would have been selected if the form had been designed for a printout.

- Exit Word. (If Word asks if you want to save the modified styles, click the Don't Save button.)

- If the File Explorer window still is open, close it.

BTW

Linking a Form to a Database

If you want to use or analyze the data that a user enters into a form in an Access database or an Excel worksheet, you could save the form data in a comma-delimited text file. This file separates each data item with a comma and places quotation marks around text data items. Then, you can use Access or Excel to import the comma-delimited text file for use in the respective program. To save form data, open Backstage view, click Save As in Backstage view, and then display the Save As dialog box. Click the Tools button (Save As dialog box) and then click Save Options on the Tools menu to display the Word Options dialog box. Click Advanced in the left pane (Word Options dialog box), scroll to the Preserve fidelity when sharing this document area in the right pane, place a check mark in the 'Save form data as delimited text file' check box, and then click OK. Next, be sure the file type is Plain Text (Save As dialog box) and then click the Save button to save the file as a comma-delimited text file. You can import the resulting comma-delimited file in an Access database or an Excel worksheet. To convert successfully, you should use the legacy controls (i.e., text form field, check box form field, etc.), which are available through the Legacy Tools button (Developer tab | Controls group).

Working with Templates

If you want to modify a protected template, open it by clicking Open in Backstage view, clicking the template name, and then clicking the Open button in the dialog box. Then, you must **unprotect a form** by clicking the Restrict Editing button (Developer tab | Protect group) and then clicking the Stop Protection button in the Restrict Editing pane.

When you created the template in this module, you saved it on your local storage location. In environments other than an academic setting, you would not save the template on your own storage location; instead, you would save the file in the Custom Office Templates folder. When you save a template in the Custom Office Templates folder, you can locate the template by opening Backstage view, clicking New to display the New screen, and then clicking the Personal tab in the New screen, which displays the template in the New screen (Figure 10–72).

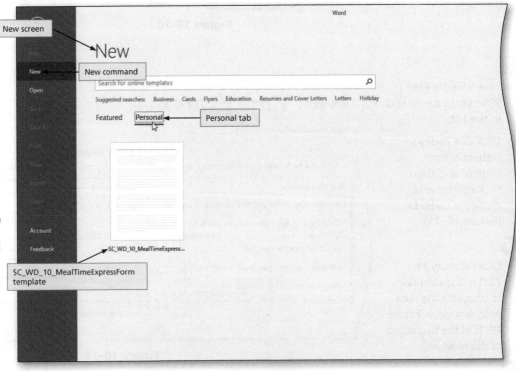

Figure 10–72

Summary

In this module, you learned how to create an online form. Topics covered included saving a document as a template, changing paper size, using a table to control layout, showing the Developer tab, inserting and formatting content controls, editing placeholder text, changing properties of content controls, and protecting a form.

What decisions will you need to make when creating online forms?
Use these guidelines as you complete the assignments in this module and create your own online forms outside of this class.

1. Design the form.

   a) To minimize the time spent creating a form while using a computer or mobile device, consider sketching the form on a piece of paper first.

   b) Design a well-thought-out draft of the form — being sure to include all essential form elements, including the form's title, text and graphics, data entry fields, and data entry instructions.

2. For each data entry field, determine its field type and/or list of possible values that it can contain.

3. Save the form as a template, instead of as a Word document, to simplify the data entry process for users of the form.

4. Create a functional and visually appealing form.

   a) Use colors that complement one another.

   b) Draw the user's attention to important sections.

   c) Arrange data entry fields in logical groups on the form and in an order that users would expect.

   d) Data entry instructions should be succinct and easy to understand.

   e) Ensure that users can enter and edit data only in designated areas of the form.

5. Determine how the form data will be analyzed.

   a) If the data entered in the form will be analyzed by a program outside of Word, create the data entry fields so that the entries are stored in separate fields that can be shared with other programs.

6. Test the form, ensuring it works as you intended.

   a) Fill in the form as if you are a user.

   b) Ask others to fill in the form to be sure it is organized in a logical manner and is easy to understand and complete.

   c) If any errors or weaknesses in the form are identified, correct them and test the form again.

7. Publish or distribute the form.

   a) Not only does an online form reduce the need for paper, it saves the time spent making copies of the form and distributing it.

   b) When the form is complete, post it on social media, the web, or your company's intranet, or email it to targeted recipients.

Apply Your Knowledge

Reinforce the skills and apply the concepts you learned in this module.

Working with an Online Form

Note: To complete this assignment, you will be required to use the Data Files. Please contact your instructor for information about accessing the Data Files.

Instructions: Start Word. Open the template, SC_WD_10-1.dotx, which is located in the Data Files. The template is a draft of an online survey created by Carter's Recycling Service, a new recycling facility, that will be emailed to community members by the community relations coordinator at the New Town Village Hall requesting feedback on potential upcoming village services. You are to modify the template. The final template is shown in Figure 10–73.

Figure 10–73

Perform the following tasks:

1. Click File on the ribbon and then click Save As and save the document using the new file name, SC_WD_10_RecyclingCommunitySurvey.

2. Add the page color Turquoise, Accent 1, Lighter 80% to the template. Apply the Small grid pattern fill effect to the template. (*Hint:* Use the Page Color button (Design tab | Page Background group).)

3. Remove the table border from each of the two tables in the form. (*Hint:* One at a time, select each table using the Select button (Table Tools Layout tab | Table group) and then use the Borders arrow (Table Tools Design tab | Borders group).)

4. If necessary, use the View Gridlines button (Table Tools Layout tab | Table group) to show table gridlines.

5. If necessary, show the Developer tab on the ribbon.

6. In the 2 × 1 table in the data entry area, in the cell to the right of the First Name content control, enter the text, Last Name:, followed by a space as the label and then use the Developer tab to insert a plain text content control in the cell after the label.

7. Select the inserted plain text content control and then turn on Design mode. Edit the placeholder text so that it reads: Click here and type your last name. Turn off Design mode.

8. Change the properties of the plain text content control as follows: enter Last Name as the tag, select the 'Use a style to format text typed into the empty control' check box, select the Intense Emphasis style for the text to be typed in the content control, and select the 'Content control cannot be deleted' check box.

9. Use the Styles group in the Home tab to format the placeholder text in the plain text content control to the Intense Emphasis style.

10. In the data entry area, to the right of the type of recycling services question, insert a drop-down list content control.

11. Select the inserted drop-down list content control and then turn on Design mode. Edit the placeholder text so that it contains two sentences that read: Click here. Click arrow and select from list. When you have finished editing the placeholder text, turn off Design mode.

12. Change the properties of the drop-down list content control as follows: enter Recycling Services as the tag, select the 'Use a style to format text typed into the empty control' check box, select the Intense Emphasis style for the text to be typed in the content control, select the 'Content control cannot be deleted' check box, and set these four choices for the list: Fee-Based Curbside Recycling, Free Drop-Off Locations, Both, Neither (be sure to delete the default choice of Choose an item.).

13. Use the Styles group on the Home tab to format the placeholder text in the drop-down list content control to the Intense Emphasis style.

14. In the 5 × 1 table in the data entry area, in the cell to the right of the Glass content control, insert a check box content control.

15. Change the properties of the check box content control as follows: enter Plastic as the tag, select the Show as box and then select None, and select the 'Content control cannot be deleted' check box.

16. One blank space to the right of the inserted check box content control, enter Plastic as the label.

17. In the 5 × 1 table in the data entry area, in the cell to the right of the Plastic content control, insert a check box content control.

18. Change the properties of the check box content control as follows: enter Yard Waste as the tag, select the Show as box and then select None, and select the 'Content control cannot be deleted' check box.

19. One space to the right of the inserted check box content control, enter the text, Yard Waste, as the label.

20. In the data entry area, to the right of the Other (please specify): check box, insert a rich text content control.

21. Select the inserted rich text content control and then turn on Design mode. Edit the placeholder text so that it reads: Click here and type other items you would recycle. Turn off Design mode.

22. Change the properties of the rich text content control as follows: enter Other Recycle Items as the tag, select the 'Use a style to format text typed into the empty control' check box, select the Intense Emphasis style for the text to be typed in the content control, and select the 'Content control cannot be deleted' check box.

Continued >

Apply Your Knowledge *continued*

23. Use the Styles group on the Home tab to format the placeholder text in the rich text content control to the Intense Emphasis style.

24. In the data entry area, to the right of the frequency of recycling yard waste question, insert a combo box content control.

25. Select the inserted combo box content control and then turn on Design mode. Edit the placeholder text so it contains two sentences that read: Click here. Click arrow and select from list, or type your preference. When you have finishing editing the placeholder text, turn off Design mode.

26. Change the properties of the combo box content control as follows: enter Yard Waste Frequency as the tag, select the 'Use a style to format text typed into the empty control' check box, select the Intense Emphasis style for the text to be typed in the content control, select the 'Content control cannot be deleted' check box, and set these four choices for the list: Twice a year, Four times a year, Monthly, Never. (Be sure to delete the default choice of Choose an item.)

27. Use the Styles group in the Home tab to format the placeholder text in the combo box content control to the Intense Emphasis style.

28. At the bottom of the data entry area, to the right of the Today's Date: label, insert a Date Picker content control.

29. Select the inserted date picker content control and then turn on Design mode. Edit the placeholder text so that it contains two sentences that read: Click here. Click arrow and select today's date. When you have finished editing the placeholder text, turn off Design mode.

30. Change the properties of the date picker content control as follows: enter Today's Date as the tag, select the 'Use a style to format text typed into the empty control' check box, select the Intense Emphasis style for the text to be typed in the content control, select the 'Content control cannot be deleted' check box, and select the date in this format: February 13, 2021.

31. Use the Styles group on the Home tab to format the placeholder text in the date picker content control to the Intense Emphasis style.

32. If table gridlines show, hide them. (*Hint*: Position the insertion point in one of the two tables in the form and the use the View Gridlines button (Table Tools Layout tab | Table group).)

33. Collapse the ribbon. If necessary, adjust spacing above and below paragraphs as necessary so that all contents fit on a single screen with the ribbon collapsed.

34. Use the Restrict Editing pane to set editing restrictions to filling in forms and then start enforcing protection (do not use a password). Close the Restrict Editing pane.

35. Save the form again with the same file name and then submit it in the format specified by your instructor. Close the template and exit Word.

36. Open a File Explorer window. Locate the SC_WD_10_RecyclingCommunitySurvey.dotx template you just created and then double-click the template in File Explorer to create a new document based on the template.

37. When Word displays a new document based on the template, if necessary, collapse the ribbon, hide formatting marks, and change the zoom to page width. Your screen should look like Figure 10–73 and display Document1 (or a similar name) on the title bar instead of the file name.

38. Test your form as follows:

   a. With the First Name content control selected, enter your first name.

   b. Press TAB and then enter your last name in the last name content control.

   c. Click the Recycling Services content control, click its arrow, and then click Both in the list.

   d.   Click the Cardboard, Glass, and Plastic check boxes to select them.

   e.   Click the Other check box. If necessary, click the Other text box and then enter Steel in the text box.

   f.   Click the Recycle Yard Waste Frequency content control to select it, click its arrow, press ESC because none of these choices answers the question, and enter the text, Every other month, as the response.

   g.   Click the Today's Date content control, click the arrow to display a calendar, and then select today's date in the calendar.

   h.   Close the form without saving it. (If any content controls do not work as intended, use Word to open the SC_WD_10_RecyclingCommunitySurvey.dotx template, unprotect the template, modify it as appropriate, protect the template again, save it, and then retest it as described in this step.)

39. ✸ If the recycling service wanted the community member's middle name on the same line as the first and last names, how would you evenly space the three items across the line?

Extend Your Knowledge

Extend the skills you learned in this module and experiment with new skills. You may need to use Help to complete the assignment.

Working with Icons, Picture Content Controls, Passwords, and More

Note: To complete this assignment, you will be required to use the Data Files. Please contact your instructor for information about accessing the Data Files.

Instructions: Start Word. Open the template, SC_WD_10-2.dotx, which is located in the Data Files. This template is a draft of an online freshman orientation feedback form, written by the campus life coordinator at Harper View College.

    You will unprotect the form, insert and format icons, group images, insert a picture content control in a text box, practice inserting repeating section and building block gallery content controls, change a shape's shadow color, customize theme colors, and protect a document (form, in this case) with passwords.

Perform the following tasks:
1. Use Help to review and expand your knowledge about these topics: unprotecting documents, picture content controls, text boxes, grouping objects, shadows, shape fill effects, changing theme colors, and protecting forms with passwords.

2. Click File on the ribbon, click Save As, and then save the template using the new file name, SC_WD_10_FreshmanOrientationForm.

3. Unprotect the document. (*Hint*: Use the Developer tab on the ribbon or the Info screen in Backstage view.)

4. Change the paper size to a width of 8.5 inches and a height of 4 inches.

5. Insert two appropriate icons of your choice in the template. (*Hint*: Use the Icons button (Insert tab | Illustrations group). If your version of Word does not include the Icons button, insert two appropriate images using the Online Picture button or insert the images that are called Support_WD_10_Backpack.png and Support_WD_10_Books.png from the Data Files.)

6. Change the wrapping of each of the inserted images to In Front of Text. For only one of the images, change the color, fill, outline, effects, or style to options of your choice. Move the two images on the page so that they overlap each other. Select the image on the top and send it

Continued >

Extend Your Knowledge *continued*

backward. (*Hint*: Right-click the image and then use commands on the submenu or use buttons in the Arrange group on the ribbon.) Select the image on the bottom and bring it forward. Select the image on top and send it to the back. Select the image on the bottom and bring it to the front.

7. For the image you have not yet formatted, change its color, fill, outline, effects, or style to options of your choice.

8. Move one image on one side of the college name and the other image on the other side. Resize the images as appropriate.

9. Group the two images at the top of the form together. Move the grouped graphics. Return them to their original location.

10. Select the college name and then use the 'Text Effects and Typography' button (Home tab | Font group) to add a reflection of your choice to the college name. Adjust spacing above and below paragraphs as necessary so that the entire form fits on a single page.

11. Change the Orientation Start Date content control to a format other than M/d/yyyy (i.e., 2/16/2021).

12. Insert a simple text box into the empty space on the right side of the data entry area by clicking the Text Box button (Insert tab | Text group) and then clicking 'Simple Text Box' in the Text Box gallery. Change the wrapping of the inserted text box to In Front of Text. Resize the text box so that it fits completely in the data entry area. Remove space after the paragraph. Delete the placeholder in the text box.

13. In the text box, type the label, Student Photo:, and then resize the text as necessary. Below the label, insert a picture content control in the text box. Resize the picture content control so that it fits in the text box and then center both the picture and label in the text box (Figure 10–74). Remove the border from the text box.

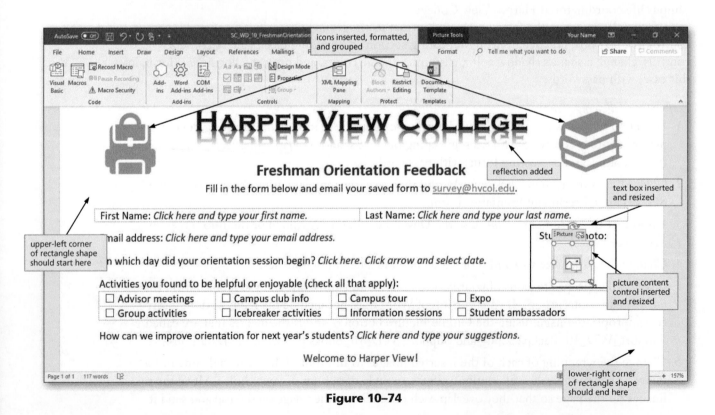

Figure 10–74

14. Select one of the tables in the data entry area. Insert a repeating section content control. Click the insert control (the plus sign) at the far-right edge of the table with the repeating section content control. What happens when you click the insert control? Click the Undo button on the Quick Access Toolbar to undo the added duplicate table row. Click the Undo button again to undo the insert of the repeating section content control or delete the content control manually.

15. Click to the right of the last line on the template. Insert a building block gallery content control. Click the Properties button (Developer tab | Controls group) to display the Content Control Properties dialog box. Change the value in the Gallery box in the Document Building Block Properties area to Equation and then click OK. In the template, click the 'Explore Quick Parts' button attached to the top of the building block gallery content control. What is displayed when you click this button? Delete the building block gallery content control by right-clicking it and then clicking 'Remove Content Control' on the shortcut menu.

16. Hide table gridlines, if they are showing.

17. Add a page color of your choice to the template. Apply a pattern fill effect of your choice to the page color background.

18. Insert a rectangle shape around the data entry area (starting in the upper-left corner by the First Name label and ending in the lower-right corner to the right of the Orientation Suggestions rich text content control).

19. Send the rectangle shape backward, which sends the shape back one layer. Send the rectangle shape behind text. Note that in this case, these two commands yield the same result.

20. Change the shape fill in the rectangle shape to a color of your choice. Change the shape outline on the rectangle shape to a color or style of your choice. If necessary, change the font color or style of text in the data entry area so that it is readable on the background color.

21. Add a shadow to the rectangle and then change the color of the shadow on the rectangle to a color other than the default.

22. Customize the theme colors for the hyperlink to a color of your choice (*Hint*: Use the Customize Colors command in Colors gallery (Design tab | Document Formatting group).) Save the modified theme colors.

23. Make any necessary formatting changes to the form.

24. If requested by your instructor, change the email address above the data entry area to your email address.

25. Restrict formatting in the document using the 'Limit formatting to a selection of styles' check box. Click the Settings link (Restrict Editing pane) and then select document formatting restrictions. Remove the formatting restrictions just set in the form.

26. Restrict editing in the document to tracked changes. Change the restrict editing selection to comments. Finally, restrict editing to filling in the form and protect the unencrypted form using the word, fun, as the password in the Start Enforcing Protection dialog box. What is the purpose of this password?

27. If requested by your instructor, use the Info screen in Backstage view to encrypt the document with a password. Use the word, fun, as the password. (*Hint*: You will need to use the Restrict Editing pane to remove the password added in the previous step before you can complete this step.) What is the purpose of this password? (Note that to delete the password, you would remove the password in the Password text box in the Encrypt Document dialog box.)

28. Save the form again with the same name and then submit it in the format specified by your instructor. Close the template and exit Word.

Continued >

Extend Your Knowledge *continued*

29. Test the form using your own data for the responses. When filling in the form, use your own photo for the student photo or the use the picture called Support_WD_10_FaceShot in the Data Files for the picture content control. If required by your instructor, save the filled-in form and then submit it in the format specified by your instructor.

30. If your document had multiple pages with headers and footers and did not want the same headers or footers to appear on different pages, what button would you click to break the link between the sections?

31. ✳ Answer the questions posed in #14, #15, #26, #27, and #30. What is the advantage of grouping graphics? Besides changing the color of the shadow, what other shadow settings can you adjust?

Expand Your World

Create a solution that uses cloud or web technologies by learning and investigating on your own from general guidance.

Using Microsoft Forms to Create an Online Survey

Instructions: You will use Microsoft Forms, which is part of Office 365, to prepare an online form. As a marketing coordinator at Harkin Realtors, you will create an online client survey. Figure 10–75 shows a portion of the survey. You will enter the questions Microsoft Forms and then use its tools to enter settings for the responses.

Perform the following tasks:

1. Start a browser. Search for the text, Microsoft Forms, using a search engine. Visit websites to learn about Microsoft Forms. Navigate to the Microsoft Forms website. You will need to sign in to your OneDrive account.

2. Create a new form using Microsoft Forms. Use SC_WD_10_HarkinRealtors.docx as the file name.

3. Enter the text, Client Survey, as the description.

4. Click the Add question button. Select Text as the type of question. Enter the text, Who was your agent?, in the text box. Make this question required.

5. Click the Add question button. Select Rating as the type of question. Enter the text, How would you rate your agent (with five stars being this highest rating)?, in the text box. Make this question required.

6. Click the Add question button. Select Choice as the type of question. Enter the text, Which type of real estate did you purchase or sell through our agency?, in the text box. Enter these three options: Single-family home, Condominium, Land. Add an 'Other' option. Make this question required.

7. Click the Add question button. Select Date as the type of question. Enter the text, On what date was your closing held?, in the text box. Make this question required.

8. Add an appropriate theme to the form.

9. Preview the form on a computer (Figure 10–75). (*Hint*: Adjust the zoom in the browser window to see more of the form in the window at once.) If requested by your instructor, take a screenshot of the preview and submit the screenshot in the format requested by your instructor. Save the screenshot with the file name, SC_WD_10_HarkinRealtors.

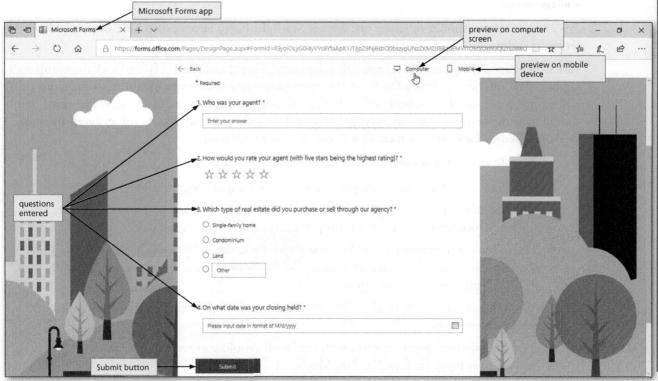

Figure 10–75

10. Preview the form on a mobile device. Click the Back button to return to the form design screen.

11. Click the 'More form settings' button in the upper-right corner of the screen, click Settings on the menu, and review the additional form settings options.

12. Click the Share button and review the sharing options.

13. If requested by your instructor, copy the form link and email it to your instructor.

14. If requested by your instructor, click the 'Get a link to view and edit' button (or a similar button), copy this link, and email it to your instructor.

15. Copy the form link. Open a new browser tab and paste the link into the browser address bar. Fill in the form in the new browser window using responses of your choice and then click the Submit button.

16. Redisplay your form window and then click the Responses tab to see how Microsoft Forms tabulates results.

17. Close the Microsoft Forms window. If necessary, sign out of your OneDrive account.

18. ✸ What is Microsoft Forms? Do you prefer using Microsoft Forms or the Word desktop app to create online forms? Why?

In the Lab

Design and implement a solution using creative thinking and problem-solving skills.

Create an Online Form for a Ferry Service

Note: To complete this assignment, you may be required to use the Data Files. Please contact your instructor for information about accessing the Data Files.

Continued >

In the Lab *continued*

Problem: As the customer relations manager at Starlight Ferry Service, you have been asked to create an online customer satisfaction survey.

Part 1: Create a template that contains the company name (Starlight Ferry Service), the company's tag line (Smooth Sailing Every Day!), and an appropriate image that you obtain from the icons or online images, or use the Support_WD_10_FerryBoat.png image in the Data Files. The third line should have the text, Satisfaction Survey. The fourth line should read: Please fill in the form below, save the filled-in form, and then email it to survey@starlightfs.org.

The data entry area should contain the following:

- First Name and Last Name are plain text content controls within a table.
- A combo box content control with the label, How often do you use our services?, has these choices: Once or twice a year, Monthly, Weekly, More than once a week.
- The following instruction should appear above these check boxes: What do you like best about our services (check all that apply)?; the check boxes are Food selection, Friendly staff, Price, Cleanliness, and Other (please specify).
- A rich text content control after the Other (please specify) label allows customers to enter their own response.
- A drop-down list content control with the label, Would you recommend Starlight Ferry Service?, has these choices: Yes, No, Maybe.
- A date picker content control with the label, What date did you last use our service?

On the line below the data entry area, include the text: Thank you for your time!

Use the concepts and techniques presented in this module to create and format the online form. Use meaningful placeholder text for all content controls. (For example, the placeholder text for the First Name plain text content control could be as follows: Click here and type your first name.) Apply a style to the placeholder text. Assign names, styles, and locking to each content control (so that the content controls cannot be deleted). Draw a rectangle around the data entry area of the form and format the rectangle appropriately. Add a page color. Be sure to change the page size and margins, and adjust spacing as necessary above and below paragraphs, so that the entire form fits in the document window.

When you are finished creating the form, protect it so that editing is restricted to filling in the form and then save it as a template with the file name, SC_WD_10_StarlightSatisfactionSurvey. Test the form and make any necessary corrections. Submit the form in the format specified by your instructor.

Part 2: ✳ You made several decisions while creating the online form in this assignment: placeholder text to use and how to organize and format the online form (fonts, font sizes, styles, colors, etc.). What was the rationale behind each of these decisions? When you proofread and tested the online form, what further revisions did you make, and why? How would you recommend publishing or distributing this online form?

11 | Enhancing an Online Form and Using Macros

Objectives

After completing this module, you will be able to:

- Unprotect a document
- Specify macro settings
- Convert a table to text
- Insert and edit a field
- Create a character style
- Apply and modify fill effects
- Change a shape
- Remove a background from a graphic
- Apply an artistic effect to a graphic
- Insert and format a text box
- Group objects
- Record and execute a macro
- Customize the Quick Access Toolbar
- Edit a macro's VBA code
- Work with 3-D models

Introduction

Word provides many tools that allow you to improve the appearance, functionality, and security of your documents. This module discusses tools used to perform the following tasks:

- Modify text and content controls.
- Enhance with color, shapes, effects, and graphics.
- Automate a series of tasks with a macro.

Project: Online Form Revised

This module uses Word to improve the visual appearance of and add macros to the online form created in Module 10, producing the online form shown in Figure 11–1a. This project begins with the Meal Time Express Consultation Request online form created in Module 10 and then enhances it and improves its functionality. Thus, if you created the online form template in Module 10, you will use that file in this module. If you did not create the online form template in Module 10, see your instructor for a copy.

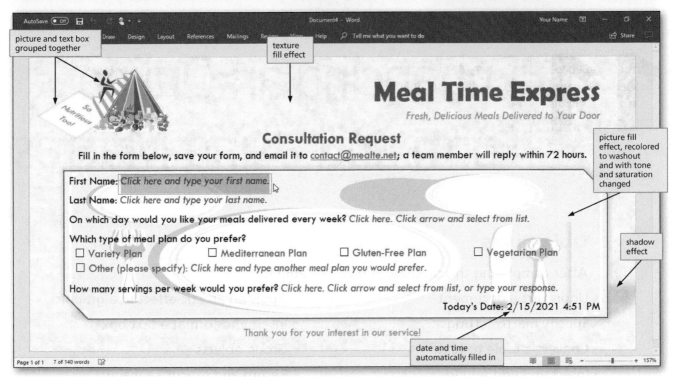

(a) Modified and Enhanced Online Form

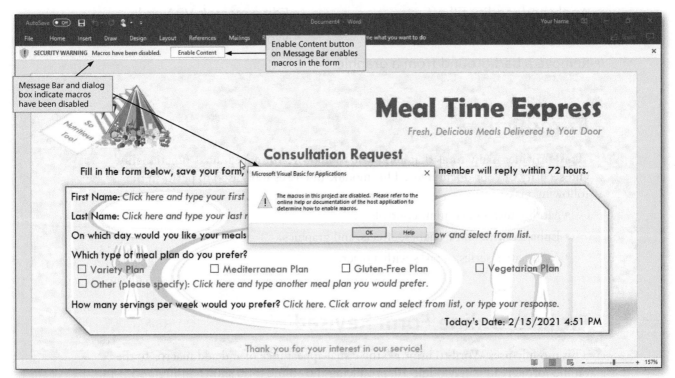

(b) Macros in Online Form Generate Security Warning

Figure 11–1

This project modifies the fonts and font colors of the text in the Meal Time Express Consultation Request online form and enhances the contents of the form to include a texture fill effect, a picture fill effect, and a text box and picture grouped together. The date in the form automatically displays the computer or mobile device's system date, instead of requiring the user to enter the date.

This form also includes macros to automate tasks. A **macro** is a named set of instructions, written in the Visual Basic programming language, that performs tasks automatically in a specified order. One macro allows the user to hide formatting marks and the ruler by pressing a keyboard shortcut (sometimes called a shortcut key) or clicking a button on the Quick Access Toolbar. Another macro specifies how the form is displayed initially on a user's Word screen. As shown in Figure 11–1b, when a document contains macros, Word may generate a security warning. If you are sure the macros are from a trusted source and free of viruses, then enable the content. Otherwise, do not enable the content, which protects your computer from potentially harmful viruses or other malicious software.

You will perform the following general tasks as you progress through this module:

1. Save a document as a macro-enabled template.
2. Modify the text and form content controls.
3. Enhance the form's visual appeal.
4. Create macros to automate tasks in the form.
5. Insert and format a 3-D model.

To Start Word and Specify Settings

If you are using a computer to step through the project in this module and you want your screens to match the figures in this book, you should change your screen's resolution to 1366 × 768. The following steps start Word, hide formatting marks, ensure rulers are not displayed, change the zoom to page width, and verify ruler and Mouse mode settings.

1 Start Word and create a blank document in the Word window. If necessary, maximize the Word window.

2 If the Print Layout button on the status bar is not selected, click it so that your screen is in Print Layout view.

3 If the 'Show/Hide ¶' button (Home tab | Paragraph group) is selected, click it to hide formatting marks because you will not use them in this project.

4 If the rulers are displayed on the screen, click the Ruler check box (View tab | Show group) to remove the rulers from the Word window because you will not use the rulers in this project.

5 If the edges of the page do not extend to the edge of the document window, display the View tab and then click the Page Width button (View tab | Zoom group).

6 If you are using a mouse and you want your screens to match the figures in the book, verify that you are using Mouse mode by clicking the Touch/Mouse Mode button on the Quick Access Toolbar and then, if necessary, clicking Mouse on the menu. (If your Quick Access Toolbar does not display the Touch/Mouse Mode button, click the 'Customize Quick Access Toolbar' button on the Quick Access Toolbar and then click Touch/Mouse Mode on the menu to add the button to the Quick Access Toolbar.)

BTW
The Ribbon and Screen Resolution
Word may change how the groups and buttons within the groups appear on the ribbon, depending on the screen resolution of your computer. Thus, your ribbon may look different from the ones in this book if you are using a screen resolution other than 1366 × 768.

To Save a Macro-Enabled Template

The project in this module contains macros. Thus, the first step in this module is to open the Meal Time Express Consultation Request template created in Module 10 and then save the template as a macro-enabled template. *Why? To provide added security to templates, a basic Word template cannot store macros. Word instead provides a specific type of template, called a* **macro-enabled template,** *in which you can store macros.*

- **sam**↓ Open the template named SC_WD_10_MealTimeExpressForm.dotx that you created in Module 10. If you did not create the online form template in Module 10, see your instructor for a copy.

- Open Backstage view, click Save As to display the Save As screen, display the Save As dialog box, and navigate to the desired save location.

- Type `SC_WD_11_MealTimeExpressFormModified` in the File name text box (Save As dialog box) to change the file name.

- Click the 'Save as type' arrow to display the list of available file types and then click 'Word Macro-Enabled Template' in the list to change the file type (Figure 11–2). (Before proceeding, verify that your file type changed to Word Macro-Enabled Template.)

- Click the Save button (Save As dialog box) to save the file using the entered file name as a macro-enabled template.

Q&A

How does Word differentiate between a Word template and a Word macro-enabled template?
A Word template has an extension of .dotx, whereas a Word macro-enabled template has an extension of .dotm. Also, the icon for a macro-enabled template contains an exclamation point.

Figure 11–2

To Show the Developer Tab

Many of the tasks you will perform in this module use commands on the Developer tab. Thus, the following steps show the Developer tab on the ribbon.

1. Open Backstage view and then click Options in the left pane of Backstage view to display the Word Options dialog box.

2. Click Customize Ribbon in the left pane (Word Options dialog box) to display associated options in the right pane.

3. If it is not selected already, place a check mark in the Developer check box in the Main Tabs list.

4. Click OK to show the Developer tab on the ribbon.

To Unprotect a Document

The SC_WD_11_MealTimeExpressFormModified.dotm template is protected. In a protected form, users enter data only in designated areas, specifically, the content controls. The following steps unprotect a document. *Why? Before this form can be modified, it must be unprotected. Later in this project, after you have completed the modifications, you will protect it again.*

- Display the Developer tab.
- Click the Restrict Editing button (Developer tab | Protect group) to open the Restrict Editing pane (Figure 11–3).

- Click the Stop Protection button in the Restrict Editing pane to unprotect the form.
- Click the Close button in the Restrict Editing pane to close the pane.

Figure 11–3

Other Ways

1. Click File on ribbon, if necessary, click Info in Backstage view, click Protect Document button, click Restrict Editing on Protect Document menu, click Stop Protection button in Restrict Editing pane

---

How do you protect a computer from macro viruses?

A **computer virus** is a type of malicious software, or malware, which is a potentially damaging computer program that affects, or infects, a computer or mobile device negatively by altering the way the computer or mobile device works, usually without the user's knowledge or permission. Millions of known viruses and other malicious programs exist. The increased use of networks, the Internet, and email has accelerated the spread of computer viruses and other malicious programs.

- To combat these threats, most computer users run an **antivirus program** that locates viruses and other malware and destroys the malicious programs before they infect a computer or mobile device. Macros are known carriers of viruses and other malware. For this reason, you can specify a macro setting in Word to reduce the chance your computer or mobile device will be infected with a macro virus. These macro settings allow you to enable or disable macros. An **enabled macro** is a macro that Word (or any other Office application) will execute, and a **disabled macro** is a macro that is unavailable to Word (or any other program).

- As shown in Figure 11–1b at the beginning of this module, you can instruct Word to display a security warning on a Message Bar if it opens a document that contains a macro(s). If you are confident of the source (author) of the document and macros, enable the macros. If you are uncertain about the reliability of the source of the document and macros, then do not enable the macros.

CONSIDER THIS

To Specify Macro Settings in Word

Why? *When you open the online form in this module, you want the macros enabled. At the same time, your computer or mobile device should be protected from potentially harmful macros. Thus, you will specify a macro setting that allows you to enable macros each time you open this module's online form or any document that contains a macro from an unknown source.* The following steps specify macro settings.

- Click the Macro Security button (Developer tab | Code group) to display the Trust Center dialog box.
- If it is not selected already, click the 'Disable all macros with notification' option button (Trust Center dialog box), which causes Word to alert you when a document contains a macro so that you can decide whether to enable the macro(s) (Figure 11–4).

Figure 11–4

- Click OK to close the dialog box.

Other Ways

1. Click File on ribbon, click Options in Backstage view, click Trust Center in left pane (Word Options dialog box), click 'Trust Center Settings' button in right pane, if necessary, click Macro Settings in left pane (Trust Center dialog box), select desired setting, click OK in each dialog box

Modifying Text and Form Content Controls

The form created in Module 10 is enhanced in this module by performing these steps:

1. Delete the current image.
2. Change the fonts, colors, and alignments of the first four lines of text and the last line.
3. Convert the 2 × 1 table containing the First Name and Last Name content controls to text so that each of these content controls is on a separate line.
4. Delete the date picker content control and replace it with a date field.
5. Modify the color of the hyperlink and the check box labels.

The following pages apply these changes to the form.

To Delete a Graphic, Format Text, and Change Paragraph Alignment

The online form in this module contains a different image. It also has different formats for the company name, business tag line, form name, form instructions, date line, and thank you line. The following steps delete the image, format text, and change paragraph alignment.

1 Click the image of the fork and knife to select it and then press DELETE to delete the selected image.

2 Change the color of the first line of text, Meal Time Express, and the third line of text, Consultation Request, to 'Orange, Accent 2, Darker 25%' (sixth color in fifth row).

3 Change the color of the business tag line and the last line on the form, Thank you for your interest in our service!, to Aqua, Accent 1 (fifth color in first row).

4 Right-align the first and second lines of text (company name and business tag line).

5 Italicize the business tag line.

6 Right-align the line of text containing the Today's Date content control.

7 If necessary, widen the text box surrounding the data entry area to include the entire date placeholder (Figure 11–5).

BTW
Touch Mode
Differences
The Office and Windows interfaces may vary if you are using Touch mode. For this reason, you might notice that the function or appearance of your touch screen differs slightly from this module's presentation.

Figure 11–5

BTW
Saving and Resetting Themes
If you have changed the theme colors or theme fonts and want to save this combination for future use, save it as a new theme by clicking the Themes button (Design tab | Document Formatting group), clicking 'Save Current Theme' in the Themes gallery, entering a theme name in the File name box (Save Current Theme dialog box), and then clicking Save. If you want to reset the theme template to the default, you would click the Themes button (Design tab | Document Formatting group) and then click 'Reset to Theme from Template' in the Themes gallery.

To Change the Properties of a Plain Text Content Control

In this online form, the First Name and Last Name content controls are on separate lines. In Module 10, you selected the 'Content control cannot be deleted' check box in the Content Control Properties dialog box so that users could not delete the content control accidentally while filling in the form. With this check box selected, however, you cannot move a content control from one location to another on the form. Thus, the following steps change the locking properties of the First Name and Last Name content controls so that you can rearrange them.

1. Display the Developer tab.

2. Click the First Name content control to select it.

3. Click the Properties button (Developer tab | Controls group) to display the Content Control Properties dialog box.

4. Remove the check mark from the 'Content control cannot be deleted' check box (Content Control Properties dialog box) (Figure 11–6).

5. Click OK to assign the modified properties to the content control.

6. Click the Last Name content control to select it and then click the Properties button (Developer tab | Controls group) to display the Content Control Properties dialog box.

7. Remove the check mark from the 'Content control cannot be deleted' check box (Content Control Properties dialog box) and then click OK to assign the modified properties to the content control.

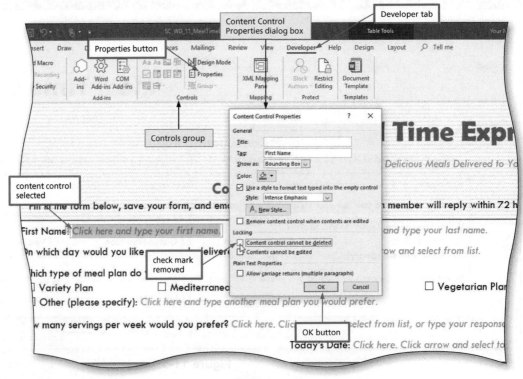

Figure 11–6

To Convert a Table to Text

The First Name and Last Name content controls currently are in a 2 × 1 table. The following steps convert the table to regular text, placing a paragraph break at the location of the second column. *Why? In this online form, these content controls are on separate lines, one below the other. That is, they are not in a table.*

- Position the insertion point somewhere in the table.

- Display the Table Tools Layout tab.

- Click the 'Convert to Text' button (Table Tools Layout tab | Data group) to display the Convert Table To Text dialog box.

- Click Paragraph marks (Convert Table To Text dialog box), which will place a paragraph mark at the location of each new column in the table (Figure 11–7).

Figure 11–7

- Click OK to convert the table to text, separating each column with the specified character, a paragraph mark in this case.

Why did the Last Name content control move below the First Name content control?

The Separate text with area (Convert Table To Text dialog box) controls how the table is converted to text. The Paragraph marks setting converts each column in the table to a line of text below the previous line. The Tabs setting places a tab character where each column was located, and the Commas setting places a comma where each column was located.

- With the First Name and Last Name lines selected, using either the ruler or the Layout tab, change the left indent to 0.06" so that the text aligns with the text immediately below it (that is, the O in On), as shown in Figure 11–8.

- Click anywhere to remove the selection from the text.

Figure 11–8

To Change the Properties of a Plain Text Content Control

You are finished moving the First Name and Last Name content controls. The following steps reset the locking properties of these content controls.

1 Display the Developer tab.

2 Click the First Name content control to select it and then click the Properties button (Developer tab | Controls group) to display the Content Control Properties dialog box.

BTW
Document Properties
If you wanted to insert document properties in a document, you would click the 'Explore Quick Parts' button (Insert tab | Text group) to display the Explore Quick Parts menu, point to Document Property on the Explore Quick Parts menu, and then click the property you want to insert on the Document Property menu. To create a custom document property for a document, open Backstage view, if necessary, click Info to display the Info screen, click the Properties button in the far right pane to display the Properties menu, click Advanced Properties on the Properties menu to display the Document Properties dialog box, click the Custom tab (Document Properties dialog box) to display the Custom sheet, enter the name of the new property in the Name text box, select its type and enter its value in the dialog box, click the Add button to add the property to the document, and then click OK to close the dialog box.

3 Place a check mark in the 'Content control cannot be deleted' check box (Content Control Properties dialog box) and then click OK to assign the modified properties to the content control.

4 Repeat Steps 2 and 3 for the Last Name content control.

To Adjust Paragraph Spacing and Resize the Rectangle Shape

With the First Name and Last Name content controls on separate lines, the thank you line moved to a second page, and the rectangle outline in the data entry area now is too short to accommodate the text. The following steps adjust paragraph spacing and extend the rectangle shape downward so that it surrounds the entire data entry area.

1 Position the insertion point in the first line of text on the form (the company name) and then adjust the spacing after to 0 pt (Layout tab | Paragraph group).

2 Position the insertion point in the second line of text on the form (the business tag line) and then adjust the spacing after to 6 pt (Layout tab | Paragraph group).

3 Adjust the spacing after to 6 pt for the First Name and Last Name lines.

4 Adjust the spacing before and after to 6 pt for the line that begins, On which day would you like..., and the line that begins, How many servings per week...

5 Adjust the spacing before to 12 pt for the thank you line.

6 Scroll to display the entire form in the document window. If necessary, reduce spacing after other paragraphs so that the entire form fits in a single document window.

7 Click the rectangle shape to select it.

8 Position the pointer on the bottom-middle sizing handle of the rectangle shape.

9 Drag the bottom-middle sizing handle downward so that the shape includes the bottom content control, in this case, the Today's Date content control (Figure 11–9). If necessary, resize the other edges of the shape to fit the text.

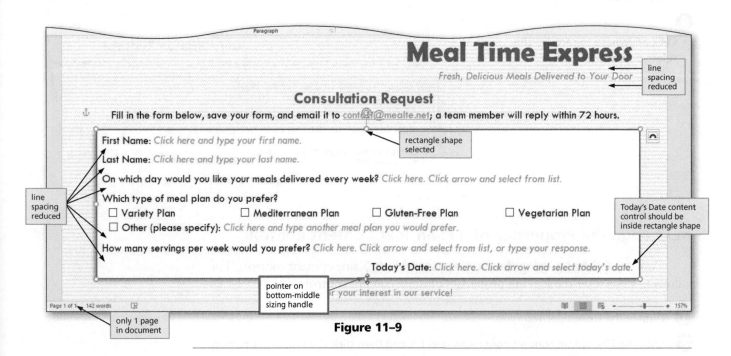

Figure 11–9

To Change the Properties of a Date Picker Content Control

In this online form, instead of the user entering the current date, the computer or mobile device's system date will be filled in automatically by Word. Thus, the Today's Date content control is not needed and can be deleted. To delete the content control, you first will need to remove the check mark from the 'Content control cannot be deleted' check box in the Content Control Properties dialog box. The following steps change the locking properties of the Today's Date content control and then delete the content control.

1 Display the Developer tab.

2 Click the Today's Date content control to select it.

3 Click the Properties button (Developer tab | Controls group) to display the Content Control Properties dialog box.

4 Remove the check mark from the 'Content control cannot be deleted' check box (Content Control Properties dialog box) (Figure 11–10).

Figure 11–10

5 Click OK to assign the modified properties to the content control.

6 Right-click the Today's Date content control to display a shortcut menu and then click 'Remove Content Control' on the shortcut menu to delete the selected content control.

BTW

Field Formats
If you wanted to create custom field formats, you would click the Field Codes button (Field dialog box) (shown in Figure 11–15) to display advanced field properties in the right pane in the dialog box, click the Options button to display the Field Options dialog box, select the format to apply in the Formatting list, click the 'Add to Field' button, and then click OK in each open dialog box.

To Insert a Date Field

The following steps insert the date and time as a field in the form at the location of the insertion point. *Why? The current date and time is a field so that the form automatically displays the current date and time. Recall that a field is a set of codes that instructs Word to perform a certain action.*

- Display the Insert tab.

- With the insertion point positioned as shown in Figure 11–11, which is the location for the date and time, click the 'Explore Quick Parts' button (Insert tab | Text group) to display the Explore Quick Parts menu.

Figure 11–11

- Click Field on the Explore Quick Parts menu to display the Field dialog box.

- Scroll through the Field names list (Field dialog box) and then click Date, which displays the Date formats list in the Field properties area.

- Click the date in the format of 2/15/2021 1:58:56 PM in the Date formats list to select a date format — your date and time will differ (Figure 11–12).

Q&A What controls the date that appears?

Your current computer or mobile device date appears in this dialog box. The format for the selected date shows in the Date formats box. In this case, the format for the selected date is M/d/yyyy h:mm:ss am/pm, which displays the date as month/day/year hours:minutes:seconds AM/PM.

Figure 11–12

3

- Click OK to insert the current date and time that automatically will be filled in at the location of the insertion point (Figure 11–13).

How do I delete a field?

Select it and then press DELETE or click the Cut button (Home tab | Clipboard group), or right-click the field and then click Cut on the shortcut menu or Mini toolbar.

Figure 11–13

Other Ways

1. Click 'Insert Date and Time' button (Insert tab | Text group), select date format (Date and Time dialog box), place check mark in Update automatically check box, click OK

To Edit a Field

The following steps edit the field. **Why?** *After you see the date and time in the form, you decide not to include the seconds in the time. That is, you want just the hours and minutes to be displayed.*

1

- Right-click the date field to display a shortcut menu (Figure 11–14).

Figure 11–14

2

- Click Edit Field on the shortcut menu to display the Field dialog box.

- If necessary, scroll through the Field names list (Field dialog box) and then click Date to display the Date formats list in the Field properties area.

- Select the desired date format, in this case 2/15/2021 2:02 PM (Figure 11–15).

Figure 11–15

3

- Click OK to insert the edited field at the location of the insertion point (Figure 11–16).

Figure 11–16

To Modify a Style Using the Styles Pane

In this online form, the hyperlink should be the same color as the company name so that the hyperlink is noticeable. The following steps modify a style using the Styles pane. *Why? The Hyperlink style is not in the Styles gallery. To modify a style that is not in the Styles gallery, you can use the Styles pane.*

1

- Position the insertion point in the hyperlink in the form.
- Display the Home tab.
- Click the Styles Dialog Box Launcher (Home tab | Styles group) to open the Styles pane.

Q&A What if the Styles pane is floating in the window?
Double-click its title bar to lock it to the right edge of the document window.

- If necessary, click Hyperlink in the list of styles in the pane to select it and then click the Hyperlink arrow to display the Hyperlink menu (Figure 11–17).

Q&A What if the style I want to modify is not in the list?
Click the Manage Styles button at the bottom of the pane, locate the style, and then click the Modify button in the dialog box.

Figure 11–17

- Click Modify on the Hyperlink menu to display the Modify Style dialog box.
- Click the Font Color arrow (Modify Style dialog box) to display the Font Color gallery (Figure 11–18).

Figure 11–18

- Click 'Orange, Accent 2, Darker 25%' (sixth color in fifth row) as the new hyperlink color.
- Click OK to close the dialog box. Close the Styles pane (Figure 11–19).

Figure 11–19

To Modify a Style

In this online form, the placeholder text is to be the same color as the company name. Currently, the placeholder text is formatted using the Intense Emphasis style, which uses a shade of aqua as the font color. Thus, the following steps modify the color of the Intense Emphasis style to a shade of orange.

1. Scroll through the Styles gallery (Home tab | Styles group) to locate the Intense Emphasis style.

2. Right-click Intense Emphasis in the Styles gallery to display a shortcut menu and then click Modify on the shortcut menu to display the Modify Style dialog box.

3. Click the Font Color arrow (Modify Style dialog box) to display the Font Color gallery (Figure 11–20).

BTW

Hidden Styles and Text
Some styles are hidden, which means they do not appear in the Styles pane. You can display all styles, including hidden styles, by clicking the Manage Styles button in the Styles pane (Figure 11–17), which displays the Manage Styles dialog box. Click the Edit tab, if necessary, and then locate the style name in the Select a style to edit list. To format text as hidden, select the text, click the Font Dialog Box Launcher (Home tab | Font group) to display the Font dialog box, select the Hidden check box in the Effects area, and then click OK (Font dialog box). To see hidden text on the screen, show formatting marks. Hidden text does not print.

Figure 11–20

4️⃣ Click 'Orange, Accent 2, Darker 25%' (sixth color in fifth row) as the new color.

5️⃣ Click OK to change the color of the style, which automatically changes the color of every item formatted using this style in the document.

BTW

Assign a Shortcut Key to a Style
If you wanted to assign a shortcut key to a style, you would right-click the style name in the Styles gallery (Home tab | Styles group) or open the Styles pane and then click the style arrow, click Modify Style on the menu to display the Modify Style dialog box, click the Format button (Modify Style dialog box), click Shortcut key on the Format menu to display the Customize Keyboard dialog box, press the desired shortcut key(s) (Customize Keyboard dialog box), click the Assign button to assign the shortcut key to the style, click the Close button to close the Customize Keyboard dialog box, and then click OK to close the Modify Style dialog box.

To Modify the Default Font Settings

You can change the default font so that the current document and all future documents use the new font settings. That is, if you exit Word, restart the computer or mobile device, and start Word again, documents you create will use the new default font. If you wanted to change the default font from 11-point Calibri to another font, font style, font size, font color, and/or font effects, you would perform the following steps.

1. Click the Font Dialog Box Launcher (Home tab | Font group) to display the Font dialog box.

2. Make desired changes to the font settings in the Font dialog box.

3. Click the 'Set As Default' button to change the default settings to those specified in Step 2.

4. When the Microsoft Word dialog box is displayed, select the desired option button and then click OK.

TO RESET THE DEFAULT FONT SETTINGS

To change the font settings back to the default, you would follow the steps in the previous section, using the default font settings when performing Step 2. If you do not remember the default settings, you would perform the following steps to restore the original Normal style settings.

1. Exit Word.
2. Use File Explorer to locate the Normal.dotm file (be sure that hidden files and folders are displayed and include system and hidden files in your search), which is the file that contains default font and other settings.
3. Rename the Normal.dotm file to oldnormal.dotm file so that the Normal.dotm file no longer exists.
4. Start Word, which will recreate a Normal.dotm file using the original default settings.

BTW

Advanced Character Attributes

If you wanted to set advanced character attributes, you would click the Font Dialog Box Launcher (Home tab | Font group) to display the Font dialog box, click the Advanced tab (Font dialog box) to display the Advanced sheet, select the desired Character Spacing or OpenType Features settings, and then click OK.

To Create a Character Style

In this online form, the check box labels are to be the same color as the placeholder text. The following steps create a character style called Check Box Labels. *Why? Although you could select each of the check box labels and then format them, a more efficient technique is to create a character style.* If you decide to modify the formats of the check box labels at a later time, you simply change the formats assigned to the style to automatically change all characters in the document based on that style.

- Position the insertion point in one of the check box labels.
- Click the Styles Dialog Box Launcher (Home tab | Styles group) (shown in Figure 11–20) to open the Styles pane.
- Click the Manage Styles button in the Styles pane to display the Manage Styles dialog box (Figure 11–21).

Figure 11–21

- Click the New Style button (Manage Styles dialog box) to display the Create New Style from Formatting dialog box.

- Type **Check Box Labels** in the Name text box (Create New Style from Formatting dialog box) as the name of the new style.

- Click the Style type arrow and then click Character so that the new style does not contain any paragraph formats.

- Click the Font Color arrow to display the Font Color gallery and then click 'Orange, Accent 2, Darker 25%' (sixth color in fifth row) as the new color (Figure 11–22).

Figure 11–22

- Click OK in each open dialog box to create the new character style, Check Box Labels in this case, and insert the new style name in the Styles pane (Figure 11–23).

Q&A What if I wanted the style added to the Styles gallery?

You would place a check mark in the 'Add to the Styles gallery' check box (Create New Style from Formatting dialog box), shown in Figure 11–22.

Figure 11–23

BTW

Character vs. Paragraph Styles
In the Styles pane, character styles display a lowercase letter a to the right of the style name, and paragraph styles show a paragraph mark. If a style has character and paragraph settings, then both a lowercase letter a and the paragraph mark are displayed to the right of the style name. With a character style, Word applies the formats to the selected text. With a paragraph style, Word applies the formats to the entire paragraph.

To Apply a Style

The next step is to apply the Check Box Labels style just created to the first row of check box labels in the form. The following steps apply a style.

1. Drag through the check box label, Variety Plan, to select it and then click 'Check Box Labels' in the Styles pane to apply the style to the selected text.

2. Repeat Step 1 for these check box labels (Figure 11–24): Mediterranean Plan, Gluten-Free Plan, Vegetarian Plan, and Other (please specify):.

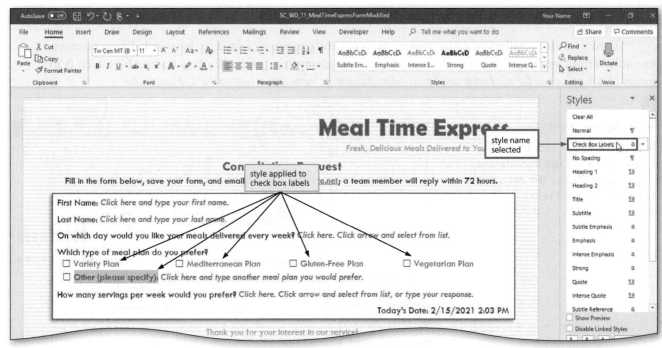

Figure 11–24

Q&A Do I have to drag through one word labels to apply a style?

No. You simply can position the insertion point in the word before clicking the desired style to apply.

3 Close the Styles pane.

4 If necessary, click anywhere to remove the selection from the check box label.

5 Save the template again on the same storage location with the same file name.

Break Point: If you want to take a break, this is a good place to do so. You can exit Word now. To resume later, start Word, open the file called SC_WD_11_MealTimeExpressFormModified.dotm, and continue following the steps from this location forward.

Enhancing with Color, Shapes, Effects, and Graphics

You will enhance the form created in Module 10 by performing these steps:

1. Apply a texture fill effect for the page color.
2. Change the appearance of the shape.
3. Change the color of a shadow on the shape.
4. Fill a shape with a picture.
5. Insert a picture, remove its background, and apply an artistic effect.
6. Insert and format a text box.
7. Group the picture and the text box together.

The following pages apply these changes to the form.

To Use a Fill Effect for the Page Color

Word provides a gallery of 24 predefined textures you can use as a page background. These textures resemble various wallpaper patterns. The following steps change the page color to a texture fill effect. *Why? Instead of a simple color for the background page color, this online form uses a texture for the page color.*

- Display the Design tab.
- Click the Page Color button (Design tab | Page Background group) to display the Page Color gallery (Figure 11–25).

Figure 11–25

- Click Fill Effects in the Page Color gallery to display the Fill Effects dialog box.
- Click the Texture tab (Fill Effects dialog box) to display the Texture sheet.
- Scroll to, if necessary, and then click the Parchment texture in the Texture gallery to select the texture (Figure 11–26).

Figure 11–26

3

- Click OK to apply the selected texture as the page color in the document (Figure 11–27).

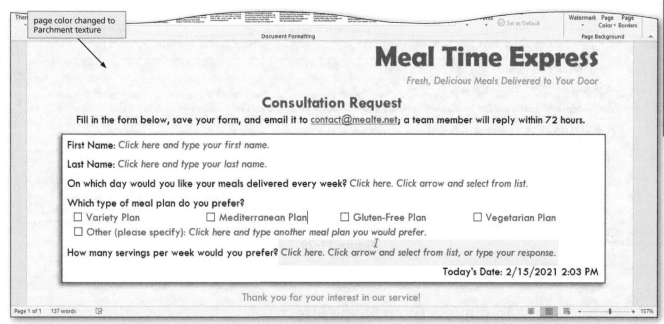

Figure 11–27

Q&A

How would I remove a texture page color?
You would click the Page Color button (Design tab | Page Background group) and then click No Color in the Page Color gallery.

To Change a Shape

The following steps change a shape. *Why? This online form uses a variation of the standard rectangle shape.*

- Click the rectangle shape to select it.

- Display the Drawing Tools Format tab.

- Click the Edit Shape button (Drawing Tools Format tab | Insert Shapes group) to display the Edit Shape menu.

- Point to Change Shape on the Edit Shape menu to display the Change Shape gallery (Figure 11–28).

Figure 11–28

2

• Click 'Rectangle: Diagonal Corners Snipped' in the Rectangles area in the Change Shape gallery to change the selected shape (Figure 11–29).

Fill in the form below, save your form, and email it to contact@mealte.net; a team member will reply within 72 hours.

First Name: *Click here and type your first name.*

Last Name: *Click here and type your last name.*

On which day would you like your meals delivered every week? *Click here. Click arrow and select from list.*

Which type of meal plan do you prefer?

☐ Variety Plan ☐ Mediterranean Plan ☐ Gluten-Free Plan ☐ Vegetarian Plan

☐ Other (please specify): *Click here and type another meal plan you would prefer.*

How many servings per week would you prefer? *Click here. Click arrow and select from list, or type your response.*

Today's Date: 2/15/2021 2:03 PM

Thank you for ...

shape changed to Rectangle: Diagonal Corners Snipped

Figure 11–29

To Apply a Glow Shape Effect

The next step is to apply a glow effect to the rectangle shape. You can apply the same effects to shapes as to pictures. That is, you can apply shadows, reflections, glows, soft edges, bevels, and 3-D rotations to pictures and shapes. The following steps apply a shape effect.

1 With the rectangle shape selected, click the Shape Effects button (Drawing Tools Format tab | Shape Styles group) to display the Shape Effects menu.

2 Point to Glow on the Shape Effects menu to display the Glow gallery.

3 Point to 'Glow: 5 point; Aqua, Accent color 1' in the Glow Variations area (first glow in first row) to display a Live Preview of the selected glow effect applied to the selected shape in the document window (Figure 11–30).

4 Click 'Glow: 5 point; Aqua, Accent color 1' in the Glow gallery (first glow in first row) to apply the shape effect to the selected shape.

Figure 11–30

To Apply a Shadow Shape Effect

The following steps apply a shadow effect and change its color. ***Why?*** *The rectangle in this online form has a shadow with a similar color to the placeholder text.*

- With the rectangle shape still selected, click the Shape Effects button (Drawing Tools Format tab | Shape Styles group) again to display the Shape Effects menu.

- Point to Shadow on the Shape Effects menu to display the Shadow gallery.

- Point to 'Perspective: Upper Right' in the Perspective area at the bottom of the Shadow gallery to display a Live Preview of that shadow applied to the shape in the document (Figure 11–31).

 Experiment

- Point to various shadows in the Shadow gallery and watch the shadow on the selected shape change.

Figure 11–31

- Click 'Perspective: Upper Right' in the Shadow gallery to apply the selected shadow to the selected shape.

- Click the Shape Effects button (Drawing Tools Format tab | Shape Styles group) again to display the Shape Effects menu.

- Point to Shadow in the Shape Effects menu to display the Shadow gallery.

- Click Shadow Options in the Shadow gallery to open the Format Shape pane.

- Click the Shadow Color button (Format Shape pane) and then click 'Aqua, Accent 1' (fifth color in first row) in the Shadow Color gallery to change the shadow color.

- Click the Transparency down arrow as many times as necessary until the Transparency box displays 60% to change the amount of transparency in the shadow (Figure 11–32).

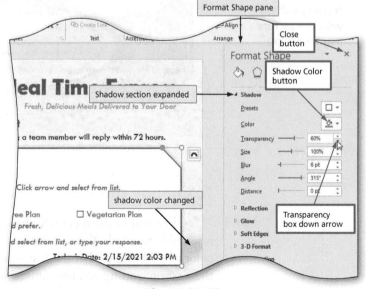

3

- Click the Close button to close the Format Shape pane.

Figure 11–32

To Fill a Shape with a Picture

The following steps fill a shape with a picture. *Why? The rectangle in this online form contains a picture of a table setting.* The picture, called Support_WD_11_TableSetting.png, is located on the Data Files. Please contact your instructor for information about accessing the Data Files.

1

- With the rectangle shape still selected, click the Shape Fill arrow (Drawing Tools Format tab | Shape Styles group) to display the Shape Fill gallery (Figure 11–33).

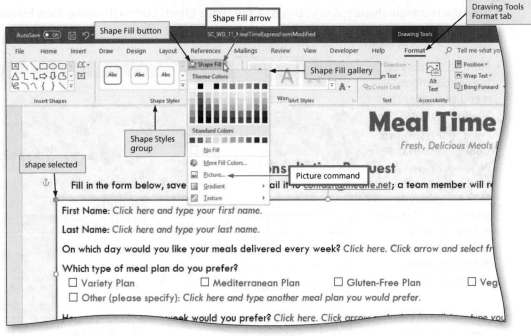

Q&A

My Shape Fill gallery did not appear. Why not?

You clicked the Shape Fill button instead of the Shape Fill arrow. Repeat Step 1.

Figure 11–33

2

- Click Picture in the Shape Fill gallery to display the Insert Pictures dialog box.

- Click the 'From a File' button (Insert Pictures dialog box) to display the Insert Picture dialog box. Locate and then select the file called Support_WD_11_TableSetting.png (Insert Picture dialog box).

- Click the Insert button (Insert Picture dialog box) to fill the rectangle shape with the picture (Figure 11–34).

Figure 11–34

To Change the Color of a Picture

The text in the rectangle shape is difficult to read because the picture just inserted is too dark. You can experiment with adjusting the brightness, contrast, and color of a picture so that the text is readable. In this project, the color is changed to the washout setting and the saturation and tone are changed so that the text is easier to read. The following steps change the color, tone, and saturation of the picture.

1 Display the Picture Tools Format tab.

2 With the rectangle shape still selected, click the Color button (Picture Tools Format tab | Adjust group) to display the Color gallery.

3 Click Washout in the Recolor area in the Color gallery to apply the selected color to the selected picture.

4 Click the Color button again (Picture Tools Format tab | Adjust group) and then click Temperature: 11200K in the Color Tone area in the Color gallery to apply the selected temperature to the selected picture.

5 Click the Color button again (Picture Tools Format tab | Adjust group) and then point to Saturation: 0% in the Color Saturation area to display a Live Preview of the selected saturation applied to the selected picture (Figure 11–35).

6 Click Saturation: 0% in the Color gallery to apply the selected saturation to the selected picture.

Figure 11–35

To Insert, Change Wrapping Style, and Resize a Picture

The top of the online form in this module contains a picture of a food pyramid. The picture, called Support_WD_11_FoodPyramid.png, is located in the Data Files. Please contact your instructor for information about accessing the Data Files.

You will change the wrapping style of the inserted picture so that it can be positioned in front of the text. Because the graphic's original size is too large, you also will resize it. The following steps insert a picture, change its wrapping style, and resize it.

1 Position the insertion point in a location near where the picture will be inserted, in this case, near the top of the online form.

2 Display the Insert tab. Click the Pictures button (Insert tab | Illustrations group) to display the Insert Picture dialog box.

3 Locate and then click the file called Support_WD_11_FoodPyramid.png (Insert Picture dialog box) to select the file.

BTW
Drawing Canvas
Some users prefer inserting graphics on a drawing canvas, which is a rectangular boundary between a shape and the rest of the document; it also is a container that helps you resize and arrange shapes on the page. To insert a drawing canvas, click the Shapes button (Insert tab | Illustrations group) and then click 'New Drawing Canvas' in the Shapes gallery. You can use the Drawing Tools Format tab to insert objects in the drawing canvas or format the appearance of the drawing canvas.

④ Click the Insert button to insert the picture at the location of the insertion point.

⑤ With the picture selected, click the Wrap Text button (Picture Tools Format tab | Arrange group) and then click 'In Front of Text' so that the graphic can be positioned on top of text.

⑥ Change the value in the Shape Height box (Picture Tools Format tab | Size group) to 1.01" and the value in the Shape Width box (Picture Tools Format tab | Size group) to 1.31".

⑦ If necessary, scroll to display the online form in the document window (Figure 11–36).

Figure 11–36

To Change a Picture

If you wanted to change an existing picture in a document to another picture, you would perform the following steps.

1. Select the picture and then click the Change Picture button (Picture Tools Format tab | Adjust group) or right-click the picture to be changed and then point to Change Picture on the shortcut menu.

2. Click the desired option (From a File, From Online Sources, From Icons, or From Clipboard) on the Change Picture menu or submenu.

3. Locate the desired replacement picture and then click OK.

To Remove a Background

In Word, you can remove a background from a picture. The following steps remove a background. *Why? You remove the sky and bottom banner in the background from the picture of the food pyramid.*

• With the food pyramid picture selected, click the Remove Background button (Picture Tools Format tab | Adjust group) (shown in Figure 11–36), to display the Picture Tools Background Removal tab and show the proposed area to be deleted in purple (Figure 11–37).

◁| What is the Picture Tools Background Removal tab?
Q&A You can draw around areas to keep or areas to remove by clicking the respective buttons on the Picture Tools Background Removal tab. If you mistakenly mark too much, use the 'Mark Areas to Remove' button. When finished marking, click the Keep Changes button, or to start over, click the 'Discard All Changes' button.

Figure 11–37

- Click the 'Mark Areas to Keep' button (Picture Tools Background Removal tab | Refine group) and then use the pointer to drag over areas that should remain in the image. If necessary, click the 'Mark Areas to Remove' button (Picture Tools Background Removal tab | Refine group) and use the pointer to drag over areas that should be deleted from the image. Your resulting areas to keep and delete should look similar to Figure 11–38.

Figure 11–38

Q&A How can you tell from the image which areas will be removed?
The areas in purple will be removed from the image.

- Click the Keep Changes button (Picture Tools Background Removal tab | Close group) to remove the area shaded purple and to close the Background Removal tab (Figure 11–39).

Figure 11–39

To Apply an Artistic Effect

Word provides several different artistic effects, such as blur, line drawing, and paint brush, that alter the appearance of a picture. The following steps apply an artistic effect to the picture. *Why? You want to soften the look of the picture a bit.*

- With the picture still selected, click the Artistic Effects button (Picture Tools Format tab | Adjust group) to display the Artistic Effects gallery (Figure 11–40).

- Click Crisscross Etching (third effect in the fourth row) in the Artistic Effects gallery to apply the selected effect to the selected picture.

Figure 11–40

To Move the Graphic

In this project, the graphic is to be positioned on the left edge of the form. The following step moves the graphic.

 Drag the graphic to the approximate location shown in Figure 11–41.

To Draw a Text Box

The picture of the food pyramid in this form has a text box with the words, So Nutritious Too!, positioned near the lower-left corner of the pyramid. The following steps draw a text box. *Why? The first step in creating the text box is to draw its perimeter. You draw a text box using the same procedure as you do to draw a shape.*

- Position the insertion point somewhere in the top of the online form.
- Display the Insert tab.
- Click the Text Box button (Insert tab | Text group) to display the Text Box gallery (Figure 11–41).

Figure 11–41

2
- Click 'Draw Text Box' in the Text Box gallery, which removes the gallery and changes the shape of the pointer to a crosshair.

- Drag the pointer to the right and downward to form the boundaries of the text box, similar to what is shown in Figure 11–42.

Q&A
What if I am using a touch screen?
A text box is inserted in the document window. Proceed to Step 4.

Figure 11–42

3
- Release the mouse button so that Word draws the text box according to your drawing in the document window.

4

- Verify your shape is the same approximate height and width as the one in this project by changing the values in the Shape Height and Shape Width boxes (Drawing Tools Format tab | Size group) to 0.76" and 0.83", respectively (Figure 11–43).

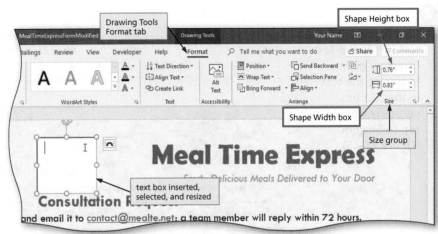

Figure 11–43

To Add Text to a Text Box and Format the Text

The next step is to add the phrase, So Nutritious Too!, centered in the text box using a text effect. You add text to a text box using the same procedure you do when adding text to a shape. The following steps add text to a text box.

1 Display the Home tab. With the text box selected, click the Center button (Home tab | Paragraph group) so that the text you enter is centered in the text box.

2 With the text box selected, click the 'Text Effects and Typography' button (Home tab | Font group) and then click 'Fill: Aqua, Accent 1; Shadow' (second effect in first row) in the Text Effects and Typography gallery to specify the format for the text in the text box.

3 If your insertion point is not positioned in the text box (shape), right-click the shape to display a shortcut menu and the Mini toolbar and then click Edit Text on the shortcut menu or Mini toolbar to place an insertion point centered in the text box.

4 Type `So Nutritious Too!` as the text for the text box (shown in Figure 11–44). (If necessary, adjust the height of the text box to fit the text.)

To Change Text Direction in a Text Box

The following steps change text direction in a text box. *Why? The direction of the text in the text box should be vertical instead of horizontal.*

1

- Display the Drawing Tools Format tab.

- With the shape still selected, click the Text Direction button (Drawing Tools Format tab | Text group) to display the Text Direction gallery (Figure 11–44).

Q&A What if my text box no longer is selected?
Click the text box to select it.

Figure 11–44

- Click 'Rotate all
  text 90°' in the Text
  Direction gallery
  to display the text
  in the text box
  vertically from
  top to bottom
  (Figure 11–45).

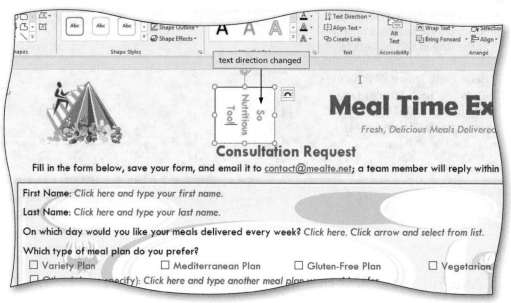

Figure 11–45

To Apply a Shadow Shape Effect to a Text Box

The text box in this online form has an inside shadow that is in the same color as the business tag line. The following steps apply a shadow effect and change its color.

1 Move the text box to the right so that it is visible when you change the shadows and colors.

2 With the text box still selected, click the Shape Effects button (Drawing Tools Format tab | Shape Styles group) to display the Shape Effects menu.

3 Point to Shadow in the Shape Effects menu to display the Shadow gallery and then click Inside: Center in the Inner area of the Shadow gallery to apply the selected shadow to the selected shape.

4 Click the Shape Effects button (Drawing Tools Format tab | Shape Styles group) again to display the Shape Effects menu.

5 Point to Shadow in the Shape Effects menu to display the Shadow gallery and then click Shadow Options in the Shadow gallery to display the Format Shape pane.

6 Click the Shadow Color button (Format Shape pane) and then click 'Aqua, Accent 1' (fifth color in first row) in the Color gallery to change the shadow color (shown in Figure 11–46).

7 Click the Close button to close the Format Shape pane.

To Change a Shape Outline of a Text Box

You change an outline on a text box (shape) using the same procedure as you do with a picture. The following steps remove the shape outline on the text box. *Why? The text box in this form has no outline.*

1

- With the text box still selected, click the Shape Outline arrow (Drawing Tools Format tab | Shape Styles group) to display the Shape Outline gallery (Figure 11–46).

 The Shape Outline gallery did not display. Why not?

You clicked the Shape Outline button instead of the Shape Outline arrow. Repeat Step 1.

Experiment

- Point to various colors in the Shape Outline gallery and watch the color of the outline on the text box change in the document.

Figure 11–46

2

- Click No Outline in the Shape Outline gallery to remove the outline from the selected shape.

Other Ways

1. Click Shape Styles Dialog Box Launcher (Drawing Tools Format tab | Shape Styles group); expand Line section (Format Shape pane); click No line to remove line, or click Solid line, click Outline color button, and select desired color to change line color; click Close button

2. Right-click text box (or, if using touch, tap 'Show Context Menu' button on Mini toolbar), click Format Shape on shortcut menu, expand Line section (Format Shape pane), click No line to remove line, or click Solid line, click Outline color button, and select desired color to change line color; click Close button

To Apply a 3-D Effect to a Text Box

Word provides 3-D effects for shapes (such as text boxes) that are similar to those it provides for pictures. The following steps apply a 3-D rotation effect to a text box. **Why?** *In this form, the text box is rotated using a 3-D rotation effect.*

1

- Move the text box to the left so that you can see it when you change to a 3-D effect.

- With the text box selected, click the Shape Effects button (Drawing Tools Format tab | Shape Styles group) to display the Shape Effects gallery.

- Point to '3-D Rotation' in the Shape Effects gallery to display the 3-D Rotation gallery.

- Point to 'Isometric: Top Up' in the Parallel area (third rotation in first row) to display a Live Preview of the selected 3-D effect applied to the text box in the document window (Figure 11–47).

Figure 11–47

Experiment

- Point to various 3-D rotation effects in the 3-D Rotation gallery and watch the text box change in the document window.

2

- Click 'Isometric: Top Up' in the 3-D Rotation gallery to apply the selected 3-D effect.

Other Ways
1. Click Shape Styles Dialog Box Launcher (Drawing Tools Format tab | Shape Styles group), click Text Options tab (Format Shape pane), click Text Effects button, if necessary expand 3-D Rotation Section, select desired options, click Close button
2. Right-click text box (or, if using touch, tap 'Show Context Menu' button on Mini toolbar), click Format Shape on shortcut menu, click Text Options tab (Format Shape pane), click Text Effects button, if necessary expand 3-D Rotation Section, select desired options, click Close button

To Move the Text Box

In this project, the text box is to be positioned near the lower-left of the graphic. The following steps move the text box.

1 With the text box selected, click the Send Backward arrow (Drawing Tools Format tab | Arrange group) and then click 'Send to Back' on the Send Backward menu to send the text box behind the pyramid image.

2 Drag the text box to the location shown in Figure 11–48. (You may need to drag the text box a couple of times to position it as shown in the figure.)

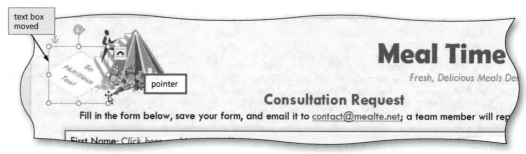

Figure 11–48

To Group Objects

When you have multiple graphics, such as pictures, shapes, and text boxes, positioned on a page, you can group them so that they are a single graphic instead of separate graphics. The following steps group the food pyramid image and the text box together. *Why? Grouping the graphics makes it easier to move them because they all move together as a single graphic.*

1

- With the text box selected, hold down CTRL while clicking the food pyramid image (that is, CTRL+click), so that both graphics are selected at the same time.

Q&A What if I had more than two graphics (i.e., pictures, shapes, text boxes, etc.) that I wanted to group?
For each subsequent graphic to select, CTRL+click the graphic, which enables you to select multiple objects at the same time.

- Click the Group Objects button (Drawing Tools Format tab | Arrange group) to display the Group Objects menu (Figure 11–49).

Figure 11–49

- Click Group on the Group Objects menu to group the selected objects into a single selected object (Figure 11–50).

What if I wanted to ungroup grouped objects (i.e., pictures, shapes, text boxes, etc.)?
Select the object to ungroup, click the Group Objects button (Drawing Tools Format tab | Arrange group), and then click Ungroup on the Group Objects menu.

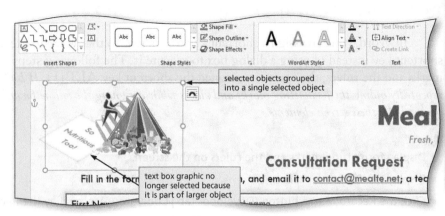

Figure 11–50

❸

- Click outside of the graphic to position the insertion point in the document and deselect the graphic.

- Save the template again on the same storage location with the same file name.

Break Point: If you want to take a break, this is a good place to do so. You can exit Word now. To resume later, start Word, open the file called SC_WD_11_MealTimeExpressFormModified.dotm, and continue following the steps from this location forward.

Using a Macro to Automate a Task

A macro consists of a series of Word commands or instructions that are grouped together as a single command. This single command is a convenient way to automate a difficult or lengthy task. Macros often are used to simplify formatting or editing activities, to combine multiple commands into a single command, or to select an option in a dialog box using a shortcut key.

To create a macro, you can use the macro recorder or the Visual Basic Editor. With the macro recorder, Word generates the VBA instructions associated with the macro automatically as you perform actions in Word. If you wanted to write the VBA instructions yourself, you would use the Visual Basic Editor. This module uses the macro recorder to create a macro and the Visual Basic Editor to modify it.

The **macro recorder** creates a macro based on a series of actions you perform while the macro recorder is recording. The macro recorder is similar to a video camera: after you start the macro recorder, it records all actions you perform while working in a document and stops recording when you stop the macro recorder. To record a macro, you follow this sequence of steps:

1. Start the macro recorder and specify options about the macro.
2. Execute the actions you want recorded.
3. Stop the macro recorder.

After you record a macro, you can execute the macro, or play it, any time you want to perform the same set of actions.

BTW
Naming Macros
If you give a new macro the same name as an existing built-in command in Microsoft Word, the new macro's actions will replace the existing actions. Thus, you should be careful not to assign a macro a name reserved for automatic macros (see Table 11–1) or any Word commands. To view a list of built-in macros in Word, click the Macros button (View tab | Macros group) to display the Macros dialog box. Click the Macros in arrow and then click Word commands.

To Record a Macro and Assign It a Shortcut Key

In Word, you can assign a shortcut key to a macro so that you can execute the macro by pressing the shortcut key instead of using a dialog box to execute it. The following steps record a macro that hides formatting marks and the rulers; the macro is assigned the shortcut key, ALT+H. *Why? Assume you find that you are repeatedly hiding the formatting marks and rulers while designing the online form. To simplify this task, the macro in this project hides these screen elements.*

1

- Display formatting marks and the rulers on the screen.
- Display the Developer tab.
- Click the Record Macro button (Developer tab | Code group) to display the Record Macro dialog box.
- Type **HideScreenElements** in the Macro name text box (Record Macro dialog box).

Q&A Do I have to name a macro?

If you do not enter a name for the macro, Word assigns a default name. Macro names can be up to 255 characters in length and can contain only numbers, letters, and the underscore character. A macro name cannot contain spaces or other punctuation.

- Click the 'Store macro in' arrow and then click 'Documents Based On SC_WD_11_MealTimeExpressFormModified'. Note that, depending on settings, your file name also may show the extension .dotm at the end.

Q&A What is the difference between storing a macro with the document template versus the Normal template?

Macros saved in the Normal template are available to all future documents; macros saved with the document template are available only with a document based on the template.

- Before proceeding, verify that your Store macro in location is set to 'Documents Based On SC_WD_11_MealTimeExpressFormModified'.
- In the Description text box, type this sentence (Figure 11–51): **Hide formatting marks and the rulers.**

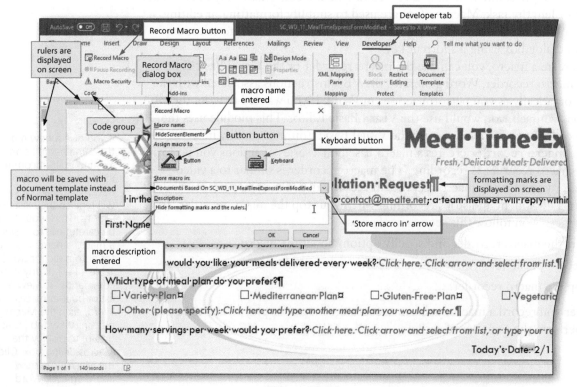

Figure 11–51

2

- Click the Keyboard button (shown in Figure 11–51) to display the Customize Keyboard dialog box.

- Press ALT+H to display the characters, ALT+H, in the 'Press new shortcut key' text box (Customize Keyboard dialog box) (Figure 11–52).

Q&A Can I type the letters in the shortcut key (ALT+H) in the text box instead of pressing them?
No. Although typing the letters places them in the text box, the shortcut key is valid only if you press the shortcut key combination itself.

Figure 11–52

3

- Click the Assign button (Customize Keyboard dialog box) to assign the shortcut key, ALT+H, to the macro named HideScreenElements.

- Click the Close button (Customize Keyboard dialog box), which closes the dialog box, displays a Macro Recording button on the status bar, and starts the macro recorder (Figure 11–53).

Q&A How do I record the macro?
While the macro recorder is running, any action you perform in Word will be part of the macro — until you stop or pause the macro.

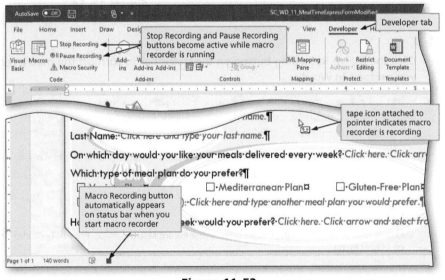

Figure 11–53

What is the purpose of the Pause Recording button (Developer tab | Code group)?
If, while recording a macro, you want to perform some actions that should not be part of the macro, click the Pause Recording button to suspend the macro recorder. The Pause Recording button changes to a Resume Recorder button that you click when you want to continue recording.

4

- Display the Home tab.

Q&A What happened to the tape icon?
While recording a macro, the tape icon might disappear from the pointer when the pointer is in a menu, on the ribbon, or in a dialog box.

- Click the 'Show/Hide ¶' button (Home tab | Paragraph group) to hide formatting marks.
- Display the View tab. Remove the check mark from the Ruler check box (View tab | Show group) to hide the rulers (Figure 11–54).

Figure 11–54

- Click the Macro Recording button on the status bar to turn off the macro recorder, that is, to stop recording actions you perform in Word.

Q&A

What if I made a mistake while recording the macro?
Delete the macro and record it again. To delete a macro, click the Macros button (Developer tab | Code group), select the macro name in the list (Macros dialog box), click the Delete button, and then click the Yes button.

What if I wanted to assign the macro to a button instead of a shortcut key?
You would click the Button button in the Record Macro dialog box (shown in Figure 11–51) and then follow Steps 4 and 5 in this section.

Other Ways

1. Click Macros arrow (View tab | Macros group), click Record Macro on Macros menu
2. Press ALT+F8, click Create button (Macros dialog box)

To Run a Macro

BTW

Running Macros
You can run a macro by clicking the Macros button (Developer tab | Code group or View tab | Macros group) or by pressing ALT+F8 to display the Macros dialog box, selecting the macro name in the list, and then clicking the Run button (Macros dialog box).

The next step is to execute, or run, the macro to ensure that it works. Recall that this macro hides formatting marks and the rulers, which means you must be sure the formatting marks and rulers are displayed on the screen before running the macro. Because you created a shortcut key for the macro in this project, the following steps show formatting marks and the rulers so that you can run the HideScreenElements macro using the shortcut key, ALT+H.

① Display formatting marks on the screen.

② Display rulers on the screen.

③ Press ALT+H, which causes Word to perform the instructions stored in the HideScreenElements macro, that is, to hide formatting marks and rulers.

To Add a Command and a Macro as Buttons on the Quick Access Toolbar

Word allows you to add buttons to and delete buttons from the Quick Access Toolbar. You also can assign a command, such as a macro, to a button on the Quick Access Toolbar. The following steps add an existing command to the Quick Access Toolbar and assign a macro to a new button on the Quick Access Toolbar. *Why? This module shows how to add the New File command to the Quick Access Toolbar and also shows how to create a button for the HideScreenElements macro so that instead of pressing the shortcut keys, you can click the button to hide formatting marks and the rulers.*

1

- Click the 'Customize Quick Access Toolbar' button on the Quick Access Toolbar to display the Customize Quick Access Toolbar menu (Figure 11–55).

Q&A What happens if I click the commands listed on the Customize Quick Access Toolbar menu?
If the command does not have a check mark beside it and you click it, Word places the button associated with the command on the Quick Access Toolbar. If the command has a check mark beside it and you click (deselect) it, Word removes the command from the Quick Access Toolbar.

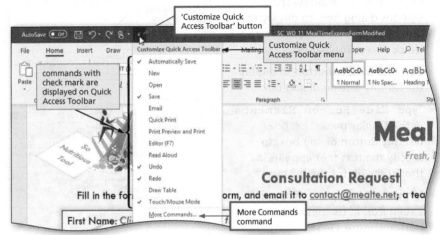

Figure 11–55

2

- Click More Commands on the Customize Quick Access Toolbar menu to display the Word Options dialog box with Quick Access Toolbar selected in the left pane.

- Scroll through the list of popular commands (Word Options dialog box) and then click New File to select the command.

- Click the Add button to add the selected command (New File, in this case) to the Customize Quick Access Toolbar list (Figure 11–56). Note that the built-in ScreenTip for the New File command is New Blank Document.

Figure 11–56

3

- Click the 'Choose commands from' arrow to display a list of categories of commands (Figure 11–57).

Figure 11–57

4

- Click Macros in the Choose commands from list to display the macro in this document.
- If necessary, click the macro to select it.
- Click the Add button (Word Options dialog box) to display the selected macro in the Customize Quick Access Toolbar list.
- Click the Modify button to display the Modify Button dialog box.
- Type **Hide Screen Elements** in the Display name text box (Modify Button dialog box) to specify the text that appears in the ScreenTip for the button.
- In the list of symbols, click the screen icon as the new face for the button (Figure 11–58).

Figure 11–58

5

- Click OK (Modify Button dialog box) to change the button characteristics in the Customize Quick Access Toolbar list (Figure 11–59).

Figure 11–59

● Click OK (Word Options dialog box) to add the buttons to the Quick Access Toolbar (Figure 11–60).

Figure 11–60

Other Ways

1. Right-click Quick Access Toolbar, click 'Customize Quick Access Toolbar' on shortcut menu

To Use the New Buttons on the Quick Access Toolbar

The next step is to test the new buttons on the Quick Access Toolbar, that is, the 'New Blank Document' button and the 'Hide Screen Elements' button, which will execute, or run, the macro that hides formatting marks and the rulers. The following steps use buttons on the Quick Access Toolbar.

1 Click the 'New Blank Document' button on the Quick Access Toolbar to display a new blank document window. Close the new blank document window.

2 Display formatting marks on the screen.

3 Display rulers on the screen.

4 Click the 'Hide Screen Elements' button on the Quick Access Toolbar, which causes Word to perform the instructions stored in the HideScreenElements macro, that is, to hide formatting marks and the rulers.

To Delete Buttons from the Quick Access Toolbar

The following steps delete the 'New Blank Document' button and the 'Hide Screen Elements' button from the Quick Access Toolbar. *Why? If you no longer plan to use a button on the Quick Access Toolbar, you can delete it.*

● Right-click the button to be deleted from the Quick Access Toolbar, in this case the 'Hide Screen Elements' button, to display a shortcut menu (Figure 11–61).

● Click 'Remove from Quick Access Toolbar' on the shortcut menu to remove the button from the Quick Access Toolbar.

3

● Repeat Steps 1 and 2 for the 'New Blank Document' button on the Quick Access Toolbar.

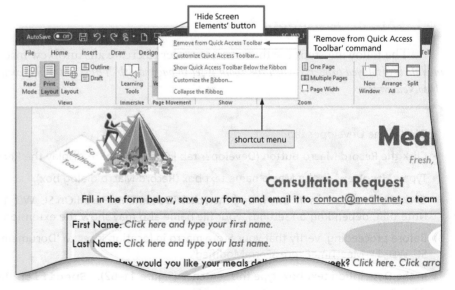

Figure 11–61

TO DELETE A MACRO

If you wanted to delete a macro, you would perform the following steps.

1. Click the Macros button (Developer tab | Code group) to display the Macros dialog box.
2. Click the macro to delete and then click the Delete button (Macros dialog box) to display a dialog box asking if you are sure you want to delete the macro. Click Yes in the dialog box.
3. Close the Macros dialog box.

Automatic Macros

The previous section showed how to create a macro, assign it a unique name (HideScreenElements) and a shortcut key, and then add a button that executes the macro on the Quick Access Toolbar. This section creates an **automatic macro**, which is a macro that executes automatically when a certain event occurs. Word has five prenamed automatic macros. Table 11–1 lists the name and function of these automatic macros.

Table 11-1 Automatic Macros	
Macro Name	**Event That Causes Macro to Run**
AutoClose	Closing a document that contains the macro
AutoExec	Starting Word
AutoExit	Exiting Word
AutoNew	Creating a new document based on a template that contains the macro
AutoOpen	Opening a document that contains the macro

The automatic macro you choose depends on when you want certain actions to occur. In this module, when a user creates a new Word document that is based on the SC_WD_11_MealTimeExpressFormModified.dotm template, you want to be sure that the zoom is set to page width. Thus, the AutoNew automatic macro is used in this online form.

To Create an Automatic Macro

The following steps use the macro recorder to create an AutoNew macro. *Why? The online form in this module is displayed properly when the zoom is set to page width. Thus, you will record the steps to zoom to page width in the AutoNew macro.*

- Display the Developer tab.
- Click the Record Macro button (Developer tab | Code group) to display the Record Macro dialog box.
- Type **AutoNew** in the Macro name text box (Record Macro dialog box).
- Click the 'Store macro in' arrow and then click 'Documents Based On SC_WD_11_MealTimeExpressFormModified'. Note that, depending on settings, your file name also may show the extension .dotm at the end.
- Before proceeding, verify that your Store macro in location is set to 'Documents Based On SC_WD_11_MealTimeExpressFormModified'.
- In the Description text box, type this sentence (Figure 11–62): **Specifies how the form initially is displayed.**

Figure 11–62

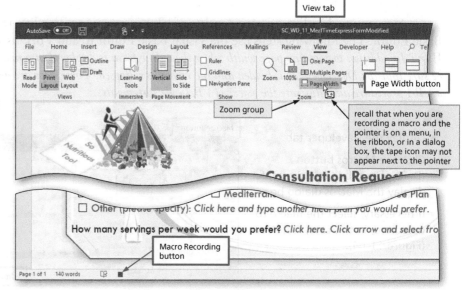

2

- Click OK to close the Record Macro dialog box and start the macro recorder.
- Display the View tab.
- Click the Page Width button (View tab | Zoom group) to zoom page width (Figure 11–63).

3

- Click the Macro Recording button on the status bar to turn off the macro recorder, that is, stop recording actions you perform in Word.

Q&A How do I test an automatic macro?

Activate the event that causes the macro to execute. For example, the AutoNew macro runs whenever you create a new Word document that is based on the template.

Figure 11–63

BTW
Display Macros
If you wanted to display macros in a document, you would click the Macros button (View tab | Macros group or Developer tab | Code group) and review the list in the Macro name area (Macros dialog box). To restrict the list to macros saved in only this document or to see all macros in Word, click the Macros in arrow and select the desired option. You also can click the Organizer button (Macros dialog box) to see a list of macros in a document or in Word.

To Run the AutoNew Macro

The next step is to execute, or run, the AutoNew macro to ensure that it works. To run the AutoNew macro, you need to create a new Word document that is based on the SC_WD_11_MealTimeExpressFormModified.dotm template. This macro contains instructions to zoom page width. To verify that the macro works as intended, you will change the zoom to 100% before testing the macro. The following steps run a macro.

1 Use the Zoom Out button on the status bar to change the zoom to 100%.

2 Save the template with the same file name, SC_WD_11_MealTimeExpressFormModified.

3 Click the File Explorer button on the taskbar to open the File Explorer window.

4 Locate and then double-click the file SC_WD_11_MealTimeExpressFormModified.dotm to display a new document window that is based on the contents of the SC_WD_11_MealTimeExpressFormModified.dotm template, which should be zoomed to page width as shown in Figure 11–1a at the beginning of this module. (If Word displays a dialog box about disabling macros, click OK. If the Message Bar displays a security warning, click the Enable Content button.)

5 Close the new document that displays the form in the Word window. Click the Don't Save button when Word asks if you want to save the changes to the new document.

6 Close the File Explorer window.

7 Change the zoom back to page width.

To Edit a Macro's VBA Code

As mentioned earlier, a macro consists of VBA instructions. To edit a recorded macro, you use the Visual Basic Editor. The following steps use the Visual Basic Editor to add VBA instructions to the AutoNew macro. *Why? In addition to zooming page width when the online form is displayed in a new document window, you would like to be sure that the Developer tab is hidden and the ribbon is collapsed. These steps are designed to show the basic composition of a VBA procedure and illustrate the power of VBA code statements.*

- Display the Developer tab.

- Click the Macros button (Developer tab | Code group) to display the Macros dialog box.

- If necessary, select the macro to be edited, in this case, AutoNew (Figure 11–64).

Figure 11–64

2

- Click the Edit button (Macros dialog box) to open the Visual Basic Editor window and display the VBA code for the AutoNew macro in the Code window — your screen may look different depending on previous Visual Basic Editor settings (Figure 11–65).

Figure 11–65

Q&A What if the Code window does not appear in the Visual Basic Editor?

In the Visual Basic Editor, click View on the menu bar and then click Code. If it still does not appear and you are in a network environment, this feature may be disabled for some users.

What are the lines of text (instructions) in the Code window?

The named set of instructions associated with a macro is called a **procedure**. It is this set of instructions — beginning with the word, Sub, and continuing sequentially to the line with the words, End Sub — that executes when you run the macro. The instructions within a procedure are called **code statements**.

3

- Position the insertion point at the end of the second-to-last line in the AutoNew macro (that is, after the text, wdPageFitBestFit) and then press ENTER to insert a blank line for a new code statement.

- On a single line aligned below the code statement on the previous line, type `Options.ShowDevTools = False` and then press ENTER, which enters the VBA code statement that hides the Developer tab.

Q&A What are the lists that appear in the Visual Basic Editor as I enter code statements?

The lists present valid statement elements to assist you with entering code statements. Because they are beyond the scope of this module, ignore them.

- On a single line aligned below the code statement on the previous line, type `If Application.CommandBars.Item("Ribbon").Height > 100 Then` and then press ENTER, which enters the beginning VBA if statement that determines whether to collapse the ribbon.

- On a single line, press TAB, type `ActiveWindow.ToggleRibbon` and then press ENTER, which enters the beginning VBA code statement that collapses the ribbon.

- On a single line, press SHIFT+TAB and then type `End If` to enter the ending VBA code statement that determines whether to collapse the ribbon (Figure 11–66).

4

- Click the Close button on the right edge of the Microsoft Visual Basic window title bar.

Figure 11–66

To Run the AutoNew Macro

The next step is to execute, or run, the AutoNew macro again to ensure that it works. To be sure the macro works as intended, ensure the Developer tab is displayed on the ribbon. The AutoNew macro should hide the Developer tab. The following steps run the automatic macro.

1 Save the template with the same file name, SC_WD_11_MealTimeExpressFormModified.

2 Click the File Explorer button on the taskbar to open the File Explorer window.

3 Locate and then double-click the file SC_WD_11_MealTimeExpressFormModified.dotm to open a new document that is based on the contents of the this template, which should be zoomed to page width, show a collapsed ribbon, and display no Developer tab. (If Word displays a dialog box about disabling macros, click OK. If the Message Bar displays a security warning, click the Enable Content button.)

4 Close the new document that displays the form in the Word window. Click the Don't Save button when Word asks if you want to save the changes to the new document.

5 Close the File Explorer window.

BTW

VBA

VBA includes many more statements than those presented in this module. You may need a background in programming if you plan to write VBA code instructions in macros you develop and if the VBA code instructions are beyond the scope of those instructions presented in this module. If you wanted to create a macro using VBA in the Visual Basic window, you would click the Macros button (View tab | Macros group or Developer tab | Code group), enter the macro name in the Macro name text box (Macros dialog box), select where you want the macro to be saved in the Macros in list, and click the Create button to open the Visual Basic window, where you can enter VBA code statements.

VBA

As shown in the previous steps, a VBA procedure begins with a Sub statement and ends with an End Sub statement. The Sub statement is followed by the name of the procedure, which is the macro name (AutoNew). The parentheses following the macro name in the Sub statement are required. They indicate that arguments can be passed from one procedure to another. Passing arguments is beyond the scope of this module, but the parentheses still are required. The End Sub statement signifies the end of the procedure and returns control to Word.

Comments often are added to a procedure to help you remember the purpose of the macro and its code statements at a later date. Comments begin with an apostrophe (') and appear in green in the Code window. The macro recorder, for example, placed four comment lines below the Sub statement. These comments display the name of the macro and its description, as entered in the Record Macro dialog box. Comments have no effect on the execution of a procedure; they simply provide information about the procedure, such as its name and description, to the developer of the macro.

For readability, code statement lines are indented four spaces. Table 11–2 explains the function of each element of a code statement.

Table 11–2 Elements of a Code Statement		
Element	**Code Statement** **Definition**	**Examples**
Keyword	Recognized by Visual Basic as part of its programming language; keywords appear in blue in the Code window	Sub End Sub
Variable	An item whose value can be modified during program execution	ActiveWindow.ActivePane.View.Zoom.PageFit
Constant	An item whose value remains unchanged during program execution	False
Operator	A symbol that indicates a specific action	=

To Protect a Form Using Backstage View and Exit Word

You now are finished enhancing the online form and adding macros to it. Because the last macro hid the Developer tab on the ribbon, you will use Backstage view to protect the form. The following steps use Backstage view to protect the online form so that users are restricted to entering data only in content controls.

1 Open Backstage view and then, if necessary, display the Info screen.

2 Click the Protect Document button to display the Protect Document menu.

3 Click Restrict Editing on the Protect Document menu to open the Restrict Editing pane.

4 In the Editing restrictions area, if necessary, place a check mark in the 'Allow only this type of editing in the document' check box, click its arrow, and then select 'Filling in forms' in the list.

5 Click the 'Yes, Start Enforcing Protection' button and then click OK (Start Enforcing Protection dialog box) to protect the document without a password.

6 Close the Restrict Editing pane.

7 Save the template again on the same storage location with the same file name.

8 **sam↑** If the File Explorer window still is open, close it.

BTW
Allowing No Changes in a Document
You can use the Restrict Editing pane to allow no changes to a document. To do this, place a check mark in the 'Allow only this type of editing in the document' check box and then change the associated text box to 'No changes (Read only)', which instructs Word to prevent any editing to the document.

Working with 3-D Models

Some versions of Word enable you to insert and format 3-D models into documents. You can rotate and tilt 3-D models in any direction. This section replaces the graphic currently in the SC_WD_11_MealTimeExpressFormModified.dotm file with a 3-D model and then formats the 3-D model. If your version of Word does not include the capability of working with 3-D models, read the steps in these sections without performing them. In the following sections, you will perform these tasks:

1. Save the macro-enabled template with a new file name and then unprotect the template.
2. Delete a graphic.
3. Insert a 3-D model.
4. Format the 3-D model by resizing it, tilting and rotating it, applying a 3-D model view to it, and resetting it.
5. Save and protect the template.

To Save the Template with a New File Name and Unprotect It

The following steps save the macro-enabled template with a new file name and then unprotect the template so that you can modify it.

1 With the SC_WD_11_MealTimeExpressFormModified.dotm file still open, click File on the ribbon, click Save As, and then save the template using the new file name, SC_WD_11_MealTimeExpressFormModified_3-DModel.

Q&A What if my SC_WD_11_MealTimeExpressFormModified.dotm no longer is open?
Open it and then perform Step 1.

BTW
Unsaved Document Versions
If you wanted to open a previous unsaved version of a document, you could open an automatically saved copy of your document if one is available. To do this, open Backstage view and then, if necessary, click Info to display the Info screen, and then click the desired (autosave) file listed. Or, click the Manage Document button, click 'Recover Unsaved Documents' in the Manage Document list, select the document to open, and then click the Open button (Open dialog box). To change the autosave frequency, open Backstage view, click Options, click Save in the left pane (Word Options dialog box), enter the desired number of minutes in the 'Save AutoRecover information every' box, and then click OK. To compare two versions of a document, you could recover them or open automatically saved copies and then use the Compare button (Review tab | Compare group) to identify differences.

2 If necessary, display the Developer tab and then click the Restrict Editing button (Developer tab | Protect group) to open the Restrict Editing pane.

3 Click the Stop Protection button in the Restrict Editing Pane to unprotect the form.

4 Close the Restrict Editing pane.

To Delete a Graphic

The following steps delete the grouped graphic that contains the text box and the food pyramid image so that you can insert a 3-D model in its location.

1 Click the grouped graphic that contains the text box and the food pyramid image to select the graphic.

2 Press DELETE to delete the selected graphic.

To Insert a 3-D Model

The next step is to insert a 3-D model in the template. Microsoft Office applications can access a collection of free 3-D models in an online catalog called Remix 3D.

The following steps insert a 3-D model of a table setting from the Remix 3D online catalog. *Why? You want to add a 3-D model to the template for visual appeal.* If your version of Word does not support Remix 3D or 3-D models, read these steps in this section without performing them.

1

- If necessary, position the insertion point at the location where you want to insert the picture (in this case, near the top of the online form).
- Display the Insert tab.
- Click the 3D Models arrow (Insert tab | Illustrations group) to display the 3D Models menu (Figure 11–67).

Q&A What if the Online 3D Models dialog box is displayed instead of the 3D Models menu? You clicked the 3D Models button instead of the 3D Models arrow. Proceed to Step 3.

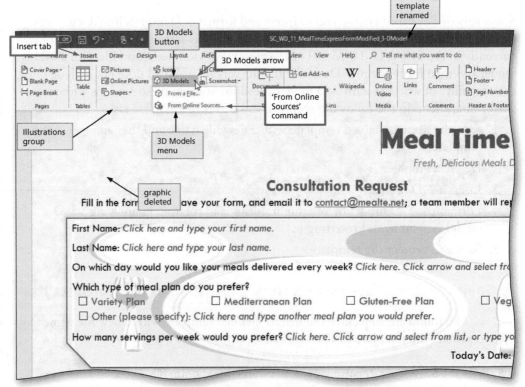

Figure 11–67

2

- Click 'From Online Sources' on the 3D Models menu to display the Online 3D Models dialog box with categories of online 3-D models displayed in the dialog box (Figure 11–68).

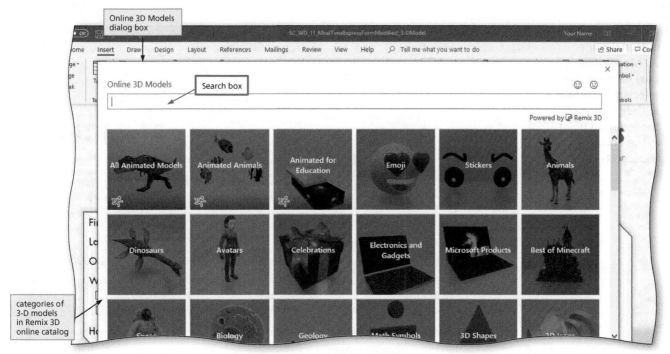

Figure 11–68

Q&A | Can I click the categories to see 3-D models?
Yes, you can click categories or type search text in the Search box.

3

- Type **dinner party** in the Search box (Online 3D Models dialog box) to specify the search text.
- Press ENTER to display a list of online 3-D models that matches the entered search text.
- Scroll through the search results and then click the desired 3-D model to select it (Figure 11–69).

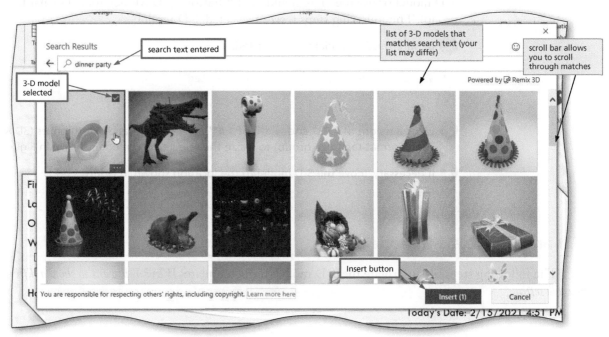

Figure 11–69

What if I cannot locate the exact 3-D model selected in Figure 11–69?
Select any 3-D model so that you can practice using 3-D models.

4
- Click the Insert button (Online 3D Models dialog box) to insert the selected 3-D model at the location of the insertion point in the document (Figure 11–70).

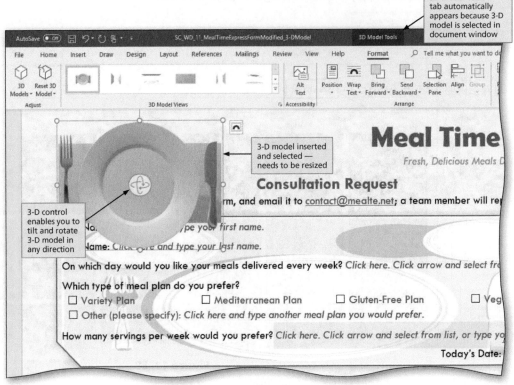

Figure 11–70

To Resize a 3-D Model

You resize a 3-D model the same way you resize any other graphic. You can drag its sizing handles that appear at the corner or middle locations of the selected 3-D model or use the Height and Width buttons (3D Model Tools Format tab | Size group). The following steps resize a selected 3-D model.

1 Be sure the 3-D model still is selected.

What if the object (3-D model) is not selected?
To select a 3-D model, click it.

2 Enter a height of 1.03" and width of 1.41" in the Height and Width boxes (3D Model Tools Format tab | Size group) to resize the selected 3-D model (shown in Figure 11–71).

3 If necessary, move the 3-D model to the location shown in Figure 11–71.

To Tilt and Rotate a 3-D Model

The following steps tilt and rotate the 3-D model in the template. *Why? You want to show a different view of the table setting.*

- Position the pointer on the 3-D control in the 3-D model (shown in Figure 11–70) and then drag the 3-D control up and to the right in a clockwise motion so that the view resembles Figure 11–71.

Figure 11–71

- Continue to drag the 3-D control clockwise down and to the left so that the view resembles Figure 11–72.

Figure 11–72

To Apply a 3-D Model View

Word provides more than 15 different views of 3-D models. *Why? The 3-D model views enable you to select a tilted and rotated view of a 3-D model without dragging the 3-D control.* The following steps apply a 3-D model view to the selected 3-D model.

- Ensure the 3-D model still is selected and that the 3D Model Tools Format tab is displayed on the ribbon.

Q&A | What if the 3-D model is not selected?
Click it to select it.

- Click the More button in the 3D Model Views gallery (3D Model Tools Format tab | 3D Model Views group) (shown in Figure 11–72) to expand the gallery.

- Point to 'Above Front Left' in the 3D Model Views gallery to display a Live Preview of that view applied to the 3-D model in the template (Figure 11–73).

🔎 **Experiment**

- Point to various 3-D model views in the 3D Model Views gallery and watch the view of the 3-D model change in the document window.

Figure 11–73

2
- Click 'Above Front Left' in the 3D Model Views gallery to apply the view to the selected 3-D model.

Q&A What if I wanted to format the 3-D model further?
You could open the Format 3D Model pane by clicking the 3D Model Views Dialog Box Launcher (shown in Figure 11-72) and then selecting desired options in the Format 3D Model pane.

Other Ways

1. Right-click 3-D model (or, if using touch, tap 'Show Context Menu' button on Mini toolbar), click 'Format 3D Model' on shortcut menu, if necessary, click 3D Model button (Format 3D Model pane), select desired options, click Close button

2. Click 3D Model Views Dialog Box Launcher (3D Model Tools Format tab | 3D Model Views group), if necessary, click 3D Model button (Format 3D Model pane), select desired options, click Close button

To Reset a 3-D Model

You can reset a 3-D model by discarding all formatting changes. The following steps reset a selected 3-D model.

1 Be sure the 3-D model still is selected.

2 Click the 'Reset 3D Model' arrow (3D Model Tools Format tab | Adjust group) to display the Reset 3D Model menu (Figure 11–74).

3 Click 'Reset 3D Model' on the Reset 3D Model menu to discard all formatting changes.

Q&A What is the purpose of the 'Reset 3D Model and Size' command on the Reset 3D Model menu?
In addition to discarding all formatting changes, it resets the size to the 3-D model's original size.

Figure 11–74

To Save the Template, Protect It, and Exit Word

You now are finished with the 3-D model in the online form and with this project. The following steps save the form again, protect it, and then exit Word.

1 Open Backstage view and then, if necessary, display the Info screen.

2 Click the Protect Document button to display the Protect Document menu.

3 Click Restrict Editing on the Protect Document menu to open the Restrict Editing pane.

4 In the Editing restrictions area, if necessary, place a check mark in the 'Allow only this type of editing in the document' check box, click its arrow, and then select 'Filling in forms' in the list.

5 Click the 'Yes, Start Enforcing Protection' button and then click OK (Start Enforcing Protection dialog box) to protect the document without a password.

6 Close the Restrict Editing pane.

7 Save the template again on the same storage location with the same file name.

8 Exit Word.

Supplementary Word Tasks

If you plan to take the certification exam, you should be familiar with the skills in the following sections.

Adding a Digital Signature to a Document

Some users attach a **digital signature** to a document to verify its authenticity. A digital signature is an electronic, encrypted, and secure stamp of authentication on a document. This signature confirms that the file originated from the signer (file creator) and that it has not been altered.

A digital signature references a digital certificate. A **digital certificate** is code attached to a file, macro project, email message, or other digital content that verifies the identity of the creator of the file. Many users who receive online forms enable the macros based on whether they are digitally signed by a developer on the user's list of trusted sources. You can obtain a digital certificate from a commercial certification authority or from your network administrator.

Once a digital signature is added, the document becomes a read-only document, which means that modifications cannot be made to it. Thus, you should create a digital signature only when the document is final. In Word, you can add two types of digital signatures to a document: (1) an invisible digital signature or (2) a signature line.

To Add an Invisible Digital Signature to a Document

An invisible digital signature does not appear as a tangible signature in the document. If the status bar displays a Signatures button, the document has an invisible digital signature. If you wanted to add an invisible digital signature to a document, you would perform the following steps.

1. Open Backstage view and then, if necessary, display the Info screen.
2. Click the Protect Document button to display the Protect Document menu and then click 'Add a Digital Signature' on the Protect Document menu to display the Sign dialog box. (If a dialog box appears indicating you need a digital ID,

BTW

Removing Metadata
If you wanted to remove document metadata, such as personal information and comments, you would do the following with the document open in a document window: open Backstage view, if necessary, click Info in Backstage view to display the Info screen, click the 'Check for Issues' button in the Info screen to display the Check for Issues menu, click Inspect Document on the Check for Issues menu to display the Document Inspector dialog box, click the Inspect button (Document Inspector dialog box) to instruct Word to inspect the document, review the results (Document Inspector dialog box), and then click the Remove All button(s) for any item that you do not want to be saved with the document. When you have finished removing information, click the Close button to close the dialog box.

BTW
Password-Protecting Documents
You can save documents with a password to keep unauthorized users from accessing files. To do this, open Backstage view, click Info, click the Protect Document button, click 'Encrypt with Password' on the Protect Document menu, type the password in the Encrypt Document dialog box, type the password again (Confirm Password dialog box), and click OK; or open Backstage view, click Save As, display the Save As dialog box, click the Tools button (Save As dialog box), click General Options on the Tools menu, type the password in the appropriate text box (General Options dialog box), type the password again (Confirm Password dialog box), and then click OK and the Save button (Save As dialog box). As you type a password in the text box, Word displays a series of dots instead of the actual characters so that others cannot see your password as you type it. To remove a password from a document, follow these steps except leave the password text box blank.

Be sure to keep the password confidential. Choose a password that is easy to remember and that no one can guess. Do not use any part of your first or last name, Social Security number, birthday, and so on. Use a password that is at least six characters long, and if possible, use a mixture of numbers and letters.

click the Yes button and then follow the on-screen instructions. If a dialog box about signature services appears, click OK.)

3. Type the purpose of the digital signature in the 'Purpose for signing this document' text box.

4. Click the Sign button to add the digital signature, show the Signatures button on the status bar, and display Marked as Final on a Message Bar.

Q&A How can I view or remove the digital signatures in a document?
Open Backstage view, if necessary, display the Info screen, and then click the View Signatures button to open the Signatures pane. To remove a digital signature, click the arrow beside the signature name, click Remove Signature on the menu, and then click Yes in the dialog box.

TO ADD A SIGNATURE LINE TO A DOCUMENT

A **digital signature line**, which resembles a printed signature placeholder, allows a recipient of the electronic file to type a signature, include an image of his or her signature, or write a signature using the ink feature on a mobile computer or device. Digital signature lines enable organizations to use paperless methods of obtaining signatures on official documents, such as contracts. If you wanted to add a digital signature line to a document, you would perform the following steps.

1. Position the insertion point at the location for the digital signature.

2. Display the Insert tab. Click the 'Add a Signature Line' button (Insert tab | Text group) to display the Signature Setup dialog box. (If a dialog box appears about signature services, click OK.)

3. Type the name of the person who should sign the document in the appropriate text box.

4. If available, type the signer's title and email address in the appropriate text boxes.

5. Place a check mark in the 'Allow the signer to add comments in the Sign dialog' check box so that the recipient can send a response back to you.

6. Click OK (Signature Setup dialog box) to insert a signature line in the document at the location of the insertion point.

Q&A How does a recipient insert his or her digital signature?
When the recipient opens the document, a Message Bar appears that contains a View Signatures button. The recipient can click the View Signatures button to open the Signatures pane, click the requested signature arrow, and then click Sign on the menu (or double-click the signature line in the document) to display a dialog box that the recipient then completes.

Copying and Renaming Styles and Macros

If you have created a style or macro in one document or template, you can copy the style or a macro to another so that you can use it in a second document or template.

TO COPY A STYLE FROM ONE TEMPLATE OR DOCUMENT TO ANOTHER

If you wanted to copy a style from one template or document to another, you would perform the following steps.

1. Open the document or template into which you want to copy the style.

2. If necessary, click the Styles Dialog Box Launcher (Home tab | Styles group) to open the Styles pane, click the Manage Styles button at the bottom of the Styles pane to display the Manage Styles dialog box, and then click the

Import/Export button (Manage Styles dialog box) to display Styles sheet in the Organizer dialog box. Or, click the Document Template button (Developer tab | Templates group) to display the Templates and Add-ins dialog box, click the Organizer button (Templates and Add-ins dialog box) to display the Organizer dialog box, and then, if necessary, click the Styles tab to display the Styles sheet in the dialog box. Notice that the left side of the dialog box displays the style names in the currently open document or template.

3. Click the Close File button (Organizer dialog box) to clear the right side of the dialog box.

Q&A What happened to the Close File button?
It changed to an Open File button.

4. Click the Open File button (Organizer dialog box) and then locate the file that contains the style you wish to copy. Notice that the styles in the located document or template appear on the right side of the dialog box.

5. On the right side of the dialog box, select the style you wish to copy and then click the Copy button to copy the selected style to the document or template on the left. You can continue to copy as many styles as necessary.

6. When finished copying styles, click the Close button to close the dialog box.

TO RENAME A STYLE

If you wanted to rename a style, you would perform the following steps.

1. Open the document or template that contains the style to rename.

2. If necessary, click the Styles Dialog Box Launcher (Home tab | Styles group) to open the Styles pane, click the Manage Styles button at the bottom of the Styles pane to display the Manage Styles dialog box, and then click the Import/Export button (Manage Styles dialog box) to display the Styles sheet in the Organizer dialog box. Or, click the Document Template button (Developer tab | Templates group) to display the Templates and Add-ins dialog box, click the Organizer button (Templates and Add-ins dialog box) to display the Organizer dialog box, and then, if necessary, click the Styles tab to display the Styles sheet in the dialog box. Notice that the left side of the dialog box displays the style names in the currently open document or template.

3. Select the style you wish to rename and then click the Rename button (Organizer dialog box) to display the Rename dialog box.

4. Type the new name of the style in the text box and then click OK (Rename dialog box).

Q&A Can I delete styles too?
Yes, click the Delete button (Organizer dialog box) to delete any selected styles.

5. When finished renaming styles, click the Close button (Organizer dialog box) to close the dialog box.

TO COPY A MACRO FROM ONE TEMPLATE OR DOCUMENT TO ANOTHER

If you wanted to copy a macro from one template or document to another, you would perform the following steps.

1. Open the document or template into which you want to copy the macro.

2. If necessary, click the Macros button (Developer tab | Code group or View tab | Macros group) to display the Macros dialog box and then click the Organizer button (Macros dialog box) to display Macro Project Items sheet in the Organizer dialog box. Or, click the Document Template button (Developer tab | Templates group) to display the Templates and Add-ins dialog box, click the Organizer button (Templates and Add-ins dialog box) to display the Organizer dialog box, and then, if necessary, click the Macro Project Items tab to

BTW
Fields
In addition to using content controls where users can enter data into a form, you can insert fields from the Fields dialog box so that Word will automatically fill in and display the field's value on the form. If you are working with a mail merge document instead of an online form and wanted to prompt users to fill in a field value, you could use the ASK or FILLIN fields in the main document for the form letter.

display the Macro Project Items sheet in the dialog box. Notice that the left side of the dialog box displays the macro names in the currently open document or template.

3. Click the Close File button (Organizer dialog box) to clear the right side of the dialog box.

Q&A What happened to the Close File button?
It changed to an Open File button.

4. Click the Open File button (Organizer dialog box) and then locate the file that contains the macro you wish to copy. Notice that the macros in the located document or template appear on the right side of the dialog box.

5. On the ride side of the dialog box, select the macro you wish to copy and then click the Copy button to copy the selected macro to the document or template on the left. You can continue to copy as many macros as necessary.

6. When finished copying macros, click the Close button (Organizer dialog box) to close the dialog box.

TO RENAME A MACRO

If you wanted to rename a macro, you would perform the following steps.

1. Open the document that contains the macro to rename.

2. If necessary, click the Macros button (Developer tab | Code group or View tab | Macros group) to display the Macros dialog box and then click the Organizer button (Macros dialog box) to display Macro Project Items sheet in the Organizer dialog box. Or, click the Document Template button (Developer tab | Templates group) to display the Templates and Add-ins dialog box, click the Organizer button (Templates and Add-ins dialog box) to display the Organizer dialog box, and then, if necessary, click the Macro Project Items tab to display the Macro Project Items sheet in the dialog box. Notice that the left side of the dialog box displays the macro names in the currently open document or template.

3. Select the macro you wish to rename and then click the Rename button (Organizer dialog box) to display the Rename dialog box.

4. Type the new name of the macro in the text box and then click OK (Rename dialog box).

Q&A Can I delete macros, too?
Yes, click the Delete button (Organizer dialog box) to delete any selected macros.

5. When finished renaming macros, click the Close button to close the dialog box.

Preparing a Document for Internationalization

Word provides internationalization features you can use when creating documents and templates. Use of features should be determined based on the intended audience of the document or template. By default, Word uses formatting consistent with the country or region selected when installing Windows. In addition to inserting symbols, such as those for currency, and using date and time formats that are recognized internationally or in other countries, you can set the language used for proofing tools and other language preferences.

TO SET THE LANGUAGE FOR PROOFING TOOLS

If you wanted to change the language that Word uses to proof documents or templates, you would perform the following steps.

1. Click the Language button (Review tab | Language group) to display the Language menu.
2. Click 'Set Proofing Language' on the Language menu to display the Language dialog box. (If you want to set this language as the default, click the 'Set As Default' button.)
3. Select the desired language to use for proofing tools and then click OK.

TO SET LANGUAGE PREFERENCES

If you wanted to change the language that Word uses for editing, display, Help, and ScreenTips, you would perform the following steps.

1. Click the Language button (Review tab | Language group) to display the Language menu and then click Language Preferences on the Language menu to display the language settings in the Word Options dialog box. Or, open Backstage view, click Options in the left pane to display the Word Options dialog box, and then click Language in the left pane (Word Options dialog box) to display the language settings.
2. Select preferences for the editing language, display language, and Help language, and then click OK.

Working with XML

You can convert an online form to the XML format so that the data in the form can be shared with other programs, such as Microsoft Access. XML is a popular format for structuring data, which allows the data to be reused and shared. **XML**, which stands for Extensible Markup Language, is a language used to mark up structured data so that it can be more easily shared between different computer programs. An **XML file** is a text file containing XML tags that identify field names and data. Each data item is called an **element**. Businesses often create standard XML file layouts and tags to describe commonly used types of data.

In Word, you can save a file in a default XML format, in which Word parses the document into individual components that can be used by other programs. Or, you can identify specific sections of the document as XML elements; the elements then can be used in other programs, such as Access. This feature may not be available in all versions of Word.

TO SAVE A DOCUMENT IN THE DEFAULT XML FORMAT

If you wanted to save a document in the XML format, you would perform the following steps.

1. Open the file to be saved in the XML format (for example, a form containing content controls).
2. Open Backstage view and then click Save As to display the Save As screen.
3. Navigate to the desired save location and then display the Save As dialog box.
4. Click the 'Save as type' arrow (Save As dialog box), click 'Word XML Document' in the list, and then click the Save button to save the template as an XML document.

BTW

Opening Files
In addition to current and previous versions of Word documents and templates, XML and PDF files, and webpage files, you can open a variety of other types of documents through the Open dialog box, including rich text format, text files, OpenDocument text, and WordPerfect files. To open these documents, open Backstage view, click Open to display the Open screen, click the Browse button to display the Open dialog box, click the file type arrow (Open dialog box), click the desired file type to open, locate the file, and then click the Open button to open the file and display its contents in a Word window. Through the Save dialog box, you can save the open file in its native format or save it as a Word document or template.

Q&A How can I identify an XML document?
XML documents typically have an .xml extension.

TO ATTACH A SCHEMA FILE

To identify sections of a document as XML elements, you first attach an XML schema to the document, usually one that contains content controls. An **XML schema** is a special type of XML file that describes the layout of elements in other XML files. Word users typically do not create XML schema files. Software developers or other technical personnel create an XML schema file and provide it to Word users. XML schema files, often simply called **schema files**, usually have an extension of .xsd. Once the schema is attached, you can use the 'XML Mapping Pane' button (Developer tab | Mapping group) to insert controls from the schema into the document. If you wanted to attach a schema file to a document, such as an online form, you would perform the following steps.

1. Open the file to which you wish to attach the schema, such as an online form that contains content controls.
2. Open Backstage view and then use the Save As command to save the file with a new file name, to preserve the contents of the original file.
3. Click the Document Template button (Developer tab | Templates group) to display the Templates and Add-ins dialog box.
4. Click the XML Schema tab (Templates and Add-ins dialog box) to display the XML Schema sheet and then click the Add Schema button to display the Add Schema dialog box.
5. Locate and select the schema file (Add Schema dialog box) and then click the Open button to display the Schema Settings dialog box.
6. Enter the URI and alias in the appropriate text boxes (Schema Settings dialog box) and then click OK to add the schema to the Schema Library and to add the namespace alias to the list of available schemas in the XML Schema sheet (Templates and Add-ins dialog box).

Q&A | What is a URI and an alias?
Word uses the term, URI, also called a **namespace**, to refer to the schema. Because these names are difficult to remember, you can define a namespace alias. In a setting outside of an academic environment, a computer administrator would provide you with the appropriate namespace entry.

7. If necessary, place a check mark in the desired schema's check box.
8. Click OK, which causes Word to attach the selected schema to the open document and open the XML Structure pane in the Word window.

TO DELETE A SCHEMA FROM THE SCHEMA LIBRARY

To delete a schema from a document, you would remove the check mark from the schema name's check box in the XML Schema sheet in the Templates and Add-ins dialog box. If you wanted to delete a schema altogether from the Schema Library, you would do the following.

1. Click the Document Template button (Developer tab | Templates group) to display the Templates and Add-ins dialog box.
2. Click the XML Schema tab (Templates and Add-ins dialog box) to display the XML Schema sheet and then click the Schema Library button to display the Schema Library dialog box.
3. Click the schema you want to delete in the Select a schema list (Schema Library dialog box) and then click the Delete Schema button.
4. When Word displays the Schema Library dialog box asking if you are sure you want to delete the schema, click Yes.
5. Click OK (Schema Library dialog box) and then click the Cancel button (Templates and Add-ins dialog box).

Summary

In this module, you learned how to enhance the look of text and graphics, automate a series of tasks with a macro, and work with 3-D models. You also learned about several supplementary tasks that you should know if you plan to take the certification exam.

CONSIDER THIS: PLAN AHEAD

What decisions will you need to make when creating macro-enabled and enhanced online forms?

Use these guidelines as you complete the assignments in this module and create your own online forms outside of this class.

1. Save the form to be modified as a macro-enabled template, if you plan to include macros in the template for the form.

2. Enhance the visual appeal of a form.

   a) Arrange data entry fields in logical groups on the form and in an order that users would expect.

   b) Draw the user's attention to important sections.

   c) Use colors and images that complement one another.

3. Add macros to automate tasks.

   a) Record macros, if possible.

   b) If you are familiar with computer programming, write VBA code to extend capabilities of recorded macros.

4. Determine how the form data will be analyzed.

   a) If the data entered in the form will be analyzed by a program outside of Word, create the data entry fields so that the entries are stored in a format that can be shared with other programs.

Apply Your Knowledge

Reinforce the skills and apply the concepts you learned in this module.

Working with Images, Shapes, and Fields

Note: To complete this assignment, you will be required to use the Data Files. Please contact your instructor for information about accessing the Data Files.

Instructions: Start Word. Open the template called SC_WD_10_RecyclingCommunitySurvey.dotx that you created in the Apply Your Knowledge Student Assignment in Module 10. If you did not complete the Apply Your Knowledge Student Assignment in Module 10, see your instructor for a copy. In this assignment, you enhance the Carter's Recycling Service online form created in Module 10 by changing colors and pictures, removing an image background, adding an artistic effect to an image, changing saturation and tone, grouping images, using a texture fill effect, changing a shape, inserting a date field, rotating text in a shape, and applying 3-D effects to a shape (Figure 11–75).

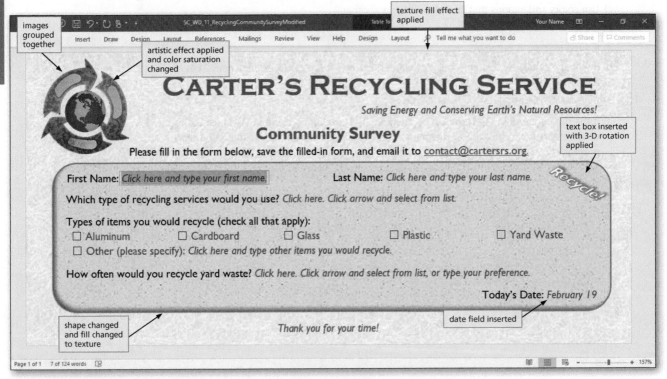

Figure 11–75

Perform the following tasks:

1. Click File on the ribbon, click Save As, and then save the template using the new file name, SC_WD_11_RecyclingCommunitySurveyModified.

2. Unprotect the template.

3. Change the font color of the title (Carter's Recycling Service), the third line (Community Survey), and the last line on the form (Thank you for your time!) to Blue, Accent 2, Darker 25%.

4. Change the font color of the tag line (Saving Energy and Conserving Earth's Natural Resources!) and the email address (contact@cartersrs.org) to Dark Green, Accent 5, Darker 25%.

5. Select the image in the upper-right corner and then open the Selection pane, which you may use throughout this assignment. Use the Layout Options button attached to the image or the Wrap Text button (Picture Tools Format tab | Arrange group) to change the layout to In Front of Text.

6. Move the image in the upper-right corner of the form to the upper-left corner. Right-align the first two lines of text (the company name and the tag line).

7. Modify the Intense Emphasis style to use the color, Dark Green, Accent 5, Darker 25%.

8. Create a character style with the name Check Box Labels for all check boxes in the data entry area that uses an 11-point Gill Sans MT (Body) font and a color of Dark Green, Accent 5, Darker 25%. Apply the new character style to the check box labels in the form: Aluminum, Cardboard, Glass, Plastic, Yard Waste, Other (please specify):.

9. Change the image in the upper-left corner of the form with the earth image called Support_WD_11_WorldInHands.png, which is located in the Data Files. (*Hint*: Use the Change Picture button (Picture Tools Format tab | Adjust group) and then click 'From a File' on the Change Picture menu, or right-click the image, point Change Picture on the shortcut menu, and then click 'From a File' on the Change Picture submenu.)

10. Use the Bring Forward arrow (Picture Tools Format tab | Arrange group) to bring the selected image to the front (so that the earth image can be positioned in front of the recycle image later in this assignment).

11. Use the Remove Background button (Picture Tools Format tab | Adjust group) to remove the background from the new image so that just the earth remains; that is, remove the hands from the image. Note that you may need to use the 'Mark Areas to Keep' button on the image of the earth.

12. Also in the upper-left corner of the form but in a separate location from the earth image, insert the recycle image called Support_WD_11_RecycleSymbol.png, which is located in the Data Files. Change the size of the inserted image to a height of 1.3" and a width of 1.23".

13. Use the Layout Options button attached to the recycle image or the Wrap Text button (Picture Tools Format tab | Arrange group) to change the wrap style to In Front of Text. Use the Send Backward arrow (Picture Tools Format tab | Arrange group) to send the selected image to the back (so that the earth image can be positioned in front of the recycle image).

14. First move the recycle image and then move the earth image to the center and on top of the recycle image as shown in Figure 11–75.

15. Apply the Watercolor Sponge artistic effect to the recycle symbol image and then change the color saturation of the same image (the recycle symbol) to 400% and the color tone to Temperature: 8800 K.

16. Group the recycle and earth images together. Ungroup the images. Regroup the images. If necessary, move the grouped images so that they appear as shown in Figure 11–75.

17. Change the page color to the Blue tissue paper texture fill effect.

18. Change the shape around the data entry area to Rectangle: Rounded Corners.

19. Change the fill of the rectangle shape to the Recycled paper texture fill effect.

20. Apply the Inside: Bottom Left shadow to the rectangle shape.

21. Display the Developer tab. Change the properties of the date picker content control so that its contents can be deleted and then delete the content control. Use the 'Explore Quick Parts' button (Insert tab | Text group) to insert a date field after the Today's Date: label in the format month day (i.e., September 13), so that the date field is automatically filled in on the form.

Continued >

Apply Your Knowledge *continued*

Right-align the line containing the date. If necessary, change the format of the displayed date field to Intense Emphasis. Hide the Developer tab.

22. Draw a text box that is approximately 1.15" × 0.73" that contains the text, Recycle!, centered in the text box. Remove the outline from the text box (shape). Change the direction of text in the text box (shape) to Rotate all text 90°. Select the text and use the 'Text Effects and Typography' button (Home tab | Font group) to apply the effect called Fill: White, Outline: Blue, Accent color 2; Hard Shadow: Blue, Accent color 2. Increase the font size to 18 point. Select the text box and then apply the 3-D rotation shape effect called 'Isometric: Top Up' to the text box (shape). Then, apply the Offset: Right shadow shape effect to the text box. Remove the fill from the text box (shape). Move the text box to the upper-right corner of the data entry area as shown in Figure 11–75.

23. Select the text box, click the Send Backward arrow (Drawing Tools Format tab | Arrange group), and then click 'Send Behind Text' on the Send Backward menu to send the text box behind text. (Note this step is necessary so that you can group the rectangle and text box shapes together.) Select the rectangle shape and then the text box shape. With both shapes selected, group the two shapes together. Ungroup the shapes. Regroup the shapes. If necessary, close the Selection pane.

24. If requested by your instructor, change the email address on the form to your email address.

25. If necessary, adjust spacing above and below paragraphs so that all contents fit on a single screen.

26. Protect the form to restrict editing to filling in forms. Save the form again with the same file name and then submit it in the format specified by your instructor. Collapse the ribbon.

27. Access the template through File Explorer and test it using your own data for the responses. If necessary, make necessary corrections to the form.

28. ✸ What is the advantage of creating a style for the check box labels?

Extend Your Knowledge

Extend the skills you learned in this module and experiment with new skills. You may need to use Help to complete the assignment.

Enhancing a Form and Working with Macros

Note: To complete this assignment, you will be required to use the Data Files. Please contact your instructor for information about accessing the Data Files.

Instructions: Start Word. Open the template called SC_WD_10_FreshmanOrientationForm.dotx that you created in the Extend Your Knowledge Student Assignment in Module 10. If you did not complete the Extend Your Knowledge Student Assignment in Module 10, see your instructor for a sample solution file. In this assignment, you enhance the Harper View College online form created in Module 10 by changing colors and pictures, converting a table to text, and working with macros.

Perform the following tasks:

1. Click File on the ribbon and then click Save As and save the template as a macro-enabled template using the new file name, SC_WD_11_FreshmanOrientationFormModified.

2. Unprotect the password-protected template. Enter the password, fun, when prompted.

3. Select the grouped graphics at the top of the form and delete them.

4. Use the 'Text Effects and Typography' button (Home tab | Font group) to remove the reflection from the school name at the top of the form.

5. In the rectangle that surrounds the data entry area, use the Shape Fill arrow (Drawing Tools Format tab | Shape Styles group) to insert the picture called Support_WD_11_Books.png, which is located in the Data Files, in the rectangle shape. Change the color of the picture in the rectangle to Washout.

6. Convert the table to text for the 2 × 1 table containing the First Name: and Last Name: labels and associated First Name and Last Name content controls. (*Hint*: You will need to change the properties of the content controls so that their contents can be deleted before you can convert the table to text. When finished, reset the content controls so that their contents cannot be deleted.) Change the left indent to 0.06" on these two lines.

7. Delete the Student Photo content control and its text box shape.

8. If necessary, adjust spacing above and below paragraphs so that all contents fit on a single screen.

9. Adjust the size of the rectangle shape so that it covers all content controls in the data entry area.

10. Change the page background to a texture or color of your choice.

11. Change the font color of the school name (Harper View College) and the last line on the form (Welcome to Harper View!) to a color of your choice. If desired, change the color of other text on the form.

12. Customize macro security settings to the 'Disable all macros with notification' option.

13. Show formatting marks and the ruler on the screen. Record a macro that hides the formatting marks and the rulers. Name it HideScreenElements. Store it in Documents Based On SC_WD_11_FreshmanOrientationFormModified template (Figure 11–76). Assign it the shortcut key, ALT+H. Run the macro to test it.

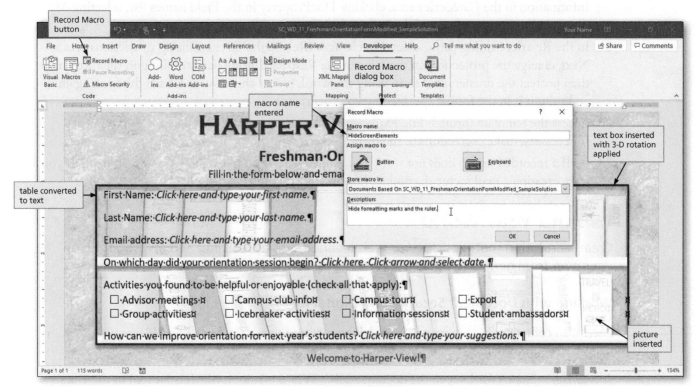

Figure 11–76

Continued >

Extend Your Knowledge *continued*

14. Add a button to the Quick Access Toolbar for the macro created in Step 13. Test the button and then delete the button from the Quick Access Toolbar.

15. Create an automatic macro called AutoNew using the macro recorder. Store it in Documents Based On SC_WD_11_FreshmanOrientationFormModified template. The macro should change the view to page width. While recording the macro, pause the recording and then resume recording the macro.

16. Edit the AutoNew macro so that it also hides the Developer tab and the ribbon. (*Hint:* You will need to open the Visual Basic Editor window from the Macros dialog box to display the VBA code for the AutoNew macro and then enter the appropriate VBA code statements in the Visual Basic Editor.)

17. Display all macros.

18. If requested by your instructor, create a macro of your choice using the Visual Basic window.

19. If requested by your instructor, display the Organizer dialog box. Close the file on the right side and then open another template of your choice. Copy the Intense Emphasis style from the SC_WD_11_FreshmanOrientationFormModified file to the template you opened on the right side. Then, delete the Intense Emphasis style from the template on the right side. Copy the macros from the SC_WD_11_FreshmanOrientationFormModified file to the template on the right side. Then, delete the copied macros from the template on the right side. Close the Organizer dialog box.

20. If requested by your instructor, add a custom document property by opening Backstage view, clicking Info, clicking the Properties button in the right pane, clicking Advanced Properties, entering the text, My Name, in the Name text box, selecting Text in the Type box if necessary, typing your name as the value, clicking the Add button, and then clicking OK. Then, in the form, in place of the school name (Harper View), insert the custom field by clicking the 'Explore Quick Parts' button (Insert tab | Text group), clicking Field, selecting Document Information in the Categories area, clicking DocProperty in the Field names list, selecting My Name in the Property list, and then clicking OK.

21. In the Restrict Editing pane, select 'No changes (Read only)' in the Editing restrictions area. Next, change the protection on the form in the Restrict Editing pane to filling in the form and then protect the unencrypted form using the word, fun, as the password. Save the form again and submit it in the format specified by your instructor.

22. Access the template through File Explorer and test it using your own data for the responses. If necessary, make corrections to the form.

23. ✴ If a recorded macro does not work as intended when you test it, how would you fix it? If you were creating a mail merge document, how would you insert a fill-in field?

Expand Your World

Create a solution that uses cloud or web technologies by learning and investigating on your own from general guidance.

Working with Document Security and Digital IDs

Note: To complete this assignment, you will be required to use the Data Files. Please contact your instructor for information about accessing the Data Files.

Instructions: Start Word. Open the document, SC_WD_11-1.docx, which is located in the Data Files. You will add a digital signature line, encrypt the document with a password, remove the password, digitally sign the document, mark the document as final.

Perform the following tasks:

1. Use Help to review and expand your knowledge about these topics: signature lines, passwords, document encryption, marking the document as final, and digital IDs.

2. Click File on the ribbon, click Save As, and then save the document using the new file name, SC_WD_11_AddressChangeRequest.

3. Position the insertion point on the blank line at the end of the document and then click the 'Add a Signature Line' button (Insert tab | Text group) to display the Signature Setup dialog box. Fill in the information to add a signature line to the document. If requested by your instructor, use your personal information in the signature line; otherwise, use the recipient name and title.

4. Encrypt the document with the password, fun.

5. Save the document again on the same storage location with the same file name. Then, close the document and reopen it. Enter the password when prompted.

6. Click the View Signatures button on the Signatures Bar that appears in the document to open the Signatures pane. Close the Signatures pane.

7. Remove the password from the document. (*Hint*: To delete a password, follow the same steps as to add a password, except delete all content from the password text box so that it is blank.)

8. Double-click the digital signature to sign the document.

9. Click the Edit Anyway button on the Message Bar.

10. Select the signature line in the document and then use the Font dialog box to format the text as hidden. If formatting marks are showing, hide formatting marks so that the hidden text is not visible in the document. Show formatting marks, select the hidden signature line, and then use the Font dialog box to unhide the text.

11. Click the 'Add a Signature Line' arrow (Insert tab | Text group) and then click 'Add Signature Services' on the Protect Document menu, which starts a browser and opens an Office Help window with a list of services that issue digital IDs (Figure 11–77). (If Word displays a Get a Digital ID dialog box, click Yes.)

Figure 11–77

12. Click the link beside each service to learn more about each one.

Continued >

Expand Your World continued

13. Use a search engine to read reviews about these services and determine which digital ID service you would recommend. Close the browser window.

14. Use Backstage view to add a digital signature to the document.

15. If requested by your instructor, set the proofing language to English.

16. Mark the document as final. (*Hint*: Use the Protect Document button in Backstage view.)

17. Submit the document in the format specified by your instructor.

18. ☀ Which digital ID services did you evaluate? When you read the reviews, were there other services not listed on the Office website? If so, what were their names? Which digital ID service would you recommend? Why? When you marked the document as final, what text appeared on the title bar? What text appeared in the Message Bar? What appeared on the status bar?

In the Lab

Design and implement a solution using creative thinking and problem-solving skills.

Modifying an Online Form for a Ferry Service

Problem: As customer relations manager at Starlight Ferry Service, you created the online customer satisfaction survey that was defined in the In the Lab Student Assignment in Module 10. Although you were pleased with the initial design, you believe the form can be improved by enhancing its appearance and adding macros to it.

Part 1: Open the template called SC_WD_10_StarlightSatisfactionSurvey.dotx that you created in the In the Lab Student Assignment in Module 10. If you did not complete the In the Lab Student Assignment in Module 10, see your instructor for a sample solution file. Click File on the ribbon and then click Save As and save the template as a macro-enabled template using the new file name, SC_WD_11_StarlightSatisfactionSurveyModified.

In this assignment, enhance the Starlight Ferry Service online form by changing the font and color of the service name, tag line, and form title; changing the page color to a texture; and changing the font and color of the last line. Apply an artistic effect to the image that you used on the form. Change the rectangle shape around the data entry area. In the rectangle, add a picture fill effect using the image of the ferry boat (if desired, one is available in the Data Files for use called Support_WD_11_FerryBoat.png) and recolor it as necessary. Change the color of the shadow in the rectangle. Draw a text box with the text, See you again soon!, and apply a 3-D effect to the text box.

Specify the appropriate macro security level. Record a macro that hides screen elements and then assign the macro to a button on the Quick Access Toolbar. Record another macro of your choice for a task you would like to automate. Add a button to the Quick Access Toolbar for any Word command not on the ribbon.

Use the concepts and techniques presented in this module to modify the online form. Be sure to save it as a macro-enabled template. Protect the form, test it, and submit it along with the answers to the Part 2 critical thinking questions in the format specified by your instructor.

If working with a 3-D model is required by your instructor, save the form using a new file name, SC_WD_11_StarlightSatisfactionSurveyModified_3-DModel. Delete the current image at the top of the form and the insert an appropriate 3-D model in its place. Resize and position the 3-D model as needed. Practice rotating and tilting the 3-D model. Format the 3-D model using additional formatting options of your choice. Protect the form, test it, and submit it in the format specified by your instructor.

Part 2: ☀ You made several decisions while creating the online form in this assignment: formats to use (i.e., fonts, font sizes, colors, styles, etc.), graphics to use, which task to automate, and which button to add to the Quick Access Toolbar. What was the rationale behind each of these decisions? When you proofread and tested the online form, what further revisions did you make, and why?

8 | Creating Photo Albums and Delivering Presentations

Objectives

After completing this module, you will be able to:

- Create a custom slide show
- Save a slide as a picture
- Create handouts by exporting to Word
- Record slide timings and narration
- Save a presentation as a PowerPoint show

- Check a presentation for compatibility and accessibility
- Encrypt a presentation with a password
- Print handouts and notes
- Create and edit a photo album
- Change slide orientation and resolution
- Insert a summary zoom slide

Introduction

BTW
Using Photographs
A carefully selected image can convey an engaging message that your audience will remember long after the presentation has ended. One picture can evoke emotions and create a connection between the speaker and the listeners. The adage, "A picture is worth a thousand words," is relevant when audience members view PowerPoint slides.

Sharing pictures has become a part of our everyday lives. We often use smartphones, digital cameras, and mobile devices, and we visit social media websites to share our adventures, special occasions, and business activities. PowerPoint has the ability to create custom slide shows with these pictures so you can show particular slides to specific audiences. For example, one large presentation created for community residents interested in maintaining their homes can be separated into custom shows describing tasks that should be performed monthly, semi-annually, and yearly.

In addition, the PowerPoint photo album feature allows you to organize and enhance your pictures. These photo albums can be shared with people who do not have PowerPoint installed on their computers. You can create custom handouts to distribute to audience members and develop notes to help you deliver your presentation effectively.

Project: Presentation with a Custom Slide Show and Photo Album

In this module's project, you will follow proper design guidelines and learn to use PowerPoint to create the slides and printouts shown in Figure 8–1a through 8–1g. The objective is to produce a presentation for a seminar at the local home improvement center concerning taking preventive measures to spot potential problems before they become complete disasters. You will create a custom slide show highlighting the vital maintenance tasks residents should perform monthly. You will save one slide as a picture, create handouts to distribute to audience members, and save the presentation as a PowerPoint show. You then will create a photo album with all the slides in the presentation.

(a) Custom Slide Show Title Slide

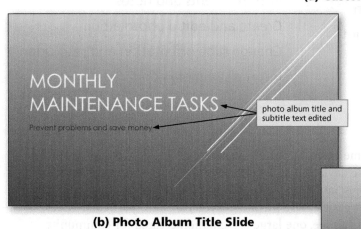

(b) Photo Album Title Slide

(c) Photo Album Slide

iStock.com/Kameleon007

(d) Summary Zoom Slide

(e) Microsoft Word Handout

(f) Handout in Landscape Orientation

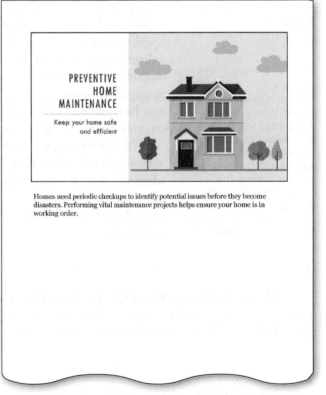

Homes need periodic checkups to identify potential issues before they become disasters. Performing vital maintenance projects helps ensure your home is in working order.

(g) Speaker Notes in Portrait Orientation

Figure 8–1

BTW
**Ribbon and Screen
Resolution**
PowerPoint may change
how the groups and buttons
within the groups appear on
the ribbon, depending on
the screen resolution of your
computer. Thus, your ribbon
may look different from the
ones in this book if you are
using a screen resolution
other than 1366 × 768.

In this module, you will learn how to create the slides shown in Figure 8–1. You will perform the following general tasks as you progress through this module:

1. Select specific slides to create a custom slide show.
2. Share a presentation by saving the presentation as a PowerPoint show.
3. Check presentation compatibility and accessibility.
4. Customize handout and notes pages.
5. Create a photo album.
6. Insert a summary zoom slide.

To Start PowerPoint and Save a File

You can begin the project by starting PowerPoint and then saving the presentation with a new file name. The following steps start PowerPoint and then save a file.

1 **sam** ↓ Start PowerPoint. If necessary, maximize the PowerPoint window.

2 Open the presentation, SC_PPT_8_Home.pptx, from the Data Files.

3 Save the presentation using **SC_PPT_8_Home_Maintenance** as the file name.

BTW
**Touch Screen
Differences**
The Office and Windows
interfaces may vary if you are
using a touch screen. For this
reason, you might notice that
the function or appearance
of your touch screen differs
slightly from this module's
presentation.

BTW
**Hyperlinking Custom
Shows**
You can hyperlink to a
custom show with slides
relating to a specific topic in
your presentation. Click the
Hyperlink button (Insert tab |
Links group), if necessary
click the 'Place in This
Document' button in the Link
to area, and then select the
custom show in the 'Select a
place in this document' area.

Creating a Custom Slide Show

Quality PowerPoint presentations are tailored toward specific audiences, and experienced presenters adapt the slides to meet the listeners' needs and expectations. Speakers can develop one slide show and then modify the content each time they deliver the presentation. For example, the director of human resources may present one set of slides for new employees, another set for potential retirees, and a third for managers concerned with new regulations and legislation. Slides for all these files may be contained in one file, and the presenter can elect to show particular slides to accompany specific speeches.

A **custom show** is a subset of slides in a presentation that can be reordered without affecting the order of slides in the original presentation. This can be useful when you want to show slides in a different order than in the original presentation. For example, you may desire to show a title slide and Slides 2, 4, 5, 10, and 12, in that order. One PowerPoint presentation can have several custom shows to adapt to specific audiences.

To Select Slides for a Slide Show

Many presenters deliver their speeches in front of targeted audiences. PowerPoint allows you to create a custom show that displays only selected slides for these people. The following steps select the slides for a custom show. *Why? You decide to use the slides that showcase maintenance tasks that should be performed every month.*

- Click the Slide Show tab and then click the 'Custom Slide Show' button (Slide Show tab | Start Slide Show group) to display the 'Custom Slide Show' menu (Figure 8–2).

Figure 8–2

- Click Custom Shows to open the Custom Shows dialog box (Figure 8–3).

Figure 8–3

- Click the New button (Custom Shows dialog box) to display the 'Define Custom Show' dialog box.

- Click '1. Preventive Home Maintenance' in the 'Slides in presentation' area to place a check mark in the check box and select this slide (Figure 8–4).

Figure 8–4

- Click the Add button ('Define Custom Show' dialog box) to add this slide to the 'Slides in custom show' area.

- Click the check boxes for Slide 2, Slide 4, and Slide 5 in the 'Slides in presentation' area.

- Scroll down and then click the check boxes for Slide 10 and Slide 12 (Figure 8–5).

Figure 8–5

To Create a Custom Slide Show

Once you have selected the slides, you can add them and name the slide show. The following steps create this show. *Why? Your specific slides are ready to add to the presentation.*

- Click the Add button (Define Custom Show dialog box) to add these slides to the 'Slides in custom show' area.

- Select the text in the 'Slide show name' text box ('Define Custom Show' dialog box) and then type **Monthly Maintenance Tasks** as the new name (Figure 8–6).

Figure 8–6

- Click OK ('Define Custom Show' dialog box) to create the new Monthly Maintenance Tasks custom show and display the Custom Shows dialog box (Figure 8–7).

- Click Close (Custom Shows dialog box) to close the dialog box.

Figure 8–7

To Open and Edit a Custom Slide Show

A PowerPoint file can have several custom slide shows. You can elect to display one of them at any time. *Why? If you need to reorder the slides based on the particular needs of your audience, you can change the sequence easily.* The following steps open a custom show and edit the slide sequence.

• With the Slide Show tab displaying, click the 'Custom Slide Show' button (Slide Show tab | Start Slide Show group) to display the 'Custom Slide Show' menu (Figure 8–8).

<table>
<tr><td>◀ Q&A</td><td>Why does 'Monthly Maintenance Tasks' display in the 'Custom Slide Show' menu?</td></tr>
</table>

The names of any custom shows will be displayed in the menu. If desired, you could click this custom show name to run the slide show and display the selected slides.

Figure 8–8

• Click Custom Shows to display the Custom Shows dialog box (Figure 8–9).

Figure 8–9

❸

• With the Monthly Maintenance Tasks custom show selected in the Custom shows area, click the Edit button (Custom Shows dialog box) to display the 'Define Custom Show' dialog box.

• Click '3. Inspect electrical cords for wear' in the 'Slides in custom show' area to select it (Figure 8–10).

Figure 8–10

- Click the Up button to move Slide 3 below Slide 1 as the second slide in the custom show (Figure 8–11).

Figure 8–11

- Click '4. Trip circuit breakers and ground fault interrupters' in the 'Slides in custom show' area to select it and then click the Up button to move Slide 4 below Slide 2 as the third slide in the custom show.

- Click '5. Change furnace filter' in the 'Slides in custom show' area to select it and then click the Down button to move Slide 5 as the last slide in the custom show (Figure 8–12).

Figure 8–12

- Click OK ('Define Custom Show' dialog box) to create the revised Monthly Maintenance Tasks custom show and display the Custom Shows dialog box (Figure 8–13).

Figure 8–13

To Run a Custom Slide Show

Once the custom show is created, you can run the show from within the Custom Shows dialog box. **Why?** *You want to review the slides to ensure they are in the desired order.* The following step runs the custom slide show.

- Click the Show button (Custom Shows dialog box) to run the Monthly Maintenance Tasks custom show.

- Display all the slides and then exit the custom show.

Other Ways

1. While running main slide show, click Options button on Slide Show toolbar, click Custom Shows, select desired custom show

3D Models

If you have an Office 365 subscription, you can enhance your creativity and productivity by embedding 3D models in your presentations. **3D models** are illustrations created using 3D animation techniques, which you can rotate in three dimensions. The Remix 3D online catalog contains hundreds of free 3D models in a wide variety of categories. Once you have inserted your model into your slide, you can rotate and tilt the images. You also can engage your audience even more by adding animation. The 3D objects can be matched with 2D content to illustrate your points.

TO INSERT A 3D MODEL

You insert 3D images into your slide in the same manner that you insert pictures or other content. To insert a 3D model, you would perform the following steps.

1. Click the Insert tab and then click the 3D Models arrow (Insert tab | Illustrations Group) to display the 3D Models menu. If you have a model already created, click 'From a File'. Otherwise, click 'From Online Sources' to display the 'Online 3D Models' dialog box.

2. Select a category and then click a picture to place a check mark in that model.

3. Click the Insert button to insert the model into your slide.

TO MODIFY A 3D MODEL

PowerPoint's controls help you manipulate a 3D model to focus on an area you want to highlight. These controls are available on the contextual tab that is displayed when you insert the image. The 3D Model Views gallery has a collection of views you can use, such as head-on or top-down. The Align tool helps you position the image in a precise area of the slide, in the same manner that you position pictures and other slide objects. The Pan & Zoom control allows you to click and drag the object within the frame, and the Zoom arrow on the right side of the frame makes the object larger or smaller within the frame. If you want to modify a 3D model, you would perform the following steps.

1. With the model selected, click a view (3D Model Tools Format tab | 3D Model Views group) to change the view.

2. Click the 'Pan & Zoom' button (3D Model Tools Format tab | Size group) and then click the Pan & Zoom 3D control in the middle of the image to rotate and tilt the model in any direction.

3. Click the Zoom arrow on the right side of the image to increase or decrease the size of the image

TO ANIMATE A 3D MODEL

You can add animation effects to your 3D model. Along with the effects available to animate 2D content, new 3D options include Arrive or Leave, Turntable, Swing, and Jump & Turn. All the animations have options to adjust the direction, intensity, or movement. The Turntable animation allows you to showcase the object slowly and smoothly. You also can have two animations play simultaneously. To animate a 3D model, you would perform the following steps.

1. Display the Animations tab and then click one of the animation effects (Animations tab | Animation group) to see a preview of that animation and apply the animation to the model.

2. Click the Effect Options button to view the Effect Options menu and then choose a property related to the movement direction, intensity, or rotation axis.

3. Click the Preview button to view the effect.

BTW
**Embedding
Animated 3D
Graphics**
Office 365 subscribers can embed an animated 3D graphic in Word or PowerPoint for Windows. Each one has preset animations, or scenes. When you display the 'Online 3D Models' dialog box, look for the categories that have a runner badge, which indicates the graphics in it are animated. Each graphic has multiple scenes, or animations, to choose from.

Saving and Sharing a Presentation

Many people design PowerPoint presentations to accompany a speech given in front of an audience, and they also develop slide shows to share with family, work associates, and friends in a variety of ways. PowerPoint saves files by default as a PowerPoint Presentation with a .pptx file extension. You can, however, select other file types that allow other computer users to view your slides if they do not have one of the newer PowerPoint versions installed. You also can save the file as a PowerPoint show so that it runs automatically when opened and does not require the user to have the PowerPoint program. Another option is to save one slide as an image that can be inserted into another program such as Word, or emailed.

To Save a Slide as a Picture

To create visually interesting slides, you insert pictures, clips, and video files into your presentation. Conversely, you may want to insert a PowerPoint slide into another document, such as a file you created in Word. *Why? A slide may have information that you want to share with an audience and include with other material that is not part of the PowerPoint presentation.* You can save one slide as an image and then insert this file into another document. The following steps save Slide 1 as a JPEG File Interchange Format (.jpg) image.

- With Slide 1 of the SC_PPT_8_Home_ Maintenance presentation displaying, open Backstage view, display the Export tab, and then click 'Change File Type' in the Export section to display the 'Change File Type' section.

- Click 'JPEG File Interchange Format (*.jpg)' in the 'Image File Types' section (Figure 8–14).

Figure 8–14

- Click the Save As button to display the Save As dialog box.

- Change the file name to `SC_ PPT_8_Home_ Maintenance_ Slide` in the File name box (Figure 8–15).

Figure 8–15

- Click the Save button (Save As dialog box) to display the Microsoft PowerPoint dialog box (Figure 8–16).

Figure 8–16

- Click the 'Just This One' button to save only Slide 1 as a file in JPEG (.jpg) format.

Q&A What would happen if I clicked All Slides?
PowerPoint would save each slide as a separate file in a folder with the file name you specified.

Other Ways

1. Click File on ribbon, click Save As in Backstage view, click Browse button to locate save location, click 'Save as type' arrow, select 'JPEG File Interchange Format (*.jpg)', click Save button

To Create Handouts by Exporting to Word

The handouts you create using PowerPoint are useful to distribute to audiences. Each time you need to create these handouts, however, you need to open the file in PowerPoint and then print from Backstage view. As an alternative, it might be convenient to save, or export, the file as a Word document if you are going to be using Word to type a script or lecture notes. ***Why?*** *The handout can have a variety of layouts; for example, the notes you type in the Notes pane can be displayed to the right of or beneath the slide thumbnails, blank lines can be displayed to the right of or beneath the slide thumbnails, or just an outline can be displayed.* The following steps export the presentation to Word and then create a handout.

- Open Backstage view, display the Export tab, and then click Create Handouts in the Export section to display the 'Create Handouts in Microsoft Word' section (Figure 8–17).

Figure 8–17

- Click the Create Handouts button to display the 'Send to Microsoft Word' dialog box.

- Click 'Blank lines next to slides' to add blank lines next to the slides when the handout is printed (Figure 8–18).

Figure 8–18

- Click OK to save the file with this layout.

- If the handout does not display in a new Word window, click the Word program button on the Windows taskbar to see a live preview of the first page of the handout (Figure 8–19).

Figure 8–19

iStock.com/LoveTheWind

- If you print the handouts, the first page will resemble the handout shown in Figure 8–20.

BTW

Conserving Ink and Toner

If you want to conserve ink or toner, you can instruct PowerPoint to print draft quality documents by clicking File on the ribbon to open Backstage view, clicking Options in Backstage view to display the PowerPoint Options dialog box, clicking Advanced in the left pane (PowerPoint Options dialog box), scrolling to the Print area in the right pane, verifying there is no check mark in the High quality check box, and then clicking OK. Then, use Backstage view to print the document as usual.

BTW

Printing Document Properties

PowerPoint 2019 does not allow you to print document properties. This feature, however, is available in other Office 2019 apps, including Word and Excel.

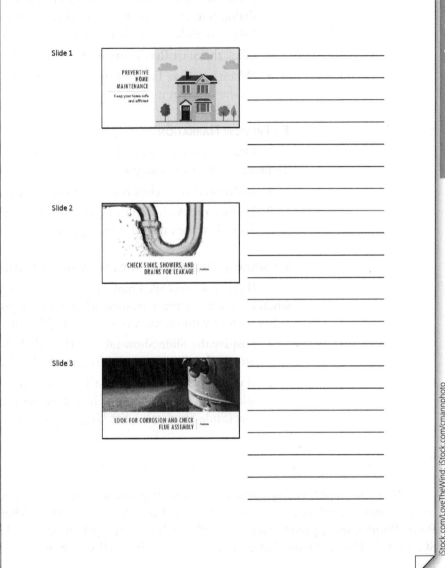

Figure 8–20 Handout – Page 1

iStock.com/LoveTheWind; iStock.com/cmannphoto

- Save the Word file using the file name, `SC_PPT_8_Word`.

- Close the Word file and, if necessary, exit Word.

To Record Slide Timings and Narration

In some situations, you may want your viewers to hear recorded narration that accompanies slides. You can record narration separately and then add this file to the slide. You also can record narration while the slide show is running. To record this narration, you would perform the following steps.

1. Display the Slide Show tab and then click the 'Record Slide Show' arrow (Slide Show tab | Set Up group).

2. Click 'Start Recording from Beginning' if you want to begin with the first slide or click 'Start Recording from Current Slide' if you want to begin with the slide that is displaying on your screen.

3. Click the 'Narrations, ink, and laser pointer' check box ('Record Slide Show' dialog box) and, if appropriate, click the 'Slide and animation timings' check box ('Record Slide Show' dialog box) to select or remove the check mark.

4. Click the Start Recording button ('Record Slide Show' dialog box).

5. When you have finished speaking, right-click the slide and then click End Show on the shortcut menu.

TO PREVIEW NARRATION

Once you have recorded narration, you can play the audio to review the sound. To preview this narration, you would perform the following steps.

1. In Normal view, click the sound icon on the slide.

2. Display the 'Audio Tools Playback' tab and then click the Play button (Audio Tools Playback tab | Preview group).

TO SHOW A PRESENTATION WITH OR WITHOUT NARRATION

If you have recorded narration to accompany your slides, you can choose whether to include this narration when you run your slide show. To run the slide show either with or without narration, you would perform the following steps.

1. Display the Slide Show tab and then click the Play Narrations check box (Slide Show tab | Set Up group) to remove the check from the box.

2. If you have chosen to show the presentation without narration and then desire to allow audience members to hear this recording, click the Play Narrations check box (Slide Show tab | Set Up group) to check this option.

To Save a Presentation as a PowerPoint Show

Why? *To simplify giving a presentation in front of an audience, you may want to start your slide show without having to start PowerPoint, open a file, and then click the Slide Show button.* When you save a presentation as a **PowerPoint Show (.ppsx)**, it automatically begins running when opened. The following steps save the SC_PPT_8_Home_Maintenance presentation as a PowerPoint show.

- Open Backstage view, display the Export tab, and then click 'Change File Type' to display the 'Change File Type' section.

- Click PowerPoint Show in the Presentation File Types section (Figure 8–21).

Figure 8–21

Click the Save As button to display the Save As dialog box.

• Change the file name to **SC_ PPT_8_Home_ Maintenance_ Show** in the File name box (Figure 8–22).

Figure 8–22

• Click the Save button to close the Save As dialog box.

Other Ways
1. Click Save As, click Browse, click 'Save as type' arrow, select PowerPoint Show, click Save

TO SHARE A PRESENTATION ON ONEDRIVE

You can save a presentation in your OneDrive account and then share this file with specific individuals. To share a presentation, you first upload it to your OneDrive account and then determine the individuals who can access this file. To share a presentation, you would perform the following steps.

1. Display Backstage view and then click the Share tab or click the Share button in the upper-right corner of the tabs.
2. Select your OneDrive account and if necessary choose a permission level then click Apply.
3. Enter the names of the individuals with whom you want to share the file and then add a message.
4. Click Send.

To Close a Presentation

The PowerPoint show is complete. You will use the SC_PPT_8_Home_ Maintenance file for the remainder of this module, so you can close the PowerPoint show presentation. The following step closes the SC_PPT_8_Home_Maintenance_ Show file.

1 Open Backstage view and then click Close to close the SC_PPT_8_Home_Maintenance_ Show file without exiting PowerPoint.

Checking and Securing a Presentation

When your slides are complete, you can perform additional functions to finalize the file and prepare it for distributing to other users or running on a computer other than the one used to develop the file. For example, the **Compatibility Checker** reviews the file for any feature that will not work properly or display on computers running a previous PowerPoint version. In addition, the **Document Inspector** locates inappropriate information, such as comments, in a file and allows you to delete these slide elements. You also can set passwords so only authorized people can distribute, view, or modify your slides. When the review process is complete, you can indicate this file is the final version.

To Check Presentation Compatibility

PowerPoint 2019 has many new features not found in some previous versions of PowerPoint, especially versions older than PowerPoint 2007. If you give your file to people who have a previous PowerPoint version installed on their computers, they will be able to open the file but may not be able to see or edit some special features and effects. The following steps run the Compatibility Checker. *Why? You can use the Compatibility Checker to see if any presentation elements will not function in earlier versions of PowerPoint and display a summary of any elements in your presentation that will be lost if your file is opened in some earlier PowerPoint versions.*

- Open the SC_PPT_8_Home_Maintenance presentation.

- Open Backstage view, if necessary click the Info tab, and then click the 'Check for Issues' button to display the 'Check for Issues' menu (Figure 8–23).

Figure 8–23

- Click Check Compatibility to display the 'Microsoft PowerPoint Compatibility Checker' dialog box.

- If any features are not supported by earlier versions of PowerPoint, they would be displayed in the Summary box (Figure 8–24).

Figure 8–24

- Click OK ('Microsoft PowerPoint Compatibility Checker' dialog box) to close the dialog box and return to the presentation.

To Check Presentation Accessibility

An effective PowerPoint presentation is highly visual, so a good designer creates slides that people with disabilities such as low vision can understand easily. PowerPoint includes an **Accessibility Checker** to identify potential issues. This feature scans the slides and finds missing alternative text, possible problems with the reading order, insufficient color contrast, slides without titles, and complex tables. The following steps run the Accessibility Checker. ***Why?*** *This feature can identify slide elements that may not be accessible and provide advice on how to fix these issues.*

- Open Backstage view and then click the 'Check for Issues' button in the Info tab to display the Check for Issues menu (Figure 8–25).

Figure 8–25

- Click Check Accessibility to display the Accessibility Checker pane (Figure 8–26).

Figure 8–26

- Click the 'Missing alternative text' error and review the Why Fix? paragraph in the Additional Information area (Figure 8–27).

Figure 8–27

- Scroll down, click the 'Check reading order' warning, click Slide 1 in the list, and then review the Why Fix? paragraph (Figure 8–28).

BTW
Office Intelligent Services
Office Intelligent Services brings the power of the cloud to Office 365 apps. Features include PowerPoint Designer, Smart Lookup, Translator, Office Tell Me, and Office Dictate.

Figure 8–28

- Scroll down, click the 'Suggested alternative text' message in the Intelligent Services area, and then scroll down and click Picture Placeholder 11 to display Slide 2 and Why Fix? information (Figure 8–29).

Q&A What if I don't see Intelligent Services? Depending upon how your computer is configured, you may not see this feature.

Figure 8–29

- Close the Accessibility Checker pane.

What types of passwords are best for security?

A password should be at least 8 characters (some experts recommend at least 20 characters) and contain a combination of letters, numbers, and other characters. Using both uppercase and lowercase letters is advised. Do not use a password that someone could guess, such as your first or last name, spouse's or child's name, telephone number, birth date, street address, license plate number, or Social Security number.

Once you develop this password, write it down in a secure place. Underneath your keyboard is not a secure place, nor is your middle desk drawer. You also can use a password manager program for added security.

CONSIDER THIS

To Encrypt a Presentation with a Password

You can prohibit a user from modifying a file without entering the password. ***Why?*** *You can protect your slide content by using a password.* The following steps set a password for the SC_PPT_8_Home_Maintenance file.

- Display Backstage view, if necessary click the Info tab, and then click the Protect Presentation button to display the Protect Presentation menu (Figure 8–30).

Figure 8–30

- Click 'Encrypt with Password' to display the Encrypt Document dialog box.
- Type **Home_365#** in the Password box (Figure 8–31).

Figure 8–31

- Click OK to display the Confirm Password dialog box.
- Type **Home_365#** in the Reenter password box (Figure 8–32).

Q&A
What if I forget my password?
You will not be able to open your file. For security reasons, Microsoft or other companies cannot retrieve a lost password.

Figure 8–32

- Click OK in the Confirm Password dialog box to encrypt the file with a password and display a message that the file is protected (Figure 8–33).

Q&A
When does the password take effect?
You will need to enter your password the next time you open your presentation.

Figure 8–33

TO OPEN A PRESENTATION WITH A PASSWORD

To open a file that has been protected with a password, you would perform the following steps.

1. Display the Open dialog box, locate the desired file, and then click the Open button to display the Password dialog box.

2. When the Password dialog box appears, type the password in the Password box and then click OK to display the presentation.

To Change or Remove Password Protection

You can change a password that you added to a file or remove all password protection from the file. *Why? Another password may be more secure or password protection may be unnecessary.* The following steps remove the password from the SC_PPT_8_Home_Maintenance file.

- With Backstage view open, click Save As to display the Save As gallery (Figure 8–34).

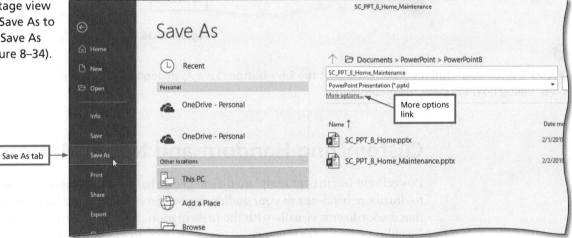

Figure 8–34

2

- Click the More options link to display the Save As dialog box. Click the Tools button to display the Tools list (Figure 8–35).

Figure 8–35

- Click General Options in the Tools list to display the General Options dialog box.
- Delete the contents of the 'Password to open' box (Figure 8–36).

Figure 8–36

- Click OK (General Options dialog box), click the Save button (Save As dialog box), and then click Yes ('Confirm Save As' dialog box) to resave the presentation.

Customizing Handout and Notes Masters

PowerPoint has master template files to create handouts and notes. If you are going to distribute handouts to your audience, you can customize the handout master so that it coordinates visually with the presentation slides and reinforces your message. In addition, if you are going to use speaker notes to guide you through a presentation, you can tailor the notes master to fit your needs.

To Switch to Handout Master View

You can create a specific handout master to determine the layout and graphics that will display on the printed handout. **Why?** *You can customize handouts for your audience's needs.* The following steps change the view to Handout Master.

- Display the View tab (Figure 8–37).

- Click the Handout Master button (View tab | Master Views group) to display the Handout Master tab.

Figure 8–37

To Customize the Handout Master

The Handout Master tab has buttons and controls that allow you to design a custom handout master. *Why? You can format the header and footer placeholders, set the page number orientation, add graphics, and specify the number of slides to print on each page.* The following steps customize the handout master to create a custom handout.

- With the Handout Master tab displaying, click the 'Slides Per Page' button (Handout Master tab | Page Setup group) to display the Slides Per Page gallery (Figure 8–38).

Is 6 Slides the default layout for all themes?
Yes. If you have fewer than six slides in your presentation or want to display slide details, then choose a handout layout with 1, 2, 3, or 4 slides per sheet of paper.

Figure 8–38

- Click 4 Slides in the list to change the layout from 6 slides to 4 slides.
- Click the Handout Orientation button (Handout Master tab | Page Setup group) to display the Handout Orientation gallery (Figure 8–39).

Figure 8–39

- Click Landscape in the gallery to display the page layout in landscape orientation (Figure 8–40).

Q&A How do I decide between portrait and landscape orientation?
If your slide content is predominantly vertical, such as an athlete running or a skyscraper in a major city, consider using the default portrait orientation. If, however, your slide content has long lines of text or pictures of four-legged animals, landscape orientation may be more appropriate.

Figure 8–40

To Insert a Header for Handouts

The handout master contains a header placeholder. You can add and format text in that box and also position it on the slide. **Why?** *The header informs your audience that the presentation's topic concerns vital maintenance tasks.* The following steps insert a header for the custom handout.

- Click the Header placeholder and then type **Preventive Home Maintenance** as the header text (Figure 8–41).

Figure 8–41

- Click the Fonts button (Handout Master tab | Background group) to display the Fonts gallery (Figure 8–42).

BTW

Formatting the Date Placeholder

The Date header can have a variety of formats. If you click the Update automatically arrow in the 'Header and Footer' dialog box, you can choose among formats that display the date in a variety of combinations.

Figure 8–42

- Click Candara to apply that font to the text in the placeholders.

- Click the Date check box (Handout Master tab | Placeholders group) to clear the check box and remove the date display (Figure 8–43).

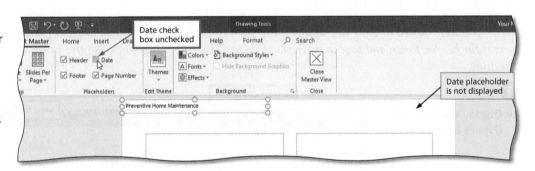

Figure 8–43

To Switch to Notes Page View

If you type notes in the Notes pane, you can print them for yourself or for your audience. The basic format found in Backstage view generally suffices for handouts. *Why? This format includes placeholders for the header, date, slide image, footer, body, and page number.* The following steps change the view to Notes Page.

- Display the View tab (Figure 8–44).

Figure 8–44

- Click the Notes Page button (View tab | Presentation Views group) to display Notes Page view.

- Press RIGHT ARROW repeatedly to view all 12 notes pages (Figure 8–45).

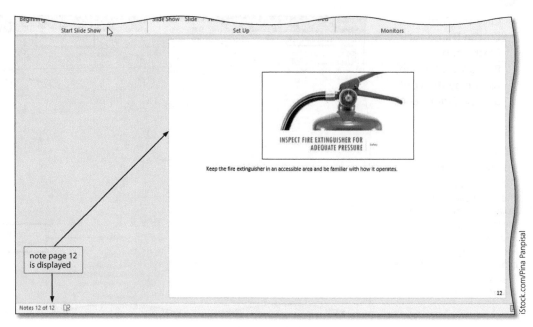

Figure 8–45

To Switch to Notes Master View

You may desire to alter the layout using the notes master. **Why?** *You can add graphics and rearrange and format the header, footer, and page number placeholders.* The following steps use the notes master to create a custom handout.

- Display the View tab (Figure 8–46)

Figure 8–46

- Click the Notes Master button (View tab | Master Views group) to display the Notes Master tab (Figure 8–47).

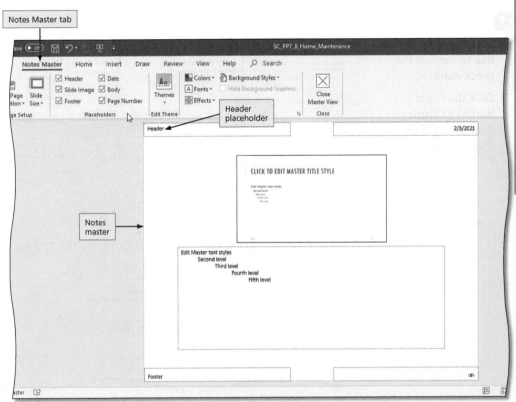

Figure 8–47

To Insert a Header for Notes

The notes master contains a header placeholder. You can add and format text in that box and also position it on the slide. *Why? You can view the header and quickly see your presentation's topic or other information that you added to this box.* The following step inserts a header for the custom handout.

- Click the Header placeholder, delete the text, and then type **Keep your home safe and efficient** as the new header text (Figure 8–48).

Figure 8–48

To Customize the Notes Master

The notes master contains placeholders for the header, slide image, footer, date, body, and page number. You can hide any of these placeholders, change the page orientation to portrait or landscape, alter the slide size, edit the theme, and change the fonts and colors. *Why? It is not important to view the date. You also want to change the font and change the page orientation to portrait.* The following steps customize the notes master by hiding the date, changing the font, and changing the page orientation to portrait.

1

- Click the Date check box to remove the check mark.

- Click the Fonts button to display the Fonts gallery (Figure 8–49).

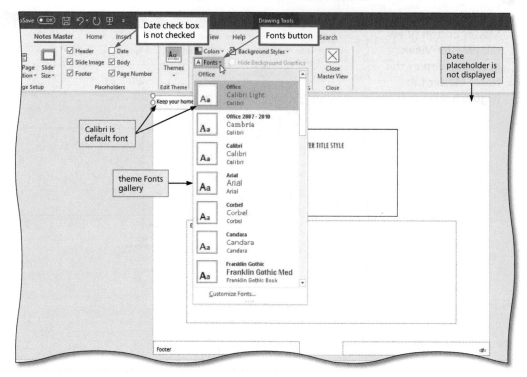

Figure 8–49

2

- Scroll down and then click Georgia in the Fonts gallery to apply that font to the text in the header and page number placeholders.

- Click the 'Notes Page Orientation' button (Notes Master tab | Page Setup group) to display the 'Notes Page Orientation' gallery (Figure 8–50).

Figure 8–50

• Click Portrait in the gallery to display the page layout in portrait orientation (Figure 8–51).

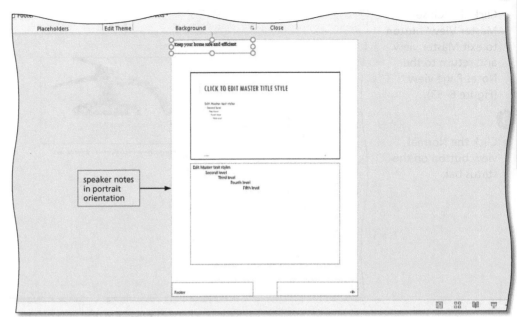

Figure 8–51

To Close Master View

You now can exit Master view and return to Normal view. **Why?** *All the changes to the handout master and notes master are complete.* The following steps close Master view.

• With the Notes Master tab displaying, point to the 'Close Master View' button (Notes Master tab | Close group) (Figure 8–52).

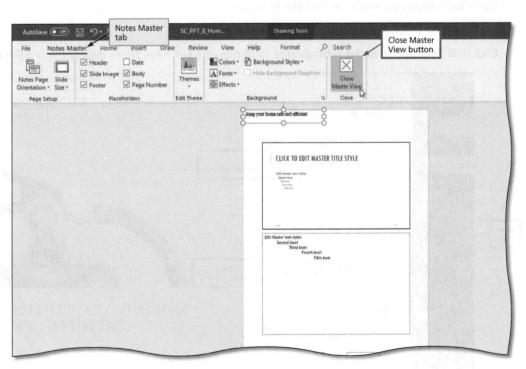

Figure 8–52

2

- Click the 'Close Master View' button to exit Master view and return to the Notes Page view (Figure 8–53).

3

- Click the Normal view button on the status bar.

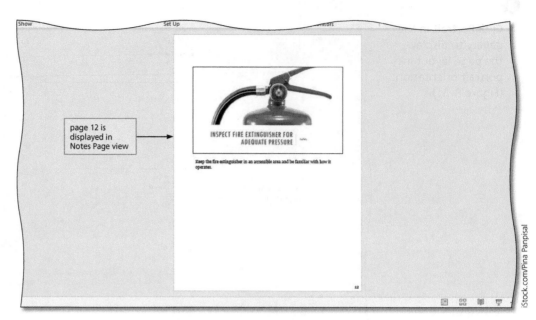

Figure 8–53

To Print Handouts

In the previous steps you customized the handout master and notes master by adding and formatting header text. You now can print handouts easily using these masters. *Why? You want to print customized handouts.* The following steps print handouts and speaker notes pages.

1

- Open Backstage view and then click the Print tab.

2

- Click 'Full Page Slides' in the Settings area to display the Full Page Slides gallery (Figure 8–54).

Figure 8–54

3

- Click '4 Slides Horizontal' in the Handouts area.

- Click Portrait Orientation in the Settings area to display the Orientation gallery (Figure 8–55).

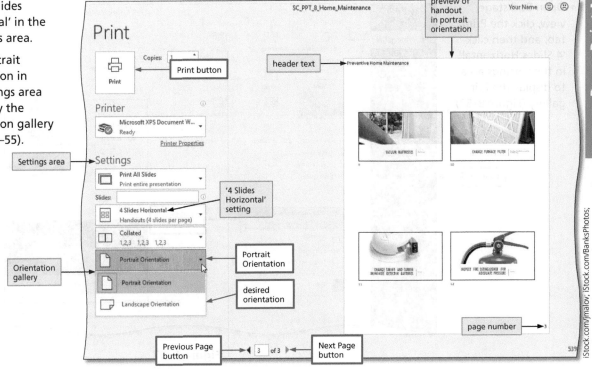

Figure 8–55

4

- Click Landscape Orientation to change the setting.

- Verify that '4 Slides Horizontal' is selected as the option in the Settings area and that the preview shows the header text, page number, and four slides in landscape orientation.

- Click the Previous Page and Next Page buttons to display previews of the other pages and then display Page 1.

- Click the Print button in the Print gallery to print the handout. Figure 8–56 shows the first page of the printout.

BTW

Printing Selections

When you are developing slides or creating handouts for a particular audience, you may not want to print every slide in your presentation. To print specific slides, select the desired slides in the Slide pane. Then, open Backstage view, display the Print tab, click the first button in the Settings area, click Print Selection in the list to specify you want to print the slides you have selected, and then click the Print button in the Print gallery to print these slides.

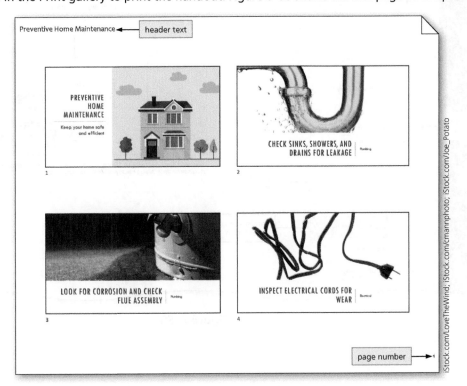

Figure 8–56 Handout in Landscape Orientation – Page 1

5

- Open Backstage view, click the Print tab, and then click '4 Slides Horizontal' in the Settings area to display the Print gallery (Figure 8–57).

Figure 8–57

6

- Click Notes Pages in the Print Layout area.
- Click Landscape Orientation in the Settings area (Figure 8–58).

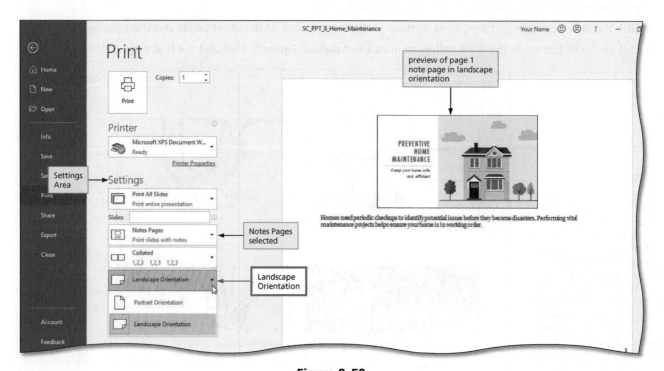

Figure 8–58

7
- Click Portrait Orientation in the gallery to change the setting.
- Verify that the page preview shows the speaker notes and page number in portrait orientation (Figure 8–59).

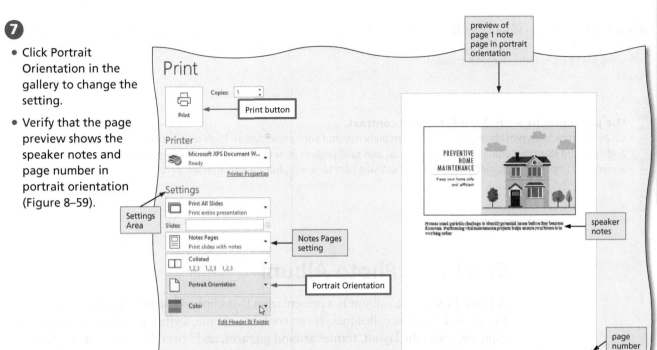

Figure 8–59

8
- Click the Previous Page and Next Page buttons to display previews of the other pages.
- Click the Print button to print the notes. Figure 8–60 shows the first page of the printout.

BTW

Printing in Grayscale
If you desire to keep your images in color but you do not have a color printer or do not require a color printout, choosing Grayscale will print all the slide objects in shades of gray. In grayscale, some objects on the slides will appear crisper and cleaner than if you choose the Color option on a non-color printer. Open Backstage view, click the Print tab to display the Print pane, click the Color button in the Settings area, click Grayscale, and then click Print. If you then want to print in color, click the Grayscale button and then click Color.

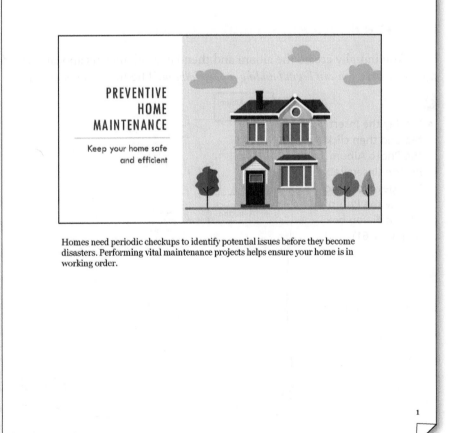

Figure 8–60

Break Point: If you wish to take a break, this is a good place to do so. Be sure the Home Maintenance file is saved and then you can exit PowerPoint. To resume later, start PowerPoint, open the file called SC_PPT_8_Home_Maintenance.pptx, and continue following the steps from this location forward.

CONSIDER THIS

Use photographs with sharp focus and contrast.

Clear, sharp pictures provide details that draw an audience into your presentation. High-quality photographs impress your audience and state that you have an eye for detail and take pride in your work. When your slides are projected on a large screen, any imperfection is magnified, so you must take care to select photographs that are in focus and have high contrast.

Creating a Photo Album

A PowerPoint photo album is a presentation that contains pictures to share with friends and business colleagues. It can contain a theme, a vibrant background, custom captions, a specific layout, frames around pictures, and boxes. You can enhance the quality of the pictures by increasing or decreasing brightness and contrast, and you can rotate the pictures in 90-degree increments. You also can change color pictures to display in black and white.

You can share your photo album in a variety of ways. You can, for example, email the file, publish it to the web, or print the pictures as handouts.

To Start a Photo Album and Add Pictures

You initially create the album and then later enhance its appearance. *Why? Once you have gathered files of digital pictures, you can begin building a photo album.* The following steps start a photo album and add pictures.

1

- Display the Insert tab and then click the Photo Album button (Insert tab | Images group) to display the Photo Album dialog box (Figure 8–61).

Q&A Why am I viewing a menu with the 'New Photo Album' and 'Edit Photo Album' commands instead of the Photo Album dialog box?
You mistakenly clicked the 'New Photo Album' arrow instead of the 'New Photo Album' button.

Figure 8–61

iStock.com/Pina Panpisal

- Click the File/Disk button to display the 'Insert New Pictures' dialog box.

- If necessary, navigate to the location where your Data Files are stored (Figure 8–62).

Figure 8–62

- If necessary, display only the picture file names by clicking the 'Change your view.' arrow (shown in Figure 8–62), on the toolbar ('Insert New Pictures' dialog box) to display the view settings (Figure 8–63).

- Click List in the view settings to change the view setting and display only the picture file names.

Figure 8–63

- Click Support_PPT_8_Breakers to select the file name. Press and hold down CTRL and then select the file names Support_PPT_8_Cord, Support_PPT_8_Detector, Support_PPT_8_Drain, Support_PPT_8_Extinguisher, and Support_PPT_8_Refrigerator as additional files to insert (Figure 8–64).

BTW

Selecting Slides or Other Items
To select sequential or adjacent files or items, select the first item, press and hold down SHIFT, and then select the last item. All items between the first and last item will be highlighted. To select nonadjacent files or items, select the first item and then press and hold down CTRL. While holding down CTRL, select additional items.

Q&A

If I mistakenly select a file name, how can I remove the selection?
Click the file name again to remove the check mark.

I'm using a touch screen and am having trouble selecting multiple files. What can I do?
You may need to use a mouse in combination with onscreen keyboard CTRL, or you can select and insert each file individually.

Figure 8–64

 5

- Click Insert ('Insert New Pictures' dialog box) to add the pictures to the album.

To Reorder Pictures in a Photo Album

PowerPoint inserted the pictures in alphabetical order, which may not be the desired sequence for your album. You easily can change the order of the pictures in the same manner that you change the slide order in a custom show. The following steps reorder the photo album pictures. *Why? You want to emphasize that checking the smoke detector is one of the more important tasks that should be performed every month.*

1

- Click the check box for the third picture, Support_PPT_8_ Detector, to select it (Figure 8–65).

Figure 8–65

2

- Click the Move Up button two times to move the Support_ PPT_8_Detector picture upward so that it now is the first picture (picture 1) in the album (Figure 8–66).

Q&A
I clicked the Move Up button, but the photo is not moving. What should I do?
Be patient. The photo eventually will move.

Figure 8–66

iStock.com/Karneleon007; iStock.com/Pina Panpisal

3

- Click the Support_ PPT_8_Detector check box to remove the check mark.

- Select the fourth picture, Support_ PPT_8_Drain, and then click the Move Down button two times to move this picture downward so that it now is the last picture (picture 6) in the album.

- Click the Support_ PPT_8_Drain check box to remove the check mark (Figure 8–67).

Figure 8–67

iStock.com/LoveTheWind; iStock.com/Pina Panpisal

To Format Photos in an Album

A picture you insert may need correcting to enhance its visual appeal. You can adjust the difference between the darkest and lightest areas of the picture by increasing or decreasing the contrast. If a picture in the photo album is too light or too dark, you can adjust its brightness to enhance its appearance. The following steps adjust the brightness and contrast of a photo album picture. *Why? The breakers picture is somewhat light, so decreasing the brightness would help the colors stand out on the slide and give more depth to the image. In addition, it lacks contrast and would be more dramatic if it had a wide variety of dark and light regions.*

- Click the check box for the second picture, Support_PPT_8_Breakers, to select it and display a preview (Figure 8–68).

Figure 8–68

2

- Click the Increase Contrast button (Photo Album dialog box) three times to increase the contrast of this picture.

3

- With the Support_PPT_8_Breakers picture selected, click the Decrease Brightness button (Photo Album dialog box) two times to intensify the colors in the picture (Figure 8– 69).

- Click the Support_PPT_8_Breakers check box to remove the check mark.

Figure 8–69

To Change a Photo Album Layout

PowerPoint inserts each photo album picture so that it fills, or fits, one entire slide. You can modify this layout to display two or four pictures on a slide, display a title, or add white space between the image and the slide edges. You also can add a white or black frame around the perimeter of each picture. The following steps change an album layout. *Why? You want to display only one picture on each slide so that you can discuss each maintenance task thoroughly during your presentation. Adding a frame provides contrast between the photos and the background.*

- With the Photo Album dialog box displayed, click the Picture layout arrow in the Album Layout area (Photo Album dialog box) to display the Picture layout list (Figure 8–70).

Figure 8–70

- Click 1 picture in the Picture layout list to change the layout so that one picture is displayed on each slide and a rectangular frame is displayed around each picture.
- Click the Frame shape arrow in the Album Layout area (Photo Album dialog box) to display the Frame shape list (Figure 8–71).

Figure 8–71

- Click 'Compound Frame, Black' in the Frame shape list to show a preview and add a compound black frame around each picture.

To Add a Photo Album Theme

The themes that are used to design a presentation also are available to add to a photo album. These themes determine the colors and fonts that complement each other and increase the visual appeal of the slides. The following steps add a theme to the photo album. *Why? You want to select a simple theme that has an uncluttered layout and font that will complement the pictures.*

● Click the Browse
  button in the Album
  Layout area (Photo
  Album dialog box) to
  display the Choose
  Theme dialog box.

● Click Slice in the
  theme list to
  select this theme
  (Figure 8–72).

Figure 8–72

● Click the Select
  button (Choose
  Theme dialog box)
  to apply this theme
  to the presentation
  (Figure 8–73).

Figure 8–73

To Create a Photo Album

Once you have inserted the pictures and determined the picture sequence, layout, frame shape, and theme,
you are ready to make the photo album. *Why? You have specified all the information PowerPoint needs to create this
album.* The following step creates the photo album.

1

- Click the Create button (Photo Album dialog box) to close the dialog box and create a photo album with a title slide and six pictures (Figure 8–74).

- If the Design Ideas pane is displayed, close it.

iStock.com/Kameleon007; iStock.com/melissabrock1; iStock.com/Joe_Potato; iStock.com/Pina Panpisal

Figure 8–74

Why does a particular name display below the Photo Album title?

PowerPoint displays the user name that was entered when the program was installed. To see this name, display Backstage view, click Options to display the 'PowerPoint Options' dialog box, and then view or change the name entered in the User name box in the Personalize your copy of Microsoft Office area.

To Edit a Photo Album

Once you review the photo album PowerPoint creates, you can modify the contents by adding and deleting pictures, changing the layout and frames, and adding transitions. The following steps edit the photo album. *Why? The Slice theme has white accent lines on the right side of the slide, so you want a white picture frame to coordinate with this slide element. You also want to add the Clock transition that relates to the timeliness nature of performing household maintenance tasks.*

1

- With Slide 1 displaying, select the title text, Photo Album, and then type **Monthly Maintenance Tasks** as the replacement text.

- Increase the font size of the title text to 54 point.

- Select the subtitle text, by Your Name, and change it to **Prevent problems and save money** as the replacement text (Figure 8–75).

Figure 8–75

- Display the Insert tab and then click the Photo Album arrow (Insert tab | Images group) to display the Photo Album menu (Figure 8–76).

Figure 8–76

- Click 'Edit Photo Album' in the menu to display the 'Edit Photo Album' dialog box.
- Click the Frame shape arrow to display the Frame shape list and then click 'Simple Frame, White' in the list to change the frame from a double black border to a single white border (Figure 8–77).

Figure 8–77

- Click the Update button (Edit Photo Album dialog box) to make the frame change to the photo album.
- If the Design Ideas pane is displayed, close it.
- Apply the Clock transition and then change the duration to 03.00 seconds for all slides.
- Save the file using **SC_PPT_8_Photo_Album** as the file name.
- Close the SC_PPT_8_Photo_Album presentation to return to the open Home Maintenance presentation.

Modifying and Presenting Slides

BTW
Zoom Availability
Zoom for PowerPoint is available only in Office 365 and PowerPoint 2019. Summary zoom is also supported for Office 365 for Mac.

PowerPoint's default settings generally suffice for most presentations. At times, however, the slide content can be presented more effectively in a different perspective or in a different resolution. You easily can modify these settings to tailor the slides to your specific needs. In addition, many designers create one comprehensive slide deck and then elect to display particular parts of that file when presenting to varied audiences. They create a **summary zoom** slide as the first slide in their presentation, which allows them to jump to a specific slide or section and then return to this initial slide.

Speakers often deliver a presentation using two monitors: one to display their speaker notes privately, and a second to display the slides and project them on a large screen for the audience to view. PowerPoint's **Presenter view** supports the use of two monitors connected to one computer so presenters can view the slide currently being projected while viewing the slide thumbnails, seeing a preview of the next slide or animation, reading their speaker notes, viewing the elapsed time, lightening or darkening the audience's screen, or customizing the presentation by skipping the next slide or reviewing a slide previously displayed. A computer must support the use of multiple monitors and must be configured to use this feature.

Use hyperlinks to show slides with landscape and portrait orientations.

When you are creating your presentation, you have the option to display all your slides in either the default landscape orientation or portrait orientation. You may, however, desire to have slides with both orientations during a single presentation. Using hyperlinks is one solution to mixing the orientations. Apply a hyperlink to an object on the last slide in one orientation and then hyperlink to another presentation with slides in the other orientation. If you desire to hyperlink to one particular slide in a second presentation, click the Bookmark button in the Insert Hyperlink dialog box and then select the title of the slide you want to use as your link. Once you have displayed the desired slides in the second presentation, create another hyperlink from that presentation back to a slide in your original presentation.

To Change the Slide Orientation

By default, PowerPoint displays slides in landscape orientation, where the width dimension is greater than the height dimension. You can change this setting to specify that the slides display in portrait orientation. *Why?* *In portrait orientation, the height dimension is greater than the width dimension, so it is useful to display tall objects, people who are standing, or faces.* The following steps change the slide orientation.

- If necessary, turn AutoSave off.

- With the SC_PPT_8_Home_Maintenance presentation open, display the Design tab and then click the Slide Size button (Design tab | Customize group) to display the Slide Size gallery (Figure 8–78).

Figure 8–78

- Click 'Custom Slide Size' to display the Slide Size dialog box and then click Portrait in the Slides area of the Orientation section to change the slide orientation from Landscape to Portrait (Figure 8–79).

Figure 8–79

- Click OK to display the Microsoft PowerPoint dialog box (Figure 8–80).

- Click Ensure Fit to scale the slide content to fit on each slide.

Q&A I see an Ensure Fit icon and an Ensure Fit button. Can I click either one to scale the slide content? Yes.

Figure 8–80

To Change the Slide Show Resolution

Screen resolution affects the number of pixels that are displayed on your screen. When screen resolution is increased, more information is displayed, but it is decreased in size. Conversely, when screen resolution is decreased, less information is displayed, but that information is increased in size. You can change the resolution you want to use to display your presentation. This feature is valuable when your computer is connected to two different monitors, when you are delivering your presentation using a computer other than the one used to create the slides, or when the projector does not support the resolution you specified when you saved the presentation. Throughout this book, the screen resolution has been set to 1366 × 768. The following steps change the presentation resolution to 800 × 600. **Why?** *You may need to run your presentation on a monitor that has a different resolution.*

- Display the Slide Show tab and then click the 'Set Up Slide Show' button (Slide Show tab | Set Up group) to display the 'Set Up Show' dialog box.

- If necessary, click the 'Slide show monitor' arrow in the Multiple monitors section and then choose Primary Monitor.

- Click the Resolution arrow in the Multiple monitors section to display the Resolution list (Figure 8–81).

Figure 8–81

- Click 800 x 600 to change the slide show resolution setting.

- If necessary, click the 'Use Presenter View' check box to clear the check box (Figure 8–82).

Q&A What is Presenter view?

When you use Presenter view, you control the slide show using one screen only you can see, but your audience views the slides on another main screen.

Figure 8–82

- Click OK to close the 'Set Up Show' dialog box and apply the new resolution to the slides.

- Save the presentation using **SC_PPT_8_Home_Maintenance_Portrait** as the file name.

To Insert a Summary Zoom Slide

Speakers often use their PowerPoint files in many venues for different types of audiences. They may, for example, need to condense the presentation and display only a few slides when time is short. Or, in another situation, the audience may be familiar with the topic and need to know only specific information located on slides near the end of the slide deck. When a Zoom is created in PowerPoint, a speaker can decide which slides, sections, and portions of a presentation to display in a nonlinear way depending upon the audience's needs. The following steps insert a summary zoom slide in the SC_PPT_8_Home_Maintenance_Portrait file. *Why? When this slide is displayed during the presentation, you will see thumbnails of all the slides on one slide and then can interactively decide which slide to display next in any order.*

- Display the Insert tab and then click the Zoom button (Insert tab | Links group) to display the Zoom menu (Figure 8–83).

Figure 8–83

- Click Summary Zoom to display the 'Insert Summary Zoom' dialog box.

◄ **Q&A** | When would I use Slide Zoom or Section Zoom?
Slide Zoom shows specific slides that you select, and Section Zoom shows slides contained in a single section.

- Click the check boxes to the left of all 12 slide numbers (Figure 8–84).

Figure 8–84

- Click the Insert button ('Insert Summary Zoom' dialog box) to create the summary zoom slide and insert it as the new Slide 1 in the slide deck.

- Click the text box at the top of the summary zoom slide and then type **Preventive Home Maintenance** as the slide title (Figure 8–85).

- Save the presentation again.

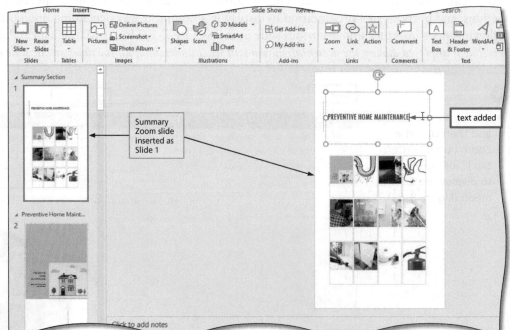

Figure 8–85

Rehearse, rehearse, rehearse.
Speakers should spend as much time practicing their presentations as they do preparing their PowerPoint slides. Frequently, however, they use the majority of their preparation time designing and tweaking the slides. Audience members expect to see a presenter who is prepared, confident, and enthusiastic. Practicing the presentation helps convey this image. As you rehearse, focus on a strong introduction that grasps the audience's attention and previews the main points of your talk. You have only one chance to make a good first impression, so begin the speech by establishing eye contact with audience members in various parts of the room. Resist the urge to stare at the slides projected on the screen. Your audience came to your presentation to hear you speak, and rehearsing will help you deliver a high-quality talk that exceeds their expectations.

TO CREATE AND INSERT SCREEN RECORDINGS

You can create screen recordings in your PowerPoint presentations if you have a sound card, microphone, and speakers. To create and insert a screen recording in your presentation, you would perform the following steps.

1. Display the slide you would like to record at the beginning of the presentation.
2. Display the Insert tab, click the Screen Recording button (Insert tab | Media group), select an area of your screen to record, and then click the Record button.
3. Capture the desired information, including voice narrations, slide timings, and ink and laser pointer gestures.
4. When you have finished recording, save the presentation.
5. The recording is directly inserted into your presentation in the desired area of the slide.

TO RECORD AUDIO

You can record narration and play back the sound within PowerPoint if you have a sound card, microphone, and speakers. To record audio and add it to a slide, you would perform the following steps.

1. Display the slide for which you want to record audio.
2. Display the Insert tab, click the Audio button (Insert tab | Media group) to display the Audio menu, and then click Record Audio.
3. Type a file name for the audio segment in the Name box.
4. Click the Record button and capture the desired sound through the microphone (such as your voice or other audio).
5. Click the Stop button to stop recording.
6. Click OK to save the sound and insert it directly into your presentation in the desired area of the slide.
7. Drag the audio icon to the desired location on the slide.

TO PRESENT A SLIDE SHOW ONLINE

Microsoft's Office Presentation Service feature allows you to share your presentation remotely with anyone having an Internet connection. As you display your slides, they see a synchronized view of your slide show in their web browser, even if they do not have PowerPoint installed on their computers. To present your presentation online, you would perform the following steps.

1. Click the Present Online arrow (Slide Show tab | Start Slide Show group) to display the Present Online menu.

BTW
Updating Summary Zoom
If you make changes to your presentation after you have created the summary zoom, you can update the summary zoom by clicking the Edit Summary button (Zoom Tools Format tab | Zoom Options), selecting the sections you want to include in your summary zoom, and then clicking the Update button.

BTW
Turning Off Slide Timings
If you recorded narration with slide timings, you might decide to play the narration for your audience but want to advance the slides manually. PowerPoint gives you the option to turn slide timings off and then turn them back on without having to recreate them. Click the 'Set Up Slide Show' button (Slide Show tab | Set Up group) and then click Manually in the Advance slides area ('Set Up Show' dialog box). To turn the slide timings back on, click 'Using timings, if present' in the Advance slides area ('Set Up Show' dialog box).

BTW
Restricting Permissions
You can allow PowerPoint users to see your presentation but not allow them to change the slide content, copy the slides, or print the presentation. To protect your presentation, open Backstage view, display the Info tab, click the Protect Presentation button, click the Restrict Access button, and then click 'Connect to Rights Management Servers and get templates'.

2. Click 'Office Presentation Service' to display the Present Online dialog box. If you wanted viewers to be able to download the presentation, you would check the box for 'Enable remote viewers to download the presentation'.

3. Click the CONNECT button (Present Online dialog box) to agree to the service terms, then, if necessary, sign in to your Microsoft account, and then click the Next button (Sign in dialog box).

4. After PowerPoint has connected to the service and completed preparing the presentation, share the presentation link with up to 50 remote viewers and then click the START PRESENTATION button (Present Online dialog box). People visiting the website can view your presentation with any annotations you make.

5. When you have displayed the last slide, click the 'End Online Presentation' button (Present Online tab | Present Online group) and then click the 'End Online Presentation' button (Microsoft PowerPoint dialog box).

To Display All Slides in Presenter View

Presenter view allows a speaker to use dual monitors: one that displays what the audience is seeing, and another with controls to aid the presenter. You can rehearse using Presenter view with one monitor so that you are comfortable using the features. You will not be able to edit the slides while using Presenter view. To use Presenter view, you would perform the following steps.

1. Display the Slide Show tab and then click the 'Use Presenter View' check box (Slide Show tab | Monitors group).

2. Press ALT+F5.

To Zoom Using the Magnifying Glass in Presenter View

While using Presenter view, you can magnify part of the slide on the screen. When you click the magnifying glass icon, a bright rectangle is displayed on the slide and the mouse pointer changes to a hand. To zoom using this magnifying glass, you would perform the following steps.

1. In Slide Show view, click the magnifying glass icon in the lower-left corner of Presenter view.

2. Position your mouse pointer over the area of the slide that you want to magnify and then click to zoom in on that location.

3. Press ESC or click the magnifying glass icon again to turn off the zoom effect.

To Run a Presentation with Slide Zoom Links

All changes are complete. You now can view the Home Maintenance Portrait presentation with zoom links. The following steps run the slide show.

1 Display Slide 1 and then run the presentation.

2 Click the circuit breaker slide to display it and then click the slide to return to Slide 1.

3 Click the title slide and then click this slide to return to Slide 1.

4 Continue displaying the slides in the presentation using the summary zoom slide. When the last slide (the fire extinguisher) is displayed, press ESC to end the presentation.

To Save the Presentation

With the presentation completed, you should save the file. The following steps save the Home Maintenance Portrait file and then exit PowerPoint.

1 Save the presentation again in the same storage location with the same file name.

2 sam↑ Because the project now is complete, you can exit PowerPoint.

Summary

In this module you learned how to create a custom slide show by selecting specific slides and then reordering their sequence. You also saved a slide as a .jpg file and saved a presentation as a PowerPoint show. You created handouts by exporting the file to Word and customized handouts and notes pages. You checked the presentation for compatibility and accessibility and then protected it with a password. Next, you created a photo album, formatted a photo, and changed the album theme and slide borders. Finally, you modified the slide show orientation and resolution and also inserted a summary zoom slide.

What decisions will you need to make when creating your next presentation?
Use these guidelines as you complete the assignments in this module and create your own slide show decks outside of this class.

1. **Use secure passwords.** A password should be at least 8 characters and contain a combination of letters, numbers, and other characters. Using both uppercase and lowercase letters is advised. Do not use a password that someone could guess, such as your first or last name, spouse's or child's name, telephone number, birth date, street address, license plate number, or Social Security number. Once you develop this password, write it down in a secure place. Underneath your keyboard is not a secure place, nor is your middle desk drawer. You also can use a password manager program for added security.

2. **Use photographs with sharp focus and contrast.** The adage, "A picture is worth a thousand words," is relevant in a PowerPoint presentation. When your audience can see a visual representation of the concept you are describing during your talk, they are apt to understand and comprehend your message. Be certain your pictures are sharp and clear.

3. **Use hyperlinks to show slides with landscape and portrait orientations.** All slides in one presentation must be displayed in either landscape or portrait orientation. If you want to have variety in your slide show or have pictures or graphics that display best in one orientation, consider using hyperlinks to mix the two orientations during your presentation.

4. **Rehearse, rehearse, rehearse.** Outstanding slides lose their value when the presenter is unprepared to speak. Always keep in mind that the visual aspects are meant to supplement a speaker's verbal message. Practice your presentation before different types of audiences to solicit feedback and use their comments to improve your speaking style.

Apply Your Knowledge

Reinforce the skills and apply the concepts you learned in this module.

Creating a Custom Show and Notes

Note: To complete this assignment, you will be required to use the Data Files. Please contact your instructor for information about accessing the Data Files.

Instructions: Start PowerPoint. Open the presentation called SC_PPT_8-1.pptx, which is located in the Data Files.

The benefits of regular physical exercise coupled with mindfulness and healthy eating have been linked to boosting energy, decreasing stress, and combating health conditions and diseases. Most communities have a variety of gyms and wellness centers for residents, and they vary in cost, amenities, and programs. Your local hospital has an onsite fitness center, and the director wants to inform the community about the programs available for all ages. You have received a PowerPoint presentation with 10 slides, and you need to develop two custom shows and the notes shown in Figure 8–86.

Perform the following tasks:

1. Create a custom slide show with slides 1, 2, 5, 7, and 9.
2. Type **Popular Classes for Everyone** as the new custom show name.
3. Edit the custom show by moving the last slide (5. Fitness for Kids) up below the title slide (Slide 1) and Slide 4 (Personal Training) down to the end of the custom show.
4. Create a second custom show with slides 1, 8, 9, and 10.
5. Type **Classes for Kids** as the new custom show name (Figure 8–86a).
6. Edit the custom show by moving Slide 2 (Family Fitness) down to the end of the custom show.
7. Display the notes master. Change the font to Century Schoolbook and do not display the date.
8. Display the notes page in Landscape orientation and then print the notes pages (Figure 8–86b).
9. Create a handout in Word with notes below the slides. Save the Word file using the file name, **SC_PPT_8_Fitness_Word** (Figure 8–86c).
10. Save Slide 1 as a .jpg picture using the file name, **SC_PPT_8_Fitness_Slide** (Figure 8–86d).
    If requested by your instructor, insert the time of day you were born after the word, Boxing, in the title text placeholder on the last slide.
11. Insert a summary zoom slide with all 10 slides in the presentation. Type **Fitness for Everyone** as the title text for the new slide and then center this text in the placeholder (Figure 8–86e).
12. Check the presentation accessibility and compatibility.
13. Run the presentation using the summary zoom slide to display various slides.
14. Run the presentation showing the two custom slide shows.
15. Save the presentation using the file name, **SC_PPT_8_Fitness**.
16. Submit the presentation in the format specified by your instructor.
17. ✹ Where would a presenter use the two custom shows? What were the Accessibility Checker's inspection results? Did the Compatibility Checker summary display any features not supported by earlier versions of PowerPoint? If so, what were they?

Figure 8–86 (a) Custom Slide Shows

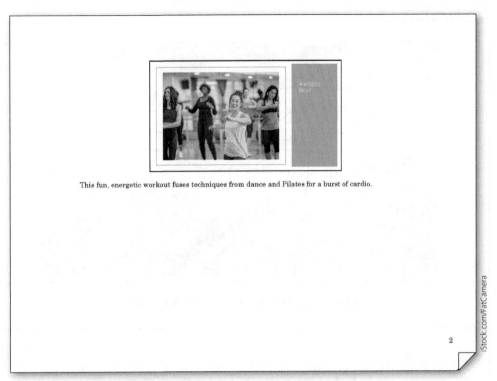

iStock.com/FatCamera

Figure 8–86 (b) Speaker Notes in Landscape Orientation – Page 2

iStock.com/FatCamera

Figure 8–86 (c) Microsoft Word Handout – Page 2

Continued >

Apply Your Knowledge *continued*

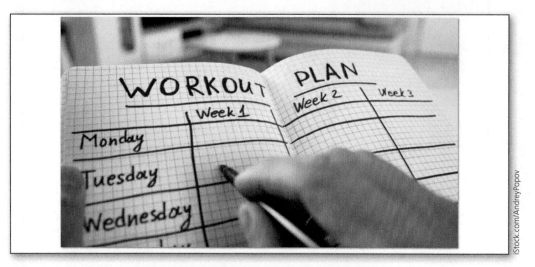

iStock.com/AndreyPopov

Figure 8–86 (d) Slide 1 Saved as a Picture

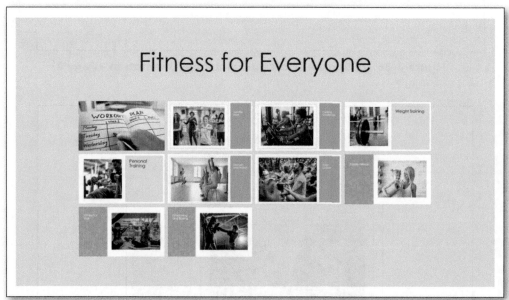

iStock.com/AndreyPopov; iStock.com/FatCamera; iStock.com/skynesher; iStock.com/Pekic; iStock.com/FatCamera; iStock.com/SilviaJansen; iStock.com/skynesher; iStock.com/FatCamera; iStock.com/FatCamera; iStock.com/skynesher

Figure 8–86 (e) Summary Zoom Slide

Extend Your Knowledge

Extend the skills you learned in this module and experiment with new skills. You may need to use Help to complete the assignment.

Inserting, Modifying, and Animating 3D Models

Note: To complete this assignment, you will be required to use the Data Files. Please contact your instructor for information about accessing the Data Files. You will need Internet access and an Office 365 subscription to obtain the 3D models and complete this assignment. If you do not have Internet access and the subscription, read this assignment without performing the instructions.

Instructions: Start PowerPoint. Open the presentation called SC_PPT_8-2.pptx, which is located in the Data Files.

The background of the slide in this presentation is the .jpg file created in this module's project. You will insert two 3D models in this slide and then modify and animate these objects, as shown in Figure 8–87.

Perform the following tasks:

1. Display the Insert tab and then click the 3D Models arrow to display the 3D models menu. Click 'From Online Sources' to display the 'Online 3D Models' dialog box.

2. Click the Animated Animals gallery to view the models and then click the black and white dog (or a similar animal) to place a check mark in that model.

3. Click the Insert button on the search results page to insert the selected dog model on the slide. Resize the dog height to approximately 4.5" and position it near the tree on the left side of the house.

4. With the dog selected, click the Left 3D model view (second model in first row) to turn the dog and have it face the right side of the slide.

5. Display the Animations tab and then change the Delay to 2 seconds.

6. Display the Insert tab, click the 3D Models button, type **bird** in the search box, and then press ENTER to display models. Click the yellow and black bird (or a similar bird) to place a check mark in that model and then click the Insert button.

7. Resize the bird's height to approximately 0.7". Click the 'Above Front Right' 3D model view (fifth view in second row) and then position the bird on a branch in one of the trees on the right side of the house. (*Hint:* Use the ARROW keys to adjust the bird's location.)

8. With the bird selected, display the Animations tab and then click the Swing animation (Animations tab | Animation group). Click the Effect Options button (Animations tab | Animation group) and then click Strong in the Intensity area. Change the Start option to After Previous and the Duration to 10.00 seconds. Click Preview (Animations tab | Preview group) to view the animations.

   If requested by your instructor, add the city in which you were born to the Notes pane.

9. Save the presentation using the file name, **SC_PPT_8_Home_3D**.

10. Submit the revised document in the format specified by your instructor.

11. ✳ In this assignment, you searched for and selected two 3D models. Were these models appropriate for this presentation? Which other models would be suitable? Does the animation add interest to the slide or is it a distraction? What are the advantages and disadvantages of adding 3D models to a slide?

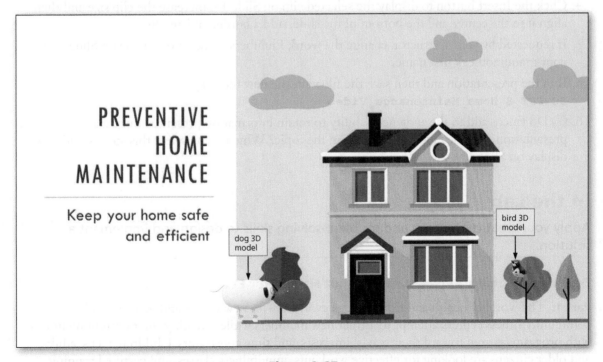

Figure 8–87

Expand Your World

Create a solution that uses cloud or web technologies by learning and investigating on your own from general guidance.

Linking to a YouTube Video

Note: You will need Internet access to complete this assignment. If you do not have Internet access, read this assignment without performing the instructions.

Instructions: You have created a presentation and want to play a video from an online website, such as YouTube or a news or sports organization, as part of your slide show. Some websites encourage users to share video clips, while others restrict users from performing this process. The videos are not downloaded and inserted, or embedded, in the file; instead, they are linked to the presentation so that when the slide show is running and an Internet connection is present, the user can click the Play button to begin watching the video. PowerPoint includes commands on the Insert Video dialog box to insert a video clip from YouTube and from other websites.

Perform the following tasks:

1. Start PowerPoint and then open the SC_PPT_8_Home_Maintenance presentation you created in this module. At the end of the presentation, insert one slide using the Title and Content layout and then type the title text, **Maintenance Advice** on Slide 13.

2. Display the Insert tab and then click the Video button (Insert tab | Media group) to display the Video menu. Click Online Video in the menu to display either the Insert Video or the Online Video dialog box.

3. If the Insert Video box is displayed, click the Search YouTube box, type **Home Maintenance Checklist** as the search text, and then click the Search button (the magnifying glass) or press ENTER. Watch several videos on the website and then select one you desire to link to your PowerPoint presentation. If the Online Video box is displayed, locate a video in your web browser, copy the web address of the webpage from the browser's Address bar, switch back to PowerPoint, and then paste the web address in the Online Video dialog box.

4. Click the Insert button to display the selected clip on Slide 13. Increase the clip size and then align it in the center and the bottom of the slide. Add a border and an effect.

   If requested by your instructor, change the word, Plumbers, in the Notes pane on Slide 3 to your grandmother's first name.

5. Run the presentation and then save the file with the new file name, **SC_PPT_8_Home_Maintenance_Video.**

6. ✳ Do videos add to the audience's ability to retain information presented during a presentation? Do they increase interest in the topic? Why did you select this specific video to display on Slide 13?

In the Lab

Apply your creative thinking and problem-solving skills to design and implement a solution.

Design and Create a Presentation about Fitness for Everyone

Part 1: The world of health and fitness keeps evolving with new trends and gadgets, and community fitness centers attempt to attract new members while retaining their current members with programs geared toward their needs, interests, and time constraints. Children, teens, adults, and older citizens are looking for effective workouts, mindfulness classes, and certified training as part of their wellness regimen. The Apply Your Knowledge exercise in this module featured a presentation with 10 pictures, and these files are available in your Data Files folder. The marketing manager at your community fitness center is creating a new campaign directed toward residents of all ages, and she has asked you to create a PowerPoint photo album highlighting the variety of classes offered.

Perform some research to learn about fitness trends, such as 30-minute workouts, small group training, apps, and strength training. Use the pictures in the Data Files folder and other pictures to create a photo album. Format at least two pictures in the album by changing the contrast and brightness. Add a frame and a theme. Review and revise your presentation as needed and then save the file as a PowerPoint show using the file name, **SC_PPT_8_Fitness_Show**. Submit your assignment in the format specified by your instructor.

Part 2: You made several decisions while creating the presentation in this assignment: what content to include, how to format the album with a frame and theme, and which pictures to format. What was the rationale behind each of these decisions? Where would you recommend distributing this album? When you reviewed the document, what changes did you make?

8 | Working with Trendlines, PivotTables, PivotCharts, and Slicers

Objectives

After completing this module, you will be able to:

- Analyze worksheet data using a trendline
- Create a PivotTable report
- Format a PivotTable report
- Apply filters to a PivotTable report
- Create a PivotChart report
- Format a PivotChart report
- Apply filters to a PivotChart report

- Analyze worksheet data using PivotTable and PivotChart reports
- Create calculated fields
- Create slicers to filter PivotTable and PivotChart reports
- Format slicers
- Examine other statistical and process charts
- Create a Box and Whisker Chart

Introduction

In both academic and business environments, people are presented with large amounts of data that need to be analyzed and interpreted. Data are increasingly available from a wide variety of sources and gathered with ease. Analysis of data and interpretation of the results are important skills to acquire. Learning how to ask questions that identify patterns in data is a skill that can provide businesses and individuals with information that can be used to make decisions about business situations.

Project: Bell & Rodgers Accounting

Bell & Rodgers Accounting is a firm that began six years ago with 50 employees who perform a wide variety of accounting and tax services. They keep records on clients, employees, billable hours, and revenue, among other things. Over the six years, they have hired several more accountants at their two locations in Durante and Jamison.

The owners at Bell & Rodgers are interested in reviewing billable hours for the past six years. They also have requested a comparison of the last two years of revenue figures for the different service types. In this module, you will learn how to use the trendline charting feature in Excel to examine data for trends. You also will analyze revenue data for Bell & Rodgers Accounting using PivotTable and PivotChart reports. The results of this analysis are shown in Figure 8–1.

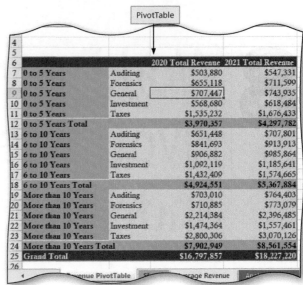

(a) Trendline

(b) PivotTable Report

(c) PivotChart Report

(d) Slicers

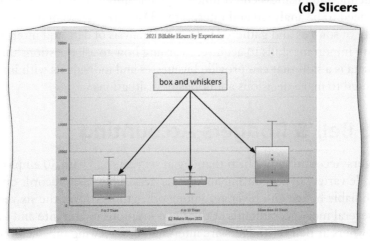

(e) Box and Whisker Chart

Figure 8–1

A **trendline** (Figure 8–1a) is a line that represents the general direction in a series of data. Trendlines often are used to represent changes in one set of data over time. Excel can overlay a trendline on certain types of charts, allowing you to compare changes in one set of data with overall trends.

In addition to trendlines, PivotTable reports and PivotChart reports provide methods to manipulate and visualize data. A **PivotTable report** (Figure 8–1b) is a workbook table designed to create meaningful data summaries that analyze worksheets containing large amounts of data. As an interactive view of worksheet data, a PivotTable report lets users summarize data by selecting and grouping categories. When using a PivotTable report, you can change, or pivot, selected categories quickly without needing to manipulate the worksheet itself. You can examine and analyze several complex arrangements of the data and may spot relationships you might not otherwise see. For example, you can look at years of experience for each employee, broken down by type of accounting service, and then look at the yearly revenue for certain subgroupings without having to reorganize your worksheet.

A **PivotChart report** (Figure 8–1c) is an Excel feature that lets you summarize worksheet data in the form of a chart, and rearrange parts of the chart structure to explore new data relationships. Also called simply PivotCharts, these reports are visual representations of PivotTables. For example, if Bell & Rodgers wanted to view a pie chart showing percentages of total revenue for each service type, a PivotChart could show that percentage categorized by city without having to rebuild the chart from scratch for each view. When you create a PivotChart report, Excel creates and associates a PivotTable with that PivotChart.

Slicers (Figure 8–1d) are graphic objects that you click to filter the data in PivotTables and PivotCharts. Each slicer button clearly identifies its purpose (the applied filter), making it easy to interpret the data displayed in the PivotTable report.

Figure 8–1e displays a box and whisker chart. You will create that chart later in this module as you learn about various kinds of statistical and process charts.

Using trendlines, PivotTables, PivotCharts, slicers, and other charts, a user with little knowledge of formulas, functions, and ranges can perform powerful what-if analyses on a set of data.

Figure 8–2 illustrates the requirements document for the Bell & Rodgers accounting analysis. It includes the needs, source of data, calculations, and other facts about the worksheet's development.

Worksheet Title	Bell & Rodgers Accounting Analysis
Needs	Evaluate different sets of data:
	1. Total billable hours for 2016–2021. Provide a visual representation of billing over the past six years and a forecast for the next two years based on the current trend.
	2. Revenue data for 2020 and 2021 for both locations, with details identifying years of employee experience, accounting type, billable hours, and revenue. For this data, use PivotTables and PivotCharts to look for patterns and anomalies in the data, based on different arrangements of data to discover relationships. Some specific items of interest include Total Revenue and Average Revenue for Employee Experience and Accounting Type by City.
	3. Set up slicers to facilitate easy examination of various subgroupings for users with little or no Excel experience.
	4. Create a box and whisker chart to look at the distribution of numerical data, including the highs and lows for 2021 billable hours by experience.
Calculations	In addition to total revenue for the various groupings, calculations will include product comparisons of average revenue for groupings. Create calculations of the average revenue for various combinations.
Source of Data	The owners will supply the data in the workbook SC_EX_8-1.xlsx.

Figure 8–2

To Start Excel and Open a Workbook

The following steps start Excel and open a workbook named SC_EX_8-1.xlsx. The workbook currently has two worksheets, one showing detailed billing and revenue, named Analysis Figures, and one summarizing the data, named 6-Year Billable Hours.

To complete these steps, you will be required to use the Data Files. Please contact your instructor for information about accessing the Data Files.

1 **sam** ⬇ Start Excel.

2 Open the file named SC_EX_8-1.xlsx from the Data Files.

3 If the Excel window is not maximized, click the Maximize button on its title bar to maximize the window. If necessary, change the magnification to 120%.

4 Save the file on your storage device with the name, SC_EX_8_Bell&RodgersAccountingAnalysis.

Line Charts and Trendlines

A **line chart** is a chart that displays data as lines across categories. A line chart illustrates the amount of change in data over a period of time, or it may compare multiple items. Some line charts contain data points that usually are plotted in evenly spaced intervals to emphasize the relationships between the points. A 2-D line chart has two axes but can contain multiple lines of data, such as two data series over the same period of time. A 3-D line chart may include a third axis, illustrated by depth, to represent the second data series or even a new category.

Using a trendline on certain Excel charts allows you to illustrate the behavior of a set of data to determine if there is a pattern. Trends most often are thought about in terms of how a value changes over time, but trends also can describe the relationship between two variables, such as height and weight. In Excel, you can add a trendline to most types of charts, such as unstacked 2-D area, bar, column, line, inventory, scatter (X, Y), and bubble charts, among others. Chart types that do not examine the relationship between two variables, such as pie and doughnut charts that examine the contribution of different parts to a whole, cannot include trendlines.

How do you determine which trends to analyze?
Before you add a trendline to a chart, you need to determine which data series to analyze. If the chart displays only one data series, Excel uses it automatically. If the chart involves more than one data series, you select the one you want to use as a trendline. Then you can analyze current or future trends.

To analyze a current trend, make sure you have enough data available for the period you want to analyze. For example, two years of annual sales totals might not provide enough data to analyze sales performance. Five years of annual sales totals or two years of monthly sales totals are more likely to present a trend.

To analyze a future trend, you use a trendline to project data beyond the values or scope of the data set in a process called forecasting. **Forecasting** is an analysis tool that helps predict data values that are outside of a data set. For example, if a data set is for a 10-year period and the data show a trend in that 10-year period, Excel can predict values beyond that period or estimate what the values may have been before that period.

When you add a trendline to a chart, you can set the number of periods to forecast forward or backward in time. For example, if you have six years of sales data, you can forecast two periods forward to show the trend for eight years: six years of current data and two years of projected data. You also can display information about the trendline on the chart itself to help guide your analysis. For example, you can display the equation used to calculate the trend and show the **R-squared value**, which is a number from 0 to 1 that measures the strength of the trend. An R-squared value of 1 means the estimated values in the trendline correspond exactly to the actual data.

To Create a 2-D Line Chart

Why? *Line charts are suited to charting a variable, in this case billable hours, over a number of time periods.* The following steps create a 2-D line chart of the Bell & Rodgers billing data. You will add a trendline to the chart later in the module.

- If necessary, click the '6-Year Billable Hours' sheet tab.
- Select cells A4:G5 to select the range to be charted (Figure 8–3).

Figure 8–3

- Click Insert on the ribbon to display the Insert tab.
- Click the 'Insert Line or Area Chart' button (Insert tab | Charts group) to display the Insert Line and Area Chart gallery (Figure 8–4).

Figure 8–4

3

- Click 'Line with Markers' in the 2-D Line area to insert a 2-D line chart with data markers (Figure 8–5).

Q&A

What are data markers?
A data marker is the symbol in a chart that represents a single value from a worksheet cell. In this case, the data markers are circles that represent the six years of billable hours.

Why do the selected cells appear with colored fill?
Excel uses colors to identify chart elements when preparing to create a chart. In this case, the red cell is the chart title, the purple cells are the x-axis or category values (in this case, years), and the blue cells are the data or values.

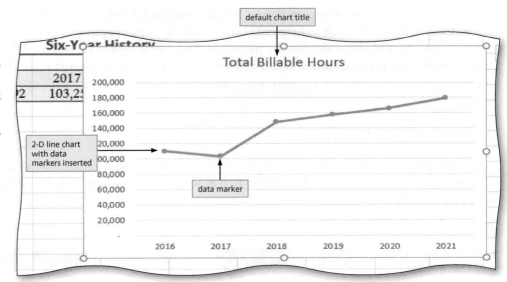

Figure 8–5

4

- If necessary, display the Chart Tools Design tab.

- Click the Move Chart button (Chart Tools Design tab | Location group) to display the Move Chart dialog box.

- Click New sheet (Move Chart dialog box) to select the option button.

- If necessary, double-click the default text in the New sheet box to select the text, and then type **Trendline Chart** to enter a name for the new worksheet (Figure 8–6).

5

- Click OK (Move Chart dialog box) to move the chart to a new worksheet.

Figure 8–6

Other Ways

1. Click Quick Analysis button, click Charts tab, click Line button

To Format a 2-D Line Chart

You can format 2-D line charts by editing various chart elements, changing the style or color of the chart, or formatting the data series. In the following steps you will edit the title, format the y-axis, and change the chart style. **Why?** *Customizing the chart will make the data easier to read.* You also will change the **bounds** of the chart axis, which are the beginning or ending values on an axis.

- Click the chart title.

- Edit the title to read **Total Billable Hours 2016 – 2021** to enter the new chart title.

- Bold the text (Figure 8–7).

Figure 8–7

- Double-click the y-axis to display the Format Axis pane.

- If necessary, click the Axis Options tab.

- In the Minimum box (Axis Options area), type **100000** and then press ENTER to set a lower value for the y-axis (Figure 8–8).

Q&A

Why should I change the minimum value?

If you adjust the minimum value to a position slightly below the lowest data point, you will have less white space in your chart, making it more legible. Be aware, however, that trends represented in line charts may appear exaggerated when the lowest data point is not zero. Do not change the value if you are confident your data will change.

What is the purpose of the Reset button?

When you click the Reset button, Excel automatically adjusts the lower bounds to back to zero.

Figure 8–8

3

- Display the Chart Tools Design tab if necessary.

- Click the More button (Chart Tools Design tab | Chart Styles group) to display the Chart Styles Gallery (Figure 8–9).

Q&A What is the purpose of the Chart Styles button on the chart?
The Chart Styles button on the chart displays the same styles as on the ribbon, as well as a Color gallery from which you may choose.

Figure 8–9

4

- Click Style 14 if necessary to choose a chart style (Figure 8–10).

Q&A What is the difference between a theme and style?
Both formatting options change the color, fonts, effects, and overall look and feel. A theme changes your entire workbook. A style only affects a specific element in a worksheet; for example, a chart style might change the graph lines from horizontal to vertical.

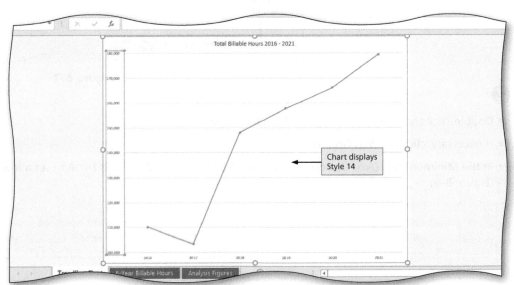

Figure 8–10

To Add a Trendline to a Chart

The following steps add a trendline to the Total Billable Hours 2016 – 2021 chart. *Why? You add a trendline to a chart to analyze current and/or future trends. A trendline can only be added to an existing chart.* The chart will predict the billable hours two years beyond the data set in the six-year figures worksheet.

- Click the 'Add Chart Element' button (Chart Tools Design tab | Chart Layouts group) to display the Add Chart Element menu.

- Point to Trendline to display the Trendline gallery (Figure 8–11).

Figure 8–11

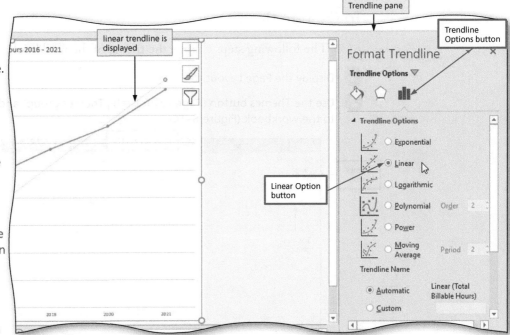

- Click 'More Trendline Options' (Trendline gallery) to display the Format Trendline pane.

- If necessary, click the Trendline Options button.

- If necessary, click Linear in the Trendline Options area to select a linear trendline type (Figure 8–12).

Q&A Why should I select the Linear option button in this case?
The 2-D line chart you created is a basic line chart, so it is appropriate to apply a linear trendline, which shows values that are increasing or decreasing at a steady rate.

My trendline runs off the chart. Did I do something wrong?
It may be that your chart did not adjust the bounds automatically. Right-click the vertical axis, click Format Axis on the shortcut menu, and then click the upper bounds Reset button.

Figure 8–12

③

- If necessary, scroll down in the Format Trendline pane until the Forecast area is visible.
- Select the text in the Forward box, type **2.0**, and press ENTER to add a trendline to the chart with a two-period forward forecast.

Q&A
What does it mean to enter a two-period forward forecast?
A two-period forward forecast estimates the values for the two time periods that follow the data you used to create the line chart. In this case, it will estimate total billable hours for the next two years.

- Click the 'Display R-squared value on chart' check box to display the R-squared value on the chart (Figure 8–13).

Q&A
What is the R-squared value?
The R-squared value is a measure of how well the trendline describes the relationship between total billable hours and time. The closer the value is to 1, the more accurate the trendline.

Figure 8–13

④

- Click the Close button (Format Trendline pane) to close the pane.

Other Ways

1. Right-click graphed line, click Add Trendline on shortcut menu

To Change the Theme

The following steps change the theme of the workbook.

1 Display the Page Layout tab.

2 Use the Themes button (Page Layout tab | Themes group) and apply the Slate theme to the workbook (Figure 8–14).

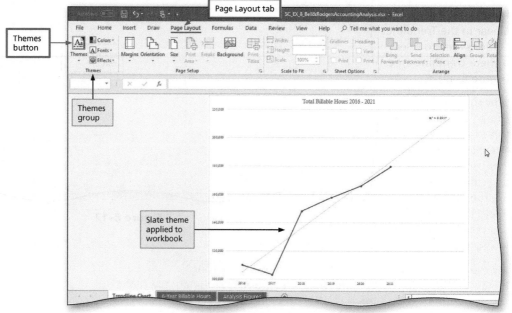

Figure 8–14

More about Trendlines

It is important to take note of the axes when looking at trendlines. Charts with trendlines are often reformatted to start the vertical axis at a number other than zero, particularly when the values on the vertical axis are high. When interpreting a trendline, you should look at the vertical axis to see if it starts at zero. If it does not, be aware that trends represented by the trendline may appear exaggerated. Figure 8–15 shows a chart with a trendline that uses the same data as the chart in Figure 8–14. The difference between the two charts is in the vertical axis, which starts at zero in Figure 8–15 and at 100,000 in Figure 8–14. The difference between the projected values for 2020 and 2021 appears much larger in Figure 8–14 where the axis starts at 100,000. When looking at charts, always check the axes to be sure that the differences shown in the chart are not being overstated visually.

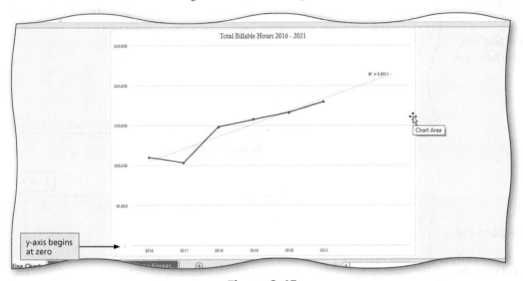

Figure 8–15

To Change the Format of a Data Point

The following steps change the format of the 2018 data point. *Why? When graphing data, you may want to call visual attention to a particular data point or points.*

1

- Slowly click the 2018 data point twice to select the single point. Do not double-click.

- Right-click the selected data point to display the shortcut menu (Figure 8–16).

Figure 8–16

- Click 'Format Data Point' on the shortcut menu to display the Format Data Point pane.
- Click the 'Fill & Line' button (Format Data Point pane) to display the Fill & Line options.
- Click Marker, and then if necessary, click Marker Options to expand the section.
- Click the Built-in option button to enable changes to the data point (Figure 8–17).
- Select the contents of the Size box, and then type **12** as the new size.

Figure 8–17

- If necessary, click Fill to expand the Fill section.
- Click the Color button and then click 'Black, Text 1' in the Standard Colors area to change the color of the data point to black.
- Click away from the data point to view the change (Figure 8–18).
- Close the Format Data Point pane and click the Save button (Quick Access Toolbar) to save the workbook with the same name in the same location.

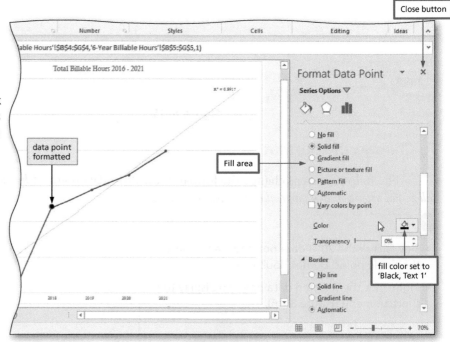

Figure 8–18

Break Point: If you want to take a break, this is a good place to do so. You can exit Excel now. To resume later, start Excel, open the file called SC_EX_8_Bell&RodgersAccountingAnalysis.xlxs, and continue following the steps from this location forward.

Creating and Formatting PivotTable Reports

A PivotTable report, also called a PivotTable, is an interactive tool that summarizes worksheet data. It uses filter buttons in the cells and a pane to change the way the data is presented without changing any of the original data. Normally, when working with data tables or lists of data, each different reorganization of the data requires a new table or list. In contrast, you can reorganize data and examine summaries in a PivotTable report with a few clicks. PivotTable reports allow you to view different summaries of the data quickly and easily, using just a single table.

When creating a PivotTable report, you can use categories in the data to summarize different groups or totals. PivotTables use two types of fields: data fields, which contain values that the PivotTable will summarize, and category fields, which describe the data by categorizing it. Category fields typically correspond to columns in the original data, and data fields correspond to summary values across categories. You can change row and column groupings quickly to summarize the data in different ways or to ask new questions. Reorganizing the table reveals different levels of detail and allows you to analyze specific subgroups.

One PivotTable created in this project is shown in Figure 8–19. It summarizes the Bell & Rodgers data to show the total revenue and average revenue in 2020 and 2021 for each level of experience by accounting type (Auditing, Forensics, General, Investment, and Taxes). The filter button in cell A4 filters the results by experience, and the filter button in cell B4 filters the results by accounting type. Columns C and D show the values for the total revenue in 2020 and 2021, and columns E and F show the values for the average revenue in 2020 and 2021.

BTW

Selecting PivotTable Ranges

When creating PivotTables, you can click anywhere in the range that contains the data. You do not have to select the range.

Figure 8–19

CONSIDER THIS

How do you determine which fields to use in a PivotTable?

You can create PivotTable and PivotChart reports in almost any configuration of your existing data. To use this powerful tool effectively, you need to create these reports with various questions in mind. Look at the categories you can use to describe your data and think about how the various categories can interact. Common questions relate to how the data changes over time and how the data varies in geographical locations, such as states or regions, different functional groups within an organization, different product groupings, and demographic groupings, such as age and gender.

To Create a Blank PivotTable

The following steps create a blank PivotTable report using the ribbon. *Why? Creating a blank PivotTable allows you to create a framework within which to analyze the available data.* When you create a PivotTable, each column heading from your original data will represent a field accessible via the Field List (formerly called the PivotTable Fields task pane).

- Click the Analysis Figures sheet tab to make the worksheet active.

- Click cell B3 to select a cell containing data for the PivotTable.

- Display the Insert tab.

Experiment

- Click the Recommended PivotTables button (Insert tab | Tables group). Scroll down the list to view the various ways the data might be represented as a PivotTable. Click Cancel (Recommend PivotTables dialog box) to continue.

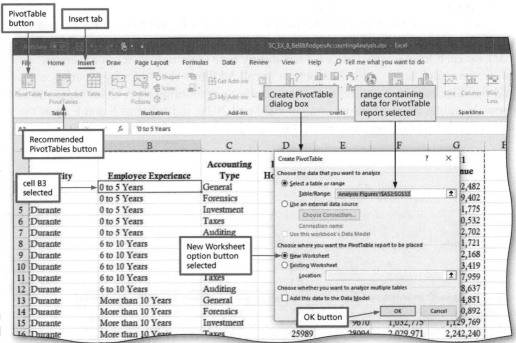

Figure 8–20

- Click the PivotTable button (Insert tab | Tables group) to display the Create PivotTable dialog box (Figure 8–20).

 ❷

- Click OK (Create PivotTable dialog box) to create a blank PivotTable report on a new worksheet and display the Field List (Figure 8–21).

Q&A

Why is the PivotTable blank?

When you create a PivotTable, you first create the structure. The resulting PivotTable is blank until you add fields to it, which you will do in the next set of steps.

My Field List just disappeared. What happened?

If you click outside of the PivotTable, the pane no longer will appear. To redisplay the pane, click in the PivotTable.

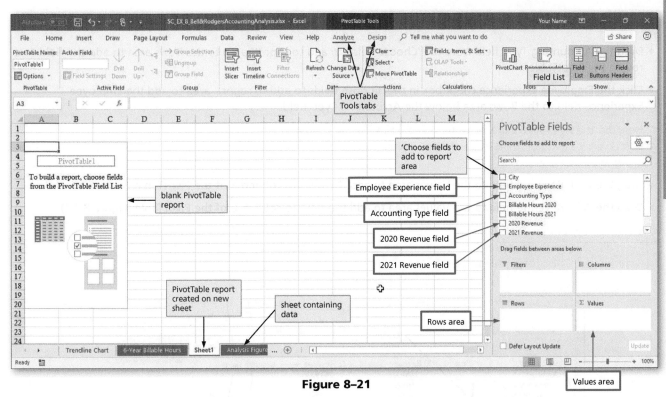

Figure 8–21

Other Ways

1. Click cell in range, click Recommended PivotTables (Insert tab | Tables group), click Blank PivotTable button (Recommended PivotTables dialog box), click OK

To Add Data to the PivotTable

Why? Once the blank PivotTable is created, it needs to be populated using any or all of the fields in the Field List. You can add data by selecting check boxes in the Field List or by dragging fields from the Choose fields area to the one of the four boxed areas in the lower part of the pane. Once you add a field, it becomes a button in the pane, with its own button menu. Table 8–1 describes the four areas in the Field List and their common usage.

Table 8–1 Field Areas in the PivotTable Fields Pane

Areas	Use
Filters	Fields added to the Filters area create a report filter and filter button in the PivotTable, representing a subset that meets a selection criterion.
Columns	Normally, Excel creates a field in the Columns area when multiple fields are dragged to the Values area. Fields directly added to the Columns fields should contain summary numeric data.
Rows	Fields added to the Rows area become rows in the PivotTable. Subsequent fields added to the Rows area become subsets of the first field.
Values	Fields added to the Values area must contain numeric data from the source data.

The following step adds data to the PivotTable. The rows will show the accounting type and, within that, the years of employee experience. As you add the 2020 Total Revenue and 2021 Total Revenue fields to the Values area, Excel will create columns.

1

- Drag the Accounting Type field from the 'Choose fields to add to report' area to the Rows area to add the field to a row in the PivotTable.

- Click the Employee Experience check box in the 'Choose fields to add to report' area to add the Employee Experience field to the Rows area below the Accounting Type field.

Q&A How did the Employee Experience field end up in the Rows area?
Excel places a checked field in the group it determines is correct for that field. You can drag the field to a different group if you choose.

- Drag the 2020 Revenue field to the Values area to add the field to column B of the PivotTable.

- Drag the 2021 Revenue field to the Values area to add the field to column C of the PivotTable (Figure 8–22).

Q&A What is shown in the PivotTable?
Excel displays the Accounting Type and Employee Experience fields as rows in the PivotTable. The 2020 Total Revenue and 2021 Total Revenue display as columns.

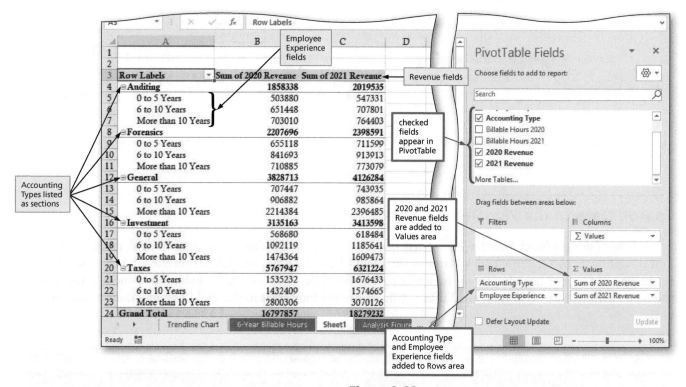

Figure 8–22

Other Ways

1. Click check box for each field name (Field List)

To Change the Layout of a PivotTable

You can display a PivotTable in one of three layouts; however, sometimes you may want to change the layout. *Why? When using multiple row labels, a different layout can make identifying the groups and subgroups easier for the reader.* By default, PivotTable reports are presented in a compact layout. The following steps change the layout of the PivotTable report to the tabular layout and then add item labels to all rows. The tabular layout will display totals below each accounting type.

- If necessary, display the PivotTable Tools Design tab.

- Click the Report Layout button (PivotTable Tools Design tab | Layout group) to display the Report Layout menu (Figure 8–23).

Figure 8–23

- Click 'Show in Tabular Form' to display the PivotTable report in a tabular format (Figure 8–24).

Experiment

- Click all the layout options to review the differences in the layout. When done, click 'Show in Tabular Form' once again.

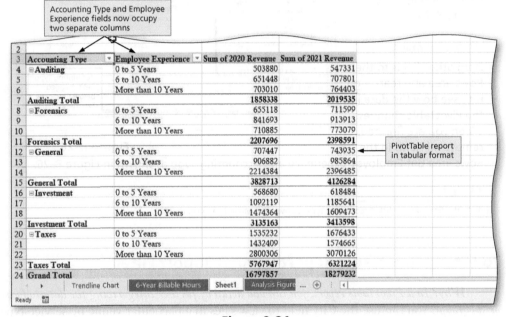

Accounting Type	Employee Experience	Sum of 2020 Revenue	Sum of 2021 Revenue
Auditing	0 to 5 Years	503880	547331
	6 to 10 Years	651448	707801
	More than 10 Years	703010	764403
Auditing Total		1858338	2019535
Forensics	0 to 5 Years	655118	711599
	6 to 10 Years	841693	913913
	More than 10 Years	710885	773079
Forensics Total		2207696	2398591
General	0 to 5 Years	707447	743935
	6 to 10 Years	906882	985864
	More than 10 Years	2214384	2396485
General Total		3828713	4126284
Investment	0 to 5 Years	568680	618484
	6 to 10 Years	1092119	1185641
	More than 10 Years	1474364	1609473
Investment Total		3135163	3413598
Taxes	0 to 5 Years	1535232	1676433
	6 to 10 Years	1432409	1574665
	More than 10 Years	2800306	3070126
Taxes Total		5767947	6321224
Grand Total		16797857	18279232

Figure 8–24

- Click the Report Layout button (PivotTable Tools Design tab | Layout group) again, and then click 'Repeat All Item Labels' to display Accounting Type labels for all Employee Experience entries (Figure 8–25).

Experiment

- Point to any cell in column C or D to see the ScreenTip that displays information about the value.

Accounting Type	Employee Experience	Sum of 2020 Revenue	Sum of 2021 Revenue
Auditing	0 to 5 Years	503880	547331
Auditing	6 to 10 Years	651448	707801
Auditing	More than 10 Years	703010	764403
Auditing Total		1858338	2019535
Forensics	0 to 5 Years	655118	711599
Forensics	6 to 10 Years	841693	913913
Forensics	More than 10 Years	710885	773079
Forensics Total		2207696	2398591
General	0 to 5 Years	707447	743935
General	6 to 10 Years	906882	985864
General	More than 10	2214384	2396485
General Total		3828713	4126284
Investment	0 to 5 Years	568680	618484
Investment	6 to 10 Years	1092119	1185641
Investment	More than 10 Years	1474364	1609473
Investment Total		3135163	3413598
Taxes	0 to 5 Years	1535232	1676433
Taxes	6 to 10 Years	1432409	1574665
Taxes	More than 10 Years	2800306	3070126
Taxes Total		5767947	6321224
Grand Total		16797857	18279232

Figure 8–25

To Change the View of a PivotTable Report

If you use the sort and summary features in Excel, comparing the revenue for each service type and region would require many steps. With PivotTable reports, this comparison is accomplished quickly. The PivotTable report in the SC_EX_8_Bell&RodgersAccountingAnalysis workbook currently shows the sum of the revenue for each year by accounting type and then by employee experience. (See Figure 8–25.) The following step changes the view of the PivotTable. *Why? You decide to show the total revenue by level of experience for each accounting type.*

- In the Rows area (Field List), drag the Accounting Type button below the Employee Experience button to group total sales by Employee Experience (rather than by Accounting Type) (Figure 8–26).

 Experiment

- Drag other fields to the Rows area and rearrange it to see how the data in the PivotTable changes. When you are finished, remove all fields in the Rows area but Employee Experience and Accounting Type as shown in Figure 8–26.

Figure 8–26

Other Ways

1. In the Rows area, click Accounting Type arrow, click Move Down on menu

To Filter a PivotTable Report Using a Report Filter

Why? In a PivotTable report, you can add detail by further categorizing the data to focus on a particular subgroup or subgroups. You can use the City field to view sales in a particular venue by service type and region. Viewing a PivotTable report for a subset of data that meets a selection criterion is known as filtering. The following steps add a report filter to change the view of the PivotTable and then filter the PivotTable by City.

1

- Drag the City field from the 'Choose fields to add to report' area (Field List) to the Filters area to create a report filter in the PivotTable (Figure 8–27).

Figure 8–27

- Click the filter button in cell B1 to display the filter menu for column B, City in this case.

- Click Durante on the filter menu to select the Durante criterion (Figure 8–28).

filter button

	A	B	C	D	E	F	G
1	City	(All)					
2							
3	Employe	Search	um of 2020 Revenue	Sum of 2021 Revenue			
4	⊟0 to 5	(All)	503880	547331			
5	0 to 5	Durante	655118	711599			
6	0 to 5	Jamison	707447	743935			
7	0 to 5		568680	618484			
8	0 to 5		1535232	1676433			
9	0 to 5 Ye		3970357	4297782			
10	⊟6 to 10		651448	707801			
11	6 to 10		841693	913913			
12	6 to 10		906882	985864			
13	6 to 10	☐ Select Multiple Items	1092119	1185641			
14	6 to 10		1432409	1574665			
15	6	OK Cancel	4924551	5367884			
16	⊟More than 10 Years	Auditing	703010	764403			
17	More than 10 Years	Forensics	710885	773079			

Durante filter option

OK button

Figure 8–28

- Click OK to display totals for Durante only (Figure 8–29).

Q&A

What is shown now in the PivotTable report?
Now the PivotTable shows total revenue for each level of experience and accounting type for Durante only.

applied filter is displayed

filter button shows filter is applied

	A	B	C	D	E	F	G
1	City	Durante					
2							
3	Employee Experience	Accounting Type	Sum of 2020 Revenue	Sum of 2021 Revenue			
4	⊟0 to 5 Years	Auditing	389183	422702			
5	0 to 5 Years	Forensics	487179	529402			
6	0 to 5 Years	General	462891	502482			
7	0 to 5 Years	Investment	424464	461775			
8	0 to 5 Years	Taxes	857550	940532			
9	0 to 5 Years Total		2621267	2856893			
10	⊟6 to 10 Years	Auditing	182687	198637			
11	6 to 10 Years	Forensics	398080	432168			
12	6 to 10 Years	General	507329	551721			
13	6 to 10 Years	Investment	583512	633419			
14	6 to 10 Years	Taxes	882856	977959			
15	6 to 10 Years Total		2554464	2793904			
16	⊟More than 10 Years	Auditing	398363	433167			
17	More than 10 Years	Forensics	350261	380892			
18	More than 10 Years	General	1578500	1714851			
19	More than 10 Years	Investment	1032775	1129769			
20	More than 10 Years	Taxes	2029971	2242240			
21	More than 10 Years Total		5389870	5900919			
22	Grand Total		10565601	11551716			
23							

PivotTable displays revenue for employee experience then by service type for Durante only

Figure 8–29

To Filter a PivotTable Report Using Multiple Selection Criteria

Why? *You may need to identify a subset that is defined by more than one filter criterion.* The following steps change the filter field and select multiple criteria on which to filter.

1

- Drag the Accounting Type button from the Rows area to the Filters area.

- Drag the City button from the Filters area to the Rows area below Employee Experience (Figure 8–30).

Q&A

What does the PivotTable now show?
Excel now filters the entire report by Accounting type and does not show that as a detail line within the report.

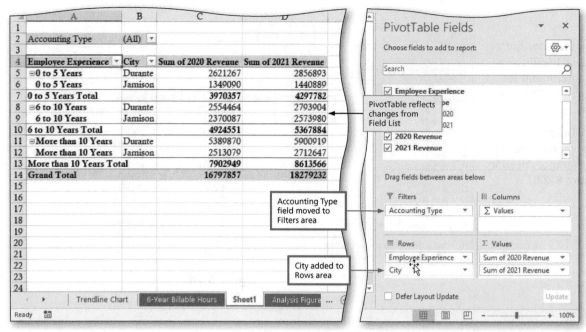

Figure 8–30

2

- Click the filter button in cell B2 to display the filter menu for the Accounting Type field.

- Click the 'Select Multiple Items' check box to prepare to select multiple criteria.

- Click to remove the check mark in each of the Auditing, Forensics, and Investment check boxes to deselect these criteria and leave only the General and Taxes service plans selected (Figure 8–31).

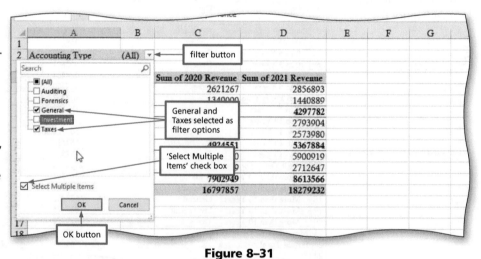

Figure 8–31

3

- Click OK to display revenue totals for General and Taxes accounting types in the cities of Durante and Jamison (Figure 8–32).

Q&A
How do I know which criteria have been selected?
With a multiple item filter, you need to click the filter button to see which criteria have been selected.

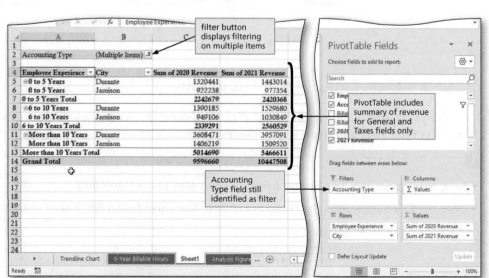

Figure 8–32

To Remove a Report Filter from a PivotTable Report

Why? *When you no longer need to display filtered data in a PivotTable, you can remove the filter easily.* The following step removes the Accounting Type report filter from the PivotTable report.

- Click the filter button in cell B2 and then click the (All) check box to include all service type criteria in the PivotTable report.

- Click OK.

- Drag the Accounting Type button out of the Filters area (Field List) to remove the field from the PivotTable report (Figure 8–33).

Q&A Should I drag it to a specific location?
No. You can drag it out of the box to any blank area on the worksheet.

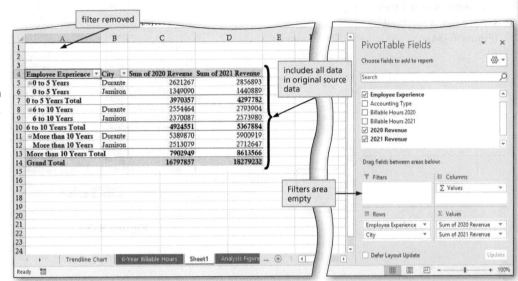

Figure 8–33

To Remove and Add Data to the PivotTable Report

The following steps remove the City field from the Rows area and add the Accounting Type field.

1 In the Field List, drag the City button out of the Rows area to remove the field from the report.

2 Click the Accounting Type check box in the 'Choose fields to add to report' area to add the Accounting Type field to the Rows area below the Employee Experience field.

To Filter a PivotTable Report Using the Row Label Filter

Report filters are added to the PivotTable report by adding a field to the Filters area of the Field List. **Why?** *In a PivotTable report, you may want to look at a subset of data based on fields that are already in use.* When the field of interest is already part of the PivotTable and included in the Rows area of the Field List, you can use row label filters to view a subset of the data. Like other filter buttons, row label filters display within the column heading. When you click the filter button, Excel displays a menu of available fields. The following steps use a row label filter for Accounting Type to restrict data in the PivotTable to the General and Taxes accounting types.

- Click the filter button in cell B4 to display the filter menu for the Accounting Type field.

Q&A I do not have a filter button in cell B4. How do I access the filter?
The filter buttons may be hidden. Click the Field Headers button (PivotTable Tools Analyze tab | Show group) to turn on the field headers and make the filter buttons visible.

Why does cell B4 not appear selected when I use the filter button?
Filtering happens independently of cell selection. You do not need to select the cell in which the filter button is located in order to use the filter.

- Click the Auditing, Forensics, and Investment check boxes on the filter menu to leave only the General and Taxes service plans selected (Figure 8–34).

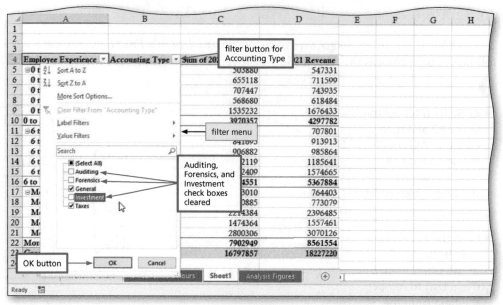

Figure 8–34

2

- Click OK to display totals for General and Taxes only, categorized by experience (Figure 8–35).

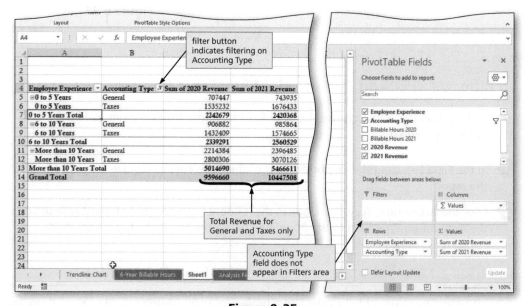

Figure 8–35

To Clear the Filter

Why? *Once you have reviewed the subset of data, you may want to remove the criteria using the Row Label filter to display all records.* The following steps clear the filter in order to display all records.

1

- Click the filter button in cell B4 again to display the filter menu for the Accounting Type field (Figure 8–36).

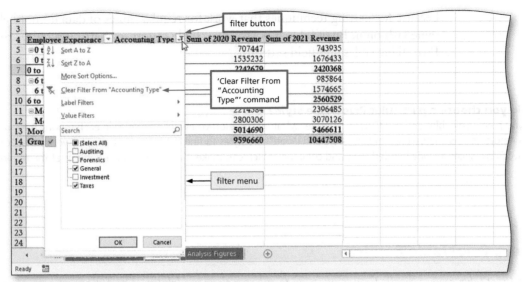

Figure 8–36

②

- Click 'Clear Filter From "Accounting Type"' on the filter menu to display totals for all service types in all regions (Figure 8–37).

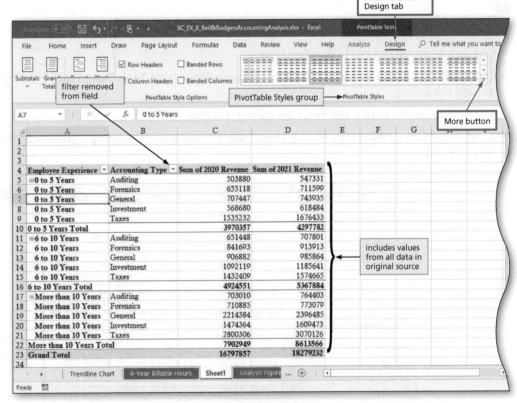

Figure 8–37

Other Ways

1. Click filter button, click (Select All) check box on filter menu, click OK

Formatting PivotTable Reports

You can use several formatting options to enhance the appearance of PivotTable reports and make the content easier to read. Excel includes a number of preset PivotTable report styles to simplify this task. These styles function in a similar fashion to the Excel table styles. Take care when formatting PivotTable reports, however, because formatting techniques that work for regular tables of data do not behave in the same fashion in PivotTable reports. PivotTable report formatting requires the use of PivotTable styles and field settings.

CONSIDER THIS

How do you choose a particular PivotTable style?

When you plan PivotTables and PivotCharts, consider what information you want to display in each report. As you are developing a report, review the galleries of PivotTable and PivotChart styles to find the best one to display your data. For example, some PivotTable styles include banded rows and columns, which can make it easier to scan and interpret the report.

To Format a PivotTable Report

Why? *PivotTable reports benefit from formatting to enhance their readability.* The following steps format a PivotTable report by applying a PivotTable style and specifying number formats for the fields.

1

- Name the Sheet1 tab, **Revenue PivotTable**, and set the color to Tan, Accent 2.
- Click cell A7 to select a cell in the PivotTable.
- Click the More button in the PivotTable Styles group (PivotTable Tools Design tab | PivotTable Styles group) to expand the gallery.
- Scroll down until the Dark section of the gallery is visible.
- Point to 'Dark Gray, Pivot Style Dark 9' (PivotTable Styles gallery) to display a preview of the style in the PivotTable (Figure 8–38).

Figure 8–38

- Click 'Dark Gray, Pivot Style Dark 9' in the PivotTable Styles gallery to apply the style to the PivotTable report.

- Right-click cell C6 and then click Number Format on the shortcut menu to display the Format Cells dialog box.

- Click Currency in the Category list (Format Cells dialog box) to select the Currency number format.

Figure 8–39

- Type 0 in the Decimal places box to specify no decimal places (Figure 8–39).

Q&A Can I use the formatting options on the Home tab?
Yes, but you would have to highlight all of the cells first and then apply the formatting. The Number Format command is easier.

- Click OK to apply the Currency style with no decimal places to all 2020 revenue values in the PivotTable report.

Q&A Why does the number format change apply to all Revenue values?
In a PivotTable, when you format a single cell using Number Format, that formatting is applied to the entire set of values to which that single cell belongs.

- Right-click cell D6 and then apply the Currency number format with zero decimal places to all 2021 revenue values.

- Click cell E24 to deselect the PivotTable report.

- Click the Save button on the Quick Access Toolbar to save the workbook (Figure 8–40).

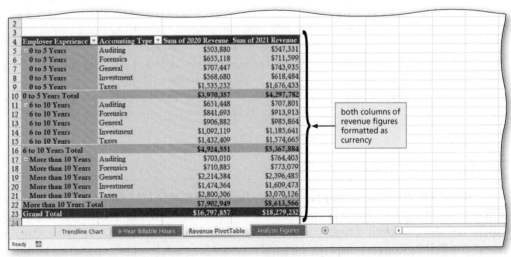

Figure 8–40

Break Point: If you want to take a break, this is a good place to do so. You can exit Excel now. To resume later, start Excel, open the file called SC_EX_8_Bell&RodgersAccountingAnalysis, and continue following the steps from this location forward.

Summary Functions

In PivotTable reports, you easily can change the **summary function**, the function that determines the type of calculation applied to PivotTable data, such as SUM or COUNT. For example, in Figure 8–40, the data is totaled for 2020 and 2021 using a SUM function. You can change that to other summary functions. Summary functions can be inserted in one of three ways: by using the shortcut menu of a cell in the PivotTable, by using the field button menu in the Values area (Field List), or by using the Field Settings button (PivotTable Tools Analyze tab | Active Field group).

Table 8–2 lists the summary functions Excel provides for analysis of data in PivotTable reports. These functions also apply to PivotChart Reports.

Table 8–2 Summary Functions for PivotTable Report and PivotChart Report Data Analysis	
Summary Function	**Description**
Sum	Sum of the values (default function for numeric source data)
Count	Number of data values
Average	Average of the values
Max	Largest value
Min	Smallest value
Product	Product of the values
Count Numbers	Number of data values that contain numeric data
StdDev.s	Estimate of the standard deviation of all of the data to be summarized, used when data is a sample of a larger population of interest
StdDev.p	Standard deviation of all of the data to be summarized, used when data is the entire population of interest
Var.s	Estimate of the variance of all of the data to be summarized, used when data is a sample of a larger population of interest
Var.p	Variance of the data to be summarized, used when data is the entire population of interest

To Switch Summary Functions

Why? *The default summary function in a PivotTable is the SUM function.* For some comparisons, using a different summary function will yield more useful measures. In addition to analyzing the total revenue by experience and accounting type, you are interested in looking at average revenue. Currently, the PivotTable report for Bell & Rodgers displays the total revenue for each level of experience by accounting type. Average revenue by accounting type and then by experience might be a better measure for comparing the revenue. The following steps switch summary functions in a PivotTable using the shortcut menu.

1

- Right-click cell C5 to display the shortcut menu and then point to 'Summarize Values By' to display the Summarize Values By submenu (Figure 8–41).

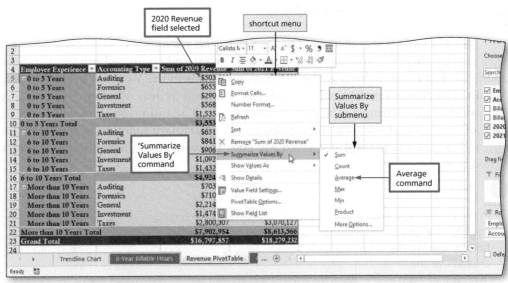

Figure 8–41

2

- Click Average on the Summarize Values By submenu to change the summary function from Sum to Average (Figure 8–42).

Q&A Why did the column title in cell C4 change? When you change a summary function, the column heading automatically updates to reflect the new summary function chosen.

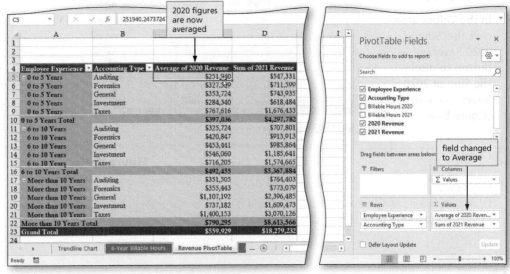

Figure 8–42

3

- Repeat Steps 1 and 2 to change the summary function used in column D from Sum to Average (Figure 8–43).

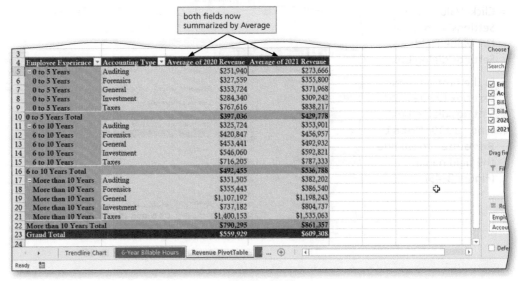

Figure 8–43

To Insert a New Summary Function

Why? *In addition to changing summary functions, you may need to add new fields to analyze additional or more complex questions.* You have been asked to review and compare both total and average sales for 2020 and 2021. Earlier you changed the two Revenue fields in the Values area (Field List) to display averages. Because you now want the totals as well, you will need to drag another copy of the two Revenue fields to the Values area, creating a total of four sets of data. The following steps add a second value calculation for each of the two years and use these fields to add a summary function in the PivotTable report. This time, you will use the menu displayed when you click the value field button to access the Value Field Settings dialog box.

- In the Field List, drag the 2020 Revenue field to the Values area above the 'Average of 2020 Revenue' button to add a third field to the PivotTable.

- In the Values area, click the 'Sum of 2020 Revenue' button to display the Sum of 2020 Revenue menu (Figure 8–44).

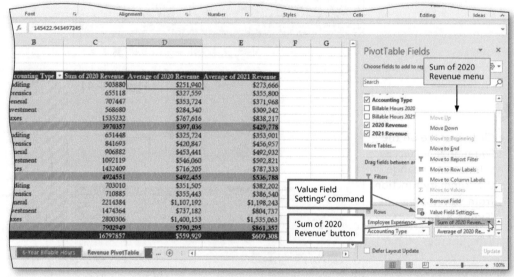

Figure 8–44

Q&A

Why did I place the new field above the other items in the Values area?

Dragging the new field to a location above the other fields will place the data in a new column before the others in the PivotTable report, in this case in column C.

- Click 'Value Field Settings' to display the Value Field Settings dialog box.

- In the Custom Name text box (Value Field Settings dialog box), type `2020 Total Revenue` to change the field name (Figure 8–45).

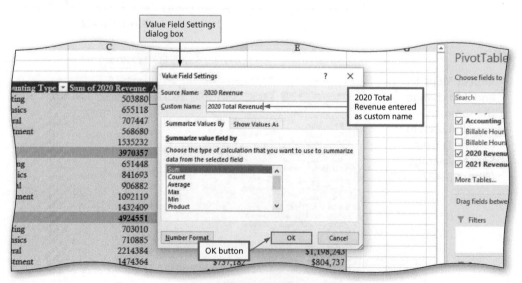

Figure 8–45

3

- Click OK (Value Field Settings dialog box) to apply the custom name.

- In the Field List, drag the 2021 Revenue field to the Values area to add a fourth field. Place it between the '2020 Total Revenue' button and the 'Average of 2020 Revenue' button.

- In the Values area, click the 'Sum of 2021 Revenue' button to display its menu, and then click 'Value Field Settings' to display the Value Field Settings dialog box.

- In the Custom Name text box, type `2021 Total Revenue` and then click OK (Value Field Settings dialog box) to rename the field.

- Using the buttons in the Values area, rename the other two fields to customize the column headings in cells E4 and F4 as shown in Figure 8–46.

- Using the shortcut menu, format the values in columns C and then D to the Currency category, 0 decimal places, and the $ symbol (Figure 8–46).

Q&A

How many items should I have in the Values area now?
You can use the scroll buttons in the Values area to see the four fields: 2020 Total Revenue, 2021 Total Revenue, 2020 Average Revenue, and 2021 Average Revenue.

My format change did not change all of the cells. What did I do wrong?
You may have formatted a single cell using the ribbon. To format all numbers in the column, use the Number Format command on the shortcut menu.

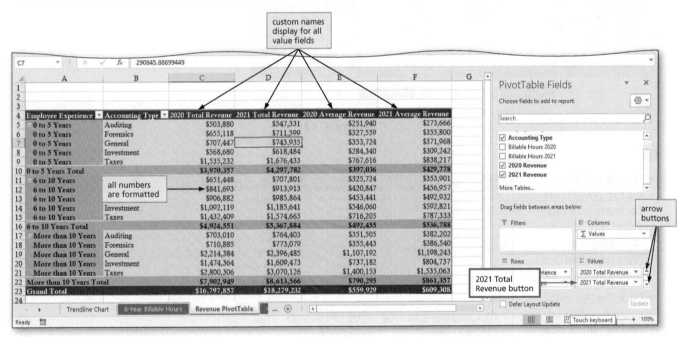

Figure 8–46

To Customize the Field Headers and Field List

The following steps hide the Field List, hide the field headers, and then turn off column autofitting. *Why? Customizing the display of the field headers and the field list can provide a less cluttered worksheet.*

1

- Display the PivotTable Tools Analyze tab.

- Click the Field List button (PivotTable Tools Analyze tab | Show group) to hide the Field List.

- Click the Field Headers button (PivotTable Tools Analyze tab | Show group) to hide the field headers.

● If necessary, click the '+/– Buttons' button to display the expand and collapse buttons in the PivotTable (Figure 8–47).

Q&A How can I display the Field List and field headers after hiding them?
The Field List and Field Headers buttons (PivotTable Tools Analyze tab | Show group) are toggle buttons—clicking them again turns the display back on.

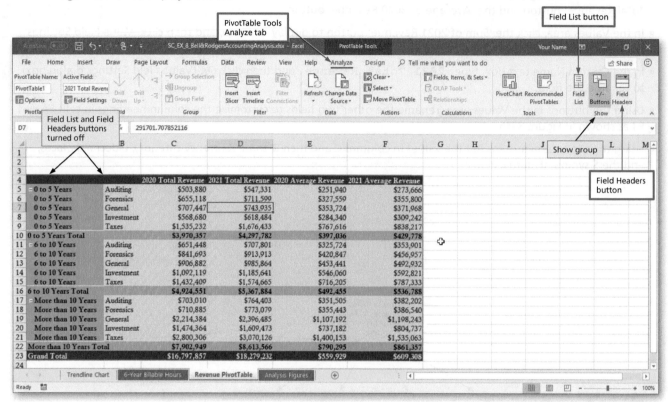

Figure 8–47

2

● Click the Options button (PivotTable Tools Analyze tab | PivotTable group) to display the PivotTable Options dialog box.

● Click the 'Autofit column widths on update' check box to remove the check mark (Figure 8–48).

3

● Click OK (PivotTable Options dialog box) to turn off the autofitting of column widths if updates should take place.

Figure 8–48

To Expand and Collapse Categories

The Expand and Collapse buttons expand and collapse across categories, reducing the amount of detail visible in the report without removing the field from the report. The following steps expand and collapse categories using the buttons and shortcut menus, and then suppress the display of the Expand and Collapse buttons in the report. **Why?** *In some instances, the report may be more visually appealing without the Expand or Collapse buttons in the report.*

1

- Click the Collapse button in cell A5 to collapse the '0-5 Years' of experience information (Figure 8–49).

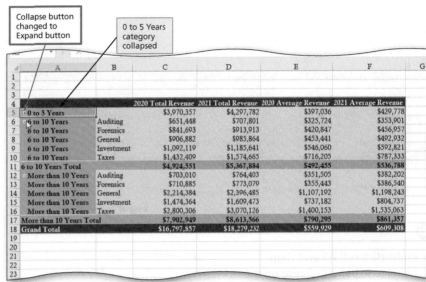

Figure 8–49

2

- Right-click cell A12 to display the shortcut menu and then point to Expand/Collapse to display the Expand/Collapse submenu (Figure 8–50).

Q&A Which method should I use to expand and collapse? Either way is fine. Sometimes the Collapse button is not visible, in which case you would have to use the shortcut menu.

Figure 8–50

3

- Click Collapse on the Expand/Collapse submenu to collapse the 'More than 10 Years' data.

- Click the '+/– Buttons' button (PivotTable Tools Analyze tab | Show group) to hide the Expand and Collapse buttons in the PivotTable (Figure 8–51).

Figure 8–51

 4

- Right-click cell A5 and then point to Expand/Collapse on the shortcut menu to display the Expand/Collapse submenu.

- Click 'Expand Entire Field' on the Expand/Collapse submenu to redisplay all data (shown in Figure 8–52).

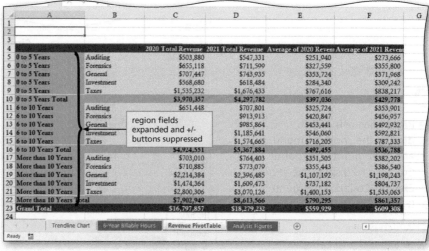

Figure 8–52

To Create a Title

The following steps insert two blank rows and create a title for the PivotTable. You must insert new rows because Excel requires the two rows above the PivotTable to be reserved for extra filters.

1 Insert two blank rows above row 1 for the title and subtitle.

2 In cell A1, enter the title **Bell & Rodgers Accounting Report** and then enter the subtitle **2020 and 2021** in cell A2.

3 Merge and center the text in cell A1 across A1:F1.

4 Merge and center the text in cell A2 across A2:F2.

5 Apply the Title style to cell A1 and bold the cell.

6 Apply the Heading 4 style to cell A2.

To Update a PivotTable

When you update cell contents in Excel, you also update related tables, formula calculations, and charts; however, this does not work for PivotTables. *Why? PivotTables do not update automatically when you change the underlying data for the PivotTable report. You must update the PivotTable manually to recalculate summary data in the PivotTable report.* Two figures in the original data worksheet are incorrect: the 2021 Billable Hours and Total Revenue at the Durante location for accountants with more than 10 years' experience working with investments. The following steps correct the typographical errors in the underlying worksheet, and then update the PivotTable report.

- Click the Analysis Figures sheet tab to make it the active worksheet.

- Click cell E15 and then type **9225** as the new value.

- Click cell G15, type **1077757**, and then press ENTER to change the contents of the cell (Figure 8–53).

Q&A What data will this change in the PivotTable?
Upon updating the PivotTable, the 2021 total revenue and the 2021 average revenue will change, reflected in cells D22 and F22.

	City	Employee Experience	Accounting Type	Billable Hours 2020	Billable Hours 2021	2020 Revenue	2021 Revenue
3	Durante	0 to 5 Years	General	4650	5020	462,891	502,482
4	Durante	0 to 5 Years	Forensics	4788	5175	487,179	529,402
5	Durante	0 to 5 Years	Investment	5061	5470	424,464	461,775
6	Durante	0 to 5 Years	Taxes	8177	8920	857,550	940,532
7	Durante	0 to 5 Years	Auditing	3477	3758	389,183	422,702
8	Durante	6 to 10 Years	General	5610	6064		551,721
9	Durante	6 to 10 Years	Forensics	3243	3505		432,168
10	Durante	6 to 10 Years	Investment	4536	4903	58,12	633,419
11	Durante	6 to 10 Years	Taxes	12459	13468	82,856	977,959
12	Durante	6 to 10 Years	Auditing	1992	2153	182,687	198,637
13	Durante	More than 10 Years	General	14350	15512	1,578,500	714,851
14	Durante	More than 10 Years	Forensics	3843	413	350,261	80,892
15	Durante	More than 10 Years	Investment	8946	9225	1,032,775	1,077,757
16	Durante	More than 10 Years	T	25989	28094	2,029,971	2,242,240
17	Durante	More than 10 Years		4272	4618	398,363	433,167
18	Jamison	0 to 5 Years		3305	3410	244,556	241,453
19	Jamison	0 to 5 Years	Forensics	1308	1413	167,939	182,197
20	Jamison	0 to 5 Years	Investment	1491	1611	144,216	156,709

updated values

Analysis Figures sheet tab

Trendline Chart | 6-Year Billable Hours | Revenue PivotTable | **Analysis Figures**

Figure 8–53

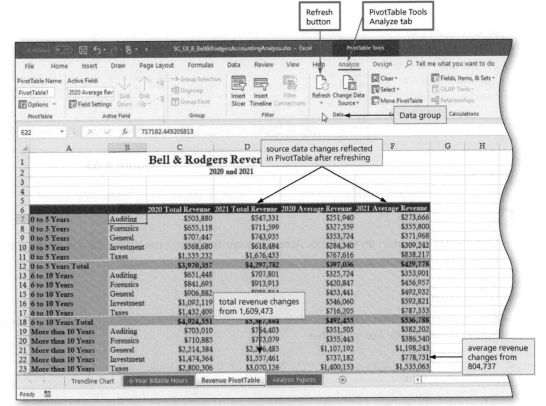

Refresh button

PivotTable Tools Analyze tab

- Click the Revenue PivotTable sheet tab to make it the active worksheet.

- If necessary, click inside the PivotTable report to make it active.

- Display the PivotTable Tools Analyze tab on the ribbon.

- Click the Refresh button (PivotTable Tools Analyze tab | Data group) to update the PivotTable report to reflect the change to the underlying data (Figure 8–54).

E22 | fx | 737182.449205813

Bell & Rodgers Rever
source data changes reflected in PivotTable after refreshing
2020 and 2021

	2020 Total Revenue	2021 Total Revenue	2020 Average Revenue	2021 Average Revenue
7 0 to 5 Years	Auditing	$503,880	$547,331	$251,940	$273,666
8 0 to 5 Years	Forensics	$655,118	$711,599	$327,559	$355,800
9 0 to 5 Years	General	$707,447	$743,935	$353,724	$371,968
10 0 to 5 Years	Investment	$568,680	$618,484	$284,340	$309,242
11 0 to 5 Years	Taxes	$1,535,232	$1,676,433	$767,616	$838,217
12 0 to 5 Years Total		$3,970,357	$4,297,782	$397,036	$429,778
13 6 to 10 Years	Auditing	$651,448	$707,801	$325,724	$353,901
14 6 to 10 Years	Forensics	$841,693	$913,913	$420,847	$456,957
15 6 to 10 Years	General	$906,882		$453,441	$492,932
16 6 to 10 Years	Investment	$1,092,119		$546,060	$592,821
17 6 to 10 Years	Taxes	$1,432,409		$716,205	$787,333
18 6 to 10 Years Total		$4,924,551		$492,455	$536,788
19 More than 10 Years	Auditing	$703,010	$764,403	$351,505	$382,202
20 More than 10 Years	Forensics	$710,885	$773,079	$355,443	$386,540
21 More than 10 Years	General	$2,214,384	$2,396,485	$1,107,192	$1,198,243
22 More than 10 Years	Investment	$1,474,364	$1,557,461	$737,182	$778,731
23 More than 10 Years	Taxes	$2,800,306	$3,070,126	$1,400,153	$1,535,063

total revenue changes from 1,609,473

average revenue changes from 804,737

Trendline Chart | 6-Year Billable Hours | **Revenue PivotTable** | Analysis Figures

Figure 8–54

Do I always have to refresh the data?
Yes. The contents of a PivotTable are not refreshed when the data from which they are created changes. This means you must refresh the PivotTable manually when underlying data changes.

If I add rows or columns to the data, will refreshing update the PivotTable?
If your data is in a data table, yes. Otherwise, you will have to create a new PivotTable.

To Drill Down into PivotTable

An easy way to view the underlying data associated with a PivotTable value is to drill down, a visualization that lets the user drill into, or go to deeper levels in, the data. To drill down, you simply double-click a PivotTable value. Excel creates a new worksheet with the details of the value. The following steps drill down into the PivotTable. *Why? You want to see detailed information about a value, in this case, all of the 2021 investment accounting for employees with 6 to 10 years of experience.*

1

- In the Revenue PivotTable report, double-click cell D16 to drill down in the data. Click away from the data to remove the selection (Figure 8–55).

What did Excel do?
Excel found all of the data related to the value in D16 and displayed it in a new worksheet.

What should I do with the data?
Sometimes you may just want to view the data or use the filter buttons to drill down further; other times, you may want to print it. If it important to have a permanent record of the data behind a value, rename the new worksheet and save it with the workbook.

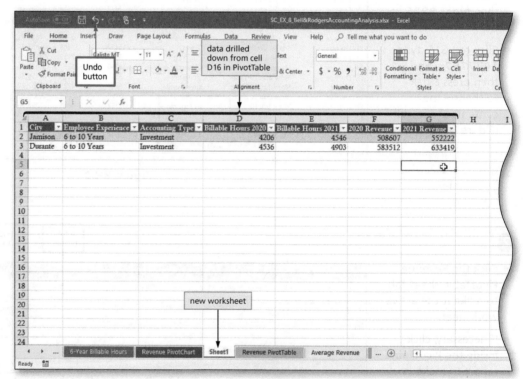

Figure 8–55

2

- Click the Undo button on the Quick Access Toolbar to remove the drilled data worksheet and return to the PivotTable report.

Experiment

- One at a time, double-click other cells in the PivotTable to view the underlying data. After each, click the Undo button on the Quick Access Toolbar.

Could I use the Drill Down and Drill Up buttons on the PivotTable Tools Analyze tab?
No. Those buttons are only available with Power Pivot or for PivotTables associated with a data model. You will learn about data models in a later module.

- Click the Save button on the Quick Access Toolbar to save the workbook.

Break Point: If you want to take a break, this is a good place to do so. You can exit Excel now. To resume later, start Excel, open the file called SC_EX_8_Bell&RodgersAccountingAnalysis, and continue following the steps from this location forward.

Creating and Formatting PivotChart Reports

A PivotChart report, also called a PivotChart, is an interactive chart that allows users to change, with just a few clicks, the groupings that graphically present the data in chart form. As a visual representation of PivotTables, each PivotChart Report must be associated or connected with a PivotTable report. Most users create a PivotChart from an existing PivotTable; however, you can create a new PivotTable and PivotChart at the same time. If you create the PivotChart first, Excel will create the PivotTable automatically.

To Create a PivotChart Report from an Existing PivotTable Report

If you already have created a PivotTable report, you can create a PivotChart report for that PivotTable using the PivotChart button (PivotTable Tools Analyze tab | Tools group). The following steps create a 3-D clustered column PivotChart report from the existing PivotTable report. *Why? The PivotChart will show the two-year data for each accounting type side by side.*

- If necessary, click cell A7 to select it in the PivotTable report.

- Click the Field List button (PivotTable Tools Analyze tab | Show group) to display the Field List.

- Click the PivotChart button (PivotTable Tools Analyze tab | Tools group) to display the Insert Chart dialog box.

- Click '3-D Clustered Column' in the Column Chart gallery to select the chart type (Figure 8–56).

Figure 8–56

2

- Click OK (Insert Chart dialog box) to add the chart to the Revenue PivotTable worksheet (Figure 8–57).

Q&A My chart does not display field buttons across the top. Did I do something wrong? No. It may be that they are turned off. Click the Field Buttons button (PivotChart Tools Analyze tab | Show/Hide Group) to turn them on.

Figure 8–57

Other Ways

1. Click Insert PivotChart button (Insert tab | Charts group), select chart type (Insert Chart dialog box), click OK
2. Select data for PivotChart, press F11 to create default chart

To Move the PivotChart Report

By default, a PivotChart report will be created on the same page as the associated PivotTable report. The following steps move the PivotChart report to a separate worksheet and then change the tab color to match that of the PivotTable report tab.

1 Display the PivotChart Tools Design tab.

2 With the 3-D Clustered Column chart selected, use the Move Chart button (PivotChart Tools Design tab | Location group) and move the chart to a new worksheet named **Revenue PivotChart**.

3 Set the tab color to Brown, Accent 1.

To Remove Fields

The following step deletes the average revenue data from the PivotTable and PivotChart reports. Because the PivotTable and PivotChart are connected, removing the fields from one worksheet automatically removes the fields from the other. You will use the Field List related to PivotCharts, which is slightly different from the Field List displayed when using a PivotTable. The areas labeled Columns and Rows become Legend and Axis areas in the Field List, respectively.

1 In the Field List, drag 2020 Average Revenue and 2021 Average Revenue out of the Values area to remove the average revenue data from the PivotChart report and PivotTable report (Figure 8–58).

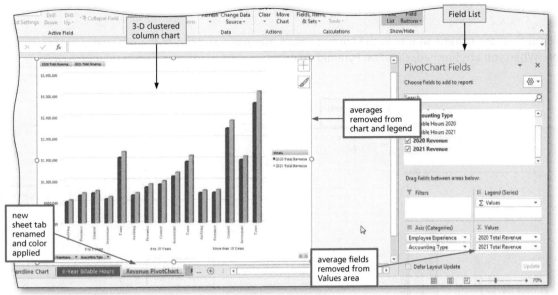

Figure 8–58

To Change the PivotChart Type and Reset Chart Elements

Why? *Selecting a chart type instead of using the default type provides variety for the reader.* The default chart type for a PivotChart is a clustered column chart. However, PivotCharts can support most chart types, except scatter (X, Y), stock, and bubble. The following steps change the PivotChart type to Full Pyramid, add a title to the PivotChart report, and apply formatting options to the chart.

- Click one of the reddish-brown '2020 Total Revenue' columns to select the data series.
- Right-click to display the shortcut menu (Figure 8–59).

Figure 8–59

- Click 'Format Data Series' on the shortcut menu to open the Format Data Series pane.
- If necessary, click the Series Options button.
- In the Column shape section (Series Options area), click Full Pyramid (Figure 8–60).

Experiment

- One at a time, click each of the column shapes in the Format Data Series pane and notice the difference in the PivotChart column. When you are finished, click Full Pyramid again.

Figure 8–60

3

- Repeat the process to change the 2021 Total Revenue column to a full pyramid and then close the Format Data Series pane.

- Click the Chart Elements button to display the menu and then click to place a check mark in the Chart Title check box.

- Select the chart title and then type **Bell & Rodgers** as the first line in the chart title. Press ENTER to move to a new line.

Figure 8–61

- Type **Total Revenue by Employee Experience and Accounting Type** as the second line in the chart title and then press ENTER to move to a new line.

- Type **2020 and 2021** as the third line in the chart title.

- Select all of the text in the title and change the font color to 'Black, Text 1' (Figure 8–61).

4

- Display the PivotChart Tools Format tab.
- Click the Chart Elements arrow (PivotChart Tools Format tab | Current Selection group) to display the Chart Elements menu (Figure 8–62).

Figure 8–62

5

- Click Back Wall on the Chart Elements menu to select the back wall of the chart.

- Click the Shape Fill arrow (PivotChart Tools Format tab | Shape Styles group) to display the Shape Fill gallery and then click Light Blue in the Standard Colors.

- Click the Shape Fill arrow again and then point to Gradient in the Shape Fill gallery to display the Gradient submenu (Figure 8–63).

Figure 8–63

- Click From Center in the Light Variations area to apply a gradient fill to the back wall of the chart (Figure 8–64).

Figure 8–64

- Select Side Wall on the Chart Elements menu and then repeat Steps 5 and 6 (Figure 8-65).

- Close the Format Wall pane.

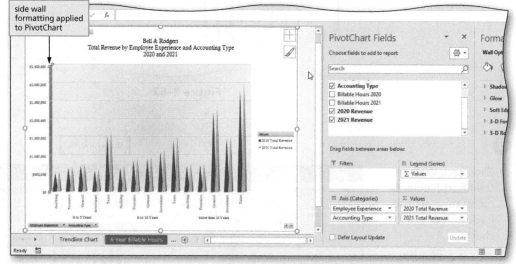

Figure 8–65

To Change the View of a PivotChart Report

Why? Changing the view of the PivotChart lets you analyze different relationships graphically. Changes made to the view of the PivotChart are reflected automatically in the view of the PivotTable. The following steps change the view of the PivotChart report that causes a corresponding change in the view of its associated PivotTable report.

- Display the PivotChart Tools Analyze tab.

- If necessary, click the Field List button (PivotChart Tools Analyze tab | Show /Hide group) to display the Field List.

- Click the Employee Experience check box in the 'Choose fields to add to report' area to deselect the Employee Experience field.

- Place a check mark in the City check box to select the field and add it to the Axis area (Figure 8–66).

Figure 8–66

2

● Click the Revenue PivotTable sheet tab to view the changes in the corresponding PivotTable report (Figure 8–67).

Q&A What usually happens when the view of the PivotChart report changes?
Changes to the PivotChart are reflected automatically in the PivotTable. Changes to category (x-axis) fields, such as City, are made to row fields in the PivotTable. Changes to series (y-axis) fields appear as changes to column fields in the PivotTable.

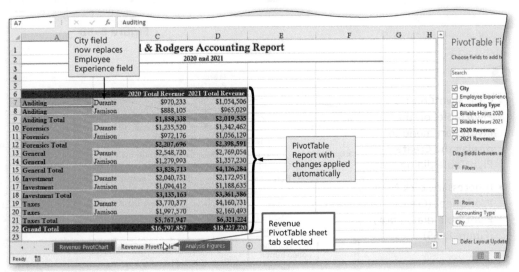

Figure 8–67

3

● Click the Save button on the Quick Access Toolbar to save the workbook.

To Create a PivotChart and PivotTable Directly from Data

The requirements document included a request to create a second PivotChart and PivotTable that examine the average revenue amount, controlling for different variables. *Why? Creating a second PivotChart and PivotTable offers a platform for pursuing multiple inquiries of the data simultaneously.* The following steps create a PivotChart report and an associated PivotTable report directly from the available data.

1

• Click the Analysis Figures sheet tab to display the worksheet.

• Click cell A3 and then display the Insert tab.

• Click the PivotChart arrow (Insert tab | Charts group) to display the PivotChart menu (Figure 8–68).

Q&A Can I select specific data for a PivotChart?
Yes, you can highlight the cells before creating the PivotChart. By default, Excel includes the table around the chosen cell; or, if the data is not a table, Excel assumes all contiguous data.

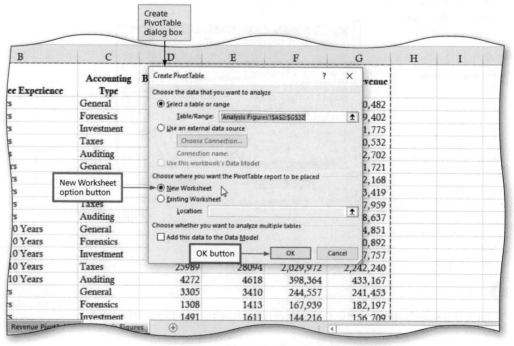

Figure 8–68

2

• Click 'PivotChart & PivotTable' on the PivotChart menu to display the Create PivotTable dialog box.

• If necessary, click New Worksheet (Create PivotTable dialog box) (Figure 8–69).

Figure 8–69

3

- Click OK to add a new worksheet containing a blank PivotTable and blank PivotChart (Figure 8–70).

Q&A What does the Field List display when creating a blank PivotChart?
Based on the location of your selected cell when you started the process, the Field List displays the available fields for you to place in the Filters and Axis areas.

Figure 8–70

4

- Use the Field List to add the Employee Experience and City fields to the Axis area.

- Add the 2020 Revenue and 2021 Revenue fields to the Values area in the Field List (Figure 8–71).

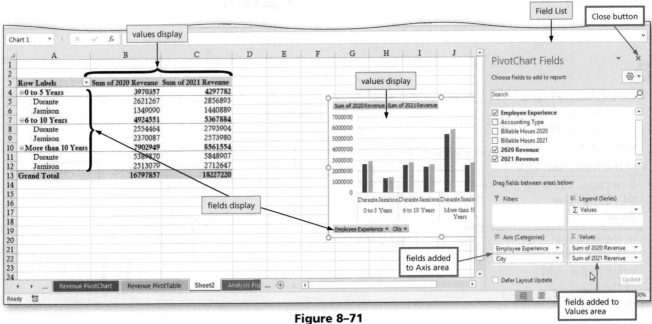

Figure 8–71

5

- Close the Field List.

- Rename the new worksheet, **Average Revenue**, in preparation for creating averages in the next steps, and choose the Yellow tab color in the Standard Colors area.

To Create a Calculated Field to a PivotTable Report

The following steps create calculated fields to use in the PivotTable and PivotChart reports. ***Why?** You would like to review the average revenue by city and experience for 2020 and 2021, but this information currently is not part of the data set with which you are working.* You will need to calculate the values you need through the use of a calculated field. A **calculated field** is a field or table column whose values are not entered but are calculated based on other fields. A calculated field may contain a formula, function, cell reference, structured reference, or condition. In this case, Average 2020 Billing and Average 2021 Billing will be new calculated fields, based on dividing the existing values of the 2020 Revenue and 2021 Revenue by the billable hours for 2020 and 2021, respectively.

- If necessary, click the PivotTable to make it active and then display the PivotTable Tools Analyze tab.

- Click the 'Fields, Items, & Sets' button (PivotTable Tools Analyze tab | Calculations group) to display the Fields, Items, & Sets menu (Figure 8–72).

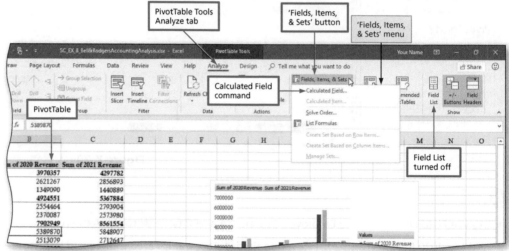

Figure 8–72

2

- Click Calculated Field to display the Insert Calculated Field dialog box.

- In the Name box, type **Average 2020 Billing per Hour**.

- In the Formula box, delete the value to the right of the equal sign, in this case, 0.

- In the Fields list, double-click the 2020 Revenue field to insert it in the Formula text box.

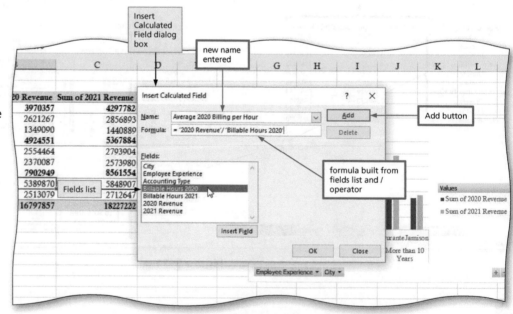

Figure 8–73

- Type / (slash) and then double-click the 'Billable Hours 2020' field to complete the formula, which should read = '2020 Revenue' / 'Billable Hours 2020' (Figure 8–73).

- Click the Add button (Insert Calculated Field dialog box) to add the calculated field to the Fields list.

- Repeat Step 2 to create a calculated field named Average 2021 Billing per Hour, calculated using 2021 Revenue divided by Billable Hours 2021 (Figure 8–74).

Figure 8–74

- Click the Add button (Insert Calculated Field dialog box) and then click OK to close the dialog box.

- If necessary, drag the PivotChart to the right so it does not cover the PivotTable (Figure 8–75).

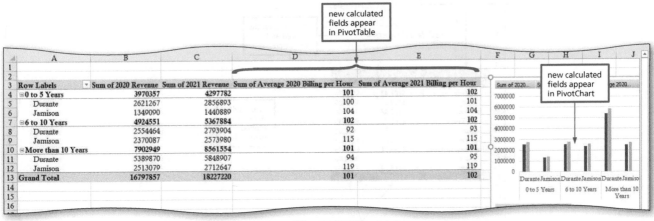

Figure 8–75

To Format the PivotTable

Now that you have added a calculated field, you can format the PivotTable and PivotChart so they look professional and are easy to interpret. The following steps format the PivotTable report.

1 If necessary, click the Field List button (PivotTable Tools Analyze tab | Show/Hide group) to display the Field List and then click to remove the check mark in the 2020 Revenue check box and the 2021 Revenue check box to remove these fields from the PivotTable and PivotChart.

2 If necessary, click cell A3 to select it. Display the PivotTable Tools Design tab and then apply 'Tan, Pivot Style Medium 19' to the PivotTable.

3 Insert two blank rows above the PivotTable. In cell A1, enter the title `Bell & Rodgers`. In cell A2, enter the subtitle `Average Billing per Hour, 2020 and 2021`.

4 Merge and center the text across A1:C1 and A2:C2. Apply the Title style to cell A1 and bold the text. Apply the Heading 4 style to cell A2.

5 Change the field name in cell B5 to `Average 2020 Hourly Billing`. Change the field name in cell C5 to `Average 2021 Hourly Billing`.

6 Apply the Currency number format with two decimal places and the $ symbol to the Average 2020 Hourly Billing and Average 2021 Hourly Billing fields.

7 Change the column widths for columns B and C to 12.00, and change the width for column D, which is currently blank, to 50.

8 Wrap and center the field names in cells B5 and C5.

9 Use the Field List button, the '+/– Buttons' button, and the Field Headers button (PivotTable Tools Analyze tab | Show group) to hide the field list, the Expand/Collapse buttons, and the field headers (Figure 8–76).

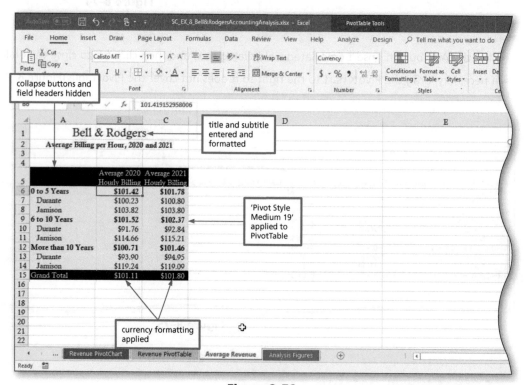

Figure 8–76

To Format the PivotChart

The following steps format the PivotChart report.

1 If necessary, click in the PivotChart report to select it.

2 Move and resize the PivotChart report so that it fills the range D1:D15.

3 Apply Style 12 in the Chart Styles gallery (PivotChart Tools Design tab | Chart Styles group).

4 Use the 'Change Colors' button (PivotChart Tools Design tab | Chart Styles group) to change the colors to 'Colorful Palette 3' in the Colorful area.

5 If necessary, position the legend at the top of the PivotChart report.

6 Click the Field Buttons button (PivotChart Tools Analyze tab | Show/Hide group) to hide the field buttons.

7 Increase the magnification to 120%.

8 Save the workbook (Figure 8–77).

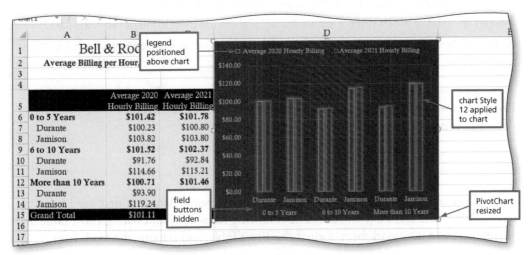

Figure 8–77

More About PivotCharts

If you need to make a change to the underlying data for a PivotChart, you can click the Change Data button (PivotChart Tools tab | Data group). You also can refresh PivotChart data after the change by clicking the Refresh button (PivotChart Tools tab | Data group).

As you have seen, Excel automatically creates a legend when you create a PivotChart. The legend is from the fields in the Values area of the Field List. To move the legend in a PivotChart, right-click the legend and then click Format Legend on the shortcut menu. The Format Legend pane will display options for placing the legend at various locations in the chart area.

As with tables and PivotTables, you can filter the data in a Pivot Chart. Any fields in the Axis (Categories) area of the Field List, display as filter buttons in the lower-left corner of the chart area. To filter a PivotChart, click one of the buttons; the resulting menu will allow you to sort, search, and select.

Working with Slicers

One of the strengths of PivotTables is that you can ask questions of the data by using filters. Being able to identify and examine subgroups is a useful analytical tool; however, when using filters and autofilters, the user cannot always tell which subgroups have the filters and autofilters selected without clicking filter buttons. Slicers are easy-to-see buttons that you can click to filter the data in PivotTables and PivotCharts, making the data easier to interpret. With slicers, the subgroups are immediately identifiable and can be changed with a click of a button or buttons.

BTW
Distributing a Workbook
Instead of printing and distributing a hard copy of a workbook, you can distribute the workbook electronically. Options include sending the workbook via email; posting it on cloud storage (such as OneDrive) and sharing the file with others; posting it on social media, a blog, or other website; and sharing a link associated with an online location of the workbook. You also can create and share a PDF or XPS image of the workbook so that users can view the file in Acrobat Reader or XPS Viewer instead of in Excel.

BTW
Printing
If you want to improve the quality of Excel printouts that contain graphical elements, such as images, charts, and tables, you can instruct Excel to print draft quality workbooks by clicking File on the ribbon to open Backstage view, clicking the Options tab in Backstage view to display the Excel Options dialog box, clicking Advanced in the left pane (Excel Options dialog box), scrolling to the Print area in the right pane, placing a check mark in the 'High quality mode for graphics' check box, and then clicking OK. Then use Backstage view to print the workbook as usual.

CONSIDER THIS

Why would you use slicers rather than row, column, or report filters?
One effective way to analyze PivotTable data is to use slicers to filter the data in more than one field. They offer the following advantages over filtering directly in a PivotTable:

- In a PivotTable, you use the filter button to specify how to filter the data, which involves a few steps. After you create a slicer, you can perform this same filtering task in one step.

- You can filter only one PivotTable at a time, whereas you can connect slicers to more than one PivotTable to filter data.

- Excel treats slicers as graphic objects, which means you can move, resize, and format them as you can any other graphic object. As graphic objects, they invite interaction.

- Slicers are intuitive—users without knowledge of Excel can use them to interact with the data.

- Slicers make it easy for users to understand exactly what is shown in a filtered PivotTable or PivotChart.

The owner of Bell & Rodgers has asked you to set up a PivotChart and PivotTable with a user-friendly way for anyone to explore the average hourly billing data. You can use slicers to complete this task efficiently.

To Copy a PivotTable and PivotChart

To create a canvas for exploratory analysis of revenue data, you first need to create a new PivotTable and a PivotChart. The following steps copy an existing PivotTable and PivotChart to a new worksheet, format the PivotTable, and rename the worksheet.

1 Create a copy of the Average Revenue worksheet and then move the copy so that it precedes the Average Revenue worksheet.

2 Rename the new worksheet, `Slicers`, and apply the Green tab color from the Standard Colors area.

3 Apply chart Style 8 to the PivotChart.

4 Set the column width of column E to 18 and column F to 19.00.

5 If necessary, turn off the display of field headers and +/– buttons for the PivotTable (Figure 8–78).

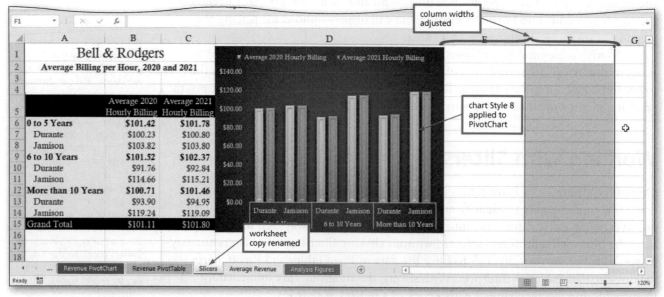

Figure 8–78

To Add Slicers to the Worksheet

The following steps add slicers that provide an easier way to filter the new PivotTable and PivotChart. **Why?** *To analyze sales data for specific subgroups, you can use slicers instead of PivotTable filters.*

- If necessary, click to make the PivotChart active and then display the PivotChart Tools Analyze tab.

- Click the Insert Slicer button (PivotChart Tools Analyze tab | Filter group) to display the Insert Slicers dialog box.

- Click to place check marks in the City, Employee Experience, and Accounting Type check boxes (Figure 8–79).

Figure 8–79

- Click OK (Insert Slicers dialog box) to display the selected slicers on the worksheet (Figure 8–80).

Figure 8–80

To Format Slicers

You can format slicers in a variety of ways. Using the Slicer Tools Options tab, you can customize slicer settings, resize slicer buttons to exact dimensions, change the number of columns in a slicer, or connect a slicer to a different PivotChart using the Report Connections button (Slicer Tools Options tab | Slicer group). The following steps move the slicers to the right of the PivotChart and then format them. **Why?** *The slicers need to be moved and formatted so that they do not obscure the PivotTable or PivotChart, and are easy to read and use.*

1

- Click the title bar of the City slicer and then drag the slicer to column E. Use the sizing handles to adjust the length of the slicer so that it ends at the bottom of row 6 and fits the width of the slicer so that it ends at the right edge of column E.

- Click and drag the Accounting Type slicer to column F. Use the sizing handles to adjust the length of the slicer so that it ends at the bottom of row 15 and the width so that it fits in column F.

- Click and then drag the Employee Experience slicer to column E, just below the City slicer. Use the sizing handles to change the length of the slicer so that it ends at the bottom of row 15 and the width so that it fits in column E.

- Hold down CTRL and then, one at a time, click each of the slicer title bars to select all three.

- Select the text in the Height box (Slicer Tools Options tab | Buttons group), type `.4` and then press ENTER to set the button height (Figure 8–81).

Figure 8–81

2

- Click the 'Tan, Slicer Style Light 4' Slicer style (Slicer Tools Options tab | Slicer Styles group) to apply it to the slicers (Figure 8–82).

Figure 8–82

- Click any cell to deselect the slicers.

Q&A How do you resize slicers and slicer buttons to exact dimensions?
Use the Height and Width boxes (Slicer Tools Options tab | Size group and Buttons group) to change the size of a slicer or of slicer buttons.

To Use the Slicers

Why? *Slicers provide you with a visual means of filtering data by simply clicking subgroups of interest to change the data displayed in the PivotTable and PivotChart.* Slicers based on row label fields provide the same results as filters in a PivotTable. They narrow the table down to a visible subgroup or subgroups. Clicking a slicer button displays only the data that corresponds to the variable name on the slicer. You can select multiple fields by using the Multi-Select button in the slicer title bar or by using CTRL+click to add a button (in the same slicer) to the display. Note that slicers filter data in both the PivotTable and the PivotChart.

The following steps use slicers to review average sales for different combinations of Employee Experience and City.

- Click Durante in the City slicer to display only the data for Durante in the PivotTable and PivotChart calculations.

- Hold down CTRL and then click '0 to 5 Years' in the Employee Experience slicer to remove that data and show the 6 to 10 Years and More than 10 Years data only (Figure 8–83).

Figure 8–83

- Release CTRL if necessary. Click Jamison in the City slicer to see the data for Jamison from the 6 to 10 Years and More than 10 Years data only (Figure 8–84).

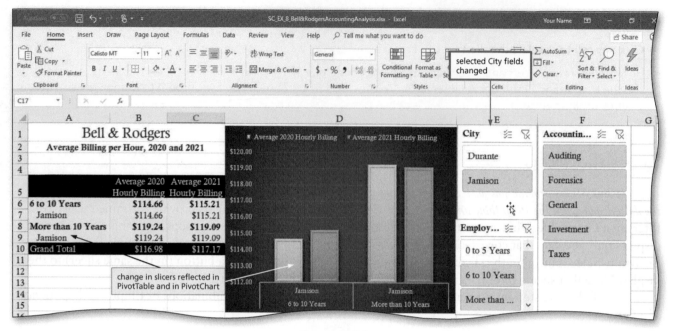

Figure 8–84

To Use Slicers to Review Data Not in a PivotTable

You can look for possible explanations of patterns by using slicers to analyze data other than that which displays in the PivotTable. *Why? Slicers based on fields not included in the PivotTable provide the same results as report filters.* Slicers regroup and narrow the PivotTable content to groups not visible in the PivotTable. The following steps use slicers to review data not currently visible in the PivotTable.

1

- Click the Clear Filter button on the City slicer and on the Employee Experience slicer to remove the filters and return the PivotTable and PivotChart to their unfiltered states.

- Click the Taxes button in the Accounting Type slicer to see the aggregate data for the average hourly billing for customers who chose the Taxes service, broken down by City and Employee Experience (Figure 8–85).

Experiment

- Click different service types and combinations of service types to see how the aggregate data changes.

Figure 8–85

- If necessary, click the Taxes button in the Accounting Type slicer to select it, click the Multi-Select button in the slicer header, and then click the Investment button in the Accounting Type slicer to view the aggregate data for both Taxes and Investments, broken down by City and Employee Experience (Figure 8–86).

Q&A How can I save a particular PivotTable setup?
PivotTables are dynamic by nature. To save a particular configuration, make a copy of the worksheet, and use the Protect Sheet command (Review tab | Protect group) to keep changes from being made to the worksheet copy. You can continue to use the PivotTable on the original worksheet to analyze the data.

3

- Save the workbook.

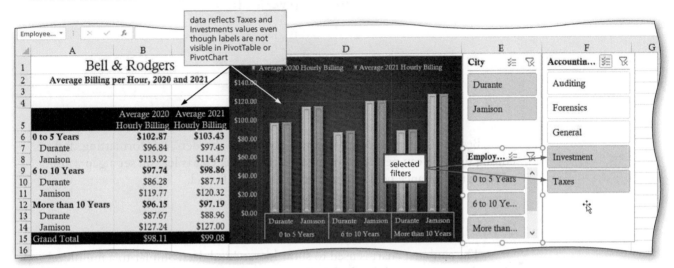

Figure 8–86

Other Excel Charts

Large amounts of data, while sometimes crucial for data management, can be cumbersome and hard to read, especially when you are trying to see data trends and relationships. Earlier in this module you created PivotCharts from a PivotTable report and from the data itself, also called raw data. Excel provides many additional chart types to help you create easy-to-read, intuitive overviews of your data. Deciding which kind of chart to use depends on what data you want the chart to portray, how the data is grouped, the relationship of the data to totals, and sometimes personal preference.

Recall that most charts have two buttons near the upper-right corner to specify chart elements and chart styles. Advanced formatting usually involves the use of the Format pane or the Chart Tools Format ribbon.

Funnel Charts

Funnel charts show values across various stages in a process as progressively smaller horizontal bars creating a funnel-like effect. Types of data used for funnel charts might include the process of narrowing down a pool of job applicants to hired employees, a sales pipeline, or an order fulfillment process. Figure 8-87 uses data from an ecommerce software website to show how website hits drill down into licensed users.

Figure 8–87

Besides the typical color schemes, styles, fills, borders, axis formatting, and editing that you can perform on most charts, funnel charts let you set a gap width, which is the distance between bars or levels in the funnel.

Sunburst Charts

The sunburst chart is used to show hierarchical data. Similar to a multilevel pie or donut chart, each level of the hierarchy is represented by a ring or circle. The innermost circle is the top of the hierarchy; relationships are shown via the outer rings. Types of data used for sunburst charts might include the reporting relationships in an organization, taxonomies, or sales or events shown by time (month-weeks-days) or locations (country-state-city). Figure 8–88 uses a sunburst chart to demonstrate online learning component relationships, and the focus on interactivity.

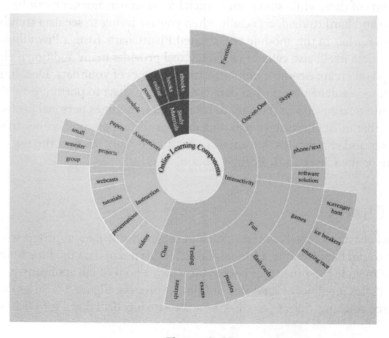

Figure 8–88

Colors in a sunburst chart are based on the theme and color style of the worksheet. Interesting effects can be created by adjusting the size of shadows, soft edges, and glows. With numeric data, you can add values to the sunburst chart in the same manner you do with a treemap.

Waterfall Charts

A waterfall chart shows how an initial value is affected by a series of positive and negative changes. The initial and the final value columns often start on the horizontal axis, while the intermediate values are floating columns. A waterfall chart shows how one data point grew or declined over a period of time, allowing users to see which categories within the data point improved and which ones declined. Typically, columns are color-coded so you quickly can tell positive numbers from negative ones. Waterfall charts can be used for company growth, profit/loss, or inventory. Figure 8–89 uses a waterfall chart to show changes in regional sales over a six-month period. Data labels appear as percentages on the floating columns.

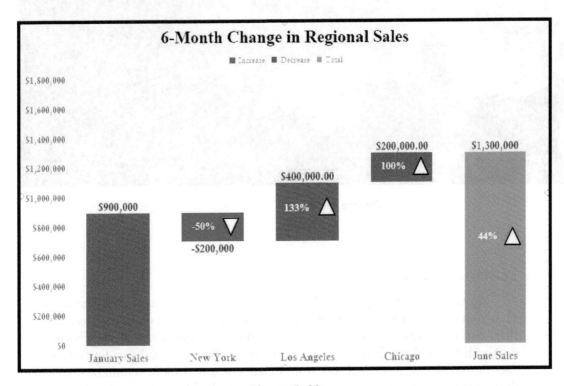

Figure 8–89

Map Charts

If your data has geographical regions or postal codes, you can create a map chart to compare values and show categories across those regions. To do so, highlight the list of locations and the matching data such as populations, land masses, or other statistical information. Then, when you choose to insert a map chart, Excel executes a Bing search to create a map. Figure 8–90 displays a map of the United States with statistical data about heart-related deaths.

Formatting options include cartographic projections (including flat, spherical, and others), area (displays of data, regions, world), and labels (names of countries, states, etc.). You even can format individual locations by clicking them and then making changes in the Format pane. The chart in Figure 8–90 displays a solid color chart area (background) and a gradient legend.

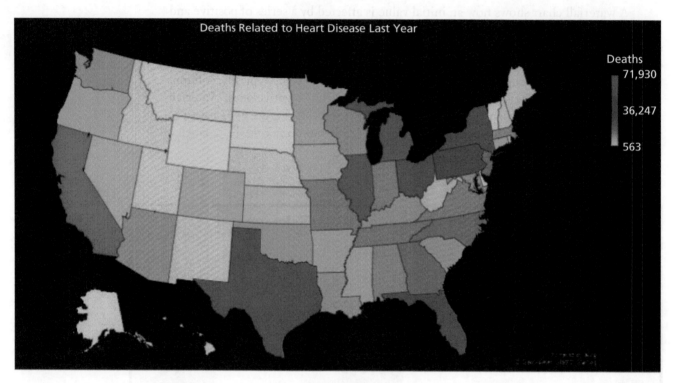

Figure 8–90

Scatter Charts

Scatter charts displays two value axes to show one set of numerical data along a horizontal (x) axis and another set of numerical values along a vertical (y) axis. The chart displays points at the intersection of x and y numerical values. These data points may be distributed evenly or unevenly across the horizontal axis, depending on the data. Scatter charts, also called X-Y scatter charts or scatter plots, should be used when there are many different data points and you want to highlight the similarities or see the distribution of your data.

Figure 8–91 shows sales data—the days of the month along the horizontal axis at the bottom, and the amount of sales on the vertical axis on the side. The plot area (area inside the chart) displays an Excel built-in texture.

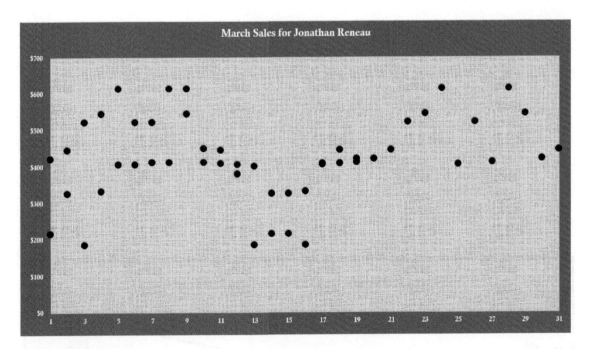

Figure 8–91

Histogram Chart

A histogram is a type of column chart that shows the frequency of data. It consists of rectangles whose height is proportional to the frequency of a variable. The x-axis across the bottom contains ranges of data values called bins. The y-axis is the frequency. Figure 8–92 displays the average winter temperature in Los Angeles and displays a picture chart area (background). You can set a gap width between columns. Like many charts, you also can set alternative text, which is added descriptive text available to screen readers.

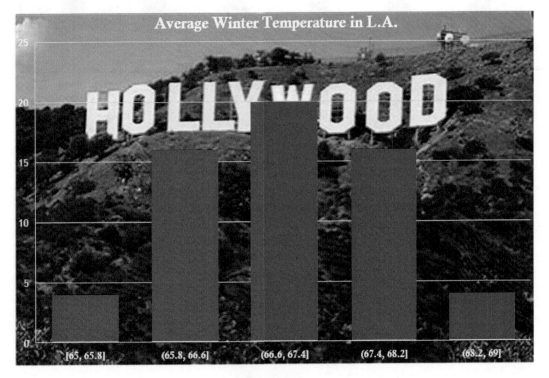

Figure 8–92

Combo Charts

A **combo chart** is a chart consisting of two charts, such as a column chart combined with a line chart, that together graph related but dissimilar data. Other combinations might include bar charts or area charts. Combo charts emphasize the differences between sets of data; for example, in-store sales are down but online sales are up, or comparing projections versus actual figures. Figure 8–93 uses a column chart to display attendance at an amusement park for 2019 and a line chart to display attendance for 2020. While a clustered column chart could show the same data, a combo chart emphasizes the difference by presenting the data in a completely different way. Figure 8–93 displays a gradient background in the chart area as well as a thick border with mitered corners.

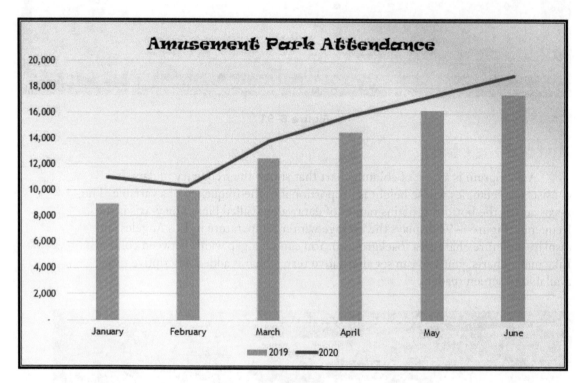

Figure 8–93

Box and Whisker Charts

A box and whisker chart (Figure 8–94) is a statistical graph that shows distribution of numerical data into quartiles. A **quartile** is a way to divide ordered data into equal groups based on finding the median. Simply put, the box part of the chart shows the median and the two groups around the median with equal sets of numbers. The high and low values in the ordered data are displayed by lines extending vertically, called whiskers. Any value that is 1.5 times below or above the box is called an outlier and is represented by a dot in the box and whisker chart.

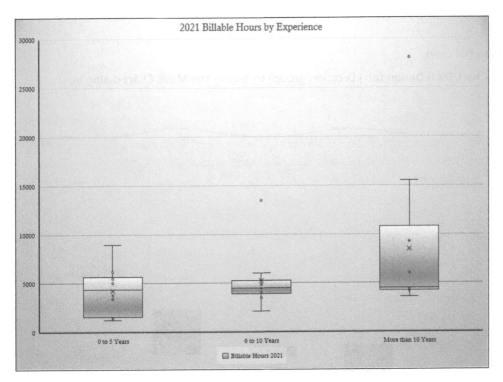

Figure 8–94

To Create a Box and Whisker Chart

The Bell & Rodgers company would like to compare the billable hours in 2021 by using the years of employee experience: 0 to 5 years, 6 to 10 years, and more than 10 years. In each category, the company would like to see the box and whisker notation. *Why? The company is looking for the median billable hours by experience and any billable hours that are extremely high or low in each category.* The following steps create a box and whisker chart.

1

- Click the Analysis Figures tab to display the Analysis Figures sheet.

- Select cells B2:B32. CTRL+drag cells E2:E32 to add the range to the selection.

- Click the 'Insert Statistic Chart' button to display its gallery (Insert tab | Charts group (Figure 8–95).

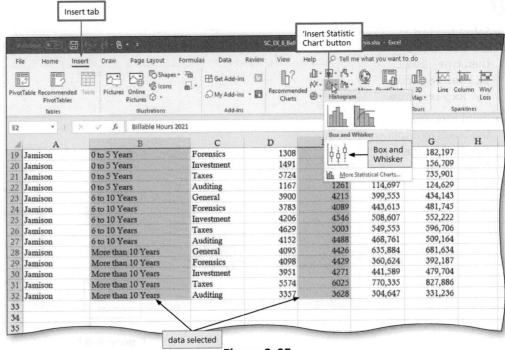

Figure 8–95

2

- Click Box and Whisker to create the chart.
- Click the Move Chart button (Chart Tools Design tab | Location group) to display the Move Chart dialog box.
- Click New sheet (Move Chart dialog box) to select the option button.
- If necessary, double-click the default text in the New sheet box to select the text, and then type **Box and Whisker Chart** to enter a name for the new worksheet.
- Click OK (Move Chart dialog box) to move the chart to a new worksheet.
- Color the worksheet tab Light Blue in the Standard Colors area (Figure 8–96).

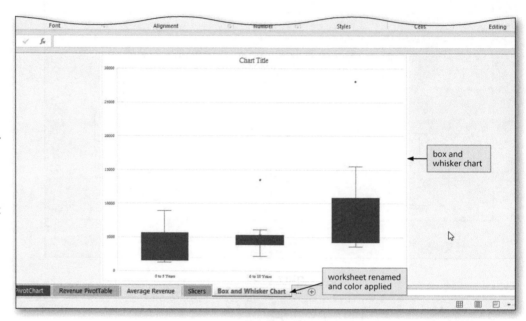

Figure 8–96

To Format a Box and Whisker Chart

The following steps edit the chart title, apply a chart style, and format the box and whisker data series.

- Select the text in the chart title and then type **2021 Billable Hours by Experience**.
- Right-click any of the boxes to display the shortcut menu (Figure 8–97).

Figure 8–97

- Click 'Format Data Series' to display the Format Data Series pane.
- If necessary, click the Series Options button to display the Series Options sheet.
- Click the 'Show Inner Points' check box to display the various data values as dots on the chart (Figure 8–98).

Experiment
- Click other combinations of check boxes to see how the chart changes. When you are finished, click the check boxes shown in Figure 8–98.

Figure 8–98

- In the Format Data Series pane, click the 'Fill & Line' button to display the Fill & Line sheet.
- Click Fill if necessary to display the choices for filling the boxes in the chart.
- Click the Gradient fill option button (Figure 8–99).

Experiment
- One at a time, click each of the other option buttons to see how the chart changes. When you are finished, click the Gradient option button.

Q&A What are the other gradient settings?
You can choose from various preset gradients and types. The Gradient stops bar lets you customize the amount of color from darkest to lightest. As you click each stop, you can set its color, position, amount of transparency, and brightness.

Figure 8–99

4

- Click the Chart Style 3 in the Chart Styles gallery (Chart Tools Design tab | Chart Styles group) (Figure 8–100).

5

- **sam↑** Save the file again and exit Excel.

Figure 8–100

Summary

In this module, you learned how to create a 2-D line chart and add a trendline to extend the trend to two more time periods. You added an R-squared (R^2) value to the trendline to measure the strength of the trend and formatted a data point. You created and formatted a PivotTable report based on raw data. Using the Field List, you added row fields and columns to the PivotTable. You created calculated fields in the PivotTable using summary functions. To see the power of the PivotTable, you inserted, deleted, and organized fields to view the data in different ways. You created and formatted a PivotChart Report from a PivotTable, filtering and analyzing data. You then created both a PivotTable and PivotChart from scratch and added a calculated field. Finally, you created slicers to make manipulating PivotTables and PivotCharts easier and added a box and whisker chart.

What decisions will you need to make when creating your next worksheet to analyze data using trendlines, PivotCharts, and PivotTables?

Use these guidelines as you complete the assignments in this module and create your own worksheets for evaluating and analyzing data outside of this class.

1. Identify trend(s) to analyze with a trendline.

    a. Determine data to use.

    b. Determine time period to use.

    c. Determine type and format of trendline.

2. Identify questions to ask of your data.

    a. Determine which variables to combine in a PivotTable or PivotChart.

3. Create and format PivotTables and PivotCharts.

    a. Add all fields to the field list.

    b. Use formatting features for PivotTables and PivotCharts.

4. Manipulate PivotTables and PivotCharts to analyze data.

    a. Select fields to include in PivotTables and PivotCharts.

    b. Use filters to review subsets of data.

    c. Use calculated fields and summary statistics to look at different measures of data.

    d. Create and use slicers to look at subsets of data.

CONSIDER THIS: PLAN AHEAD

Apply Your Knowledge

Reinforce the skills and apply the concepts you learned in this module.

Creating a PivotTable and PivotChart

Note: To complete these steps, you will be required to use the Data Files. Please contact your instructor for information about accessing the Data Files.

Instructions: Start Excel. Open the workbook SC_EX_8-2.xlsx, which is located in the Data Files. The workbook you open contains an order entry sheet for a restaurant supply company. You are to create a PivotTable and PivotChart from the Order Database. Figure 8–101 shows the completed Inventory worksheet.

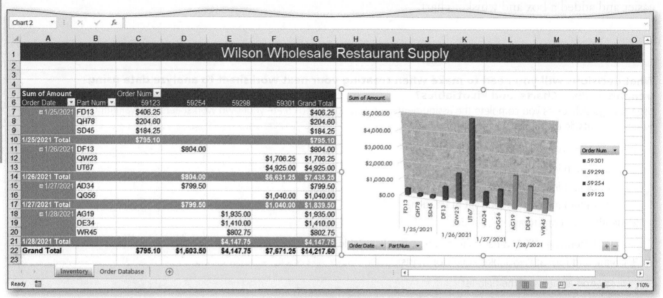

Figure 8–101

Perform the following tasks:

1. Save the workbook as SC_EX_8_RestaurantSupplyComplete. Select cell A3 and then click the PivotTable button (Insert tab | Tables group) to display the Create PivotTable dialog box. Make sure New Worksheet is selected and then click OK.

2. Drag the Order Num and Description fields from the 'Choose fields to add to report' area to the Rows area to add the fields to the PivotTable.

3. Drag the Amount field from the 'Choose fields to add to report' area to the Values area to add the sum of the Amount field to the PivotTable.

4. Drag the Order Date field from the 'Choose fields to add to report' area to the Filters area.

5. Click the More button (PivotTable Design tab | PivotTable Styles group) and choose the 'Rose, Pivot Style Medium 7' style.

6. Format the Total data as currency with dollar signs and two decimal places. If necessary, widen columns so all data and headings display correctly.

7. Click the Report Layout button (PivotTable Tools Design tab | Layout group) to display the Report Layout menu. Change the PivotTable report layout to tabular.

8. Click the filter button in cell B1 to display the filter menu. Click the 'Select Multiple Items' check box to select it. Select only orders from January 25 and January 26.

9. Click the filter button again and select all dates.

10. Move the Order Num field to the Columns Area. Remove the Description field from the Rows area. Move the Order Date and add the Part Num fields to the Rows area.

11. If necessary, format any remaining dollar amounts as currency.

12. Click the PivotChart button (PivotTable Analyze tab | Tools group) and select the 3-D Clustered Column.

13. Move the PivotChart to a location beside the PivotTable and resize it as shown in Figure 8–101. In the PivotChart, click the OrderNum filter button and then click 'Sort Smallest to Largest' on the menu.

14. Insert two more blank lines at the top of the worksheet. Type `Wilson Wholesale Restaurant Supply` as the title. Merge and center it across both the PivotTable and PivotChart. Change the font color and fill color to match the PivotTable headers. Change the font size to 20.

15. Click the PivotChart. Click the Chart Elements arrow (PivotChart Tools Format tab | Current Selection group) and choose Back Wall. Click the Shape Fill button (PivotChart Tools Format tab | Shape Styles group), click Texture, and then click 'Pink tissue paper' in the Texture gallery. Click the Shape Effects button (PivotChart Tools Format tab | Shape Styles group), click 3-D Rotation, and then, in the Perspective area, click 'Perspective: Contrasting Left'.

16. Right-click the vertical axis labels, and then click Format Axis on the shortcut menu. In the Axis Options area, change the Major Units to 1000.

    If requested by your instructor, in cell L2, type `Data Analyzed by`, followed by your name.

17. Name the worksheet Inventory and change the tab color to Pink, Accent 1. Save the workbook again, and then close the workbook.

18. Submit the revised workbook in the format specified by your instructor and exit Excel.

19. ✸ List two changes you would make to the PivotTable report to make it more easily interpreted by the user and explain why you would make these changes. These changes could be to the formatting, layout, or both.

Extend Your Knowledge

Extend the skills you learned in this module and experiment with new skills. You may need to use Help to complete the assignment.

Grouping Content in PivotTables

Note: To complete this assignment, you will be required to use the Data Files. Please contact your instructor for information about accessing the Data Files.

Instructions: Start Excel. Open the workbook SC_EX_8-3.xlsx from the Data Files. The workbook you open contains data about the number of books sold via an ecommerce website for each day of the year. You are to create a PivotTable and PivotChart for Sophie's Online Books that analyzes books sold in 2020.

Perform the following tasks:

1. Save the workbook using the file name, SC_EX_8_OnlineBooksComplete.

2. Use Help to learn to group or ungroup data in a PivotTable.

Continued >

Extend Your Knowledge *continued*

3. Select the data in the Sales Data worksheet (cells A3:B257). Create a PivotTable on a new worksheet. Use Date as the Rows field and use Books Sold as the Values field. Note that Excel breaks the date field down into months and days.

4. Name the new worksheet **Books Sold PivotTable.** Color the sheet tab green. Change the PivotTable style to 'Light Green, Pivot Style Medium 21'.

5. In cell A1, type **Sophie's Online Books** to create a title. In cell A2, type **Books Sold 2020** to create a subtitle. Merge and center the titles across columns A and B. Format cell A1 using the Title cell style and A2 using the 'Light Green, 20% - Accent6' cell style. Change the font color in both cells to black, if necessary.

6. Format the Books Sold data values to be Number with commas, but no decimal places. Remove the Field Header for column A.

7. Click cell A4 and use the Group Field command (PivotTable Tools Analyze tab | Group group) to group the daily figures by months and quarters.

8. Change the width of columns A and B to 17 (Figure 8–102).

9. Create a PivotChart and locate it on the same worksheet as the PivotTable. Use the 3-D Clustered Column chart type and set up the chart to have no legend.

10. Right-click the chart area, and then choose '3-D Rotation' on the shortcut menu. In the Format Chart Area pane, set the X rotation to 100° and Y rotation to 50°.

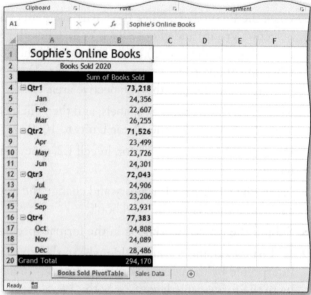

Figure 8–102

11. Edit the chart title text to match the PivotTable title and subtitle. Format the data series in the chart to use a solid fill, light green fill color. Resize the chart to fill the area between cell D2 and K20.

If requested by your instructor, add a worksheet header with your name and course number.

12. Because Excel changes the column width of the PivotTable as you change the grouping, double-check that the column widths of A and B are still 17.

13. Preview and then print the PivotTable worksheet in landscape orientation.

14. Save the workbook.

15. Submit the revised document in the format specified by your instructor.

16. ✵ What other chart type would you use to present this data for the user? Why would you choose that particular chart type?

Expand Your World

Create a solution that uses cloud and web technologies by learning and investigating on your own from general guidance.

Creating PivotTable Reports and PivotCharts with Web Data

Instructions: Start Excel. You are to create a PivotTable, PivotChart, and map chart from data you obtain from the web.

Perform the following tasks:

1. Open a browser and navigate to https://www.data.gov/, a searchable, open database of files stored by the U.S. government.

2. In the search box, type **Leading Causes of Death in the United States** and then press ENTER.

3. In the search results, navigate to the link, '**NCHS - Leading Causes of Death: United States**', and then click the CSV (Comma Separated Values) button. Save the file on your storage device.

4. Start Excel and open a blank workbook. Import the CSV file. *Hint:* Use the 'From Text/CSV' button (Data tab | Get & Transform Data group). Load the data into the existing worksheet.

5. Save the workbook using the file name, SC_EX_8_CausesOfDeath.

6. Delete the column named 113 Cause Name, leaving the columns for Year, Cause Name, State, Deaths, and Age-adjusted Death Rate. If necessary, close the Queries & Connections pane.

7. Use the Cause Name filter button to hide the All Causes records from the list. Use the State filter button to remove the United States field from the list.

8. Click any cell in the data and insert a PivotTable on a separate worksheet and perform the following analysis:

    a. Using the Field list, drag the State field to the Columns area, the Cause Name field to the rows area, and Deaths to the Values area. Filter the data to show deaths from Heart disease, Stroke, and Diabetes.

    b. Format the numbers with the comma separator and no decimal places.

    c. Apply a PivotTable Style.

    d. Experiment by dragging fields to various PivotTable areas to show different views of the data.

9. Create a Line PivotChart from the PivotTable and do the following:

    a. Move the chart to a new worksheet.

    b. If necessary, use the filter button on the Line Chart to edit out the United States numbers, so you are seeing just the 50 states and the District of Columbia.

    c. Format the PivotChart with a title, style, and an appropriate legend.

    d. Filter the PivotChart to show only data for your state and the states that border it, or a region of the United States.

Continued >

Expand Your World *continued*

e. Give each worksheet a descriptive name and color (Figure 8–103).

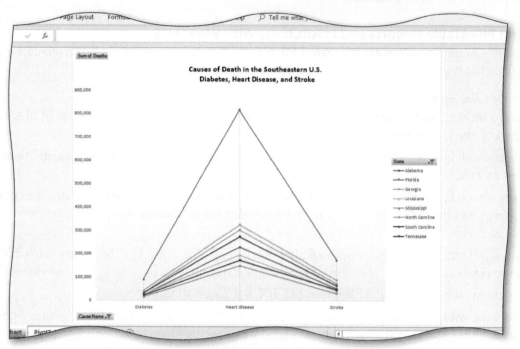

Figure 8–103

f. Experiment by clicking the Cause Name filter button to choose other diseases.

g. Return to the PivotTable and experiment with drilling down into the data.

10. Go back to the original web data. Use the Year filter button to select only the most recent year. Filter the Cause Name for Heart disease only. Filter the State column with the region you chose in Step 9.

11. Select the resulting State and Deaths data. Create a map chart similar to Figure 8–90 from the filtered data. *Hint:* Click the Maps button (Insert tab | Charts group).

   a. If Bing prompts you to allow its search, click the I Accept button.

   b. Move the map to a new worksheet. Name the worksheet, Regional Map.

   c. Display the Format Data Series Pane and the Series Options sheet. Click the Map Area button and then click 'Only Regions with Data'.

   d. Edit the title, color, and series name. *Hint:* To change the series name, right-click the legend, click Select Data, and click the Edit button.

   e. Format the data labels to display both Category Name and Value. If the entire state name will not display, reduce the font size of the label. Change the font color as necessary to ensure readability.

12. Save the workbook again.

13. Submit the revised workbook as specified by your instructor.

14. ✸ In this data, you dealt with 50 states and 10 diseases. With large amounts of data, what are the advantages to using PivotTables? What are the problems with PivotCharts?

In the Lab

Design and implement a solution using creative thinking and problem-solving skills.

Create Charts

Note: To complete this assignment, you will be required to use the Data Files. Please contact your instructor for information about accessing the Data Files.

Problem: The Saint Luke School District would like summary results from the latest round of statewide student testing in 4th, 7th, 10th, and 12th grade. Data has been compiled for the three testing areas, Math, Science, and English, for each of the 10 schools in the district.

Perform the following tasks:

Part 1: Open the workbook SC_EX_8-4.xlsx from the Data Files and then save the workbook using the file name, SC_EX_8_ SaintLukeSchoolDistrictComplete. The data includes both the average score for each grade and school combination and the test goals. Create a PivotTable with slicers and instructions for use. The PivotTable should show averages and goals organized by school and grade. Format the columns headings as necessary. Submit your assignment in the format specified by your instructor.

Part 2: ✳ How did the data from the Saint Luke School District pose a special challenge when creating the PivotTable? How might you address that challenge? What slicers did you decide to use? Why?

9 | Formula Auditing, Data Validation, and Complex Problem Solving

Objectives

After completing this module, you will be able to:

- Use formula auditing techniques to analyze a worksheet
- Trace precedents and dependents
- Use error checking to identify and correct errors
- Add data validation rules to cells
- Use trial and error to solve a problem on a worksheet
- Use goal seeking to solve a problem
- Circle invalid data on a worksheet
- Enable the Solver add-in
- Use Solver to solve a complex problem
- Use the Scenario Manager to record and save sets of what-if assumptions
- Create a Scenario Summary report
- Create a Scenario Summary PivotTable
- Draw with inking techniques

Introduction

Excel offers many tools that can be used to solve complex problems. In previous modules, simple what-if analyses have shown the effect of changing one value on another value of interest. This module introduces you to auditing the formulas in a worksheet, validating data, and solving complex problems. **Formula auditing** allows you to examine formulas to determine which cells are referenced by those formulas and examine cells to determine which formulas are built upon those cells. Auditing the formulas in a worksheet can give insight into how a worksheet is structured and how cells are related to each other. Formula auditing is especially helpful when you are working with a workbook created by someone else.

    Data validation allows you to set cells so that the values they accept are restricted in terms of type and range of data. This feature can be set up to display prompts and error messages when users select a cell or enter invalid data. You also can use data validation to circle cells containing data that does not meet the criteria you specified.

When trying to solve some problems, you can make an educated guess if you are familiar with the data and the structure of the workbook. **Trial and error** is a way to perform what-if analysis by changing one or more of the input values to see how they affect the other cells in the workbook. For simpler problems, you may find a solution using this process. For more complex problems, you might need to use the error and validation techniques in Excel to find a satisfactory solution.

One of the tools that Excel provides to solve complex problems is **Solver**, which allows you to specify up to 200 cells that can be adjusted to find a solution to a problem. Solver also lets you place limits or constraints on allowable values for some or all of those cells. A **constraint** is a limitation on the possible values that a cell can contain. Solver will try many possible solutions to find one that solves the problem subject to the constraints placed on the data.

Project: Instrument Logistics Analysis

In this module, you will learn how to use the Instrument Logistics Analysis workbook shown in Figure 9–1. Instrument Logistics is a small company that receives shipments of musical instruments from manufacturers, which it then distributes to wholesalers around the country. To ship its goods, the company purchases extra space on trucks from trucking firms. This week they are wanting to ship three types of instruments currently in stock: guitars, drum sets, and keyboards. Typically, the company deals with the instrument's physical volume in cubic feet, the weight in pounds, the profit per instrument, and the number of instruments in stock. The company will need to enter the number of each instrument to ship, making sure it is more than one and less than the number in stock. The objective is to maximize the profit while filling up as much of the truck as possible.

The Weekly Shipment worksheet, shown in Figure 9–1a, was created to determine the most cost-effective way of scheduling trucks to meet existing needs. The worksheet includes the details of the requirements for the three instruments, taking into account the truck capacities as well as the weight and volume of the instruments.

The details of the first solution determined by Solver are shown in Figure 9–1b. Solver was given the goal of maximizing the total profits (cell E13) while also accommodating the following constraints: the number of instruments assigned to each truck (range B9:D9) cannot be negative or fractional. The total volume and weight must not exceed the truck constraints shown in cells B16:B17. The company wants to ship at least one of each instrument per truck. Applying these constraints, Solver calculated the optimal instruments to ship shown in the range B9:D9 to achieve the goal of maximizing total profit and filling the truck. Solver modified the shipping quantities for each instrument (B9:D9) that resulted in changes in the total volume and weight per truck (E11:E12). If you applied a different set of constraints, Solver would determine a new solution.

When Solver finishes solving a problem, you can create an Answer Report. An Answer Report (Figure 9–1c) summarizes the answer found by Solver, identifying which constraints were in place and which values in the worksheet were manipulated in order to solve the problem within the constraints.

The Excel **Scenario Manager** is a what-if analysis tool that allows you to record and save different sets, or scenarios, of what-if assumptions for the same worksheet. In this case, you will use Scenario Manager to manage the two sets of Solver data for the Weekly Shipment Worksheet. The Scenario Manager also allows you to create

BTW
Ribbon and Screen Resolution
Excel may change how the groups and buttons within the groups appear on the ribbon, depending on the screen resolution of your computer. Thus, your ribbon may look different from the ones in this book if you are using a screen resolution other than 1366 × 768.

BTW
Touch Mode Differences
The Office and Windows interfaces may vary if you are using Touch mode. For this reason, you might notice that the function or appearance of your touch screen differs slightly from this module's presentation.

reports that summarize the scenarios on your worksheet. Both the Scenario Summary report (Figure 9–1d) and the Scenario PivotTable (Figure 9–1e) concisely present the differences among different shipping scenarios. Like any PivotTable, the Scenario PivotTable allows you to interact with the data easily.

(a) Scheduling Plan Worksheet

(b) Solver Solution
Figure 9–1 (Continued)

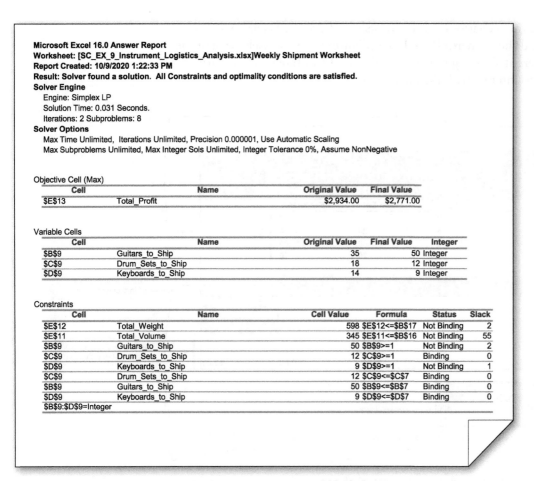

Microsoft Excel 16.0 Answer Report
Worksheet: [SC_EX_9_Instrument_Logistics_Analysis.xlsx]Weekly Shipment Worksheet
Report Created: 10/9/2020 1:22:33 PM
Result: Solver found a solution. All Constraints and optimality conditions are satisfied.
Solver Engine
  Engine: Simplex LP
  Solution Time: 0.031 Seconds.
  Iterations: 2 Subproblems: 8
Solver Options
  Max Time Unlimited, Iterations Unlimited, Precision 0.000001, Use Automatic Scaling
  Max Subproblems Unlimited, Max Integer Sols Unlimited, Integer Tolerance 0%, Assume NonNegative

Objective Cell (Max)

Cell	Name	Original Value	Final Value
$E$13	Total_Profit	$2,934.00	$2,771.00

Variable Cells

Cell	Name	Original Value	Final Value	Integer
$B$9	Guitars_to_Ship	35	50	Integer
$C$9	Drum_Sets_to_Ship	18	12	Integer
$D$9	Keyboards_to_Ship	14	9	Integer

Constraints

Cell	Name	Cell Value	Formula	Status	Slack
$E$12	Total_Weight	598	$E$12<=$B$17	Not Binding	2
$E$11	Total_Volume	345	$E$11<=$B$16	Not Binding	55
$B$9	Guitars_to_Ship	50	$B$9>=1	Not Binding	2
$C$9	Drum_Sets_to_Ship	12	$C$9>=1	Binding	0
$D$9	Keyboards_to_Ship	9	$D$9>=1	Not Binding	1
$C$9	Drum_Sets_to_Ship	12	$C$9<=$C$7	Binding	0
$B$9	Guitars_to_Ship	50	$B$9<=$B$7	Binding	0
$D$9	Keyboards_to_Ship	9	$D$9<=$D$7	Binding	0
$B$9:$D$9=Integer					

(c) Scheduling Plan Answer Report

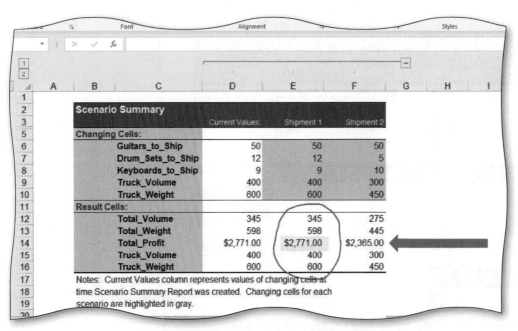

(d) Scheduling Scenario Summary Table
Figure 9–1 (Continued)

(e) Scenario PivotTable
Figure 9–1

Figure 9–2 illustrates the requirements document for the Instrument Logistics Analysis workbook. It includes the needs, source of data, and other facts about its development.

Worksheet Title	Instrument Logistics Analysis
Needs	Evaluate three different sets of instrument data to determine the optimal scheduling distribution to minimize total cost and maximize profits.
Data	• Three types of instruments: guitars, drum sets, and keyboards. • Data related to each instrument includes volume, weight, profit, and number in stock.
Constraints	• Constraints related to the truck include spare volume in cubic feet and spare weight in pounds. • Each shipment must include at least one of each instrument. • Instrument numbers cannot be fractional or negative.
Source of Data	All instrument information is available in the SC_EX_9-1.xlsx workbook on the Weekly Shipment Worksheet.
Calculations	All formulas are set up in the workbook with some errors. The worksheets in the workbook should be reviewed to familiarize yourself with the following calculations. • Total Shipment Volume is volume times number of instruments to ship. • Total Weight Volume is weight times number of instruments to ship. • Total Profit is profit per item times number of instruments to ship.
Other Requirements	Create a Shipment Scenario Summary. Create a Shipment Scenario Pivot Table. Create two Shipment Plan Answer Reports.

Figure 9–2

With a good understanding of the requirements document and an understanding of the necessary decisions, the next step is to use Excel to create the workbook. In this module, you will learn how to create the Instrument Logistics Analysis workbook shown in Figure 9–1.

To Start Excel and Open a Workbook

The following steps start Excel and open a workbook named SC_EX_9-1. The Weekly Shipment Worksheet tab shows the overall shipping plan and constraints for the instruments and trucks. To complete these steps, you will be required to use the Data Files. Please contact your instructor for information about accessing the Data Files.

1 **sam⁷ ↓** Start Excel.

2 Open the file named SC_EX_9-1.xlsx from the Data Files.

3 If the Excel window is not maximized, click the Maximize button on its title bar to maximize the window.

4 Save the workbook on your hard drive, OneDrive, or other storage location using SC_EX_9_InstrumentLogisticsAnalysis as the file name (Figure 9–3).

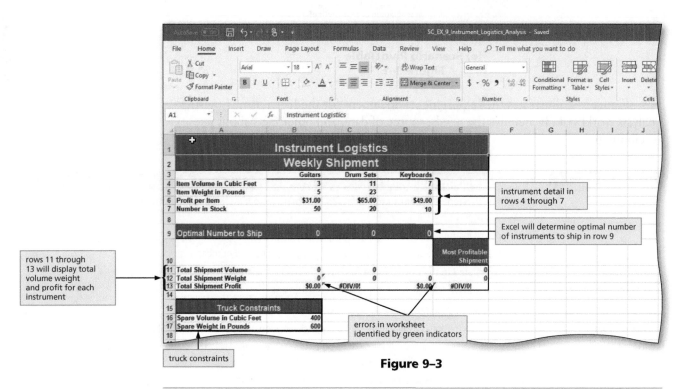

Figure 9–3

About the Weekly Shipment Worksheet

BTW

Getting Familiar with a Worksheet
When working with a new worksheet, you should try to become familiar with formulas, functions, and errors. You also should click the Name Manager button (Formula tab | Defined Names group) to see what ranges or cells may have useful predefined names.

The Weekly Shipment Worksheet shown in Figure 9–3 provides information about three instruments and four types of data: volume, weight, stock levels, and profits. Rows 4 and 5 contain the volume and weight for each of the three instruments. Row 6 contains the profit per item; row 7 shows the number in stock. The range B9:D9 will show the optimal number of instruments to ship that maximizes the total profit to Instrument Logistics, which is the problem that needs to be solved in this module. The total volume, weight, and profits for each instrument (rows 11 to 13) are based on the number of instruments to ship—shown in the range B9:D9—multiplied by the corresponding values in rows 4 through 6. As the number of instruments changes, the values in the range B11:D13 are updated.

Your goal is to determine the optimal number of instruments to ship in each category without exceeding the maximum volume and weight per truck, 400 and 600, respectively (cells B16:B17), while maximizing total profits for the company (cell E13).

As outlined in the requirements document in Figure 9–2, a second set of constraints also must be analyzed. Thus, the information in the range B16:B17 will be modified to reflect the constraints associated with the different scenario, with a volume of 300 and a weight of 450.

The worksheet also contains some errors which will be addressed in the following sections.

To View Named Cells

In workbooks prepared by others, it is always a good idea to double-check for named cells and ranges. The Weekly Shipment Worksheet contains several named cells. Named cells help identify concepts in the worksheet and can be used in formulas, for data validation, and as bookmarks. Later in the module, you will see that named cells are used by Excel to make constraints and answer reports easier to read. The following steps view named cells.

1 Click the Name Manager button (Formulas tab | Defined Names Group) to display the Name Manager dialog box.

2 To see the full name of each named cell, widen the first column by pointing to the border between the column headings until the pointer changes to a double-headed arrow, then double-click.

3 Review the named cells and their location (Figure 9–4).

4 Close the Name Manager dialog box.

Figure 9–4

Formula Auditing

Formula auditing is the process of tracking errors, checking worksheet logic, and reviewing formulas for errors. Errors may be obvious, with results that indicate that a formula is incorrect. For example, in Figure 9–3, cells C12, C13, and E13 display error codes. These errors are flagged by the error indicator, a green triangle, in the upper-left corner of those cells, and two of the three errors display an error code, #DIV/0!.

BTW
Naming Cell Ranges
Naming ranges for use with input variables is helpful when dealing with multiple input variables. Assign names to all the input variables before creating your first scenario. Named ranges will make scenario reports easier to understand and interpret.

BTW
Tracing Precedents and Dependents
When all levels of precedents or dependents have been identified, Excel will sound a beep if you try to trace another level.

Errors also may be less obvious, introduced through formulas that, while technically correct, result in unintended results in the worksheet or formulas that are inconsistent with other similar formulas. Error indicators with no accompanying error code, such as that found in cell C12, should be examined for these less-obvious errors. A complex worksheet should be reviewed to correct obvious errors and to correct formulas that do not produce error indicators but still do not produce the intended results.

Excel provides formula auditing tools, found in the Formula Auditing group on the Formulas tab, that can be used to review the formulas in a worksheet. Some tools, such as the Error Checking command, deal with identified errors. Other auditing tools provide visual cues to identify how cells in a worksheet are related to each other. **Tracer arrows** are blue, worksheet auditing arrows that point from cells that might have caused an error to the active cell containing an error. Tracer arrows identify cells that are related to other cells through their use in a formula. Red tracer arrows indicate that one of the referenced cells contains an error.

BTW
Tracer Arrow Lines
If a tracer arrow line appears as a black dashed line connected to a small worksheet icon, it indicates that precedent cells exist on another worksheet. You can double-click a dashed tracer line to move to the connected worksheet.

A formula that references other cells is said to have precedents. A **precedent** is a cell referenced in a formula that references other cells. For example, cell C24 might contain the formula, = C23/$B$1. Cells C23 and B1 are precedents of cell C24. Cells C23 and B1 may contain their own precedents, and these cells also would be precedents of cell C24. Oppositely, cell C24 is considered dependent upon C23 and B1. A **dependent** cell relies on references to another cell, and usually contains a formula whose value changes depending on the values in the input cells. Tracing precedents and dependents can indicate where a formula may be incorrect.

To Trace Precedents

Why? *Tracing precedents in Excel allows you to identify upon which cells a particular formula is based, not only directly by the formula in the cell, but indirectly via precedents.* The following steps trace the precedent cells for cell E13, which displays the Total Shipment Profit for accommodating the shipping needs.

1

- Display the Formulas tab if necessary, and then select cell E13.

- Click the Trace Precedents button (Formulas tab | Formula Auditing group) to draw a tracer arrow across precedents of the selected cell (Figure 9–5).

Q&A
How do I interpret the precedent arrows?
The arrow in Figure 9–4 terminates with an arrowhead on the traced cell, in this case cell E13. The arrow that runs through the range of cells B13:D13 indicates that all cells in the range are precedents of the traced cell.

Is it always red?
No. If a referenced cell contains a formula and that formula also contains an error, then a red line is drawn between the formula cells; otherwise the arrow is blue.

Figure 9–5

- Click the Trace Precedents button (Formulas tab | Formula Auditing group) again to draw arrows indicating precedents of cells B13:D13 (Figure 9–6).

Q&A How do I interpret the new precedent arrows?
The new arrows in Figure 9–6 have arrowheads on traced cells and dots on cells that are direct precedents of the cells with arrowheads. For instance, cell B13 has a tracer arrow pointing to it with a blue line appearing in the range B6:B12 and dots in cell B6 and B9. This indicates that the cells containing dots are precedents of cell B12, while the other cells, without dots, are not.

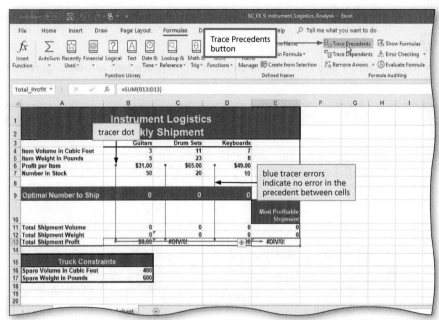

Figure 9–6

To Remove the Precedent Arrows

Why? Reducing visual clutter makes the worksheet easier to edit. The following steps remove the precedent arrows level by level and then correct the formula in cell C12.

- Click the 'Remove Arrows' arrow (Formulas tab | Formula Auditing group) to display the 'Remove Arrows' menu (Figure 9–7).

Figure 9–7

2

● Click 'Remove Precedent Arrows' on the Remove Arrows menu to remove precedent arrows.

3

● Repeat steps 1 and 2 to remove any remaining precedent arrows (Figure 9–8).

Figure 9–8

TO REVIEW PRECEDENTS ON A DIFFERENT WORKSHEET USING THE GO TO COMMAND

You can use precedent arrows to navigate directly to precedents on a different worksheet or different workbook. If you choose to use this feature, you would use the following steps:

1. Double-click on the dashed precedent arrow to display the Go To dialog box.
2. Select the cell reference you wish to navigate to, from the Go To list (Go To dialog box).
3. Click OK (Go To dialog box) to navigate to the selected cell reference.

To Trace Dependents

Why? *Identifying dependents highlights where changes will occur in the worksheet as a result of changing the value in the referenced cell.* The following steps trace the dependents of cell C9, which will display the optimal number of drum sets to ship.

1

- Select cell C9.

- Click the Trace Dependents button (Formulas tab | Formula Auditing group) to draw arrows to dependent cells (Figure 9–9).

 Q&A What is the meaning of the dependent arrows?
As shown in Figure 9–8, the arrowheads indicate which cells directly depend on the selected cell. In this case, cell C9 is explicitly referenced in formulas located in cells C11, C12, and C13, indicated by the arrow tips.

Figure 9–9

2

- Click the Trace Dependents button again to draw arrows indicating the indirectly dependent cells—cells that depend directly or indirectly on the selected cell (Figure 9–10).

Q&A How do I know when I have identified all remaining dependents?
You can click the Trace Dependents button again. If no additional dependents are present, Excel does not draw additional arrows but plays an error tone.

Figure 9–10

How can I tell the difference between dependents and precedents?
The tracer arrows always point in the direction of the data flow.

To Remove the Dependent Arrows

The following step clears the dependent arrows from the worksheet.

 Click the 'Remove Arrows' button (Formulas tab | Formula Auditing group) as necessary to remove all of the dependent arrows.

To Use the Trace Error Button

Another way to trace errors is to the use the Trace Error button that appears in the worksheet itself. *Why?* *The Trace Error button offers commands that may help identify the error further.* The following steps use the Trace Error button and the Trace Error command to identify the error.

1

- Select cell E13 to display the Trace Error button.
- Click the Trace Error button to display its menu (Figure 9–11).

Experiment

- Click Error Checking Options on the Trace Error menu to open the Excel Options dialog box. Read the Error checking rules. When you are finished, click Cancel to close the Excel Options dialog box without any changes. Click the Trace Error button again.

Figure 9–11

2

- Click Trace Error on the menu to display precedent arrows directly involved in the error (Figure 9–12).

Q&A How is tracing the error different from tracing precedents? The Trace Error command displays only the precedent arrows involved in the error. Depending on the kind of error, the Trace Error command also moves the selection to the probable erroneous cell.

Figure 9–12

3

- Click the Remove Arrows button (Formulas tab | Formula Auditing group) to remove all of the arrows.

Other Ways

1. Click Error Checking arrow (Formula tab | Formula Auditing Group), click Trace Error on menu

To Use Error Checking to Correct Errors

After tracing the precedents and dependents, and using the Trace Error command, you decide to correct the #DIV/0! in cell C13 first. *Why? All the arrows indicate that C13 may be causing the error shown in E13.*

The following steps use error checking features to find the source of these errors and correct them.

1

- Select cell C13.

- Click the Error Checking button (Formulas tab | Formula Auditing group) to display the Error Checking dialog box. If necessary, drag the dialog box away from the figures on the worksheet so the figures are visible.

- Read the message in the Error Checking dialog box that identifies that the formula is dividing by zero or empty cells (Figure 9–13).

Q&A What is the purpose of the Next button? Excel will move to the next cell in which it finds an error code or an error indicator. Excel moves forward or backward through the workbook, row by row, when you click the Next or Previous button. Clicking the Next button does not move to a precedent or dependent cell.

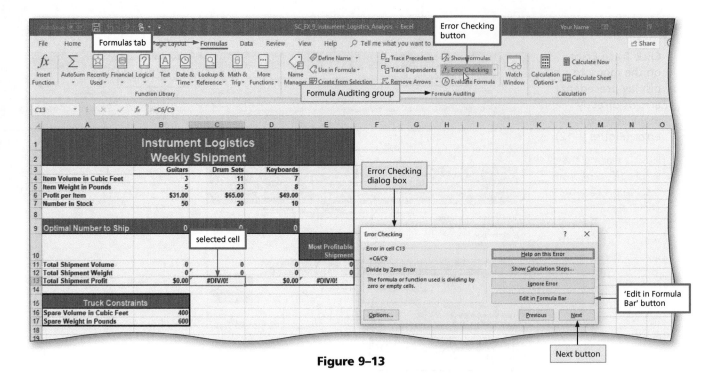

Figure 9–13

2

- Look at the formula in cell C13. Rather than dividing, it should multiply C6 by C9, which is the 'Profit per Item' by the 'Optimal Number to Ship'.

- Click the 'Edit in Formula Bar' button (Error Checking dialog box) and edit cell C13 to read =C6*C9 (Figure 9–14).

Q&A | Why are some cells highlighted in different colors?
Excel highlights the cells involved in the current formula. The cell highlighted in red indicates a possible error.

Figure 9–14

3

- Click the Enter button in the formula bar to complete the edit of the cell and to correct the error in cell C13 and the dependent error in cell E13 (Figure 9–15).

Why did correcting one error in cell C13 correct the other #DIV/0! error in the worksheet?

The other cell containing a #DIV/0! error was directly or indirectly dependent on the value in cell C13; thus correcting the error in cell C13 provided a valid value for use in the other formulas.

Figure 9–15

4

- Click the Resume button (Error Checking dialog box) to continue checking errors. Excel will move to the error in cell C12 (Figure 9–16).

Experiment

- Click the 'Help on this Error' button (Error Checking dialog box) and read about the error in the browser window that Excel opens. When you are finished, close the browser window.

Figure 9–16

- Click the Trace Precedents button (Formula tab | Formula Auditing group) to display the tracer arrow (Figure 9–17).

Experiment

- Look at the formula in the Formula Bar. Notice the formula and the tracer arrow both reference C2, which is text and is incorrect.

Figure 9–17

- Because the Error Checking dialog box suggests copying the formula from the cell on the left, click cell B12 to view the suggested formula (Figure 9–18).

Experiment

- Notice this formula is =B9*B5, which correctly multiples the 'Optimal Number to Ship' by the 'Item Weight in Pounds'.

Figure 9–18

7

• Click the Resume button (Error Checking dialog box) to move to the error in cell C12 (Figure 9–19).

Figure 9–19

8

• Click the 'Copy Formula from Left' button (Error Checking dialog box) to fix the error (Figure 9–20).

Figure 9–20

- Click OK (Microsoft Excel dialog box) as the error correction is complete.
- Save the workbook again on the same storage location with the same file name.

More about the Formula Auditing Group

BTW

Setting Iterative Calculation Options
In certain situations, you will want Excel to recalculate a formula that contains a circular reference, to enable Excel to converge upon an acceptable solution. Changing the iterative calculation option allows Excel to recalculate a formula a specified number of times after the initial circular reference error message is dismissed. To allow Excel to recalculate a formula, display the Excel Options dialog box and then click the Formulas tab. In the Calculation options area, click to select the `Enable iterative calculation` check box. You can specify the maximum number of iterations and maximum amount of change between iterations. Be aware that turning on this option will slow down the worksheet due to the additional computations.

In the previous steps, you used some of the buttons in the Formula Auditing group on the Formulas tab to identify and correct errors in your worksheet. You already have used the Trace Precedents, Trace Dependents, and 'Remove All Arrows' buttons to gain insight into the structure of the worksheet. You used the Trace Error button in the worksheet and the Trace Error command to display red arrows to highlight the precedents of the selected cell, to help you identify the source of the error. You also used the Error Checking button to check for errors throughout the worksheet. When the Error Checking button is clicked, Excel highlights each error in the worksheet in sequence and displays options for correcting the error.

If you click the Error Checking arrow (Formula tab | Formula Auditing group), you have an option to fix a Circular Reference, if your worksheet contains one. A **circular reference** occurs when one of the defining values in a cell is itself. For example, if you type =B2/A2 in cell B2, you have created a circular reference. Excel displays an error message when you create a circular reference and provides you with access to the appropriate Help topic. In complex worksheets with multiple precedent levels, these errors are not uncommon.

Table 9–1 lists other common error codes identified in Excel.

Table 9-1 Common Excel Error Codes	
Error Code	**Description**
#DIV/0!	Indicates that a formula divides a number by zero
#N/A!	Indicates that a formula cannot locate a referenced value
#NAME?	Indicates use of an invalid function name
#NULL!	Indicates that a formula incorrectly contains a space between two or more cell references
#NUM!	Indicates that a formula contains invalid numeric values
#REF!	Indicates that a cell reference in a formula is not valid; it may be pointing to an empty cell, for instance
#VALUE!	Indicates that a calculation includes nonnumeric data

The Formula Auditing group contains three other commands you can use when auditing formulas. The Evaluate Formula button allows you to move through a formula step by step, which can be a useful tool when working with long, complex formulas. The Show Formulas button displays the formulas instead of values in the active worksheet. The Watch Window button opens a separate window that displays values and formulas for specific cells that you choose to monitor.

Using the Watch Window

The **Watch Window** (Figure 9–21a) displays values of cells located throughout the workbook and allows you to keep an eye on cells that you have identified as being related; this allows you to observe changes to the cells even when viewing a different worksheet or workbook. For example, if you were watching cell E13, which displays 'Total Shipment Profit' for the most profitable shipment, and you changed the value in cell B13, the

Watch Window would display the updated value of cell E13 on the Weekly Shipment Worksheet. You add cells to the Watch Window using the Add Watch button and the Add Watch dialog box (Figure 9–21b). The Watch Window continues to show the values of watched cells even as you navigate the worksheet and the cells no longer are in view. Similarly, if you change the view to another worksheet or workbook, the Watch Window allows you to continue to monitor the cell values.

(a) Watch Window   (b) Add Watch dialog box

Figure 9–21

TO OPEN THE WATCH WINDOW

If you wanted to open the Watch Window, you would perform the following steps:

1. If necessary, display the Formulas tab.
2. Click the Watch Window button (Formulas tab | Formula Auditing group) to open the Watch Window (Figure 9–21a).
3. If necessary, move the Watch Window to a location where it does not obscure cells you want to edit.

TO ADD CELLS TO THE WATCH WINDOW

If you wanted to add cells to the Watch Window, you would perform the following steps:

1. Click the Add Watch button on the Watch Window toolbar to display the Add Watch dialog box (Figure 9–21b).
2. Select the cell or cells to be watched.
3. Click the Add button (Add Watch dialog box) to add the selected cells to the Watch Window.

TO DELETE CELLS FROM THE WATCH WINDOW

If you wanted to delete cells from the Watch Window, you would perform the following steps:

1. In the Watch Window dialog box, select the cell you want to stop watching.
2. Click the Delete Watch button in the Watch Window to delete the selected cell from the Watch Window (Figure 9-21a).

Data Validation

When creating advanced worksheets, some user-entered values my need to fall within certain ranges or contain specific types of data. For example, cells B9:D9 in the Weekly Shipment Worksheet display the optimal number of instruments to ship. Recall from the requirements that shipment amounts must be whole numbers and at least one of each type of instrument must be included in each shipment but no more than are in stock of each type of instrument. Excel provides you with tools to restrict the values that can be placed in cells to valid values. You can place restrictions on values, provide a message to the user when a cell with restrictions is selected, and create an error message that is displayed when an invalid value is entered.

Excel data validation rules apply only when you enter data into the cell manually. Excel does not check the validation rules if a cell is calculated by a formula or set in a way other than by direct input by the user.

The types of data validation criteria you can use include specific values, whole numbers, a value in a list (such as a text value), dates, and custom values. When using the custom validation type, you can use a formula that evaluates to either true or false. If the value is false, users may not enter data in the cell. Suppose, for example, you have a cell that contains an employee's salary. If the salary is zero, which indicates the employee no longer is with the company, you may want to prohibit a user from entering a percentage in another cell that contains the employee's raise for the year.

To Add Data Validation to Cells

Why? In the Weekly Shipment Worksheet, the numbers of each type of instrument to ship must be nonnegative whole numbers. The cells that need to be restricted are cells B9:D9. You can use data validation to apply these conditions and restrictions to the cells. The following steps add data validation to cells in the range B9:D9.

- Display the Data tab and then select cells B9:D9.

- Click the Data Validation button (Data tab | Data Tools group) to display the Data Validation dialog box.

- Click the Allow arrow (Data Validation dialog box | Settings tab) to view the list of allowed restrictions on the input data (Figure 9–22).

Figure 9–22

What are the allowed restrictions?
The Any value selection allows you to enter any value but still allows you to specify an input message for the cell. The Whole number, Decimal, Date, and Time selections permit only values of those types to be entered in the cell. The List selection allows you to specify a range that contains a list of valid values for the cell. The Text length selection allows only a certain length of text string to be entered in the cell. The Custom selection allows you to specify a formula that validates the data entered by the user. Each selection displays its own set of options.

2

- Click Whole number in the Allow list to display options for whole numbers.
- Click the Data arrow to view its list (Figure 9–23).

 What is in the Data list?
The Data list includes the standard logical operators for numeric, date, and time data. The list is not available for other data types.

Figure 9–23

3

- Click between in the Data list to select it.
- Type 1 in the Minimum box to specify that the values in the selected cells must be whole numbers greater than or equal to one (Figure 9–24).

 What am I entering 1?
Recall that the requirements document specifies that at least one of each instrument should be shipped.

Figure 9–24

4

- Click the 'Maximum: Collapse Dialog' button to collapse the dialog box and go to the worksheet (Figure 9–25).

 Why is the dialog box collapsed?
When you click a Collapse Dialog button associated with any input box, you are telling Excel that you want to choose the value from the worksheet rather than type it in yourself. Excel collapses the dialog box to get it out of the way.

Figure 9–25

- In the worksheet, click cell B7 to choose the cell for the Maximum value.

- Click the Restore Dialog button (Data Validation dialog box) to maximize the dialog box (Figure 9–26).

Q&A Will all three values in the validation range (B9:D9) be compared to B7?
No. Excel will apply a relative reference; in other words, B9 will be compared to B7, C9 will be compared to C7, and D9 will be compared to D7. If you wanted to compare to an absolute, non-changing reference, you would input =$B$7.

Figure 9–26

- Click the Input Message tab (Data Validation dialog box) to display the Input Message sheet.

- Type **Item to Ship** in the Title box to enter a title for the message displayed when cell B9, C9, or D9 is selected.

- Type **Enter the number of items to include in this shipment. The number must be greater than zero and less than or equal to the quantity in stock.** in the Input message box to enter the text for the message (Figure 9–27).

Figure 9–27

7

- Click the Error Alert tab (Data Validation dialog box) to display the Error Alert sheet.

- If necessary, Click the Style arrow and then click Stop to select the Stop error style.

- Type **Input Error** in the Title box to enter a title for the error message displayed if invalid data is entered in cell B9, C9, or D9.

- Type **You must enter a whole number that is greater than zero and less than or equal to the quantity in stock.** in the Error message box to enter the for the error message (Figure 9–28).

Q&A What is a Stop error style?
You can select one of three types of error styles. Stop prevents users from entering invalid data in a cell. Warning displays a message that the data is invalid and lets users accept the invalid entry, edit it, or remove it. Information displays a message that the data is invalid but still allows users to enter it.

Figure 9–28

8

- Click OK (Data Validation dialog box) to accept the data validation settings for cells B9:D9.
- Click outside the data range to remove the selection.

To Test the Validation

The following steps test the validation rules. *Why? It is always a good idea to test validation rules to make sure they work as you expect them to.*

1

- Click cell B9 to make it the active cell and display the 'Items to Ship' input message (Figure 9–29).

Experiment

- Click cells C9 and D9 to make sure the same input message appears. Click cell B9.

Figure 9–29

- Type **47.5** and then press ENTER to enter the number of guitars to ship and to display the Input Error dialog box (Figure 9–30).

Q&A

Why does the Input Error dialog box appear after entering 47.5 in cell B9?

You set a data validation rule in cell B9 that accepts only whole numbers greater than or equal to zero. Because 47.5 is not a whole number, Excel displays the Input Error dialog box with the title and error message you specified when you set the data validation rule.

Figure 9–30

- Click Retry (Input Error dialog box) to return to cell B9.

Experiment

- Repeat Step 1 using values that are negative and values that are more than the number in stock. When you are finished, click Cancel (Input Error dialog box).

- Save the workbook again on the same storage location with the same file name. If Excel displays an Input Error dialog box, click Cancel.

Break Point: If you want to take a break, this is a good place to do so. You can exit Excel now. To resume later, start Excel, open the file called SC_EX_9_InstrumentLogisticsAnalysis.xlsx, and continue following the steps from this location forward.

BTW

Copying Validation Rules

You can copy validation rules from one cell to other cells using the Paste Special command. Select the cell that contains the validation rules you want to copy and then click Copy. Select the cell or cells to which you want to apply the validation rules, click the Paste button arrow, and then click Paste Special. Click Validation in the Paste area and then click the OK button (Paste Special dialog box).

Solving Complex Problems

In the Instrument Logistics Analysis workbook, the problem of determining how to schedule trucks to maximize weight, volume, and profit within the constraints provided is not straightforward due to the number of variables involved. You can attempt to solve the problem manually through trial and error, or you can use an Excel tool to automate some or all of the solution. To solve the problem manually, you could try adjusting values in the ranges B9, C9, and D9 until the goal for the schedule is met. Remember that Instrument Logistics wants to identify the best logistics of instruments to trucks that will maximize the company's total profit. Because so many possible combinations could meet the criteria, you could hold one or more of the cells affected by constraints constant and adjust the other cells to attempt to meet the rest of the criteria.

How should you approach solving a complex problem?

When considering an approach to a complex problem in Excel, start with the least complex method of attempting to solve the problem. In general, the following methods can be useful in the order shown:

1. **Use trial and error** to modify the values in the worksheet. Use a commonsense approach, and keep in mind the range of acceptable answers to your problem. For example, the number of instruments should not be a negative number.

2. **Use the Excel Goal Seek feature** to have Excel automatically modify a cell's value in a worksheet in an attempt to reach a certain goal in a dependent cell.

3. **Use the Excel Solver feature** to provide Excel with all of the known rules, or constraints, of your problem as well as the goal you are seeking. Allow Solver to attempt as many different solutions to your problem as possible.

To Use Trial and Error to Attempt to Solve a Complex Problem

Trial and error is not making blind guesses; rather, it is a process of making incremental changes in order to observe the impact on the desired result. *Why? With an understanding of how the worksheet is set up and how the various values interact, you can make informed changes, or trials, based on how each decision affects the worksheet.* In the first trial for the Instrument Logistics workbook, you will enter valid data for each of the instruments; then you will compare the total weight and volume to that allowed on the truck. The following steps use trial and error to attempt to solve a complex problem. In this case, you are trying to maximize the profit while filling the truck without going over.

- Enter   **47**   in cell B9 as the number of guitars to ship, then press TAB.

- Enter   **18**   in cell C9 as the number of drum sets to ship, and then press TAB.

- Enter   **9**   in cell D9 as the number of keyboards to ship, and then press ENTER (Figure 9–31).

◁ | Do the values entered in Step 1 solve the scheduling problem?
Q&A | No. Both the Volume and Weight in cells E11:E12 exceed the truck constraints shown in cells B16:B17.

Figure 9–31

2

- Click cell B9 to make it the active cell.

- Enter **35** and then press ENTER to reduce the number of guitars to ship (Figure 9–32).

 Q&A

Does the value entered in Step 2 solve the scheduling problem?
No. The weight is still too heavy. Compare cells E12 and B17.

What are some problems with using trial and error?
While trial and error can be used on simple problems, it has many limitations when used to solve complex problems. Endless combinations of values could be entered in cells B7, C7, D7, C9, B9, and D9 to try to come up with a solution. Using trial and error, it is difficult to determine if a solution you reach satisfies the goal of maximizing the total profit.

Figure 9–32

To Use Goal Seek to Attempt to Solve a Complex Problem

If you know the result you want a formula to produce, recall that you can use **Goal Seek** to determine the value of a cell on which a formula depends. Goal seeking takes trial and error one step further by automatically changing the value of a cell until a single criterion is met in another cell.

In the Weekly Shipment Worksheet, the number of shipped instruments cannot exceed the number in stock, and, with the various weights and volumes, the shipment must fit in the truck. With Goal Seek, you can manipulate one of these precedent cells to find a solution that meets the constraints. You decide to have Goal Seek manipulate the number of keyboards. ***Why?*** *You want to try to achieve the goal of 400 cubic feet, the total volume for the shipment.*

The following steps use Goal Seek to change the number of keyboards to keep the total volume close to but under or equal to 400 cubic feet.

1

- If necessary, display the Data tab.

- Click the 'What-If Analysis' button (Data tab | Forecast group) to display the What-If Analysis menu (Figure 9–33).

Figure 9–33

- Click Goal Seek on the What-If Analysis menu to display the Goal Seek dialog box. Drag the dialog box so that it does not cover the data on the worksheet.

- Type **$E$11** in the Set cell box (Goal Seek dialog box) to specify which cell should contain the goal value.

- Type **400** in the To value box as the goal value.

- Type **$D$9** in the 'By changing cell' box (Figure 9–34).

Q&A | Could I have clicked those cells in the worksheet instead of typing them?
Yes, just be sure that Excel applies the absolute reference $ before both the row and column so no replications are made.

Figure 9–34

- Click OK (Goal Seek dialog box) to seek the goal of 400 cubic feet in cell E11 and display the Goal Seek Status dialog box (Figure 9–35).

Figure 9–35

Experiment

• Watch Excel create iterations in trying to come close to 400.

Q&A How can the number of keyboards to ship (D9) be more than the number is stock (D7) when the data validation rule disallowed numbers greater than the number in stock?

Data validation rules are applied only to data that is entered into a cell. Entries that are the result of calculations and goal seeking will not produce a data validation error.

4

• Click OK (Goal Seek Status dialog box) to close the dialog box and display the updated worksheet.

To Circle Invalid Data

The 'Circle Invalid Data' command checks for invalid data entered as the result of a formula or automated tool, such as Goal Seek. In this case, Goal Seek found a solution that satisfied the criteria specified for the goal, but that solution violated the conditions specified for data validation. It is good practice to check your worksheet for invalid data periodically through use of the 'Circle Invalid Data' command. *Why? The previous set of steps illustrates how the data validation rules apply only to data directly entered into a cell, not to the results of actions such as Goal Seek.* The following steps check for and circle any invalid data on the Weekly Shipment Worksheet.

1

• Click the Data Validation arrow (Data tab | Data Tools group) to display the Data Validation menu (Figure 9–36).

Q&A What are some limitations of using goal seeking?

Goal seeking allows you to manipulate only one cell in order to reach a goal. In this example, Goal Seek produced a result that is acceptable mathematically, but not logically, as is the case here.

Figure 9–36

2

- Click 'Circle Invalid Data' on the Data Validation menu to place a red validation circle around any invalid data, in this case cell D9 (Figure 9–37).

Q&A How does Excel determine invalid data?

Excel only can identify data you have specified in the data validation process earlier in the module. In this case, the optimal number to ship is greater than the quantity in stock.

Now that I have identified invalid data, what do I do with that information?

Once you identify invalid data in a worksheet, you should determine how to correct the data.

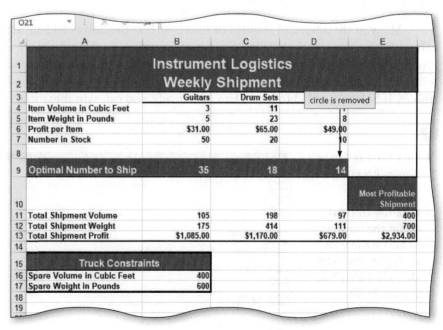

Figure 9–37

To Clear Validation Circles

Why? *Once the invalid data has been identified, it is easier to work when the worksheet is clear of extraneous marks.* The following step clears the validation circles.

1

- Click the Data Validation arrow (Data tab | Data Tools group) to display the Data Validation menu (shown in Figure 9-36).

- Click 'Clear Validation Circles' on the Data Validation menu to remove the red validation circle (Figure 9–38).

Q&A Has the scheduling problem been solved?

No. As noted previously, the number of keyboards is more than the number in stock. Also, the weight is significantly over the truck constraint.

2

- Save the workbook again on the same storage location with the same file name.

Figure 9–38

Customizing Excel Add-Ins

Excel provides optional commands and features to solve complex problems through the inclusion of add-ins. An **add-in** is software that adds commands and features to Microsoft Office applications. Although some add-ins are built into Excel, including the Solver add-in used in this module, you may need to download and install others as needed. In any case, add-ins for Excel must be installed before they are available for use.

Add-ins are managed through the Add-ins tab accessible through the Excel Options dialog box. Once activated, the add-in and related commands are accessible through the ribbon, often in custom tabs or groups. If installed, the Solver and Analysis ToolPak add-ins are represented by buttons in the Analyze group on the Data tab. Euro Currency Tools, another built-in add-in for Excel, appears as commands in the Solutions group on the Formulas tab.

The Solver Add-In

The Solver add-in is a tool you use to generate the best possible solution for complex problems from a wide range of possibilities. Solver works to optimize a specific cell, called an objective cell, by maximizing, minimizing, or setting it to a specific value. For example, you want to maximize the total profit (cell E13). Because of the number of precedents, it can be difficult to determine which values should change. When you decrease the number of items to ship for one instrument, you have to increase the number assigned to another instrument to ensure that all trucks are full. This change has an impact on costs and resulting profit. Solver considers all of the various constraints when determining the best solution. The countless options make it difficult to identify the best solution to the problem using other methods of what-if analysis such as trial and error or Goal Seek.

To Enable the Solver Add-In

Many of the advanced features of Excel, such as the Solver add-in, are hidden until the user adds the feature to the user interface. **Why?** *Excel is a powerful application with many features that the average user does not need to access on a regular basis. These features are hidden to keep the interface from becoming too overwhelming.* The following steps will add the Solver add-in to Excel and verify the additional features on the Data tab of the ribbon. If Solver is added to your Data tab already, you can skip these steps.

- Click the File tab to display Backstage view.

- Click the Options tab at the bottom of Backstage view to display the Excel Options dialog box (Figure 9–39).

Figure 9–39

2

- Click the Add-ins tab to display the 'View and manage Microsoft Office Add-ins' screen (Figure 9–40).

Q&A Why is my list of add-ins different? Depending on the applications installed and enabled for use in Excel, the list of active, inactive, and available add-ins may be different.

Figure 9–40

3

- Click the Manage button to display the list (Figure 9–41).

Figure 9–41

4

- Click Excel Add-ins in the Manage list to select it as the add-in type.

- Click Go to display the Add-ins dialog box.

- If necessary, click to select the Solver Add-in check box in the Add-ins available list (Add-ins dialog box) (Figure 9–42).

Figure 9–42

5

- Click OK to apply the setting and to close the Add-ins dialog box.

- If necessary, display the Data tab to verify the addition of the Analyze group and the Solver button (Figure 9–43).

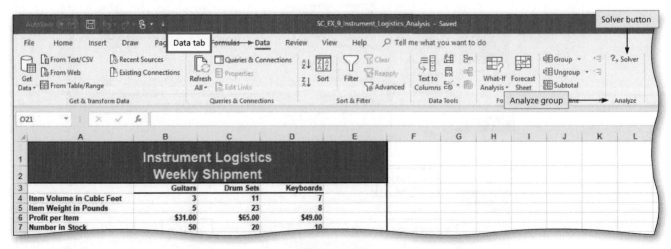

Figure 9–43

Solver Requirements

Regardless of the technique Solver uses to solve a problem, it requires three different types of input from the user: the objective, or the result you need for the target cell; variable cells, the values that can change; and constraints, the conditions that the solution has to meet.

The technique Solver uses to solve a problem depends on the model that the user selects as best representing the data. For the current scheduling problem, you will use LP Simplex, a technique in Solver associated with linear programming. **Linear programming** is a complex mathematical process used to solve problems that include multiple variables and the minimizing or maximizing of result values. Solver essentially tries as many possible combinations of solutions as it can. On each attempt to solve the problem, Solver checks to see if it has found a solution. The other two techniques are beyond the scope of this book.

In order for Solver to solve the scheduling problem, Solver must modify data until an optimum value is reached for the selected cell. The cells modified by Solver are called **decision variable cells**, also known as changing cells or adjustable cells. In this case, these are cells in the ranges B9:D9. The cell that Solver is working to optimize, either by finding its maximum or its minimum value, is known as the **objective cell**, or target cell. In this case, Solver is trying to maximize the total profit of the shipment, which makes cell E13 the objective cell. Solver will attempt to maximize the value of cell E13 by varying the values in the decision variable cells within the constraints set by Instrument Logistics.

Recall that constraints have been placed on certain values in the problem and are listed in the requirements document. For example, one constraint in the Weekly Shipment Worksheet is that each truck must contain at least one of each instrument. Other constraints include the truck volume and weight limits as well as the number of instruments in stock. The constraints are summarized in Table 9–2. In the table, the word, int, applies an integer constraint which means Solver must use a positive whole number.

BTW
Using Solver to Solve Complex Problems
Solver allows you to solve complex problems where a number of variables can be changed in a worksheet in order to meet a goal in a particular cell. Unlike Goal Seek, Solver is not restricted to changing one cell at a time and can efficiently evaluate many combinations for a solution.

Table 9–2 Constraints for Solver		
Cell or Range or Named Cell	**Operator**	**Constraint**
$B$9:$D$9	>=	1
$B$9:$D$9	int	integer
Guitars_to_Ship	<=	Guitars_in_Stock
Drum_Sets_to_Ship	<=	Drum_Sets_in_Stock
Keyboards_to_Ship	<=	Keyboards_in_Stock
$E$11	<=	$B$16
$E$12	<=	$B$17

When Solver reaches a solution to a problem, it generates an Answer Report. An **Answer Report** is a Solver report summarizing the results of a successful solution. It shows the answer for the objective cell, the values used in the changing cells to arrive at that answer, and the constraints that were applied to the calculation. By creating an Answer Report, you satisfy the requirement to document the results of the scheduling calculation.

To Enter Constraints with Solver

To solve the shipping problem for Instrument Logistics, you give Solver the goal of maximizing the total profit of the shipment, shown in cell E13, within the constraints set in the requirements document. To accomplish this goal, Solver can modify the number of instruments of each type (represented by the ranges B9, C9, and D9). *Why use Solver? Solver allows Excel to evaluate multiple combinations of values and constraints for changing variables to find an optimal solution to a complex problem.*

The following steps use Solver to find the optimal solution to the scheduling problem in the Weekly Shipment Worksheet within the given constraints.

1

- Click the Solver button (Data tab | Analysis group) to display the Solver Parameters dialog box. Drag the title bar to move the dialog box so you can see the figures in the worksheet.

- If necessary, click the Set Objective box (Solver Parameters dialog box) and then, in the worksheet, click cell E13 to set the objective cell, in this case the total profit (Figure 9–44).

Q&A Are there any restrictions on which cell can be the objective?
The value in the Set Objective box must be a single cell reference or name, and the cell must contain a formula.

Figure 9–44

2

- Click the Max option button in the To area (Solver Parameters dialog box) if necessary to specify that the value of the target cell should be as large as possible, maximizing the total profit.

- Click the 'By Changing Variable Cells' box and then, in the worksheet, select the range B9:D9 to set the cells that you want Solver to manipulate (Figure 9–45).

Q&A Can you save the constraints you add to the Solver?
Yes. You can click the Load/Save button (Solver parameters dialog box) to load constraints you have saved previous or to save a new one, called a Solver model. Models are saved to an empty part of the worksheet, but do not print or display.

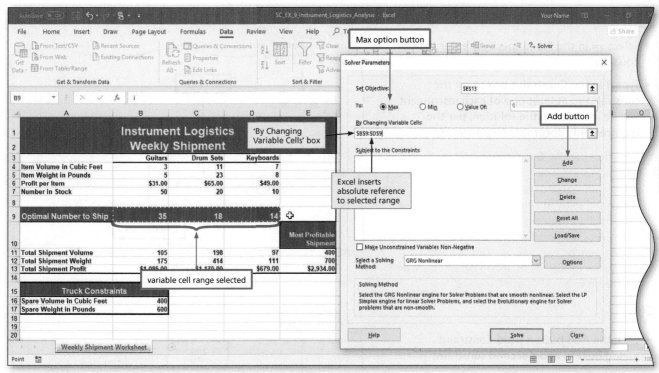

Figure 9–45

3

- Click the Add button (Solver Parameters dialog box) to display the Add Constraint dialog box.

- If necessary, click the 'Cell Reference: Collapse Dialog' button. Select the range B9:D9 to set the value of the Cell Reference box. Click the Expand Dialog button, if necessary.

- Click the middle arrow to display the list of constraint operators (Figure 9–46).

Q&A   What does the Add Constraint dialog box do?
It is a way to set limitations on the possible values that a cell or range can contain.

What happened to the dialog box while I selected the range?
Excel collapsed the dialog box to give you more room to select cells.

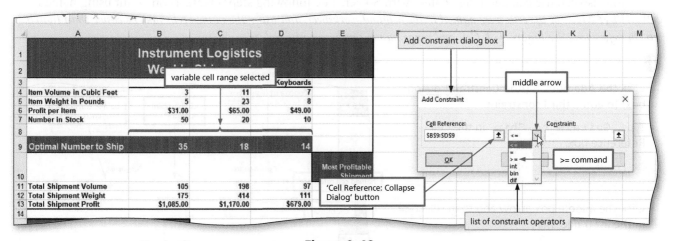

Figure 9–46

④

- Select >= in the list to specify greater than or equal to.

- Type 1 in the Constraint box to set the constraint so at least one of each instrument will be included in the solution, per the requirements document (Figure 9–47).

How do I use the Constraint box?

After entering a cell reference, you must select an operator. If the operator is <=, >=, or =, then you enter a constraint value or cell reference. Other valid operators are int, for an integer value; bin, for cells that contain a binary value of only one of two values, such as yes/no or true/false; or dif, for an all different constraint where no two values are the same.

Figure 9–47

⑤

- Click the Add button (Add Constraint dialog box) to add a second constraint.

- Select the range B9:D9 to set the value of the Cell Reference box.

- Click the middle box arrow and then select int in the list to set a constraint on the cells in the range B9:D9 to be assigned only integer values.

- Do not close the Add Constraint dialog box (Figure 9–48).

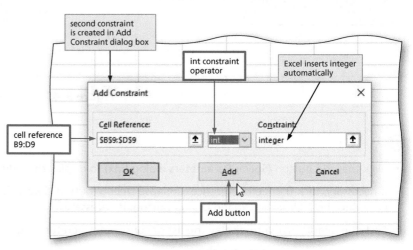

Figure 9–48

To Enter Constraints with Named Cells

You also can use cell and range names with Solver. The following steps create a constraint using named cells. **Why?** *Many of the cells were named in the original worksheet, and using the named cells may be easier than figuring out the references. See Figure 9–4. Cell and range names carry over into Solver.*

①

- Click the Add button (Add Constraint dialog box) to add a third constraint.

- Type **Guitars_to_Ship** in the Cell Reference box.

Do I have to type the underscores?

Yes. Named cells and ranges cannot have spaces.

- Click the middle box arrow and then select <= in the list if necessary.

- Click the Constraint box, and then type **Guitars_in_Stock** to specify that the number to ship should be less than or equal to the number in stock (Figure 9–49).

Figure 9–49

2

- Click the Add button (Add Constraint dialog box) to add the next constraint.

Q&A Nothing happened when I clicked the Add button. Did I do something wrong?
No. The constraint is added behind the scenes and will display in the Solve Parameters dialog box after you add the last constraint.

- Enter the remaining constraints as shown in Table 9–2, beginning with the constraint for Drum_Sets_to_Ship.

- After entering the last constraint, click OK (Add Constraint dialog box) to close the dialog box and display the Solver Parameters dialog box.

- Do not close the Solver Parameters dialog box. (Figure 9–50).

Q&A What should I do if a constraint does not match the ones shown in Figure 9–49?
Your order may differ, but the constraints should be the same. If they are not, select the constraint in error, click the Change button (Solver Parameters dialog box), and then enter the constraint as shown in Table 9–2. To delete a constraint, select the constraint you want to delete, and then click the Delete button.

Figure 9–50

To Set Solver Options

Now that you have entered all of the constraints for the problem, the following steps set options in order to obtain the optimal solution. You will choose the Simplex LP solving method. LP stands for linear progression, and Simplex refers to the basic problem-solving method used to solve linear problems. Linear problems are ones in which a "straight-line" approach of cause and effect can seek to determine a goal value by modifying values that impact the goal. For example, a decrease in costs results in an increase in profits.

To ensure that Solver finds the true optimal solution—possibly at the expense of more solution time—you will set the Integer Optimality % tolerance to zero. **Why?** *Setting the value to zero will help Solver to find an optimal solution when one of the constraints says that a value must be an integer.*

- With the Solver Parameters dialog box still open, click the 'Select a Solving Method' arrow to display the choices (Figure 9–51).

Figure 9–51

- Click Simplex LP in the list to select the linear progression method (Figure 9–52).

Q&A

What are the other choices?
GRG Nonlinear is the Generalized Reduced Gradient optimizing algorithm in which the change of the objective cell is not proportional to the change of the dependent cells. The Evolutionary method finds a better solution, but because it does not rely on derivative or gradient information, it usually requires running Solver several times as you search for the best one.

Figure 9–52

2

- Click the Options button (Solver parameters dialog box) to display the Options dialog box.

- If necessary, click the 'Use Automatic Scaling' check box to select it.

- Set the 'Integer Optimality (%)' to 0 to extend the amount of time that Solver takes to find an optimal solution.

- Verify that all other dialog box settings match those in Figure 9–53.

- In particular, ensure that only the Use Automatic Scaling option is selected.

Figure 9–53

3

- Click OK (Options dialog box) to return to the Solver Parameters dialog box (Figure 9–54).

 Experiment

- Click the Help button (Solver Parameters dialog box) to open Help related to Solver in a browser window. Read the general explanation and click on various links to read specific instruction. When you are finished, close the browser window and return to Excel.

Figure 9–54

To Find the Optimal Solution

The following steps find the optimal solution that considers the constraints and options that you entered earlier. Solver will produce an answer report. *Why? You may want to view a summary of how Solver came up with the solution.*

• Click the Solve button (Solver Parameters dialog box) to display the Solver Results dialog box, indicating that Solver found a solution to the problem.

• Click Answer in the Reports list (Solver Results dialog box) to select the report to generate (Figure 9–55).

 I received an error message or a non-optimal solution. What should I do?

You may have made an error in one of the constraints. Click the Cancel button to return to the worksheet. Click the Solver button (Data tab | Analyze group) and look closely at the constraints. They should match Figure 9–51. Edit them as necessary.

Figure 9–55

• Click OK (Solver Results dialog box) to display the values found by Solver and the newly recalculated totals (Figure 9–56).

 What is the result of using Solver?

Solver found a solution to the shipping problem that meets the constraints and maximizes the total profit of the shipment. The solution ships 50 guitars, 12 drum sets, and 9 keyboards, with a total volume of 345 cubic feet and a total weight of 598 pounds.

My solution lists a different number of instruments to ship. Did I do something wrong?

It may be that someone has turned off integer constraints. Return to the Solver Parameters dialog box, click the Options button, and then click the All Methods tab. Remove the checkmark for 'Ignore Integer Constraints'. The 'Use Automatic Scaling' check box should be checked. Click OK and then solve again.

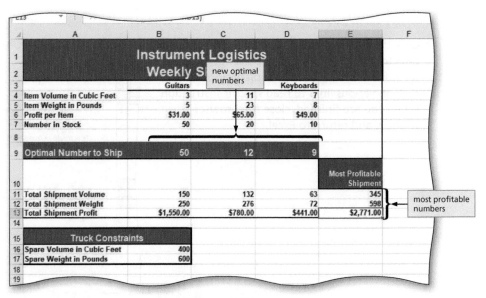

Figure 9–56

To View the Solver Answer Report

Solver generates the requested Answer Report on a separate worksheet after it finds a solution. The Answer Report summarizes the problem that you have presented to Solver. It shows the original and final values of the objective cell along with the original and final values of the changing cells that Solver modified to find the answer. Additionally, it lists all of the constraints that you entered.

Why? *The Answer Report documents that a particular problem has been solved correctly. Because it lists all of the relevant information in a concise format, you can use the Answer Report to make certain that you have entered all of the constraints and allowed Solver to modify all the necessary values to solve the problem. You also can use the report to reconstruct the Solver model in the future.*

The following steps view the Solver Answer Report.

- Click the Answer Report 1 sheet tab to display the Solver Answer Report (Figure 9–57).

Q&A What is shown in the Answer Report?

The Answer Report shows additional information about the constraints and how they were used to solve the problem. The Status column, beginning in cell F28, indicates whether a constraint was binding. A constraint that is **binding** is one that limits the final solution in some way and must be included in the Solver model. A constraint that is not binding is one that is not a limiting factor in the solution that Solver provides.

Figure 9–57

- Drag the Answer Report 1 sheet tab to the right of the Weekly Shipment Worksheet tab to move the worksheet in the workbook.

- Double-click the Answer Report 1 sheet tab to select the name.

- Type **Shipment Plan Answer Report 1** and then press ENTER to rename the worksheet.

- Change the color of the sheet tab to 'Gold, Accent 2'.

- Save the workbook again on the same storage location with the same file name.

More about Solver Options

BTW
Viewing Other Solutions
If you want to view solutions other than the one Solver identifies as optimal, select the Show Iteration Results check box in the Solver Parameters dialog box. After each iteration, the Show Trial Solution dialog box will be displayed, and you will have the option of saving that scenario and then stopping Solver or continuing on to the next solution.

When you selected the Simplex LP method of solving the production problem in the Solver Parameters dialog box, you selected a linear programming method that assumes the problem follows a cause and effect relationship. Changes to one value have a direct impact on another value. After choosing the Solver method, you can select various options to further configure the inner workings of Solver. Note that Excel saves the most recently used Solver parameters and options. Table 9–3 presents some of the more commonly used Solver options.

Table 9–3 Commonly Used Solver Parameters	
Parameter	**Meaning**
Max Time	The total time that Solver should spend trying different solutions, expressed in seconds
Iterations	The number of possible answer combinations that Solver should try
Constraint Precision	Instructs Solver in how close it must come to the target value in order to consider the problem to be solved. For example, if the target value is 100 and you set tolerance to 5%, then generating a solution with a target value of 95 is acceptable.
Use Automatic Scaling	Selected by default, specifies that Solver should internally rescale values of variables, constraints, and the objective to reduce the effect of outlying values

When using Solver, three issues must be kept in mind. First, some problems do not have solutions. The constraints may be constructed in such a way that Solver cannot find an answer that satisfies all of the constraints. Second, sometimes multiple answers solve the same problem. Solver does not indicate when this is the case, and you will have to use your own judgment to determine if you should seek another solution. As long as you are confident that you have given Solver all of the constraints for a problem, however, all answers should be equally valid. Finally, if Solver fails to find a solution, more time or more iterations may be required to solve the problem.

Break Point: If you want to take a break, this is a good place to do so. You can exit Excel now. To resume later, start Excel, open the file called SC_EX_9_InstrumentLogisticsAnalysis.xlsx, and continue following the steps from this location forward.

Using Scenarios and Scenario Manager to Analyze Data

BTW
Baseline Scenarios
For each model, it is helpful to define a baseline scenario that represents the starting assumptions. Even if the results of the baseline scenario do not figure prominently in the final analysis, they represent the starting point and should be saved.

A **scenario** is a named set of values you use in a what-if analysis; the Excel Scenario Manager lets you store and manage different scenarios. In this project, you will create different shipping plans—scenarios—based on different assumptions. For example, you have created a shipping plan that required finding the optimal number of instruments to ship based on several constraints, one of which was the free space on the truck. Changing the truck volume or weight would create a new scenario. Each set of values in these examples represents a what-if assumption. You use the Scenario Manager to keep track of various scenarios and produce a report detailing the what-if assumptions and results for each scenario.

The primary uses of the Scenario Manager are to:

1. Create different scenarios with multiple sets of changing cells.
2. Build summary worksheets that contain the different scenarios.
3. View the results of each scenario on your worksheet.

You will use the Scenario Manager for each of these three applications. After you create the scenarios, you will instruct Excel to build the summary worksheets, including a Scenario Summary worksheet and a Scenario PivotTable worksheet.

To Save the Current Data as a Scenario

Why? *The current data on the Weekly Shipment Worksheet consists of constraints and values that correctly solve the shipping problem.* These values can be saved as a scenario that can be accessed later or compared with other scenarios. The following steps save the current data using the Scenario Manager dialog box.

- Make the Weekly Shipment Worksheet the active sheet.
- Click the 'What-If Analysis' button (Data tab | Forecast group) to display the What-If Analysis menu (Figure 9–58).

Figure 9–58

- Click Scenario Manager on the What-If Analysis menu to display the Scenario Manager dialog box, which indicates that no scenarios are defined (Figure 9–59).

Figure 9–59

- Click the Add button (Scenario Manager dialog box) to open the Add Scenario dialog box.

- Type **Shipment 1** in the Scenario name box (Add Scenario dialog box) to provide a name for the scenario (Figure 9–60).

Q&A I have information in the Comment box. Is that OK?
Yes. Excel may add information about your user name and the date in the Comment box.

Figure 9–60

- Click the 'Changing Cells: Collapse Dialog' button (Add Scenario dialog box) to collapse the dialog box.

- Select the range B9:D9, type **,** (comma), and then select the range B16:B17 to enter the ranges in the Changing cells box (Figure 9–61).

Figure 9–61

5

- Click the Expand Dialog button (Add Scenario dialog box) to display the expanded Edit Scenario dialog box (Figure 9–62).

Figure 9–62

- Click OK (Edit Scenario dialog box) to accept the settings and display the Scenario Values dialog box.

- Click OK (Scenario Values dialog box) to display the Scenario Manager dialog box with the Shipment 1 scenario selected in the Scenarios list. (Figure 9–63).

Q&A | What can I do with the scenario? After the scenario has been saved, you can recall it at any time using the Scenario Manager or create a Scenario Summary, as you will do later in this module.

Figure 9–63

- Click Close (Scenario Manager dialog box) to save the Shipment 1 scenario in the workbook.

Other Ways

1. When running Solver, click Save Scenario (Solver Results dialog box), enter scenario name, click OK (Save Scenario dialog box), click OK (Solver Results dialog box)

Creating a New Scenario

After saving the Shipment 1 scenario, you will enter new data for the Shipment 2 scenario directly in the worksheet and then use Solver to solve the problem in the same way that you solved the Shipment scenario. Because both scenarios are based on the same model, you do not need to reenter the constraints into the Scenario Manager. A second Answer Report will solve the needs of the requirements document.

To Add the Data for a New Scenario

A truck with less room has become available. The shipping manager would like to see the difference in profit should the company fill this smaller load. The constraints for the Shipment 2 scenario therefore require a change in available truck volume and weight. These values must be entered into the appropriate cells before you can use Solver. The following steps add the data for a new scenario.

1 Click cell B16 and then type   300   as the truck volume.

2 Click cell B17 and then type   450   as the truck weight.

3 Click cell C17 to deselect cell B17 (Figure 9–64).

Figure 9–64

To Use Solver to Find a New Solution

Why? *After entering the new values, the total volume and weight shown in the range B16:B17 no longer satisfy the shipping constraints for the new scenario.* You now must use Solver again to determine if a solution exists for the constraints of Shipment 2. The following steps use Solver to seek a solution.

1

- Click the Solver button (Data tab | Analysis group) to display the Solver Parameters dialog box with the objective cell, changing cells, and constraints used with the previous scenario (Figure 9–65).

Q&A

Why am I not updating the constraints?

When you set up the constraints in Solver for Shipment 1, you used cell references and named cells rather than actual values for the number of each type of instrument. Entering the new values in cells B16:B17 automatically updated the constraints.

Figure 9–65

- Click the Solve button (Solver Parameters dialog box) to solve the problem and display the Solver Results dialog box.

- Click Answer in the Reports list to select a report type (Figure 9–66).

Figure 9–66

- Click OK (Solver Results dialog box) to display the solution found by Solver (Figure 9–67).

Q&A What did Solver accomplish? Solver found a solution that satisfies all of the constraints and maximizes the total profit. In this new scenario, total profit will be $2,365.00.

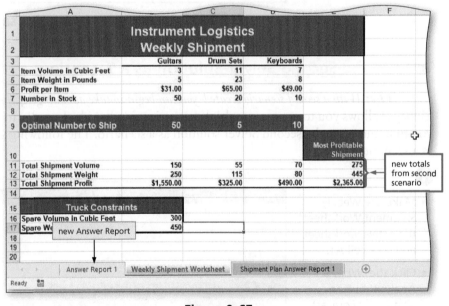

Figure 9–67

To View the Solver Answer Report for the Shipment 2 Solution

The next step views the Answer Report for the Shipment 2 solution.

1. Drag the new Answer Report 1 sheet tab to the right of the Shipment Answer Report 1 sheet tab to move the worksheet.

2. Rename the Answer Report 1 worksheet as **Shipment Plan Answer Report 2**.

3. Change the sheet tab color to 'Green, Accent 4' (Figure 9–68).

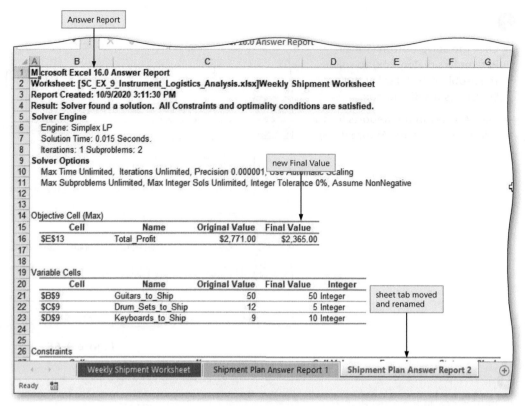

Figure 9–68

To Save the Second Solver Solution as a Scenario

Why? *With a second scenario created, you can begin to take advantage of the Scenario Manager.* The Scenario Manager allows you to compare multiple scenarios side by side. In order to use the Scenario Manager for this, you first must save the second Solver solution as a scenario. The following steps save the second Solver solution as a scenario.

• Make the Weekly Shipment Worksheet the active worksheet and click cell A1.

• Click the 'What-If Analysis' button (Data tab | Forecast group) and then click Scenario Manager on the What-If Analysis menu to display the Scenario Manager dialog box (Figure 9–69).

Figure 9–69

2

- Click the Add button (Scenario Manager dialog box) to display the Add Scenario dialog box.

- Type **Shipment 2** in the Scenario name box to name the new scenario (Figure 9–70).

Q&A Do I have to make any other changes?

No. The new figures will be saved automatically with the scenario.

3

- Click OK (Add Scenario dialog box) to display the Scenario Values dialog box with the current values.

- Click OK (Scenario Values dialog box) to display the updated Scenarios list in the Scenario Manager dialog box.

- Click the Close button (Scenario Manager dialog box) to save the Shipment 2 scenario and close the dialog box.

Figure 9–70

To Show a Saved Scenario

Why? *You can display and review any scenario in the workbook by using the Show button in the Scenario Manager dialog box.* The following steps display the Shipment 1 scenario created earlier.

1

- Click the 'What-If Analysis' button (Data tab | Forecast group) to display the What-If Analysis menu.

- Click Scenario Manager on the What-If Analysis menu to display the Scenario Manager dialog box.

- Click the scenario of interest, Shipment 1 in this case, to select it (Figure 9–71).

Q&A Can I edit a scenario?

Yes. Select the scenario (Scenario Manager dialog box) and then click the Edit button. Excel will display the Edit Scenario dialog box, allowing you to change the scenario name, edit the cells, or add a comment.

Figure 9–71

- Click the Show button (Scenario Manager dialog box) to display the data for the selected scenario in the worksheet.
- Click the Close button (Scenario Manager dialog box) to close the dialog box (Figure 9–72).

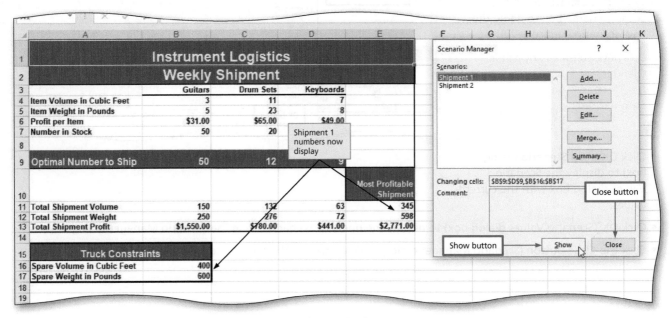

Figure 9–72

Summarizing Scenarios

BTW

Scenario Summary Details
Clicking the show detail button on the Scenario Summary worksheet will display any information entered in the Comments box of the Scenario Manager dialog box, along with creation and modification information.

You can create a Scenario Summary worksheet or a Scenario PivotTable worksheet to review and analyze various what-if scenarios when making decisions. A Scenario Summary worksheet, generated by the Scenario Manager, is a worksheet in outline format that you can print and manipulate just like any other worksheet. Recall that you worked with outlines in a previous module.

The Scenario PivotTable worksheet generated by the Scenario Manager also is a worksheet that you can print and manipulate like other worksheets. PivotTables summarize large amounts of data and can be rearranged and regrouped to show the data in various forms. Recall that you worked with PivotTables in a previous module. The Scenario PivotTable worksheet allows you to compare the results of multiple scenarios.

To Create a Scenario Summary Worksheet

Why? A Scenario Summary worksheet is a useful decision-making tool. The Scenario Summary worksheet will show the number of each type of instrument scheduled and total profit of the shipment for the current worksheet values, followed by the Shipment 1 and Shipment 2 scenarios. The optimal number of each type of instrument to be shipped, as calculated by Solver, is shown for both shipping plans. The following steps create a Scenario Summary worksheet.

1

- Click the 'What-If Analysis' button (Data tab | Forecast group) to display the What-If Analysis menu.

- Click Scenario Manager on the What-If Analysis menu to display the Scenario Manager dialog box (Figure 9–73).

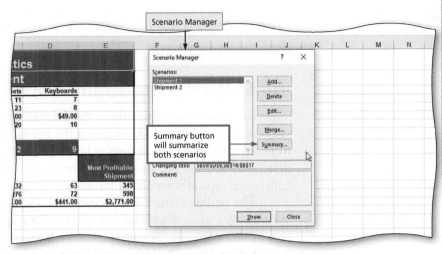

Figure 9–73

2

- Click the Summary button (Scenario Manager dialog box) to display the Scenario Summary dialog box.

- If necessary, click the Scenario summary option button in the Report type area (Scenario Summary dialog box).

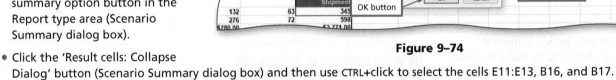

Figure 9–74

- Click the 'Result cells: Collapse Dialog' button (Scenario Summary dialog box) and then use CTRL+click to select the cells E11:E13, B16, and B17.

- Click the Expand Dialog button to return to the Scenario Summary dialog box (Figure 9–74).

3

- Click OK (Scenario Summary dialog box) to generate a Scenario Summary report.

- Rename the Scenario Summary sheet tab as **Shipment Scenario Summary** to provide a descriptive name for the sheet.

- Change the sheet tab color to 'Rose, Accent 6'.

- Drag the Shipment Scenario Summary sheet tab to the right of the Shipping Plan Answer Report 2 sheet tab to reposition the worksheet in the workbook (Figure 9–75).

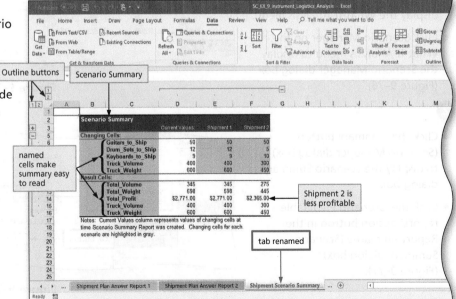

Figure 9–75

Working with an Outlined Worksheet

Excel automatically outlines the Scheduling Scenario Summary worksheet. The symbols for expanding and collapsing the rows appear above and to the left of the worksheet. You can hide or display levels of detail by using the hide detail and show detail symbols. You can also use the row- and column-level show detail buttons to collapse or expand rows and columns.

The outline feature is especially useful when working with very large worksheets. With smaller worksheets, the feature may not provide any real benefits. You can remove an outline by clicking the Ungroup arrow (Data tab | Outline group), and then clicking Clear Outline on the Ungroup menu.

To Create a Scenario PivotTable Worksheet

Excel also can create a Scenario PivotTable report worksheet to help analyze and compare the results of multiple scenarios. *Why? A Scenario PivotTable report worksheet gives you the ability to summarize the scenario data and reorganize the rows and columns to obtain different views of the summarized data.* The Scenario PivotTable summarizes the Shipment 1 and Shipment 2 scenarios and displays the result cells for the two scenarios for easy comparison. The following steps create the Scenario PivotTable worksheet.

- Click the Weekly Shipment Worksheet tab to make it active. You may have to scroll through the sheet tabs to locate the worksheet.

- Click the 'What-If Analysis' button (Data tab | Forecast group) to display the What-If Analysis menu.

- Click Scenario Manager on the What-If Analysis menu to display the Scenario Manager dialog box (Figure 9–76).

Figure 9–76

- Click the Summary button (Scenario Manager dialog box) to display the Scenario Summary dialog box.

- Click the 'Scenario PivotTable report' option button in the Report type area (Scenario Summary dialog box) (Figure 9–77).

Figure 9–77

3

- Click OK (Scenario Summary dailog box) to create the Scenario PivotTable (Figure 9–78).

🔍 **Experiment**

- Examine the various boxes, sections, and settings in the Field List.

Figure 9–78

4

- Rename the Scenario PivotTable worksheet as **Shipment Scenario PivotTable** to provide a descriptive name for the worksheet.

- Change the sheet tab color for the Shipment Scenario PivotTable worksheet to 'Aqua, Accent 5'.

- Drag the Shipment Scenario PivotTable sheet tab to the right of the Shipment Scenario Summary sheet tab to reposition the worksheet in the workbook.

- Format cells D4:D5 using the Accounting number format.

- Click cell A2 to deselect any other cell (Figure 9–79).

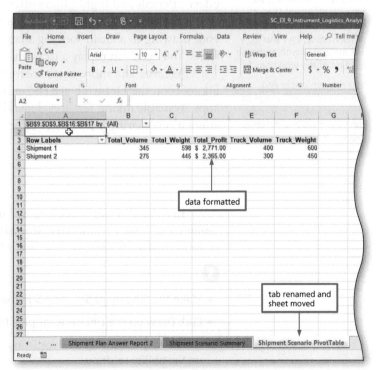

Figure 9–79

Q&A How can I use the PivotTable?

After creating the PivotTable, you can treat it like any other worksheet. Thus, you can print or chart a PivotTable. If you update the data in one of the scenarios, click the Refresh All button (Data tab | Queries & Connections group) to update the PivotTable. Note that if you merely change values on a scenario worksheet, it is not the same as changing the scenario. If you want to change the data in a scenario, you must enter the new data using the Scenario Manager.

● Save the workbook again on the same storage location with the same file name.

Ink Annotations

One of the new features in Office 2019 is digital inking. **Ink annotations** or **inking** is the process of freehand drawing on the screen with your finger, a digital pen, or a mouse. While digital inking tools have been available in previous versions, Microsoft has added them to a new Draw tab on the ribbon in Excel (Figure 9–80).

Figure 9–80

BTW
Distributing
Workbooks
Instead of printing and distributing a hard copy of a workbook, you can distribute the workbook electronically. Options include sending the workbook via email; posting it on cloud storage (such as OneDrive) and sharing the file with others; posting it on social media, a blog, or other website; and sharing a link associated with an online location of the workbook.

You also can create and share a PDF or XPS image of the workbook so that users can view the file in Acrobat Reader or XPS Viewer instead of in Excel

The Pens gallery includes pens, pencils, and highlighters. When you click a pen, Excel displays five thickness settings as well as sixteen solid colors and eight special effects. Pencils and highlighters offer color choices only. An 'Ink to Shape' button (Draw tab | Convert group) allows you to draw shapes roughly; Excel then will change your drawing to a clean-looking shape for creating things such as diagrams and process flows. You even can replay a drawing.

As more and more users create worksheets on mobile devices, the pen and ink tools on the Draw tab are becoming primary input mechanisms across the apps. Available inking features depend on the type of device you are using. Use ink annotations sparingly for better effects.

To Draw with a Pen

In the following steps, you will use the Draw tab to circle Shipment 1 on the 'Shipment Scenario Summary' worksheet. *Why? You will mark which Shipment you want to use by circling the shipment that has a larger profit.*

● Make the 'Shipment Scenario Summary' worksheet active.

● Click Draw on the ribbon to display the Draw tab.

● If necessary, click the Draw (or Draw with Touch) button (Draw tab | Tools group) to turn on the ability to draw.

Experiment

- One at a time, point to each drawing implement to display its ScreenTip.

- Click the second pen, 'Pen: Red, 0.5 mm', in the gallery to select it. If your pen ScreenTip is different, click the pen arrow to display its gallery and then click. 0.5 mm and Red.

- In the worksheet, draw a rough circle around the Shipment 1 results (Figure 9–81).

What if I make a mistake or want to redo my circle?

Press CTRL+Z and try again. Or, you can click the Eraser button (Draw tab | Tools group) and then click the drawing.

Figure 9–81

To Use the 'Ink to Shape' Tool

In the following steps, you will use the Draw tab to draw a rough arrow. *Why? You want to point out the profit line on the summary.* Excel then will convert the rough drawing to a distinctive arrow shape.

1

- If necessary, click the second pen, labelled 'Pen: Red, 0.5 mm', to display its arrow.

- Click the pen arrow to display the pen gallery (Figure 9–82).

Experiment

- Point to various items in the pen gallery to view the ScreenTips.

Figure 9–82

- In the Thickness area, click the 2 mm pen size to increase the diameter of the pen tip.

- Click the 'Ink to Shape' button (Draw tab | Convert group) to select it.

- In a blank area of the worksheet, draw a rough arrow using one motion. Do not lift your finger or mouse button (Figure 9–83).

Q&A What other shapes can I draw and convert?

You can draw squares, rectangles, diamonds, pentagons, ellipses, connectors, and others. Look up 'Convert ink to shapes' in Excel Help for a complete listing.

Figure 9–83

- Lift your finger or release the mouse button.

- When Excel converts your drawing into a shape, click the Draw (or Draw with Touch) button (Draw tab | Tools group) to turn it off.

- Use the sizing handles to resize the arrow as necessary.

- Drag the arrow so it points at line 14 (Figure 9–84).

Q&A How do you use the Lasso Select tool (Draw tab | Tools group)?

After you create an ink effect, you can use the Lasso Select tool to draw around all, or part, of the annotation. Excel will convert the lassoed area to an object with sizing handles and the ability to move, delete, or cut the object.

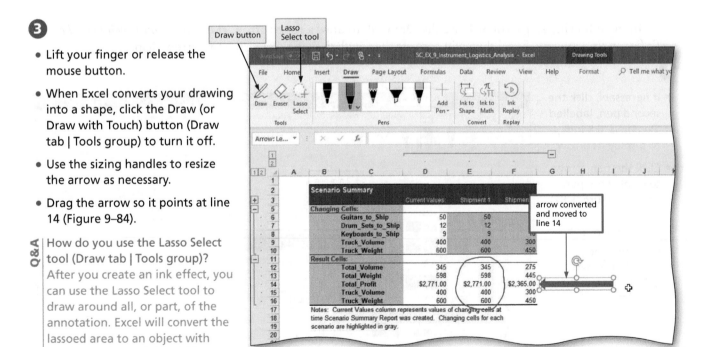

Figure 9–84

To Highlight with Ink

In the following steps, you will use the Drawing toolbar to highlight an area on the worksheet. *Why? Highlighting the bigger profit will draw attention to your choice even further.*

1

- In the Pens group, click 'Highlighter: Yellow 6 mm'.
- Drag through the profit for Shipment 1 to highlight the figure (Figure 9–85).

Experiment

- Click the Ink Replay button (Draw tab | Replays group) to watch Excel replay your inking annotations.

2

- **sam'** Because the project is now complete, you can save the file again and exit Excel.

Figure 9–85

Summary

In this module, you learned how to analyze a worksheet using formula auditing techniques and tracer arrows. You used error checking features to determine how to fix errors in the worksheet. You established data validation rules and informed users with input messages about the validation rules. You solved a complex problem with Excel, using trial and error, Goal Seek, and Solver. You used the Scenario Manager to manage different problems on the same worksheet and then summarized the results of the scenarios with a Scenario Summary worksheet and a Scenario PivotTable worksheet. Finally, you added ink annotations to the worksheet using the new Draw tab.

What decisions will you need to make when creating your next worksheet to solve a complex problem?
Use these guidelines as you complete the assignments in this module and create your own worksheets for evaluating and analyzing data outside of this class.

1. Review and analyze workbook structure and organization.

   a) Review all formulas.

   b) Use precedent and dependent tracing to determine dependencies.

   c) Use formula auditing tools to correct formula errors.

2. Establish data validation rules.

   a) Identify changing cells.

   b) Determine data restrictions to address using data validation.

3. Configure useful add-ins.

   a) Identify missing add-ins.

   b) Use Excel Options to enable necessary add-ins.

   c) Verify inclusion on the ribbon.

4. Determine strategies for problem solving.

   a) Use trial and error to modify input or changing values.

   b) Use Goal Seek.

   c) Use Solver to address multiple constraints and changing cells.

5. Create and store scenarios.

   a) Use the Scenario Manager to keep track of multiple scenarios.

   b) Use a Scenario Summary worksheet to present and compare multiple scenarios.

   c) Use a Scenario PivotTable report to manipulate and interpret scenario results.

6. Annotate your worksheet using the Draw tab.

   a) Use the pen, pencil, and highlighter sparingly for better effects.

   b) When you need a quick shape, use the 'Ink to Shape' tool.

Apply Your Knowledge

Reinforce the skills and apply the concepts you learned in this module.

Using Solver to Plan Festival Advertising

Note: To complete this assignment, you will be required to use the Data Files. Please contact your instructor for information about accessing the Data Files.

Instructions: Start Excel. Open the workbook called SC_EX_9-2.xlsx, which is located in the Data Files. The workbook you open contains information about your town's two annual festivals, one in June and one in October. You are to determine how best to promote the festivals, making the most of the town's advertising budget. Figure 9–86a shows the completed Answer Report. Figure 9–86b shows the completed Scenario Summary.

(a) Answer Report

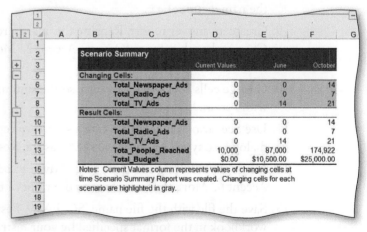

(b) Scenario Summary

Figure 9–86

Continued >

Apply Your Knowledge *continued*

Perform the following tasks:

1. Trace precedents and dependents on the two cells with errors: F9 and E7.

2. Use Error Checking to evaluate the error in cell F9. Use the solution suggested by Error Checking.

3. Trace the error in cell E7. Because the Social Media cost of zero is valid, the division error appears. In cell E7, type `=E5` because all people might be reached by Social Media with no cost.

4. Use Solver to determine the best mix of advertising for the advertising dollars. The costs for the month of June are already in the worksheet (B6:D6).

   a. The objective is an advertising budget of $10,500 (the Value Of parameter), which will display in cell F11.

   b. Set the Value Of parameter to 10500.

   c. The changing variables cells are B9:D9.

   d. The constraints are as follows: the newspaper allows a maximum of 14 ads per week, the radio station allows a maximum of 30 advertisement spots per week, and the TV station allows a maximum of 21 advertisements per week. The Ads Placed values must be positive whole numbers (*Hint*: Use the int operator as well as the >= operator.)

   e. Use the Simplex LP solving method.

5. After you click the Solve button (Solver Parameters dialog box), use the Save Scenario button (Solver Results dialog box) to save the scenario with the name, **June**.

6. Instruct Solver to create the Answer Report for your solution. Rename the answer report tab, **June Advertising Report**. Change the tab color to 'Blue, Accent 1.' Move the worksheet to the right of the 'Festival Ads Placement' worksheet.

7. Create a second solution using Solver. This solution is for the larger, October festival and will have an advertising budget of $25,000.

8. After you click the Solve button (Solver Parameters dialog box), if the Solver Results dialog box says it cannot find a solution, click the 'Solve Without Integer Constraints' option button and solve again. Use the Save Scenario button (Solver Results dialog box) to save the scenario with the name, **October**.

9. Create an answer report. Rename the answer report tab, **October Advertising Report**. Change the tab color to 'Orange, Accent 2.' Move the worksheet to the right of the other worksheets.

10. Change cells B9:D9 back to zero, so the summary report you create in the next step will begin with zeroes.

11. Use Scenario Manager to create a summary report. When Excel displays the Scenario Summary dialog box, type **B9:D9,F10:F11** as the Result cells box.

12. Name the resulting summary tab, **Advertising Summary**. Change the tab color to 'Green, Accent 6.' Move the worksheet to the right of the other worksheets.

13. Save the file with the file name, SC_EX_9_FestivalAdvertising, and submit the revised workbook in the format specified by your instructor.

14. Exit Excel.

15. ✷ How would you determine which scenario makes the best use of the advertising dollars? If the budget was a secondary concern, what cell might you use as an objective? Would it be a max, min, or value?

Extend Your Knowledge

Extend the skills you learned in this module and experiment with new skills. You may need to use Help to complete the assignment.

Validating Car Loan Calculator Data

Note: To complete this assignment, you will be required to use the Data Files. Please contact your instructor for information about accessing the Data Files.

Instructions: Start Excel. Open the workbook SC_EX_9-3.xlsx, which is located in the Data Files. The workbook you open contains a template that calculates the monthly payment for a car loan. The workbook has some errors. You are to correct these errors and create data validation rules. Figure 9–87 shows the worksheet with the errors fixed and an input message for the price of the car.

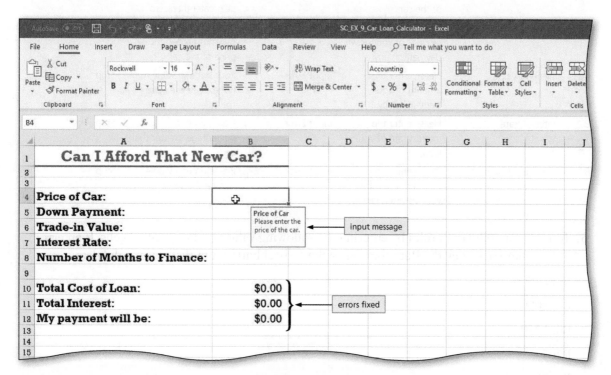

Figure 9–87

Perform the following tasks:

1. To validate the data in cells B10:B12, first do the following:

   a. Examine the formula in cell B10. Trace the error. Check for both precedent and dependent cells. Remove the tracer arrows.

   b. Examine the formula in cell B11. Trace the error. Check for both precedent and dependent cells. Remove the tracer arrows.

   c. Examine the formula in cell B12. Trace the error. Check for both precedent and dependent cells. Remove the tracer arrows.

2. Use Help to review the IF() function. In cells B10 and B11, use the IF( ) function to execute the formula only when the dependent value is greater than 0. (*Note:* Cell B10 may still show a #NUM error until you fix other errors.)

Continued >

Extend Your Knowledge *continued*

3. Use Help to review the IFERROR() function, and then use it in cell B12 to display zero if any other errors occur. (*Hint:* Use the current PMT() function as the first argument in the IFERROR() function and use 0 as the second argument.)

4. Create data validation constraints and messages for each of the cells in Table 9–4. (*Hint:* B4:B6 should be formatted in Accounting style with two decimal places.) Use the Error message column to help you determine the constraint.

Table 9–4 Data Constraints and Messages

Cell	Input Message Title	Input Message	Error Alert Title	Error Message	Error Alert Style
B4	Price of Car	Please enter the price of the car.	Input Error	The price of the car must be greater than zero.	Stop
B5	Down Payment	Please enter the amount of your down payment, if any.	Input Error	Your down payment may not exceed the price of the car.	Stop
B6	Trade-in Value	Please enter the amount of your trade-in, if any.	Input Error	Your trade-in value may not exceed the price of the car.	Stop
B7	Interest Rate	Please enter the interest rate of your loan.	Input Error	Please enter a percentage greater than zero.	Stop
B8	Number of Months	Please enter the number of months you wish to finance.	Input Error	Please enter a whole number between 1 and 72.	Stop

5. Test the data validation rules by entering the following values in the specified cells. If an error message appears, click the Retry button or the Cancel button and then enter valid data.

    B4: 25000

    B5: 1000

    B6: 1250

    B7: 5

    B8: 60

6. Save the file with the file name, SC_EX_9_CarLoanCalculator, and submit the revised workbook in the format specified by your instructor.

7. ☀ In step 3, why did you need to use the IFERROR() function, rather than the IF function? Was there another way you could have solved the errors other than using those functions? What effect would locking the cells with the formulas have on the rest of the spreadsheet?

Expand Your World

Create a solution that uses cloud and web technologies by learning and investigating on your own from general guidance.

Add-Ins for Excel Online

You use Excel Online through your OneDrive account and understand that there are limitations to the online versions of the Office apps compared to the desktop applications. You are interested in discovering add-ins that can improve your overall productivity with Excel Online.

Instructions:

1. Sign into OneDrive and create a new workbook using Excel Online.

2. Explore the Office Add-ins collection available from the Insert tab of the ribbon in the new workbook.

3. Browse options in the Education and Productivity categories of the Store as well as those in another category of your choice.

4. Create a document that summarizes the features of an add-in from each of the three categories.

5. Save the file with the file name, SC_EX_9_ExcelAddIns, and submit the revised workbook in the format specified by your instructor.

6. ✲ Compare the add-ins available in Excel 2019 to those available for Excel Online. Choose two add-ins and evaluate the strengths and weaknesses of each. Which would you recommend, and why?

In the Lab

Design and implement a solution using creative thinking and problem-solving skills.

Do You Want to Be a Millionaire?

Note: To complete this assignment, you will be required to use the Data Files. Please contact your instructor for information about accessing the Data Files.

Problem: You decide to use a financial calculator to see how much you might have to save each year to retire a millionaire!

Perform the following tasks:

Part 1: Start Excel and open the file named SC_EX_9-4.xlsx. Examine the Retirement Schedule worksheet and examine the various calculations. The worksheet, shown in Figure 9–88, makes the following assumptions:

a. The starting balance deposited in the retirement account is stored in cell B3.

b. The first annual contribution is in cell C3. The calculator assumes a $200 increase in contributions each year.

c. The rate of return (column D) is based on a fairly aggressive investment strategy, 8%, until the age of 60. It then reduces to a moderate investment strategy of 5%.

Use Goal Seek to set the final ending balance (E38) to $1,000,000 by changing cell B3, the initial starting balance. Write down the new B3 value on a piece of paper. Click Cancel to undo the changes and return to the original values.

Use Goal Seek again by changing cell C3, the annual contribution. Write down the new value in cell C3. Click Cancel to undo the changes.

Use Solver to set the objective in cell E38 to 1000000 by changing the values in cells B3:D3. Set constraints for cells B3 and C3 to be greater than or equal to one. Set a constraint for cell D3 to be less than or equal to .08 (8 percent) and greater than or equal to zero. Select the GRG Nonlinear solving method (because you are dealing with a percentage rate of return). When Excel displays the Solver Results dialog box, choose to produce an answer report. Move the new worksheet to the right of the original one, and change the tab color to 'Brown, Accent 2'.

Continued >

In the Lab *continued*

Age	Starting Balance	Annual Contribution	Return	Ending Balance
30	$ 25,000.00	$ 500.00	8%	$ 27,540.00
31	27,540.00	700.00	8%	$ 30,499.20
32	30,499.20	900.00	8%	$ 33,911.14
33	33,911.14	1,100.00	8%	$ 37,812.03
34	37,812.03	1,300.00	8%	$ 42,240.99
35	42,240.99	1,500.00	8%	$ 47,240.27
36	47,240.27	1,700.00	8%	$ 52,855.49
37	52,855.49	1,900.00	8%	$ 59,135.93
38	59,135.93	2,100.00	8%	$ 66,134.80
39	66,134.80	2,300.00	8%	$ 73,909.59
40	73,909.59	2,500.00	8%	$ 82,522.35
41	82,522.35	2,700.00	8%	$ 92,040.14
42	92,040.14	2,900.00	8%	$ 102,535.35
43	102,535.35	3,100.00	8%	$ 114,086.18
44	114,086.18	3,300.00	8%	$ 126,777.08
45	126,777.08	3,500.00	8%	$ 140,699.24
46	140,699.24	3,700.00	8%	$ 155,951.18
47	155,951.18	3,900.00	8%	$ 172,639.28
48	172,639.28	4,100.00	8%	$ 190,878.42
49	190,878.42	4,300.00	8%	$ 210,792.69
50	210,792.69	4,500.00	8%	$ 232,516.11
51	232,516.11	4,700.00	8%	$ 256,193.40
52	256,193.40	4,900.00	8%	$ 281,980.87
53	281,980.87	5,100.00	8%	$ 310,047.34
54	310,047.34	5,300.00	8%	$ 340,575.13
55	340,575.13	5,500.00	8%	$ 373,761.14
56	373,761.14	5,700.00	8%	$ 409,818.03
57	409,818.03	5,900.00	8%	$ 448,975.47
58	448,975.47	6,100.00	8%	$ 491,481.51
59	491,481.51	6,300.00	8%	$ 537,604.03
60	537,604.03	6,500.00	5%	$ 571,309.23
61	571,309.23	6,700.00	5%	$ 606,909.69
62	606,909.69	6,900.00	5%	$ 644,500.17
63	644,500.17	7,100.00	5%	$ 684,180.18
64	684,180.18	7,300.00	5%	$ 726,054.19
65	726,054.19	7,500.00	5%	$ 770,231.90

Figure 9–88

Experiment with other constraints. For example, suppose the most you can start the account with is $25,000. Perhaps you can only add a maximum of $500 a year. Will Solver find a solution with those constraints? Write down your answers; do not save the file.

Save the file with the file name, SC_EX_9_RetirementCalculator. Submit the revised workbook and answers to the Part 2 critical thinking questions in the format specified by your instructor.

Part 2: ✳ You made several decisions while creating the worksheet in this assignment: initial starting balance, annual contribution, constraints. What was the rationale behind each of these decisions? Which of the solutions seemed the most feasible to you? Why?

10 | Data Analysis with Power Tools and Creating Macros

Objectives

After completing this module, you will be able to:

- Explain the Excel power tools
- Customize the ribbon and enable data analysis
- Use the Get & Transform data commands
- Create a query using Power Query Editor
- Build a PivotTable using Power Pivot
- Explain data modelling
- Create a measure
- View cube functions
- Use Power View
- Create tiles in a Power View report
- Use 3D Maps
- Save a tour as an animation
- Explain Power BI
- Create hyperlinks
- Use the macro recorder to create a macro
- Execute a macro

Introduction

Excel has a wide range of interlinked power tools for data analysis—Get & Transform, Power Pivot, Power View, 3D Maps, and Power BI (Business Intelligence)—whether you need to export data for business intelligence, pivot or manipulate data to find trends, create data models, or show data more visually.

Table 10–1 describes the five power tools available with Excel 2019. In this module, you will only touch on each of the power tools. The topic is vast and would require a lot of time and data modelling experience to explore all of the features associated with each tool. Power Pivot and Power View may not be available in all versions of Excel. While you may have limited access to these tools, you will be able to work through the majority of the steps in this module.

Table 10–1 Power Tools

Tool	Purpose
Get & Transform (formerly called Power Query)	The Get & Transform commands enable you to extract, connect, refine, and transform large amounts of data into an accessible Excel file. You can use Get & Transform to exert greater control over columns, formulas, and filtering tools, and also to modify data types and extract PivotTables.
Power Pivot	Power Pivot enables you to import and compare large amounts of data from multiple sources to analyze relationships between tables of data. You can use Power Pivot to create and model data tables, feed data to other Power Tools, and use data analysis expressions. Power Pivot is not available with all versions of Excel.
Power View	Power View is an interactive visualization tool used to provide a drag-and-drop interface for rapid model building. You can use Power View to connect to different data models within the same workbook, create new relationships among current data, and introduce key performance indicators (KPIs) based on those relationships. Power View can group (or smart group) data automatically to create advanced pie charts, maps, data cards, and other data visualizations.
3D Maps (formerly called Power Map)	3D Maps let you plot and visualize geographic or temporal data on a three-dimensional map. With filtering, you can compare how different factors affect your data. You can use a 3D Map to build custom regions, capture screenshots, and build cinematic time tours or animations through your data.
Power BI	Power BI, or Power Business Intelligence, is an Excel-based cloud tool that combines the other Power Tools with some additional features to enable you to find and visualize data, share, and collaborate. Power BI includes a wide range of forecasting tools, a drag-and-drop canvas, dashboards, report generation, and data modelling. Currently Power BI is available only to businesses, Office 365 subscribers, or as a download.

In addition to using Excel power tools, you will create hyperlinks to move quickly to other parts of the workbook, animations, and external websites. You also will record a macro to automate a task.

Project: Business Decisions Demographics

The project in this module follows proper design guidelines and uses Excel to create the workbook shown in Figures 10–1 and 10–2. The Rural Hospital Advancement Commission (RHAC) of the state health department in Missouri wants to address the needs of rural counties by building a new hospital. They are hiring a business analytics firm to find the best location based mainly on population. The business analytics firm specializes in examining raw data, looking for patterns, correlations, and other associations to help companies and organizations make better business decisions. Using data from the U.S. Census Bureau, the firm plans to present several forms of visual data to its client using Excel power tools.

Figure 10–1a shows the opening worksheet that includes a screen capture, a symbol, and hyperlinks to the other pages. Figure 10–1b queries the external data to display the 10 least populous counties. Figure 10–1c lists all counties, along with the number of housing units and total area from a different data table.

(a) Homepage with Hyperlinks

(b) 10 Least Populous Counties

(c) Housing Units by County

Figure 10–1

EX 10-3

Figure 10–2a displays a PivotTable that merges the two data sources to display the population, number of housing units, and occupancy rates per county. Figure 10–2b displays a Power View report. Figure 10–2c displays the data represented in Power BI. **Power BI** (pronounced bee-eye), or Business Intelligence, is a powerful web-based tool used to visualize and share data. Finally, the data then will be transformed into an interactive map. The 3D Maps window is shown in Figure 10–2d.

(a) PivotTable

(b) Power View

(c) Power BI

(d) 3D Maps

Figure 10–2

Figure 10–3 illustrates the requirements document for the Hospital Proposal workbook. It includes the needs, source of data, and other facts about its development.

Worksheet Title	Demographic Analysis for Proposed Rural Hospital
Needs	The business analytics firm would like to present a variety of data visualizations to the client, including: 1. The 10 least populous counties in order from least to most, and income for each. 2. A list of all of the counties in the state, along with the number of housing units in each, and the total area represented in square miles. 3. A Power Pivot report combining the data sources to show the relationship between county, population, and housing units. 4. A Power View report showing the population, housing units, and occupancy rate for each county. 5. An animated map showing the counties with the least population. 6. An attractive opening worksheet with hyperlinks to each of the above items, 1 through 5, a hyperlink to the Power BI website, and a symbol.
Source of Data	Data is available in two external sources, downloaded from the U.S. Census Bureau: Support_EX_10_MOHousingSqMiles.xlsx and Support_EX_10_MOPopulationIncomeByCounty.xlsx.
Calculations	Average occupancy rate for each county, which is calculated by taking the population of the county divided by the number of housing units. This calculation will appear in the Power Pivot report.

Figure 10–3

Workflow

Recall that in previous modules you imported data from a variety of sources including an Access database, a Word table, a comma-delimited text file, and a table from the web. The workflow to create connections for use with the power tools is similar:

- **Connect to the data:** Make connections to data in the cloud, in a service, or from local sources. You can work with the connected data by creating a permanent connection from your workbook to that data source, ensuring that the data you work with is always up to date.

- **Transform the data:** Shape the data locally to meet your needs; the original source remains unchanged.

- **Combine data from various sources:** Create a data model from multiple data sources and get a unique view into the data.

- **Share the data:** Save, share, or use transformed data for reports and presentations.

With a good understanding of the requirements and an understanding of the necessary decisions, the next step is to use Excel to create the workbook. In this module, you will learn how to create the workbook shown in Figure 10–1 and Figure 10–2.

BTW
The Ribbon and Screen Resolution
Excel may change how the groups and buttons within the groups appear on the ribbon, depending on the computer's screen resolution. Thus, your ribbon may look different from the ones in this book if you are using a screen resolution other than 1366 x 768.

To Create a Workbook

The following steps start Excel and open a blank workbook. Then, after changing the color scheme, you will use the Save As dialog box to save the workbook on your storage device.

1 **sam**⬇ Start Excel.

2 Click the Blank workbook from the template gallery in Backstage view.

3 If necessary, maximize the Excel window.

4 Set the color scheme to Violet.

5 Display Backstage view, click Save As, and then click Browse to open the Save As dialog box.

6 Browse to your storage device.

7 In the File name box, type SC_EX_10_HospitalProposal as the file name.

8 Click Save (Save As dialog box) to save the file.

To Copy Data Files

Sometimes data sources move to different locations. You probably have noticed while surfing the web that some webpages no longer exist or have been redirected. On your computer, you may have links that no longer work after moving a file to a different folder. Therefore, if you are using local data—that is, the data stored on your computer—it is a good idea to store the workbook and any connected data sources in the same folder location.

The following steps copy two files from the Data Files to your storage location. See your instructor for more information about this process. If you already have downloaded the Data Files to the same storage location that you are using to create and save files in this module, you can skip these steps.

To complete these steps, you will be required to use the Data Files. Please contact your instructor for information about accessing the Data Files.

1 Click the File Explorer button on the Windows taskbar to open a File Explorer window.

2 Navigate to the location of the Data Files for this module.

3 Select both the Support_EX_10_MOHousingSqMiles.xlsx file and the Support_EX_10_MOPopulationIncomeByCounty.xlsx file, and then copy and paste the files into your storage location folder.

4 Close the File Explorer window.

To Enable Data Analysis

The following steps verify that Data Analysis has been enabled in the version of Excel that you are running. *Why? Data analysis commands are required in order to use the power tools and they are not enabled by default in a standard Excel installation.*

1

- Display Backstage view and then click Options to open the Excel Options dialog box.

- In the left pane of the dialog box, click Data to display the Data options area.

- If necessary, click to display a check mark in the 'Enable Data Analysis add-ins: Power Pivot, Power View and 3D Maps' check box (Figure 10–4).

 Q&A I do not see the Enable option. What should I do?
You may have a version of Excel that does not support data analysis and the power tools. Continue with the steps and contact your instructor or IT administrator.

Figure 10–4

2

- Click OK (Excel Options dialog box) to close the dialog box and enable the data analysis tools.

Q&A Should I see a change in Excel?
No. Changing the setting ensures that you will not see an error message when you try to use the power tools later in the module.

To Add in Power Map

If you could not enable data analysis in the previous steps, you may need to add Power Map to your version of Excel in order to run 3D Maps. Recall from a previous module that you used the Add-ins option to add Solver to Excel. The following steps add in Power Map.

1 Display Backstage view and then click Options to open the Excel Options dialog box.

2 In the left pane of the dialog box, click Add-ins to display the Add-ins Options.

3 Near the bottom of the dialog box, click the Manage arrow and then click COM Add-ins.

4 Click the Go button to open the COM Add-ins dialog box.

5 Click to display a check mark in the 'Microsoft Power Map for Excel' check box. If you have check boxes for Power View or Power Pivot, select those as well.

6 Click OK (COM Add-ins dialog box).

Customizing the Ribbon

It is easy to **customize**, or personalize, the ribbon the way that you want it. You can

- Create custom groups and custom tabs to contain frequently used commands.
- Rearrange or rename buttons, groups, and tabs to fit your work style.
- Rename or remove buttons and boxes from an existing tab and group.
- Add new buttons to a custom group or to the Quick Access Toolbar.

When you add new buttons to the ribbon, you can choose from a list that includes 1) commands that you use elsewhere in Excel, such as those on shortcut menus; 2) commands from Backstage view; or 3) other commands that are not on the ribbon. Or, you can create a new button that executes a command or set of commands that you record. In this module, you will enable the Power Pivot tab on the ribbon, add the 'Insert a Power View' button to the Insert tab, and then enable the Developer tab.

You can customize the ribbon in all of the Microsoft Office applications, but the customizations only apply to the application you are using. The changes you make to the Excel ribbon will not change the ribbon in any other Microsoft Office application. When you no longer need the customization, it can be removed individually, or the entire ribbon can be reset to its default settings, removing all customizations.

CONSIDER THIS

What should I keep in mind when customizing the ribbon?

- Customize the ribbon when you need to access new features of Excel, or when you regularly need to access commands that are not part of the ribbon already.
- If the new command will be used at various times, with different tabs, consider adding the command or button to the Quick Access Toolbar.
- If you need to add a single command to the ribbon, choose a tab with plenty of room to hold the new command and its new group.
- If you need to add several commands, consider creating a new tab on the ribbon.
- If you are using a computer in a lab situation, you may not have permission to change the ribbon. Check with your instructor or IT administrator.
- If you are using a computer in a lab situation, reset the ribbon when you are done.

To Customize the Ribbon

The following steps customize the ribbon. *Why? Due to space constraints on the ribbon and the advanced nature of the power tools, some of the commands do not appear automatically.* You will enable the Power Pivot tab on the ribbon, add the 'Insert a Power View' button to the Insert tab, and then enable the Developer tab that you will use later in the module.

The Power Pivot tool is not available in all versions of Excel. If you do not see the Power Pivot tab in the following steps, contact your instructor or IT administrator to see if your version of Excel can run Power Pivot; you may have to use an Add-in process.

- Right-click a blank area of the ribbon to display the shortcut menu (Figure 10–5).

Figure 10–5

2

- Click the 'Customize the Ribbon' command on the shortcut menu to display the Customize Ribbon area of the Excel Options dialog box.

- In the Main Tabs area, scroll as necessary, and then click to display a check mark in both the Developer and the Power Pivot check boxes, if necessary (Figure 10–6).

Q&A I do not see Power Pivot. What should I do?
Contact your instructor or IT administrator to see if your version of Excel can run Power Pivot. If not, you can still continue with these steps and use the Developer ribbon.

Figure 10–6

3

- In the Main Tabs area, click Insert (not its check box) to select the Insert tab.

- Click the New Group button to insert a new group on the selected tab (in this case, the Insert tab) (Figure 10–7).

Q&A Why am I adding this command to the Insert tab?
The Insert tab will be easy to remember when you want to insert a Power View report.

Figure 10–7

• Click the 'Choose commands from' button to display the menu (Figure 10–8).

Q&A Can I add a command directly to a tab?

No. You only can add commands to new groups.

Figure 10–8

• Click 'Commands Not in the Ribbon' to display only those commands.

• Scroll down and click 'Insert a Power View Report' to select it.

• Click the Add button to add the command to the new group (Figure 10–9).

Figure 10–9

6

- Click OK (Excel Options dialog box) to display the customization on the ribbon (Figure 10–10).

Experiment

- Click the Insert tab and look at the new group and new button. Click the Home tab.

two new tabs appear on ribbon

Figure 10–10

Other Ways

1. Display Backstage view, click Options, click Customize Ribbon (Excel Options dialog box), click appropriate check box in Main Tabs list, add necessary commands, click OK

TO RENAME A NEW GROUP

If you wanted to rename a new group to customize the ribbon further, you would perform the following steps.

1. Right-click a blank area of the ribbon to display the shortcut menu.
2. Click the 'Customize the Ribbon' command on the shortcut menu to display the Excel Options dialog box.
3. In the Main Tabs area, navigate to and then click 'New Group (Custom)' to select it.
4. Click the Rename button to display the Rename dialog box.
5. Choose an appropriate symbol and enter a display name.
6. Click OK (Rename dialog box).
7. Click OK (Excel Options dialog box).

Get & Transform

Also called Power Query, the Get & Transform commands located on the Data tab allow you to extract, connect, clean, and transform large amounts of data into an accessible Excel table. Recall that when you get data using a Get & Transform command, Excel provides advanced editing and querying techniques to use with that data. When you use the Power Query Editor, you are provided with tools to group rows, filter, replace values, remove duplicates, and edit columns to facilitate transformations. The resulting query table then becomes a displayed subset of the actual data. When loaded into your workbook, the Queries & Connections pane shows all of the files connected to your workbook.

To Get Data

The following steps connect to a table with data provided by the U.S. Census Bureau for the state of Missouri. The table is located in the Data Files. ***Why? Connecting with the U.S. Census Bureau website is somewhat cumbersome and requires many steps.*** You will use the Get Data button (Data tab | Get & Transform group) to connect to the data. When you bring the data into Excel, you are working with a local copy; you will not change the original data source in any way. Should the data source be updated externally, however, you easily can refresh your local copy. The local data becomes a table, also called a query.

BTW

Getting Data from Access Databases
When you click the New Query button (Data Tab | Get & Transform group) and choose an Access database, the Navigator window appears so you can select which table (or tables) you want to use in your query. When you select a table, a preview of its data is shown in the right pane of the Navigator window.

To complete these steps, you will be required to use the Data Files. Please contact your instructor for information about accessing the Data Files.

1

- Display the Data tab.

- Click the Get Data button (Data tab | Get & Transform group) to display the Get Data menu.

- Point to the From File command to display the From File submenu (Figure 10–11).

Experiment

- Point to the other commands on the Get Data menu and look at the various sources from which you can get data. When you are done, point to From File again.

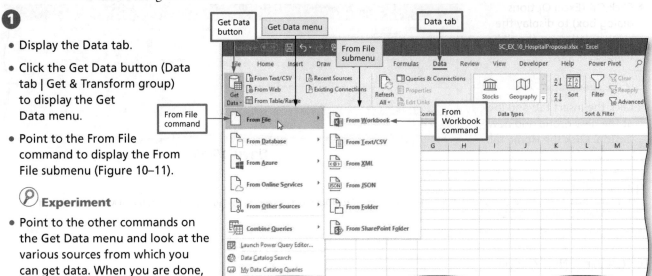

Figure 10–11

2

- Click From Workbook on the From File submenu to display the Import Data dialog box.

- If necessary, navigate to your storage location to display the files (Figure 10–12).

Q&A Could I have clicked From Web and navigated to the Census data?
Yes; however, you would have had to perform many additional steps to drill down to the desired data for this project.

Figure 10–12

3

- Double-click the file named Support_EX_10_MOPopulationIncomeByCounty.xlsx to display the Navigator dialog box.

- Click the table named Population & Income to preview the data (Figure 10–13).

Q&A What does the Edit button do?
If you know that you want to edit the data before creating the query, you can click the Edit button to display the Power Query Editor window.

Figure 10–13

4

- Click the Load button (Navigator dialog box) to import the data (Figure 10–14).

Q&A How is the data displayed?
Excel shows column headings and 117 rows of data for the counties in Missouri in a table format, using colors from the chosen color scheme.

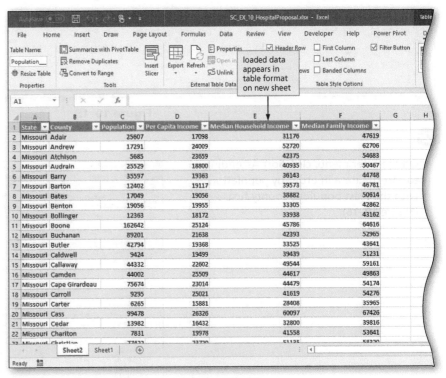

Figure 10–14

To Edit Data Using the Power Query Editor

In the following steps you will use the Power Query Editor to sort the data and only display the 10 least populous counties. *Why? The RHAC wants to narrow down the counties to the places with the least people.*

1

- On the right side of the screen, double-click the 'Population & Income' query in the Queries & Connections pane to display the Power Query Editor window.

- In the third column, click the Population column filter button to display the filter menu (Figure 10–15).

Q&A Is the Power Query Editor a separate app?
The Power Query Editor window is like an app within an app; it has its own ribbon, tabs, and groups and is navigated independently from Excel. The Query Settings pane on the right allows you to make changes to the data and keeps track of each change in order.

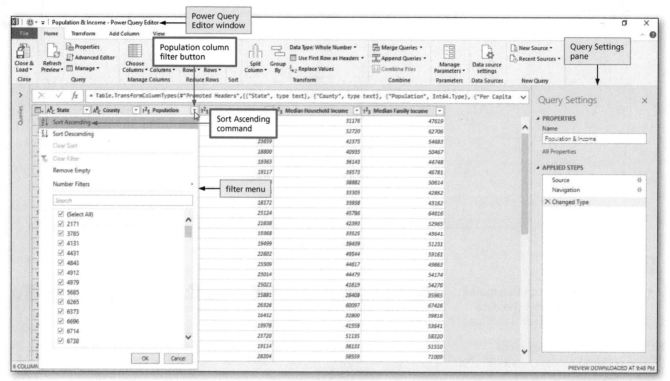

Figure 10–15

2

- On the filter menu, click Sort Ascending to sort the data in order by population with the least populous county first (Figure 10–16).

Figure 10–16

- Click the Keep Rows button (Home tab | Reduce Rows group) to display the menu (Figure 10–17).

Figure 10–17

- Click the 'Keep Top Rows' command to display the Keep Top Rows dialog box.

- Type 10 in the 'Number of rows' box (Figure 10–18).

Q&A
Could I have just deleted the rows in the main Excel window?
You could have; however, that would permanently delete the local copy of the data. Using the Power Query Editor, you can restore the data if you need it later.

Figure 10–18

- Click OK (Keep Top Rows dialog box) to return to the Power Query Editor window (Figure 10–19).

Q&A
What happens if my source data moves?
If you suspect that your source data has moved, display the Power Query Editor window and then click the Refresh Preview button (Power Query Editor window | Home tab | Query group). If an error message appears, click the 'Go To Error' button, click the Edit Details button, and then navigate to the new location of the file. When your table appears, click the final step in the Applied Steps area. You may have to click the Expand Data filter button in the Data column and remove extraneous columns.

Figure 10–19

6

- Click the 'Close & Load' button (Home tab | Close group) to load the transformed data into the worksheet in the Excel window.

- Rename the sheet tab with the name **10 Least Counties**.

- Recolor the sheet tab with the color Lavender, Accent 1 (Figure 10–20).

Experiment

- Point to the file on the Queries & Connections pane to see the preview window.

Q&A | What is the new tab on the ribbon?
It is the Query Tools Query tab (shown in Figure 10–22), which allows you to make additional queries easily. The tab appears when you click anywhere in the data itself.

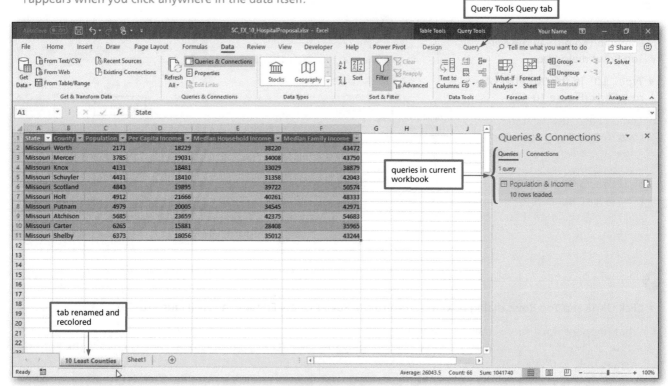

Figure 10–20

Other Ways

1. Click Edit button (Query Tools Query tab | Edit group), filter data, edit columns and rows, click 'Close & Load' button

2. Right-click table in Queries & Connections pane, click Edit (shortcut menu), filter data, edit columns and rows, click 'Close & Load' button

To Get Another Data Source

The following steps add a second data source to the workbook.

1 In the Excel window, click the Get Data button (Data tab | Get & Transform group), point to From File to display the From File submenu, and then click From Workbook to display the Import Data dialog box.

2 If necessary, navigate to your storage location.

3 Click the file named Support_EX_10_MOHousingSqMiles.xlsx to select it and then click the Import button to display the Navigator dialog box.

4 Click the 'Housing & Area' table to preview the data.

5 Click the Load button (Navigator dialog box) to import the data (Figure 10–21).

Figure 10–21

To Edit Data Using the Query Tools Query Tab

The following steps edit the query to remove a heading from the imported data and to convert the second row into column headings. This time you will use the Query Tools Query tab to access the Power Query Editor window. *Why? Depending on where you in the process of getting and transforming your data, the Query Tools Query tab may be more convenient than using the Queries & Connections pane.* You also will save the file again.

1

- Click any cell in the data and then display the Query Tools Query tab.

- Click the Edit button (Query Tools Query tab | Edit group) to display the Power Query Editor window.

- In the Power Query Editor window, click the Remove Rows button (Power Query Editor Home tab | Reduce Rows group) to display the Remove Rows menu (Figure 10–22).

Q&A | How can I delete columns using the Power Query Editor?
You can delete columns using the Remove Columns button (Power Query Editor Home tab | Manage Columns group).

Figure 10–22

2

- Click the 'Remove Top Rows' command to display the Remove Top Rows dialog box.

- Type 1 in the Number of rows box (Figure 10–23).

Q&A | Why am I removing the first row?
The first row is the title of the imported worksheet; it is not part of the data itself.

Figure 10–23

3

- Click OK (Remove Top Rows dialog box) to remove the first row.

- Click the 'Use First Row as Headers' button (Home tab | Transform group) to use the imported table's column headings (Figure 10–24).

Q&A | What is the Applied Steps area in the Query Settings pane?
The Applied Steps area displays each manipulation that you performed on the data, in order. You can click a step to return to that view of the data or delete the step. Your list of steps may vary.

Figure 10–24

- Click the 'Close & Load' button (Home tab | Close group) to load the transformed data into the worksheet.
- Rename the sheet tab with the name Housing Units.
- Recolor the sheet tab with the color Blue-Gray, Accent 3 (Figure 10–25).
- Save the file.

Figure 10–25

Other Ways

1. Double-click 'Housing & Area' query (Queries & Connections pane), filter data, edit columns and rows, click 'Close & Load' button

2. Right-click table in Queries & Connections pane, click Edit (shortcut menu), filter data, edit columns and rows, click 'Close & Load' button

Break Point: If you want to take a break, this is a good place to do so. You can exit Excel now. To resume later, start Excel, open the file called SC_EX_10_HospitalProposal.xlsx, and continue following the steps from this location forward.

Power Pivot

Power Pivot is a tool that extends the analytical functionality of PivotTables in Excel. It includes the capability to combine data from multiple data sources into one PivotTable. Valued as a business intelligence (BI) tool by the business community, Power Pivot especially is helpful when analyzing large, complex sets of related tables. Using Power Pivot, you can import some or all of the tables from a relational database into Excel in order to analyze the data using PivotTables and the enhanced features.

Data Models

Power Pivot, along with the other power tools, provides a data modelling tool to help you explore, analyze, and manage your data. **Data modelling** is the process of creating a model, simulation, or small-scale representation of data and the relationships

BTW
The SUMIFS Function
Besides adding fields to the PivotTable report, another way to find multi-criteria sums is to use the SUMIFS function with arguments of range, criteria, range, criteria, etc.

among pieces of data. Data modelling often includes multiple ways to view the same data and ensure that all data and processes are identified. A **data model** documents the processes and events to capture and translate complex data into easy-to-understand information. It is an approach for integrating data from multiple tables, effectively building a relational database inside Excel. A **relational database** consists of a collection of tables that can be joined through a common field and that can be accessed or reassembled without having to reorganize the tables.

CONSIDER THIS

Are data models unique to Power Pivot?

No. You used the concept of a data model when you created PivotTable and PivotChart reports; a field list is a visual representation of a data model. The difference between Power Pivot and a PivotTable is that you can create a more sophisticated data model using Power Pivot. When importing relational data, the creation of a data model occurs automatically when you select multiple tables. However, if the tables are from different sources, they may have to be added to the data model manually.

To Add a Query to a Data Model

Recall that a query is a request for information from a data source. The following steps add a query to the data model. *Why? You cannot create the Power Pivot PivotTable unless queries are added to the data model.* You will use the 'Add to Data Model' command. If you do not have Power Pivot, simply read these steps.

- If necessary, display the Housing Units worksheet and then click in the table to make it active.

- Click Power Pivot on the ribbon to display the Power Pivot tab (Figure 10–26).

Figure 10–26

- Click the 'Add to Data Model' button (Power Pivot tab | Tables group) to add the data on the current worksheet to the data model, and to display the Power Pivot for Excel window. Maximize the window, if necessary (Figure 10–27).

Q&A What window is displayed?
Excel displays the maximized Power Pivot for Excel window that contains tabs and groups used when working with multiple tables from multiple sources.

My column headings do not display the entire name. Is that a problem?
No. You can widen the column, however, by dragging the column heading border to the right.

Figure 10–27

- Close the Power Pivot for Excel window to return to the regular Excel window.

Q&A Did anything change on the screen?
No, but behind the scenes Excel added the file to the data model.

To Add Another Query to the Data Model

The following steps add another query to the data model. If you do not have Power Pivot, skip these steps.

1 Click the 10 Least Counties tab to display the worksheet.

2 Click any cell in the data.

3 Click the 'Add to Data Model' button (Power Pivot tab | Tables group) to add a second query to the data model. Do not close the Power Pivot for Excel window (Figure 10–28).

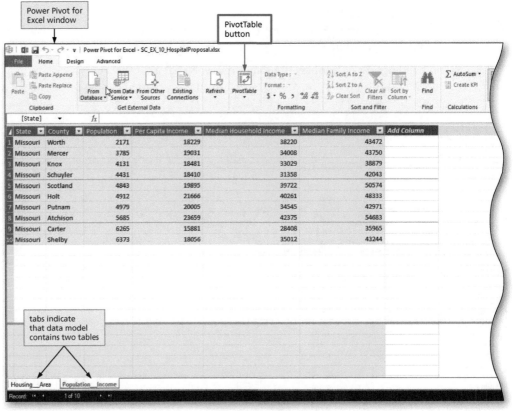

Figure 10–28

To Build a PivotTable Using Power Pivot

The following steps create a PivotTable using Power Pivot, based on the two queries. *Why? Using Power Pivot provides you with the most flexibility and functionality when building a PivotTable.* Once created, you can update a Power PivotTable in the same way you update regular PivotTables. Simply click the Refresh button (Power PivotTable Tools Analyze tab | Data group). If you do not have access to Power Pivot, you can create a regular PivotTable report.

• With the Power Pivot for Excel window still open and any table cell selected, click the PivotTable button (Power Pivot for Excel | PivotTable group) to display the Create PivotTable dialog box.

• If necessary, click the New Worksheet option button to select it (Figure 10–29).

Can I make a PivotTable without Power Pivot?
Yes. Click the PivotTable button (Insert tab | Tables group). In the Create PivotTable dialog box, click to display a check mark in the 'Add this data to the Data Model' check box.

Figure 10–29

2

- Click OK (Create PivotTable dialog box) to create a PivotTable on a new sheet and to display the PivotTable Fields pane.

- Close the Queries & Connections pane, if necessary (Figure 10–30).

Q&A Why do I not see both of my tables?
In the PivotTable Fields pane, click the All tab.

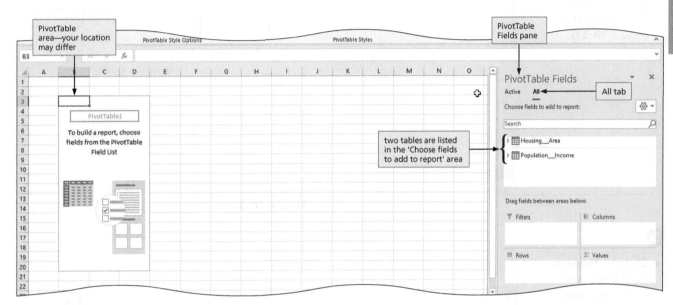

Figure 10–30

3

- In the PivotTable Fields pane, click Population__Income to display the fields from the query table.

- Click the check boxes beside State and County to add the fields to the Rows area.

- Click the Population check box to add the field to the Values area (Figure 10–31).

Figure 10–31

Q&A Why do the query tables use two underscore symbols in their name?
Database structures rarely allow spaces in the names of files or fields. Excel wants to make sure the data can be used in many kinds of databases.

4

● Scroll up in the
'Choose fields to add
to the report' area
(PivotTable Fields
pane) and then click
Housing__Area to
display the fields
from the query
(Figure 10–32).

Figure 10–32

5

● Click the Housing
Units check box
to add the field
to the Values area
(Figure 10–33) and
display a yellow
message about table
relationships.

Q&A

Why do all of the
counties have the
same number of
housing units?
The PivotTable
does not associate
the housing units
with the counties
automatically. You
will create that
relationship in the
next series of steps.

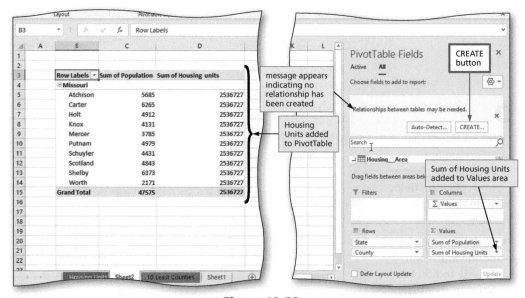

Figure 10–33

To Create a Relationship

A **relationship** is a field or column that two data sources have in common. For example, a payroll file
and a human resource file might each have a field named employee_number. Sometimes that field is named
identically in the two files and has the same number of rows; other times the name is different. One file might
use the field name last_name and another file might call it LastName. Those two fields would have to be
manually associated.

When the number of rows is different, the relationship is said to be **one-to-many**; in that case, the
relationship between two tables is created by a common field that links the tables together, and one table value

can have many options from another table. For example, both a client file and an employee file might have a field named salesperson. In the employee file, there is only one record for each salesperson; however, in the client file, several clients might be assigned to the same salesperson.

The following steps create a relationship using the County field. **Why?** *Both query tables have a column named County.*

- Click the CREATE button in the yellow relationships message to display the Create Relationship dialog box (Figure 10–34).

Q&A I do not have a CREATE button, or it did not work. What should I do?
Click the Relationships button (Data tab | Data Tools) to display the Manage Relationships dialog box. Click the New button.

Figure 10–34

- Click the Table button and then click Data Model Table: Housing__Area.

- Click the Related Table button and then click Data Model Table: Population__Income (Figure 10–35).

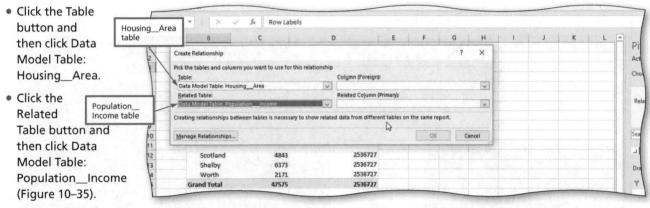

Figure 10–35

❸

- Click the Column (Foreign) button and then click County (Figure 10–36).

Q&A Why is it called a foreign column?
Foreign, or foreign key, refers to a field in one table that uniquely identifies a row in a different table. Even though the names may be the same, the field is foreign to the second table. For most Excel purposes, it does not matter which table you use for the foreign versus primary key.

Figure 10–36

• Click OK (Create Relationship dialog box) to create the relationship between the tables and adjust the numbers in the PivotTable.

Other Ways
1. Click Detect Relationships button (Power Pivot tab | Relationship group), select relationships

To Manage Table Relationships

The following steps graphically display the relationship that you created in the previous steps using the Power Pivot window. *Why? Sometimes looking at a picture makes the concept clearer.* If you do not have Power Pivot, simply read these steps.

• Click the Manage button (Power Pivot tab | Data Model group) to make the Power Pivot for Excel window active.

• Click the Diagram View button (Home tab | View group) to see a visual display.

• Resize each of the table views to display all of the data, and then drag the tables by their title bars to show the relationship, as shown in Figure 10–37. Your field order may differ.

Figure 10–37

• Click the Data View button (Home tab | View group) to return to the Data View.

TO MANAGE RELATIONSHIPS

You may need to add, edit, or delete relationships at some point. You can set up multiple relationships using Power Pivot. To do this, you would use the Manage Relationships command in the Power Pivot window, as shown in the following steps.

1. Click the 'Go to the Power Pivot window' button (Power Pivot tab | Data Model group) to make the Power Pivot for Excel window active.

2. Display the Design tab and then click the Manage Relationships button in the Power Pivot for Excel window (Design tab | Relationships group) to display the Manage Relationships dialog box.

3. Use the Create, Edit, or Delete button to make changes to the selected relationship and then click Close (Manage Relationships dialog box) to close the dialog box.

4. Minimize the Power Pivot for Excel window.

To Create a Measure

A **measure** is a calculated, named field in Power Pivot. Measures are created by a special set of functions and commands called **data analysis expressions (DAX).** Measures have several advantages over simple formulas and other calculated fields. *Why? With measures, you can create aggregate formulas that use one or multiple rows from multiple sources, which will adjust as you rearrange the pivot. You can format measures as you create them for global formatting benefits. Measures become fields in pivot field lists and can be used in multiple reports and across multiple worksheets. In regular PivotTables, you cannot create calculated fields using multiple data sources.*

The following steps create a measure to calculate the average number of people in each household. If you do not have Power Pivot, simply read these steps.

 1

- If necessary, minimize the Power Pivot for Excel window.

- Click any cell in the Sum of Population column and then click the Measures button (Power Pivot tab | Calculations group) to display the menu (Figure 10–38).

Figure 10–38

 2

- Click New Measure in the Measures menu to display the Measure dialog box. If necessary, click the Table name arrow and then click Population_ Income in the list.

- In the Measure name box, select any default text and then type `Occupancy Rate` to name the column.

- In the Description box, select any default text and then type `number of people per housing unit` to create a description.

- In the Formula box, following the equal sign, type `[` (left bracket) to prompt Excel to display the available fields that exist in the PivotTable (Figure 10–39).

Figure 10–39

3

- Double-click the [Sum of Population] field to insert it into the formula.

- Type / [to enter the division symbol and to display again the available fields.

- Double-click the [Sum of Housing Units] field to insert it into the formula.

- In the Category box, click Number (Figure 10–40).

 Experiment

- Click the Format button and then look at the various number formats that are available.

Figure 10–40

Q&A Could I obtain the same result by creating a calculated field in the PivotTable?
No. The Calculated Field option is unavailable to PivotTable data with multiple data sources.

4

- Click OK (Measure dialog box) to create the measure and display the new column (Figure 10–41).

Q&A How do I edit or manage the measures I have created?
Click the Measures button (Power Pivot tab | Calculations group) to display the Manage Measures dialog box. Then select the measure and click the Edit button.

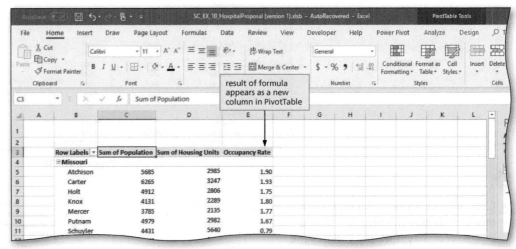

Figure 10–41

To Finish Formatting the PivotTable

The following steps format the other columns of numbers, insert a heading for the page, add a footnote, and save the file.

1 Right-click any number in the 'Sum of Population' column and then click Number Format on the shortcut menu to display the Format Cells dialog box.

2 In the Category area (Format Cells dialog box), click Number. Change the decimal places to 0 and then click to select the 'Use 1000 Separator' check box.

3 Click OK (Format Cells dialog box) to return to the PivotTable.

4 Repeat Steps 1 through 3 for the numbers in the Sum of Housing Units column.

5 Click cell A1. If necessary, change the font color to black. Change the font size to 20. Type **Number of Housing Units per County** and then press the ENTER key to complete the text.

6 Drag through cells A1 through F1 and then click the Merge & Center button (Home tab | Alignment group) to merge and center the title.

7 Click cell F18. Type ***blank represents counties not in the lowest 10** to create a footnote.

8 Rename the worksheet tab with the name, **Power Pivot**.

9 Recolor the worksheet tab with the color, Yellow.

10 Move the Power Pivot worksheet to the left of the Housing Units worksheet and click inside the PivotTable.

11 Save the file again (Figure 10–42).

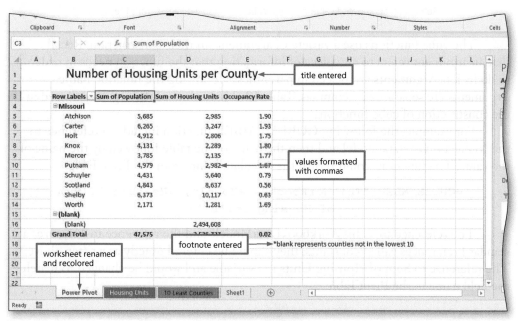

Figure 10–42

Cube Functions

Normally if you want to reference a piece of data, you use a cell reference such as B4. If the data in that cell changes, your reference will reflect that change as well. And when you want to replicate a formula containing a reference that should not change, you use an absolute reference, such as $B$4. In PivotTables, however, neither of those cell references work. The data is prone to change dramatically, from numeric to text, from field to field, or even to blank. Formulas or other references to that data immediately become invalid or display errors when the data is pivoted.

The solution to that problem is to use cube functions. **Cube functions** are a set of advanced analytic functions that you can use with multidimensional data, also called **data cubes**. A Power Pivot report is considered a data cube because of its 3-D cube-like structure. With a cube function, you can reference any piece of data in the

BTW
The COUNTIFS Function
The COUNTIFS function is an easy way to count data using multiple criteria sets. For example, in the 10 Least Counties worksheet, you could count the number of cities in York county with more than 1000 housing units by entering=COUNTIFS (A2:A395, "York", C2:C395, ">1000"). Criteria that includes operands or text must be enclosed within quotations marks.

PivotTable to use in formulas or in other functions, or merely to display the data in other places in the workbook. The cube function will adjust automatically if you change the way your data pivots.

Table 10–2 lists the cube functions.

Table 10–2 Cube Functions		
Function	**Return Value**	**Purpose**
CUBEKPIMEMBER	Returns the name of a key performance indicator (KPI)	Produces a quantifiable measure such as net income
CUBEMEMBER	Returns a member or tuple from the cube	Validates that the member or tuple exists in the cube
CUBEMEMBERPROPERTY	Returns the value of a member property from the cube	Validates that a member name exists within the cube and returns the specified property for this member
CUBERANKEDMEMBER	Returns the nth, or ranked, member in a set	Returns one or more elements in a set, such as the top salesperson or the top 10 athletes
CUBESET	Defines a set of members by sending an expression to the cube	Identifies sets for use in other cube functions
CUBESETCOUNT	Returns the number of items in a set	Finds how many entries are in a set
CUBEVALUE	Returns an aggregated value from the cube	Displays values from the cube

The cube functions use a variety of arguments in their construction. Recall that an argument refers to any piece of information that the function needs in order to do its job. Arguments are placed in parentheses following the function name. Arguments are separated by commas. Table 10–3 lists some of the arguments used in the construction of cube functions.

For example, the following CUBEMEMBER function includes a reference to the connection or data model and then the name of the table followed by the name of the value. The function would return the calculated sum from the PivotTable.

$$\texttt{=CUBEMEMBER("ThisWorkbookDataModel"," [Measures] . [Sum of Housing Units]")}$$

The reference to "ThisWorkbookDataModel" and the reference to Measures are standard references called constants; they should be entered exactly as written above. The reference to Sum of Housing Units is a variable and would be changed to match the field name in the PivotTable.

Table 10–3 Cube Function Arguments	
Argument	**Definition**
Caption or property	An alternate text to display in the cell that is perhaps more user-friendly than the database, field, or row name
Connection	Names the table, query, or data model
Key performance indicator (KPI)	A quantifiable measurement, such as net profit, used to monitor performance
Measures	A pivot calculation such as sum, average, minimum, or maximum
Member expression	Uses database field-like references to the data rather than cell references
Rank	An integer to represent which piece of data to return in an ordered list
Set	A string to represent a set of values that has been defined or returned by another cube function
Sort by	A field name to sort by when a function returns a set of values
Sort order	An integer to represent how the data should be ordered when a function returns a set of values
Tuple	A row of values in a relational database

To View Cube Functions

The following steps use the 'Convert to Formulas' command. ***Why?*** *The command converts the cells in a Power Pivot report or a PivotTable report to cube references, allowing you to see the functions behind the scenes.*

- Click cell E3 in the Power Pivot PivotTable.

- Display the PivotTable Tools Analyze tab.

- Click the OLAP Tools button (PivotTable Tools Analyze tab | Calculations group) to display the menu (Figure 10–43).

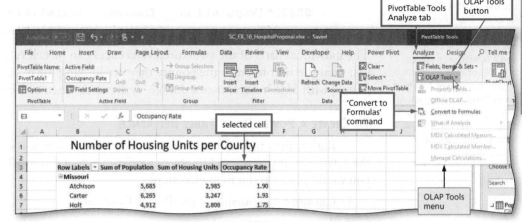

Figure 10–43

What does OLAP stand for?

OLAP stands for Online Analytical Processing, which is an advanced analytic tool to assist users in data warehousing and data mining, especially with multidimensional data such as a PivotTable with two outside sources.

- Click 'Convert to Formulas' on the OLAP Tools menu to view the cube function in the formula bar (Figure 10–44).

  Experiment

- Click various cells in the table, including the row and column headings, while watching the formula bar. Note the various cube functions that make up the PivotTable.

Figure 10–44

- Click the Undo button on the Quick Access Toolbar to hide the cube functions and display the PivotTable.

The GETPIVOTDATA function

Another way to access data in a PivotTable is to use the GETPIVOTDATA function. The function takes the following arguments:

```
= GETPIVOTDATA (data field, location of pivot table,
            search field, search item)
```

In a regular PivotTable, an example might be:

```
= GETPIVOTDATA ("Population", $B$3, "County", "Knox")
```

The specific names of the fields are in quotation marks when not referencing a cell location.

BTW
The GETPIVOTDATA Function
Another way to extract data stored in a PivotTable is to use the GETPIVOTDATA function. The function takes at least two arguments: the name of the data field and a reference to any cell in the PivotTable report. It returns the sum of that field. An optional third argument allows you to enter a search term. The GETPIVOTDATA function also can search calculated fields.

However, because the PivotTable in this module is a Power Pivot PivotTable, based on two different imported files, the reference is more complex and must include structured references to the file, field, and data, as shown in the following:

```
=GETPIVOTDATA("[Population___Income].[Sum of Housing Units]",
     $B$3,"[Population___Income].[State].&[Missouri]",
          "[Population___Income].[County].&[Knox]")
```

The individual parts of the structured references can be cell references. For example, if you want the user to enter the county they are looking for in cell H3, you could replace [Knox] with $H$3. Excel uses a double-underscore when naming the pivot data tables.

TO CREATE A POWER PIVOT TABLE REFERENCE

Rather than typing in a long, complicated function, it is easier to let Excel define the reference. If you wanted to create a reference to a cell in a Power Pivot PivotTable, you would perform the following steps.

1. Choose a cell outside of the Power Pivot table.
2. Type = (equal sign).
3. Click a cell in the Power Pivot table to create the reference and then click the Enter button.
4. Replicate or copy the function if necessary.

BTW
Enabling Data
After you save and close the file, subsequent openings will display a yellow bar asking you to enable the content. Click the Enable Content button to complete the connection the external files.

Power View

Power View is another of the interactive visualization power tools. Power View uses a drag-and-drop interface to create a variety of visualizations. A **visualization** is a chart, map, tile, filter data card, or other image that is created as a representation of an object, situation, or set of information. Power View supports multiple visualizations within the same view or report.

Power View relies on an updated version of Silverlight. **Silverlight** is an operating system and browser plug-in that enables interactive media experiences and advanced business applications. Some versions of Office may block updates to Silverlight. Microsoft offers registry keys to enable the update of Silverlight if your system displays an error.

To Start Power View

Earlier in this module, you added the Power View button to the Insert tab. The following steps use the new button to start Power View. Power View will display two new tabs on the ribbon. *Why? Power View uses many tools and needs its own tabs to display the buttons and menus.* The Power View tab helps you add data to the view. Once you add data to the view, the DESIGN tab appears with access to charts and many formatting tools. If you could not enable the data analysis features earlier in this module, you may not have access to Power View.

- Display the tab containing the New Group you added earlier in the module (in this case, the Insert tab) (Figure 10–45).

- Click a cell within the table.

Figure 10–45

- Click the Power View button (Insert tab | New Group group) to open Power View and to display the Power View sheet tab.
- If your Power View Fields pane does not appear, click the Field List button (Power View tab | View group).
- If your Filters area does not appear, click the Filters Area button (Power View tab | View group).
- If necessary, click ALL in the Power View Fields pane to display both data connections.
- Close the Workbook Queries pane, if necessary (Figure 10–46).

Q&A

My Power View button did not work. What should I do?
Make sure you have selected a cell within the table. See your instructor or IT administrator regarding access to Power View. If you do not have access, read through these steps and study the figures.

I received an 'OLEObject class failed' error. What should I do?
You may need to add a Silverlight registry key. See your instructor or IT administrator, or search the web for 'registry key to enable Silverlight'.

Experiment

- Point to each of the buttons on the Power View tab to view the associated ScreenTip.

Figure 10–46

To Create a Power View Report

The following steps add data to the Power View data visualization area to create a Power View table that shows the 10 least populous counties and their square miles. *Why? As with PivotTables, the report is blank until you identify fields of data.* You also will create a second Power View table to display a different visualization with all of the counties. If you do not have Power View, simply read these steps.

- Click the expand triangle beside the Population__Income table to display the fields.
- Click the check boxes for County and Population to move them to the Fields area in the Power View Fields pane and to display them in the report (Figure 10–47).

Figure 10–47

2

- In the report, drag the lower-right corner of the table to fill approximately two-thirds of the pane (Figure 10–48).

Q&A My table will not resize. What did I do wrong?
Try resizing the tiles area or resize using the upper-right sizing handle.

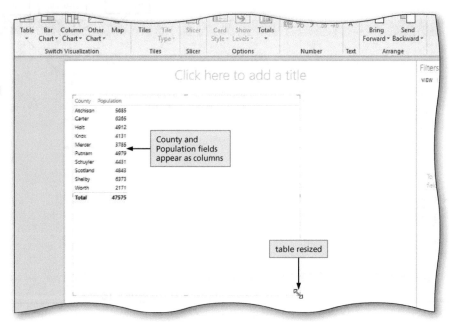

Figure 10–48

3

- In the report area, click outside of the table to deselect it.

- In the Power View Fields pane, click the expand triangle next to Housing__Area to display its fields.

- Click to display a check mark in the Housing Units field and then click to display a check mark in the County field to the report pane to create a second table to the right of the first one (Figure 10–49).

Q&A Does the order matter?
Yes. The order in which you click the fields determines the order in the visualization.

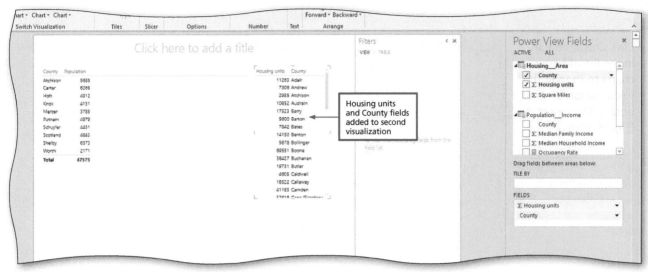

Figure 10–49

To Switch Visualizations

The following steps convert the left table to a bar chart visualization and convert the right table to a card visualization. *Why? Different kinds of visualizations add variety and aid in reading the data.* You have created various types of bar charts before. A **card** is a visualization that displays the data from each row of the table laid out in a card format, like an index card. Cards have two styles. The default Card style displays the default label more prominently; the Callout style displays the first field name in large text. You also can add images on each card and in the banner. If you do not have Power View, simply read these steps.

- Click any item in the left table to select the table.

- Click the Bar Chart button (DESIGN tab | Switch Visualization group) to display the bar chart choices (Figure 10–50).

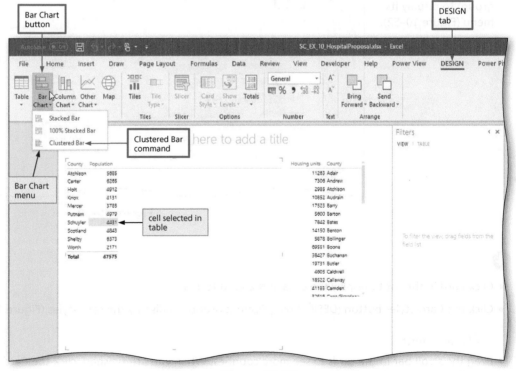

Figure 10–50

2

- Click Clustered Bar in the list of bar charts to change the visualization of the data in the report (Figure 10–51).

Q&A Can I add a legend to a Power View Report?
Yes. In the Power View Fields pane, drag a field to the Legend area.

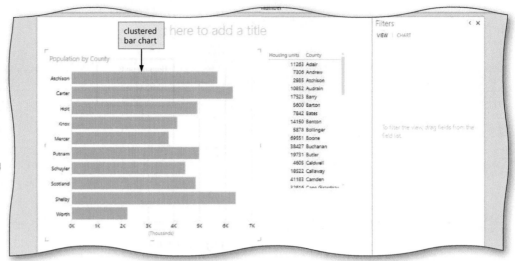

Figure 10–51

3

- Click any cell in the right visualization to select the table.

- Click the Table button (DESIGN tab | Switch Visualization group) to display its menu (Figure 10–52).

Figure 10–52

4

- Click Card in the list to display the data in the Card format.

- Click the Card Styles button (DESIGN tab | Options group) to display the card styles (Figure 10–53).

Experiment

- Drag the scroll bar in the cards to see more counties. When you are finished, click the Card Style button (DESIGN tab | Options group) again.

Figure 10–53

5

- Click Callout to change the style.

- Resize the card to display only one county at a time.

- Click the value in the data card and then click the Comma Style button (DESIGN tab | Number group). Click the value again and click the Decrease Decimal button (DESIGN tab | Number group) twice to display the number with a comma and no decimal places (Figure 10-54).

Figure 10–54

Q&A Why does the data card show Adair county when it is not one of the 10 least populous counties?
The data card visualization draws its data from the Housing__Units table which includes all 117 counties. Later, as you click the bars in the bar chart, the data card will display each of the appropriate counties.

To Format the Power View Report

The following steps format the Power View report. *Why? Adding a theme, title, background, and image enhance the report and improves comprehension.* You also will format the numbers. If you do not have Power View, simply read these steps.

- Display the Power View tab.

- Click the Themes button (Power View tab | Themes group) to display the Power View themes (Figure 10–55).

Figure 10–55

- Click the Executive theme (sixth row, fourth column) to change the colors in the Power Pivot report.

- In the report pane, click the title area. Type **Power View for Least Populated Counties** to enter the title text (Figure 10–56).

Q&A Could I add a background to the report?
Yes. You can use the Background button (Power View tab | Themes group) to add a colored or gradient background. You also can change the text size and font of the visualization.

Figure 10–56

- Click the Set Image button (Power View tab | Background Image group) to display its menu (Figure 10–57).

Figure 10–57

- Click the Set Image command to display the Open dialog box. Navigate to the data files for Module 10 (Figure 10-58).

Q&A Where are my other data files?
Excel only displays picture files when you click Set Image.

Figure 10–58

- Double-click the file named Support_EX_10_ MissouriOutline. png to create a background image (Figure 10–59).

Q&A What other format changes could I make?
You can change the image position of the background image or change the transparency.

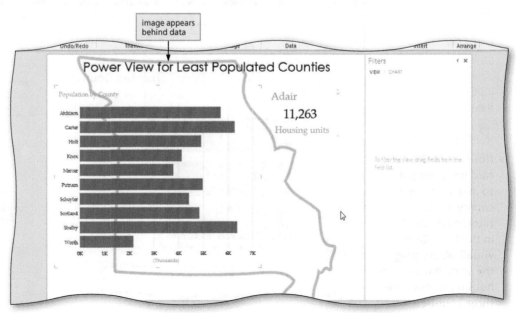

Figure 10–59

To Add a Filter in Power View

The following steps add a filter to the Power View visualization. You will filter the data to display only median incomes greater than $45,000. **Why?** *Filtering for income is another measure that the client may want to use in determining the location for the new hospital.* The Filters pane has three modes: List filter mode with a draggable slider bar, Advanced filter mode to select specific data, and Range filter mode for searching within ranges.

If you do not have Power View, simply read these steps.

1

- In the Power View Fields pane, drag the Median Family Income field to the Filters area (Figure 10–60).

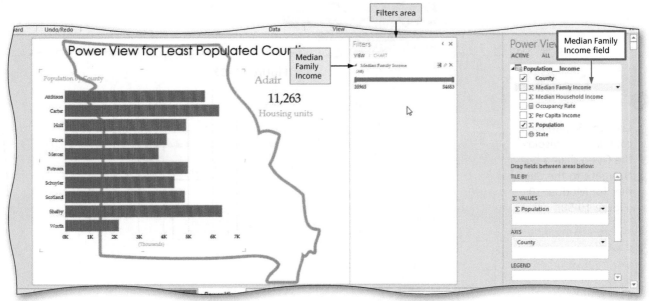

Figure 10–60

2

- In the Filters area, slowly click the 'List filter mode' button twice to display the Range filter mode.

- In the box below the 'is greater than or equal to' box, type **45000** and then click the Apply Filter button (Figure 10–61).

Q&A

What is the data showing?
Excel displays only three counties, out of 10 least populous counties, with median incomes of $45,000 or more.

Experiment

- Notice that the data card has changed to match the first county in the filtered bar chart. In the Data Card visualization, drag the scroll bar to view housing units in the three counties.

Figure 10–61

- Click the Delete Filter button (Filters pane).
- Click the Filters Area button (Power View tab | View group) to hide the pane.

To Use the Bar Chart

The following steps use the bars on the chart to highlight specific data items. **Why?** *Sometimes when presenting data, you may want to focus in on a piece of data (in this case, one county).* You also will save the file. If you do not have Power View, simply read these steps.

- In the bar chart, click the fourth bar to view the information for Knox county (Figure 10–62).

Figure 10–62

- Click the Undo button (Power View tab | Undo/Redo group).

Experiment

- Display the LAYOUT tab. Click the Data Labels button (LAYOUT tab | Labels group) and then click Outside end to view the population data associated with each county. Press CTRL+Z to undo.

- Save the file again.

To Create an External Link

If you wanted to create an external link to the data, rather than a query or connection, you would perform the following steps. (If you created earlier modules, you already may have learned to create an external link.)

1. Open both the source and destination files.
2. In the destination file, select a cell to receive the data.
3. If it is a cell reference, type   =   and then click the cell in the source file. Excel will create an absolute reference to the source file. An example might be:

```
='[Support_EX_10_MOHousingSqMiles.xlsx]Housing & Area'!$C$3
```

BTW

Distributing a Workbook
Instead of printing and distributing a hard copy of a workbook, you can distribute the workbook electronically. Options include sending the workbook via email; posting it on cloud storage (such as OneDrive) and sharing the file with others; posting it on a social networking site, blog, or other website; and sharing a link associated with an online location of the workbook. You also can create and share a PDF or XPS image of the workbook, so that users can view the file in Acrobat Reader or XPS Viewer instead of in Excel.

4. If it is a range, such as those used in functions, type = followed by the function name and opening parenthesis; then, drag the range in the source file. Excel will create an absolute link to the range. An example might be:

```
=SUM('[Support_EX_10_MOHousingSqMiles.xlsx]Housing &
Area'!$C$3:$C$116)
```

5. Save the destination file.

TO UPDATE DATA ASSOCIATED WITH EXTERNAL LINKS

If you wanted to update the data associated with external links, you would perform the following steps.

1. Close all workbooks and then open only the destination workbook, such as SC_EX_10_HospitalProposal.xlsx.
2. Click the Edit Links button (Data tab | Connections group) to display the Edit Links dialog box.
3. Click the Update Values button (Edit Links dialog box).
4. Click Close (Edit Links dialog box).

Break Point: If you want to take a break, this is a good place to do so. You can exit Excel now. To resume later, start Excel, open the file called SC_EX_10_HospitalProposal.xlsx, and continue following the steps from this location forward.

BTW

Accessing 3D Maps
You cannot create a direct hyperlink to the 3D Maps window. You must click the 3D Map arrow (Insert tab | Tours group) and then click the 'Open 3D Maps' command on the menu. You can create a macro that opens the 3D Maps window or create a hyperlink to a saved tour.

3D Maps

The 3D Maps power tool, formerly called Power Map, helps show your data in relation to a geographical area on a map. You can create a single map or several maps that become an animation focusing in on your data. The animation is called a tour, and each map is called a scene. If you are going to create a tour, you should plan out each scene and decide what data you want to display in each one.

The 3D Maps command opens a new window that uses a lot of your computer's resources. It is a good idea to close any apps other than Excel while working with 3D Maps.

To Open the 3D Maps Window

The following steps open the 3D Maps window. **Why?** *The 3D Maps windows has the tools to create a map or tour.*

- Click the Housing Units sheet tab and click anywhere within the data.
- Display the Insert tab (Figure 10–63).

Q&A Do I have to be in a specific worksheet to access 3D Maps?
No. 3D Maps can be accessed from any worksheet or window. However, if you want tables to appear in the Field List, it is best to start from a worksheet associated with the data model.

Figure 10–63

2

- Click the 3D Map button (Insert tab | Tours group) to open the 3D Maps window (Figure 10–64).

Q&A

I do not see two tables in my field list. What should I do?

It is possible that the second table was not added to the data model. Minimize the 3D Map window and return to the main Excel window. Click the sheet tab of the missing data and click any cell in the table. Click the 3D Map arrow (Insert tab | Tours group) and then click 'Add the Selected Data to 3D Maps' on the menu.

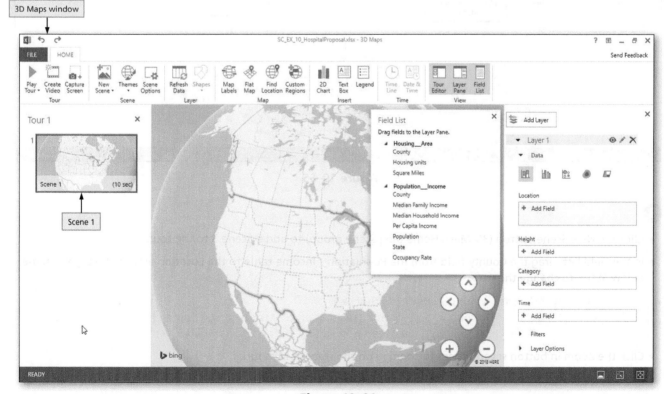

Figure 10–64

To Create Scenes

If you want to create more than just a single static map, you must add scenes to the tour. The following steps add four scenes to the tour. *Why? The first scene will focus in on the state, the second one will focus on the counties, the third will display the population for each of the 10 least populous counties, and the fourth will annotate the chosen county for the new hospital.* When you add a new scene, it temporarily duplicates the previous scene until you customize its settings.

- In the 3D Maps window, click the New Scene button (3D Maps Home tab | Scene group) to add Scene 2 to the tour.
- In the Field List, drag the State field from the Population__Income table to the Location area in the Layer 1 pane to focus in on the state.
- Click the Map Labels button (3D Maps Home tab | Map group) to display state labels on the map (Figure 10–65).

Q&A Does the map have its own worksheet tab in Excel?
3D Maps opens in a new window accessible only via the 3D Map button. If you close the window without saving, you will have to start over. To revisit a saved map, click the 3D Map button (Insert tab | Tours group). Excel will display a 3D Map dialog box from which you can choose the specific map you have created.

Figure 10–65

- Click the New Scene button (3D Maps Home tab | Scene group) to add a Scene 3 to the tour.
- In the Field List, drag the County field from the Population__Income table to the Location area in the Layer 1 pane, below State, to change the map.

Q&A Does it make any difference which County field I choose?
Yes. The County field from the Population__Income table has only 10 records. The County field from the Housing__ Area table has 117. If you chose the latter, all counties would be indicated on the map.

- Click the Zoom in button several times to zoom in on the state of Missouri.
- If necessary, drag in the map and use the tilt buttons to better position the state (Figure 10–66).

Figure 10–66

❸

- Click the New Scene button (3D Maps Home tab | Scene group) to add a Scene 4 to the tour.
- Scroll as necessary in the Layer Pane to show the Data icons.
- Click the 'Change the visualization to Region' icon.

 Experiment

- One at a time, click each of the icons in the Layer 1 pane and see how the map changes. When you are finished, click the 'Change the visualization to Region' icon again.

- In the Field List, drag the Population field from the Population__Income table to the Value area in the Layer 1 pane to change the map. If a legend appears, select the legend and then press DELETE.

- In the Field List, drag the County field from the Population__Income table to the Category area in the Layer pane to change the map (Figure 10–67).

Experiment

- On the map itself, point to any of the colored county regions to display its data card.

Figure 10–67

- Click the Field List button (3D Maps Home tab | View group) to close the Field List.

- Click the Layer Pane button (3D Maps Home tab | View group) to close the Layer 1 pane.

Q&A
My 3D Maps window suddenly closed. What should I do?
In the Excel window, click the 3D Map button (Insert tab | Tours group) and continue with these steps.

- Drag in the map to position the state slightly to the left of center. Make sure you can see all the edges of the state outline.

- Click the Legend button (3D Maps Home tab | Insert group) to display the legend.

- Right-click the legend to display the shortcut menu (Figure 10–68).

Figure 10–68

- Click Edit on the legend shortcut menu to display the Edit Legend dialog box.

- Click to remove the check mark in the Show Title check box.

- Change the font size of the Categories to 8 (Figure 10–69).

Figure 10–69

- Click OK (Edit Legend dialog box) to close it.

- Resize the legend to make it very narrow, just wide enough to see the name of the county and the population.

- Resize the legend to be as tall as the map itself.

- Drag the legend to the far-right side of the map (Figure 10–70).

Figure 10–70

- Click the Text Box button (3D Maps Home tab | Insert group) to display the Add Text Box dialog box.

- In the TITLE box, type **Population of the 10 Least Populated Counties** to enter the title (Figure 10–71).

Figure 10–71

8

- Click the Create button (Add Text Box dialog box) to create a text box title for the map.

- Resize the text box so the title appears on one line.

- Drag the text box to the center of the map.

- Adjust the size of the map and center as necessary (Figure 10–72).

Figure 10–72

9

- Click the New Scene button (3D Maps Home tab | Scene group) to add a Scene 5 to the tour.

- Right-click the tan-colored county in the top right corner to display the shortcut menu (Figure 10–73).

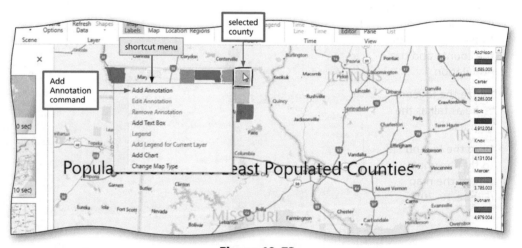

Figure 10–73

10

- Click Add Annotation to display the Add Annotation dialog box.

- Type **Chosen Location** in the TITLE box. Type **SCOTLAND COUNTY** in the DESCRIPTION box (Figure 10–74).

Q&A What do the PLACEMENT option buttons do?

You can choose on which side of the selected item the annotation will appear.

Figure 10–74

• Click OK (Add Annotation dialog box) to add the annotation to the map (Figure 10–75).

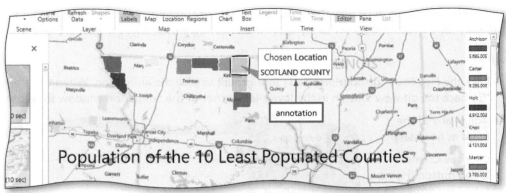

Figure 10–75

To Format Scene Options

The following steps format scene options. ***Why?*** *To make the animation smoother, you will change the duration of each scene and then select a scene effect.*

• Select the text, Tour 1, at the top of the Tour pane. Type **Chosen Location** to replace the text.

• Click Scene 1 in the Tour pane.

• Click the Scene Options button (Home tab | Scene group) to display the Scene Options dialog box.

• Select the text in the Scene duration box and then type **2** to change the scene to a length of two seconds.

• In the Scene Name box type **United States** to change the name.

• Click the Effect button to display the list of effects (Figure 10–76).

• Click Push In to select the effect.

• Repeat Steps 2 and 3 for Scene 2. Use the name State.

• Repeat Steps 2 and 3 for Scene 3. Use the name Region.

• Repeat Steps 2 and 3 for Scene 4. Use the name County.

• Repeat Steps 2 and 3 for Scene 5. Use the name Chosen Location.

• Click the Scene Options button (3D Maps Home tab | Scene group) to close the Scene Options dialog box.

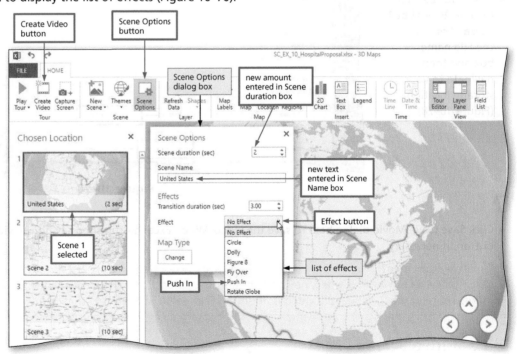

Figure 10–76

To Finish the Animation Steps

The following steps play the tour, save a copy of the tour, and take a screenshot of the final map. **Why?** *You will paste the screenshot to Sheet1 in preparation for creating a home page for the workbook.* You also will save the file.

- Click the Play Tour button (Home tab | Tour group) to play the animation. When the animation is finished, click the 'Go back to Edit view' button in the lower-left corner of the animation window to return to the 3D Maps window.

- Adjust any of the maps as necessary.

- Click the Create Video button (Home tab | Tour group) to display the Create Video dialog box.

- Click the 'Quick Export & Mobile' option button (Figure 10–77).

Figure 10–77

- Click the Create button (Create Video dialog box) to display the Save Movie dialog box.

- Type **SC_EX_10_ChosenHospital Location** in the File name box and then navigate to your storage location. (Figure 10–78).

Figure 10–78

- Click Save (Save Movie dialog box) to save the video. When Excel has finished saving the video, click the Close button, if necessary.

Q&A

Can I play the video?

Yes, if you wish to view the video, navigate to the storage location, right-click the file, and then click Open or Play on the shortcut menu. When the video is finished, click the Close button in the video window.

To Capture a Screen

The following steps capture a screen. **Why?** *A screen capture is a picture that can be used in other places in the workbook and in other applications because it is stored on the clipboard.*

- If necessary, click the Close button of any open dialog boxes. Close the Field List.
- If necessary, select Scene 5 and then click the Capture Screen button (Home tab | Tour group) to place a copy of the map on the clipboard (Figure 10–79).

Figure 10–79

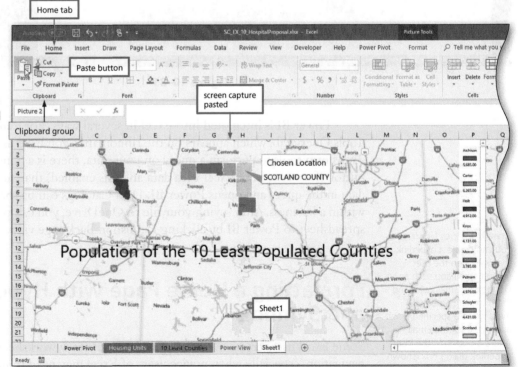

- Close the 3D Maps window and navigate to Sheet1 in the workbook.
- Click the Paste button (Home tab | Clipboard group) to paste the map to Sheet1 (Figure 10–80).

- Save the file.

Figure 10–80

Power BI

Microsoft's Power BI is a business intelligence tool to visualize and share data. It is a web-based tool designed to help business users gain insights from their data. Power BI can generate reports with a wide variety of tools including the Excel power tools. Currently, Power BI is available as a free downloadable desktop app. There are also paid professional versions available for corporate and power users.

In Power BI, a **dashboard** is the file management system where you can upload many different types of files. You can create multiple dashboards. Files in the dashboard are then used to create reports. Figure 10–81 displays a map chart using the Missouri demographic information. Notice the tools in the Visualizations pane are similar to those in the various Power Tool panes.

Figure 10–81

Power BI is integrated into Excel in several ways. For example, on the Query Tools Query tab, which appears on the ribbon after you have used the Get & Transform tools to perform a query on your data, there is a Send to Data Catalog button (for versions of Excel with data analysis enabled) that automatically loads the data in the query and opens Power BI. Data Catalogs can be shared with everyone within a business. After saving your file to OneDrive, you can publish the entire spreadsheet to Power BI by clicking Publish in Backstage view.

Formatting a Home Page with Hyperlinks and Symbols

Some Excel users create a home page or introductory worksheet to help with navigation, especially when novice users of Excel may need to interact with complex workbooks. A home page should display a title, links to other worksheets or pertinent materials, and perhaps a graphic.

A **hyperlink** is a specially formatted word, phrase, or graphic which, when clicked or tapped, lets you display a webpage on the Internet, another file, an email, or another location within the same file; also called hypertext or a link. Users click links to navigate or browse to the location. In Excel, hyperlinks can be created using cell data or linked to a graphic.

To Format the Home Page

1 If necessary, change the magnification to 100%.

2 Scroll down until you can see the lower-right corner sizing handle of the screen capture. Resize the graphic to fill the left two-thirds of the screen.

3 Turn off gridlines.

4 Change the name of the worksheet tab to Homepage. Change the tab color to Orange. Drag the tab to the far left so it becomes the first page.

To Insert a Hyperlink

To create a hyperlink in Excel, you select the cell or graphic and then decide from among four type of hyperlinks: links to places in the workbook, links to files or webpages, a link to create a new file, or links to email addresses. Table 10–4 displays the text and hyperlinks that you will enter on the home page of the SC_EX_10_HospitalProposal workbook.

Table 10–4 Homepage Text and Hyperlinks			
Cell	**Text**	**Hyperlink location**	**Hyperlink**
O6	Missouri Demographics	<none>	<none>
O8	Links:	<none>	<none>
P9	10 Least Counties by Population and Income	Place in This Document	10 Least Counties
P10	Housing Units	Place in This Document	Housing Units
P11	Power Pivot	Place in This Document	Power Pivot
P12	Power View	Place in This Document	Power View
P13	Map Animation	Existing File or Web Page	SC_EX_10_ChosenHospitalLocation.mp4
P14	Power BI	Existing File or Web Page	http://powerbi.microsoft.com
P15	Contact	E-mail Address	businessanalytics@missouri.biz

The following steps create hyperlinks on the home page. **Why?** *Creating links to other tabs, files, and websites will help users navigate through the workbook.*

- Change the width of column P to 40.
- Enter the text from Table 10–4 into the appropriate cells. Change cell O6 to Title Style.
- Change cells O8:P15 to be font size 14.
- Bold the title in cell O6 (Figure 10–82).

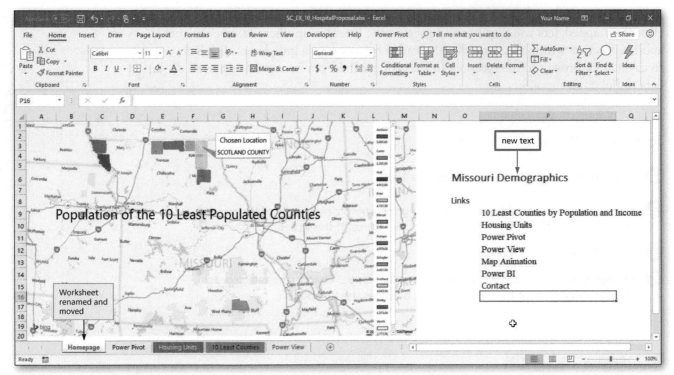

Figure 10–82

2

- Display the Insert tab.

- Select the cell you wish to make a hyperlink (in this case, cell P9) and then click the Link button (Insert tab | Links group) to display the Insert Hyperlink dialog box.

- In the Link to area, click the 'Place in This Document' button to identify the type of hyperlink.

- In the 'Or select a place in this document' area, click '10 Least Counties' (Figure 10–83).

Figure 10–83

- Click OK (Insert Hyperlink dialog box) to assign the hyperlink.

- Repeat the process for cells P10, P11, and P12, referring to Table 10–4 as necessary.

- Click cell P13 to select it (Figure 10–84).

Q&A

How can I tell if a cell is hyperlinked?
Excel will underline a hyperlink, and, when a user hovers over a hyperlink, the pointer will appear as a hand.

How do I edit a hyperlink if I make a mistake?
Right-click the hyperlink to display the shortcut menu and then click Edit Hyperlink to display the Edit Hyperlink dialog box.

Figure 10–84

- Click the Link button (Insert tab | Links group) again and then click the 'Existing File or Web Page' button to identify the type of hyperlink.

- If necessary, click Current Folder in the Look in area.

- Click SC_EX_10_ Chosen HospitalLocation.mp4 to select the file (Figure 10–85).

Figure 10–85

- Click OK (Insert Hyperlink dialog box) to apply the hyperlink.

- Click cell P14, click the Link button (Insert tab | Links group), and then click 'Existing File or Web Page' to identify the last hyperlink.

- In the Address box, type `http://powerbi.microsoft.com/en-us/` to enter the webpage address (Figure 10–86).

Figure 10–86

6

- Click OK (Insert Hyperlink dialog box) to apply the hyperlink.

- Click cell P15, click the Link button (Insert tab | Links group), and then click the E-mail Address button to identify the last hyperlink.

- In the E-mail address box, type **businessanalytics @missouri.biz** to enter the link to the email.

Figure 10–87

- In the subject box, type **presentation link** to enter the email subject line (Figure 10–87).

7

- Click OK (Insert Hyperlink dialog box) to apply the hyperlink.

- Select cells P8:P16. Change the font size to 14 and the font color to Blue.

Q&A Why am I selecting P8:P16 rather than just the hyperlink cells?
If you click cell P9 to start the selection, the hyperlink is clicked; it will transfer you to another worksheet.

- One at a time, point to each of the hyperlinks to view the ScreenTip and then click the hyperlink to verify its functionality.

Other Ways

1. Right-click cell, click Link, enter settings and hyperlink address (Insert Hyperlink dialog box), click OK

2. Press CTRL+K, enter settings and hyperlink address (Insert Hyperlink dialog box), click OK

To Customize a Hyperlink's ScreenTip

When you point to a hyperlink, Excel displays a ScreenTip with the name or location of the hyperlink and instructions for clicking or selecting. *Why? Users are accustomed to seeing ScreenTips on hyperlinks in browsers, sometimes beside the hyperlink, other times on the browser status bar.* The following steps change or customize the ScreenTip.

- Right click the Map Animation hyperlink and then click Edit Hyperlink on the shortcut menu.
- Click the ScreenTip button (Edit Hyperlink dialog box) to display the Set Hyperlink ScreenTip dialog box.
- In the ScreenTip text box, type `Click to play this MP4 movie.` to enter the new text (Figure 10–88).

Figure 10–88

- Click OK (Set Hyperlink ScreenTip dialog box).
- Click OK (Edit Hyperlink dialog box).
- Copy the text formatting from one of the other hyperlinks to the Map Animation hyperlink.
- Point to the hyperlink to display the new ScreenTip (Figure 10–89).

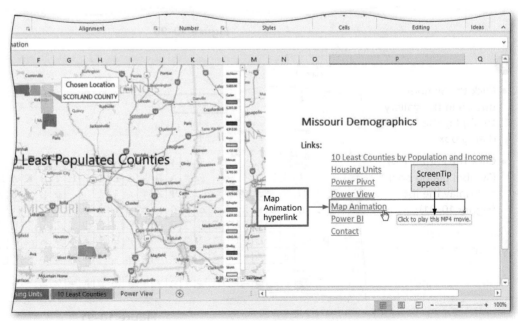

Figure 10–89

TO REMOVE A HYPERLINK

If you wanted to delete a hyperlink, you would perform the following steps.

1. Right-click the hyperlink you wish to delete.
2. On the shortcut menu, click Remove Hyperlink.

To Insert a Symbol

A **symbol** is a character that is not on your keyboard, such as ½ and ©, or **special characters**, such as an em dash (—) or ellipsis (…). Some special symbols use ASCII characters or Unicode characters. **ASCII** and **Unicode** are coding systems that represent text and symbols in computers, communications equipment, and other devices that use text. The following steps insert a link symbol on the homepage.

- Select cell P8. Click the Symbols button (Insert tab | Symbols group) to display the gallery (Figure 10–90).

Figure 10–90

- Click the Symbol button in the gallery to display the Symbol dialog box.

- Click the Font arrow (Symbol dialog box) to display the list (Figure 10–91).

◁ | What does the
Q&A | Equation button do?
The Equation button opens the Equation Tools Design tab that displays mathematical, statistical, and other symbols to help you with formulas and scientific equations.

Figure 10–91

3

- Scroll as necessary and then click 'Segoe UI Emoji' in the list.

- Scroll down more than halfway and then click the Link Symbol, character code 1F517 (Figure 10–92). Your symbol may differ slightly, as symbols are printer-dependent.

Q&A Could I enter the character code to find the character faster?
Yes.

Figure 10–92

4

- Click the Insert button (Symbol dialog box) to insert the symbol and then click Close (Symbol dialog box) to return to the worksheet (Figure 10–93).

Figure 10–93

5

- With the Homepage sheet selected, save the file.

Break Point: If you wish to take a break, this is a good place to do so. Exit Excel. To resume at a later time, start Excel, open the file called SC_EX_10_HospitalProposal, and then continue following the steps from this location forward.

Macros

A **macro** is a named set of instructions, written in the Visual Basic programming language, that performs tasks automatically in a specified order. It is a set of commands and instructions grouped together to allow a user to accomplish a task automatically. Because Excel does not have a command or button for every possible worksheet task, you can create a macro to group together commonly used tasks, which then can be reused later. People also use macros to record commonly used text, to ensure consistency in calculations and formatting, or to manipulate nonnumeric data. In this module, you will learn how to create a macro using the macro recorder. After recording a macro, you can play it back, or execute it, as often as you want to repeat the steps you recorded with the macro recorder.

Three steps must be taken in preparation for working with macros in Excel. First, you must display the Developer tab (which you did earlier in the module). Second, a security setting in Excel must be modified to enable macros whenever you use Excel. Finally, Excel requires that a workbook which includes macros be saved as an Excel Macro-Enabled Workbook file type; the file extension is .xlsm.

CONSIDER THIS

Should you customize applications with macros?
Casual Microsoft Office users do not know that customization is available. Creating special macros, events, or buttons on the ribbon can help a user to be more productive. Creating a macro for repeating tasks also saves time and reduces errors. If you understand how to do so, customization is an excellent productivity tool.

To Enable Macros

The following steps enable macros in the workbook. **Why?** *Enabling macros allows the workbook to open with executable macros.*

- Click the Developer tab to make it the active tab.

- Click the Macro Security button (Developer tab | Code group) to display the Trust Center dialog box.

- Click 'Enable all macros' to select the option button (Figure 10–94).

Figure 10–94

2

- Click OK (Trust Center dialog box) to close the dialog box and enable macros.

Recording Macros

A macro is created by recording a set of steps as they are performed. The steps and their order should be determined and rehearsed before creating the macro. When you create a macro, you assign a name to it. A macro name can be up to 255 characters long; it can contain numbers, letters, and underscores, but it cannot contain spaces or other punctuation. The name is used later to identify the macro when you want to execute it. Executing a macro causes Excel to perform each of the recorded steps in order.

Entering a cell reference always directs the macro to that specific cell. Navigating to a cell using keyboard navigation, however, requires the use of relative cell addressing. If you will be using keyboard navigation, you must ensure that the 'Use Relative References' button (Developer tab | Code group) is selected so that the macro works properly. For example, suppose you record a macro in cell C1 that moves to cell C4 and enters text. If the 'Use Relative References' button is not selected, the macro will always move to C4 and enter text; C4 would be considered an absolute reference. If the 'Use Relative References' button is selected while recording, the macro will move three cells to the right of the current position (which will not always be cell C4) and enter text.

As you record a macro, you do not have to hurry. The macro executes by keystroke, not the time between keystrokes during the creation process.

You can copy macros to other workbooks by copying the macro code. You will learn more about coding in the next module.

BTW
Starting Macros
Before recording a macro, you should select your starting cell. If you select it after you begin recording the macro, the macro always will start in that particular cell, which may limit the macro's usefulness.

BTW
Shortcut Keys
Macro shortcut keys take precedence over existing Excel shortcut keys. If you assign an existing shortcut key to a macro, it no longer will work for its original purpose. For instance, assigning CTRL+C to a macro means that you no longer will be able to use that shortcut key to copy content.

To Record a Macro

The following steps record a macro named Address_Block, with the shortcut key CTRL+M to execute the macro. *Why? The company wants to be able to use the shortcut to display company information.*

- Select cell P17.
- Click the 'Use Relative References' button (Developer tab | Code group) to indicate relative references.
- Click the Record Macro button (Developer tab | Code group) to display the Record Macro dialog box.
- In the Macro name box, type `Address_Block` to enter the macro name.
- Type `m` in the Shortcut key box to set the shortcut key for the macro to CTRL+M.
- In the Description box, type `This macro prints the name of the company and the address in a block of three cells.` to enter the text (Figure 10–95).

Q&A | Where are macros stored?
In this module, the macro will be stored in the current workbook. If you want a macro to be available in any workbook, you would click the 'Store macro in' button and then select Personal Macro Workbook.

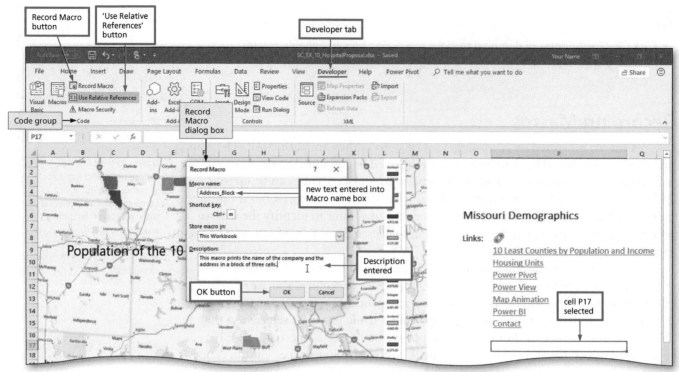

Figure 10–95

2

• Click OK (Record Macro dialog box) to begin recording the macro and to change the Record Macro button to the Stop Recording button

Q&A | What will be included in the macro?
Any task you perform in Excel will be part of the macro. When you are finished recording the macro, clicking the Stop Recording button on the ribbon or on the status bar ends the recording.

What is the purpose of the Record Macro button on the status bar?
You can use the Record Macro button on the status bar to start or stop recording a macro. When you are not recording a macro, this button is displayed as the Record Macro button. If you click it to begin recording a macro, the button changes to become the Stop Recording button.

• Type **Business Analytics** and press the DOWN ARROW key.

• Type **8325 N. Broadway** and press the DOWN ARROW key.

• Type **Rossburg, MO 64115** and press the DOWN ARROW key to complete the text (Figure 10–96).

Figure 10–96

- Click the Stop Recording button (Developer tab | Code group) to stop recording the worksheet activities.

What if I make a mistake while recording the macro?

If you make a mistake while recording a macro, delete the macro and record it again.

TO DELETE A MACRO

If you wanted to delete a macro, you would perform the following steps.

1. Click the Macros button (Developer tab | Code group).
2. Click the name of the macro in the Macro dialog box.
3. Click the Delete button (Macro dialog box). If Excel displays a dialog box asking if you are sure, click the Yes button.

Other Ways

1. Click Record Macro button on status bar, enter macro information (Record Macro dialog box), click OK, enter steps, click Stop Recording button on status bar

To Run a Macro

The following steps run (or execute) or play back the macro on the other worksheet pages. *Why?* *The company wants their name and address on each sheet.* You will use the shortcut key to execute the macro on the Power Pivot worksheet. You will use the View Macros button to execute the macro for the 10 Least Counties worksheet.

- Click the Power Pivot sheet tab and then click cell F19.

- Press CTRL+M to execute the macro with the shortcut key (Figure 10–97).

Figure 10–97

- Click the '10 Least Counties' sheet tab and then click cell A14.
- Click the Macros button (Developer tab | Code group) to display the Macro dialog box (Figure 10–98).

Figure 10–98

- Click Run (Macros dialog box) to execute the macro (Figure 10–99).

Figure 10–99

- Repeat the process for cell E1 on the Housing Units tab. Because the Power View worksheet is a chart, it has no specific cells. Do not apply the macro on that worksheet.

Other Ways

1. Press ALT+F8, select macro, click Run (Macro dialog box)

TO CREATE A MACRO BUTTON ON THE QUICK ACCESS TOOLBAR

If you wanted to create a button on the Quick Access Toolbar to run the macro, you would perform the following steps.

1. Right-click anywhere on the Quick Access Toolbar to display the shortcut menu.
2. Click 'Customize Quick Access Toolbar' on the shortcut menu to display the Customize the Quick Access Toolbar options in the Excel Options dialog box.
3. Click the 'Choose commands from' arrow in the right pane to display a list of commands to add to the Quick Access Toolbar.
4. Click Macros in the Choose commands from list to display a list of macros.
5. Click the name of the macro in the Macros list to select it.
6. Click Add (Excel Options dialog box) to add the macro to the Customize Quick Access Toolbar list.
7. Click OK (Excel Options dialog box) to close the dialog box.

TO ASSIGN A MACRO TO A SHAPE

If you wanted to assign a macro to a shape, you would perform the following steps.

1. Right-click the shape to display the shortcut menu.
2. Click Assign Macro on the shortcut menu to display the Assign Macro dialog box.
3. Click the desired macro.
4. Click OK (Assign Macro dialog box).

BTW

Storing Macros
In the Record Macro dialog box, you can select the location to store the macro in the 'Store macro in' box. If you want a macro to be available to use in any workbook whenever you use Excel, select 'Personal Macro Workbook' in the 'Store macro in' list. This selection causes the macro to be stored in the Personal Macro Workbook, which is part of Excel. If you click New Workbook in the 'Store macro in' list, then Excel stores the macro in a new workbook. Most macros created with the macro recorder are workbook-specific and thus are stored in the active workbook.

To Save a Workbook as a Macro-Enabled Workbook

The following steps save the workbook as a macro-enabled workbook. *Why? Workbooks with macros must be saved as macro-enabled.*

- Click File to display Backstage view, click Save As, click Browse, and then navigate to your storage location if necessary.

- Click the 'Save as type' button (Save As dialog box) and then click 'Excel Macro-Enabled Workbook (*.xlsm)' to select the file format (Figure 10–100).

Figure 10–100

- Click the Save button (Save As dialog box) to save the workbook as an Excel Macro-Enabled Workbook file.

To Reset the Ribbon

It is a good idea to reset the ribbon when you are finished using the customized tools. *Why? Other Excel users may not expect to see new tabs and new button groups, especially in lab situations.* The following steps reset the ribbon, removing all customization, and then exit Excel.

- Right-click a blank area of the ribbon and then click 'Customize the Ribbon' on the shortcut menu to display the Excel Options dialog box.

- Click the Reset button to display its menu (Figure 10–101).

Figure 10–101

- Click 'Reset all customizations' in the Reset menu.

- When Excel displays a Microsoft Office dialog box asking if you want to delete all customizations, click the Yes button.

- Click OK to close the Excel Options dialog box.

- **sam** ↑ Exit Excel. If the Microsoft Office Excel dialog box is displayed, click the Don't Save button.

Summary

In this module, you learned how to use Excel power tools. You learned how to enable data analysis in workbooks and customize the ribbon to display different tabs. You imported data by using the Get & Transform commands to create query tables. You used the Power Query Editor window to make changes to the data before using it as a table. Using Power Pivot, you added tables to the data model, created a PivotTable with relationships, and used a measure to create a calculated column. You also viewed the cube functions in Power Pivot.

You used Power View to create a report with tiles. You learned how to switch visualizations and highlight data in the Power View report. After opening the 3D Maps window, you create scenes with different map views and map labels, and displayed data related to geography. You created a tour animation and saved it.

You learned that Power BI is a tool that is used to create visualizations of your data to share in the cloud.

Finally, you created a home page with a captured screenshot and hyperlinks to the other tabs and webpages. You inserted a symbol. You recorded a reusable macro with the company information.

What decisions will you need to make when using Power Tools, creating hyperlinks, inserting symbols, and recording macros?
Use these guidelines as you complete the assignments in this module and create your own worksheets for evaluating and analyzing data outside of this class.

1. Select your data carefully. Make sure it is in a tabular format. If the original data could possibly move, copy the data in a new folder and create your spreadsheet in that folder.

2. Choose the kind of visualization you wish to create.

3. If you want to create a PivotTable from multiple sources of data, use Power Pivot.

4. If you want to create a chart with multiple data sources, or to use interactive tiles or data card visualizations, use Power View.

5. If you have data that is geographic in nature, use 3D Maps.

6. Design a user interface to access your data more conveniently. Include hyperlinks, macro instructions, screen captures, symbols, and graphics.

7. Determine any actions you want to automate and create a macro. The steps and their order should be determined and rehearsed before creating the macro.

8. Test the user interface. The final step in creating a user interface is to verify that the interface behaves as designed and as a user expects.

CONSIDER THIS : PLAN AHEAD

Apply Your Knowledge

Reinforce the skills and apply the concepts you learned in this module.

Using Power Pivot and Power View

Note: To complete this assignment, you will be required to use the Data Files. Please contact your instructor for information about accessing the Data Files.

Instructions: Start Excel and open a blank workbook. You are to create a Power Pivot PivotTable and a Power View report from two data files related to locations and occupancy of residence halls at a local college.

Perform the following tasks:

1. If necessary, customize the ribbon as described in the module to include the Power Pivot tab. Save the file on your storage location with the file name SC_EX_10_ResidencePivotTable.

2. Using File Explorer, copy the Data Files named Support_EX_10_Halls.xlsx and Support_EX_10_Locations.xlsx, and paste them to your storage location.

3. Use the Get Data button (Data tab | Get & Transform Data group) to import the workbook named Support_EX_10_Halls.xlsx and load the Halls table.

4. Rename the tab Halls.

5. Use the Get Data button (Data tab | Get & Transform Data group) to import the workbook named Support_EX_10_Locations.xlsx and load the Locations table.

6. Click Edit (Query Tools Query tab, Edit group) to open the Power Query Editor window. Click the 'Use First Row as Headers' button (Power Query Editor Home tab | Transform group). Close and load.

7. Rename the tab Locations.

8. Create a Power Pivot PivotTable as follows:

   a. Display the Power Pivot tab. Click the 'Add to Data Model' button (Power Pivot tab | Tables group) to add the Locations table to the data model. Close and load, if necessary.

   b. Click the Halls tab and then click the 'Add to Data Model' button (Power Pivot tab | Tables group) to add the Halls table to the data model. Use the Power Pivot for Excel window to create a Power PivotTable on a new worksheet.

   c. In the Excel window, in the PivotTable Fields pane, place check marks in the Residence, # of Rooms, and Max Occupancy check boxes from the Halls table. Drag the Location field from the Locations table to the Filters area. Create a relationship using the Residence field common to both tables.

   d. Click the Measures button (Power Pivot tab | Calculations group) and then click New Measure on the menu. Apply the new measure to the Halls table. Name the new measure, Total Occupancy, and use the left bracket key ([ ) to help you multiply the Number of Rooms times the Max Occupancy per Room. If Excel displays a Relationships yellow box, close it.

   e. Format the grand total with a comma and no decimal points.

   f. Format the PivotTable with the Dark Yellow, Pivot Style Dark 5. Use the Value Field Settings dialog box to rename the columns to remove the words, 'Sum of', and the space after. Name the sheet tab, Power Pivot (Figure 10–102a).

   g. Experiment with the filter buttons.

9. Create a Power View report as follows:

   a. Display the Insert tab. Click the Power View button (Insert tab | New Group).

   b. Display the Power View Fields pane, if necessary. Click the Residence field check box in the Locations table to add it to the visualization. Click the Total Occupancy check box to add it to the visualization.

   c. Click the Column Charts button (Power View Design tab | Switch Visualizations group) and then click Stacked Column. Resize the chart horizontally to display all of the residences.

   d. Drag the Location field to the Legend area.

   e. Change the title to Total Occupancy.

   f. Using the buttons in the Background Image group, set the image to the data file named Support_EX_10_Apartment.jpg. Set the Image position to Tile. Set the transparency to 60%.

   g. Click the Text Size button (Power View tab | Themes group) and change the text size to 125% (Figure 10–102b).

Figure 10–102a Power PivotTable

Row Labels	# of Rooms	Max Occupancy	Total Occupancy
Armstrong	25	1	25
Brown	25	1	25
Bryant	24	6	144
Campbell	4	8	32
Cooper	15	2	30
Freeman	15	2	30
Hopkins	25	3	75
Johnson	4	8	32
Kee	4	8	32
Kellogg	25	4	100
Kimball	16	6	96
Miles	4	8	32
Neely	50	2	100
Penfield	24	6	144
Perry	16	6	96
Stevenson Arms	64	2	128
Wright	12	2	24
Grand Total	**352**	**75**	**26,400**

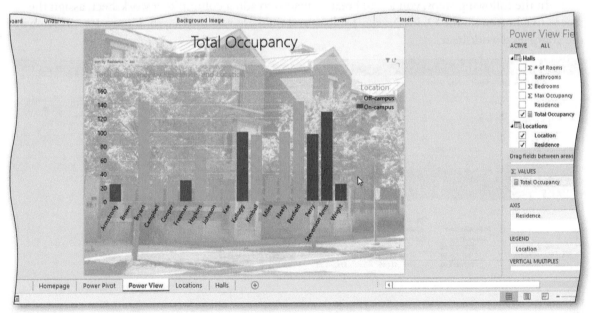

Figure 10–102b Power View report

Continued >

Apply Your Knowledge *continued*

10. On Sheet 1, insert the title Halls, Locations, Pivot Table, and Power View, and bold it. Insert hyperlinks to each of the other sheets. Format the hyperlinks to be blue, and with a font size of 18, if necessary. Rename the sheet, Homepage, and move it to the left of the other worksheet tabs. Arrange all other tabs as shown in Figure 10–102b.

If instructed to do so, create a home page with a picture of your school, and your name and course number.

11. On the homepage, click cell A1. Save the workbook. Remove the ribbon customization. Submit the revised document in the format specified by your instructor.

12. ⊛ What other measure might you create with this data? How would the housing office use this data to manage room assignments?

Extend Your Knowledge

Extend the skills you learned in this module and experiment with new skills. You may need to use Help to complete the assignment.

Creating a Macro, Editing a Macro, and Assigning It to a Button

Note: To complete this assignment, you will be required to use the Data Files. Please contact your instructor for information about accessing the Data Files.

Instructions: Start Excel. Open the workbook SC_EX_10-1.xlsx from the Data Files and then save the workbook as an Excel Macro-Enabled Workbook file type using the file name, SC_EX_10_CoolPools.xlsm.

In the following steps, you are to create a macro to add a column to a worksheet, assign the macro to a button on the Quick Access Toolbar, and then execute the macro. Figure 10–103 shows the completed worksheet.

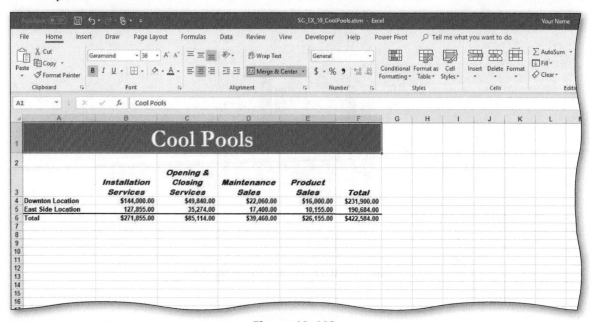

Figure 10–103

Perform the following tasks:

1. If the Developer tab is not displayed on the ribbon, display Backstage view, click Options in the left pane to display the Excel Options dialog box, click Customize Ribbon, click the Developer check box in the Customize the Ribbon area, and then click OK (Excel Options dialog box).

2. Create a macro that adds a column before the Product Sales column by doing the following:

   a. Click the Record Macro button (Developer tab | Code group).

   b. When the Record Macro dialog box appears, name the macro, AddColumn, and assign the keyboard shortcut CTRL+N. Store the macro in this workbook, enter your name in the Description box, and then click OK (Record Macro dialog box) to start the macro recording process.

   c. Select cell C3, click the Insert arrow (Home tab | Cells group), and then click the 'Insert Sheet Columns' command from the Insert Cells menu.

   d. Select cell C6, sum the cell range C4:C5, set the column width to 15, and then click the Stop Recording button (Developer tab | Code group).

3. In the newly added column, enter `Maintenance Sales` in cell C3, `22060` in cell C4, and `17400` in cell C5.

4. Right-click anywhere on the Quick Access Toolbar and then click 'Customize Quick Access Toolbar' on the shortcut menu. When the Excel Options dialog box is displayed, click the 'Choose commands from' arrow and click Macros. Click AddColumn, click the Add button, and then click OK to add a Macro button to the Quick Access Toolbar.

5. While still in column C, run the macro by clicking the AddColumn button on the Quick Access Toolbar. Enter the following data: `Opening & Closing Services,49840`, and `35274`.

   If requested by your instructor, add the following text to the end of the text in cell A1: `(EST. <year of birth>),` replacing <year of birth> with your year of birth.

6. Right-click the AddColumn button on the Quick Access Toolbar and then click 'Remove from Quick Access Toolbar' on the shortcut menu.

7. Use Help to learn how to access the VBA window. In the VBA window, click File on the menu bar and then click Print to print the AddColumn macro.

8. Save the workbook. Submit the revised workbook and the macro printout in the format specified by your instructor.

9. ✳ How would using the 'Use Relative References' button when recording your macro change how you insert columns using the AddColumn macro?

Expand Your World

Create a solution that uses cloud and web technologies by learning and investigating on your own from general guidance.

Creating a Treemap in Power BI

Note: To complete this assignment, you will be required to use the file you created in this module, named SC_EX_10_HospitalProposal.xlsx. If you did not create this file, please contact your instructor for information about accessing the file. You must be connected to the Internet to perform these steps. If you are working in a lab situation, your IT administrator must have turned on access to Power BI. If you are working from home, you will need access to your Office 365 account.

Instructions: Start Power BI by opening a browser and navigating to https://powerbi.microsoft.com. If you have an Office 365 account, sign in. If not, you can start a free trial, which involves downloading the Power BI app, or see your instructor or IT administrator for login assistance. You are to create a Power BI visualization (Figure 10–104).

Continued >

Expand Your World *continued*

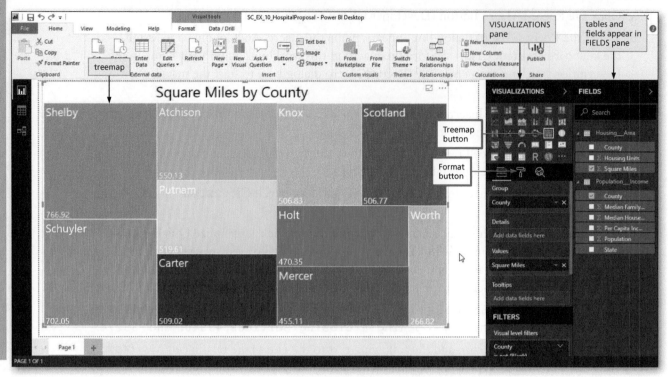

Figure 10–104

Perform the following tasks:

1. In the left pane, click File; in the right panel, click Excel. Click the Connect button (Get Data dialog box). Navigate to your storage location and double-click the file named SC_EX_10_HospitalProposal.xlsx. If you did not create this file in the module itself, please see your instructor.

2. When Power BI opens the Navigator dialog box, click to display a check mark in the two tables, Housing__Area and Population__Income. Click the Load button (Navigator dialog box).

3. In the VISUALIZATIONS pane, click the Treemap button. In the FIELDS pane, click the Expand button beside Population__Income and then click the County check box. Click the Expand button beside Housing__Area and then click the Square Miles check box.

4. If your treemap displays a blank county, scroll to the FILTERS pane. Click the Expand arrow beside County. Click the Select all check box to select all counties, then click the (Blank) check box to turn off the blank county, if any.

5. In the visualization, drag the lower-right sizing handle down and right so that the treemap fills the workspace.

6. In the Visualizations pane, click the Format button. Click to the right of the word, Title, to turn it on. If necessary, also turn on Data labels and Category. Scroll to turn on Tooltip and Visual header, if you have those fields listed.

7. Click the word Title in the Visualizations Pane Format area to display title formatting options. Change the Font color to Black, the Alignment to Center, and the Text size to 32. Scroll as necessary and click the word Title again to hide the formatting options.

8. Click the words Data labels in the Visualizations Pane Format area. Change the Text size to 18. Scroll as necessary and click the words Data labels again to hide the formatting options.

9. Click the word Category in the Visualizations Pane Format area. Change the Text size to 24. Scroll as necessary and click the word Category again to hide the formatting options.

10. Point to each of the counties to display the ScreenTip for each one.

11. Save the file with the file name, SC_EX_10_HospitalProposal.pbix, and submit the file in the format specified by your instructor.

12. Experiment with other visualization types.

13. Close Power BI. Do not save any experimental visualizations you created.

14. ✻ How was creating a visualization in Power BI different than creating a Power View report in Excel?

In the Lab

Design and implement a solution using creative thinking and problem-solving skills.

Create a Visual Report and Video

Note: To complete this assignment, you will be required to use the Data Files. Please contact your instructor for information about accessing the Data Files.

Problem: The State of Utah wants a visual report displaying the number of visitors to its five large national parks in a recent year. They also would like to be able to access the National Park Service website within the report. You decide to create a workbook with a home page and 3D Map.

Perform the following tasks:

Part 1:   Using File Explorer, copy the Data File named Support_EX_10_UtahParks.xlsx and paste it to your storage location. Start Excel and open a blank workbook. Save the file on your storage location with the name, SC_EX_10_UtahParksComplete. Get the data from Support_EX_10_UtahParks.xlsx and the Parks table. Using the Power Query Editor window, remove the first row, which is a title. Make the next row the header row. Close and load the query. Format the data. Click the 3D Map button (Insert tab | Tours group) to open the 3D Maps window and create the scenes shown in Table 10–5.

Table 10–5 Utah National Parks					
Scene	Scene Name	Layer Pane	Instructions	Zoom & Position	Scene Options
1	United States	Remove any locations		Zoom to entire United states	3 seconds duration, 1 second Fly Over effect
2	Utah	Add State field	Create a text box with the word Utah	Zoom to Utah	3 seconds duration, 1 second Fly Over effect
3	Parks	Click the 'Change the visualization to Region' icon. Add the Postal Code field to the Location area. Add the Visitors in 2017 field to the Value area. Add the National Park field to the Category area. Right-click the Legend and then click Remove.	Remove the Utah text box and turn on Map Labels. One at a time, right click each region on the map and then click Add Annotation. Click Fields button (Add Annotation dialog box), and then click National Park. Change the font size to 12.	Zoom in as close as possible, while keeping all of the regions on the map.	3 seconds duration, 1 second Fly Over effect

Continued >

In the Lab *continued*

Play the tour and then make any adjustments necessary. Capture a screenshot of scene 3. Save a video of the tour with the name, SC_EX_10_UtahParks.

Create a homepage with your screen capture. Add a hyperlink to your PivotTable. Add a hyperlink to your saved map animation. Add a hyperlink to the appropriate website on the National Park Service (http://www.nps.gov/state/ut/index.htm).

Part 2:   Would you use Excel for a presentation? What are the advantages and disadvantages of using visualizations in Excel versus apps like PowerPoint or Prezi?

11 User Interfaces, Visual Basic for Applications (VBA), and Collaboration Features

Objectives

After completing this module, you will be able to:

- Create custom color and font schemes and save them as an Excel theme
- Add and configure worksheet form controls
- Record user input to another location on the worksheet
- Understand Visual Basic for Applications (VBA) code and explain event-driven programs
- Explain sharing and collaboration techniques

- Use passwords to assign protected and unprotected status to a worksheet
- Compare workbooks
- Review a digital signature on a workbook
- Insert and edit comments in a workbook
- Format a worksheet background
- Enhance charts and sparklines
- Save a custom view of a worksheet

Introduction

This module introduces you to user interface design using form controls and ActiveX controls in a worksheet, the Visual Basic for Applications (VBA) programming environment, sharing and collaboration features of worksheets and workbooks, the use of comments in Excel, and the process of finalizing workbooks.

With Excel, you can design a user-friendly interface that permits users to enter information into the workbook easily, regardless of their experience with the app. Form controls include interface elements such as option buttons, check boxes, and group boxes. ActiveX controls, including the label and command button controls used in this module, provide the same core functionality as the form controls but allow you, as the designer, greater power to customize the appearance of the control. The VBA programming environment is used to program the functionality of the ActiveX controls.

When you are working on a team, the sharing features of Excel make it easy to provide team members access to worksheet data and protect information as necessary. Distributing a workbook through OneDrive, Exchange, Office 365, or SharePoint maintains ownership of the file while providing all members of the team access to the most current version of the data at all times. Commenting features of Excel encourage feedback on specific content within the worksheet.

Additional collaboration tools permit users to view multiple versions of the same workbook side by side for comparison.

Project: National Injection Molding Sales Analysis

The project in this module follows proper design guidelines and uses Excel to create the workbooks shown in Figure 11–1. National Injection Molding (NIM) develops and markets large, injection-molded products such as prefabricated steps, trays, chairs, and casings for the transportation industry. Because NIM's reach is national, members of the sales team are located in offices throughout the United States. The head of sales wants to use advanced features of Excel to share information about NIM's prospective clients and projected revenue among the sales team. The NIM Sales Analysis workbook consists of three worksheets—Prospect Recorder, Sales Data Analysis, and a hidden Prospect List. The NIM Events workbook consists of two worksheets—Event Expenses and Prior Years.

The Prospect Recorder worksheet (Figure 11–1a) in the NIM Sales Analysis workbook provides a framework for recording information about sales prospects. You will add form controls and ActiveX controls to finish the interface development. You then will create VBA code to add functionality to the command button controls added to the worksheet. The functionality added through the VBA programming environment will present a series of dialog boxes instructing the salesperson to enter the prospect's contact information, and then will copy the prospect's information into the Prospect List worksheet (Figure 11–1b), which will be hidden from casual users.

The Sales Data Analysis worksheet (Figure 11–1c) in the NIM Sales Analysis workbook provides production details for 2020 and 2021 related to the three production lines (production facilities are located in Oklahoma, Florida, and Louisiana) and four product types (trays, steps, chairs, and casings). You will co-author the workbook and add comments.

The Event Expenses worksheet (Figure 11–1d) in the NIM Events workbook contains estimated costs for three sales events throughout the year 2021. You will add a watermark to this worksheet.

The Prior Years worksheet (Figure 11–1e) in the NIM Events workbook contains attendance figures for prior events (2014 through 2020) and a chart representing the data. You will add a background to this worksheet. You will add finishing touches to the existing chart and add sparklines for each event. You also will create a custom view for the worksheet and prepare the workbook for distribution to users of older versions of Excel.

(a) Prospect Recorder Form

(b) Hidden Prospect List

(c) Sales Data Analysis

(d) Event Expenses

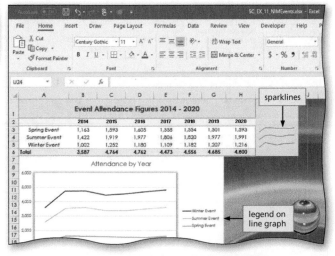

(e) Prior Year's Event Attendance

Figure 11–1

The requirements document for the National Injection Molding Sales Analysis and Events workbooks is shown in Figure 11–2. It includes the needs, source of data, calculations, and other facts about the worksheets' development.

Worksheet Titles	Prospect Recorder, Sales Data Analysis, Event Expenses, and Prior Years
Needs	National Injection Molding (NIM) develops and markets four types of large injection molding items (trays, steps, chairs, and casings) to the transportation industry nationwide. NIM has three production facilities in Oklahoma, Florida, and Louisiana.
	The company would like a workbook to record information about sales prospects and maintain current information regarding scheduled production and sales. Additionally, a second workbook is needed to maintain current data on the upcoming 2021 sales events and consolidate historic attendance information on events held from 2014 through 2020.
	The information recorded from the prospects has been structured in a hidden Prospect List worksheet, but the sales manager wants a form created to make data entry easier. Changes need to be made to sales analysis data in a shared copy of the workbook.
	Finally, three copies of the shared events workbook exist with different cost values for the events. These values need to be merged into a single workbook, and visual enhancements to the worksheets are desired for presentation purposes.
Source of Data	A workbook has been developed with Sales Data Analysis and the start of a form.
	A master copy and two employee copies of the Events workbook exist.
Calculations	All formulas are set up in the workbooks. The worksheets in each workbook should be reviewed to familiarize yourself with the calculations.
Other Requirements	None.

Figure 11–2 Requirements Document

To Start Excel and Open a Workbook

The following steps start Excel and open a workbook named SC_EX_11-1.xlsx. To complete these steps, you will be required to use the Data Files. Please contact your instructor for information about accessing the Data Files.

1 sam↓ Start Excel.

2 Open the file named SC_EX_11-1.xlsx from the Data Files.

3 If the Excel window is not maximized, click the Maximize button on its title bar to maximize the window.

4 Save the workbook on your hard drive, OneDrive, or other storage location as a macro-enabled workbook (.xlsm format) using SC_EX_11_NIMSalesAnalysis as the file name (Figure 11–3).

BTW
Create and Modify Custom Themes
Custom themes allow for personalization of workbooks with a custom set of colors, fonts, and effects. Use the Customize Colors option on the Colors menu (Page Layout tab | Themes group) or the Customize Fonts option on the Fonts menu (Page Layout tab | Themes group) to create custom options and select the desired effect setting from the Effects gallery. After selecting your desired options, click the Themes button and then click Save Current Theme to save your custom theme.

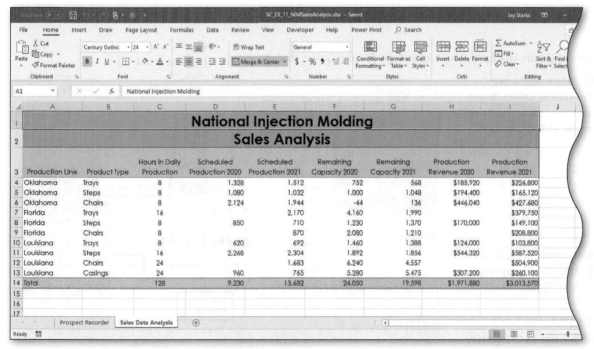

Figure 11–3

BTW
Touch Mode
Differences
The Office and Windows interfaces may vary if you are using Touch mode. For this reason, you might notice that the function or appearance of your touch screen differs slightly from this module's presentation.

Creating a Custom Theme

Excel provides an option for users to create color and font schemes rather than using one of the predefined sets. The chosen colors also will appear in the galleries related to formats, shapes, fills, and outlines. The chosen fonts will appear in the font box and in cell styles. Creating a **custom theme** means saving your own color and font schemes.

To Create a New Color Scheme

The following steps create a custom color scheme. *Why? NIM wants to use its company colors of green and brown.*

- Click the Colors button (Page Layout tab | Themes group) to display the Color Scheme gallery (Figure 11–4).

Figure 11–4

- Click Customize Colors to display the Create New Theme Colors dialog box.

- Type **NIM** in the Name box (Create New Theme Colors dialog box) to name the color scheme with the same name as the company.

Q&A What if I do not enter a name for the modified color scheme?
Excel will save your color scheme with a name that begins with the word, Custom, followed by a number (e.g., Custom 8).

- In the Theme colors area, click the Accent 1 button to display a gallery of color choices (Figure 11–5).

- Point to each color in the gallery to display its name.

Figure 11–5

- Click Green in the Standard Colors area to select the Accent 1 color.

- Click the Accent 2 button, and then click Light Green in the Standard Colors to select the Accent 2 color.

- Click the Accent 3 button, and then click 'Orange, Accent 6, Darker 50%' (in the last row of the Theme colors area, column 10) to select the Accent 3 color (Figure 11–6).

Q&A
Can I delete a color scheme once I create it?
Yes. To delete a color scheme, first display the list of color schemes, right-click the custom color scheme, and then click Delete Scheme on the shortcut menu.

Figure 11–6

- Click Save (Create New Theme Colors dialog box) to save the color scheme.

Experiment

- Click the Colors button (Page Layout tab | Themes group) to display the Color Scheme gallery. The new color scheme will be in the Custom area at the top.

Q&A
Why did the colors change immediately?
The cell styles were set previously to gray and dark gray. The new color scheme takes effect and changes all formatted cells.

To Create a Custom Font Scheme

The following steps create a custom font scheme. *Why? Some companies associate certain fonts with branding; in this case, the NIM company wants to use the Book Antiqua font.*

- Click the Fonts button (Page Layout tab | Themes group) to display the Font Scheme gallery and then click Customize Fonts to display the Create New Theme Fonts dialog box (Figure 11–7).

- In the Name box, type **NIM** to name the font scheme.

- Click the Heading font arrow and then click **Book Antiqua** in the list to choose a heading font.

Figure 11–7

- If necessary, select **Century Gothic** in the Body font box (Figure 11–8).

❷

- Click Save (Create New Theme Fonts dialog box) to save the font scheme.

Experiment

- Click the Fonts button (Page Layout tab | Themes group) to display the Font Scheme gallery. The new font scheme will be at the top.

- Apply the Title cell style to cells A1 and A2 (shown in Figure 11–9).

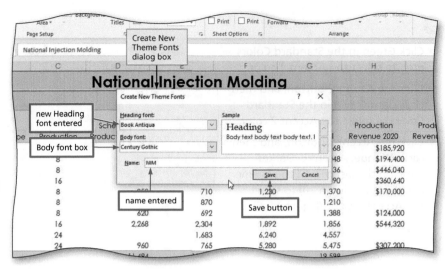

Figure 11–8

To Save a Custom Theme

The following steps save the newly created color and font schemes as an Excel theme. *Why? Saving them as a theme makes future use easier as you would not have to choose the color and font schemes individually.* Excel saves themes with the extension, .thmx. If the theme is stored in the default storage location, Microsoft Themes, the new theme will appear in the list of themes. If you are working in a lab situation, you should save new themes on your storage device. You can browse for the theme when you need it.

❶

- Click the Themes button (Page Layout tab | Themes group) to Themes gallery (Figure 11–9).

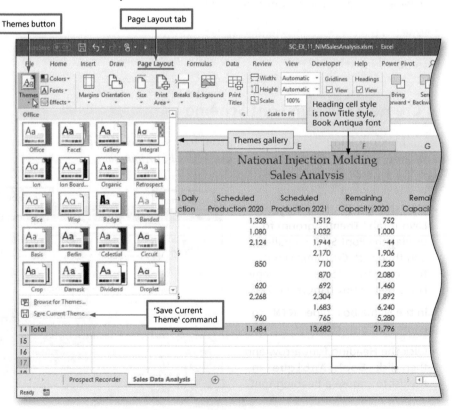

Figure 11–9

2

- Click Save Current Theme to display the Save Current Theme dialog box.

- In the File name box, type **NIM** and then browse to your Data File storage location (Figure 11–10).

◀ | Where are themes usually stored?

Q&A | By default, Microsoft themes are stored at C:\Users\Your Name\ AppData\Roaming\Microsoft\ Templates\Document Themes. You should save the NIM theme in your Data File storage location.

3

- Click Save (Current Theme dialog box).

Figure 11–10

Designing the User Interface

The NIM sales team is using Excel to maintain information on prospects and their product interests. The head of sales has requested a simple user interface that can be used by salespeople to record details about prospects in the workbook. A **user interface (UI)** is a collective term for all the ways you interact with a software program. Also called a **form**, in Excel, it is an object that provides an easy-to-use data entry screen. A form is convenient for people with little or no knowledge of Excel, who might not know which cells to select or how to navigate the worksheet. Figure 11–11 shows the approach you use to create the user interface and how the Prospect Recorder worksheet will look when complete.

When a user clicks the Step 1 - 'Click to Enter Contact Information' command button, code will trigger Excel to display a series of input dialog boxes to capture contact information. The remaining data (the prospect's preferred method of communication and how they heard about NIM's products) will be entered using check boxes and option buttons to help reduce input errors that can be caused by mistyped data. Multiple check boxes can be selected for product interests. Unlike check boxes, option buttons restrict users to one selection per group, in this case to one preferred method of contact and one source of information. Because all of the data entry will use controls and input dialog boxes, you can protect the workbook restricting the user's interaction with the worksheet to those controls and dialog boxes.

Planning Controls in the Form Design

You create a user interface or form by inserting form controls. **Form controls** are objects such as buttons and boxes that display data or make it easier for users to enter data, perform an action, or make a selection. Two types of controls are used to create the user interface: form controls and ActiveX controls. Form controls and ActiveX controls look identical in the Controls gallery. They do have functional

BTW
Managing Theme Fonts
Each theme includes two font settings: one for body text and one for headings. To manage the fonts used for each, click the Fonts button (Page Layout tab | Themes group) and then click Customize Fonts to display the Create New Theme Fonts dialog box. Select the desired heading and body font options, enter a name for the theme, and then click Save to update and apply the font selections.

BTW
Ribbon and Screen Resolution
Excel may change how the groups and buttons within the groups appear on the ribbon, depending on the screen resolution of your computer. Thus, your ribbon may look different from the ones in this book if you are using a screen resolution other than 1366 × 768.

Step 1: Design the User Interface

Step 2: Set Properties

Step 3: Write the VBA Code

Step 4: Test the Final Product

Figure 11–11

differences, however, that can help determine which one is the best choice for an object. Form controls require no knowledge of VBA to use. You can assign an Excel macro directly to a form control, allowing the macro to be run with a click. Form controls also allow you to reference cells easily and use Excel functions and expressions to manipulate data. You can customize their appearance at a rudimentary level.

ActiveX controls are controls that use a small program to enhance a user's experience or to help with tasks. ActiveX controls provide greater design flexibility than form controls. They have extensive properties used to customize their appearance. ActiveX controls cannot be assigned to an Excel macro directly. The macro code must be part of the VBA code for the control.

To create the Prospect Recorder interface, you will use form controls for the check boxes and option buttons, because of their ease of use and ability to use Excel functions with no additional code. You will use ActiveX controls for the command button and label controls to provide a more visually appealing interface than would be possible just using form controls. Figure 11–12 displays the gallery of available controls when constructing a user interface.

BTW
Copying Macros Between Workbooks
Macros consist of VBA code that can be edited or copied between workbooks using the Visual Basic Editor. To copy macros between workbooks, open the workbook containing the existing macro and the destination workbook. Open the Visual Basic Editor. In the Project pane, drag the module that you want to copy to the destination workbook.

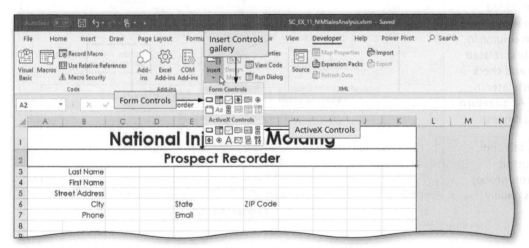

Figure 11–12

Finally, the user interface will store input in several places. It will place user input temporarily in row 40 of the Prospect Recorder worksheet, which is out of sight when the user interface is visible. It will display inputted data in the interface itself. Once the user input is recorded in row 40, an ActiveX control will display inputted data in the interface itself and then copy the input to a hidden worksheet, Prospect List. When testing the interface, you will verify the data recorded in the hidden worksheet.

To Display the Developer Tab

When you create a form, the Developer tab provides access to various VBA controls. The following steps display the Developer tab on the ribbon. If you already have the Developer tab on the ribbon, you may skip these steps.

1 Display Backstage view.

2 Click Options in the left pane to display the Excel Options dialog box.

3 Click Customize Ribbon in the left pane (Excel Options dialog box) to display the Customize the Ribbon tools.

④ Click the Developer check box in the Main Tabs list to select the Developer tab for display on the ribbon.

⑤ Click OK (Excel Options dialog box) to close the dialog box.

To Add Option Buttons to a Worksheet

Why? *You will use option buttons not only to ensure consistent data entry but also to make the final interface one that someone unfamiliar with Excel will be able to use easily.* The following steps create the option buttons. Do not be concerned about the exact placement of controls on the form. The option buttons will be aligned later in the module.

①

- Display the Prospect Recorder worksheet.

🔑 **Experiment**

- Look around the worksheet to view what has been added already. Look at the headings in row 39 and the data in column W, which displays stored text related to the option buttons and check boxes. You will use both later in the module. Click Cell A1 to return to the top of the spreadsheet.

- Display the Developer tab and then click the Insert button (Developer tab | Controls group) to display the Controls gallery (Figure 11–13).

Figure 11–13

②

- Click the Option Button button in the Form Controls area (column 6, row 1) in the Controls gallery.

- Drag in the worksheet to create an option button control in cell C9 (approximately), as shown in Figure 11–14.

- Repeat to place eight additional option buttons (Figure 11–14).

Q&A Why does my option button have more label text showing than in the figure?
The amount of text visible is determined by the size of the control. Dragging through a larger space on the worksheet will result in more label text being displayed. You can adjust the amount of visible label text by resizing the control.

My option buttons have numbers. Is that OK?
Yes, Excel may add a number in the caption or text beside the option button. You will change the caption later in the module.

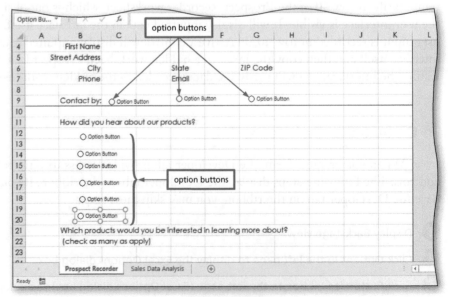

Figure 11–14

To Add Check Boxes to a Worksheet

- Click the Insert button (Developer tab | Controls group) again to display the Controls gallery, as shown in Figure 11–13.

- Click the Check Box button in the Form Controls area (column 3, row 1) in the Controls gallery.

- Drag in the worksheet to create a check box control in cell B24 (approximately), as shown in Figure 11–15.

- Repeat to place three additional check boxes (Figure 11–15).

Q&A What if I placed a control incorrectly?

If you want to reposition a control, right-click the control to select it and then drag it to its new location. You can delete a control by right-clicking the control and selecting Cut on the shortcut menu.

The check box is not the size I need it to be. What can I do?

Check boxes are resized easily. The check boxes here will be resized after the captions are changed later in this module.

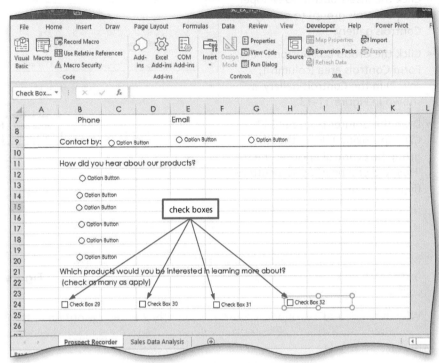

Figure 11–15

To Group Option Buttons Using a Group Box

You have grouped Excel objects, such as text boxes, pictures, and shapes for the purpose of keeping them together as they are moved, edited, or deleted. Grouping form controls has a different purpose, especially with regard to option buttons. An **option button** is a control used to display a limited list of mutually exclusive choices. In other words, users can choose only one in a set of option buttons. In the Prospect Recorder form, users should be able to choose one from the upper three 'Contact by' options buttons, as well as one from the lower six 'How did you hear' option buttons. *Why? NIM wants to know how customers would like to be contacted and how they heard about NIM products.*

To make a set of option button choices mutually exclusive, you need to group them together using the Group Box form control. In this project, you will group the lower set; users will be able to choose only one from those six option buttons. Because the lower buttons will be grouped, the upper options buttons do not need a Group Box form control to keep them together and mutually exclusive because the form itself acts as their group.

The following step first creates the Group Box form control, and then groups option buttons inside it.

1

- Click the Insert button (Developer tab | Controls group) to display the Controls gallery.

- Click the Group Box button in the Form Controls area (column 1, row 2) in the Controls gallery, as shown in Figure 11–13.

- Drag the pointer from cell B12 to C20, approximately, so that the group box control encloses the six 'How did you hear' option buttons (Figure 11–16).

Q&A How accurately do I have to draw the group box?
The Group Box control needs to enclose in the Option Button controls completely in order for it to work correctly.

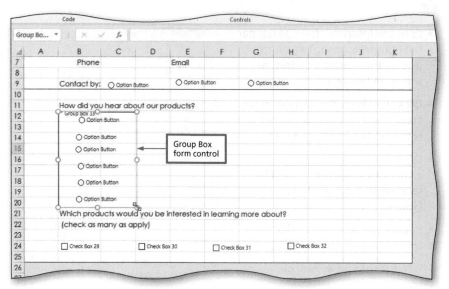

Figure 11–16

Why did I not add a group box control around the Contact by option buttons?
You could, but it is not necessary. Any option buttons not contained within a group box are treated as their own group contained by the form, so the Contact by option buttons are grouped by default. In this project, at least one group is necessary, however. Without the addition of at least one group box on the form, the user would only be able to select only one option button out of the nine option buttons.

Labels and Text Boxes

Most forms contain text: Option buttons usually need text labels that describe each option. In addition, users need to enter text information in response to question. There are two types of text controls you can add to a form. A **Label ActiveX control** (also called a label) is a box with text used to display a message, such as identifying the purpose of a cell or text box. A label can also display descriptive text, such as titles, captions, or brief instructions on the form. A label can also display a descriptive picture.

A **Text Box ActiveX control** is a rectangular box in which the user can view, enter, or edit data. A Text Box ActiveX control is different from a regular text box that you would insert using the Text Box command (Insert tab | Text group). A Text Box ActiveX control is a special text box used for data entry, programmed with code to move the data from the text box to a specific location or into a formula on the worksheet. While you are creating a Text Box ActiveX control, Excel turns on Design Mode, allowing you to set properties and write code. After you are finished, you can turn off Design Mode, allowing users to enter text in the text box. You also can use a text box to display or view text that is independent of row and column boundaries, or free-floating, preserving the layout of a grid or table of data on the worksheet.

To Add a Label Control to the Worksheet

You have added many option buttons and check boxes to the form so far, and now you need to identify them. *Why? Labels are an important part of a user interface because they guide users to select the correct controls as they enter their information.* The following step adds a label control to the worksheet.

- Click cell G12 or another cell to deselect the group box.

- Click the Insert button (Developer tab | Controls group) to display the Controls gallery.

- Click the Label button in the ActiveX Controls area (column 3, row 2) of the Controls gallery (shown in Figure 11–13).

- Drag in the worksheet from cell I13 through the lower-right corner of cell J15 to create a Label form control (Figure 11–17).

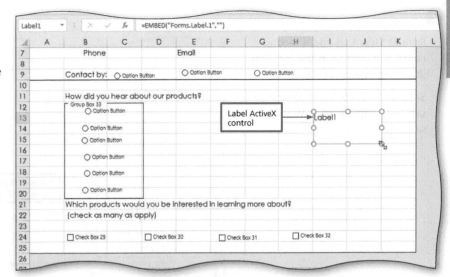

Figure 11–17

TO CREATE A TEXT BOX ACTIVEX CONTROL

In this project, you will not use a Text Box ActiveX control; the data entry will be supplied by a series of Input Boxes that you will learn about later. If you wanted to create a Text Box ActiveX control, you would do the following:

1. Click the Insert button (Developer tab | Controls group) to display the Controls gallery.
2. Click the Text Box button in the ActiveX Controls area (column 5, row 1) in the Controls gallery.
3. Drag in the worksheet to create a text box.
4. Set properties and write code as necessary.
5. Before releasing the workbook to the public, click the Design Mode button (Developer tab | Controls group) to turn it off, making the text box active.

To Add Command Buttons to the Worksheet

The use of command buttons gives the user control over the execution of each step of the process when entering data into the form. There is a difference between a Command Button form control and a Command Button ActiveX control. *Why? A Command Button ActiveX control can have Visual Basic code associated with it that accomplishes more complex actions than a macro or a Command Button form control can accommodate.* The two buttons are created in a similar manner, however. The following steps add two Command Button ActiveX controls to the worksheet.

- Click the Insert button (Developer tab | Controls group) to display the Controls gallery.
- Click the Command Button button in the ActiveX Controls area (column 1, row 1) of the Controls gallery.
- Drag in the worksheet from cell I7 through the lower-right corner of cell J9 to create a Command Button ActiveX control.

- Repeat Step 1 to add a second command button in the location shown in Figure 11–18.
- Save the workbook again in the same storage location with the same file name.

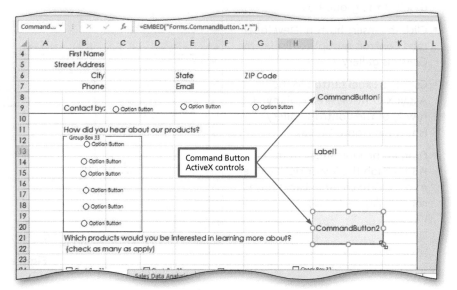

Figure 11–18

Break Point: If you want to take a break, this is a good place to do so. You can exit Excel now. To resume later, start Excel, open the file called SC_EX_11_NIMSalesAnalysis.xlsm, and continue following the steps from this location forward.

Setting Form Control Properties

Each form control in the Controls gallery has many properties, or characteristics, that can be set to determine the form control's appearance and behavior. You set these properties using the Format Control dialog box, which can be accessed by right-clicking the form control and selecting Format Control from the shortcut menu, or by selecting the control and clicking the Control Properties button (Developer tab | Controls group) on the ribbon.

The next step is to set the properties for the 13 form controls (check boxes and option buttons) in the user interface. The group box, while technically a form control, will not be formatted here; it will be formatted using VBA later in the module. The three ActiveX controls also will be formatted later in the module.

To Format the Option Buttons

Why? *The Option Button form controls must be formatted to identify their purpose for the user.* Other formatting options can be used to make the controls and the worksheet itself easier to use. The following steps change the text associated with the option button controls and resize the controls.

1

- Right-click the first option button control in the Contact by area to display the shortcut menu (Figure 11–19).

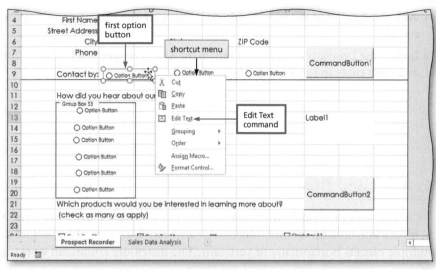

Figure 11–19

2

- Click Edit Text on the shortcut menu to edit the control text.
- Delete the text in the control and type **Email** to replace the text.
- Resize the control so that it just encloses the new text (Figure 11–20).

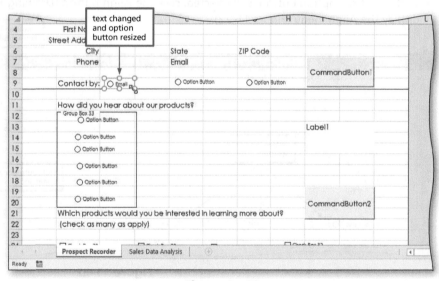

Figure 11–20

3

- Repeat Steps 1 and 2 to rename and resize the other two contact controls, with the names U.S. Mail and Telephone, respectively.
- If necessary, right-click the Telephone control to select it.
- ALT+drag the control until the right edge is aligned with the right edge of column H (Figure 11–21).

Q&A Why did I hold down the ALT key while positioning the Telephone control?
Using the ALT key aligns the controls to the Excel gridlines, making it easier to place items on the form.

Figure 11–21

- With the Telephone control still selected, CTRL+click the other two controls to select all three option button controls.
- Display the Drawing Tools Format tab. In the Shape Height box (Drawing Tools Format tab | Size group), type .2 and press ENTER to set the shape height.

Q&A

Why did I need to hold down the CTRL key while clicking the other two controls?
The CTRL key adds additional controls to the selection so that formatting and alignment options can be adjusted on the set of controls rather than individually.

To Align and Distribute

You have previously aligned objects in Excel, which means you have made either an edge or center of an object line up with another object. You also can distribute objects. The **distribute** command evenly spaces multiple objects horizontally or vertically. The distribute command works on three or more objects.

- With the three option buttons still selected, click the Align button (Drawing Tools Format tab | Arrange group) to display the Align menu (Figure 11–22).

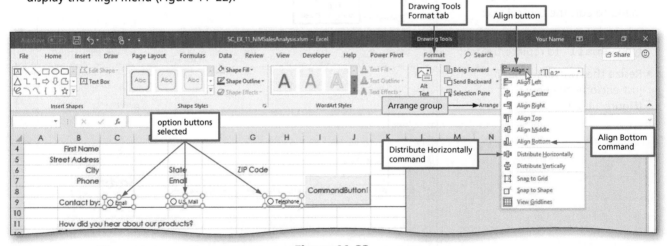

Figure 11–22

2

- Click Align Bottom on the Arrange menu to align the three controls along their bottom borders.
- Click the Align button again (Drawing Tools Format tab | Arrange group) to display the alignment options.
- Click Distribute Horizontally on the Arrange menu to space the three controls evenly between columns C and H.
- Click outside the area to deselect the option buttons.
- Click the Email option button to make it appear selected, or filled in (Figure 11–23).

Q&A

How can I make the controls more visible?
You can format the controls with borders and fill colors to make them stand out from the background. From the shortcut menu, you can select Format Control and then use the Color and Lines tab in the Format Control dialog box to apply colors and patterns.

Can I make the controls a specific size?
Yes. The size of controls also can be set using the Size tab, which you display by selecting the Format Control command on the shortcut menu.

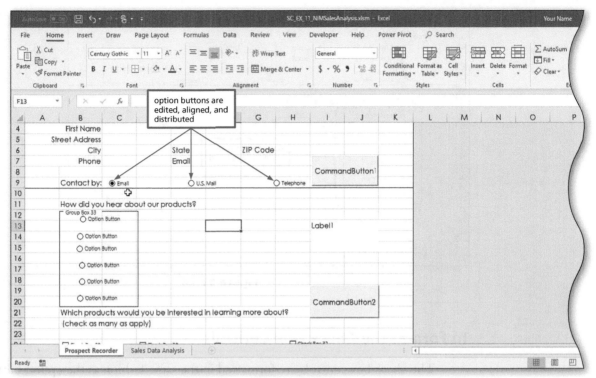

Figure 11–23

To Format the Option Buttons in the Group Box

The following steps format the option buttons in the group box control.

1 One at a time, right-click each of the six option buttons in the group box and edit the text to match the following:

Trade Show Event

Social Media

Salesperson

On the Web

Word of Mouth

Other

2 Select all six controls, and using the Shape Height and Shape Width boxes (Drawing Tools Format tab | Size group), set the height to 0.2" and the width to 1.1".

3 With the six controls still selected, click the Align Objects button (Drawing Tools Format tab | Arrange group), and then click the Align Left button.

4 Click the Align Object button again and then click Distribute Vertically to distribute the objects.

5 Click outside the option buttons to deselect them.

6 Click the Trade Show Event option button to make it appear checked, or filled in (Figure 11–24).

Q&A Can I format the Group Box control?
No. You can edit the text along the top of the group box, but to change it in any other way requires writing code, which you will do later in the module.

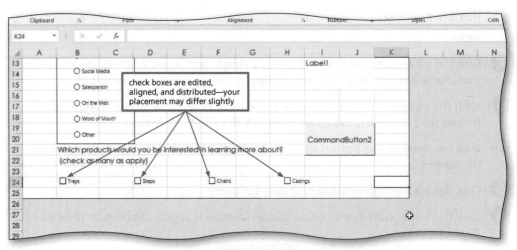

Figure 11–24

To Format the Check Box Controls

The check box controls are formatted in the same fashion as the option button controls. The following steps format and align the check box controls.

1   Select each of the four check box buttons, and in turn, type the following: Trays, Steps, Chairs, and Casings.

2   Move the leftmost check box button so that its upper-left corner aligns with the upper-left corner of cell B24, and move the rightmost check box button so that its upper-right corner aligns with the upper-right corner of cell H24.

3   Select all four controls and then, using the Shape Height and Shape Width boxes (Drawing Tools Format tab | Size group), set the height to 0.2" and the width to 1.2".

4   If necessary, select all four controls and then, using the Align Objects button (Drawing Tools Format tab | Arrange group), apply the Align Top and Distribute Horizontally formats to the group (Figure 11–25).

Figure 11–25

Setting ActiveX Control Properties

As with form controls, each ActiveX control in the Controls gallery has many properties that determine the control's appearance and behavior. You set these properties in Design Mode, which displays automatically in most cases. If you need to enter Design Mode, click the Design Mode button (Developer tab | Controls group). **Design Mode** allows the use of various tools including the Properties pane, where control properties can be set or edited. Turning off Design Mode makes the form and the command buttons ready to execute.

The Properties pane shows the name of the property on the left and the setting, text, or value on the right. When you click a property, some have an arrow button that displays a list of choices; some display an ellipsis button that opens a dialog box. For detailed information about each format property, select the property, and then press F1 to display a VBA Help topic.

The user interface contains three ActiveX controls: two command buttons and a label. The color, font, and effects for these controls will be modified by applying property values.

To Set Command Button Properties

Why? *Text on the command button helps users know what to do in the form.* You can add color, font formatting, shadow properties, and detailed captions to Command Button ActiveX controls in order to draw a user's attention. You also can give both controls user-friendly names using the Properties window. The following steps set the command button properties.

- Select the two command button controls.
- Display the Developer tab and then click the Properties button (Developer tab | Controls group) to open the Properties window.
- Click the BackColor property and then click the BackColor arrow to display the BackColor options.
- Click the Palette tab to display the color options (Figure 11–26).

Q&A Why does the Properties window look different from other dialog boxes in Excel?
The Properties window is part of the VBA interface and is used to manage ActiveX controls in Excel.

Figure 11–26

- Click gray (column 1, row 3) to add a gray background to the command buttons.
- Click the Font property to display the ellipsis button.
- Click the ellipsis button to display the Font dialog box.
- Select Segoe UI in the Font list, Bold in the Font style list, and 10 in the Size list to change the font on the command buttons and in the label (Figure 11–27).

Figure 11–27

- Click OK (Font dialog box) to apply this font to the text in the controls.
- Click the Shadow button and then click True.
- Set Height to 50.25 and Width to 140.25.
- Click the WordWrap arrow and then click True (Figure 11–28).

Experiment

- Click Mouse Pointer in the Properties pane and then click its arrow to view the different kinds of pointers that can be used with a command button. Do not change the setting.

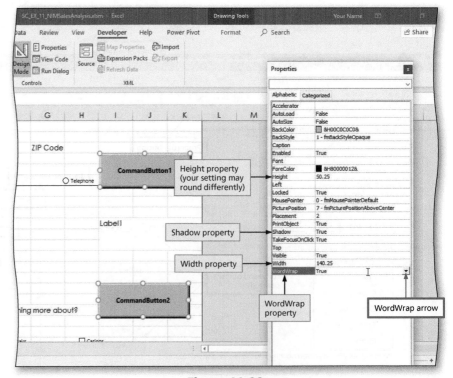

Figure 11–28

4

- Select the first command button only.

- In the Properties pane, click Name and then type `cmdStep1` to rename the control.

- Click Caption, and then type **Step 1 - Click to enter contact information** to enter the caption (Figure 11–29).

&A What are the letters, cmd, before the name, Step1?
It is common practice for developers to use a prefix with control names to indicate the type of control.

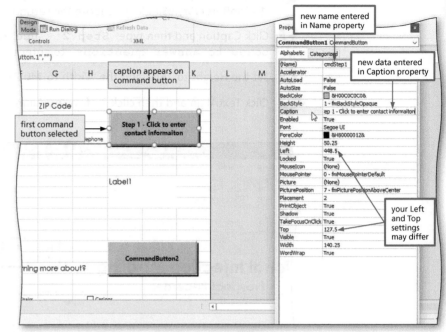

Figure 11–29

5

- Select the second command button only.

- In the Properties pane, click Name and then type `cmdStep3` to rename the control.

- Click Caption, and then type **Step 3 - Click to submit information** to enter the caption (Figure 11–30).

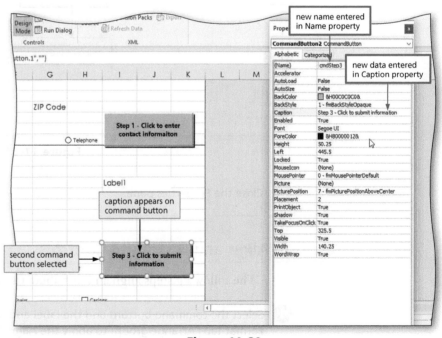

Figure 11–30

To Set Label Properties

The following steps set properties for the Label ActiveX Control.

1 Select the label control.

2 In the Properties pane, click Name and then type `lblStep2` to rename the control.

3 In the Properties pane, click BorderColor and then click the BorderColor arrow to display the BorderColor options. Click the Palette tab to display the color options. Click black (column 1, row 6) to add a black border to the label.

4 Click BorderStyle and then click the BorderStyle arrow. In the list, click '1 - frmBorderStyleSingle' to choose the setting for the border.

5 Click Caption and then type `Step 2 - Use option buttons and check boxes to answer questions` to enter the caption.

6 Set the Height to 60 and the Width to 140.25.

7 Click TextAlign and then click 2 - frm TextAlignCenter (Figure 11–31).

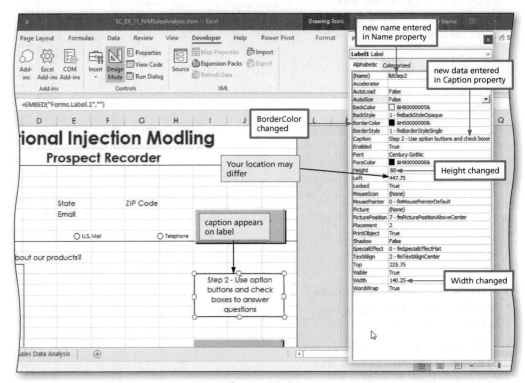

Figure 11–31

8 Close the Properties pane.

To Align and Distribute Controls

The following steps align and distribute the two command buttons and the label.

1 Select the command buttons and the label and use the Align button (Drawing Tools Format tab | Arrange group) to apply the Align Right and Distribute Vertically formats to the group.

2 Save the workbook again in the same storage location with the same file name.

Storing User Input

Once you have added the controls to the worksheet, consider where the inputted information will be stored or recorded. In most cases when you use an Excel form, you must store the information within the workbook, but it is a good idea to store it away from the form itself. You want the data to be accessible to experienced users but not distracting to users simply entering data in the form. For this project, you will store data input in row 40 of the worksheet. You then you will copy that information into a hidden Prospects List worksheet for long-term retention.

Users will be entering their name, address, and other information into the form. In this module, entering and storing data will be a three-part process. Part 1: Rather than having the users try to move to specific cells and type in data, which may or may not fit in the cell, you will program a VBA function called INPUTBOX to collect their data. Users will click option buttons and check boxes to indicate their responses. Part 2: You will program Excel to transfer the data from the INPUTBOX collection to the temporary storage location in row 40 and display it on the form. Excel also will place the values for option buttons and check boxes in row 40. Part 3: When the user clicks the Submit button, Excel will transfer the data from the temporary location in row 40 to the hidden worksheet, Prospect List, and clear the form for the next entry.

To Create from Selection

In order to make the process more user-friendly, you will name specific cells and ranges. The 'Create from Selection' command names cells based on headings or adjacent cells. Excel uses the heading to name the cell, replacing any spaces with underscores. The following steps use the headings in row 39 to name the cells in row 40. **Why?** *Row 40 will be the temporary storage location for inputted data.*

- Select the range A39:H40.

- Click the 'Create from Selection' button (Formulas tab | Defined Names group) to display the Create from Selection dialog box

- Because the headings are at the top, click the Top row check box, if necessary (Figure 11–32).

Q&A | Why am I not included columns I through N in the selection?
I40:N40 will contain formulas or functions and do not need names.

Figure 11–32

- Click OK (Create Names from Selection dialog box) to name the cells.

Experiment

- Click various cells in row 40 to verify their names in the Name Box on the formula bar.

To Assign Other Range Names

The following steps assign names to specific ranges in the form. The two ranges are in column W, which displays the captions of the option buttons.

1 Select the range W3:W5.

2 Click the Define Name button (Formulas tab | Defined Names group) to display the New Name dialog box.

3 Type **Contact_Options** in the Name text box.

4 Click OK (New Name dialog box).

5 Repeat steps 1 through 4 to name the range W7:W12 as **Source_Options**.

To Enter Cell References

The following steps enter cell references in the form. These cell references will display user input from programming later in the module. The cells and references to enter are listed in Table 11–1.

Table 11–1 Cell References	
Cell	Reference to Enter
C3	=A40
C4	=B40
C5	=C40
C6	=D40
F6	=E40
H6	=F40
C7	=G40
F7	=H40

1 On at a time, click each cell listed in column 1 of Table 11–1 and enter the cell reference listed in column 2. No data will appear on the form yet, as the reference cells have not been filled by user input.

2 Verify your entries by clicking the cell and looking in the formula bar.

Q&A My cells display an error icon triangle saying that the formula refers to empty cells. Is that OK?

You can turn off the green triangles: Click Options in Backstage view, click Formulas, and then clear the 'Formulas Referring to Empty Cells' check box in the Error checking rules area.

Evaluating Option Buttons

Recall that form users will click an option button in each group to select it. The first option button is already selected to be the default value in each group. Because those selections must be stored, you need to determine which option button of the group was clicked.

Excel maintains an index number behind the scenes for each option button; that index number is 1, 2, 3, and so on. To retrieve the option button index number, you use the Format Control dialog box to link to a cell reference that will display the index number. For example, if you link an option button to cell Z100, then during data input when the user clicks an options button, cell Z100 will display a 1, 2, or 3 to indicate which option button was selected. Excel only requires you to create a cell link for one option button per group; the cell link will work for all option buttons in the group.

Determining the caption of a selected option button is a separate process, however. Once you obtain the index number, you can look up the caption in column W, using the INDEX() function. Recall that the INDEX() function takes two arguments, a range and an index number. The function returns the cell value at that location in the range. For example, if your captions are located in cells A1, A2, and A3, you might type

`=INDEX(A1:A3, $Z$100)`

The INDEX() function would look in range A1:A3 for the specified index represented by Z100. It then would return, or display, the text at that location. Naming the range, A1:A3, would make it more user friendly.

`=INDEX(My_Captions, $Z$100)`

To Evaluate Option Button Selection

In this module, there are two option button groups: the prospect's preferred method of contact and how the prospect heard about NIM's products. In the first group, by using the INDEX function, you will have Excel record the user's selection as one of the captions stored in W3:W5, Email, U.S. Mail, or Telephone, rather than the numerical values (1, 2, or 3). *Why? User input has to be changed from a numerical value to one that salespeople can understand.* Likewise, in the second option button group, Excel will return one of the captions stored in W7:W12 rather than a number 1 through 6.

The following steps store the user's option button selections. The cell link will be established using the Form Control dialog box. The INDEX() function, entered in row 40, will use the previously named range and the index number. The function will return a caption from the range in column W.

- Right-click the Email option button control to display the shortcut menu.

- Click Format Control to display the Format Control dialog box.

- If necessary, click the Control tab (Format Control dialog box) to display the Control sheet.

- Type `$I$41` in the Cell link box (Format Control dialog box) to link the option button index number to cell I41 (Figure 11–33).

Q&A Why did I link only one of the option buttons to cell I41?
Option buttons work collectively as a group with a single identity assigned to the set of options. The specific value of the selected option button will be assigned an out-of-the-way cell, I41.

Figure 11–33

2

- Click OK (Format Control dialog box) to close the dialog box.
- Scroll down and then click cell I40 to make it the active cell.
- Type =INDEX(Contact_Options,$I$41) to record text from the named range Contact_Options rather than numbers in cell I40 (Figure 11–34).
- Click the Enter button.

 Q&A How does the INDEX function work here?

In this instance, the INDEX function looks at the value in cell I41, which identifies which option button was selected, and returns the entry associated with that value from the named range, Contact_Method. The named range is found in column W in this worksheet.

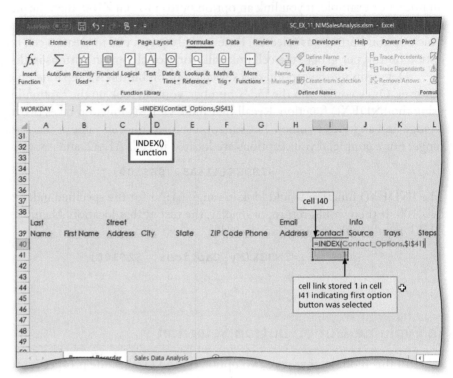

Figure 11–34

3

- Right-click the Trade Show Event option button control and then click Format Control on the shortcut menu. If necessary, click the Control tab.
- Type $J$41 in the Cell link box (Format Control dialog box) (Figure 11–35).

Figure 11–35

- Click OK (Format Control dialog box).
- Click cell J40.
- Type **=INDEX(Source_Options,$J$41)** to enter a function that returns the caption from the named range Information_Source at the index number (Figure 11–36).

⑤

- Click the Enter button.

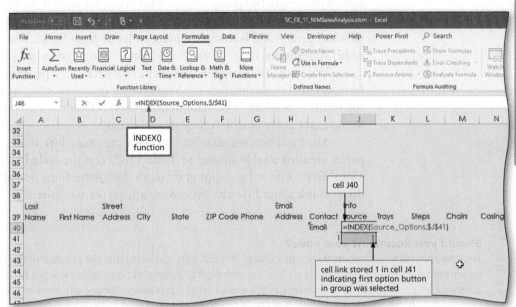

Figure 11–36

To Evaluate Check Box Control Selection

The following steps evaluate the check box selections by assigning each check box a cell link.

1 Right-click the Trays check box control. Use the shortcut menu to display the Format Control dialog box.

2 Type **$K$40** in the Cell link box (Format Control dialog box, Control tab).

3 Click OK (Format Control dialog box).

4 Repeat Steps 1 through 3 for each of the remaining three check box controls, using cells $L$40, $M$40, and $N$40 for the cell links.

5 Save the workbook again on the same storage location with the same file name.

Q&A Why do I have to link each check box control to a specific cell?

Unlike option buttons that work in groups, check box controls can each be either checked or unchecked, representing TRUE or FALSE values. Each one needs to be evaluated.

Writing Code for a Command Button

Earlier you placed two command buttons on the form. To make a button trigger an action when a user clicks it, you must write VBA code that tells Excel what to do after the command button is clicked. VBA is a vast subject; in this module you will learn only a few of its many commands and techniques.

In this section, you will write the procedure that will execute when the user clicks the 'Step 1 - Click to Enter Contact Information' button. A **procedure** is a series of statements that performs an operation or calculates an answer in response to a triggered event.

You will be using the **Visual Basic Editor**, which is a full-screen editor that lets you enter a procedure by typing lines of VBA code. Accessed from the Developer tab on the ribbon, the Visual Basic Editor is like an app within an app because it has its own ribbon, tabs, and groups and is navigated independently from Excel. You type lines of code, also called **statements**, in the Visual Basic Editor, using basic word processing techniques.

When the user triggers the event that executes a procedure, such as clicking a button, Excel steps through the Visual Basic statements one at a time, beginning at the top of the procedure. The statements should reflect the steps you want Excel to take, in the exact order in which they should occur.

After you determine what you want the procedure to do, write the VBA code on paper, creating a table similar to Table 11–2. Test the code before you enter it in the Visual Basic Editor by stepping through the instructions one at a time yourself. As you do so, think about how the procedure affects the worksheet.

The Enter Prospect Button Procedure

Table 11–2 displays the VBA code executed when users click the first command button. Lines beginning with a single quote are called comments. In VBA, a **comment** is a statement in the code that documents it. Comments are not executed, nor are they visible to form users; they are seen only by programmers and other form developers.

Table 11–2 Enter Prospect Button Procedure	
1	'Enter Prospect Button Procedure
2	'Author: SC Series
3	'Date Created: 11/12/2020
4	'Run from: Prospect Recorder worksheet by clicking Step 1 button
5	'Function: When executed, this procedure enters contact information for the prospect
6	'
7	Range("Last_Name").Value = InputBox("Last Name?", "Enter", , 800, 6000)
8	Range("First_Name").Value = InputBox("First Name?", "Enter", , 800, 6000)
9	Range("Street_Address").Value = InputBox("Street Address?", "Enter", , 800, 6000)
10	Range("City").Value = InputBox("City?", "Enter", , 800, 6000)
11	Range("State").Value = InputBox("State?", "Enter", , 800, 6000)
12	Range("ZIP_Code").Value = InputBox("Zip Code?", "Enter", , 800, 6000)
13	Range("Phone").Value = InputBox("Telephone Number?", "Enter", , 800, 6000)
14	Range("Email_Address").Value = InputBox("Email Address?", "Enter", , 800, 6000)

The rest of the procedure uses a VBA function named InputBox(). During Execution, the function displays a dialog box for user entry (Figure 11–37). The InputBox() function takes four arguments: a label or prompt, the title of the dialog box, the default value in the text box, the width, and the height. The dialog box automatically contains a text box, OK button, Cancel button, and Close button. The InputBox() function returns whatever the user enters in the text box.

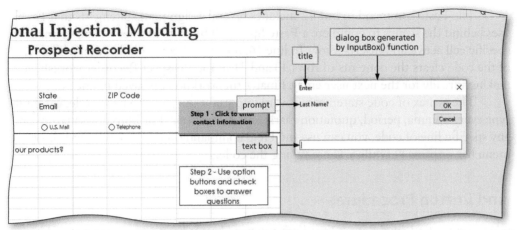

Figure 11–37

In VBA, as in other programming languages, the function and its arguments are placed to the right of an equal sign; the return location is on the left. This kind of code, that sets or resets a value, object, or location, is called an **assignment statement**. In Table 11–2, the return location is the value in a named range, in this case the single cells that were named earlier in the module.

BTW
Printing VBA Code
Some people find it easier to review and edit code by working with a printout. To print out VBA code while using the Visual Basic Editor, click File on the menu bar and then click Print on the File menu.

The Submit Button Procedure

Table 11–3 displays the VBA code executed when users click the first command button. This procedure copies the information to the hidden worksheet named Prospect List. A range is selected and copied; in this case, the range is row 40, where the user information was temporarily stored. The procedure then sets various properties of the Sheets object, short for worksheet. The code makes the worksheet visible, then active, then selects a range (lines 9–11).

Table 11–3 Submit Button Procedure
1	'Submit Button Procedure
2	'Author: SC Series
3	'Date Created: 11/12/2020
4	'Run from: Prospect Recorder worksheet by clicking Step 3 button
5	'Function: When executed, this procedure submits new information to the prospect list
6	'
7	Range("A40:O40").Select
8	Selection.Copy
9	Sheets("Prospect List").Visible = True
10	Sheets("Prospect List").Activate
11	Sheets("Prospect List").Range("A2:N2").Select
12	Selection.PasteSpecial Paste:=xlPasteValues, Operation:=xlNone, SkipBlanks:=False, Transpose:=False
13	Selection.Font.Bold = False
14	Sheets("Prospect List").Range("A2").Activate
15	ActiveCell.EntireRow.Insert
16	Sheets("Prospect List").Visible = False
17	Sheets("Prospect Recorder").Select
18	Range("I41:J41").ClearContents
19	Range("A40:H40").ClearContents
20	Range("K40:N40").ClearContents
21	Range("J8").Activate
22	ActiveWorkbook.Save

The Paste command in line 12 includes several assignment statements that Excel uses behind the scenes to complete a Paste Special. The code in lines 14 and 15 makes a specific cell active and inserts a row. In line 16, the worksheet is hidden again. The rest of the code clears the contents of rows 40 and 41 in the Prospect Recorder worksheet, making it ready for the next user entry. Finally, the workbook is saved in line 22.

The syntax of code statements is very important. As you enter the code, carefully type every comma, period, quotation mark, and parenthesis. For more information on any specific line of code, you can use the Help command on the Visual Basic Editor menu bar or press F1 while you are typing the code.

To Enter the Command Button Procedures

Why? *To enter a procedure, you use the Visual Basic Editor. Each command button has a separate procedure.* The following steps activate the Visual Basic Editor and create a procedure for each of the two command buttons.

- If necessary, display the Developer tab and then click the Design Mode button (Developer tab | Controls group) to make Design Mode active.

- Right-click the Step 1 button on the worksheet to display the shortcut menu (Figure 11–38).

Figure 11–38

- Click View Code to display the Microsoft Visual Basic for Applications editor and then, if necessary, maximize the window.

Q&A What is displayed in the code window on the right?
The beginning and the end of the procedure is created for you already.

- If necessary, click in the blank line between the beginning and end lines of code.

- Press TAB before you enter each line of VBA code from Table 11–2. Do not enter the line numbers from the table (Figure 11–39).

Q&A What is the purpose of the two commas in lines 9 through 15?
Commas must separate each argument in a function. In Lines 9 through 15, the third argument is the default text for the text box. Placing nothing between the commas indicates that nothing will appear in the text box.

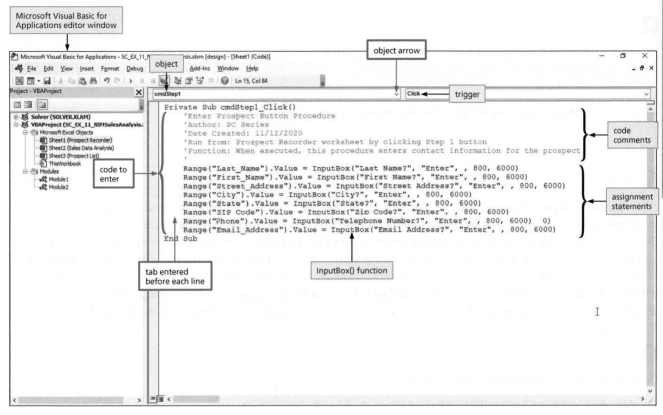

Figure 11–39

3

- Click the Object arrow and then click cmdStep3 in the list to display the beginning and ending code for the Submit button.

- Enter the VBA code shown in Table 11–3, pressing TAB at the beginning of each line (Figure 11–40).

Q&A | Do I have to press the TAB key?
No, but it is a common programming practice to do so because it improves readability.

Figure 11–40

• Verify your code by comparing it with the content of Tables 11–2 and 11–3.

Other Ways
1. Click View Code button (Excel Window | Developer tab | Controls group), enter code in Visual Basic Editor window

To Remove the Outline from the Group Box Control

Recall that the group box on the form displays a border and text. The following steps remove those from the group box control. *Why? Removing the outline will result in a more visually pleasing user interface.* Because the group box has no formatting options in the Excel window, you must set its visibility property with a line of VBA code. You will enter this in the Immediate window in the Visual Basic Editor. The **Immediate window** is a Visual Basic Editor window that lets you enter different values to test the procedures you create without changing any data in the database and often is used for debugging and executing statements during design. As its name suggests, code entered in this window is executed immediately upon exiting the Visual Basic Editor.

• Press CTRL+G to open the Immediate window.

• Type `activesheet.groupboxes.visible = false` to enter the code.

• Press ENTER to execute the code, which hides the box around the group control (Figure 11–41).

Q&A | What does the code mean?
The assignment statement code assigns the value false to the visible property of the group boxes on the active sheet.

Figure 11–41

- Click the Save button (Visual Basic Editor toolbar).
- Close the Visual Basic Editor window.
- Save the workbook again in the same storage location with the same file name.

Other Ways

1. Click View on menu bar, click Immediate window, enter code

Break Point: If you wish to take a break, this is a good place to do so. You can now exit Excel. To resume at a later time, start Excel, open the file called SC_EX_11_NIMSalesAnalysis.xlsm, and continue following the steps from this location forward.

Preparing, Protecting, and Testing Worksheets

With any worksheet that you will distribute to others, you should consider how to prepare, protect, and test it. Excel provides several ways to prepare and protect worksheets. You can turn features on or off such as page breaks, zero values, gridlines, the formula bar, or headings. You also can limit distractions for the user by hiding the ribbon, hiding row and column headers, and hiding the active cell. It is a good idea to password protect worksheets that contain forms to prevent other users from accidentally or deliberately changing, moving, or deleting data. With worksheet protection, you can make only certain parts of the sheet editable so that users will not be able to modify data in any other region in the sheet or workbook. And, of course, before sharing a document, you must thoroughly test its functionality.

To Prepare Worksheet for Distribution

The following steps prepare the worksheet for users who will only use the form. **Why?** *You are hiding the ribbon, row numbers, and columns from view to restrict what the user can do in this worksheet.*

- If necessary, click the Design Mode button (Developer tab | Controls group) to exit Design Mode.
- Display Backstage view.
- Scroll as necessary and then click Options to display the Excel Options dialog box.
- Click the Advanced tab (Excel Options dialog box) to display the advanced options.
- Scroll to the 'Display options for this worksheet' area in the right pane.
- As necessary, click to clear the 'Show row and column headers' check box, the 'Show page breaks' check box, and the 'Show a zero in cells that have zero value' check box (Figure 11–42).

Q&A What does clearing the 'Show row and column headers' check box do?
It turns that feature off, hiding the display of the row numbers and the column letters on this worksheet only. User will see only the edges of the form.

Figure 11–42

- Click OK to close the Excel Options dialog box.
- Display the View tab.
- As necessary, click to clear the Gridlines, Formula Bar, and Headings check boxes (View tab | Show group) to remove those features from the worksheet (Figure 11–43).

Figure 11–43

- Click the 'Collapse the Ribbon' button on the ribbon to hide it.

To Password Protect the Worksheet

The following steps password protect the worksheet. *Why? A password prevents users from making changes to your VBA code and calculations.* You also will choose to place the active cell in a hidden location so that it won't distract inexperienced spreadsheet users.

- Display the Review tab and then click the Protect Sheet button (Review tab | Protect group) to display the Protect Sheet dialog box.

- Type **Prospect19** in the 'Password to unprotect sheet' box (Figure 11–44).

Q&A

Should I password protect the entire workbook?
No. You will edit other sheets later in the module.

Figure 11–44

Q&A What is the purpose of the check boxes?
You can click those check boxes to allow all users of the worksheet to edit, insert, and change various kinds of cells, even when the worksheet is password protected.

- Click OK (Protect Sheet dialog box) to display the Confirm Password dialog box.

- Type **Prospect19** in the 'Reenter password to proceed' box (Figure 11–45).

Q&A Do any rules apply to passwords?
Yes. Passwords in Excel can contain, in any combination, letters, numbers, spaces, and symbols, and can be up to 15 characters long. Passwords are case sensitive. If you decide to password-protect a worksheet, make sure you save the password in a secure place. If you lose the password, you will not be able to open or gain access to the password-protected worksheet.

Figure 11–45

- Click OK (Confirm Password dialog box) to close the dialog boxes.

- Press F5 to display the Go To dialog box.

- Type **J8** in the Reference box (Go To dialog box) to enter the destination (Figure 11–46).

Q&A Why use J8 as the new active cell?
The J8 cell is hidden behind the first command button, out of the way, so as not to elicit data entry for inexperienced users.

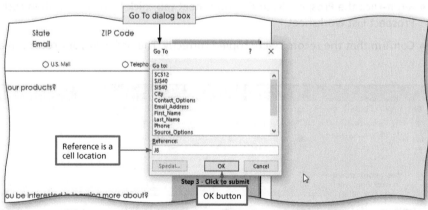

Figure 11–46

- Click OK (Go To dialog box) to make cell J8 the active cell and close the dialog box.

- Save the workbook again in the same storage location with the same file name.

To Test the Controls in the Worksheet

Why? *Before distributing the workbook for use, it is good practice to test the controls and verify the proper functionality of the VBA code.* The following steps test the controls in the Prospect Recorder worksheet using the data shown in Table 11–4.

Table 11–4 Prospect Records

Field	Record 1	Record 2
Last Name	Daniels	Stetson
First Name	Kurt	Larue
Address	572 King Street	31 Andrew Road
City	Clayton	Parkville
State	OK	LA
Zip Code	73015	70024
Phone	918-555-1212	318-555-1313
Email	kdaniels@cengage.com	lstetson@cengage.com
Contact Preference	Telephone	Email
Information Source	Social Media	Trade Show Event
Interest(s)	Steps	Trays & Casings

1

- Click the Step 1 button on the form. Answer the prompts using the data from the first record in Table 11–4.
- Check the option buttons and check boxes as shown in the table.
- Click the Step 3 button on the form to submit the data.
- Repeat the process for the second record.
- Right-click the Prospect Recorder worksheet tab, click Unhide, and then click OK (Unhide dialog box) to display the Prospect List worksheet.
- Confirm that the records were copied correctly. The order of your records may differ (Figure 11–47).

Figure 11–47

- Right-click the Prospect List worksheet tab and then click Hide on the shortcut menu.
- Make the Sales Data Analysis worksheet active.
- Save the workbook again in the same storage location with the same file name.

Sharing and Collaborating

Collaboration is the practice of sharing files with others, providing comments, and collecting feedback. Excel provides several ways to collaborate. As you have seen, you can physically distribute the workbook to others on storage media or through email using an attachment. In addition, you can save files in a variety of formats using OneDrive, Power BI, SharePoint, or other networked sites. Your storage locations commonly are listed when you click Save As or Publish in Backstage view.

In Excel 2019 you also can **co-author** or collaborate on the same workbook at the same time. When you co-author, you can see each other's changes quickly—in a matter of seconds. And with certain versions of Excel, you will see other people's selections in different colors. To co-author, rather than simply saving the file on OneDrive, you use the Share button on the Excel ribbon to distribute or save your file in a manner which allows others to access it.

BTW
Copying Comments
You can copy comments from one cell to other cells using the Paste Special command. Select the cell that contains the comment you need to copy, click the Copy button (Home tab | Clipboard group), select the cell or cells to which you want to apply the comment, click the Paste arrow, and then click Paste Special. In the Paste Special dialog box, in the Paste list, select Comments, and then click the OK button.

To Save a Copy of a Worksheet

The following steps save a copy of the Sales Data Analysis work to share with others.

1. Right-click the Sales Data Analysis worksheet tab. Click 'Move or Copy' on the shortcut menu.

2. Click the To book arrow (Move or Copy dialog box) and then click (new book).

3. Click the 'Create a copy' check box.

4. Click OK (Move or Copy dialog box) to move a copy of the worksheet to a new workbook.

5. Save the workbook with the name, SC_EX_11_Collaborate.xlsx.

Q&A | My workbook looks different. What should I do?
Depending on how you saved the color and font schemes, your new workbook may not have those schemes. Choose the NIM color scheme and the NIM font scheme (Page Layout tab | Themes group) and save again.

To Distribute via OneDrive

You can use OneDrive to distribute workbooks. Colleagues can make changes and then save the workbook on OneDrive for review. Saving workbooks for distribution on OneDrive does not differ from using OneDrive to save your own files, although you do need to make the workbook available to others by saving it in an accessible location. *Why? You may need to have a workbook reviewed by someone who does not share network access with you.* The following steps distribute the workbook via OneDrive. If you cannot access OneDrive, simply read the steps.

- If necessary, display any tab on the ribbon and then click the 'Pin the ribbon' button in the lower-right corner of the ribbon.

- In the upper-right corner of the ribbon, click Share to open the Share dialog box (Figure 11–48).

Q&A What happened to the Protect and Share Workbook command?
That command, and the Changes group on the Review tab, have been replaced by co-authoring.

What are the buttons at the bottom of the Sharing dialog box?
Those commands are shortcuts to send the file as an attachment, both as an Excel file and as a PDF file. The same commands are available in Backstage view.

Figure 11–48

- Click the OneDrive button (Share dialog box) and sign in if necessary. Or, if you have access to another network, click its button and sign in.

- When Excel displays the Send Link dialog box, enter a recipient's email address above the blue line (Figure 11–49).

Q&A Can I add a message?
Yes. Click below the blue line and type a brief message.

Experiment
- Click the 'Anyone with this link can edit' button to open the Link Settings dialog box. Look at the various groups to whom you can give permission to edit the file. Click Cancel (Link Settings dialog box) when you are finished.

Figure 11–49

- Click the Send button (Send Link dialog box).

- Close the Link Sent dialog box, if necessary.

Q&A How does the link work?
The recipient will receive an email message inviting them to open the file. They can click the link to open the workbook. A web browser will open, and the workbook will open in Excel Online.

Other Ways

1. Click Share in Backstage view, enter email address, click send.

To Co-Author a Workbook

Working together in the same workbook at the same time can improve efficiency in networked team environments. *Why? Co-authoring a workbook can provide you with a timely, interactive editing process with colleagues.* The following steps assume you have distributed the workbook to someone and that co-author has opened the file.

(a) Co-author information

- Make sure that AutoSave is on in the upper-left corner of the title bar.

- Ask the second workbook user to click the link you sent.

- When the second user comes online, click the picture or initials in the upper-right corner of the ribbon (Figure 11–50a).

- Ask the user to click cell D7 and enter 2254 as the new value, and then save the workbook (Figure 11–50b).

Q&A
Can I track the changes made by the co-author?
Excel no longer supports tracking changes; however, you can save a separate copy and compare workbooks, which you will do later in the module.

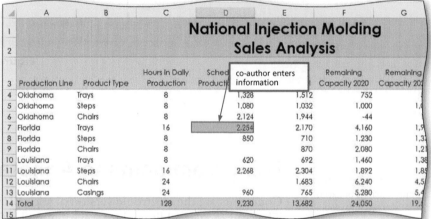

(b) Co-author editing

Figure 11–50

- In your copy of the workbook, click the Save button on the Quick Access Toolbar to display the Microsoft Excel dialog box indicating that the workbook has been updated with changes saved by another user.

- Close the workbook and ask the second user of the workbook to close his or her workbook.

To Unprotect a Password-Protected Worksheet

The Prospect Recorder worksheet in the NIM Sales Analysis workbook is protected, which restricts the changes you can make to the worksheet to unlocked cells only. You cannot make changes to locked cells or modify the worksheet itself. You will unprotect the worksheet. *Why? Unprotecting allows changes to locked cells and the worksheet itself.* Recall that a password ensures that users cannot unprotect the worksheet simply by clicking the Unprotect button. The password for the worksheet is Prospect19. The following steps unprotect the password-protected Prospect Recorder worksheet.

- If necessary, open the file named SC_EX_11_NIMSalesAnalysis.xlsm.

- Display the Prospect Recorder worksheet.

- If necessary, display the Review tab, and then click the Unprotect Sheet button (Review tab | Protect group) to display the Unprotect Sheet dialog box.

- When the Unprotect Sheet dialog box appears, type **Prospect19** in the Password box (Figure 11–51).

- Click OK (Unprotect Sheet dialog box) to unprotect the Prospect Recorder worksheet.

- Save and close the workbook.

Q&A Can I work with the entire worksheet now?
Yes. With the worksheet unprotected, you can modify the contents of cells, regardless of whether they are locked or unlocked. Cells must be both locked and the worksheet protected to restrict what users can do to cell contents.

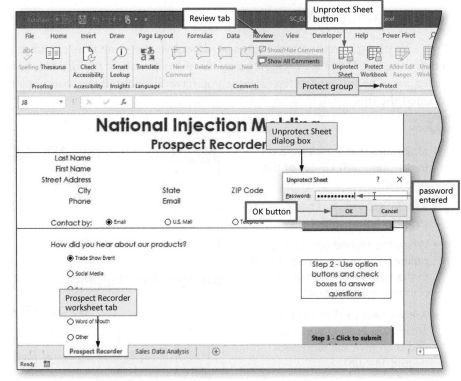

Figure 11–51

BTW
Comments and Notes
In some versions of Excel, comments are threaded, allowing you to have discussions with other people about the data. Those versions include notes for annotating the data, and they work like comments used from other versions of Excel.

Using Comments to Annotate a Worksheet

Comments are the electronic version of sticky notes or annotations in the margin. They can request additional information or clarification of existing information. Comments can provide direction to the reader about how to interpret content or describe what type of content to add. You can add a comment to any cell in a worksheet. Once you add comments, you can edit, format, move, copy, or resize them. You can choose to show comments in a worksheet, to display only a comment indicator, or to hide comments. Comments work well when multiple people are collaborating on a worksheet. Comments added by each user are identified by a name in the comment, set by the user.

Depending on the nature of the comments, you may decide to delete some or all comments after reading them and making edits to the worksheet, if appropriate.

To Add Comments to a Worksheet

Why? Comments in Excel can be used to remind the user of material that needs to be added or updated. The Sales Data Analysis worksheet in the NIM Sales Analysis workbook has some missing data. The following steps add comments to the worksheet in cells A9 and A12.

- If necessary, open the SC_EX_11_NIMSalesAnalysis.xlsm workbook and then, if necessary, click the Enable Content button in the yellow Security Warning bar below the ribbon.

- If necessary, display the Sales Data Analysis worksheet.

- Enter **2254** in cell D7.

- Display the Review tab and, if necessary, click the 'Show All Comments' button (Review tab | Comments group) to toggle the option off and hide all comments in the workbook.

- Right-click cell A9 to display the shortcut menu (Figure 11–52).

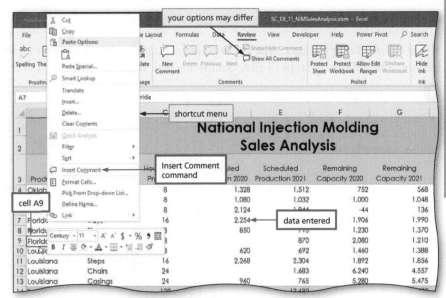

Figure 11–52

2

- Click Insert Comment on the shortcut menu to open a comment box next to the selected cell and display a comment indicator in the cell.

- Enter the text **Note to David - need accurate count of Chairs scheduled for 2020 production in Florida.** in the comment box (Figure 11–53).

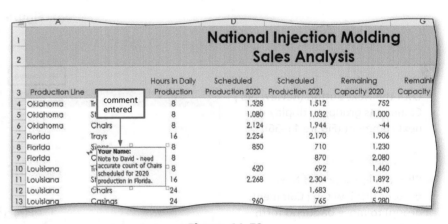

Figure 11–53

3

- Click outside the comment box to close the comment box and display only the red comment indicator in cell A9.

- Enter a comment in cell A12 with the text **Note to Amanda - need accurate count of Chairs scheduled for 2020 production in Louisiana.** (Figure 11–54).

 My comment boxes do not close when I click outside the comment box. Why?
Turn off the showing of comments by clicking the 'Show All Comments' button (Review tab | Comments group).

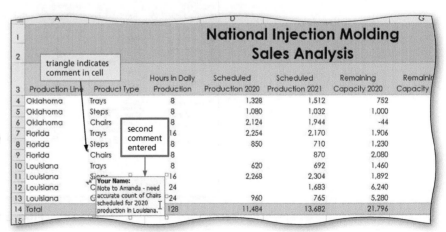

Figure 11–54

- Click outside the comment box to close the comment box and display only the red comment indicator in cell A12.

Other Ways

1. Click New Comment (Review tab | Comments group)   2. SHIFT+F2

To Display and Move among Comments

Why? While editing the worksheet, you may find it helpful to have comments visible. The comments currently are hidden. The following steps display comments one at a time and then make all comments visible.

- Point to the comment indicator in cell A9 to display the related comment (Figure 11–55).

Figure 11–55

- Click the Next button (Review tab | Comments group) to display the next comment (Figure 11–56).

🅿 **Experiment**

- Click the Previous and Next buttons (Review tab | Comments group) to move back and forth among comments.

Figure 11–56

3

- Click the 'Show All Comments' button (Review tab | Comments group) to show all comments in the workbook (Figure 11–57).

Q&A **Can I print comments?**
Yes. You can print comments where they appear on the worksheet by displaying all comments and then printing the sheet. You can print a list of comments separately using the Sheet tab in the Page Setup dialog box. To do so, click the Page Setup Dialog Box Launcher (Page Layout tab | Page Setup group), click the Sheet tab (Page Setup dialog box), click the Comments arrow, and then click 'At end of sheet' in the Comments list.

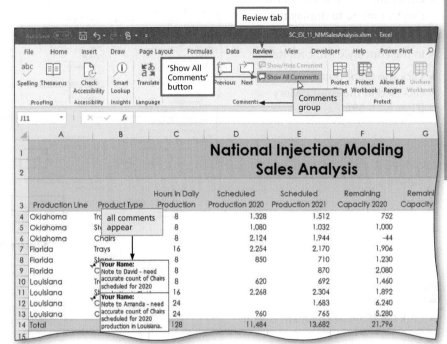

Figure 11–57

To Edit Comments on a Worksheet

You want to alert David and Amanda to the need for verification of a recorded value related to the initial comments. *Why? After adding comments to a worksheet, you may need to edit them to add or change information, or you may want to change the appearance of a particular comment to make it stand out from other comments.* The following steps edit and format the comment in cell A7.

1

- Click cell A9 to make active the cell containing the comment to format.

- Click the Edit Comment button (Review tab | Comments group) to open the comment for editing.

- Select the word, David, in the comment, and then right-click the selected text to display the shortcut menu (Figure 11–58).

Q&A **Can I delete the text?**
Yes, but if you want to delete the entire comment, right-click and then click Delete Comment on the shortcut menu.

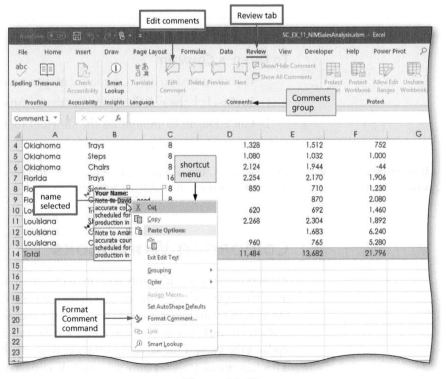

Figure 11–58

- Click Format Comment on the shortcut menu to display the Format Comment dialog box.

- In the Font style list, click Italic.

- Click the Color button and then click Red in the color gallery (Figure 11–59).

 Q&A Can I resize a comment?
Yes. To resize, point to an open comment and then drag a sizing handle.

Figure 11–59

3

- Click OK (Format comment dialog box).

- Repeat the process to change the word Amanda to red and italic, in the second comment (Figure 11–60).

- Click the 'Show All Comments' button (Review tab | Comments group) to toggle the option off and hide all comments.

- Save the workbook again in the same storage location with the same file name and close it.

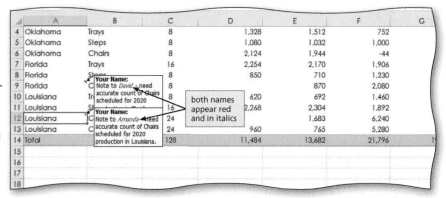

Figure 11–60

TO DELETE A COMMENT

If you wanted to delete a comment, you would perform the following steps.

1. Right-click the cell that contains the comment.

2 Click Delete Comment on the shortcut menu.

Break Point: If you want to take a break, this is a good place to do so. You can exit Excel now. To resume later, start Excel and continue following the steps from this location forward.

Comparing Workbooks

Excel provides you with a way to work with multiple versions of a workbook. You can open multiple copies of the same workbook (as long as they have different names) and move through the workbooks in a synchronized manner so that the same area of each workbook is always in view. For example, as a user scrolls down a worksheet, Excel automatically updates the view of the second worksheet to show the same rows as the first worksheet. This functionality allows for a side-by-side visual comparison of two workbooks.

To Compare Workbooks Side by Side

National Injection Molding plans to participate in three sales events in 2020. Proposed event expenditures are saved in a workbook that has been shared and copied to another member of the staff for review. To verify that there were no changes, the workbooks must be compared. ***Why?*** *They should be compared visually to note the changes made by different users.* The following steps open the master workbook, SC_EX_11-2.xlsx, and a workbook edited by a staff member, SC_EX_11-3.xlsx. The two workbooks will be compared side by side.

- Open the file SC_EX_11-2.xlsx from the Data Files.

- If the file opens in a maximized state, click the workbook's Restore Down button to resize the window.

- Open the file SC_EX_11-3.xlsx from the Data Files.

- If the file opens in a maximized state, click the workbook's Restore Down button to resize the window.

- Display the View tab and then click the 'View Side by Side' button (View tab | Window group) to display the workbooks side by side (Figure 11–61).

- Use the scroll bar in the active window to scroll the SC_EX_11-2.xlsx worksheet.

Q&A

How should the workbooks be arranged after clicking the 'View Side by Side' button?
Depending on how previous Excel windows were arranged on your computer, the workbooks may appear next to each other left to right, or with one window above the other. To change how the windows are positioned, drag one workbook window to the desired screen edge to dock it. Dock the second workbook window on the opposite edge.

What happens when I scroll the worksheet?
Because the Synchronous Scrolling button is selected, both worksheets scroll at the same time so that you can make a visual comparison of the workbooks.

Figure 11–61

- Click the 'View Side by Side' button (View tab | Window group) again to display the windows separately and turn off synchronous scrolling.
- Close the SC_EX_11-3.xlsx workbook.
- If Excel displays a Microsoft Excel dialog box, click the Don't Save button.
- Click the Maximize button in the SC_EX_11-2.xlsx window to maximize the window.

Q&A
What happened to the Compare and Merge commands?
Those commands are now legacy commands; Microsoft recommends using co-authoring instead.

To Turn Off Workbook Sharing

You have shared a workbook using OneDrive. However previous versions of Excel used a workbook sharing feature that changed the status of workbook from unshared to shared. This capability is no longer included in Excel, but you may use a workbook that was shared using an earlier version, and you can unshare it. *Why? Sometimes, turning off workbook sharing is a good idea so you will have access to all Excel features.* The following steps unshare or turn off workbook sharing so that the data can be manipulated.

- With the SC_EX_11-2.xlsx still open, display the Review tab and then click the Unshare Workbook button (Figure 11–62).

- Save the file as SC_EX_11_NIMEvents.

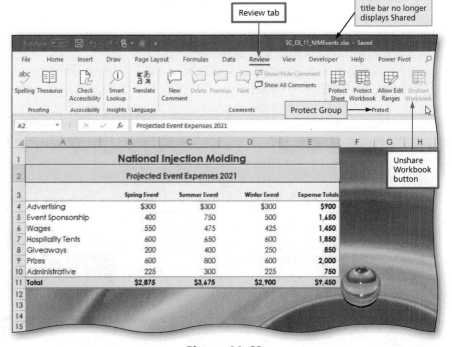

Figure 11–62

Digital Signatures

Some users prefer to attach a digital signature to verify the authenticity of a document. A **digital signature** is an electronic, encrypted, and secure stamp of authentication on a document. This signature confirms that the file originated from the signer (file developer) and that it has not been altered.

A digital signature may be visible or invisible. In either case, the digital signature references a digital certificate. A **digital certificate** is code attached to a file that verifies the identity of the creator of the file. A digital certificate vouches for the file's authenticity, provides secure encryption, or supplies a verifiable signature. Many users who receive files containing macros enable the macros based on whether they are digitally signed by a developer on the user's list of trusted sources.

You can obtain a digital certificate from a commercial certificate authority (CA), from your network administrator, or you can create a digital signature yourself. A digital certificate you create yourself is not issued by a formal certification authority. Thus, signed macros using such a certificate are referred to as self-signed projects. Certificates you create yourself are considered unauthenticated and still will generate a warning when opened if the user's security level is set to very high, high, or medium. Many users, however, consider self-signed projects safer to open than those with no certificates at all.

TO ADD A SIGNATURE BOX AND DIGITAL SIGNATURE TO A WORKBOOK

After adding a digital signature, Excel will display the digital signature whenever the document is opened. If you wanted to add a digital signature to an Excel workbook, you would perform the following steps.

1. Open the SC_EX_11_NIMSalesAnalysis.xlsm workbook and, if necessary, unprotect the Prospect Recorder worksheet using the password, Prospect19.

2. Click the Insert tab and then click the Signature Line arrow in the Text group to display the list.

3. Click the 'Microsoft Office Signature Line' command.

4. Enter your name in the Suggested signer box (Signature Setup dialog box) and then click OK to add the signature box to the workbook.

5. Right-click the signature box and then click Sign on the shortcut menu to display the Sign dialog box. If necessary, you will be prompted to get a digital ID from a Microsoft Partner.

6. In the Sign dialog box, enter your name in the signature box or click the Select Image link to select a file that contains an image of your signature.

7. Click the Sign button (Sign dialog box) to digitally sign the document. If Excel displays a dialog box, click Yes.

TO REVIEW A DIGITAL SIGNATURE ON A WORKBOOK

Excel will display the digital signature whenever the document is opened. When you open a digitally signed document, Excel displays a message announcing the signature on the status bar while the file opens. After the file is opened, Excel displays a certification icon on the status bar. You can click the icon to find out who digitally signed the document. The word, Signed, may also appear on the title bar in parentheses, indicating the document is signed digitally. If you wanted to review a digital signature on an Excel workbook, you would perform the following steps.

1. Display Backstage view. If necessary, click the Info tab and then click View Signatures to open the Signatures pane.

2. Select a name from the Valid signature list (Signature pane), click the arrow to display the shortcut menu, and then click Signature Details to display the certificate.

3. When you are finished reviewing the certificate, click the Close button (Signature Details dialog box) and then close the workbook.

BTW
Adding Alternative Text for Accessibility
Alternative text is used to assist users with disabilities. To set alternative text on form controls, right-click the control, click Format Control on the shortcut menu, and then enter the desired alternative text on the Alt Text tab of the Format Control dialog box.

Finalizing a Workbook

Once a workbook functions in the manner for which it was designed, final touches can be added to the worksheets to make them more attractive and easier to use. Excel provides several ways of finalizing a workbook that include enhancing existing objects and data, preparing custom views for multiple users, protecting your privacy, and saving the workbook in other formats. As you finalize the workbook, you should consider enhancements to charts and data that can make the information more visually appealing or easier to interpret.

For example, to improve the appearance of the Event Expenses worksheet, you will add a watermark identifying the content on the Event Expenses worksheet as a draft, to ensure that the salespeople understand that the details are subject to change. A watermark is semitransparent text overlaid on the worksheet that is used to convey something about the state of the worksheet, such as Draft or Confidential status. You will also add a background to the Prior Years worksheet. Worksheet backgrounds place an image behind the data in cells of a worksheet.

When preparing the workbook for distribution, consider establishing a custom view so that the content will display in your preferred way when you access the workbook after others have used it. In addition, regional settings in Excel allow for support of global users, so you might want to change the language settings (Excel Options dialog box), for example.

Before distributing your workbook to others, you should consider what hidden information might be in your workbook. As you learned in previous modules, rows and columns can be hidden from view, as can worksheets and workbooks. Cells also can be protected. You can use the Document Inspector to inspect and report such information, and then choose to remove the hidden information or leave the information in the workbook.

Furthermore, before distributing a workbook, you should consider whether the intended recipients have the most recent version of Excel. If this is not the case, Excel allows you to save a workbook for use in previous versions of Excel, such as Excel 97-2003. When you save a workbook in the Excel 97-2003 Workbook file format, Excel will enable the Compatibility Checker, which notifies you if any of the content of the workbook cannot be saved in that format. Additionally, the Compatibility Checker will inform you if any content will appear differently in the Excel 97-2003 Workbook format, such as cell or chart formatting.

To Add a Watermark to a Worksheet

Why? A watermark can be used to provide a reminder to the user. In this case, it will remind the users that the worksheet contains draft content. Excel does not have a watermark function, but you can use WordArt to mimic one. The following steps add a watermark to the Event Expenses worksheet.

- With the SC_EX_11_NIMEvents.xlsx workbook open, make Event Expenses the active worksheet.

- Display the Insert tab and then click the WordArt button (Insert tab | Text group) to display the Insert WordArt gallery (Figure 11–63).

Q&A I don't see a WordArt button. What should I do?
Click the Text button to expand the Text group as shown in Figure 11–66. The buttons in the Text group then should appear.

Figure 11–63

- Click 'Fill: Light Gray, Background color 2; Inner Shadow' (column 5, row 3 of the Insert WordArt gallery) to insert a new WordArt object.

- If necessary, select the text in the WordArt object and then type Draft as the watermark text.

- Point to the border of the WordArt object, and when the pointer changes to a four-headed arrow, drag the WordArt object to the center of the worksheet content, as shown in Figure 11–64. Your WordArt object may appear differently.

- With the WordArt text selected, right-click the WordArt object to display a shortcut menu (Figure 11–64).

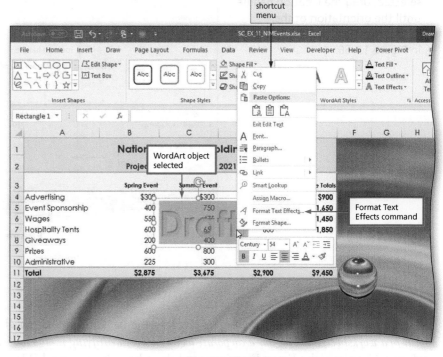

Figure 11–64

3

- Click 'Format Text Effects' on the shortcut menu to open the Format Shape pane.

- If necessary, click the Text Options tab (Format Shape pane) to display the text options.

- Click the 'Text Fill & Outline' option button (Format Shape pane) and then expand the Text Fill section.

- Set the Transparency slider to 80% to change the transparency of the WordArt (Figure 11–65).

Figure 11–65

- Click the Close button in the Format Shape pane to close it.

- With the WordArt object still selected, drag the rotation handle until the orientation of the WordArt object appears as shown in Figure 11–66.

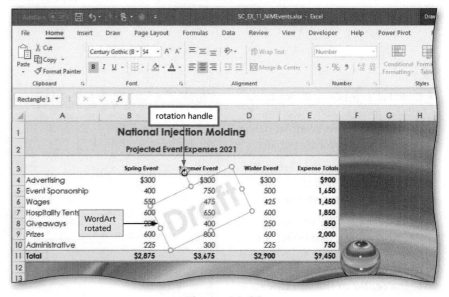

Figure 11–66

To Format a Worksheet Background

Excel allows an image to be used as a worksheet background. ***Why?*** *Worksheet backgrounds can provide visual appeal to a worksheet, allowing for a corporate logo or other identifying image to serve as the background for an entire worksheet.* Currently the Event Expenses worksheet has a background. The following steps add the same image as a worksheet background to the Prior Years worksheet.

- Display the Prior Years worksheet.

- Display the Page Layout tab and then click the Background button (Page Layout tab | Page Setup group) to display the Insert Pictures dialog box (Figure 11–67).

Figure 11–67

 2

- Click the Browse button in the From a file area to display the Sheet Background dialog box.

- Navigate to the location of the Data Files, and then select the Support_EX_11_Waterdroplet.jpg file (Figure 11–68).

Figure 11–68

 3

- Click the Insert button (Sheet Background dialog box) to display the image as the worksheet background.

- If gridlines are displayed, click the View Gridlines check box (Page Layout tab | Sheet Options group) to remove the check mark and turn off gridlines (Figure 11–69).

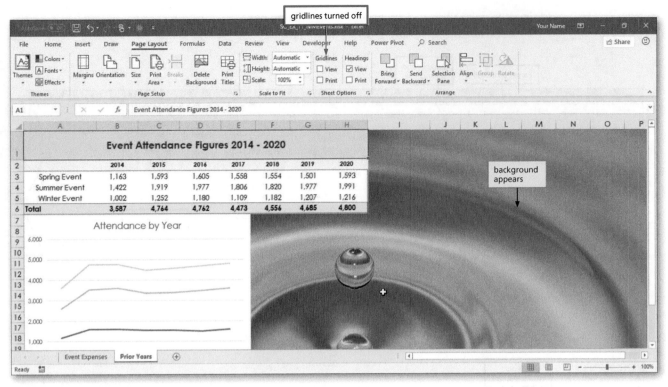

Figure 11–69

To Add a Legend to a Chart

Adding a legend to the chart will improve the readability of the chart by identifying which event each line represents. *Why? With line charts containing multiple lines, a legend is necessary for the reader to be able to understand the chart information.* The following steps add a legend to the chart and apply a color scheme.

- Click anywhere in the Attendance by Year chart to select it.
- Click the Chart Elements button (near the upper-right corner of chart) to display the Chart Elements gallery. Point to Legend to display an arrow and then click the arrow to display the Legend submenu (Figure 11–70).

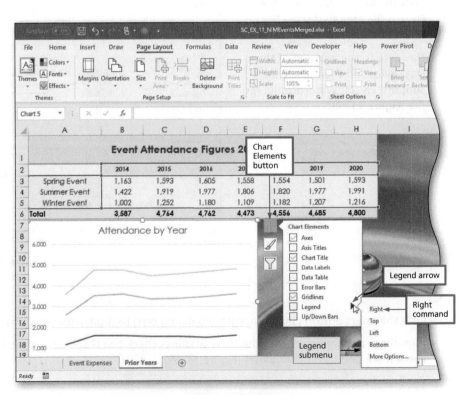

Figure 11–70

2

- Click Right (Legend submenu) to add a legend to the right side of the chart.

- Click the Chart Elements button again to close the gallery.

- Click the Colors button (Page Layout tab | Themes group) and then click the NIM color scheme (Figure 11–71).

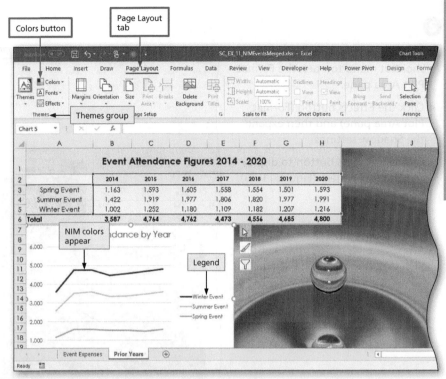

Figure 11–71

To Add a Shadow to a Chart Element

Adding a shadow to the plot area separates it from the other chart elements and improves the visual appeal of the chart. *Why? Shadows and other design features can add depth and a more professional look to your charts.* The following steps add a shadow to the plot area of the chart.

1

- Click anywhere in the plot area to select it. Do not click any of the plot lines.

- Right-click the plot area to display a shortcut menu (Figure 11–72).

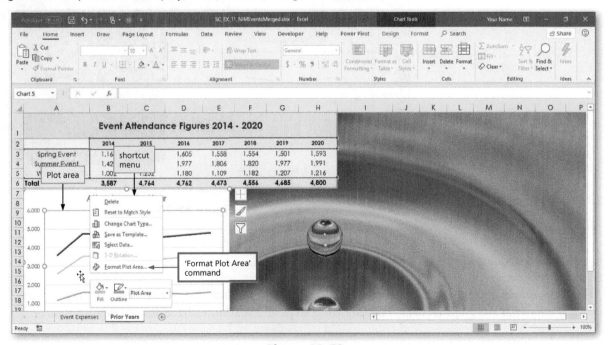

Figure 11–72

2

- Click 'Format Plot Area' on the shortcut menu to open the Format Plot Area pane.

- Click the Effects button (Format Plot Area pane) and then expand the Shadow settings.

- Click the Presets button to display the Shadow gallery (Figure 11–73).

Figure 11–73

3

- Click the Offset Center button (Outer area) to apply a shadow effect to the plot area of the chart.

- Close the Format Plot Area pane and then deselect the plot area (Figure 11–74).

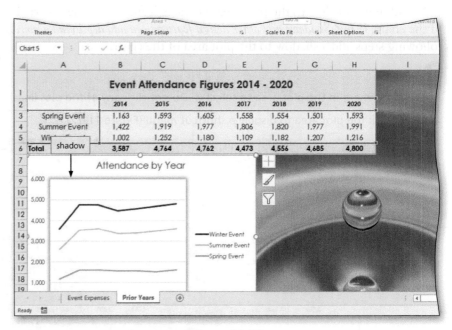

Figure 11–74

To Add Sparklines Using the Quick Analysis Gallery

Why? Sparklines are charts that are inserted immediately beside the data that creates them, allowing for easy comparison of numerical and graphical data. The following steps add sparkline charts for attendance figures.

1

- Select the range B3:H5.

- Click the Quick Analysis button to display the Quick Analysis gallery.

- Click the Sparklines tab to display the Quick Analysis gallery related to sparklines (Figure 11–75).

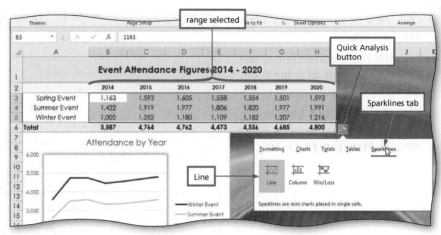

Figure 11–75

2

- Click the Line button (Quick Analysis gallery) to insert sparklines in cells I3:I5.

- Select the range I1:I6. Click the Fill Color arrow (Home tab | Font group) to display the Fill Color gallery. Click 'Lime, Accent 2, Lighter 40%' to choose a fill color.

- Make cell A1 the active cell to deselect the range (Figure 11–76).

- Save the file.

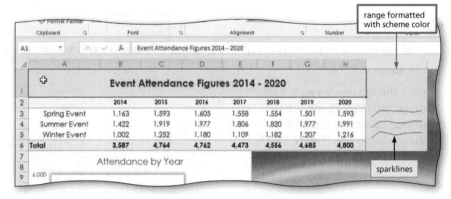

Figure 11–76

Saving Custom Views

A **custom view** allows certain layout and printing characteristics of a workbook to be saved and then used later. When a custom view of a workbook is saved, Excel stores information about the workbook's current window size and print settings. Before saving a custom view, make sure the workbook reflects the desired layout and print settings.

The Custom Views button on the View tab is used to save, delete, and display custom views. When a user saves a custom view, Excel also stores the name of the current worksheet. When a user displays a custom view by clicking the Show button in the Custom Views dialog box, Excel switches to the worksheet that was active in the workbook when the custom view was saved.

To Save a Custom View of a Workbook

Why? *If a workbook requires that you customize certain layout and printing settings to use it effectively, using a custom view allows you to save those settings with the workbook.* Whenever the workbook is opened, it will be opened with those settings active. The following steps create and save a custom view of the SC_EX_11_NIMEvents workbook.

- Click View on the ribbon to display the View tab.
- Click the Zoom button (View tab | Zoom group) to display the Zoom dialog box.
- Click the 75% option button (Zoom dialog box) to select 75% magnification (Figure 11–77).

Figure 11–77

- Click OK (Zoom dialog box) to set the zoom to 75%.
- Click the Custom Views button (View tab | Workbook Views group) to display the Custom Views dialog box (Figure 11–78).

Q&A Why does my Custom Views dialog box contain a list of views?
The views listed will reflect the authors of any open documents as well as any users signed in to Windows.

Figure 11–78

- Click the Add button (Custom Views dialog box) to display the Add View dialog box.
- Type **Event Attendance** in the Name box to provide a name for the custom view (Figure 11–79).

4

- Click OK (Add View dialog box) to close the dialog box.

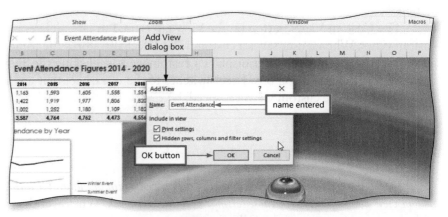

Figure 11–79

To Test the Custom View

The following steps test the previously created custom view named Event Attendance.

1 Click the Event Expenses worksheet tab.

2 Click the 100% button (View tab | Zoom group) to set the zoom to 100%.

3 Click the Custom Views button (View tab | Workbook Views group) to display the Custom Views dialog box. (Your dialog box may contain additional views.)

4 Click Event Attendance in the Views list and then click the Show button (Custom Views dialog box) to display the Event Attendance view, which includes a zoom to 75%.

5 Click the 100% button (View tab | Zoom group) to set the zoom back to 100%.

6 Save the workbook again on the same storage location with the same file name.

Q&A Can I delete a custom view?
Yes. To delete custom views, select the view you want to delete, and then use the Delete button in the Custom Views dialog box shown in Figure 11–78.

TO CUSTOMIZE HEADERS AND FOOTERS

If you decide to print the final version of your workbook, Excel offers many ways to customize the headers and footers. Not only can you include page numbers, but you can create custom headers and footers that include built-in elements such as text, graphics, and other spreadsheet data. To see the various built-in elements, click the Header & Footer button (Insert tab | Text Group) to display the Header & Footer Tools Design tab. The elements are located in the Header & Footer Elements group. For a more exact and formatted customization, use the Header/Footer sheet in the Page Setup dialog box (Figure 11–80).

Figure 11–80

If you wanted to customize your header or footer, you would perform the following steps:

1. Click the Page Setup dialog box launcher (Page Layout tab | Page setup group).
2. On the Header/Footer tab, click the Custom Header button or Custom Footer button (Page Setup dialog box).
3. Click in the desired section box and then type text or click the appropriate button to insert a built-in element code.
4. Highlight the text or code and then click the Format Text button to display the Font dialog box. Select any format changes.
5. If you have inserted a picture, highlight the &[Picture] placeholder, and then click the Format Picture button to display the Format Picture dialog box. Select any format changes.
6. Click OK (Header dialog box or Footer dialog box). Click OK (Page Setup dialog box).

Setting Internationalization Features

Excel provides internationalization features you can use when creating workbooks. Use of these features should be determined based on the intended audience of the workbook. For instance, if you are creating a workbook that will be used in European countries where decimal notation differs from that used in North America, consider setting up the workbook to use the European notation by creating custom number formats or changing the symbol used with the Currency or Accounting number formats.

By default, workbooks use formatting consistent with the country or region selected when installing Windows. Situations exist where a workbook will need to contain text or number formatting consistent with a different country or region. Several options are available for applying international formats to content.

Displaying International Symbols

You can format a cell or range of cells with international currency symbols using the Format Cells dialog box. Both the Accounting and Currency number categories provide a selection of symbols for use when formatting monetary cell entries. You also can select from the more commonly used currency symbols when applying the accounting number format by clicking the 'Accounting Number Format' arrow (Home tab | Number group) and selecting the desired currency from the list.

You can use the Symbol button (Insert tab | Symbols group) to enter international characters and monetary symbols as cell entries. To insert a character, click the Symbol button to display the Symbol dialog box, select the font you are using from the Font list, and then scroll until you see the symbol of interest. Select the symbol and then click the Insert button (Symbol dialog box) to insert the symbol at the location of the insertion point in your worksheet.

Displaying Data in Multiple International Formats

Data formatting varies from country to country and region to region, including the use of different characters to separate decimal places and differing date formats. If preparing a workbook for use in another region, consider changing the location setting in Windows to the region of your audience. Use the Windows search box to search for Region to access the Region & Language settings to set format options for a specific region. In Excel, you can click Options in Backstage view and then click Language in the left pane. In the Choose Editing Languages area in the right pane, click the 'Add additional editing languages' button. Choose the language you are interested in. The Editing language is the language in which you type and edit your content. The lower part of the right pane offers ways to change the display language, which is used for all of the buttons, menus, and controls in Excel.

Excel has other language-specific features. For example, if you want to use a European style date, you can right-click a date and click Format Cells on the shortcut menu. In the Format Cells dialog box, click Date in the left pane. On the right, click the Locale button and then choose your language or region. You also can change the proofing language by clicking Options in Backstage view. Click Proofing in the Excel Options dialog box, click the Custom Dictionary button, and then choose your language.

Collaborating with Users Who Do Not Use Excel 2019

It is not unusual to collaborate with others who are using different software versions, or different software entirely, to do their work. You even can find different versions of software being used within the same company. When collaborating with others, you should make decisions about how to save and distribute files after considering how your colleagues will be using the workbooks you create. In instances where people are working with earlier versions of software or different software, you need to provide workbooks in formats that they can use.

Before sharing a workbook with others, you can mark the workbook as being final. When another user of your workbook opens the workbook, he or she will be notified that you have marked the workbook as final. The workbook can still be edited, but only if the user clicks a button to indicate that he or she wants to edit the workbook.

To Save a Workbook in an Earlier Version of Excel

Why? *You occasionally need to save a workbook for use in previous versions of Excel.* Each version of Excel includes varying features, so you can use the Compatibility Checker to determine if the features used in your workbook are compatible with earlier versions of Excel. The following steps check the compatibility of the workbook while saving the workbook in the Excel 97-2003 Workbook file format.

- Display Backstage view, click Save As, and then navigate to the location where you store your files.

- Click the 'Save as type' arrow (Save As dialog box) to display the list of file types (Figure 11–81).

 Would saving the file using the same name overwrite the original version of the workbook?
No. It is not necessary to save the workbook with a new file name. The 'Excel 97-2003' version of the workbook will have a file extension of .xls, while the original has a file extension of .xlsx.

Figure 11–81

- Click 'Excel 97-2003 Workbook' to select the file format.

- Click the Save button (Save As dialog box) to display the Microsoft Excel - Compatibility Checker dialog box.

- Resize the dialog box so that it displays all the issues (Figure 11–82).

 What is shown in the Microsoft Excel - Compatibility Checker dialog box?
The Summary states that some of the chart elements and the sparklines used on the Prior Years worksheet are not compatible with previous versions of Excel. While the workbook still will be saved in the Excel 97-2003 file format, the sparklines will not be saved. In addition, some cell formatting is unique to Excel 2019. These formats will be converted to the nearest approximation in the earlier version of Excel.

Figure 11–82

- Click the Continue button (Microsoft Excel - Compatibility Checker dialog box) to save the workbook in the Excel 97-2003 Workbook file format.

To Mark a Workbook as Final

The following steps mark the workbook as final. *Why? The workbook is complete; marking it as final will prevent users from accidentally changing anything.*

- Display Backstage view.
- Click the Protect Workbook button in the Info gallery to display the Protect Workbook menu (Figure 11–83).

Figure 11–83

- Click 'Mark as Final' on the Protect Workbook menu to display the Microsoft Excel dialog box.
- If necessary, click the Continue button on the Microsoft Excel - Compatibility Checker dialog box.
- Click OK (Microsoft Excel dialog box) to indicate you want to mark the workbook as final (Figure 11–84).

Q&A I have saved the workbook in .xls format, but the sparklines are still showing. Why?
Although the .xls format does not support newer features such as sparklines, Excel 2019 does. If you close the file and reopen the workbook saved in the older format, the sparklines will be missing.

Figure 11–84

- Click OK to close the Microsoft Excel dialog box and mark the workbook as final. Excel will display a MARKED AS FINAL yellow bar below the ribbon tabs.
- Close the workbook.

Information Rights Management

Information Rights Management (IRM) is a feature of Excel that allows you to restrict access to workbooks. With IRM, you can restrict who can view, modify, print, forward, and copy a workbook. The types of restrictions include a variety of options. For example, expiration dates for reading or modifying a workbook are available. Before using IRM, your computer first must be configured with IRM, as should the computers or mobile devices of anyone attempting to use a document that includes IRM features.

When IRM is installed properly, the Protect Workbook menu in the Info screen in Backstage view includes several commands for limiting access to the workbook. You can limit who can access the workbook and who can make changes to the workbook. For more information about IRM, search Excel Help using the search string, information rights management.

To Inspect a Document for Hidden and Personal Information

Why? The Document Inspector should be used before sharing a workbook publicly or when you suspect extraneous information remains in hidden rows and columns, hidden worksheets, document properties, headers and footers, or worksheet comments.

The following steps make a copy of the SC_EX_11_NIMSalesAnalysis.xlsm workbook and then inspect the copy for hidden and personal information.

- If necessary, open the file named SC_EX_11_NIMSalesAnalysis.xlsm and save the workbook with the file name, SC_EX_11_NIMSalesDistribute.

- If necessary, turn off workbook sharing using the Unshare Workbook button (Review tab | Protect group).

- If necessary, make Sales Data Analysis the active worksheet.

- Display Backstage view.

- Click the 'Check for Issues' button (Info gallery) to display the Check for Issues menu (Figure 11–85).

Q&A Why did I save this workbook with a different file name?
When preparing a workbook for distribution, you may decide to use the Document Inspector to make changes to the document. Saving the workbook with a different file name ensures that you will have a copy of the workbook with all of the original information intact for your records.

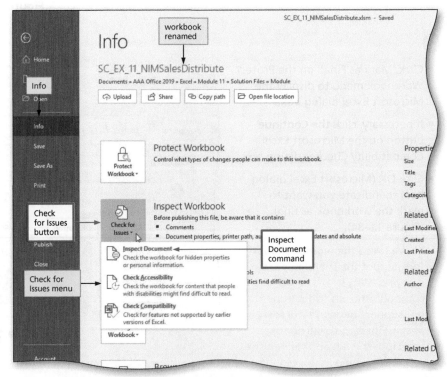

Figure 11–85

2

- Click Inspect Document (Check for Issues menu) to display the Document Inspector dialog box (Figure 11–86).

Q&A What is shown in the Document Inspector dialog box?
The Document Inspector dialog box allows you to choose which types of content to inspect. Typically, you would leave all of the items selected, unless you are comfortable with some types of content not being inspected.

Figure 11–86

3

- Click the Inspect button (Document Inspector dialog box) to run the Document Inspector and display its results (Figure 11–87).

Experiment

- Scroll in the Document Inspector to view the issues.

Q&A What did the Document Inspector find?
The Document Inspector found the hidden Prospect List worksheet, comments, and personal information (Figure 11–90), including document properties, author information, related dates, absolute path to the workbook, and printer properties. The Remove All button in the dialog box allows you quickly to remove the items found if needed. In many instances, you may want to take notes of the results and then investigate and remedy each one separately. In this workbook, all of these items found by the Document Inspector are expected and do not need to be remedied.

Figure 11–87

4

- Click the Close button (Document Inspector dialog box) to close the dialog box.
- Return to the worksheet.

To Delete Customization

The following steps delete the NIM color and font schemes. Deleting the schemes does not change the workbook.

1 Click the Colors button (Page Layout tab | Themes group) and then right-click the NIM color scheme to display the shortcut menu. Click Delete. If Excel displays a dialog box confirming the deletion, click Yes.

2 Click the Fonts button (Page Layout tab | Themes group) and then right-click the NIM color scheme to display the shortcut menu. Click Delete. If Excel displays a dialog box confirming the deletion, click Yes.

3 If desired you can reset the ribbon. Click Options in Backstage view, click 'Quick Access Toolbar' in the left pane, and then click Reset button (Excel Options dialog box). Click 'Reset all customizations'.

4 **sam** Click OK to close the Excel Options dialog box. Save the file and then quit Excel.

Summary

In this module, you developed a custom form for accepting user input, using form controls, ActiveX controls, and VBA code. You shared workbooks on OneDrive and co-authored. You used comments to provide feedback and compared worksheet data from two workbooks. You added finishing touches to worksheets, learned about internationalization, and prepared workbooks for distribution.

CONSIDER THIS: PLAN AHEAD

What decisions will you need to make when using Excel to collect information or collaborate with others?
Use these guidelines as you complete the assignments in this module and create your own worksheets for creating Excel forms and collaborating with others outside of this class.

1. Create custom fonts, schemes, and themes as necessary.

2. Determine the purpose and needs of the form data.

    a. Design a user interface with controls appropriate to the data being entered.

    b. Set control properties to give meaning and limitations to each control's use.

    c. Write the Visual Basic code associated with the user's actions, such as clicking a button.

    d. Test the user interface to prove that it behaves as expected.

3. Determine the audience, purpose, and options available for the collaboration.

4. Evaluate changes made by colleagues.

    a. With a single distributed workbook, use co-authoring.

    b. With multiple workbooks, compare workbooks side by side.

5. Add worksheet enhancements.

    a. Add watermarks and worksheet backgrounds as appropriate.

    b. Enhance charts if appropriate.

6. Prepare workbook(s) for distribution.

Apply Your Knowledge

Reinforce the skills and apply the concepts you learned in this module.

Creating a Form

Note: To complete this assignment, you will be required to use the Data Files. Please contact your instructor for information about accessing the Data Files.

Instructions: Start Excel. Open the workbook SC_EX_11-5.xlsx, which is located in the Data Files. The spreadsheet you open contains the start of a form to gather information about visitors to a museum that will display on a kiosk on the way out of the museum. Figure 11–88 shows the completed form.

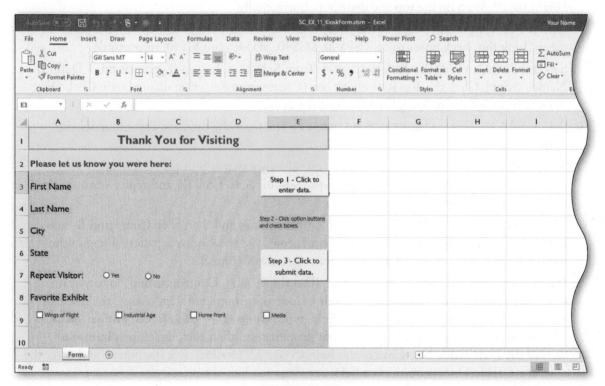

Figure 11–88

Perform the following tasks:

1. Save the workbook using the file name, SC_EX_11_KioskForm.xlsm (the macro enabled format). Examine row 39 and column W.

2. If necessary, add the Developer tab to the ribbon as described in the module.

3. Click the Insert button (Developer tab | Controls group) and then click the Option Button button in the Form Controls area (column 6, row 1) in the Controls gallery. Drag in the worksheet to create an option button control in cell B7 (approximately). Right-click the option button and click Edit Text. Change the existing text to say Yes. Resize the control as necessary.

4. Repeat Step 3 to create an option button control in cell C7 with the text No. Select both option buttons and then click the Align button (Drawing Tools Format tab | Arrange group). Align the two option buttons on the top.

Continued >

Apply Your Knowledge *continued*

5. Right-click either option button control and then click Format Control on the shortcut menu. If necessary, click the Control tab (Format Control dialog box) and then type $E$41 in the Cell link box (Format Control dialog box) to link the option button index number to cell E41.

6. Click the Insert button (Developer tab | Controls group) and then click the Check Box button in the Form Controls area (column 3, row 1) in the Controls gallery. Drag in the worksheet to create a check box control in cell A9 (approximately). Change the existing text to Wings of Flight. Resize so the check box is only slightly bigger than the text.

7. Repeat Step 6 to create a check box with the text Industrial Age in cell B9. Repeat Step 6 to create a check box with the text Home Front in cell C9. Repeat Step 6 to create a check box with the text Media in cell D9. Select all four check boxes, right-click, and then chose Format Object on the shortcut menu to open the Format Control dialog box. On the Size tab, set the height to .19. Align on the top and distribute horizontally.

8. One at a time, right-click each of the check boxes and click Format Control on the shortcut menu. Link the check boxes to cells $F$40, $G$40, $H$40, and $I$40, respectively.

9. Select the range A39:D40. Click the 'Create from Selection' button (Formulas tab | Defined Names group). Click the Top Row check box (Create from Selection dialog box). Click OK (Create from Selection dialog box) to name the cells.

10. Select cell E40. Type `=INDEX(W2:W3,$E$41)` to enter the function that evaluates the option buttons.

11. Select cell B3 and type `=A40` to enter a cell reference that will display the name during execution of the code. Select cell B4 and type `=B40`. Select cell B5 and type `=C40`. Select cell B6 and type `=D40`.

12. Click the Insert button (Developer tab | Controls group) and then click Command Button button in the ActiveX Controls area (column 1, row 1) of the Controls gallery. Drag in the worksheet in cell E3 create a Command Button ActiveX control.

13. If necessary, click the Design Mode button (Developer tab | Controls group) to turn it on. Click the Properties button (Developer tab | Controls group) and then change the name of the button to cmdStep1. In the Caption field, type `Step 1 - Click to enter data`. Change WordWrap to True. Click the Font property and then click the ellipsis button to display the Font dialog box. Change the Font to size 12. Double-click the button and enter the code from Table 11–6, pressing TAB before typing each line as necessary.

Table 11–6 Code for cmdStep1 Button
'Author: SC Series
'Date Created: 11/12/2020
'Run from: Form Worksheet, cmdStep1 Button
'Function: When executed, this procedure enters contact information for the prospect.
Range("First_Name").Value = InputBox("First Name?", "Enter", , 800, 6000)
Range("Last_Name").Value = InputBox("Last Name?", "Enter", , 800, 6000)
Range("City").Value = InputBox("City?", "Enter", , 800, 6000)
Range("State").Value = InputBox("State?", "Enter", , 800, 6000)

14. Close the VBA window.

15. Click the Insert button (Developer tab | Controls group) and then click the Command Button button in the ActiveX Controls area (column 1, row 1) of the Controls gallery. Drag in the worksheet in cell E6 create a Command Button ActiveX control.

16. If necessary click the Design Mode button (Developer tab | Controls group) to turn it on. Click the Properties button (Developer tab | Controls group) and then change the name of the button to cmdStep3. In the Caption field, type **Step 3 - Click to submit data.** Change WordWrap to True. Change the Font to size 12. Double-click the button, enter the code from Table 11–7, pressing TAB before typing each line, as necessary.

Table 11–7 Code for cmdStep3 Button
'Author: SC Series
'Date Created: 11/12/2020
'Run from: Form Worksheet, cmdStep3 Button
'Function: When executed, this procedure submits new information to the prospect list
Range("A40:I40").Select
Selection.Copy
Sheets("Data Sheet").Visible = True
Sheets("Data Sheet").Activate
Sheets("Data Sheet").Range("A2:I2").Select
Selection.PasteSpecial Paste:=xlPasteValues, Operation:=xlNone, SkipBlanks:=False, Transpose:=False
Selection.Font.Bold = False
Sheets("Data Sheet").Range("A2").Activate
ActiveCell.EntireRow.Insert
Sheets("Data Sheet").Visible = False
Sheets("Form").Select
Range("E41").ClearContents
Range("A40:D40").ClearContents
Range("F40:I40").ClearContents
Range("E3").Activate
ActiveWorkbook.Save

17. Create a Label form control between the two command buttons that says Step 2 - Click option buttons and check boxes.

18. Turn off Design Mode and test the form. Unhide the Data Sheet and check to make sure the data was recorded. If there were errors, double-check the VBA code you entered.

19. When everything runs correctly, hide the Data Sheet. Password protect the Form sheet. Save the workbook and then submit the revised workbook as specified by your instructor, along with the password. If you are working in a lab situation, delete all customization.

20. ✸ What other things could you do to this workbook to make it look more attractive or be more functional on a kiosk?

Extend Your Knowledge

Extend the skills you learned in this module and experiment with new skills. You may need to use Help to complete the assignment.

Writing VBA Code

Note: To complete this assignment, you will be required to use the Data Files. Please contact your instructor for information about accessing the Data Files.

Instructions: Start Excel. Open the file called SC_EX_11_NIMSalesDistribute.xlsm that you created earlier in this module. If you did not create the file, see your instructor for ways to complete this assignment. The document contains the Sales Data Analysis worksheet and Prospect Recorder. You are to create VBA code that will execute upon closing the file. It will include a message box shown in Figure 11–89.

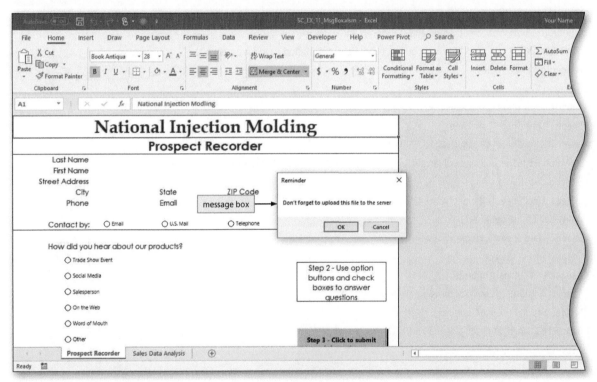

Figure 11–89

Perform the following tasks:

1. Save the file in the macro-enable format with the name, SC_EX_11_MsgBox.xlsm.

2. With the Sales Data Analysis sheet displayed, click the Visual Basic button (Developer tab | Code group) to display the Microsoft Visual Basic for Applications editor.

3. On the menu bar, click Help, and then click Microsoft Visual Basic for Applications Help in the list. Click the link for Excel VBA Reference. In the Filter by Title box in the upper-left corner, search for information about BeforeClose. Click BeforeClose in the list on the left and read about the event. Search again for information about MsgBox. Read about the MsgBox function.

4. In the Project pane (the left pane of the VBA window), double-click ThisWorkbook, so the code will apply to the entire workbook.

5. In the main window, click the Object arrow and then click Workbook. Click the Procedure arrow and then click BeforeClose. Excel will create two procedures; if necessary, click in the procedure labeled, Workbook_BeforeClose.

6. Press TAB and then type `'This procedure displays a message box when the user closes the workbook` to enter a code comment. Press ENTER to move to the next line. Enter another comment with your name and the date.

7. Create a message box by typing the code, **MsgBox "Don't forget to upload this file to the server", vbOKCancel, "Reminder"** and press ENTER.

8. Enter other comments explaining the purpose of the various parts of the MsgBox statement.

9. Save the workbook.

10. Test the workbook by clicking the Close button in the title bar. When Excel displays the message box, click the Cancel button. Test the VBA code again and this time click the OK button. If there are errors, review the VBA code and edit as necessary.

11. Submit the revised workbook in the format specified by your instructor.

12. ✳ The MsgBox function, when used with an equals sign, returns a value based on which button the user clicks in the message box (access the previous Help page and scroll down to the Return Values and Examples areas). What do you think VBA programmers do with that response value?

Expand Your World

Create a solution that uses cloud and web technologies by learning and investigating on your own from general guidance.

Preparing Surveys

Instructions: Start Excel and open a blank workbook. You are to create a survey related to either education or employment to illustrate how to use form controls and ActiveX controls in Excel to create a survey and record responses.

Perform the following tasks:

1. Open a browser and navigate to http://zoho.com/survey. Search the website for a survey template in either education or employment that you can create in Excel with form controls. Select a template that contains at least 10 questions. Right-click and print a copy, if desired.

2. Using the skills you learned in this module, create a survey that includes at least three of the questions from the survey you found on zoho.com. You should use more than one type of control in creating your survey.

3. Create a sheet named Prospect List and hide it.

4. Write a VBA procedure to collect the entered data each time the survey is completed and store it on a separate, hidden worksheet. (*Hint*: Use the code from Tables 11–6 and 11–7.)

5. Use worksheet protection and formatting to set up your survey so that a user can answer questions but not gain access to the hidden worksheet or areas on the current worksheet outside of the survey.

6. Save the file in the macro-enabled format as SC_EX_11_SurveyComplete.xlsm and submit it in the format specified by your instructor, along with the password so the instructor can view the hidden worksheet.

7. ✳ What was the hardest thing about this assignment? Why? Did you use Help at any time? If so, what did you look up?

In the Lab

Design and implement a solution using creative thinking and problem-solving skills.

Create Schemes and Themes

Problem: You have been asked to create a custom color scheme, font scheme, and workbook theme for your school or place of employment.

Perform the following tasks:

Part 1:   Start Excel and open a blank workbook. Click the Colors button (Page Layout tab | Themes group) and then click Customize Colors to open the Create New Theme Colors dialog box. Click the Accent 1 color button and then click More Colors. When Excel displays the Colors dialog box, click the Standard tab. Choose the color most closely associated with your school or business. Repeat the process for Accent 2 and Accent 3 using different colors. If your school does not have three colors, choose colors that complement the Accent 1 color. Before closing the dialog box, press ALT+PRT SC (print screen) to capture the dialog box in the clipboard. Enter a name for your color scheme. Click Save (Create New Theme Colors dialog box) and then paste the screen capture onto the worksheet.

Click the Fonts button (Page Layout tab | Themes group) and then click Customize Fonts to open the Create New Theme Fonts dialog box. Choose a heading font and body font that closely matches the fonts used in your school or company headline or logo. Before closing the dialog box, press ALT+PRT SC (print screen) to capture the dialog box in the clipboard. Enter a name for your font scheme. Click Save (Create New Theme Fonts dialog box) and then paste the screen capture onto the worksheet.

Click the Themes button (Page Layout tab | Themes group) and then click Save Current Theme to open the Save Current Theme dialog box. Enter a name of your theme and then navigate to your Data File storage location. Before clicking Save, press ALT+PRT SC (print screen) to capture the dialog box in the clipboard. Click Save (Save Current Theme dialog box) to save the theme. Paste the screen capture onto the worksheet.

Arrange the three screen captures side by side and then save the workbook with the file name SC_EX_11_Schemes. Submit the file along with your answers to the critical thinking questions in Part 2 as directed by your instructor.

Part 2:   ✸ How did you decide on the sources to use for the color and font schemes? How would your school or company use these saved schemes and themes?

8 Macros, Navigation Forms, and Control Layouts

Objectives

You will have mastered the material in this module when you can:

- Create and modify macros and submacros
- Create a menu form with command buttons
- Create a menu form with an option group
- Create a macro for the option group
- Use an IF statement in a macro
- Create datasheet forms

- Create user interface (UI) macros
- Create navigation forms
- Add tabs to a navigation form
- Create data macros
- Create and remove control layouts
- Use the Arrange tab to modify control layouts on forms and reports

Introduction

In this module, you will learn how to create and test macros that open forms and that preview reports and export reports. You will create a menu form with command buttons as well as a menu form with an **option group**, which is an object that enables you to make a selection by choosing the option button corresponding to your choice. You will also create and use user interface (UI) macros in forms. CMF Vets requires a navigation form that will allow users to open forms and reports simply by clicking appropriate tabs and buttons. You will learn about the use of data macros for ensuring that updates to the database are valid. Finally, you will learn how to use control layouts on forms and reports.

Project—Macros, Navigation Forms, and Control Layouts

CMF Vets managers would like users to be able to access forms and reports simply by clicking tabs and buttons, rather than by using the Navigation Pane. A **navigation form** like the one shown in Figure 8–1a is a form that includes tabs to display forms and reports. CMF Vets plans to use the navigation form because they believe it will improve the user-friendliness of the database, thereby improving employee satisfaction and efficiency. This navigation form contains several useful features. With the

Veterinarians tab selected, you can click the Veterinarian ID on any row to see the data for the selected veterinarian displayed in the Datasheet view. (Figure 8–1b). The form does not appear in a tabbed sheet, the way tables, queries, forms, and reports normally do. Rather, it appears as a **pop-up form**, a form that stays on top of other open objects, even when another object is active.

Figure 8–1a Navigation Form

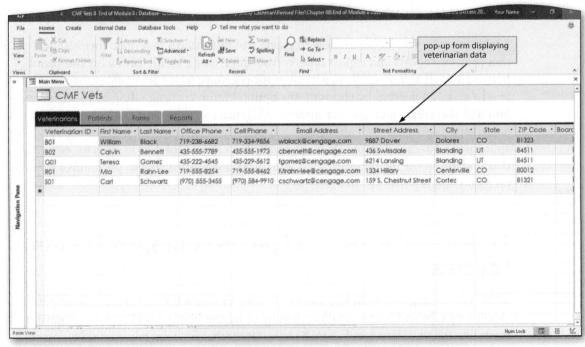

Figure 8–1b Pop-up Form Displaying Veterinarian Data

Clicking the Patients tab of the navigation form displays patient's data. As with veterinarians, clicking the patient number on any record displays data for that patient in a pop-up form.

Clicking the Forms tab in the CMF Vets navigation form displays buttons for each of the available forms (Figure 8–1c). You can open the desired form by clicking the appropriate button.

Figure 8–1c Buttons to Display Forms

Clicking the Reports tab displays an option group for displaying reports (Figure 8–1d). You can preview or export any of the reports one at a time by clicking the corresponding option button.

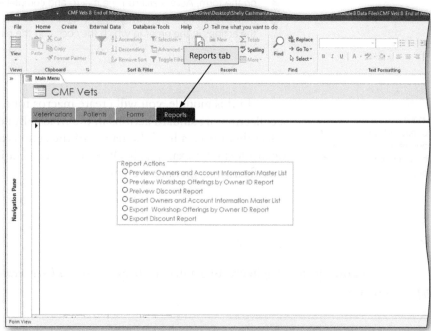

Figure 8–1d Option Buttons to Display Report Actions

Before creating the navigation form, CMF Vets managers will create **macros**, which are collections of actions designed to carry out specific tasks. To perform the actions in a macro, you run the macro. When you run a macro, Access will execute the various steps, called **actions**, in the order indicated by the macro. You run the navigation form macros by clicking certain buttons in the form.

CMF Vets managers will also create another type of macro, a data macro. A **data macro** is a special type of macro that enables you to add logic to table events such as adding, changing, or deleting data. You typically use data macros to ensure data validity.

In this module, you will learn how to create and use the navigation form shown in Figure 8–1.

Creating and Using Macros

Similar to other Office apps, Access allows you to create and use macros. A macro consists of a series of actions that Access performs when the macro is run. When you create a macro, you specify these actions. Once you have created a macro, you can simply run the macro, and Access will perform the various actions you specified. For example, the macro might open a form in read-only mode, a mode that prohibits changes to the data. Another macro might export a report as a PDF file. You can group related macros into a single macro, with the individual macros existing as submacros within the main macro.

CONSIDER THIS

How do you create macros? How do you use them?
You create a macro by entering a specific series of actions in a window called the Macro Builder window. Once a macro is created, it exists as an object in the database, and you can run it from the Navigation Pane by right-clicking the macro and then clicking Run on the shortcut menu. Macros can also be associated with buttons on forms. When you click the corresponding button on the form, Access will run the macro and complete the corresponding action. Whether a macro is run from the Navigation Pane or from a form, the effect is the same: Access will execute the actions in the order in which they occur in the macro.

In this module, you will create macros for a variety of purposes. Access provides a collection of standard actions in the Macro Builder; as you enter actions, you will select them from a list. The names of the actions are self-explanatory. The action to open a form, for example, is OpenForm. Thus, it is not necessary to memorize the specific actions that are available.

To Begin Creating a Macro

The following steps begin creating a macro. *Why? Once you have created the macro, you will be able to add the appropriate actions.*

1

• **sam** ↓ Start Access and open the database named CMF Vets from your hard drive, OneDrive, or other storage location.

• CMF Vets has decided to change the name of the Veterinarian Appointment Form to reflect practice growth. Rename this form to Veterinarians Appointment Form.

• The Appointments and Treatments query must be replaced for consistency with the change made to the Appointments table when the Treatment Number field was converted from a multi-valued field to a single-valued field.

• Delete the Appointments and Treatments query.

• Create a new query based on the Appointments and Treatment Cost tables. Include the Appointment Date field from the Appointments table and the Treatment, Animal Type, and Cost fields from the Treatment Cost table. Sort the Appointment Date and Treatment fields in Ascending order. Save the query as Appointments and Treatments.

• If necessary, close the Navigation Pane.

• Display the Create tab (Figure 8–2).

Note: To help you locate screen elements that are referenced in the instructions, such as buttons and commands, this book places a red outline around the callouts that point to these screen elements.

Figure 8–2

2

• Click the Macro button (Create tab | Macros & Code group) to create a new macro.

• Click the Action Catalog button (Macro Tools Design tab | Show/Hide group) if necessary to display the action catalog (Figure 8–3).

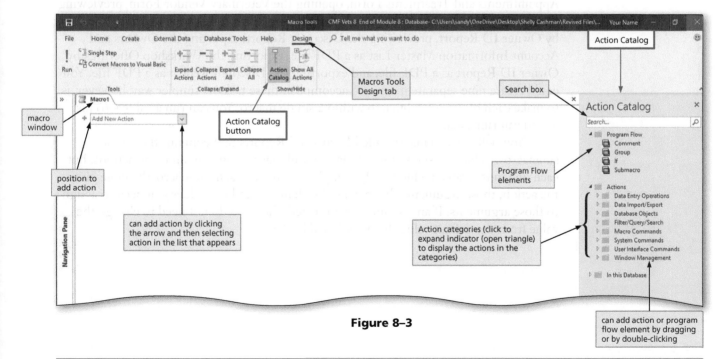

Figure 8–3

BTW
Macros
A macro is a series of commands used to automate repeated tasks. You can create macros in other Office apps, such as Word and Excel.

The Macro Builder Window

You create a macro by adding actions in the macro window, shown in Figure 8–3. You can add actions by clicking the Add New Action arrow and selecting the desired action from the list of possible actions. You can also use the Action Catalog, which is a list of macro actions organized by type. If the Action Catalog does not appear, click the Action Catalog button (Macro Tools Design tab | Show/Hide group) to display it. You can add an action by double-clicking the action in the Action Catalog or by dragging it.

Access arranges the available actions in categories. To see the actions in a category, click the **expand indicator** (the open triangle) in front of the category. The actions will appear and the expand indicator will change to a solid triangle. To hide the actions in a category, click the solid triangle.

CONSIDER THIS

How can you find an action if you are not sure which category contains the action?
You can search the list by typing in the Search box. Access will then reduce the list of actions displayed to only those actions whose names or descriptions contain the text you have typed.

Many actions require additional information, called the **arguments** of the action. For example, if the action is OpenForm, Access needs to know which form is to be opened. You indicate the form to be opened by setting the value of the Form Name argument to the desired form. If the value for the Form Name argument for the OpenForm action is Appointments and Treatments Form, then Access will open the Appointments and Treatments form when it executes this action.

BTW
Touch and Pointers
Remember that if you are using your finger on a touch screen, you will not see the pointer.

Actions can have more than one argument. For example, in addition to the Form Name argument, the OpenForm action also has a Data Mode argument. If the value of the Data Mode argument is Read Only, then the form will be opened in read-only mode, which indicates users will be able to view but not change data. When you select an action, the arguments will appear along with the action, and you can make any necessary changes to them.

In the forms you will create later in this module, you need macros for opening the Veterinarians Appointment Form as read-only (to prevent updates), opening the Appointments and Treatments Form, opening the Veterinary Vendor Form, previewing the Owners and Account Information Master List, previewing the Workshop Offerings by Owner ID Report, previewing the Discount Report, exporting the Owners and Account Information Master List as a PDF file, exporting the Workshop Offerings by Owner ID Report as a PDF file, and exporting the Discount Report as a PDF file. You could create nine separate macros to accomplish these tasks. A simpler way, however, is to make each of these a submacro within a single macro. You can run a submacro just as you can run a macro.

You will create a macro called Forms and Reports that contains these nine submacros. Table 8–1 shows the submacros. Submacros can contain many actions, but each one in this table includes only a single action. For each submacro, the table gives the action, those arguments that need to be changed, and the values you need to assign to those arguments. If an argument is not listed, then you do not need to change the value from the default value that is assigned by Access.

Table 8–1 Forms and Reports Macro		
Submacro	**Action**	**Arguments to be Changed**
Open Veterinarians Appointment Form		
	OpenForm	Form Name: Veterinarians Appointment Form
		Data Mode: Read Only
Open Appointments and Treatments Form		
	OpenForm	Form Name: Appointments and Treatments Form
Open Veterinary Vendors Form		
	OpenForm	Form Name: Veterinary Vendors Form
Preview Owners and Account Information Master List		
	OpenReport	Report Name: Owners and Account Information Master List View: Print Preview
Preview Workshop Offerings by Owner ID Report		
	OpenReport	Report Name: Workshop Offerings by Owner ID View: Print Preview
Preview Discount Report		
	OpenReport	Report Name: Discount Report View: Print Preview
Export Owners and Account Information Master List		
	ExportWithFormatting	Object Type: Report Object Name: Owners and Account Information Master List Output Format: PDF Format (*.pdf)
Export Workshop Offerings by Owner ID Report		
	ExportWithFormatting	Object Type: Report Object Name: Workshop Offerings by Owner ID Output Format: PDF Format (*.pdf)
Export Discount Report		
	ExportWithFormatting	Object Type: Report Object Name: Discount Report Output Format: PDF Format (*.pdf)

To Add an Action to a Macro

To continue creating the Forms and Reports macro, enter the actions in the Macro Builder. In these steps, you will enter actions by double-clicking the action in the Action Catalog. *Why? The actions in the Action Catalog are organized by function, making it easier to locate the action you want.* Access will add the action to the Add New Action box. If there is more than one Add New Action box, you need to ensure that the one where you want to add the action is selected before you double-click.

The following steps add the first action. They also make the necessary changes to any arguments. Finally, the steps save the macro.

1

- Double-click the Submacro element from the Program Flow section of the Action Catalog to add a submacro and then type `Open Veterinarians Appointment Form` as the name of the submacro (Figure 8–4).

Q&A How can I tell the purpose of the various actions?
If necessary, expand the category containing the action so that the action appears. Point to the action. An expanded ScreenTip will appear, giving you a description of the action.

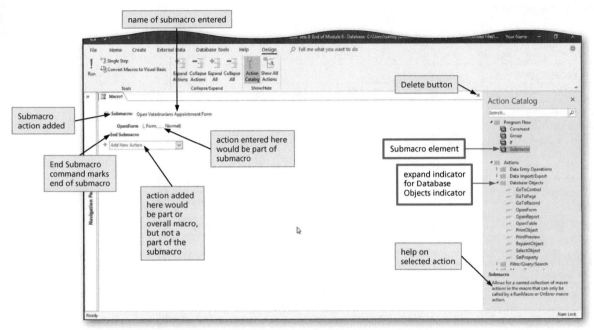

Figure 8–4

2

- Click the expand indicator for the Database Objects category of actions to display the actions within the category.

- Double-click the OpenForm action to add it to the submacro (Figure 8–5).

Q&A What should I do if I add an action in the wrong position? What should I do if I add the wrong action?
If you add an action in the wrong position, use the Move up or Move down buttons to move it to the correct position. If you added the wrong action, click the DELETE button to delete the action, and then fix the error by adding the correct action.

Figure 8–5

- Click the drop-down arrow for the Form Name argument and then select Veterinarians Appointment Form as the name of the form to be opened.

- Click the drop-down arrow for the Data Mode argument and then select Read Only to specify that users cannot change the data in the form (Figure 8–6).

◄ **Q&A** | What is the effect of the other Data Mode options?
Add allows viewing records and adding new records, but not updating records. Edit allows viewing records, adding new records, and updating existing records.

Figure 8–6

- Click the Save button on the Quick Access Toolbar, type **Forms and Reports** as the name of the macro, and then click OK to save the macro.

To Add More Actions to a Macro

To complete the macro, you need to add the additional actions shown in Table 8–1. You add the additional actions just as you added the first action. Initially, Access displays all the actions you have added with their arguments clearly visible. After you have added several actions, you might want to collapse some or all of the actions. *Why? Collapsing actions makes it easier to get an overall view of your macro.* You can always expand any action later to see details concerning the arguments. The following steps add additional actions to a macro, collapsing existing actions when necessary to provide a better view of the overall macro structure.

- Click the minus sign (–) in front of the OpenForm action to collapse the action (Figure 8–7).

◄ **Q&A** | Could I also use the buttons on the ribbon?
Yes, you can use the buttons in the Collapse/Expand group on the Macro Tools Design tab. Click the Expand Actions button to expand the selected action, or click the Collapse Actions button to collapse the selected action. You can expand all actions at once by clicking the Expand All button, or you can collapse all actions at once by clicking the Collapse All button.

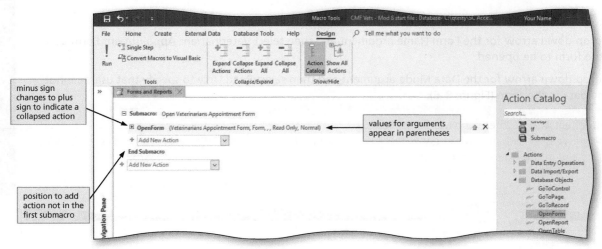

Figure 8–7

2

- Double-click the Submacro element from the Program Flow section of the Action Catalog to add a submacro, and then type **Open Appointments and Treatments Form** as the name of the submacro.

- Double-click the OpenForm action to add it to the submacro.

- Click the drop-down arrow for the Form Name argument and then select Appointments and Treatments Form.

- Double-click the Submacro element again to create a third submacro, and then type **Open Veterinary Vendors Form** as the name of the new submacro.

- Add the OpenForm action to the submacro.

- Select Veterinary Vendors Form as the value for the Form Name argument.

- Set Data Mode to Read Only and set Window Mode to Normal (Figure 8–8).

Q&A
Do I have to change the values of any of the other arguments?
No. The default values that Access sets are appropriate.

Figure 8–8

- For each of the submacros, click the minus sign in front of the submacro to collapse the submacro.
- Add a submacro named Preview Owners and Account Information Master List.
- Add the OpenReport action to the macro.
- Select Owners and Account Information Master List as the report name.
- Select Print Preview as the view (Figure 8–9).

Figure 8–9

- Collapse the Preview Owners and Account Information Master List submacro.
- Add the Preview Workshop Offerings by Owner ID Report submacro. Include the action described in Table 8–1. The report name is Workshop Offerings by Owner ID Report and the view is Print Preview.
- Add the Preview Discount Report submacro. Include the action described in Table 8–1. The report name is Discount Report and the view is Print Preview.
- Collapse the Preview Workshop Offerings by Owner ID report and Preview Discount Report submacros.
- Click the triangle to the left of Database Objects in the Action Catalog to collapse the Database Objects category, and then expand the Data Import/Export category.
- Add a submacro called Export Owners and Account Information Master List.
- Add the ExportWithFormatting action, which will export and maintain any special formatting in the process.
- Click the drop-down arrow for the Object Type argument to display a list of possible object types (Figure 8–10).

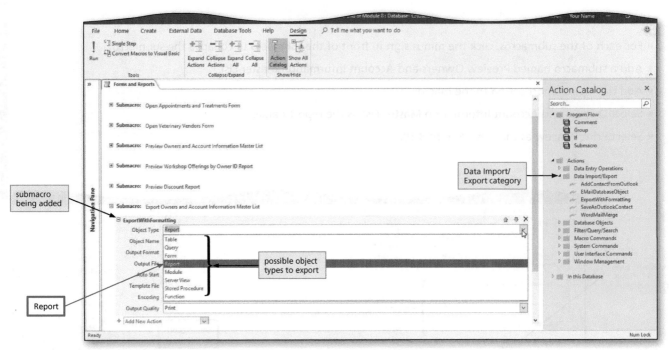

Figure 8–10

⑤
- Click Report in the list to indicate that Access is to export a report.
- Click the drop-down arrow for the Object Name argument and select Owners and Account Information Master List as the object name.
- Click the drop-down arrow for the Output Format argument and then select PDF Format (*.pdf) as the Output Format to export the report in PDF format.

⑥
- Add the Export Workshop Offerings by Owner ID Report submacro and the action from Table 8–1.
- Select Report as the Object Type and select Workshop Offerings by Owner ID as the report name.
- Select PDF Format (*.pdf) as the Output Format to export the report in PDF format.
- Add the Export Discount Report submacro and the action from Table 8–1.
- Select Report as the Object Type and Discount Report as the report name.
- Select PDF Format (*.pdf) as the Output Format to export the report in PDF format.
- Save the macro by clicking the Save button. The completed macro appears in Figure 8–11.
- Close the macro by clicking its Close button, shown in Figure 8–11.

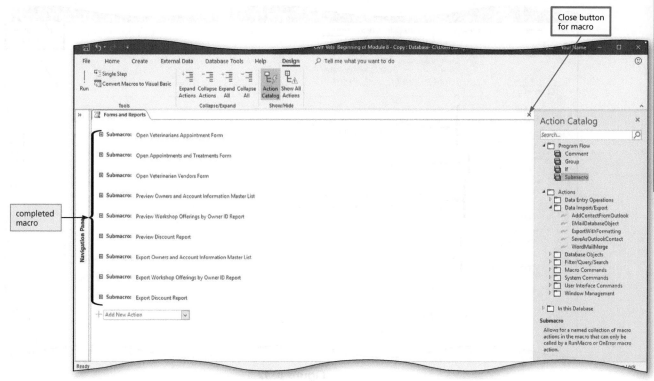

Figure 8–11

Opening Databases Containing Macros

It is possible that a macro stored in a database can contain a computer virus. By default, Access disables macros when it opens a database and displays a security warning. If the database comes from a trusted source and you are sure that it does not contain any macro viruses, click the Enable Content button. You can make adjustments to Access security settings by clicking File on the ribbon to open the Backstage view, and then clicking Options to display the Access Options dialog box, clicking Trust Center, clicking Trust Center Settings, and then clicking Macro Settings.

Errors in Macros

Macros can contain errors. The macro might open the wrong table or produce a wrong message. If you have problems with a macro, you can **single-step the macro**, that is, proceed through a macro a step at a time in Design view.

Figure 8–12 shows a macro open in Design view. This macro first has an action to open the Appointments table in Datasheet view in Read Only mode. It then changes the view to Print Preview. Next, it opens the Appointments table in Datasheet view, this time in Edit mode. Finally, it opens the Owners Query in Datasheet view in Edit mode. The macro in the figure is a common type of macro that opens several objects at once. To open all these objects, the user only has to run the macro. Unfortunately, this macro contains an error. The name of the Appointments table is written as "Appointment" in the second OpenTable action.

BTW
Converting a Macro to VBA Code
If you want to use many of the resources provided by Windows or communicate with another Windows app, you will need to convert any macros to VBA (Visual Basic for Applications) code. To convert a macro to VBA code, open the macro in Design view and click the 'Convert Macros to Visual Basic' button (Macro Tools Design tab | Tools group). When the Convert Macro dialog box appears, select the appropriate options, and then click Convert.

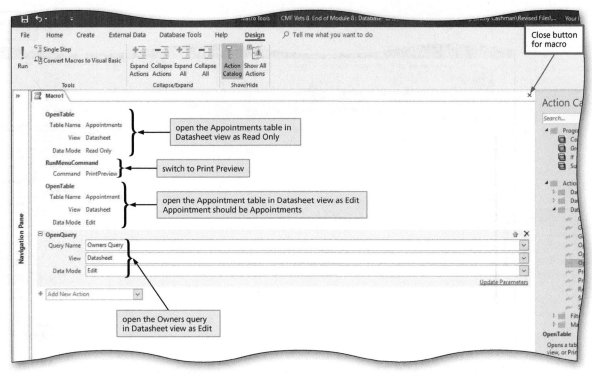

Figure 8–12

BTW

Saving a Macro as a VBA Module

You can save a macro as a VBA module using the Save Object As command in Backstage view. Open the macro in Design view, click File on the ribbon to open Backstage view, and then click Save As. When the Save As gallery appears, click 'Save Object As' in the File Types area, and then click the Save As button. When the Save As dialog box appears, click Module in the As text box and then click the OK button.

To run this macro in single-step mode, you would first click the Single Step button (Macro Tools Design tab | Tools group). You would next click the Run button (Macro Tools Design tab | Tools group) to run the macro. Because you clicked the Single Step button, Access would display the Macro Single Step dialog box (Figure 8–13). The dialog box shows the action to be executed and the values of the various arguments. You can click the Step button to proceed to the next step.

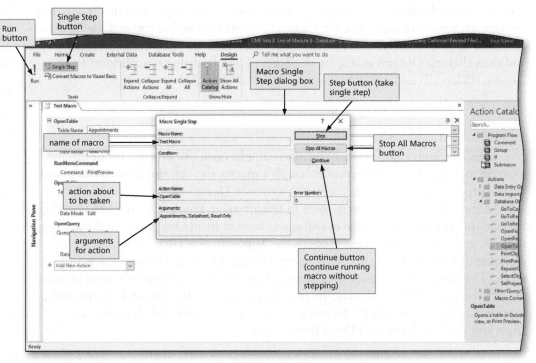

Figure 8–13

BTW
**Program Flow
Actions**
Actions in the Program
Flow category can change
the order macro actions are
executed or help structure a
macro.

With this macro, after you clicked the Step button twice, you would arrive at the screen shown in Figure 8–14. Access is about to execute the OpenTable command. The arguments are Appointment, Datasheet, and Edit. At this point, you might spot the fact that "Appointment" is misspelled. It should be "Appointments." If so, you could click the 'Stop All Macros' button and then correct the object name.

Figure 8–14

If you instead click the Step button, the misspelled name will cause the macro to terminate (abort). Access would display the appropriate error message in the Microsoft Access dialog box (Figure 8–15). This error indicates that Access could not find the object named Appointment. Armed with this knowledge, you can click the OK button, stop the macro, and then make the necessary change.

Figure 8–15

You do not need to step through a macro to discover the error. You can simply run the macro, either by clicking the Run button (Macro Tools Design tab | Tools group) with the macro open or by right-clicking the macro in the Navigation Pane and clicking Run. In either case, Access will run the macro until it encounters the error. When it does, it will display the same message shown in Figure 8–15. Just as with stepping through the macro, you would click the OK button, stop the macro, and then make the necessary change.

Once the macros are corrected, click the single-step button to turn off this feature. If this feature is not turned off, all macros will run in single-step mode.

Break Point: If you wish to stop working through the module at this point, you can resume the project later by running Access, opening the database called CMF Vets, and continuing to follow the steps from this location forward.

Creating and Using a Navigation Form

Figure 8–1a showed a navigation form for CMF Vets. A navigation form is a form that contains a **navigation control**, a control that can display a variety of forms and reports. Like the form in Figure 8–1, navigation controls contain tabs. Clicking the tab displays the corresponding form or report. The tabs can be arranged across the top and/or down the sides.

You can only include forms and reports on the tabs; you cannot include either tables or queries. The navigation form in Figure 8–1, however, appears to have a tab corresponding to the Veterinarians table. If you would find it desirable to display tables or queries on a navigation control tab, you can make it appear as though the navigation form contains these objects by creating a datasheet form based on the table or query. Figure 8–1 actually shows a datasheet form based on the Veterinarians table and does not show the Veterinarians table itself.

Before creating the navigation form, you have some other forms to create. For example, you might want the users to be able to click a tab in the navigation form and then choose from a list of forms or reports. Figure 8–16 shows a list of forms presented as buttons; the user would click the button for the desired form. Clicking the Open Veterinarians Appointment Form button, for example, would display the Veterinarians Appointment form, as shown in Figure 8–17.

Figure 8–16

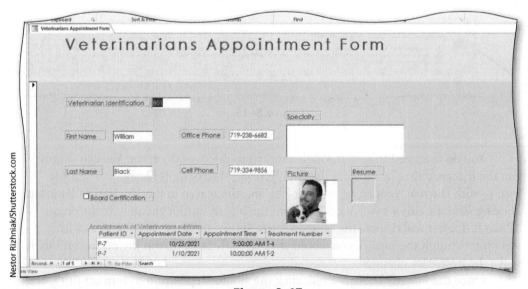

Figure 8–17

To implement options like these, you create blank forms and add either the command buttons or the option group. You then include the form you have created in the navigation form. When users click the corresponding tab, Access displays the form and users can then click the appropriate button.

To Create a Menu Form Containing Command Buttons

Why? *A menu form in which you make a selection by clicking the appropriate command button provides a convenient way to select a desired option.* You can create a menu form by adding command buttons to the form. The following steps use this technique to create a menu form with three buttons: Open Veterinarians Appointment Form, Open Appointments and Treatments Form, and Open Veterinary Vendors Form. The actions assigned to each button will run a macro that causes the desired action to occur. For example, the action for the Open Veterinarians Appointment Form button will run the Open Veterinarians Appointment Form submacro, which in turn will open the Veterinarians Appointment Form.

The following steps create a form in Design view and then add the necessary buttons.

1

- Display the Create tab.

- Click the Form Design button (Create tab | Forms group) to create a blank form in Design view.

- If a field list appears, click the 'Add Existing Fields' button (Form Design Tools Design tab | Tools group) to remove the field list.

- If a property sheet appears, click the Property Sheet button (Form Design Tools Design tab | Tools group) to remove the property sheet (Figure 8–18).

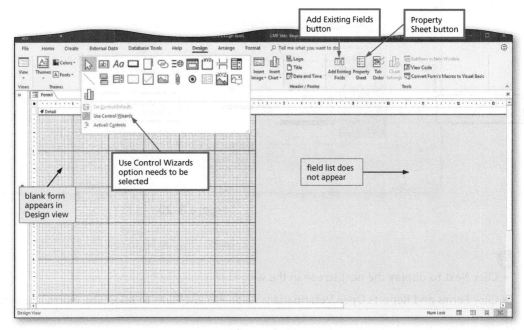

Figure 8–18

2

- If necessary, confirm that the 'Use Control Wizards' button is selected, by clicking the More button located in the Controls group.

- Click the Button tool (Form Design Tools Design tab | Controls group) and move the pointer to the approximate position shown in Figure 8–19.

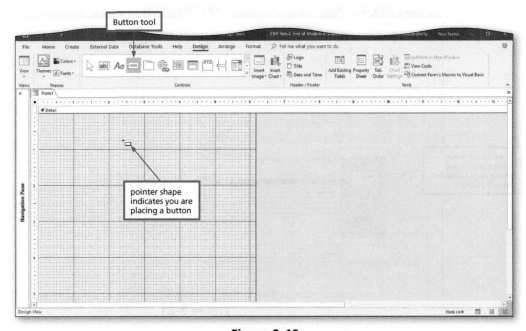

Figure 8–19

3

● Click the position shown in Figure 8–19 to display the Command Button Wizard dialog box.

● Click Miscellaneous in the Categories box, and then click Run Macro in the Actions box (Figure 8–20).

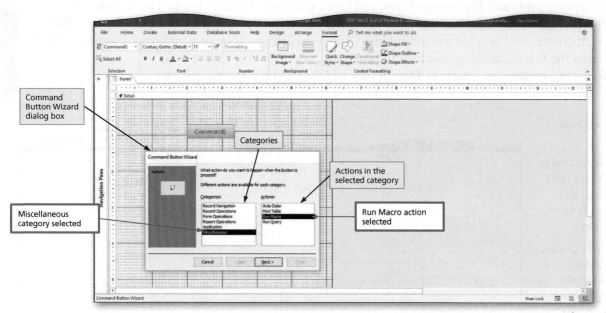

Figure 8–20

4

● Click Next to display the next screen in the wizard.

● Click Forms and Reports.Open Veterinarians Appointment Form to select the macro to be run (Figure 8–21).

Q&A **What does this notation mean?**
The portion before the period is the macro and the portion after the period is the submacro. Thus, this notation means the Open Veterinarians Appointment Form submacro within the Forms and Reports macro.

Figure 8–21

5

- Click Next to display the next Command Button Wizard screen.

- Click the Text option button to indicate that the button will display explanatory text rather than an image.

Q&A What is the purpose of these option buttons?

Choose the first option button to place text on the button. You can then specify the text to be included or accept the default choice. Choose the second option button to place a picture on the button. You can then select a picture.

- If necessary, delete the default text and then type **Open Veterinarians Appointment Form** as the text (Figure 8–22).

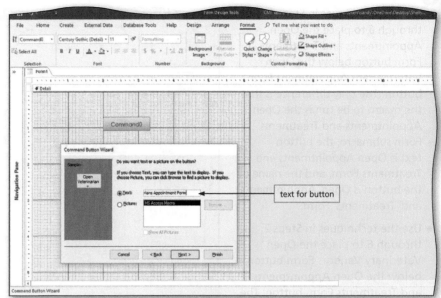

text for button

Figure 8–22

6

- Click the Next button.

- Type **Open_Veterinarians_Appointment_Form** as the name of the button (Figure 8–23).

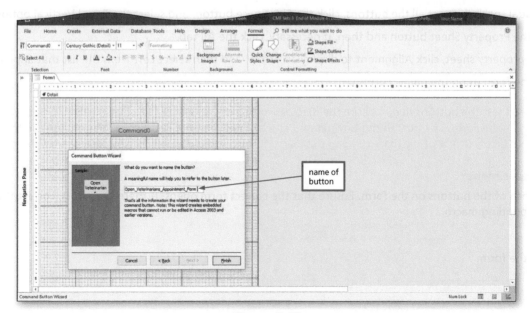

name of button

Figure 8–23

Q&A Why do you include the underscores in the name of the button?

If you are working with macros or VBA, you cannot have spaces in names. One way to avoid spaces and still make readable names is to include underscores where you would normally use spaces. Thus, Open Veterinarians Appointment Form becomes Open_Veterinarians_Appointment_Form.

- Click the Finish button to finish specifying the button.

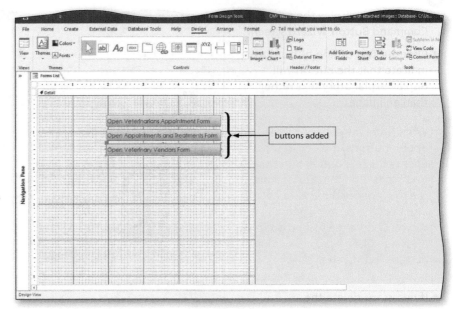

Figure 8–24

● Use the techniques in Steps 2 through 6 to place the Open Appointments and Treatments Form button below the Open Veterinarians Appointment Form button. The only difference is that the macro to be run is the Open Appointments and Treatments Form submacro, the button text is Open Appointments and Treatments Form, and the name of the button is Open_Appointments_ and_Treatments_Form.

● Use the techniques in Steps 2 through 6 to place the Open Veterinary Vendors Form button below the Open Appointments and Treatments Form button. The only difference is that the macro to be run is the Open Veterinary Vendors Form submacro, the text is Open Veterinary Vendors Form, and the name of the button is Open_Veterinary_Vendors_Form.

● Adjust the spacing of the buttons to approximately match those in Figure 8–24, using the tools on the Arrange tab.

● Move the buttons by selecting each one, pointing to its edge, and then dragging to move it.

● Resize each button by clicking the button to select it and then dragging the square handles that appear on the border of the control.

● For equal spacing, select all the buttons, click the Size/Space button, and select the Equal Vertical option.

● Click the Property Sheet button and then, if necessary, click the All tab.

● In the property sheet, click Alignment to display an arrow, and then select Left from the list that appears.

● Save the form using the name, Forms List.

Q&A How can I test the buttons to make sure the macros work?
Right-click the Forms List form in the Navigation Pane and click Open. Click each of the buttons on the form. If there are errors in any of the macros, open the macro in the Macro Builder window and correct the errors.

 Experiment

● Test each of the buttons on the form. Ensure that the correct form opens. If there are errors, correct the corresponding macro.

● Close the form.

Option Groups

You might find it useful to allow users to make a selection from some predefined options by including an option group. An **option group** is a rectangle containing a collection of option buttons. To perform an action, you simply click the corresponding option button. Figure 8–25 shows a list of reports presented in an option group where the user would click the desired option button. Notice that the user could click an option button to preview a report. The user could click a different option button to export the report as a PDF file. Clicking the 'Preview Owners and Account Information Master List Report' option button, for example, would display a preview of the Owners and Account Information Master List (Figure 8–26). Clicking the Close Print Preview button would return you to the option group.

BTW

Viewing VBA Code
You can view VBA code that is attached to a form or report. To do so, open the form or report in Design view and click the View Code button (Report Design Tools Design tab | Tools group) for reports or (Form Design Tools Design tab | Tools group) for forms.

Figure 8–25

Figure 8–26

To Create a Menu Form Containing an Option Group

The form you are creating will contain an option group. **Why?** *The option group allows users to select an option button to indicate either a report to preview or a report to export.*

The following steps use the Option Group tool to create the option group named Report Actions.

● Display the Create tab.

● Click the Form Design button (Create tab | Forms group) to create a blank form in Design view.

● If a field list appears, click the 'Add Existing Fields' button (Form Design Tools Design tab | Tools group) to remove the field list (Figure 8–27).

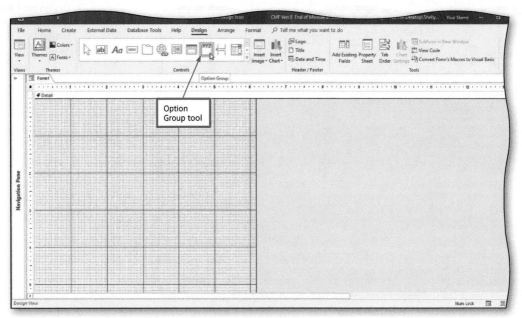

Figure 8–27

● With the 'Use Control Wizards' button selected, click the Option Group tool (Form Design Tools Design tab | Controls group) and then move the pointer to the approximate position shown in Figure 8–28.

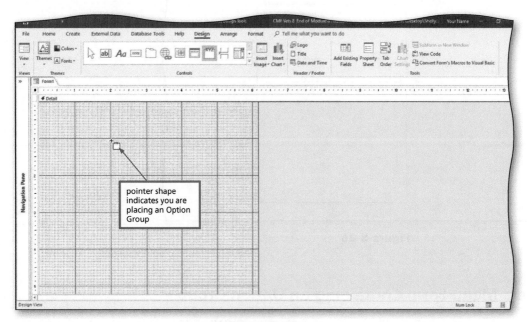

Figure 8–28

3

- Click the position shown in Figure 8–28 to place an option group and start the Option Group Wizard (Figure 8–29).

Q&A The Option Group Wizard did not start for me. What should I do?
You must not have had the 'Use Control Wizards' button selected. With the option group selected, press DELETE to delete the option group. Select the 'Use Control Wizards' button, and then add the option group a second time.

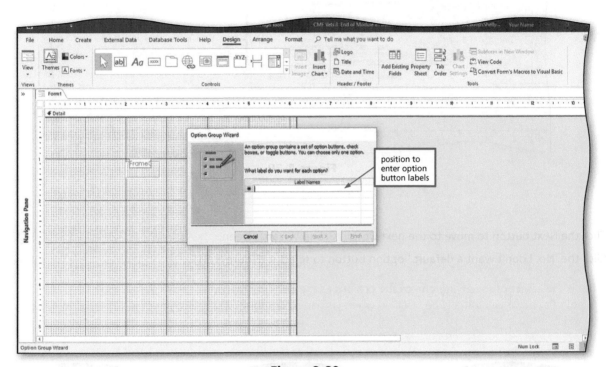

Figure 8–29

- Type **Preview Owners and Account Info Master List Report** in the first row of label names and press DOWN ARROW to specify the label for the first button in the group.

Q&A Why is the name of the form changed?
This form name is abbreviated from Information to Info here because there is not enough room for the entire name

- Type **Preview Workshop Offerings by Owner ID Report** in the second row of label names and press DOWN ARROW.

- Type **Preview Discount Report** in the third row of label names and press DOWN ARROW.

- Type **Export Owners and Account Info Master List Report** in the fourth row of label names and press DOWN ARROW.

- Type **Export Workshop Offerings by Owner ID Report** in the fifth row of label names and press DOWN ARROW.

- Type **Export Discount Report** in the sixth row of label names (Figure 8–30).

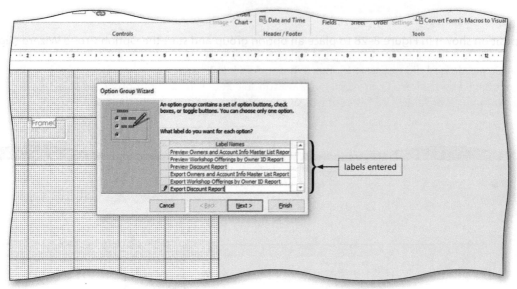

Figure 8–30

4

- Click the Next button to move to the next Option Group Wizard screen.

- Click the 'No, I don't want a default.' option button to select it (Figure 8–31).

Q&A | What is the effect of specifying one of the options as the default choice?
The default choice will initially be selected when you open the form. If there is no default choice, no option will be selected.

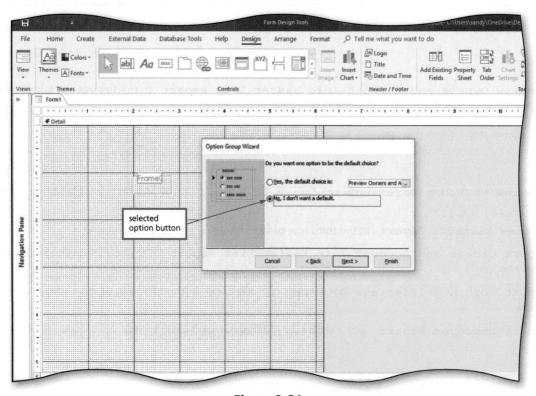

Figure 8–31

5

- Click Next to move to the next Option Group Wizard screen and then verify that the values assigned to the labels match those shown in Figure 8–32.

Q&A

What is the purpose of the values that appear for each option?

You can use the values in macros or VBA. You will use them in a macro later in this module.

Figure 8–32

6

- Click Next to move to the next Option Group Wizard screen, and then ensure that Option buttons is selected as the type of control and Etched is selected as the style (Figure 8–33).

⌕ Experiment

- Click different combinations of types and styles to see the effects on the samples shown in the dialog box. When finished, select Option buttons as the type and Etched as the style.

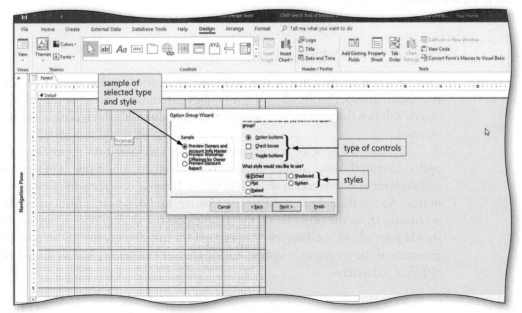

Figure 8–33

7

- Click Next to move to the next Option Group Wizard screen and then type **Report Actions** as the caption.
- Click Finish to complete the addition of the option group (Figure 8–34).

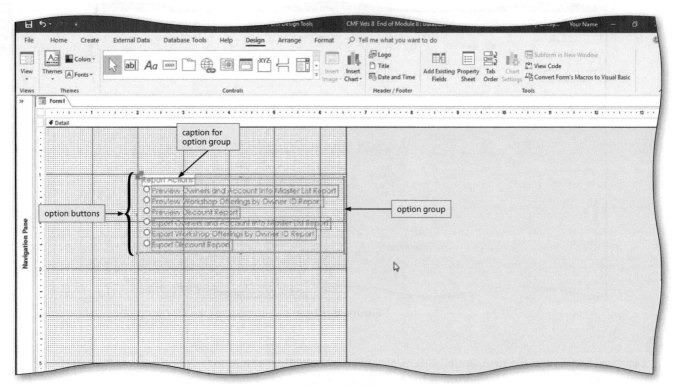

Figure 8–34

8

- Save the form using the name, Reports List.

Using an If Statement

You will create a macro that will take appropriate action when the user updates the option group, that is, when the user clicks an option button in the group. The macro will run the appropriate submacro, depending on which option the user has selected.

Because the specific actions that the macro will perform depends on the option button the user selects, the macro will contain conditions. The conditions will determine which action should be taken. If the user selects the first option button, Access should run the Preview Owners and Account Information Master List submacro. If, on the other hand, the user selects the second option button, Access should instead run the Preview Workshop Offerings by Owner ID Report submacro. For each of the six possible option buttons a user can select, Access should run a different submacro.

To instruct Access to perform different actions based on certain conditions, the macro will contain an If statement. The simplest form of an If statement is:

```
If condition Then
        action
End If
```

If the condition is true, Access will take the indicated action. If the condition is false, no action will be taken. For example, the condition could be that the user selects the first option button, and the action could be to run the Owners and Account Information Master List submacro. No action would be taken if the user selects any other button.

Another form of the If statement contains an Else clause. This form is:

```
If condition Then
        first action
Else
        second action
End If
```

If the condition is true, the first action is taken; if the condition is false, the second action is taken. For example, the condition could be that the user selects option button 1; the first action could be to run the Preview Owners and Account Information Master List submacro, and the second action could be to run the Preview Workshop Offerings by Owner ID submacro. If the user selects option button 1, Access would run the Preview Owners and Account Information List submacro. If the user selects any other option button, Access would run the Preview Workshop Offerings by Owner ID Report submacro. Because there are six option buttons, the macro needs to use an If statement with multiple Else Ifs to account for all of the options. This type of If statement has the form:

```
If first condition Then
        first action
Else If second condition Then
        second action
Else If third condition Then
        third action
    …
End If
```

The first condition could be that the user selects the first option button; the second condition could be that the user selects the second option button; the third condition could be that the user selects the third option button, and so on. The first action could be that Access runs the first submacro; the second action could be that it runs the second submacro; and the third could be that it runs the third submacro. In this case, there are six option buttons and six submacros. For six conditions, as required in this macro, the If statement will contain five Else Ifs. The If statement along with the five Else Ifs will collectively contain six conditions: one to test if the user selected option 1, one for option 2, one for option 3, one for option 4, one for option 5, and one for option 6.

To Create a Macro with a Variable for the Option Group

The following steps begin creating the macro and add an action to set a variable to the desired value. *Why? The expression that contains the option number is [Forms]![Veterinarians Appointment Form]![Form_Options]. Because this expression is fairly lengthy, the macro will begin by setting a temporary variable to this expression. A variable is a named location in computer memory. You can use a variable to store a value that you can use later in the macro. You will assign the name Optno (short for option number) as the variable name for the expression. This location can contain a value, in this case, the option number on the form. In each of the conditions, you can then use Optno rather than the full expression.*

1
- If necessary, switch to Design view and select the option group. If the Property Sheet is not displayed, click the Property Sheet button.
- If necessary, click the All tab.
- Change the name of the option group to Form_Options (Figure 8–35).

Q&A | Why this name?
The name Form_Options reflects the fact that these are options that control the action that will be taken on this form. The underscore keeps the name from containing a space.

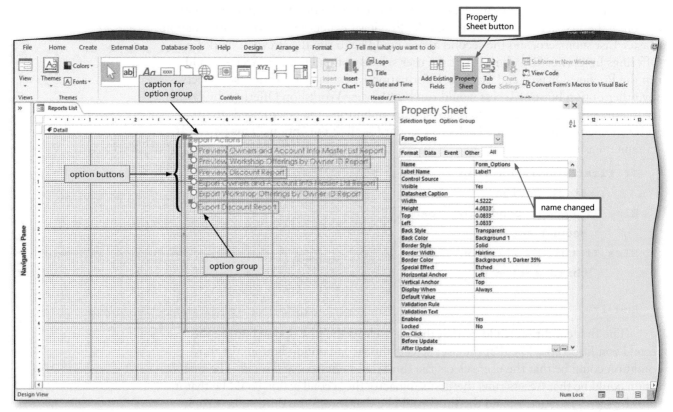

Figure 8–35

2
- Click the After Update property.
- Click the Build button to display the Choose Builder dialog box (Figure 8–36).

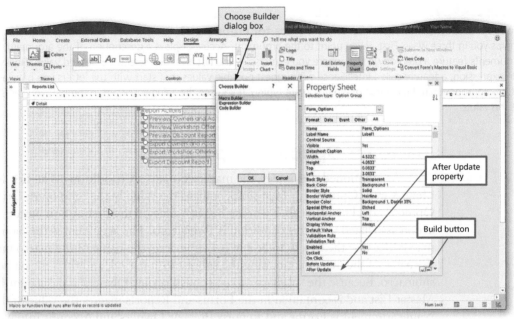

Figure 8–36

3

- With Macro Builder selected in the Choose Builder dialog box, click the OK button to create a macro.

- If necessary, click the Action Catalog button (Macro Tools Design tab | Show/Hide group) to display the Action Catalog.

- If necessary, collapse any category that is expanded.

- Expand the Macro Commands action category.

- Double-click the SetTempVar action in the Action Catalog to add the SetTempVar action to the macro.

- Type **Optno** as the value for the Name argument.

- Type **[Form_Options]** as the value for the Expression argument (Figure 8–37).

Figure 8–37

How does Access make it easier to enter values for arguments?

Access helps you in three ways. First, if you point to the argument, Access displays a description of the argument. Second, many arguments feature a drop-down List, where you can display the List and then select the desired value. Finally, if you begin typing an expression, a feature called IntelliSense will suggest possible values that start with the letters you have already typed and that are appropriate in the context of what you are typing. If you see the value you want in the List, you can simply click it to select the value.

Macro for Option Group

As mentioned previously, the macro contains six conditions. The first is [TempVars]! [Optno]=1, which simply means the value in the temporary variable Optno is equal to 1. In other words, the user selected the first option button. The action associated with this condition is RunMacro. The argument is the name of the macro. Because the macro to be run is a submacro, the name of the macro includes both the name of the macro containing the submacro, a period, and then the name of the submacro. Because the submacro to be run is Preview Owners and Account Information Master List and is contained in the Forms and Reports macro, the value of the Macro Name argument is Forms and Reports.Preview Owners and Account Info Master List. (This name needs to be shortened to fit in name space when creating the macro.)

The conditions and actions for options 2 through 6 are similar to the first submacro. The only difference is which submacro is associated with each option button. The conditions, actions, and arguments that you will change for the Form_Options macro are shown in Table 8–2. If the option number is 1, for example, the action is RunMacro. For the RunMacro action, you will change the Macro Name argument to Preview Owners and Account Info Master List submacro in the Forms and Reports macro. This name is shortened again to fit the space. On the other hand, if the option number is 2, for example, the action is again RunMacro. If the option number is 2, however, you will set the Macro Name argument to the Workshop Offerings by Owner ID submacro in the Forms and Reports macro. Similar actions take place for the other possible values for the Optno variable, that is, for option buttons 3-6. Because the temporary variable, Optno, is no longer needed at the end of the macro, the macro concludes with the RemoveTempVar command to remove this variable.

Table 8–2 Macro for After Update Property of the Option Group		
Condition	**Action**	**Arguments to be Changed**
	SetTempVar	Name: Optno Expression: [Form_Options]
If [TempVars]![Optno]=1		
	RunMacro	Macro Name: Forms and Reports.Preview Owners and Account Information Master List
Else If [TempVars]![Optno]=2		
	RunMacro	Macro Name: Forms and Reports.Preview Workshop Offerings by Owner ID Report
Else If [TempVars]![Optno]=3		
	RunMacro	Macro Name: Forms and Reports.Preview Discount Report
Else If [TempVars]![Optno]=4		
	RunMacro	Macro Name: Forms and Reports.Export Owners and Account Information Master List
Else If [TempVars]![Optno]=5		
	RunMacro	Macro Name: Forms and Reports.Export Workshop Offerings by Owner ID Report
Else If [TempVars]![Optno]=6		
	RunMacro	Macro Name: Forms and Reports.Export Discount Report
End If		
	RemoveTempVar	Name: Optno

To Add Actions to the Form Options Macro

The following steps add the conditions and actions to the Form_Options macro. *Why? The macro is not yet complete. Adding the conditions and actions will complete the macro.*

1

- Double-click the If element from the Program Flow section of the Action Catalog to add an If statement to the submacro and then type **[TempVars]![Optno]=1** as the condition in the If statement.

- With the Macro Commands category expanded, double-click RunMacro to add the RunMacro action.

- Click the drop-down arrow for the Macro Name argument and select the Preview Owners and Account Information Master List submacro within the Forms and Reports macro as the value for the argument (Figure 8–38).

Q&A What should I do if I add an action in the wrong position? What should I do if I add the wrong action?

If you add an action in the wrong position, use the Move up or Move down buttons to move it to the correct position. If you added the wrong action, click the Delete button to delete the action, and then fix the error by adding the correct action.

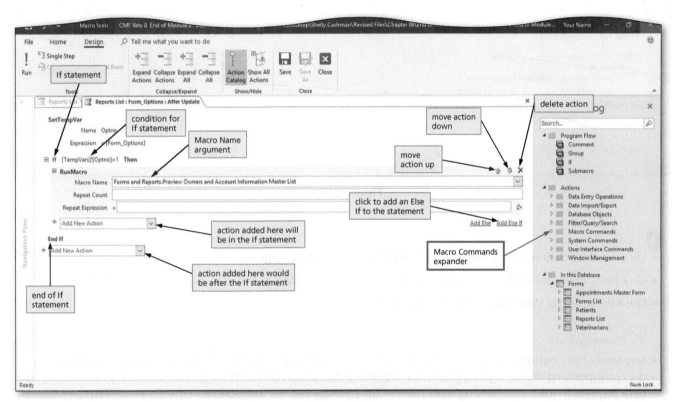

Figure 8–38

2

- Click 'Add Else If' to add an Else If clause to the If statement.

- Add the conditions and actions associated with options 2, 3, 4, 5, and 6 as described in Table 8–2, and specify the arguments for the actions. Click 'Add Else If' after adding each action except for the last one.

Q&A Do I have to enter all these actions? They seem to be very similar to the ones associated with option 1.

You can copy and paste the action for option 1. Right-click the action to select it and display a shortcut menu. Click Copy on the shortcut menu. Right-click the action just above where you want to insert the selected action and then click Paste. If the new action is not inserted in the correct position, select the new action and then click either the Move up or Move down buttons to move it to the correct location. Once the action is in the correct location, you can make any necessary changes to the arguments.

- Add the RemoveTempVar action and argument after the end of the If statement, as shown in Figure 8–39.
- Type **Optno** as the name of the TempVar to remove.

Q&A Do I need to remove the temporary variable?

Technically, no. In fact, if you plan to use this temporary variable in another macro and want it to retain the value you assigned in this macro, you would definitely not remove it. If you do not plan to use it elsewhere, it is a good idea to remove it, however.

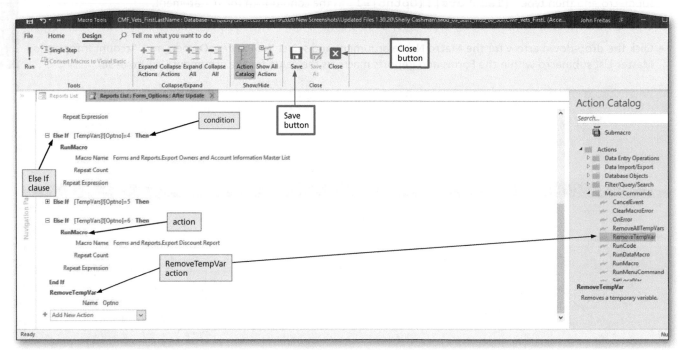

Figure 8–39

3
- Click the Save button (Macro Tools Design tab | Close group) to save the macro.
- Click the Close button (Macro Tools Design tab | Close group) to close the macro and return to the form.
- Close the property sheet, save the form, and close the form.

Experiment
- Test each of the buttons in the option group. If you do not preview or export the correct report, correct the error in the corresponding macro. If you get an error indicating that the section width is greater than the page width, you have an error in the corresponding report. Correct the error using the instructions in the Errors in Macros section of this module.

Break Point: If you wish to stop working through the module at this point, you can resume the project at a later time by running Access, opening the database called CMF Vets, and continuing to follow the steps from this location forward.

User Interface (UI) Macros

A **user interface (UI) macro** is a macro that is attached to a user interface object, such as a command button, an option group, or a control on a form. The macro you just created for the option group is thus a UI macro, as were the macros you attached to command buttons. A common use for UI macros is to associate actions with the clicking of a control on a form. In the Veterinarians form shown in Figure 8–40, for example, if you click the Veterinarian ID on the row in the datasheet where the Veterinarian ID is B01, Access displays the data for that account in a pop-up form (Figure 8–41), that is, a form that stays on top of other open objects, even when another object is active.

Figure 8–40

Figure 8–41

Similarly, in the Patients form shown in Figure 8–42, for example, if you click the patient number on the row in the datasheet where the patient number is P-1, Access displays the data for that patient in a pop-up form (Figure 8–43).

Figure 8–42

Figure 8–43

Recall that you can only use forms and reports for the tabs in a navigation form, yet the Veterinarian ID tab appears to display the Veterinarians table in Datasheet view. You can make it appear as though you are displaying the Veterinarians table in Datasheet view by creating a datasheet form that you will call Veterinarians. You will create a UI macro in this Veterinarians datasheet form. The UI macro that will be associated with the clicking of the Veterinarian ID on some record in the Veterinarians form will display the selected account in the Veterinarians Form.

To display the Veterinarians form, the UI macro will use the OpenForm action. You must set the Form Name argument of the OpenForm action to the actual name of the form to be opened, Veterinarians. (Account View and Update Form is just the form caption.) CMF Vets wants to prevent the user from updating data using this form, so the Data Mode argument is set to Read Only. The form should appear as a pop-up, which you accomplish by setting the value of the Window Mode argument to Dialog.

The form should display only the record that the user selected. If the user clicks Veterinarian ID B01 in the Veterinarian form, for example, the form should display only the data for account B01. To restrict the record that appears in the form, you include the Where Condition argument in the UI macro. The condition needs to indicate that the Veterinarian ID in the form to be opened, Veterinarians form, needs to be equal to the Veterinarian ID the user selected in the Veterinarians form.

In the Where Condition, you can simply refer to a control in the form to be opened by using its name. If the name has spaces, you must enclose it in square brackets. Thus, the name for the Veterinarian ID in the Veterinarians Form is simply [Veterinarian ID]. To reference a control that is part of any other form, the expression must include both the name of the form and the name of the control, separated by an exclamation point. Thus, the Veterinarian ID in the Veterinarians form would be [Veterinarians]![Veterinarian ID]. This declaration works correctly when you are programming a macro that simply opens the Veterinarians form. However, when you associate the Veterinarians datasheet with a tab in the navigation form, Veterinarians becomes a subform, which requires modification to the expression. This means that a form that works correctly when you open the form might not work correctly when the form is assigned to a tab in a navigation form. A safer approach avoids these issues by using a temporary variable.

Table 8–3 shows the UI macro for the Veterinarians form. It is associated with the On Click event for the Veterinarian ID control. When a user clicks a Veterinarian ID, the UI macro will display the data for the selected account in the Veterinarians Form. The main function of the macro is to open the appropriate form using the OpenForm action.

BTW
Distributing a Document
Instead of printing and distributing a hard copy of a document, you can distribute the document electronically. Options include sending the document via email; posting it on cloud storage (such as OneDrive) and sharing the file with others; posting it on a social networking site, blog, or other website; and sharing a link associated with an online location of the document. You also can create and share a PDF or XPS image of the document, so that users can view the file in Acrobat Reader or XPS Viewer instead of in Access.

Table 8–3 UI Macro Associated with On Click Event in the Veterinarians Form		
Condition	**Action**	**Arguments to Be Changed**
	SetTempVar	Name: VI Expression: [Veterinarian ID]
	OpenForm	Form Name: Veterinarians Where Condition: [Veterinarian ID]=[TempVars]![VI] Data Mode: Read Only Window Mode: Dialog
	RemoveTempVar	Name: VI

In the macro shown in Table 8–3, the first action, SetTempVar, assigns the temporary variable VI to the Veterinarian ID. The two arguments are Name, which is set to VI, and Expression, which is set to [Veterinarian ID]. The VI temporary variable refers to the Veterinarian ID in the Veterinarians form; recall that the completed macro will open the Veterinarians form. You then can use that temporary variable in the Where Condition argument. The expression is thus [Veterinarian ID]=[TempVars]![VI]. The [Veterinarian ID] portion refers to the Veterinarian ID in the Veterinarians form. The [TempVars]![VI] portion is the temporary variable that has been set equal to the Veterinarian ID in the Veterinarian form. The macro ends by removing the temporary variable.

Table 8–4 shows the macro for the Patients form, which is very similar to the macro for the Veterinarians form.

Table 8–4 UI Macro Associated with On Click Event in the Patients Form		
Condition	Action	Arguments to Be Changed
	SetTempVar	Name: PI Expression: [Patient ID]
	OpenForm	Form Name: Patients Where Condition: [Patient ID]=[TempVars]![PI] Data Mode: Read Only Window Mode: Dialog
	RemoveTempVar	Name: PI

To Create Datasheet Forms

The following steps create two datasheet forms, one for the Veterinarians table and one for the Patients table. *Why? The datasheet forms enable the Veterinarians and Patients tables to appear as if displayed in Datasheet view, despite the Access restriction that prevents tables from being used on tabs in a navigation form.*

- Open the Navigation Pane and select the Veterinarians table.

- Display the Create tab and then click the More Forms button (Create tab | Forms group) to display the More Forms gallery (Figure 8–44).

Figure 8–44

- Click Datasheet to create a datasheet form.

- Save the form using the name, Veterinarians.

Q&A Is it acceptable to use the same name for the form as for the table?
Yes. In this case, you want it to appear to the user that the Veterinarians table is open in Datasheet view. One way to emphasize this fact is to use the same name as the table.

What is the difference between this form, Veterinarians, and the form named Veterinarians Form?
The Veterinarians Form is a simple form that displays only one record at a time. The Veterinarians form you just created displays all of the veterinarian data in a datasheet.

- Use the same technique to create a datasheet form named Patients for the Patients table.

- Close both forms.

To Create UI Macros for the Datasheet Forms

The following steps create the UI macro shown in Table 8–3 for the Veterinarians datasheet form and the UI macro shown in Table 8–4 for the Patients datasheet form. *Why? The UI macros will display the appropriate pop-up forms as a result of clicking the appropriate position on the forms.*

- Open the Veterinarians form and then close the Navigation Pane.

- Click the Veterinarian ID heading to select the Veterinarian ID column in the datasheet.

- If necessary, click the Property Sheet button (Form Tools Datasheet tab | Tools group) to display a property sheet.

- Click the Event tab to display only event properties.

Q&A Why click the Event tab? Why not just use the All tab as we have before?
You can always use the All tab; however, if you know the category that contains the property in which you are interested, you can greatly reduce the number of properties that Access will display by clicking the tab for that category. That gives you fewer properties to search through to find the property you want. Whether you use the All tab or one of the other tabs is strictly a matter of personal preference.

- Click the On Click event and then click the Build button (the three dots) to display the Choose Builder dialog box (Figure 8–45).

Figure 8–45

2

- Click the OK button (Choose Builder dialog box) to display the Macro Builder window.
- Add the SetTempVar action to the macro, enter `VI` (be sure to use a capital i and not a number 1) as the value for the Name argument, and enter   `[Veterinarian ID]`   as the value for the Expression argument.
- If necessary, click the Action Catalog button on the Design tab. Add the OpenForm action to the macro, select Veterinarians as the value for the Form Name argument, leave the value of the View argument set to Form, enter `[Veterinarian ID]=[TempVars]![VI]` as the value for the Where Condition argument, select Read Only as the value for the Data Mode argument, and select Dialog as the value for the Window Mode argument.

Q&A | **What does this expression mean?**
The portion before the equal sign, [Veterinarian ID], refers to the Veterinarian ID in the form just opened, that is, in the Veterinarians form. The portion to the right of the equal sign, [TempVars]![VI_ID], is the temporary variable that was set equal to the Veterinarian ID Number on the selected record in the Veterinarians Form. This Where Condition guarantees that the record displayed in the Veterinarians Form will be the record with the same Veterinarians ID as the one selected in the Veterinarians Form.

- Add the RemoveTempVar action to the macro and enter `VI` as the value for the Name argument (Figure 8–46).

Q&A | **Why do you need to remove the temporary variable?**
Technically, you do not. It has fulfilled its function, however, so it makes sense to remove it at this point.

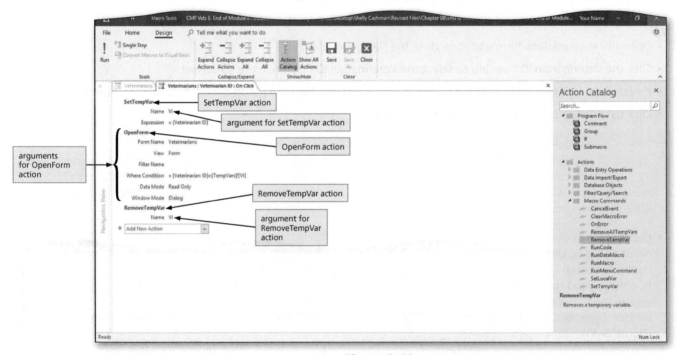

Figure 8–46

3

- Click the Save button (Macro Tools Design tab | Close group) to save the macro.
- Click the Close button (Macro Tools Design tab | Close group) to close the macro and return to the form.
- Close the property sheet.
- Save the form and then close the form.
- Use the techniques in Steps 1 through 3 to create a UI macro for the Patients datasheet form called Patients, referring to Table 8–4 for the actions. Create the macro shown in Figure 8–47 associated with clicking the Patient ID (PI) column.

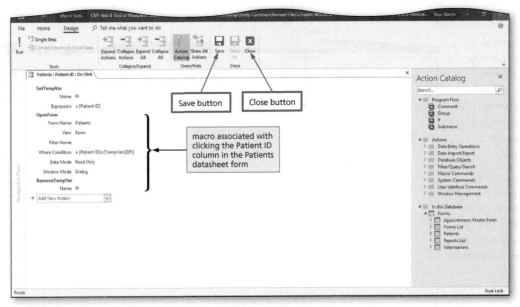

Figure 8–47

4

- Click the Save button (Macro Tools Design tab | Close group) to save the macro.

- Click the Close button (Macro Tools Design tab | Close group) to close the macro and return to the datasheet form.

- Close the property sheet.

- Save the form and then close the form.

To Create a Navigation Form

You now have all the forms you need to include in the navigation form. The following steps create the navigation form using horizontal tabs. *Why? Horizontal tabs are common on navigation forms and are easy to use. The steps then save the form and change the title.*

1

- If necessary, open the Navigation Pane.

- Click the Create tab and then click the Navigation button (Create tab | Forms group) to display the gallery of available navigation forms (Figure 8–48).

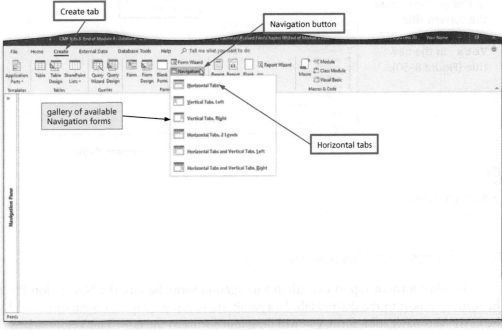

Figure 8–48

2

- Click Horizontal Tabs in the gallery to create a form with a navigation control in which the tabs are arranged horizontally in a single row.

- If necessary, click the 'Add Existing Fields' button (Form Layout Tools Design tab | Tools group) to display the field list (Figure 8–49).

Figure 8–49

3

- Save the form using the name, Main Menu.

- Click the form title twice: once to select it and the second time to produce an insertion point.

- If necessary, switch to Design view. Erase the current title and then type **CMF Vets** as the new title (Figure 8–50).

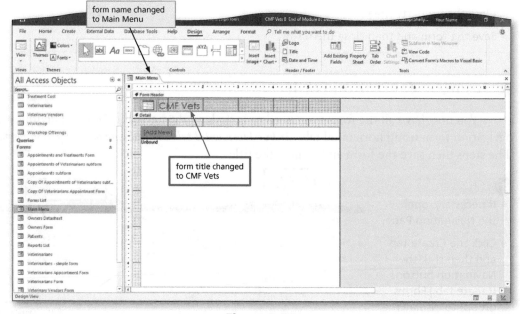

Figure 8–50

4

- Save the form.

To Add Tabs to a Navigation Form

To add a form or report to a tab in a navigation form, be sure the Navigation Pane is open, and then drag the form or report to the desired tab. As a result, users can display that form or report by clicking the tab. For the CMF Vets navigation form, you will drag four forms to the tabs. The Veterinarians datasheet form that appears to display the Veterinarians table open in Datasheet view. Similarly, the Patients form is a datasheet form that appears to display the Patients table open in Datasheet view. The Forms List form contains three buttons users can click to display the form of their choice. Finally, the Reports List form contains an option group that users can use to select a report to preview or export. The following steps add the tabs to the navigation form. They also change the name of the Forms List and Reports List tabs. *Why? The names of the tabs do not have to be the same as the name of the corresponding forms. By changing them, you can often make tabs more readable.*

1

• In Layout view, scroll down in the Navigation Pane so that the form named Veterinarians appears, and then drag the form to the position shown in the figure to add a new tab (Figure 8–51).

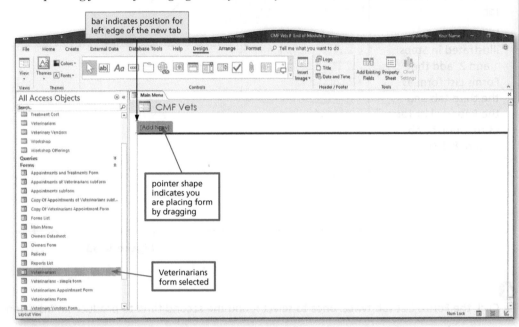

Figure 8–51

2

• Release the left mouse button to add the Veterinarians as the first tab.

• Drag the Patients form to the position shown in the figure to add a new tab (Figure 8–52).

Q&A
What should I do if I made a mistake and added a form or report to the wrong location?
You can rearrange the tabs by dragging them. Often, the simplest way to correct a mistake is to click the Undo button to reverse your most recent action, however. You can also choose to simply close the form without saving it and then start over.

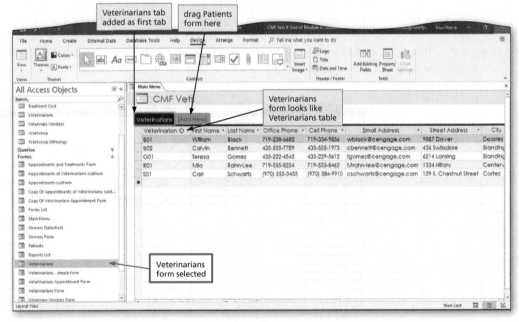

Figure 8–52

3

- Release the left mouse button to add the Patients form as the second tab.

- Using the techniques illustrated in Steps 1 and 2, add the Forms List form as the third tab and the Reports List form as the fourth tab (Figure 8–53).

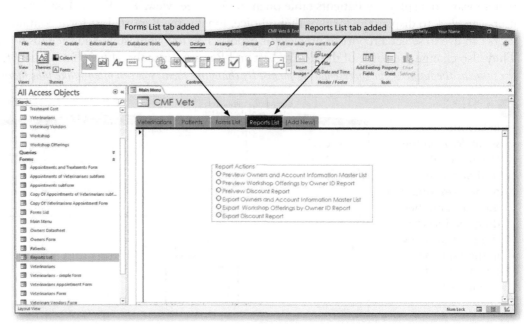

Figure 8–53

4

- Click the Forms List tab twice: once to select it and the second time to produce an insertion point.

- Change the name from Forms List to Forms.

- In a similar fashion, change the name of the Reports List tab from Reports List to Reports (Figure 8–54).

Q&A I created these two forms using the names Forms List and Reports List. Now I have changed the names to Forms and Reports. Why not call them Forms and Reports in the first place, so I would not have to rename the tabs?

Because the words, forms and reports, have specific meaning in Access, you cannot use these names when creating the forms. Thus, you needed to use some other names, like Forms List and Reports List. Because tabs within forms are not database objects, you can rename them to be any name you want.

Figure 8–54

- Save the Main Menu form.

- Open the Main Menu in Form View and click on each tab to test it for accuracy.

- If requested to do so by your instructor, rename the Main Menu form as LastName Main Menu where LastName is your last name.

- Close the form.

Using a Navigation Form

The Main Menu navigation form is complete and ready for use. To use the navigation form, right-click the form in the Navigation Pane, and then click Open on the shortcut menu. The Main Menu form then will appear with the first tabbed object (see Figure 8–1). To display the other forms, simply click the appropriate tab.

How do you determine the organization of the navigation form?
Once you decide you want a navigation form, you need to decide how to organize the form.

- **Determine which tasks should be accomplished by having the user click tabs or buttons in the navigation form.** Which forms should be opened? Which reports should be opened? Are there any tables or queries that you need to be able to open in the navigation form? If so, you must create forms for the tables or queries.

- **Determine any special requirements for the way the tasks are to be performed.** When a form is opened, should a user be able to edit data, or should the form open as read-only? Should a report be exported or simply viewed on the screen?

- **Determine how to group the various tasks.** Should forms or reports simply be assigned to the tabs in the navigation form? Should they be grouped as buttons on a menu form? Should they be placed as options within an option group? (For consistency, you would usually decide on one of these approaches and use it throughout. In this module, one menu form uses command buttons, and the other uses an option group simply to illustrate both approaches.) As far as the navigation form is concerned, is a single set of horizontal tabs sufficient, or would you also like vertical tabs? Would you like two rows of horizontal tabs?

Data Macros

A data macro is a special type of macro that is associated with specific table-related events, such as updating a record in a table. The possible events are Before Change, Before Delete, After Insert, After Update, and After Delete. Data macros allow you to add logic to these events. For example, the data macro shown in Table 8–5 is associated with the Before Change event, an event that occurs after the user has changed the data but before the change is actually made in the database.

BTW
Data Macros
Data macros are similar to SQL triggers. You attach logic to record or table events and any forms and code that update those events inherit the logic. Data macros are stored with the table.

Table 8–5 Data Macro for Before Change Event		
Condition	Action	Arguments to Be Changed
If [Hours Spent]>[Total Hours]		
	SetField	Name: [Hours Spent] Value: [Total Hours]
Else If [Hours Spent]<0		
	SetField	Name: [Hours Spent] Value: 0
End If		

This macro will examine the value in the Hours Spent field in the Workshop Offerings table. If the user's update would cause the value in the Hours Spent field to be greater than the value in the Total Hours field, the macro will change the value in the Hours Spent field so that it is equal to the value in the Total Hours field. Likewise, if the update would cause the value in the Hours Spent field to be less than zero, the macro will set the value in the Hours Spent field to 0. These changes take place after the user has made the change on the screen but before Access commits the change to the database, that is, before the data in the database is actually changed.

There are other events to which you can assign data macros. The actions in a data macro associated with the Before Delete event will take place after a user has indicated that he or she wants to delete a record, but before the record is actually removed from the database. The actions in a macro associated with the After Insert event will take place immediately after a record physically is added to the database. The actions in a macro associated with the After Update event will take place immediately after a record is physically changed in the database. The actions in a macro associated with the After Delete event will take place immediately after a record is physically removed from the database.

To Create a Data Macro

The following steps create the data macro in Table 8–5, a macro that will be run after a user makes a change to a record in the Workshop Offerings table, but before the record is updated in the database. *Why? CMF Vets management wants a way to prevent users from entering invalid data into the database.*

1

- Open the Workshop Offerings table in Datasheet view and close the Navigation Pane.

- Display the Table Tools Table tab (Figure 8–55).

Q&A What is the meaning of the events in the Before Events and After Events groups? Actions in macros associated with the Before Events group will occur after the user has taken action to change or delete a record, but before the change or deletion is made permanent in the database. Actions in macros associated with the After Events group will occur after the corresponding update has been made permanent in the database.

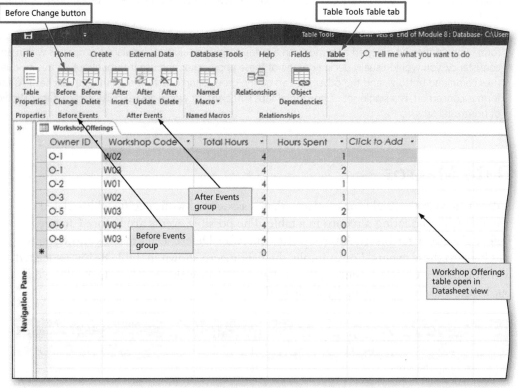

Figure 8–55

2

- Click the Before Change button (Table Tools Table tab | Before Events group).

- Double-click the IF element from the Program Flow section of the Action Catalog to add an IF statement to the macro and then type   `[Hours Spent]>[Total Hours]`   as the condition in the IF statement.

- Add the SetField action to the macro.

- Enter   `[Hours Spent]`   in the Name field and then enter   `[Total Hours]`   in the Value field.

- Add an Else If statement.

- Type   `[Hours Spent]<0`   for the Else If condition.

- Add the SetField action to the macro.

- Enter   `[Hours Spent]`   in the Name field and then enter   `0`   (zero) in the Value field.

- Confirm that your macro looks like one shown in Figure 8–56, and correct any errors if necessary.

Q&A | What happened to all the actions that were in the list? In the previous macros we created, there seemed to be many more actions available.
There are only certain actions that make sense in data macros. Only those actions appear. Therefore, the list of actions that appears is much smaller in a data macro than in other macros.

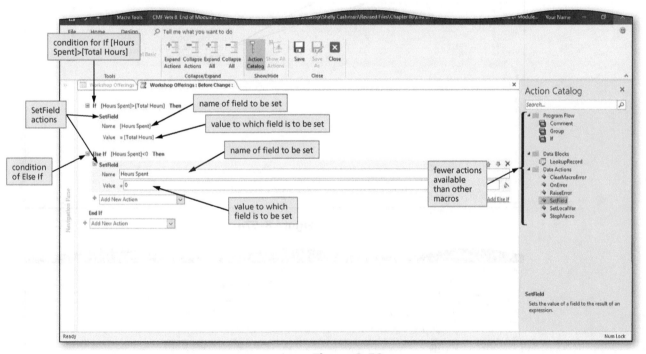

Figure 8–56

3

- Save and close the macro.

- Save and close the Workshop Offerings table.

- If desired, sign out of your Microsoft account.

- **sam** ⬆ Exit Access.

Note: Unless your instructor indicates otherwise, you are encouraged to simply read the material in this module from this point on for understanding without carrying out any operations.

Using a Table That Contains a Data Macro

If you update a table that contains a data macro, the actions in the data macro will be executed whenever the corresponding event takes place. If the data macro corresponds to the Before Change event, the actions will be executed after the user has changed the data, but before the change is saved in the database. With the data macro you just created, for example, if a user attempts to change the data in such a way that the Hours Spent is greater than the Total Hours (Figure 8–57a), as soon as the user takes an action that would require saving the record, Access makes Hours Spent equal to Total Hours (Figure 8–57b). Likewise, if a user attempts to set Hours Spent to a negative number (Figure 8–58a), as soon as the user takes an action that would require saving the record, Access will set Hours Spent to 0 (Figure 8–58b). This change will take place automatically, regardless of whether the user changes the values in Datasheet view, with a form, in an update query, or in any other fashion.

Figure 8–57a

Figure 8–57b

Figure 8–58a

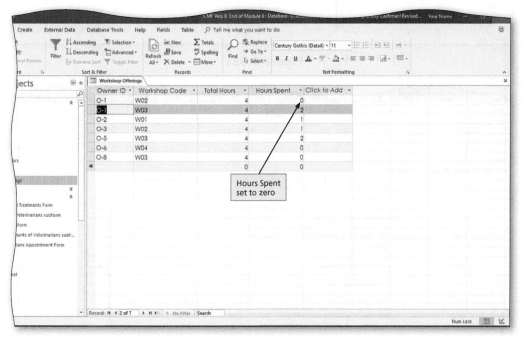

Figure 8–58b

Using Control Layouts on Forms and Reports

In earlier modules, you worked with control layouts in forms and reports. In a control layout, the data is aligned either horizontally or vertically. The two types of layouts are stacked layouts, which are most commonly used in forms, and tabular layouts, which are most commonly used in reports (Figure 8–59). Using a control layout gives you more options for moving rows or columns than you would have without the layout.

Figure 8–59a

Figure 8–59b

In working with control layouts, there are many functions you can perform using the Form Layout Tools Arrange tab. You can insert rows and columns, delete rows and columns, split and merge cells, and move rows. You can also change margins, which affects spacing within cells, and padding, which affects spacing between rows and columns. You can split a layout into two layouts and move layouts. Finally, you can anchor controls so that they maintain the same distance between the control and the anchor position as the form or report is resized. Table 8–6 gives descriptions of the functions available on the Form Layout Tools Arrange tab.

Table 8–6 Arrange Tab	
Button	**Enhanced ScreenTip**
Gridlines	Gridlines
Stacked	Create a layout similar to a paper form, with labels to the left of each field.
Tabular	Create a layout similar to a spreadsheet, with labels across the top and data in columns below the labels.
Insert Above	Insert Above
Insert Below	Insert Below
Insert Left	Insert Left
Insert Right	Insert Right
Select Layout	Select Layout
Select Column	Select Column
Select Row	Select Row
Merge	Merge Cells
Split Vertically	Split the selected layout into two rows.
Split Horizontally	Split the selected layout into two columns.
Move Up	Move Up
Move Down	Move Down
Control Margins	Control Margins
Control Padding	Control Padding
Anchoring	Tie a control to a section or another control so that it moves or resizes in conjunction with movement or resizing of the parent.

TO CREATE A LAYOUT FOR A FORM OR REPORT

If you create a form using the Form button (Create tab | Forms group), Access automatically creates a stacked layout. If you create a report using the Report button (Create tab | Reports group), Access automatically creates a tabular layout. In other cases, you can create a layout using the Form Layout Tools Arrange tab for forms or the Report Layout Tools Arrange tab for reports. If you no longer want controls to be in a control layout, you can remove the layout.

To create a layout in either a form or report, you would use the following steps.

1. Select all the controls that you want to place in a layout.
2. Click the Stacked button (Form Layout Tools Arrange tab | Table group) to create a stacked layout or the Tabular button (Form Layout Tools Arrange tab | Table group) to create a tabular layout.

TO REMOVE A LAYOUT FOR A FORM OR REPORT

To remove a layout from either a form or report, you would use the following steps.

1. Right-click any control in the layout you want to remove to produce a shortcut menu.
2. Point to Layout on the shortcut menu and then click Remove Layout on the submenu to remove the layout.

BTW
Quick Styles for Controls
To make a navigation form more visually appealing, you can change the style of a command button and/or tabs. Quick styles change how the different colors, fonts, and effects are combined. To change the style of a command button or tab, open the navigation form in Layout view. Select the control(s) for which you want to change the style and then click Quick Styles. When the Quick Styles gallery appears, select the desired style. You also can change the style of a control in Design view.

BTW
Change the Shape of a Control
Command buttons and tabs have a default shape. For example, both command buttons and tabs have a rounded rectangle shape as the default shape. You can change the shape of a button or tab control on a navigation form. To do so, open the navigation form in Layout view. Select the control(s) for which you want to change the shape and click Change Shape. When the Change Shape gallery appears, select the desired shape. You also can change the shape of a command button or tab in Design view.

Using Undo

When making changes with the Form Layout Tools Arrange tab buttons, it is not uncommon to make a change that you did not intend. Sometimes taking appropriate action to reverse the change can prove difficult. If so, remember that you can undo the change by clicking the Undo button on the Quick Access Toolbar. It is also a good idea to save your work frequently. That way, you can always close the form or report without saving. When you reopen the form or report, it will not have any of your most recent changes.

TO INSERT A ROW

You can insert a blank row either above or below a selected row (Figure 8–60). You can then fill in the row by either typing a value or dragging a field from a field List. In a similar fashion, you can insert a blank column either to the left or right of a selected column.

Figure 8–60a

Figure 8–60b

You would use the following steps to insert a blank row.

1. Select any control in the row above or below where you want to insert a new row.
2. Click the Select Row button (Form Layout Tools Arrange tab | Rows & Columns group) to select the row.
3. Click the Insert Above button (Form Layout Tools Arrange tab | Rows & Columns group) to insert a blank row above the selected row or the Insert Below button (Form Layout Tools Arrange tab | Rows & Columns group) to insert a blank row below the selected row.

As you have seen earlier in the text, you also can insert a row containing a field by simply dragging the field from the field List to the desired location.

TO INSERT A COLUMN

You would use the following steps to insert a new column.

1. Select any control in the column to the right or left of where you want to insert a new column.
2. Click the Select Column button (Form Layout Tools Arrange tab | Rows & Columns group) to select the column.
3. Click the Insert Left button (Form Layout Tools Arrange tab | Rows & Columns group) to insert a blank column to the left of the selected column or the Insert Right button (Form Layout Tools Arrange tab | Rows & Columns group) to insert a blank column to the right of the selected column.

TO DELETE A ROW

You can delete any unwanted row or column from a control layout. You would use the following steps to delete a row.

1. Click any control in the row you want to delete.
2. Click Select Row (Form Layout Tools Arrange tab | Rows & Columns group).
3. Press DELETE to delete the row.

TO DELETE A COLUMN

You would use the following steps to delete a column.

1. Click any control in the column you want to delete.
2. Click Select Column (Form Layout Tools Arrange tab | Rows & Columns group).
3. Press DELETE to delete the column.

Splitting and Merging Cells

You can split a cell into two cells either horizontally, as shown in Figure 8–61, or vertically. You can then enter contents into the new cell. For example, in Figure 8–61, you could type text into the new cell that gives information about Veterinarian IDs. You can also merge two cells into one.

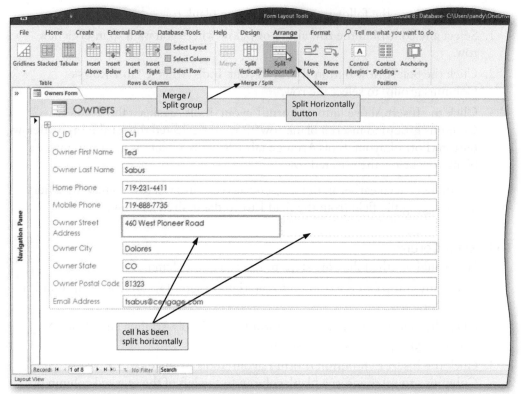

Figure 8–61

TO SPLIT A CELL

To split a cell, you would use the following steps.

1. Click the cell to be split.
2. Click the Split Vertically button (Form Layout Tools Arrange tab | Merge / Split group) to split the selected cell vertically or the Split Horizontally button (Form Layout Tools Arrange tab | Merge / Split group) to split the selected cell horizontally.

TO MERGE CELLS

You would use the following steps to merge cells.

1. Select the first cell to be merged.
2. While holding down the CTRL key, CLICK all the other cells to be merged.
3. Click the Merge button (Form Layout Tools Arrange tab | Merge / Split group) to merge the cells.

BTW
Control Padding
The term, padding, refers to the amount of space between a control's border and its contents. Effectively, you can increase or decrease the amount of white space in a control.

Moving Cells

You can move a cell in a layout by dragging it to its new position. Most often, however, you will not want to move individual cells, but rather whole rows (Figure 8–62). You can move a row by selecting the row and then dragging it to the new position or you can use the Move buttons on the Form Layout Tools Arrange tab.

Figure 8–62a

Figure 8–62b

TO MOVE ROWS USING THE MOVE BUTTONS

You would use the following steps to move a row.

1. Select any cell in the row to be moved.
2. Click the Select Row button (Form Layout Tools Arrange tab | Rows & Columns group) to select the entire row.
3. Click the Move Up button (Form Layout Tools Arrange tab | Move group) to move the selected row up one row or the Move Down button (Form Layout Tools Arrange tab | Move group) to move the selected row down one row.

Margins and Padding

You can change the spacing within a layout by changing the control margins and the control padding. The control margins, which you change with the Control Margins button, affect the spacing around the text inside a control. Figure 8–63 shows the various options as well as samples of two of the options.

Figure 8–63a

Figure 8–63b

Figure 8–63c

The control padding, which you change with the Control Padding button, affects the spacing around the outside of a control. The options are the same as those for control margins. Figure 8–64 shows samples of two of the options.

Figure 8–64a

Figure 8–64b

TO CHANGE CONTROL MARGINS

You would use the following steps to change a control's margins.

1. Select any cell in the layout.
2. Click the Select Layout button (Form Layout Tools Arrange tab | Rows & Columns group) to select the entire layout. (You also can select the layout by clicking the layout selector.)
3. Click the Control Margins button (Form Layout Tools Arrange tab | Position group) to display the available margin settings.
4. Click the desired margin setting.

TO CHANGE CONTROL PADDING

You would use the following steps to change control padding.

1. Select the layout.
2. Click the Control Padding button (Form Layout Tools Arrange tab | Position group) to display the available padding settings.
3. Click the desired padding setting.

Although you can make the margin and padding changes for individual controls, it is much more common to do so for the entire layout. Doing so gives a uniform appearance to the layout.

Splitting a Layout

You can split a single control layout into two separate layouts (Figure 8–65) and then modify each layout separately. They can be moved to different locations and formatted differently.

BTW

Gridlines
You can also add gridlines to a form. To do so, select the control(s) for which you want to add gridlines, then click the Gridlines button. When the Gridlines menu appears, select the desired option. You also can change the color, border, style, and width of gridlines using the Gridlines menu.

Figure 8–65a

Figure 8–65b

To Split a Layout

To split a layout, you would use the following steps.

1. Select all the cells that you want to move to a new layout.

2. Click the Stacked button (Form Layout Tools Arrange tab | Table group) to place the cells in a stacked layout or the Tabular button (Form Layout Tools Arrange tab | Table group) to place the cells in a tabular layout.

Moving a Layout

You can move a control layout to a different location on the form (Figure 8–66).

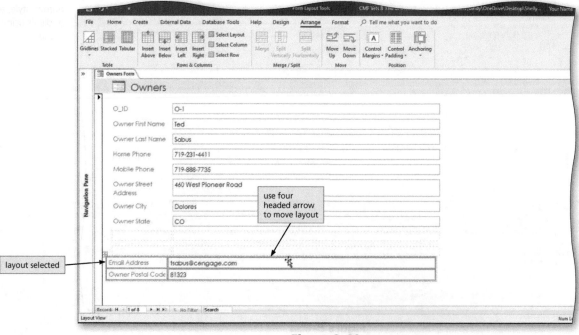

Figure 8–66

TO MOVE A LAYOUT

You would use the following steps to move a layout.

1. Click any cell in the layout to be moved and then click the Select Layout button (Form Layout Tools Arrange tab | Rows & Columns group) to select the layout.

2. Drag the layout to the new location.

Anchoring Controls

The Anchoring button allows you to tie (anchor) controls to a section or to other controls so that they maintain the same distance between the control and the anchor position as the form is resized. To anchor the controls you have selected, you use the Anchoring gallery (Figure 8–67).

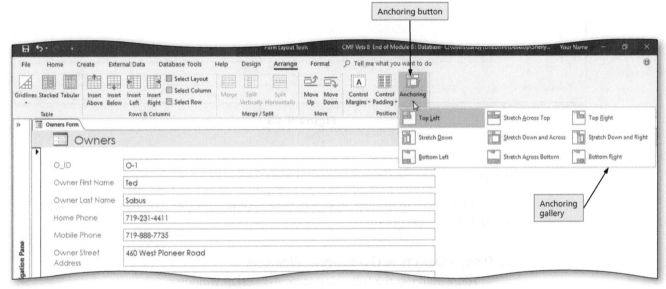

Figure 8–67

The Top Left, Top Right, Bottom Left, and Bottom Right options anchor the control in the indicated position on the form. The other five operations also stretch the controls in the indicated direction.

TO ANCHOR CONTROLS

You would use the following steps to anchor controls.

1. Select the control or controls to be anchored.

2. Click the Anchoring button (Form Layout Tools Arrange tab | Position group) to produce the Anchoring gallery.

3. Select the desired Anchoring option from the Anchoring gallery.

To see the effect of anchoring you need to display objects in overlapping windows rather than standard tabbed documents. With overlapping windows, you can resize the object by dragging the border of the object. Anchored objects keep their same relative position (Figure 8–68).

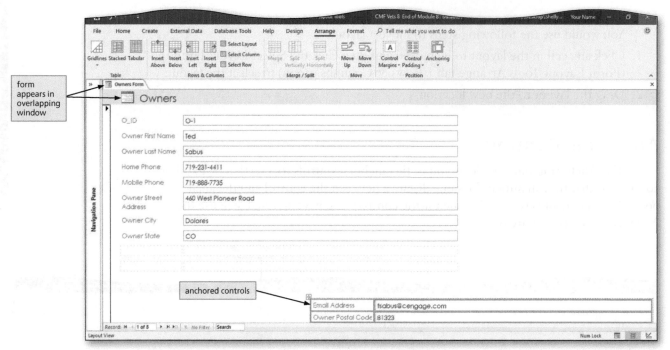

Figure 8–68

Window

If you want to display objects in overlapping windows, you have to modify the appropriate Access option.

TO DISPLAY OBJECTS IN OVERLAPPING WINDOWS

You would use the following steps to overlap windows.

1. Click File on the ribbon to open the Backstage view.
2. Click Options to display the Access Options dialog box.
3. Click Current Database to display the Current Database options.
4. In the Application Options area, click the Overlapping Windows option button.
5. Click the OK button to close the Access Options dialog box.
6. For the changes to take effect, you will need to close and then reopen the database.

You use a similar process to return to displaying objects in tabbed documents.

BTW
Overlapping
Windows
When you display objects in overlapping windows, each database object appears in its own window. When multiple objects are open, these windows overlap each other. By default, Access 2019 displays database objects in a single pane separated by tabs.

TO DISPLAY OBJECTS IN TABBED DOCUMENTS

You would use the following steps to display tabbed documents.

1. Click File on the ribbon to open the Backstage view.
2. Click Options to display the Access Options dialog box.
3. Click Current Database to display the Current Database options.
4. In the Application Options area, click the Tabbed Documents option button.
5. Click the OK button to close the Access Options dialog box.
6. For the changes to take effect, you will need to close and then reopen the database.

Summary

In this module you have learned to create and use macros, create a menu form that uses command buttons for the choices, create a menu form that uses an option group for the choices, create a macro that implements the choices in the option group, create datasheet forms that utilize user interface macros, create a navigation form, add tabs to a navigation form, and create data macros. You also learned to modify control layouts.

CONSIDER THIS

What decisions will you need to make when creating your own macros and navigation forms?
Use these guidelines as you complete the assignments in this module and create your own macros and navigation forms outside of this class.

1. Determine when it would be beneficial to automate tasks in a macro.

   a. Are there tasks involving multiple steps that would be more conveniently accomplished by running a macro than by carrying out all the individual steps? For example, opening a form in read-only mode could be accomplished conveniently through a macro.

   b. Are there tasks that are to be performed when the user clicks buttons on a menu form?

   c. Are there tasks to be performed when a user clicks a control on a form?

   d. Are there tasks to be performed when a user updates a table? These tasks can be placed in a macro that can be run when the button is clicked.

2. Determine whether it is appropriate to create a navigation form.

   a. If you want to make it easy and convenient for users to perform a variety of tasks just by clicking tabs and buttons, consider creating a navigation form.

   b. You can associate the performance of the various tasks with the tabs and buttons in the navigation form.

3. Determine the organization of the navigation form.

   a. Determine the various tasks that need to be performed by clicking tabs and buttons.

   b. Decide the logical grouping of the tabs and buttons.

CONSIDER THIS

How should you submit solutions to questions in the assignments identified with a symbol?
Every assignment in this book contains one or more questions identified with a symbol. These questions require you to think beyond the assigned database. Present your solutions to the questions in the format required by your instructor. Possible formats may include one or more of these options: write the answer; create a document that contains the answer; present your answer to the class; discuss your answer in a group; record the answer as audio or video using a webcam, smartphone, or portable media player; or post answers on a blog, wiki, or website.

Apply Your Knowledge

Reinforce the skills and apply the concepts you learned in this module.

Creating UI Macros and a Navigation Form

Note: To complete this assignment, you will be required to use the Data Files. Please contact your instructor for information about accessing the Data Files.

Instructions: Start Access. Open the Support_AC_Financial Services database and enable the content. (If you do not have the database, see your instructor for a copy of the modified database.)

Perform the following tasks:

1. Create a datasheet form for the Client table and name the form Client. Create a UI macro for the Client form. Use CN as the temporary variable name. When a user clicks a client number on a row in the datasheet form, the Client form should appear in a pop-up form in read-only mode.

2. Create a datasheet form for the Advisor table and name the form Advisor Datasheet. Create a UI macro for the Advisor Datasheet form. Use AN as the temporary variable name. When a user clicks an advisor number on a row in the datasheet form, the Advisor Datasheet form should appear in a pop-up form in read-only mode.

3. Create the navigation form shown in Figure 8–69. The purpose of the form is to display the two datasheet forms in the database as horizontal tabs. Name the form Main Menu and change the title to Financial Services Main Menu.

Figure 8–69

4. If requested to do so by your instructor, open the Advisor datasheet form and change the first and last names of advisor 110 to your first and last name.

5. Submit the revised database in the format specified by your instructor.

6. ✹ How could you add a Services Data form to the navigation form?

Extend Your Knowledge

Extend the skills you learned in this module and experiment with new skills. You may need to use Help to complete the assignment.

Creating and Modifying Navigation Forms

Note: To complete this assignment, you will be required to use the Data Files. Please contact your instructor for information about accessing the Data Files. Start Access, and then open the Support_AC_Healthy Pets database. (If you do not have this database, see your instructor for a copy of the modified database).

Instructions: Healthy Pets is a veterinary practice that is being closed due to retirements. CMF is thinking of buying the practice to expand their client base. Before the management makes any decisions on this, the Healthy Pets database needs to be updated so that it is compatible with CMF Vets and so their files may be imported into CMF Vets database. Perform the following tasks:

1. Create a form named Forms List form that contains macros to open the Clients by Technician form and the Technician form.
2. Create a form named Reports List form that contains macros to open the Client Amount Due Summary report and the Revised Client Summary report.
3. Create a Main Menu form for forms and reports. The Forms List menu should include the command buttons for the Clients and Technicians form and the Technician form. The Reports List menu should include Command Buttons for both summary reports. Test the macros and then save the changes.
4. Research how to import database objects from one database into another database. Note what changes would need to be made to the Healthy Pets database before it is imported into the CMF Vets database.
5. Open the Main Menu navigation form in Layout view. Change the shape of the Forms List tab to Oval and the shape of the Reports List tab to Snip Single Corner Rectangle.
6. If requested to do so by your instructor, add a label to the form header for the Main Menu form with your first and last name.
7. Submit the revised database in the format specified by your instructor.
8. ✸ Why would you convert a macro to Visual Basic code?

Expand Your World

Create a solution, which uses cloud and web technologies, by learning and investigating on your own from general guidance.

Problem: Support_AC_Physical Therapy is a database of clients and therapists. Therapists are required to update their national physical therapy certification annually with the American Physical Therapy Association. You will need to find colleges in the city of Madison, Wisconsin that offers these classes. Madison is the major city closest to the Wisconsin communities of Portage, Empeer, and Grant City. You will create images that display the course name and hyperlinks for these classes that you download from the Internet. Finally, you will modify the Therapist table by adding a field for these hyperlinks and images. In addition, you will add another field that displays either Yes or No to indicate whether the therapist has met the annual certification requirement.

Expand Your World *continued*

Note: To complete this assignment, you will be required to use the Data Files. Please contact your instructor for information about accessing the Data Files. Start access, and then open the Support_ AC_Physical Therapy database that you used in previous modules. (If you do not have database, see your instructor for a copy of the modified database).

Instructions: Perform the following tasks:

1. Search the Internet to locate continuing education courses for physical therapy in Madison, Wisconsin.

2. Create hyperlinks to the course information on the school's website. Enter the hyperlinks into the Therapist table.

3. Find images to enter for the courses for the Attachment field in the Therapist table. You can use images that you have found online or photos that you have taken. Note: make sure you have the appropriate permissions to use the images.

4. Add a Yes/No field into the Therapist table indicating whether the therapist has completed the annual certification.

5. Create a form based on the updated Therapist table for easy reference concerning the new fields and name the form Therapist Certification.

6. Save your changes.

7. Submit the revised database in the format specified by your instructor.

8. ✸ How did you create the images you included in the Therapist table? Why did you make those choices?

In the Labs

Design, create, modify and/or use a database following the guidelines, concepts, and skills presented in this module.

Lab: Adding a Navigation Form to the Lancaster College Database

Instructions: Open the Support_AC_Lancaster College database. (If you do not have the database, see your instructor for a copy of the modified database.)

Part 1:   The sports department of Lancaster College would like you to create a main menu that allows easy access to forms and reports.

   a. Create a form with macro buttons that opens the Coach subform and the Sport subform. Name the form List of Available Forms.

   b. Create a form with macro buttons that opens the Sport Teams and Captains report and the Sports table report. Name the form List of Available Reports.

   c. Create a Main Menu navigation form that includes the List of Available Forms form and the List of Available Reports form.

   d. Save the changes and test the navigation form.

Submit your assignment in the format specified by your instructor.

Part 2:   You made several decisions while adding the macro buttons and creating the form for this assignment. What was the rationale behind your decisions? Would you add any additional macro buttons to The Form List or The Report List?

   a. Research and document how you can have the Navigation form open automatically when the database is opened.

   b. Submit the revised database in the format specified by your instructor.

9 Administering a Database System

Objectives

You will have mastered the material in this module when you can:

- Convert a database to and from earlier versions of Access
- Use the Table Analyzer, Performance Analyzer, and Documenter
- Create custom categories and groups in the Navigation Pane
- Use table, database, and field properties
- Create indexes

- Enable and use automatic error checking
- Create custom data type parts
- Create a database for a template
- Create a custom template
- Encrypt a database and set a password
- Lock a database and split a database

Introduction

Administering a database system is an important activity that has many facets. Administration activities are an important aspect of database management because they improve the usability, accessibility, security, and efficiency of the database.

Project — Administering a Database System

CMF Vets realizes the importance of database administration, that is, the importance of administering its database system properly. An important activity in administering databases is the creation of custom templates, application parts, and data type parts. A custom template is a customized database application that can be used as a basis for additional databases. The template contains tables, forms, queries, and other objects that can be used by others to create a database based on that template. Application parts and data type parts are templates included in Access that you can add to your database to extend its functionality. Clicking an application part adds to your database a predetermined collection of objects such as tables, queries, forms, reports, and /or macros. Clicking a data type part adds a predetermined collection of fields to a table. Creating an understandable startup form gives database users easy access to the forms when the database is opened.

CMF Vets have recognized a need for a pet sitting business. Many of their clients travel and want to have their pets cared for at home during their absence. The veterinary clinic decides to organize a pet sitting database system that links the available pet sitters with those owners in need of pet care. The personnel organizing the pet sitting business at CMF Vets realize that some of pet sitters might not be familiar with operating a database and a startup menu would be extremely helpful. Figure 9-1 shows a startup form that is automatically opened when the database is opened.

Figure 9–1

BTW
Enabling the Content
For each of the databases you use in this module, you will need to enable the content.

BTW
The Ribbon and Screen Resolution
Access may change how the groups and buttons within the groups appear on the ribbon, depending on the computer's screen resolution. Thus, your ribbon may look different from the ones in this book if you are using a screen resolution other than 1366 x 768.

Figure 9–2 illustrates the range of activities involved in database administration, including the conversion of an Access database to an earlier version of Access. Database administration usually includes such activities as analyzing tables for potential problems, analyzing performance to see if changes could make the system perform more efficiently, and documenting the various objects in the database. It can include creating custom categories and groups in the Navigation Pane as well as changing table and database properties. It can also include the use of field properties in such tasks as creating a custom input mask and allowing zero-length strings. It can include the creation of indexes to speed up retrieval. The inclusion of automatic error checking is part of the administration of a database system. Understanding the purpose of the Trust Center is critical to the database administration function. Another important area of database administration is the protection of the database. This protection includes locking the database through the creation of an ACCDE file to prevent unauthorized changes from being made to the VBA source code or to the design of forms and reports. Splitting the database into a front-end and a back-end database is another way to protect the functionality and improve the efficiency of a database.

Figure 9–2

In this module, you will learn how to perform a variety of database administration tasks.

Converting Databases

Access 2007, Access 2010, Access 2013, Access 2016, and Access 2019 all use the same file format, the .accdb format. The format is usually referred to as the Access 2007 file format. Thus, in Access 2019, you can use any database created in Access 2007. You should be aware of the following changes in Access 2013, Access 2016, and Access 2019 from the earlier versions.

1. Unlike previous versions, these versions do not support PivotTables or PivotCharts.

2. The Text data type is now Short Text, and the Memo data type is now Long Text.

3. Smart Tags are no longer supported.

4. Replication is no longer available.

To convert an Access 2007 database to an earlier version, the database cannot contain any features that are specific to Access 2007, 2010, 2013, 2016, or 2019. These include attachments, multivalued fields, offline data, or links to external files not supported in earlier versions of Access. They also include objects published to the web, data macros, and calculated columns. Provided the database does not contain such features, you can convert the database by clicking the Save As tab in the Backstage view (Figure 9–3). You can then choose the appropriate format.

BTW
Converting
Databases
If you try to convert a database that contains features specific to a later version of Access, Access displays an error message alerting you that you cannot save the database as an earlier version because it contains features that require the current file format.

BTW
Maintaining
Backward
Compatibility
If you plan to share your database with users who may have an earlier version of Access, be sure to maintain backward compatibility. Do not include multivalued fields, attachment fields, or calculated fields in your database design. For example, if there is a calculation that is used frequently, create a query with the calculated field and use the query as the basis for forms and reports rather than adding the field to the table design.

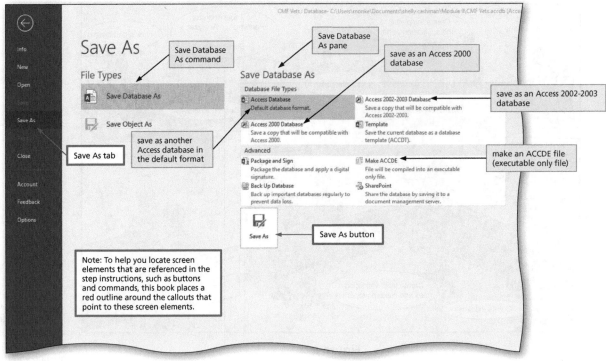

Figure 9–3

BTW
Saving Databases to External Locations
You also can save a database to an external location, such as OneDrive, and to any portable storage device, such as a USB flash drive. To do so, select the desired external location or portable storage device when you browse to specify a location for your database.

BTW
Exporting XML Data
Database administration also may include responsibility for exchanging data between dissimilar systems or apps. Extensible Markup Language (XML) is a data interchange standard for describing and delivering data on the web. With XML, you can describe both the data and the structure (schema) of the data. You can export tables queries, forms, or reports. To export a database object, select the object and click the XML File button (External Data tab | Export group). Select the appropriate options in the Export XML dialog box.

TO CONVERT AN ACCESS 2007–2016 DATABASE TO AN EARLIER VERSION

Specifically, to convert an Access 2007–2019 database to an earlier version, you would use the following steps.

1. With the database to be converted open, click File on the ribbon to open the Backstage view.
2. Click the Save As tab.
3. With the 'Save Database As' command selected, click the desired format, and then click the Save As button.
4. Type the name you want for the converted database, select a location in which to save the converted database, and click the Save button.

TO CONVERT AN ACCESS 2000 OR 2002–2003 DATABASE TO AN ACCESS 2019 DATABASE

To convert an Access 2000 or Access 2002–2003 database to the default database format for Access 2019, you open the database in Access 2019. Initially, the database is open in compatibility mode, where features that are new to Access 2019 and that cannot easily be displayed or converted are disabled. In this mode, the database remains in its original format. If you want to convert it so that you can use it in Access 2019, you use the Access Database command on the Backstage view. Once the database is converted, the disabled features will be enabled. You will no longer be able to share the database with users of Access 2000 or Access 2002–2003, however.

Specifically, to convert an Access 2000 or 2002–2003 database to the default database format for Access 2019, you would use the following steps.

1. With the database to be converted open, click File on the ribbon to open the Backstage view.
2. Click the Save As tab.

3. With the Save Database As command selected, click Access Database and then click the Save As button.

4. Type the name you want for the converted database, select a location, and click the Save button.

BTW
Creating Databases in Older Formats
To create a database in an older format, create a database and browse to select a location for the database, then click the Save As Type arrow in the File New Database dialog box, and select either 2002–2003 format or 2000 format.

Microsoft Access Analysis Tools

Microsoft Access has a variety of tools that are useful in analyzing databases. Analyzing a database gives information about how the database functions and identifies opportunities for improving functionality. You can use the Access analysis tools to analyze tables and database performance, and to create detailed documentation.

To Use the Table Analyzer

Access contains a Table Analyzer tool that performs three separate functions. This tool can analyze tables while looking for potential redundancy (duplicated data). The Table Analyzer can also analyze performance and check for ways to make queries, reports, or forms more efficient. Then, the tool will make suggestions for possible changes. The final function of the analyzer is to produce detailed documentation describing the structure and content of the various tables, queries, forms, reports, and other objects in the database.

The following steps use the Table Analyzer to examine the Account table for **redundancy,** or duplicated data. *Why? Redundancy is one of the biggest potential sources of problems in a database.* If redundancy is found, the Table Analyzer will suggest ways to split the table in order to eliminate the redundancy.

1
• **sam↓** Start Access and open the database named CMF Vets from your hard disk, OneDrive, or other storage location.

• If necessary, close the Navigation Pane.

• Display the Database Tools tab (Figure 9–4).

Figure 9–4

• Click the Analyze Table button (Database Tools tab | Analyze group) to display the Table Analyzer Wizard dialog box (Figure 9–5).

Q&A Where did the data in the figure come from? It does not look like my data. The data is fictitious. It is just intended to give you an idea of what the data might look like.

Figure 9–5

• Click Next to display the next Table Analyzer Wizard screen (Figure 9–6).

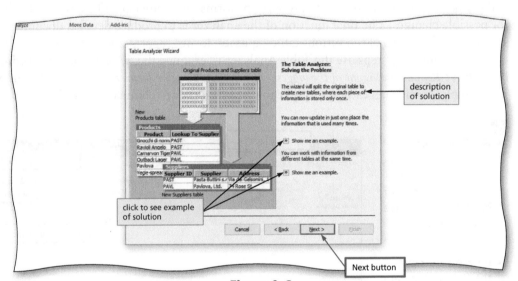

Figure 9–6

4

• Click Next to display the next Table Analyzer Wizard screen.

• If necessary, select the Treatment Cost table (Figure 9–7).

Figure 9–7

- Click Next.

- Be sure the 'Yes, let the wizard decide.' option button is selected (Figure 9–8) to let the wizard determine what action to take.

Figure 9–8

- Click Next to run the analysis (Figure 9–9), which indicates redundancy in the database.

Q&A I do not really want to put the Animal Type in a different table, even though I realize that this data does appear to be duplicated. Do I have to follow this advice?
Certainly not. This is only a suggestion.

Figure 9–9

- Because the type of duplication identified by the analyzer does not pose a problem, click the Cancel button to close the analyzer.

To Use the Performance Analyzer

The Performance Analyzer examines the database's tables, queries, reports, forms, and other objects in your system, looking for ways to improve the efficiency of database operations. These improvements could include modifications to the way data is stored, as well as changes to the indexes created for the system. (You will learn about indexes later in this module.) The following steps use the Performance Analyzer. *Why? The Performance Analyzer identifies possible areas for improvement in the CMF Vets database. Users then can determine whether to implement the suggested changes.*

- Click the Analyze Performance button, shown in Figure 9–4 (Database Tools tab | Analyze group), to display the Performance Analyzer dialog box.

- If necessary, click the Tables tab (Figure 9–10).

Figure 9–10

- Click the Select All button to select all tables.

- Click OK to display the results (Figure 9–10).

- Click OK to finish working with the Performance Analyzer (Figure 9–11).

Q&A

What do the results mean?

The data is stored correctly to optimize efficiency. If this had not been the case, you would see a set of suggestions for efficiency improvement such as changing the data types of the fields.

Figure 9–11

To Use the Database Documenter

The Database Documenter allows you to produce detailed documentation of the various tables, queries, forms, reports, and other objects in your database. Documentation is required by many organizations. It is used for backup, disaster recovery, and planning for database enhancements. Figure 9–12 shows a portion of the documentation for the Appointments table. The complete documentation is much lengthier than the one shown in the figure.

Figure 9–12

The following steps use the Database Documenter. *Why? The Database Documenter is the easiest way to produce detailed documentation for the Appointments table.*

- Click the Database Documenter button, shown in Figure 9–4 (Database Tools tab | Analyze group), to display the Documenter dialog box.

- If necessary, click the Tables tab and then click the Appointments check box to specify documentation for the Appointments table (Figure 9–13).

Figure 9–13

2

- Click OK to produce a preview of the documentation (Figure 9–14).

Q&A

What can I do with this documentation? You could print it by clicking the Print button (Print Preview tab | Print group). You could create a PDF or XPS file containing the documentation by clicking the PDF or XPS button (Print Preview tab | Data group) and following the directions. You could create a Word (RTF) file by clicking the More button (Print Preview tab | Data group), and then clicking Word and following the directions. Whatever option you choose, you might need to use this documentation later if you make changes to the database design.

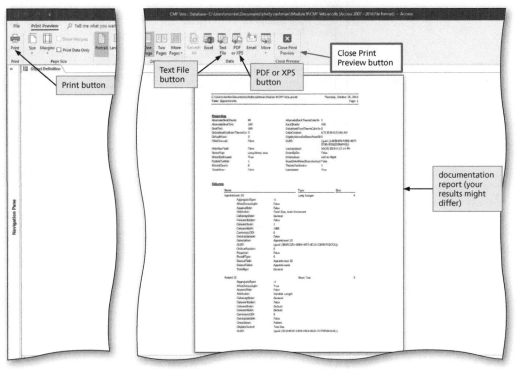

Figure 9–14

- Click the 'Close Print Preview' button (Print Preview tab | Close Preview group) to close the preview of the documentation.

Experiment

- Try other options within the Database Documenter to see the effect of your choice on the documentation produced. Each time, close the preview of the documentation.

Navigation Pane Customization

You have already learned how to customize the Navigation Pane by selecting the category and the filter as well as how to use the Search Bar to restrict the items that appear in the Navigation Pane. You can also create custom categories and groups that you can use to categorize the items in the database in ways that are most useful to you.

To Create Custom Categories and Groups

You can create custom categories in the Navigation Pane. You can further refine the objects you place in a category by adding custom groups to the categories. Why? Custom categories and groups allow you to tailor the Navigation Pane for your own specific needs. The following steps create a custom category called Veterinarian Tasks. They then add two custom groups, Appointments and Emergency and On Call, to the Veterinarian Tasks category.

1

- Display the Navigation Pane.

- Right-click the Navigation Pane title bar to display a shortcut menu (Figure 9–15).

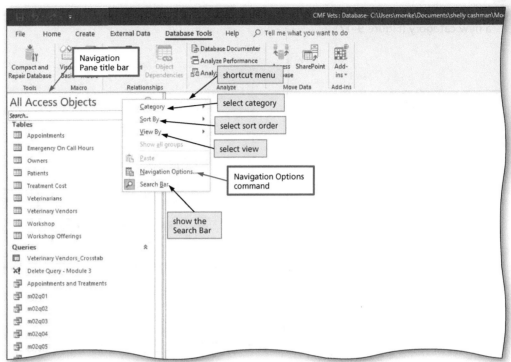

Figure 9–15

2

- Click the Navigation Options command on the shortcut menu to display the Navigation Options dialog box (Figure 9–16).

Q&A What else could I do with the shortcut menu?
You could select a category, select a sort order, or select how to view the items within the Navigation Pane.

Figure 9–16

- Click the Add Item button to add a new category (Figure 9–17).

Figure 9–17

- Type **Veterinarian Tasks** as the name of the category.

- Click the Add Group button to add a group and then type **Appointments** as the name of the group.

- Click the Add Group button to add a group and then type **Emergency and On Call** as the name of the group (Figure 9–18).

Q&A I added the groups in the wrong order. How can I change the order?
Select the group that is in the wrong position. Click the Move Up or Move Down arrow to move the group to the correct location.

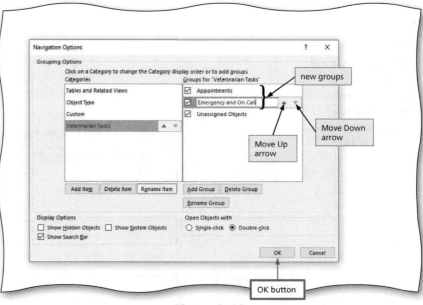

Figure 9–18

If I made a mistake in creating a new category, how can I fix it?
Select the category that is incorrect. If the name is wrong, click the Rename Item button and change the name appropriately. If you do not want the category, click the Delete Item button to delete the category and then click OK.

- Click OK to create the new category and groups.

To Add Items to Groups

Once you have created new groups, you can move existing items into the new groups. The following steps add items to the Appointments and Emergency and On Call groups in the Veterinarian Tasks category. *Why? These items are all related to the veterinarians.* Note: Before beginning this task, import the table Emergency On Call Hours from the database file called Emergency On Call Extra Table, if you did not already import it in completing Module 7. The Emergency On Call Hours database is stored with the Data Files. See your instructor for if you do not have the required files.

1

- Click the Navigation Pane arrow to produce the Navigation Pane menu and then scroll as necessary to display the Veterinarian Tasks category (Figure 9–19).

Q&A Do I have to click the arrow?
No. If you prefer, you can click anywhere in the title bar for the Navigation Pane. Clicking arrows is a good habit, however, because there are many situations where you must click the arrow.

Figure 9–19

2

- Click the Veterinarian Tasks category to display the groups within the category. Because you created the Appointments and Emergency and On Call groups but did not assign items, the table objects all appear in the Unassigned Objects area of the Navigation Pane.

- Right-click Appointments table to display the shortcut menu.

- Point to the 'Add to group' command on the shortcut menu to display the list of available groups (Figure 9–20).

Figure 9–20

Q&A I did not create an Unassigned Objects group. Where did it come from?

Access creates the Unassigned Objects group automatically. Until you add an object to one of the groups you created, it will be in the Unassigned Objects group.

What is the purpose of the New Group on the submenu?

You can create a new group using this submenu. This is an alternative to using the Navigation Options dialog box. Use whichever approach you find most convenient.

3

- Click Appointments to add the Appointments table to the Appointments group.

- Using the same technique, add the item shown in Figure 9–21 to the Emergency and On Call group.

Q&A What is the symbol that appears in front of the items in the Appointments and Emergency and On Call groups?

It is the link symbol. You do not actually add an object to your group. Rather, you create a link to the object. In practice, you do not have to worry about this. The process for opening an object in one of your custom groups remains the same.

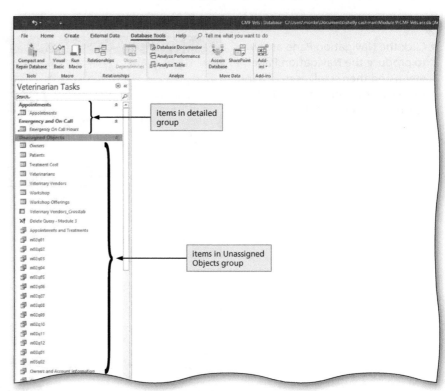

Figure 9–21

4

- Click the arrow in the Unassigned Objects bar to hide the unassigned objects (Figure 9–22).

Q&A Do I have to click the arrow?

No. Just as with the Navigation Pane, you can click anywhere in the Unassigned Objects bar.

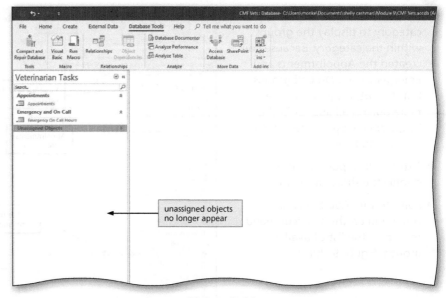

Figure 9–22

Break Point: If you wish to stop working through the module at this point, you can close Access now. You can resume the project at a later time by starting Access, opening the CMF Vets database, and continuing to follow the steps from this location forward.

What issues do you consider in determining the customization of the Navigation Pane?
The types of issues to consider are the following:

- Would a new category be useful?

- If so, are there new groups that would be useful to include in the new category?

- If you have created a new category and new groups, which items should be included in the new groups, and which should be left uncategorized?

Table and Database Properties

BTW
Touch and Pointers
Remember that if you are using your finger on a touch screen, you will not see the pointer.

You can assign properties to tables. For example, you could assign a validation rule and validation text to an entire table. You can also assign properties to the database, typically for documentation purposes.

To Create a Validation Rule for a Table

Previously, you created validation rules that applied to individual fields within a table. Some, however, apply to more than one field. In the Workshop Offerings table, you created a macro that would change the value of the Hours Spent field in such a way that it could never be greater than the Total Hours field. You can also create a validation rule that ensures this will never be the case; that is, the validation rule would require that the hours spent must be less than or equal to the total hours. To create a validation rule that involves two or more fields, you need to create the rule for the table using the table's Validation Rule property. The following steps create a **table validation rule**. *Why? This rule involves two fields, Hours Spent and Total Hours.*

- If necessary, click the arrow for Unassigned Objects to display those objects in the Navigation Pane.

- Open the Workshop Offerings table in Design view and close the Navigation Pane.

- If necessary, click the Property Sheet button (Table Tools Design tab | Show /Hide group) to display the table's property sheet.

- Click the Validation Rule property and type `[Hours Spent] < = [Total Hours]` as the validation rule.

- Click the Validation Text property and type `Hours spent cannot exceed total hours` as the validation text (Figure 9–23).

Figure 9–23

Q&A | Could I use the Expression Builder to create the validation rule?
Yes. Use whichever method you find the most convenient.

2

- Close the property sheet.
- Click the Save button on the Quick Access Toolbar to save the validation rule and the validation text.
- When asked if you want to test existing data, click the No button.
- Close the Workshop Offerings table.

To Create Custom Properties

In addition to the general database property categories, you can also use custom properties. **Why?** *You can use custom properties to further document your database in a variety of ways. If you have needs that go beyond the custom properties, you can create your own original or unique properties.* The following steps **populate** the Status custom property; that is, they set a value for the property. In this case, they set the Status property to Live Version, indicating this is the live version of the database. If the database were still in a test environment, the property would be set to Test Version. The steps also create and populate a new property, Production, which represents the date the database was placed into production.

1

- Click File on the ribbon to open the Backstage view.
- Ensure the Info tab is selected (Figure 9–24).

Figure 9–24

2

- Click the 'View and edit database properties' link to display the CMF Vets.accdb Properties dialog box.
- Click the Custom tab.
- Scroll down in the Name list so that Status appears, and then click Status.
- If necessary, click the Type arrow to set the data type to Text.
- Click the Value box and type **Live Version** as the value to create the custom property (Figure 9–25).

Figure 9–25

- Click the Add button to add the property.
- Type **Production** in the Name box.
- If requested to do so by your instructor, type your first and last name in the Name box.
- Select Date as the Type.
- Type **10/25/2021** as the value (Figure 9–26) to indicate that the database went into production on October 25, 2021.

Figure 9–26

- Click the Add button to add the property (Figure 9–27).

Q&A What if I add a property that I decide I do not want?
You can delete it. To do so, click the property you no longer want and then click the Delete button.

5

- Click OK to close the CMF Vets.accdb Properties dialog box.

Q&A How do I view these properties in the future?
The same way you created them. Click File on the ribbon, click the Info tab, and then click the 'View and edit database properties' link. Click the desired tab to see the properties you want.

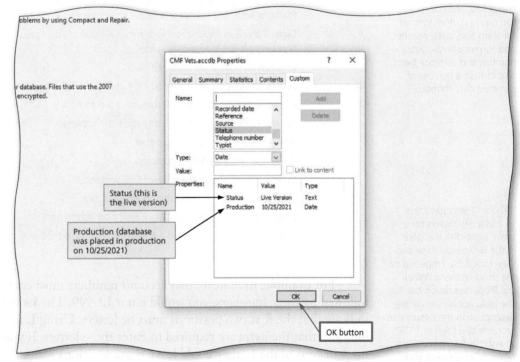

Figure 9–27

Special Field Properties

Each field in a table has a variety of field properties available. Recall that field properties are characteristics of a field. Two special field properties, the Custom Input Mask property and the Allow Zero Length property, are described in this section.

Custom Input Masks

One way to help users enter data using a certain format is to use an input mask. You have already used the Input Mask Wizard to create an input mask. Using the wizard, you can select the input mask that meets your needs. This is often the best way to create the input mask.

If the input mask you need to create is not similar to any in the list provided by the wizard, you can create a custom input mask by entering the appropriate characters as the value for the Input Mask property. In doing so, you use the symbols from Table 9–1.

BTW
Changing Data Formats
To create custom data formats, enter various characters in the Format property of a table field. The characters can be placeholders (such as 0 and #), separators (such as periods and commas), literal characters, and colors. You can create custom formats for short text, date, number, and currency fields. Date, number, and currency fields also include a number of standard data formats.

Table 9–1	Input Mask Symbols	
Symbol	**Type of Data Accepted**	**Data Entry**
0	Digits 0 through 9 without plus (+) or minus (–) sign are accepted. Positions left blank appear as zeros.	Required
9	Digits 0 through 9 without plus (+) or minus (–) sign are accepted. Positions left blank appear as spaces.	Optional
#	Digits 0 through 9 with plus (+) or minus (–) sign are accepted. Positions left blank appear as spaces.	Optional
L	Letters A through Z are accepted.	Required
?	Letters A through Z are accepted.	Optional
A	Letters A through Z or digits 0 through 9 are accepted.	Required
a	Letters A through Z or digits 0 through 9 are accepted.	Optional
&	Any character or a space is accepted.	Required
C	Any character or a space is accepted.	Optional
<	Symbol converts any letter entered to lowercase.	Does not apply
>	Symbol converts any letter entered to uppercase.	Does not apply
!	Characters typed in the input mask fill it from left to right.	Does not apply
\	Character following the slash is treated as a literal in the input mask.	Does not apply

BTW
Table Descriptions
To add a description for a table, right-click the table in the Navigation Pane and then click Table Properties on the shortcut menu. When the Properties dialog box for the table appears, enter the description in the Description property and then click OK. To enter a description for a table in Design view, click the Property Sheet button, and then enter a description in the Description property on the property sheet (see Figure 9–23).

For example, to indicate that account numbers must consist of two letters followed by three numbers, you would enter LL999. The Ls in the first two positions indicate that the first two positions must be letters. Using L instead of a question mark indicates that the users are required to enter these letters. If you had used the question mark instead of the L, they could leave these positions blank. The 9s in the last three positions indicate that the users can enter only digits 0 through 9. Using 9 instead of 0 indicates that they could leave these positions blank; that is, they are optional. Finally, to ensure that any letters entered are displayed as uppercase, you would use the > symbol at the beginning of the input mask. The complete mask would be > LL999.

To Create a Custom Input Mask

The following step creates a custom input mask for the Account Number field. Why? None of the input masks in the list meet the specific needs for the Account Number field.

- Open the Navigation Pane, open the Owners table in Design view, and then close the Navigation Pane.

- With the Owner ID field selected, click the Input Mask property, and then type >L-999 as the value (Figure 9–28). Access adds a backslash to your custom input mask, like this >L\-999.

- Save the changes and close the table.

Q&A

What is the difference between the Format property and the Input Mask property?
The Format property ensures that data is displayed consistently, for example, always in uppercase. The Input Mask property controls how data is entered by the user.

Figure 9–28

What is the effect of this input mask?
From this point on, anyone entering an owner ID will be restricted to a letter in the first position, followed by a dash and numeric digits in the last three. Further, any letter entered in the first position will be displayed as uppercase.

Can you have a field that has both a custom input mask and a format. Is this a problem?
Technically, you do not need both. When the same field has both an input mask and a format, the format takes precedence. However, if the format specified for the field is the same as the input mask (uppercase), it will not affect the data.

Creating and Using Indexes

You are already familiar with the concept of an index. The index in the back of a book contains important words or phrases along with a list of pages on which the given words or phrases can be found. An index for a table is similar. An index is a database object that is created based on a field or combination of fields. An index on the Vendor Name field, for example, would enable Access to rapidly locate a record that contains a particular veterinary vendor. In this case, the items of interest are vendor names instead of keywords or phrases, as is the case for the index in the back of this book. The field or fields on which the index is built is called the index key. Thus, in the index on account names, the Vendor Name field is the index key.

Each name occurs in the index along with the number of the record on which the corresponding account is located. Further, the names appear in the index in alphabetical order, so Access can use this index to rapidly produce a list of vendors alphabetized by account name.

BTW
Changing Default Sort Order
To display the records in a table in an order other than the primary key (the default sort order), use the Order By property on the table's property sheet (see Figure 9–23).

Another benefit of indexes is that they provide an efficient way to order records. That is, if the records are to appear in a certain order in a database object, Access can use an index instead of physically having to rearrange the records in the database. Physically rearranging the records in a different order can be a very time-consuming process.

To gain the benefits of an index, you must first create one. Access automatically creates an index on some special fields. If, for example, a table contains a field called Postal Code, Access would create an index for this field automatically. You must create any other indexes you determine would improve database performance, indicating the field or fields on which the index is to be built.

Although the index key will usually be a single field, it can be a combination of fields. For example, you might want to sort records by quantity within product type. In other words, the records are ordered by a combination of fields: Product Type and Quantity. An index can be used for this purpose by using a combination of fields for the index key. In this case, you must assign a name to the index. It is a good idea to assign a name that represents the combination of fields. For example, an index whose key is the combination of the Product Type and Quantity fields might be called TypeQuantity.

How Access Uses Indexes

Access uses indexes automatically. If you request that data be sorted in a particular order and Access determines that an index is available that it can use to make the process efficient, it will do so automatically. If no index is available, it will still sort the data in the order you requested; it will just take longer than with the index.

Similarly, if you request that Access locate a particular record that has a certain value in a particular field, Access will use an index if an appropriate one exists. If not, it will have to examine each record until it finds the one you want.

BTW
Indexes
The most common structure for high-performance indexes is called a B-tree. It is a highly efficient structure that supports very rapid access to records in the database as well as a rapid alternative to sorting records. Virtually all systems use some version of the B-tree structure.

To Create a Single-Field Index

The following steps create a single-field index on the Vendor Name field in the Veterinary Vendors table. *Why? This index will make finding vendors based on their name more efficient than it would be without the index. It will also improve the efficiency of sorting by vendor name.*

- Open the Navigation Pane, open the Veterinary Vendors table in Design view, and then close the Navigation Pane.

- Select the Vendor Name field.

- Click the Indexed property box in the Field Properties pane to select the property.

- Click the arrow that appears to display the Indexed list.

- Click Yes (Duplicates OK) in the list to specify that duplicates are to be allowed (Figure 9–29).

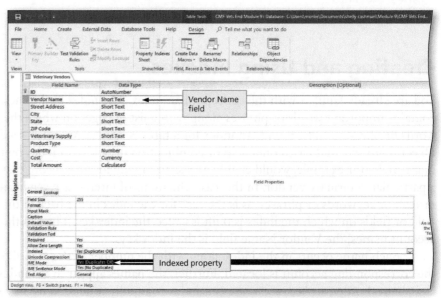

Figure 9–29

To Create a Multiple-Field Index

Creating **multiple-field indexes** — that is, indexes whose key is a combination of fields — involves a different process than creating single-field indexes. To create multiple-field indexes, you will use the Indexes button, enter a name for the index, and then enter the combination of fields that make up the index key. The following steps create a multiple-field index on the combination of Product Type and Quantity. *Why? CMF Vets needs to sort records on the combination of Product Type and Quantity and wants to improve the efficiency of this sort.* The steps assign this index the name TypeQuantity.

1

- Click the Indexes button, shown in Figure 9–29 (Table Tools Design tab | Show/Hide group), to display the Indexes: Veterinary Vendors window (Figure 9–30).

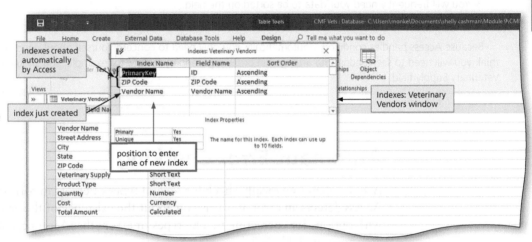

Figure 9–30

2

- Click the blank row (the row below Vendor Name) in the Index Name column in the Indexes: Veterinary Vendors window to select the position to enter the name of the new index.

- Type **TypeQuantity** as the index name, and then press TAB.

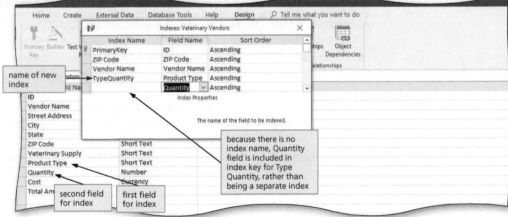

Figure 9–31

- Click the arrow in the Field Name column to produce a list of fields in the Veterinary Vendors table, and then select Product Type to enter the first of the two fields for the index.

- Press TAB three times to move to the Field Name column on the following row.

- Select the Quantity field in the same manner as the Product Type field (Figure 9–31).

3

- Close the Indexes: Veterinary Vendors window by clicking its Close button.

- Save your changes and close the table.

How do you determine when to use an index?

An index improves efficiency for sorting and finding records. On the other hand, indexes occupy space on your storage device. They also require Access to do extra work. Access must keep current all the indexes that have been created. The following guidelines help determine how and when to use indexes to their fullest advantage.

Create an index on a field (or combination of fields) if one or more of the following conditions are present:

1. The field is the primary key of the table. (Access creates this index automatically.)

2. The field is the foreign key in a relationship you have created.

3. You will frequently need your data to be sorted on the field.

4. You will frequently need to locate a record based on a value in this field.

Because Access handles condition 1 automatically, you only need to concern yourself about conditions 2, 3, and 4. If you think you will need to see vendor data arranged in order of veterinary supply, for example, you should create an index on the Veterinary Supply field.

Automatic Error Checking

Access can automatically check for several types of errors in forms and reports. When Access detects an error, it warns you about the existence of the error and provides you with options for correcting it. The types of errors that Access can detect and correct are shown in Table 9–2.

Table 9–2 Types of Errors	
Error Type	**Description**
Unassociated label and control	A label and control are selected and are not associated with each other.
New unassociated labels	A newly added label is not associated with any other control.
Keyboard shortcut errors	A shortcut key is invalid. This can happen because an unassociated label has a shortcut key, there are duplicate shortcut keys assigned, or a blank space is assigned as a shortcut key.
Invalid control properties	A control property is invalid. For example, the property contains invalid characters.
Common report errors	The report has invalid sorting or grouping specifications, or the report is wider than the page size.

To Enable Error Checking

Why? *For automatic error checking to take place, it must be enabled.* The following steps ensure that error checking is enabled and that errors are found and reported.

• Click File on the ribbon and then click the Options tab to display the Access Options dialog box.

• Click Object Designers to display the options for creating and modifying objects.

- Scroll down so that the Error checking area appears.

- Ensure the 'Enable error checking' check box is checked (Figure 9–32).

Q&A
What is the purpose of the other check boxes in the section?
All the other check boxes are checked, indicating that Access will perform all the various types of automatic error checking that are possible. If there were a particular type of error checking that you would prefer to skip, you would remove its check mark before clicking OK.

2

- Click OK to close the Access Options dialog box.

Figure 9–32

Error Indication

With error checking enabled, if an error occurs, a small triangle called an **error indicator** appears in the appropriate field or control. For example, you could change the label for Patient ID in the Appointments Master Form to include an ampersand (&) and letter A, making it a keyboard shortcut for this control. This would be a problem because A is already a shortcut for Appointment to Find. If this happens, an error indicator appears in both controls in which A is the keyboard shortcut, as shown in Figure 9–33.

Figure 9–33

BTW
Freezing Fields
The Freeze Fields command allows you to place a column or columns in a table on the left side of the table. As you scroll to the right, the column or columns remain visible. To freeze a column or columns, select the column(s) in Datasheet view, right-click and click Freeze Fields on the shortcut menu. To unfreeze fields, click the `Unfreeze All Fields' command on the shortcut menu. When you freeze a column, Access considers it a change to the layout of the table. When you close the table, Access will ask you if you want to save the changes.

Selecting a control containing an error indicator displays an 'Error Checking Options' button. Clicking the 'Error Checking Options' button produces the 'Error Checking Options' menu, as shown in Figure 9–34. The first line in the menu is simply a statement of the type of error that occurred, and the second is a description of the specific error. The Change Caption command gives a submenu of the captions that can be changed. The 'Edit Caption Property' command allows you to change the caption directly and is the simplest way to correct this error. The 'Help on This Error' command gives help on the specific error that occurred. You can choose to ignore the error by using the Ignore Error command. The final command, 'Error Checking Options', allows you to change the same error checking options shown in Figure 9–34.

Figure 9–34

The simplest way to fix the duplicate keyboard shortcut error is to edit the caption property. Clicking the 'Edit Caption Property' command produces a property sheet with the Caption property highlighted. You could then change the Caption property of one of the controls.

Data Type Parts

Access contains data type parts that are available on the More Fields gallery. Some data type parts, such as the Category part, consist of a single field. Others, such as the Address part, consist of multiple fields. In addition to the parts provided by Access, you can create your own parts. Quick Start fields act as a framework that lets you rapidly add several fields to a table in a single operation. For example, you could create a quick start field called Name-Address that consists of a Last Name field, a First Name field, a Street field, a City field, a State field, and a Postal Code field. Once you have created this quick start field, you can use it when creating tables in the future. By simply selecting the Name-Address quick start field, you will immediately add the Last Name, First Name, Street, City, State, and Postal Code fields to a table.

To Create Custom Data Parts

CMF Vets has decided that combining several address-related fields into a single data part would make future database updates easier. To create data parts in the Quick Start category from existing fields, you select the desired field or fields and then select the Save Selection as New Data Type command in the More Fields gallery. If you select multiple fields, the fields must be adjacent.

The following steps create a Quick Start field consisting of the Owner First Name, Last Name, Street, City, State, and Postal Code fields in the Owners table. *Why? Once you have created this Quick Start field, users can add this collection of fields to a table by simply clicking the Quick Start field.*

- Open the Navigation Pane, open the Owners table in Datasheet view, and then close the Navigation Pane.

- Click the column heading for the Owner First Name field to select the field.

- Hold the SHIFT key down and click the column heading for the Owner Postal Code field to select all the fields from the Owner First Name field to the Owner Postal Code field.

- Display the Table Tools Fields tab.

- Click the More Fields button (Table Tools Fields tab | Add & Delete group) to display the More Fields gallery (Figure 9–35).

Figure 9–35

- Click 'Save Selection as New Data Type' to display the Create New Data Type from Fields dialog box.

- Enter **Name-Address** as the name.

- Enter **First Name, Last Name, Street Address, City, State, Postal Code** as the description.

Q&A What is the purpose of the description?
When a user points to the Quick Start field you created, a ScreenTip will appear containing the description you entered.

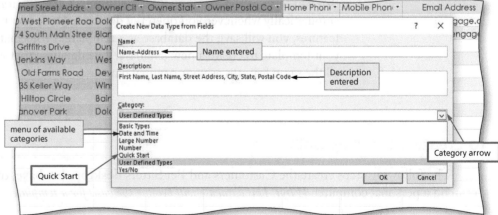

Figure 9–36

- Click the Category arrow to display a list of available categories (Figure 9–36).

- Click Quick Start to indicate the new data type will be added to the Quick Start category.

Q&A What is the difference between the Quick Start and User Defined Types category?

If you select the Quick Start category, the data type you create will be listed among the Quick Start data types that are part of Access. If you select the User Defined Types category, the data type you create will be in a separate category containing only those data types you create. In either case, however, clicking the data type will produce the same result.

- Click OK (Create New Data Type from Fields dialog box) to save the data type.

- When Access indicates that your template (that is, your Quick Start field) has been saved, click OK (Microsoft Access dialog box).

- Close the table.

- **sam** ⬆ If necessary, click No when asked if you want to save the changes to the layout of the table.

CONSIDER THIS

How do you rearrange fields that are not adjacent?

When adding new data type fields, you can hide the fields that keep your fields from being adjacent. To hide a field, right-click the field to display a shortcut menu, and then click Hide Fields on the shortcut menu. To later unhide a field you have hidden, right-click any column heading and then click Unhide Fields on the shortcut menu. You will see a list of fields with a check box for each field. The hidden field will not have a check mark in the check box. To unhide the field, click the check box for the field.

Templates

BTW

Templates and Application Parts
By default, user-created templates and application parts are stored in the C:\Users\user name\AppData\Roaming\Microsoft\Templates\Access folder.

Often, Access users find that they create and use multiple databases containing the same objects. You can use a template to create a complete database application containing tables, forms, queries, and other objects. There are many templates available for Access.

You can create your own template from an existing database. To do so, you must first ensure that you have created a database with all the characteristics you want in your template. In this module, the database you create will have two tables, a query, two single-item forms, two datasheet forms that use macros, and a navigation form that will serve as the main menu. In addition, the navigation form will be set to appear automatically whenever you open the database. Once you have incorporated all these features, you will save the database as a template. From that point on, anyone can use your template to create a new database. The database that is created will incorporate all the same features as your original database.

To Create a Desktop Database

The following steps create the Customers and Pet Sitters **desktop database**, that is, a database designed to run on a personal computer. *Why? This database will become the basis for a template.*

1

- Click File on the ribbon to open the Backstage view.

- Click the New tab.

- Click the 'Blank database' button.

- Type **Customers and Pet Sitters** as the name of the database file.

- Click the 'Browse for a location to put your database' button to display the File New Database dialog box, navigate to the desired save

location (for example, the Access folder in the CIS 101 folder), and then click OK to return to the Backstage view (Figure 9–37).

Figure 9–37

2

- Click the Create button to create the database (Figure 9–38).

Figure 9–38

To Add Fields to the Table

The tables will have an autonumber ID field as the primary key. The field that would normally be the primary key will be designated both required and unique, two characteristics of the primary key.

The following steps add the Sitter Number, Last Name, First Name, Street, City, State, Postal Code, Rate, and Commission to a table. The Rate field is a Number field and the Commission field is a Currency field.

The steps designate the Sitter Number field as both required and unique. They add the Last Name, First Name, Street, City, State, and Postal Code as a single operation by using the Quick Start field created earlier. After adding the fields, they save the table using the name, Sitter. They also change the field size for the Rate field (a Number data type field) to Single so that the field can contain decimal places.

1

- **sam** ↓ Click the 'Click to Add' column heading and select Short Text as the data type.

- Type **Sitter Number** as the field name.

- Click the white space below the field name to complete the change of the name. Click the white space a second time to select the field.

- Change the field size to 2.

Figure 9–39

- Click the Required check box (Table Tools Fields tab | Field Validation group) to make the field a required field.

- Click the Unique check box (Table Tools Fields tab | Field Validation group) so that Access will ensure that values in the field are unique (Figure 9–39).

2

- Click under the 'Click to Add' column heading to produce an insertion point in the next field.

- Click the More Fields button (Table Tools Fields tab | Add & Delete group) to display the More Fields menu (Figure 9–40).

Figure 9–40

- Scroll as necessary to display the Name-Address Quick Start field you created earlier and then click the Name-Address Quick Start field to add the Owner First Name, Owner Last Name, Owner Street Address, Owner City, Owner State, and Owner Postal Code fields (Figure 9–41).

Figure 9–41

- Delete the word "Owner" from the fields. Add the Rate and Commission fields as the last two fields. The Rate field has the Number data type and the Commission field has the Currency data type.

- Save the table, assigning `Sitter` as the table name.

- Switch to Design view, select the Rate field, and change the field size to Single so that the Rate field can include decimal places.

- Save and close the table.

Q&A What if I don't see the quick start field?

If you have switched computers since you created the custom data parts, you may not see the quick start field Name-Address. Go back and recreate that quick start field before continuing.

To Create a Second Table

The following steps create the Customer table. The steps add a lookup field for Sitter Number to relate the two tables. *Why? Because no existing field links the two tables, the relationship between the tables needs to be implemented using a lookup field.*

- Display the Create tab (Figure 9–42).

Figure 9–42

2

- Click the Table button (Create tab | Tables group) to create a new table.

- Click the 'Click to Add' column heading and select Short Text as the data type.

- Type **Customer Number** as the field name.

- Click the white space below the field name to complete

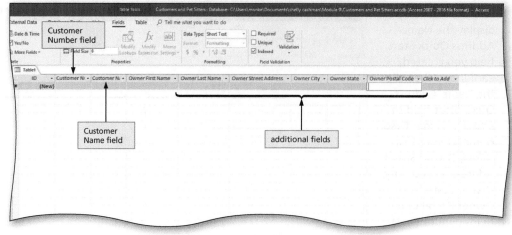

Figure 9–43

the change of the name. Click the white space a second time to select the field.

- Change the field size to 5.

- Save the table, assigning **Customer** as the table name.

- Switch to design view, make the Customer Number the key field and delete the ID field. Save your changes to the table.

- Switch back to the datasheet view.

- In a similar fashion, add the Customer Name field and change the field size to 50. Do not check the Required or Unique check boxes.

- Click under the 'Click to Add' column heading to produce an insertion point in the next field.

- Click the More Fields button (Table Tools Fields tab | Add & Delete group) to display the More Fields menu (see Figure 9–41).

- Click the Name-Address Quick Start field that you added earlier to add the Owner First Name, Owner Last Name, Owner Street Address, Owner City, Owner State, and Owner Postal Code fields (Figure 9–43).

3

- Right-click the Owner Last Name field to produce a shortcut menu, and then click Delete Field to delete the field.

- Right-click the Owner First Name field to produce a shortcut menu, and then click Delete Field to delete the field.

- Delete the word "Owner" from the other fields.

- Add the Amount Paid and Current Due fields. Both fields have the Currency data type.

- Save the table.

- Scroll, if necessary, so that the 'Click to Add' column appears on your screen.

- Click the 'Click to Add' column heading to display a menu of available data types (Figure 9–44).

Figure 9–44

4

- Click Lookup & Relationship to display the Lookup Wizard dialog box (Figure 9–45).

Figure 9–45

5

- Click the Next button to display the next Lookup Wizard screen, and then click the Sitter table to select it so that you can add a lookup field for the Sitter Number to the Customer table (Figure 9–46).

Figure 9–46

6

- Click the Next button, and then select the Sitter Number, First Name, and Last Name fields for the columns in the lookup field (Figure 9–47).

Figure 9–47

● Click Next, select the Sitter Number field for the sort order, and then click Next again (Figure 9–48).

I see the ID field listed when I am selecting the Sitter Number field for the sort order. Did I do something wrong?
No. Access automatically included the ID field.

Figure 9–48

● Ensure the 'Hide key column (recommended)' check box is selected, and then click Next.

● Type **Sitter Number** as the label for the lookup field.

● Click the 'Enable Data Integrity' check box to select it (Figure 9–49).

What is the effect of selecting Enable Data Integrity?
Access will enforce referential integrity for the Sitter Number. That is, Access will not allow a Sitter number in a customer record that does not match the number of a Sitter in the Sitter table.

Figure 9–49

● Click Finish to add the lookup field.

● Save and close the table.

To Import the Data

Now that the tables have been created, you need to add data to them. You could enter the data, or if the data is already in electronic form, you could import the data. The data for the Sitter and Customer tables is included in the Data Files as text files. The following steps import the data.

1 With the Customers and Pet Sitters database open, display the External Data tab, and then choose the New Data Source button (External Data tab | Import & Link group), point to From File and then click the Text File command.

2 Click the Browse button (Get External Data – Text File dialog box) and browse to select the location of the files to be imported (for example, the Access folder in the CIS 101 folder).

3 Select the Sitter text file, and then click the Open button.

4 Click the 'Append a copy of records to the table' option button to select it, select the Sitter table, and then click OK.

5 Ensure that the Delimited option button is selected, and then click the Next button.

6 Ensure that the Comma option button is selected, click the Next button, and then click the Finish button.

7 Click Close to close the Get External Data – Text File dialog box without saving the import steps.

8 Use the technique shown in Steps 1 through 7 to import the Customer text file into the Customer table.

To Create a Query Relating the Tables

The following steps create a query that relates the Customer and Sitter tables.

1 Display the Create tab and then click the Query Design button (Create tab | Queries group) to create a new query.

2 Click the Customer table, click the Add button, click the Sitter table, click the Add button, and then click the Close button to close the Show Table dialog box.

3 Double-click the Customer Name, and Sitter Number fields from the Customer table. Double-click the First Name and Last Name fields from the Sitter table to add the fields to the design grid.

4 Click the Save button on the Quick Access Toolbar to save the query, type `Customer-Sitter Query` as the name of the query, and then click OK.

5 Close the query.

Creating Forms

There are several types of forms that need to be created for this database. The Customer and Sitter detail forms show a single record at a time. The Customer and Sitter forms are intended to look like the corresponding table in Datasheet view. Finally, the main menu is a navigation form.

BTW

Importing Tables from Other Databases
You can import tables from other Access databases. To do so, click the Access button (External Data tab | Import & Link group) then navigate to the location containing the database and select the database. Click the Open button. Ensure that the 'Import tables, queries, forms, reports, macros, and modules into the current database' option button is selected and click OK. When the Import Object dialog box appears, select the table or tables you want to import and then click OK. You also can import other objects by clicking the appropriate object tabs.

BTW

Rearranging Fields in a Query
If you add fields to a query in the wrong order, you can select the field in the design grid, and drag it to the appropriate location.

To Create Single-Item Forms

The following steps create two single-item forms, that is, forms that display a single record at a time. The first form, called Customer Details, is for the Customer table. The second form is for the Sitter table and is called Sitter Details.

1 Select the Customer table in the Navigation Pane and then display the Create tab.

2 Click the Form button (Create tab | Forms group) to create a single-item form for the Customer table.

3 Click the Save button on the Quick Access Toolbar, type `Customer Details` as the name of the form, click OK (Save As dialog box) to save the form, and then close the form.

4 Select the Sitter table, display the Create tab, and then click the Form button (Create tab | Forms group) to create a form for the Sitter table that shows the customers using that particular sitter.

5 Save the form, using Sitter Details as the form name.

6 Close the form.

To Create a Navigation Form

The following steps create a navigation form containing a single row of horizontal tabs. The steps save the form using the name, Main Menu. ***Why?*** *This form is intended to function as a menu.* The steps change the form title and add the appropriate tabs.

1

- Display the Create tab and then click the Navigation button (Create tab | Forms group) to show the menu of available navigation forms.

- Click Horizontal Tabs in the menu to create a form with a navigation control in which the tabs are arranged in a single row, horizontally.

- If a field list appears, click the 'Add Existing Fields' button (Form Layout Tools Design tab | Tools group) to remove the field list.

Figure 9–50

- Save the navigation form, using Main Menu as the form name.

- Click the form title twice, once to select it and the second time to produce an insertion point.

- Erase the current title and then type `Customers and Sitters` as the new title (Figure 9–50).

- One at a time, drag the Customer Details form, and the Sitter Details form to the positions shown in Figure 9–51.

- Save and close the form.

What should I do if I made a mistake and added a form to the wrong location? You can rearrange the tabs by dragging. However, the simplest way to correct a mistake is to click the Undo button to reverse your most recent action. You can also choose to simply close the form without saving it and then start over.

Figure 9–51

To Select a Startup Form

If the database includes a navigation form, it is common to select the navigation form as a **startup form,** which launches when the user opens the database. *Why? Designating the navigation form as a startup form ensures that the form will appear automatically when a user opens the database.* The following steps designate the navigation form as a startup form.

1

- Click File on the ribbon to display the Backstage view (Figure 9–52).

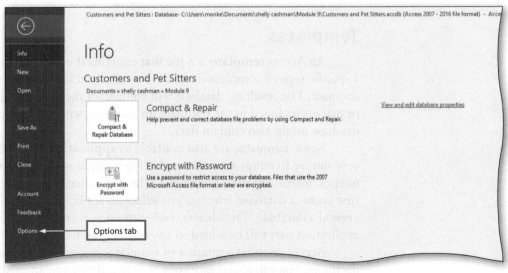

Figure 9–52

2
- Click the Options tab.
- Click Current Database (Access Options dialog box) to select the options for the current database.
- Click the Display Form arrow to display the list of available forms.
- Click Main Menu to select it as the form that will be automatically displayed whenever the database is opened (Figure 9–53).

Figure 9–53

3
- Click OK (Access Options dialog box) to save your changes.
- Click OK (Microsoft Access dialog box) when Access displays a message indicating that you must close and reopen the database for the change to take effect.
- Close the database.

Break Point: If you wish to stop working through the module at this point, you can close Access now. You can resume the project at a later time by starting Access, and continuing to follow the steps from this location forward.

Templates

An Access **template** is a file that contains the elements needed to produce a specific type of complete database. You can select a template when you create a database. The resulting database will contain all the tables, queries, forms, reports, and/ or macros included in the template. In addition, with some templates, the resulting database might also contain data.

Some templates are also available as **application parts.** Application parts are very similar to templates in that selecting a single application part can create tables, queries, forms, reports, and macros. The difference is you select a template when you first create a database, whereas you select an application part after you have already created a database. The objects (tables, queries, forms, reports, and macros) in the application part will be added to any objects you have already created.

Access provides a number of templates representing a variety of types of databases. You can also create your own template from an existing database. When you create a template, you can choose to create an application part as well. When creating templates and application parts, you can also include data if desired.

To Create a Template and Application Part

The following steps create a template from the Customers and Pet Sitters database. **Why?** *The Customers and Pet Sitters database now contains all the tables, queries, and forms you want in the template. You will then be able to use the template when you want to create similar databases.* The steps also create an application part from the database so that you can reuse the parts in other databases.

- Open the Customers and Pet Sitters database and enable the content (Figure 9–54).

Figure 9–54

- Close the Main Menu form.
- Open the Backstage view.
- Click the Save As tab.
- Click the Template button in the Save Database As area to indicate you are creating a template (Figure 9–55).

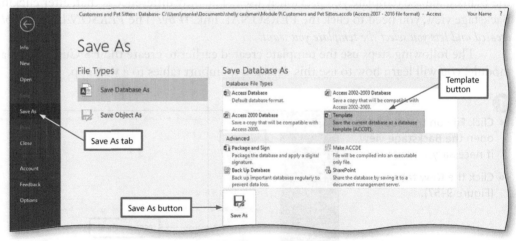

Figure 9–55

❸

- Click the Save As button to display the Create New Template from This Database dialog box.
- Type **Customers and Pet Sitters** as the name for the new template.
- Type **Database of customers and pet sitters with navigation form menu.** as the description.
- Click the Application Part check box to indicate that you also want to create an application part.
- Click the 'Include All Data in Package' check box to indicate you want to include the data in the database as part of the template (Figure 9–56).

Q&A

Why include data?

Anytime a user creates a database using the template, the database will automatically include data. This enables the users to see what any reports, forms, or queries look like with data in them. Once the users have the reports, forms, and queries the way they want them, they can delete all this data. At that point, they can begin adding their own data to the database.

 4

• Click OK (Create New Template from This Database dialog box) to create the template.

• **sam** ⬆ When Access indicates that the template has been successfully saved, click OK (Microsoft Access dialog box).

Figure 9–56

To Use the Template

You can use the Customers and Pet Sitters template just as you would use any other template, such as the Blank database template you previously used. The only difference is that, after clicking the New tab in the Backstage view, you need to click the PERSONAL link. *Why? The PERSONAL link displays any templates you created and lets you select the template you want.*

The following steps use the template created earlier to create the ES Customers database. Later in the module, you will learn how to use this database to import tables to a web app.

1

• Click File on the ribbon to open the Backstage view, if necessary.

• Click the New tab (Figure 9–57).

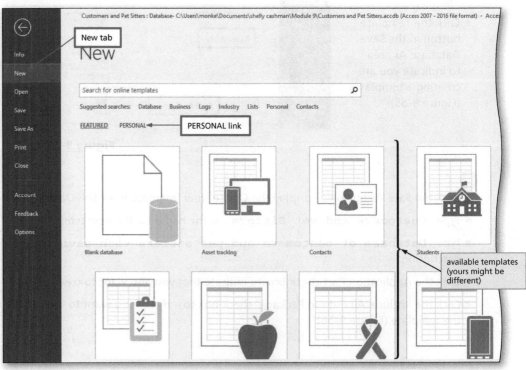

Figure 9–57

2

- Click the PERSONAL
  link to display
  the templates
  you have created
  (Figure 9–58).

3

- Click the Customers
  and Pet Sitters
  template that you
  created earlier.

- Type **ES
  Customers** as
  the name of the
  database and then
  navigate to the
  location where you
  will store the new database (for example, the Access folder in the CIS 101 folder).

- Click the Create button to create the database from the template.

- Close the database.

- If desired, sign out of your Microsoft account.

- Exit Access.

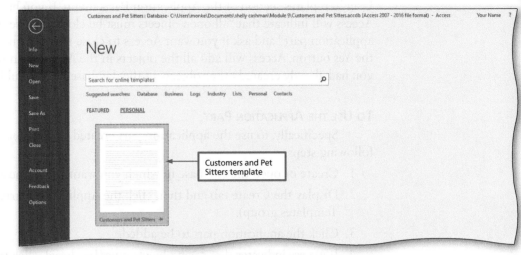

Figure 9–58

Note: Unless your instructor indicates otherwise, you are strongly encouraged to simply read the material in this module from this point on without carrying out any operations. If you decide to try it for yourself, it is important to make a backup copy of your database and store it in a secure location before performing the operation. That way, if something damages your database or you can no longer access your database, you still can use the backup copy.

Using an Application Part

To use the application part you created, you first need to create a database. After doing so, you click the Application Parts button (Create tab | Templates group) to display the Application Parts menu (Figure 9–59).

Figure 9–59

You can then click the application part you created, which will be located in the User Templates section of the Application Parts menu. If you have any open objects, Access will indicate that "all open objects must be closed before instantiating this application part" and ask if you want Access to close all open objects. After you click the Yes button, Access will add all the objects in the Application part to the database. If you had already created other objects in the database, they would still be included.

To Use the Application Part

Specifically, to use the application part created earlier, you would use the following steps.

1. Create or open the database in which you want to use the application part.
2. Display the Create tab and then click the Application Parts button (Create tab | Templates group).
3. Click the application part to be added.
4. If Access indicates that open objects must be closed, click the Yes button.

Blank Forms Application Parts

Blank Forms application parts (see Figure 9–59) represent a way to create certain types of forms. To do so, you click the Application Parts button to display the gallery of application part styles, and then click the desired type of form, for example, 1 Right. Access then creates a form with the desired characteristics and assigns it a name. It does not open the form, but you can see the form in the Navigation Pane (Figure 9–60).

Figure 9–60

You can modify the form by opening the form in Layout or Design view (Figure 9–61). This particular form automatically creates a Save button. Clicking this button when you are using the form will save changes to the current record. The form also automatically includes a Save & Close button. Clicking this button will save changes to the current record and then close the form.

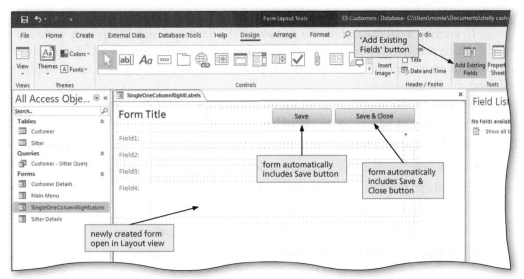

Figure 9–61

To add the specific fields you want to the form, display a field list. You can then drag a field onto the form (Figure 9–62). Once you have added the field, you can change the corresponding label by clicking the label to select it, clicking the label a second time to produce an insertion point, and then making the desired change.

Figure 9–62

Encrypting a Database

Encrypting refers to the storing of data in the database in an encoded, or encrypted, format. Anytime a user stores or modifies data in the encrypted database, the database management system (DBMS) will encode the data before actually updating the database. Before a legitimate user retrieves the data using the DBMS, the data will be decoded. The whole encrypting process is transparent to a legitimate user; that is, he or she is not even aware it is happening. If an unauthorized user attempts to bypass all the controls of the DBMS and get to the database through a utility program or a word processor, however, he or she will only be able to see the encoded, and unreadable, version of the data. In Access, you encrypt a database and set a password as part of the same operation.

BTW
Encryption and Passwords
Encryption helps prevent unauthorized use of an Access database. Consider using encryption when the database contains sensitive data, such as medical records or employee records. Passwords should be eight or more characters in length. The longer the length of the password and the more random the characters, the more difficult it is for someone to determine. Use a combination of uppercase and lowercase letters as well as numbers and special symbols when you create a password. Make sure that you remember your password. If you forget it, there is no method for retrieving it. You will be unable to open the encrypted database.

To Open a Database in Exclusive Mode

To encrypt a database and set a password, the database must be open in exclusive mode, which prevents other users from accessing the database in any way. To open a database in exclusive mode, you use the Open arrow (Figure 9–63) rather than simply clicking the Open button.

To open a database in exclusive mode, you would use the following steps.

1. If necessary, close any open databases.
2. Click Open or click 'Open Other Files' in Backstage view to display the Open screen.
3. Click Browse on the Open screen to display the Open dialog box.
4. Navigate to the location of the database to be opened.
5. Click the name of the database to be opened.
6. Click the Open arrow to display the Open button menu.
7. Click Open Exclusive to open the database in exclusive mode.

Figure 9–63

What is the purpose of the other modes?
The Open option opens the database in a mode so that it can be shared by other users. Open Read-Only allows you to read the data in the database, but not update the database.

Encrypting a Database with a Password

If you wanted to encrypt the database with a password, you would open the Backstage view (Figure 9–64).

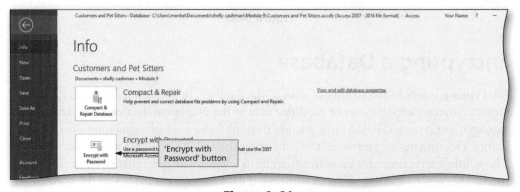

Figure 9–64

You would then click 'Encrypt with Password' to display the Set Database Password dialog box, and then enter the password you have chosen in both the Password text box and Verify text box (Figure 9–65).

Figure 9–65

To Encrypt a Database with a Password

With the database open in exclusive mode, you would use the following steps to encrypt the database with a password.

1. Click File on the ribbon to open the Backstage view and ensure the Info tab is selected.

2. Click the 'Encrypt with Password' button to display the Set Database Password dialog box.

3. Type the desired password in the Password text box in the Set Database Password dialog box.

4. Press the TAB key and then type the password again in the Verify text box.

5. Click OK to encrypt the database and set the password.

6. If you get a message indicating that row level locking will be ignored, click OK.

7. Close the database.

Is the password case sensitive?

Yes, you must enter the password using the same case you used when you created it.

CONSIDER THIS

Opening a Database with a Password

When you open a database that has a password, you will be prompted to enter your password in the Password Required dialog box. Once you have done so, click OK. Assuming you have entered your password correctly, Access will then open the database.

Decrypting a Database and Removing a Password

If the encryption and the password are no longer necessary, you can decrypt the database. The database will no longer have a password. If you later found you needed the database to be encrypted, you could repeat the steps to encrypt the database and add a password. The button to encrypt a database with a password has changed to Decrypt Database (Figure 9–66).

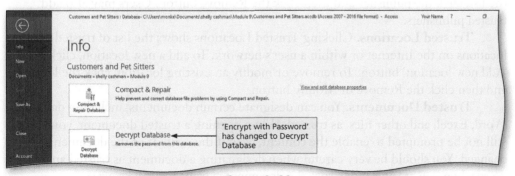

Figure 9–66

To Decrypt the Database and Remove the Password

To decrypt a database that you have previously encrypted and remove the password, you would use the following steps.

1. Open the database to be decrypted in exclusive mode, entering your password when requested.
2. Open the Backstage view and ensure the Info tab is selected.
3. Click the Decrypt Database button to display the Unset Database Password dialog box.
4. Type the password in the Password dialog box.
5. Click OK to remove the password and decrypt the database.
6. Close the database.

The Trust Center

BTW
Security
Security is the prevention of unauthorized access to a database. Within an organization, the database administrator determines the types of access individual users can have to the database. Various government rules and regulations, such as the Sarbannes-Oxley Act (SOX) and the Health Insurance Portability and Accountability Act (HIPPA), require database administrators to have strict security procedures in place to protect data from unauthorized users.

The Trust Center is a feature within Access where you can set security options and also find the latest information on technology related to privacy, safety, and security. To use the Trust Center, you click File on the ribbon and then click the Options tab to display the Access Options dialog box. You then click Trust Center to display the Trust Center content (Figure 9–67). You would then click the 'Trust Center Settings' button to display the Trust Center dialog box in which you can make changes in the following categories.

Figure 9–67

Trusted Publishers. Clicking Trusted Publishers in the Trust Center dialog box shows the list of trusted software publishers. To view details about a trusted publisher, click the publisher and then click the View button. To remove a trusted publisher from the list, click the publisher and then click the Remove button. Users may also add trusted publishers.

Trusted Locations. Clicking Trusted Locations shows the list of trusted locations on the Internet or within a user's network. To add a new location, click the 'Add new location' button. To remove or modify an existing location, click the location and then click the Remove or Modify button.

Trusted Documents. You can designate certain documents, including database, Word, Excel, and other files, as trusted. When opening a trusted document, you will not be prompted to enable the content, even if the content of the document has changed. You should be very careful when designating a document as trusted and only do so when you are absolutely sure the document is from a trusted source.

Add-ins. Add-ins are additional programs that you can install and use within Access. Some come with Access and are typically installed using the Access Setup program. Others can be purchased from other vendors. Clicking Add-ins gives you the opportunity to specify restrictions concerning Add-ins.

ActiveX Settings. When you use ActiveX controls within an Office app, Office prompts you to accept the controls. The ActiveX settings allow you to determine the level of prompting from Office.

Macro Settings. Macros written by other users have the potential to harm your computer; for example, a macro could spread a virus. The Trust Center uses special criteria, including valid digital signatures, reputable certificates, and trusted publishers, to determine whether a macro is safe. If the Trust Center discovers a macro that is potentially unsafe, it will take appropriate action. The action the Trust Center takes depends on the Macro Setting you have selected. Clicking Macro Settings enables you to select or change this setting.

Message Bar. Clicking Message Bar lets you choose whether the message bar should appear when content has been blocked.

Privacy Options. Clicking Privacy Options lets you set security settings to protect your personal privacy.

Trusted Add-in Catalogs. Use this option to specify trusted catalogs of web add-ins. You can also indicate whether Access will allow web add-ins to start.

BTW
Active X controls
Active X controls are small programs that can run within an Office app. The calendar control is an example of an Active X control.

Locking a Database

By locking a database, you can prevent users from viewing or modifying VBA code in your database or from making changes to the design of forms or reports while still allowing them to update records. When you lock the database, Access changes the file name extension from .accdb to .accde. To do so, you would use the Make ACCDE command shown in Figure 9–3.

BTW
Locked Databases
When you create a locked database, the original database remains unchanged and is still available for use.

To Create a Locked Database (ACCDE File)

To lock a database, you would use the following steps.

1. With the database open, click File on the ribbon to open the Backstage view.
2. Click the Save As tab.
3. Click Make ACCDE in the Advanced area.
4. Click the Save As button.
5. In the Save As dialog box, indicate a location and name for the ACCDE file.
6. Click the Save button in the Save As dialog box to create the file.

Using the Locked Database

You would use an ACCDE file just as you use the databases with which you are now familiar, with two exceptions. First, you must select ACCDE files in the 'Files of type' box when opening the file. Second, you will not be able to modify any source code or change the design of any forms or reports. If you right-clicked the Customer form, for example, you would find that the Design View command on the shortcut menu is dimmed, as are many other commands (Figure 9–68).

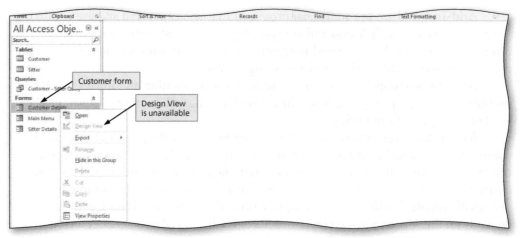

Figure 9–68

It is very important that you save your original database in case you ever need to make changes to VBA code or to the design of a form or report. You cannot use the ACCDE file to make such changes, nor can you convert the ACCDE file back to the ACCDB file format.

Record Locking

You can indicate how records are to be locked when multiple users are using a database at the same time. To do so, click File on the ribbon, click the Options tab, and then click Client Settings. Scroll down so that the Advanced area appears on the screen (Figure 9–69).

Figure 9–69

If you wanted the default open mode to be exclusive (only one user can use the database at a time) rather than shared (multiple users can simultaneously use the database), you could click the Exclusive option button. You can also select the approach you want for record locking by clicking the appropriate record locking option button. The possible approaches to record locking are shown in Table 9–3.

Table 9–3	Record Locking Approaches
Locking Type	**Description**
No locks	When you edit a record, Access will not lock the record. Thus, other users also could edit the same record at the same time. When you have finished your changes and attempt to save the record, Access will give you the option of overwriting the other user's changes (not recommended), copying your changes to the clipboard, or canceling your changes.
All records	All records will be locked as long as you have the database open. No other user can edit or lock the records during this time.
Edited record	When you edit a record, Access will lock the record. When other users attempt to edit the same record, they will not be able to do so. Instead, they will see the locked record indicator.

Database Splitting

You can split a database into two databases, one called the back-end database containing only the table data, and another database called the front-end database containing the other objects. Only a single copy of the back-end database can exist, but each user could have his or her own copy of the front-end database. Each user would create the desired custom reports, forms, and other objects in his or her own front-end database, thereby not interfering with any other user.

When splitting a database, the database to be split must be open. In the process, you will identify a name and location for the back-end database that will be created by the Access splitter. In the process, you would display the Database Splitter dialog box (Figure 9–70).

Figure 9–70

You would also have to select a location for the back-end database (Figure 9–71). Access assigns a name to the back-end database that ends with an underscore and the letters, be. You can override this name if you prefer.

Figure 9–71

TO SPLIT THE DATABASE

To split a database, you would use the following steps.

1. Open the database to be split.
2. Display the Database Tools tab.
3. Click the Access Database button (Database Tools tab | Move Data group) to display the Database Splitter dialog box.
4. Click the Split Database button to display the Create Back-end Database dialog box.
5. Type a file name to the one you want.
6. Select a location for the back-end database.
7. Click the Split button to split the database.
8. Click OK to close the dialog box reporting that the split was successful.

The Front-End and Back-End Databases

The database has now been split into separate front-end and back-end databases. The front-end database is the one that you will use; it contains all the queries, reports, forms, and other components from the original database. The front-end database only contains links to the tables, however, instead of the tables themselves (Figure 9–72). The back-end database contains the actual tables but does not contain any other objects.

Figure 9–72

Summary

In this module you have learned to convert Access databases to and from earlier versions; use Microsoft Access tools to analyze and document an Access database; add custom categories and groups to the Navigation Pane; use table and database properties; use field properties to create a custom input mask; allow zero-length strings; create indexes; use automatic error checking; create custom data parts; create and use templates and application parts; encrypt a database and set a password; understand the Trust Center; lock a database; and split a database.

What decisions will you need to make when administering your own databases?
Use these guidelines as you complete the assignments in this module and administer your own databases outside of this class.

1. Determine whether you should create any templates, application parts, or data type parts.

   a. Is there a particular combination of tables, queries, forms, reports, and/or macros that you would like to enable users to easily include in their databases? If so, you could create a template and an application part containing the specific objects you want them to be able to include.

   b. Is there a particular collection of fields that you would like to enable users to include in a table with a single click? If so, you could create a data type part containing those fields.

2. Determine whether a database needs to be converted to or from an earlier version.

   a. Do users of a previous version of Access need to be able to use the database? If so, you will need to be sure the database does not contain any features that would prevent it from being converted.

   b. Do you use a database that was created in an earlier version of Access that you would like to use in Access 2019? If so, you can convert the database for use in Access 2019.

3. Determine when to analyze and/or document the database.

   a. Once you create a database, you should use the table and performance analyzers to determine if any changes to the structure are warranted.

   b. You should also document the database.

4. Determine the most useful way to customize the Navigation Pane.

   a. Would it be helpful to have custom categories and groups?

   b. What objects should be in the groups?

   c. Would it be helpful to restrict the objects that appear to only those whose names contain certain characters?

5. Determine any table-wide validation rules.

   a. Are there any validation rules that involve more than a single field?

6. Determine any custom database properties.

   a. Are there properties that would be helpful in documenting the database that are not included in the list of database properties you can use?

7. Determine indexes.

   a. Examine retrieval and sorting requirements to determine possible indexes. Indexes can make both retrieval and sorting more efficient.

8. Determine whether the database should be encrypted.

   a. If you need to protect the security of the database's contents, you should strongly consider encryption.

   b. As part of the process, you will also set a password.

9. Determine whether the database should be locked.

   a. Should users be able to change the design of forms, reports, and/or macros?

10. Determine whether the database should be split.

   a. It is often more efficient to split the database into a back-end database, which contains only the table data, and a front-end database, which contains other objects, such as queries, forms, and reports.

How should you submit solutions to questions in the assignments identified with a symbol?
Every assignment in this book contains one or more questions identified with a symbol. These questions require you to think beyond the assigned database. Present your solutions to the questions in the format required by your instructor. Possible formats may include one or more of these options: write the answer; create a document that contains the answer; present your answer to the class; discuss your answer in a group; record the answer as audio or video using a webcam, smartphone, or portable media player; or post answers on a blog, wiki, or website.

Apply Your Knowledge

Reinforce the skills and apply the concepts you learned in this module.

Administering the Financial Services Database

Instructions: Start Access. Open the Support_AC_Financial Services database. (If you did not complete the exercise, see your instructor for a copy of the modified database.)

Perform the following tasks:

1. Open the Client table in Design view and create a custom input mask for the Client Number field. The first two characters of the client number must be uppercase letters and the last two characters must be numerical digits.

2. Create an index on the combination of Client Type and Advisor Number. Name the index TypeAdv.

3. Save the changes to the Client table.

4. Use the Database Documenter to produce detailed documentation for the Services table. Export the documentation to a Word RTF file. Change the name of the file to LastName _Documentation.rtf where LastName is your last name.

5. Use the Table Analyzer to analyze the table structure of the Client table. Open the Word RTF file that you created in Step 4 and make a note of the results of the analysis at the end of the file.

6. Use the Performance Analyzer to analyze all the tables in the database. Describe the results of your analysis in your RTF file.

7. Populate the Status custom property for the database to a Live version.

8. Add a Production version with today's date.

9. Submit the revised Financial Services database and the RTF file in the format specified by your instructor.

10. ✳ Can you convert the Financial Services database to an Access 2002–2003 database? Why or why not?

Extend Your Knowledge

Extend the skills you learned in this module and experiment with new skills. You may need to use Help to complete the assignment.

Instructions: Start Access. Open the Support_AC_Healthy Pets database. (If you did not complete the exercise, see your instructor for a copy of the modified database.)

Perform the following tasks:

1. Create a Navigation Form that is called Clients and Technicians that contains a single row with two horizontal tabs. Add two forms to the Navigation Form: Clients by Technician Form and Technician Form.

2. Change the Current Database options to ensure that the Clients and Technicians navigation form opens automatically.

3. Currently, when you open the Potential Clients table in Datasheet view, the table is ordered by Client Number. Change the property for the table so the table is in order by Client Name.

4. Create an additional table called Potential Technicians. Add the Name-Address Quick Start fields to easily create the fields. Remove the word Owner from each field name. Save the table and close it.

5. Customize the Navigation Pane by adding a custom category called Clients. Then add two custom groups, Detailed and Summary, to the Clients category.

6. Add the Client table, the Potential Clients table, and the Clients by Technician Form to the Detailed custom group under the Clients category. Add both client summary reports to the Summary custom group under the Clients category.

7. Submit the revised database in the format specified by your instructor.

8. ✹ What advantages are there to using a custom Navigation Pane as opposed to the standard Navigation Pane?

Expand Your World

Create a solution which uses cloud and web technologies by learning and investigating on your own from general guidance.

Problem: There are many ways to share an Access database. Some ways require each user to have Microsoft Access installed on their computer, while others do not. The method you select depends on factors such as need and available resources.

Instructions: Perform the following tasks:
1. Create a blog, a Google document, or a Word document on OneDrive on which to store your findings.

2. Use the web to research different ways to share an Access database such as CMF Vets with others. Be sure to note any specific resources needed, such as an Access database or a SharePoint server, any costs involved, and provide examples of different reasons for sharing a database such as CMF Vets. Record your findings in your blog, Google document, or Word document, being sure to appropriately reference your sources.

3. Submit the assignment in the format specified by your instructor.

4. ✹ Based on your research, what method would you choose to share your Access databases?

In the Labs

Design, create, modify, and/or use a database following the guidelines, concepts, and skills presented in this module.

Lab: Administering the Lancaster College Database

Part 1:   The administration at Lancaster College has asked you to perform a number of tasks. Open the Support_AC_Lancaster College database. (If you did not complete the exercise, see your instructor for a copy of the modified database.) Use the concepts and techniques presented in this module to perform each of the following tasks.

  a. Create a main menu navigation form that includes all the forms in the database. Give the main menu an appropriate title.

  b. Change the Current Database options to ensure that the Main Menu form opens automatically when the user opens the database.

c. Open the Coach table in Design view and Create an index for the LastName field that allows duplicates. Save the changes.

d. Open the Participation table in Design view and create an index named StudentIDSportName on the StudentID and the SportName.

e. Open the Sport table in Design view and create a validation rule to ensure that the minimum players are always less than the maximum players. Include validation text.

f. Open the Student table in Datasheet view and add the Quick Start Status field to the table.

g. Create a template of the database (with an application part) and call it Lancaster College Template.

h. From that template, create a new database called your initials college. Close the database.

Submit your assignment in the format specified by your instructor.

Part 2: You made several decisions while completing this project, including using an input mask and validation rule. What was the rationale behind your decisions? Would you add other input masks or validation rules to the Lancaster College database?

10 Using SQL

Objectives

You will have mastered the material in this module when you can:

- Understand the SQL language and how to use it
- Change the font or font size for queries
- Create SQL queries
- Include fields in SQL queries
- Include simple and compound criteria in SQL queries
- Use computed fields and built-in functions in SQL queries
- Sort the results in SQL queries

- Use aggregate functions in SQL queries
- Group the results in SQL queries
- Join tables in SQL queries
- Use subqueries
- Compare SQL queries with Access-generated SQL
- Use INSERT, UPDATE, and DELETE queries to update a database
- Link table to outside data source
- Change tab order in a form

Introduction

The language called **SQL (Structured Query Language)** is a very important language for querying and updating databases. It is the closest thing to a universal database language, because the vast majority of database management systems, including Access, use it in some fashion. Although some users will be able to do all their queries through the query features of Access without ever using SQL, those in charge of administering and maintaining the database system should be familiar with this important language. You can also use Access as an interface to other database management systems, such as SQL Server. Using or interfacing with SQL Server requires knowledge of SQL. Virtually every DBMS supports SQL.

Project—Using SQL

CMF Vets wants to be able to use the extended data management capabilities available through SQL. As part of becoming familiar with SQL, CMF Vets would like to create a wide variety of SQL queries.

Similar to creating queries in Design view, SQL provides a way of querying relational databases. In SQL, however, instead of making entries in the design grid, you type commands into SQL view to obtain the desired results, as shown in Figure 10–1a. You can then click the View button to view the results just as when you are creating queries in Design view. The results for the query in Figure 10–1a are shown in Figure 10–1b.

BTW

Distributing a Document
Instead of printing and distributing a hard copy of a document, you can distribute the document electronically. Options include sending the document via email; posting it on cloud storage (such as OneDrive) and sharing the file with others; posting it on a social networking site, blog, or other website; and sharing a link associated with an online location of the document. You also can create and share a PDF or XPS image of the document, so that users can view the file in Acrobat Reader or XPS Viewer instead of in Access.

Figure 10–1a Query in SQL

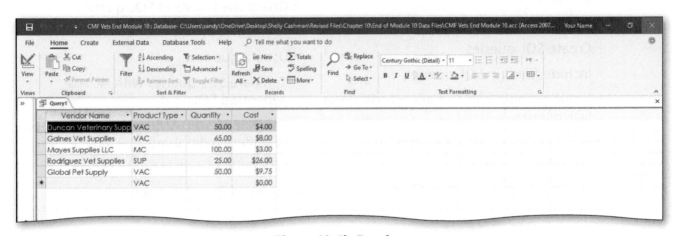

Figure 10–1b Results

In this module, you will learn how to create and use SQL queries like the one shown in Figure 10–1a.

BTW

The Ribbon and Screen Resolution
Access may change how the groups and buttons within the groups appear on the ribbon, depending on the computer's screen resolution. Thus, your ribbon may look different from the ones in this book if you are using a screen resolution other than 1366 × 768.

BTW

Enabling the Content
For each of the databases you use in this module, you will need to enable the content.

SQL Background

In this module, you query and update a database using the language called SQL (Structured Query Language). Similar to using the design grid in the Access Query window, SQL provides users with the capability of querying a relational database. Because SQL is a language, however, you must enter **commands** to obtain the desired results, rather than completing entries in the design grid. SQL uses commands to update tables and to retrieve data from tables. The commands that are used to retrieve data are usually called **queries**.

SQL was developed under the name SEQUEL at the IBM San Jose research facilities as the data manipulation language for IBM's prototype relational model DBMS, System R, in the mid-1970s. In 1980, it was renamed SQL to avoid confusion with an unrelated hardware product called SEQUEL. Most relational DBMSs, including Microsoft Access and Microsoft SQL Server, use a version of SQL as a data manipulation language.

Some people pronounce SQL by pronouncing the three letters, that is, "ess-que-ell." It is very common, however, to pronounce it as the name under which it was developed originally, that is, "sequel."

To Change the Font Size

You can change the font and/or the font size for queries using the Options button in the Backstage view and then Object Designers in the list of options in the Access Options dialog box. There is not usually a compelling reason to change the font, unless there is a strong preference for some other font. It often is worthwhile to change the font size, however. *Why? With the default size of 10, the queries can be hard to read. Increasing the font size to 11 can make a big difference.* The following steps change the font size for queries to 11.

1

- **sam** ⬇ Start Access and open the database named CMF Vets from your hard drive, OneDrive, or other storage location.

- Click File on the ribbon to open the Backstage view.

- Click Options to display the Access Options dialog box.

- Click Object Designers to display the Object Designer options.

- In the Query design area, click the Size box arrow, and then click 11 in the list to change the size to 11 (Figure 10–2).

2

- Click OK to close the Access Options dialog box.

Figure 10–2

SQL Queries

When you query a database using SQL, you type commands in a blank window rather than filling in the design grid. When the command is complete, you can view your results just as you do with queries you create using the design grid.

To Create a New SQL Query

You begin the creation of a new **SQL query**, which is a query expressed using the SQL language, just as you begin the creation of any other query in Access. The only difference is that you will use SQL view instead of Design view. *Why? SQL view enables you to type SQL commands rather than making entries in the design grid.* The following steps create a new SQL query.

1

- Close the Navigation Pane.
- Display the Create tab.
- Click the Query Design button (Create tab | Queries group) to create a query.
- Close the Show Table dialog box without adding any tables.
- Click the View button arrow (Query Tools Design tab | Results group) to display the View menu (Figure 10–3).

Q&A Why did the icon on the View button change to SQL, and why are there only two items on the menu instead of the usual five?

Without any tables selected, you cannot view any results. You can only use the normal Design view or SQL view. The change in the icon indicates that you could simply click the button to transfer to SQL view.

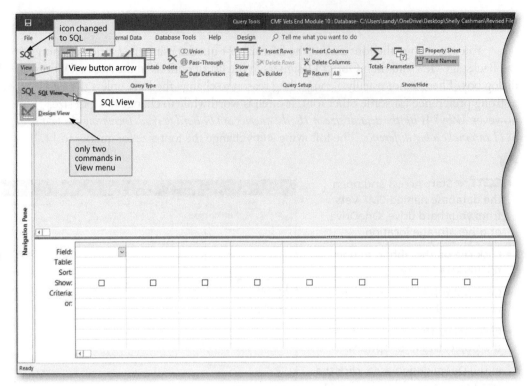

Figure 10–3

2

- Click SQL View on the View menu to view the query in SQL view (Figure 10–4).

Q&A What happened to the design grid?

In SQL view, you specify the queries by typing SQL commands rather than making entries in the design grid.

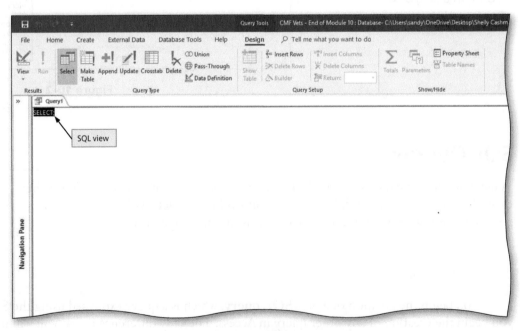

Figure 10–4

SQL Commands

The basic form of SQL expressions is quite simple: SELECT-FROM-WHERE. The command begins with a **SELECT clause**, which consists of the word, SELECT, followed by a list of those fields you want to include. The fields will appear in the results in the order in which they are listed in the expression. Next, the command contains a **FROM clause**, which consists of the word FROM followed by a list of the table or tables involved in the query. Finally, there is an optional **WHERE clause**, which consists of the word WHERE followed by any criteria that the data you want to retrieve must satisfy. The command ends with a semicolon (;), which in this text will appear on a separate line.

SQL has no special format rules for placement of terms, capitalization, and so on. One common style is to place the word FROM on a new line, and then place the word WHERE, when it is used, on the next line. This style makes the commands easier to read. It is also common to show words that are part of the SQL language in uppercase and others in a combination of uppercase and lowercase. This text formats SQL terms in uppercase letters. Because it is a common convention, and necessary in some versions of SQL, you will place a semicolon (;) at the end of each command.

Microsoft Access has its own version of SQL that, unlike some other versions of SQL, allows spaces within field names and table names. There is a restriction, however, to the way such names are used in SQL queries. When a name containing a space appears in SQL, it must be enclosed in square brackets. For example, Vendor Name must appear as [Vendor Name] because the name includes a space. On the other hand, Cost does not need to be enclosed in square brackets because its name does not include a space. For consistency, all names in this text are enclosed in square brackets. Thus, the Cost field would appear as [Cost] even though the brackets are not technically required by SQL.

To Include Only Certain Fields

To include only certain fields in a query, list them after the word, SELECT. If you want to list all rows in the table, you do not include the word, WHERE. ***Why?*** *If there is no WHERE clause, there is no criterion restricting which rows appear in the results. In that case, all rows will appear.* The following steps create a query for CMF Vets that will list the vendor name, product type, quantity, and cost of all vendors.

- Click to the right of the word, SELECT, delete the semicolon, type **[Vendor Name],[Product Type],[Quantity],[Cost]** as the first line of the command, and then press ENTER.

◁ | What is the purpose of the SELECT clause?
Q&A | The SELECT clause indicates the fields that are to be included in the query results. This SELECT clause, for example, indicates that the Vendor Name, Product Type, Quantity, and Cost fields are to be included.

- Type **FROM [Veterinary Vendors]** as the second line to specify the source table, press ENTER, and then type a semicolon (;) on the third line (Figure 10–5a).

◁ | What is the purpose
Q&A | of the FROM clause?
The FROM clause indicates the table or tables that contain the fields used in the query. This FROM clause indicates that all the fields in this query come from the Veterinary Vendors table.

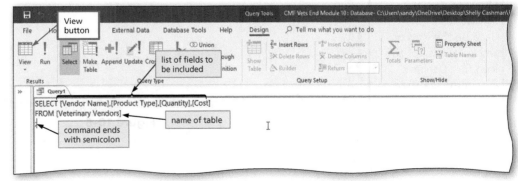

Figure 10–5a

- Click the View button (Query Tools Design tab | Results group) to view the results (Figure 10–5b).

My screen displays a dialog box that asks me to enter a parameter value. What did I do wrong?

You typed a field name incorrectly. Click Cancel to close the dialog box and then correct your SQL statement.

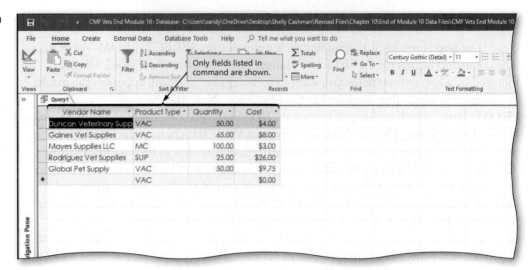

Figure 10–5b

2

- Click the Save button on the Quick Access Toolbar, type `m10q01` as the name in the Save As dialog box, and then click OK to save the query as m10q01.

To Prepare to Enter a New SQL Query

To enter a new SQL query, you could close the window, click the No button when asked if you want to save your changes, and then begin the process from scratch. A quicker alternative is to use the View menu and then select SQL View. *Why? You will be returned to SQL view with the current command appearing. At that point, you could erase the current command and then enter a new one. If the next command is similar to the previous one, however, it often is simpler to modify the current command instead of erasing it and starting over.* The following step shows how to prepare to enter a new SQL query.

1

- Click the View button arrow (Home tab | Views group) to display the View menu (Figure 10–6).

- Click SQL View to return to SQL view.

Could I just click the View button, or do I have to click the arrow?

Because the icon on the button is not the icon for SQL view, you must click the arrow.

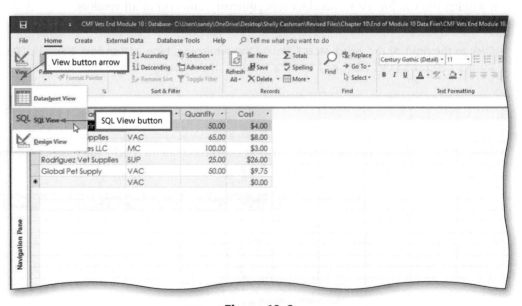

Figure 10–6

To Include All Fields

To include all fields, you could use the same approach as in the previous steps, that is, list each field in the Veterinary Vendors table after the word SELECT. There is a shortcut, however. Instead of listing all the field names after SELECT, you can use the asterisk (*) symbol. *Why? Just as when working in the design grid, the asterisk symbol represents all fields.* This indicates that you want all fields listed in the order in which you described them to the system during data definition. The following steps list all fields and all records in the Veterinary Vendors table.

- Delete the current command, type **SELECT *** as the first line of the command, and then press ENTER.

- Type **FROM [Veterinary Vendors]** as the second line, press ENTER, and type a semicolon (;) on the third line.

- View the results (Figure 10–7b).

Q&A Can I use copy and paste commands when I enter SQL commands?
Yes, you can use copy and paste as well as other editing techniques, such as replacing text.

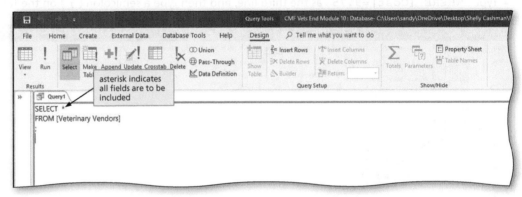

Figure 10–7a Query to List All Fields and All Records in the Veterinary Vendors Table

Figure 10–7b Results

2

- Click File on the ribbon to open the Backstage view, click the Save As tab to display the Save As gallery, click Save Object As in the File Types area, click the Save As button to display the Save As dialog box, type **m10q02** as the name for the saved query, and then click OK to save the query as m10q02 and return to the query.

Q&A Can I just click the Save button on the Quick Access Toolbar as I did when I saved the previous query?
If you did, you would replace the previous query with the version you just created. Because you want to save both the previous query and the new one, you need to save the new version with a different name. To do so, you must use Save Object As, which is available through the Backstage view.

To Use a Criterion Involving a Numeric Field

To restrict the records to be displayed, include the word WHERE followed by a criterion as part of the command. If the field involved is a numeric field, you simply type the value. In typing the number, you do not type commas or dollar signs. *Why? If you enter a dollar sign, Access assumes you are entering text. If you enter a comma, Access considers the criterion invalid.* The following steps create a query to list the name of all vendors whose current cost amount is greater than $20.00 so other lesser cost options may be reviewed.

- Return to SQL view and delete the current command.

- Type `SELECT [Vendor Name],[Product Type],[Cost]` as the first line of the command.

- Type `FROM [Veterinary Vendors]` as the second line.

- Type `WHERE [Cost]=9.75` as the third line, and then type a semicolon (;) on the fourth line.

Figure 10–8a Query to List the Vendor Name and Product Type for Those Vendors Where Cost is Equal to 9.75

Q&A

What is the purpose of the WHERE clause?

The WHERE clause restricts the rows to be included in the results to only those that satisfy the criteria included in the clause. With this WHERE clause, for example, only those rows on which Cost is equal to 9.75 will be included.

- View the results (Figure 10–8b).

Figure 10–8b Results

- Save the query as m10q03.

Simple Criteria

The criterion following the word WHERE in the preceding query is called a simple criterion. A **simple criterion** has the form: field name, comparison operator, then either another field name or a value. The possible comparison operators are shown in Table 10–1.

BTW
Context-Sensitive Help in SQL
When you are working in SQL view, you can obtain context-sensitive help on any of the keywords in your query. To do so, click anywhere in the word about which you wish to obtain help and press the F1 key.

Table 10–1 Comparison Operators

Comparison Operator	Meaning
=	equal to
<	less than
>	greater than
<=	less than or equal to
>=	greater than or equal to
<>	not equal to

To Use a Comparison Operator

In the following steps, CMF Vets uses a comparison operator to list the vendor name, product type, and cost for all vendors who have a product cost greater than $20. *Why? A comparison operator allows you to compare the value in a field with a specific value or with the value in another field.*

- Return to SQL view and delete the current command.
- Type `SELECT [Vendor Name],[Product Type],[Cost]` as the first line of the command.
- Type `FROM [Veterinary Vendors]` as the second line.
- Type `WHERE ([Veterinary Vendors].[Cost]>20)` as the third line.

Q&A Why are there parentheses in the WHERE clause?
Because this is the second time that Veterinary Vendors is shown in the query, SQL requires parentheses before the table name.

- Type a semicolon (;) on the fourth line.

Figure 10–9a Query to List the Vendor Name, Product Type and Cost for Those Vendors Where Cost is Greater Than $20

- View the results (Figure 10–9b).

Figure 10–9b Results

- Save the query as m10q04.

To Use a Criterion Involving a Text Field

If the criterion involves a text field, the value must be enclosed in quotation marks. *Why? Unlike when you work in the design grid, Access will not insert the quotation marks around text data for you in SQL view. You need to include them.* The following example lists the Vendor Name and Product Name of all of CMF Vets' vendors located in Dolores, that is, all Vendors for whom the value in the City field is Dolores.

- Return to SQL view, delete the current command, and type **SELECT [Vendor Name],[Product Type],[City]** as the first line of the command.
- Type **FROM [Veterinary Vendors]** as the second line.
- Type **WHERE [City]='Dolores'** as the third line and type a semicolon (**;**) on the fourth line.

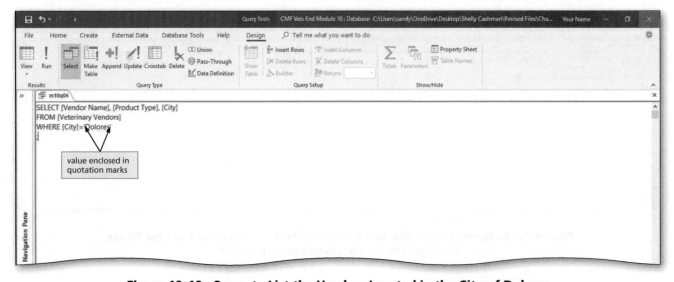

Figure 10–10a Query to List the Vendors Located in the City of Dolores

- View the results (Figure 10–10b).

Figure 10–10b Results

- Save the query as m10q05.

To Use a Wildcard

In most cases, the conditions in WHERE clauses involve exact matches, such as retrieving rows for each account located in the city of Dolores. In some cases, however, exact matches do not work. *Why? You might only know that the desired value contains a certain collection of characters.* In such cases, you use the LIKE operator with a wildcard symbol.

Rather than testing for equality, the LIKE operator uses one or more wildcard characters to test for a pattern match. One common wildcard in Access, the **asterisk** (*), represents any collection of characters. Thus, D* represents the letter, D, followed by any string of characters. Another wildcard symbol is the question mark (?), which represents any individual character. Thus, T?m represents the letter T, followed by any single character, followed by the letter, m, such as Tim or Tom.

The following steps use a wildcard to display the treatment number and treatment name for every treatment in the Treatment Cost table in CMF Vets for Felines. In case there are possible incorrect spellings, you will search for animal types starting with the letter F To be sure that Access associates the field and table correctly, you must place the table and field names in parentheses.

- Return to SQL view, delete the previous query, and type `SELECT [Treatment Number], [Treatment], [Animal Type]`.
- Type `FROM [Treatment Cost]` as the second line.
- Type `WHERE ([Treatment Cost].[Animal Type]) Like 'F*'` as the third line, and then type a semicolon (;) on the fourth line.
- View the query (Figure 10–11a) and the results (Figure 10–11b).

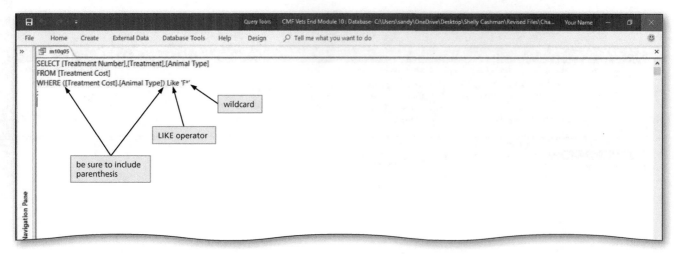

Figure 10–11a Query to List Treatment Numbers and Treatment Names for Felines

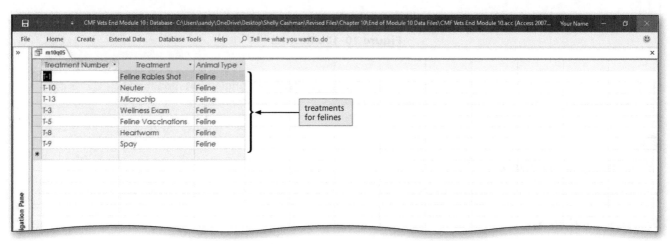

Figure 10–11b Results

2

• Save the query as m10q06.

Break Point: If you wish to stop working through the module at this point, you can close Access now. You can resume the project later by starting Access, opening the database called CMF Vets, creating a new query in SQL view, and continuing to follow the steps from this location forward.

Compound Criteria

You are not limited to simple criteria in SQL. You can also use compound criteria. **Compound criteria** are formed by connecting two or more simple criteria using AND, OR, and NOT. When simple criteria are connected by the word AND, all the simple criteria must be true in order for the compound criterion to be true. When simple criteria are connected by the word OR, the compound criterion will be true whenever any of the simple criteria are true. Preceding a criterion by the word NOT reverses the truth or falsity of the original criterion. That is, if the original criterion is true, the new criterion will be false; if the original criterion is false, the new one will be true.

BTW
Entering Field Names
Be sure to enclose field names in square brackets. If you accidentally use parentheses or curly braces, Access will display a syntax error (missing operator) message.

To Use a Compound Criterion Involving AND

The following steps use a compound criterion. *Why? A compound criterion allows you to impose multiple conditions.* In particular, these steps enable CMF Vets to display the treatments for felines whose treatment cost is greater than $20.

- Return to SQL view, delete the previous query, and type **SELECT [Treatment Number], [Treatment], [Animal Type]** as the first line.
- Type **FROM [Treatment Cost]** as the second line.
- Type **WHERE ([Treatment Cost].[Animal Type]) Like 'F*'** as the third line.
- Type **AND ([Treatment Cost].Cost)>20** on the fourth line.
- Type a semicolon (**;**) on the fifth line.

Q&A

What is the purpose of the AND clause?

The AND clause indicates that there are multiple criteria, all of which must be true. With this AND clause, only rows on which BOTH Animal Type is Feline AND Cost of the treatment is greater than 20 will be included.

- View the query (Figure 10–12a) and the results (Figure 10–12b).

Figure 10–12a Query to List Treatments for Felines and Whose Treatment Cost is Greater Than $20

Figure 10–12b Results

- Save the query as m10q07.

To Use a Compound Criterion Involving OR

The following steps use a compound criterion involving OR to enable CMF Vets to display felines or where the treatment cost is greater than $25.00. *Why? In an OR criterion only one of the individual criteria needs to be true in order for the record to be included in the results.*

- Return to SQL view, delete the previous query, and type `SELECT [Treatment Number], [Treatment], [Animal Type]` as the first line.
- Type `FROM [Treatment Cost]` as the second line.
- Type `WHERE ([Treatment Cost].[Animal Type]) Like 'F*'` as the third line.
- Type `OR ([Treatment Cost].Cost)>25` as the fourth line.
- Type a semicolon (;) on the fifth line (Figure 10–13a).

Figure 10–13a Query to List Treatments for Felines or Treatment Costs Greater Than $25

Q&A
What is the purpose of the OR clause?
The OR clause indicates that there are multiple criteria, only one of which needs to be true. With this OR clause, those rows on which EITHER Animal Type is Feline OR Treatment Cost is less than $25 (or both) will be included.

- View the results (Figure 10–13b).

Figure 10–13b Results

- Save the query as m10q08.
- Close the query.

To Use NOT in a Criterion

Why? *You can negate any criterion by preceding the criterion with the word NOT.* The following steps use NOT in a criterion to list the first names and last names of the pet owners in CMF Vets that not located in the city of Dolores.

- Click the Create tab, and then click the Query Design button (Create tab | Queries group) to create a query.
- Close the Show Table dialog box without adding any tables.
- Click the View button arrow (Query Tools Design tab | Results group) to display the View menu.

2

- Click SQL View on the View menu.
- Delete SELECT; and then type **SELECT [Owner First Name], [Owner Last Name], [Owner City]** as the first line.
- Type **FROM Owners** on the second line.
- Type **WHERE NOT [Owner City]='Dolores'** as the third line and type a semicolon (;) on the fourth line (Figure 10–14a).

Figure 10–14a Query to List the Names of Pet Owners that Do Not Live in Dolores

- View the results (Figure 10–14b).

Figure 10–14b Results

- Save the query as m10q09.

To Use a Computed Field

Just as with queries created in Design view, you can include fields in queries that are not in the database, but that can be computed from fields that are. Such a field is called a **computed** or **calculated field**. Computations can involve addition (+), subtraction (-), multiplication (*), or division (/). The query in the following steps computes the hours remaining, which is equal to the total hours minus the hours spent.

To indicate the contents of the new field (the computed field), you can name the field by following the computation with the word AS and then the name you want to assign the field. *Why? Assigning the field a descriptive name makes the results much more readable.* The following steps calculate the hours remaining for each workshop offered by subtracting the hours spent from the total hours and then assigning the name Remaining to the calculation. The steps also list the Owner ID, Workshop Code, Total Hours, and Hours Spent for all workshop offerings for which the number of hours spent is greater than 0.

1

- Return to SQL view and delete the previous query.
- Type `SELECT [Owner ID], [Workshop Code], [Total Hours], [Hours Spent], [Total Hours]-[Hours Spent] AS Remaining` as the first line.
- Type `FROM [Workshop Offerings]` as the second line.
- Type `WHERE [Hours Spent]>0` as the third line, and then type a semicolon on the fourth line (Figure 10–15a).

Figure 10–15a Query to List the Total Hours for a Workshop Less the Hours Already Spent

- View the results (Figure 10–15b).

Figure 10–15b Results

2

- Save the query as m10q10.

Sorting

Sorting in SQL follows the same principles as when using Design view to specify sorted query results, employing a sort key as the field on which data is to be sorted. SQL uses major and minor sort keys when sorting on multiple fields. By following a sort key with the word DESC with no comma in between, you can specify descending sort order. If you do not specify DESC, the data will be sorted in ascending order.

To sort the output, you include an **ORDER BY clause**, which consists of the words ORDER BY followed by the sort key. If there are two sort keys, the major sort key is listed first. Queries that you construct in Design view require that the major sort key is to the left of the minor sort key in the list of fields to be included. In SQL, there is no such restriction. The fields to be included in the query are in the SELECT clause, and the fields to be used for sorting are in the ORDER BY clause. The two clauses are totally independent.

To Sort the Results on a Single Field

The following steps list the treatment number, treatment, animal type, and cost for all treatments sorted by animal type. *Why? CMF Vets wants this data to appear in alphabetical order by treatment.*

- Return to SQL view and delete the previous query.
- Type `SELECT [Treatment Number],[Treatment], [Animal Type],[Cost]` as the first line.
- Type `FROM [Treatment Cost]` as the second line.
- Type `ORDER BY [Treatment]` as the third line and type a semicolon on the fourth line (Figure 10–16a).

Figure 10–16a Query to List the Treatment Number, Treatment, Animal Type, and Cost Sorted by Treatment

Q&A
What is the purpose of the ORDER BY clause?
The ORDER BY clause indicates that the results of the query are to be sorted by the indicated field or fields. This ORDER BY clause, for example, would cause the results to be sorted by Treatment.

- View the results (Figure 10–16b).

Figure 10–16b Results

- Save the query as m10q11.

To Sort the Results on Multiple Fields

The following steps list the treatment number, treatment, animal type, and cost for all treatments. The data is to be sorted on multiple fields. *Why? CMF Vets wants the data to be sorted by cost within treatments. That is, the data is to be sorted by treatment. In addition, within the group of treatments that have the same treatment name, the data is to be sorted further by cost.* To accomplish this sort, the Treatment field is the major (primary) sort key and the Cost field is the minor (secondary) sort key. Remember that the major sort key must be listed first.

1

- Return to SQL view and delete the previous query.
- Type **SELECT [Treatment Number],[Treatment], [Animal Type],[Cost]** as the first line.
- Type **FROM [Treatment Cost]** as the second line.
- Type **ORDER BY [Treatment],[Cost]** as the third line, and then type a semicolon on the fourth line (Figure 10–17a).

Figure 10–17a Query to List the Treatment Number, Treatment, Animal Type, and Cost Sorted by Treatment and Cost

- View the results (Figure 10–17b).

rows sorted by treatment and then by cost

Figure 10–17b Results

 Experiment

- Try reversing the order of the sort keys to see the effect. View the results to see the effect of your choice. When finished, return to the original sorting order for both fields.

2

- Save the query as m10q12.

To Sort the Results in Descending Order

Why? *To show the results in high-to-low rather than low-to-high order, you sort in descending order.* To sort in descending order, you follow the name of the sort key with the DESC operator. The following steps list the treatment number, treatment, animal type, and cost for all treatments. CMF Vets wants the data to be sorted by descending cost within treatment. That is, within the treatments having the same name, the data is to be sorted further by cost in descending order.

1

- Return to SQL view and delete the previous query.

- Type `SELECT [Treatment Number],[Treatment], [Animal Type],[Cost]` as the first line.

- Type `FROM [Treatment Cost]` as the second line.

- Type `ORDER BY [Treatment],[Cost] DESC` as the third line, and then type a semicolon on the fourth line (Figure 10–18a).

Q&A Do I need a comma between [Cost] and DESC?

No. In fact, you must not use a comma. If you did, SQL would assume that you want a field called DESC. Without the comma, SQL knows that the DESC operator indicates that the sort on the Cost field is to be in descending order.

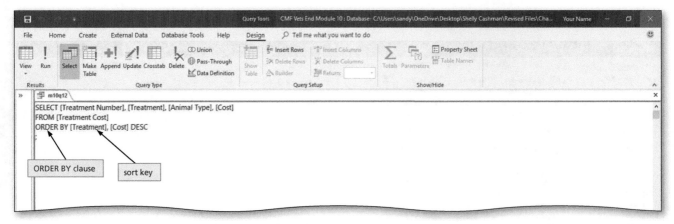

Figure 10–18a Query to List the Treatment Number, Treatment, Animal Type, and Cost with Results Sorted by Treatment and Descending Cost Order

- View the results (Figure 10–18b).

Figure 10–18b Results

- Save the query as m10q13.

To Omit Duplicates When Sorting

When you sort data, duplicates are normally included. For example, the query in Figure 10–19 sorts the Product Types in the Veterinary Vendors table. Because there are several vendors that supply vaccination products, CMF Vets does not find this useful and would like to eliminate these duplicate product types in this list. To do so, use the DISTINCT operator in the query. *Why? The DISTINCT operator eliminates duplicate values in the results of a query.* To use the operator, you follow the word DISTINCT with the field name in parentheses.

The following steps display the Product Types in the Veterinary Vendors table in Product ID order, but with any duplicates removed.

1

- Return to SQL view and delete the previous query.
- Type **SELECT DISTINCT ([Product Type])** as the first line of the command.
- Type **FROM [Veterinary Vendors]** as the second line.
- Type **ORDER BY [Product Type]** as the third line, and then type a semicolon on the fourth line (Figure 10–19a).

Figure 10–19a Query to List Product Types

- View the results (Figure 10–19b).

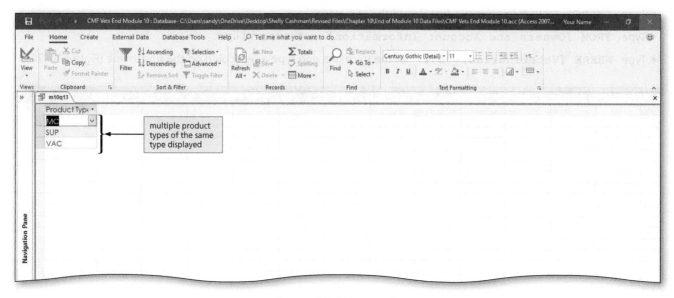

Figure 10–19b Results

2

- Save the query as m10q14. Return to the query.

How do you determine sorting when creating a query?
Examine the query or request to see if it contains words such as *order* or *sort* that would imply that the order of the query results is important. If so, you need to sort the query.

- **Determine whether data is to be sorted.** Examine the requirements for the query looking for words like *sorted by*, *ordered by*, *arranged by*, and so on.

- **Determine sort keys.** Look for the fields that follow sorted by, ordered by, or any other words that signify sorting. If the requirements for the query include the phrase, ordered by vendor name, then vendor name is a sort key.

- **If there is more than one sort key, determine which one will be the major sort key and which will be the minor sort key.** Look for words that indicate which field is more important. For example, if the requirements indicate that the results are to be ordered by cost within treatment number, Treatment Number is the more important sort key.

Break Point: If you wish to stop working through the module at this point, you can close Access now. You can resume the project later by starting Access, opening the database called CMF Vets, creating a new query in SQL view, and continuing to follow the steps from this location forward.

To Use a Built-In Function

SQL has built-in functions, also called aggregate functions, to perform various calculations. Similar to the functions you learned about in an earlier module, these functions in SQL are COUNT, SUM, AVG, MAX, and MIN, respectively. CMF Vets uses the following steps to determine the number of appointments assigned to veterinarian number B01 by using the COUNT function with an asterisk (*). *Why use an asterisk rather than a field name when using the COUNT function? You could select a field name, but that would be cumbersome and imply that you were just counting that field. You are really counting records. It does not matter whether you are counting names or street addresses or anything else.*

1

- Return to SQL view and delete the previous query.
- Type **SELECT COUNT(*)** as the first line of the command.
- Type **FROM [Owners and Account Information]** as the second line.
- Type **WHERE [Veterinarian]='B01'** as the third line and type a semicolon on the fourth line (Figure 10–20a).

Figure 10–20a Query to Count Number of Appointments for Veterinarian B01

- View the results (Figure 10–20b).

number of appointments
for veterinarian B01

Figure 10–20b Results

Q&A Why does Expr1000 appear in the column heading of the results?

Because the field is a computed field, it does not have a name. Access assigns a generic expression name. You can add a name for the field by including the AS clause in the query, and it is good practice to do so.

2

- Save the query as m10q15.

To Assign a Name to the Results of a Function

CMF Vets would prefer to have a more meaningful name than Expr1000 for the results of counting appointments. *Why? The default name of Expr1000 does not describe the meaning of the calculation.* Fortunately, just as you can assign a name to a calculation that includes two fields, you can assign a name to the results of a function. To do so, follow the expression for the function with the word AS and then the name to be assigned to the result. The following steps assign the name, Veterinarian Appointments, to the expression in the previous query.

1

- Return to SQL view and delete the previous query.

- Type `SELECT COUNT(*) AS [Veterinarian Appointments]` as the first line of the command.

- Type `FROM [Owners and Account Information]` as the second line.

- Type `WHERE [Veterinarian]='B01'` as the third line and type a semicolon on the fourth line (Figure 10–21a).

name for calculation

SELECT COUNT (*) AS [Veterinarian Appointments]
FROM [Owners and Account Information]
WHERE [Veterinarian]='B01'

Figure 10–21a Query to Count Number of Appointments for Veterinarian B01 with Results Called Veterinarian Appointments

- View the results (Figure 10–21b). If necessary, increase the width of the Veterinarian Appointments: Count column to view the entire field name.

Figure 10–21b Results

- Save the query as m10q16.

To Use Multiple Functions in the Same Command

There are two differences between COUNT and SUM, other than the obvious fact that they are computing different statistics. First, in the case of SUM, you must specify the field for which you want a total, instead of an asterisk (*); second, the field must be numeric. *Why? If the field is not numeric, it does not make sense to calculate a sum. You could not calculate a sum of names or addresses, for example.* The following steps use both the COUNT and SUM functions to count the number of appointments whose veterinarian number is B01 and calculate the sum (total) of the appointment costs. The steps use the word AS to name COUNT(*) as Veterinarian Appointments and to name SUM([Cost]) as Total Due.

- Return to SQL view and delete the previous query.
- Type **SELECT COUNT(*) AS [Veterinarian Appointments], SUM([Cost]) AS [Total Due]** as the first line of the command.
- Type **FROM [Owners and Account Information]** as the second line.
- Type **WHERE [Veterinarian]='B01'** as the third line and type a semicolon on the fourth line (Figure 10–22a).

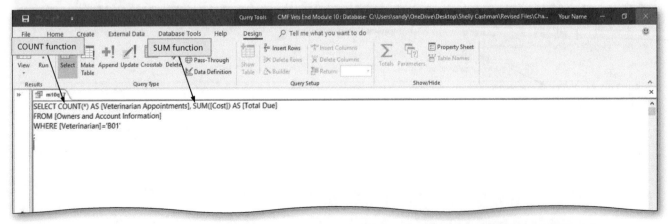

Figure 10–22a Query to Count Number of Appointments for Veterinarian B01 with Results Called Veterinarian Appointments and Calculate Cost with Results Called Total Due

• View the results (Figure 10–22b).

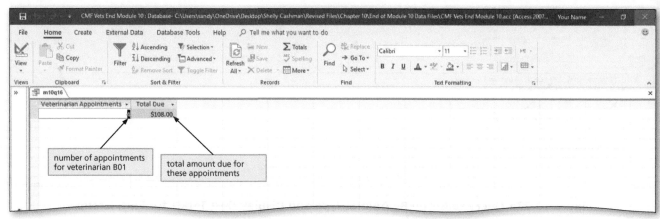

Figure 10–22b Results

Experiment

• Try using the other functions in place of SUM. The use of AVG, MAX, and MIN is similar to SUM. The only difference is that a different statistic is calculated. In each case, view the results to see the effect of your choice. When finished, once again select SUM.

• Save the query as m10q17.

Grouping

Recall that grouping means creating groups of records that share some common characteristic. When you group rows, any calculations indicated in the SELECT command are performed for the entire group.

To Use Grouping

CMF Vets wants to calculate the totals of the Cost field, for Animal Types in the Appointments and Treatments table. To calculate the totals, the command will include the calculations, SUM([Cost]). To get totals for each animal type, the command will also include a **GROUP BY clause**, which consists of the words, GROUP BY, followed by the field used for grouping, in this case, Animal Type. *Why? Including GROUP BY Animal Type will cause the types of each animal to be grouped together; that is, all costs with the same animal type will form a group. Any statistics, such as animal type totals, appearing after the word SELECT will be calculated for each of these groups.* Using GROUP BY does not mean that the information will be sorted.

The following steps use the GROUP BY clause to produce the results CMF Vets wants. The steps also rename the cost as Animal Type Total.

• Return to SQL view and delete the previous query.

• Type `SELECT [Animal Type], SUM ([Cost]) AS [Animal Type Total]` as the first line.

• Type `FROM [Appointments and Treatments]` as the second line.

• Type `GROUP BY [Animal Type]` as the third line.

• Type `;` as the fourth line (Figure 10–23a).

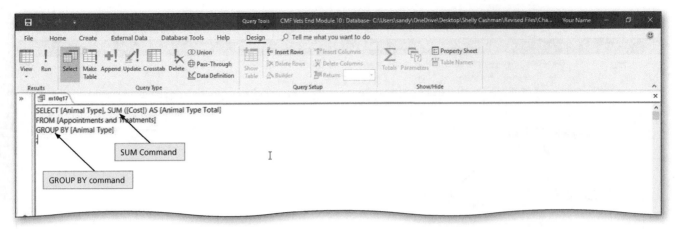

Figure 10–23a Query to Group By Animal Type and Display Cost Totals for Each Group

Q&A What is the purpose of the GROUP BY clause?

The GROUP BY clause causes the rows to be grouped by the indicated field. With this GROUP BY clause, the rows will be grouped by Account Manager Number.

- View the results (Figure 10–23b). If necessary, increase the width of the Animal Type Total column to display the entire field name.

Figure 10–23b Results

- Save the query as m10q18.

Grouping Requirements

BTW

Wildcards
Other implementations of SQL do not use the asterisk (*) and question mark (?) wildcards. In SQL for Oracle and for SQL Server, the percent sign (%) is used as a wildcard to represent any collection of characters. In Oracle and SQL Server, the WHERE clause shown in Figure 10-11a would be WHERE [City] LIKE 'G%'.

When rows are grouped, one line of output is produced for each group. The only output that SQL can display is statistics that are calculated for the group or fields whose values are the same for all rows in a group. For example, when grouping rows by animal type as in the previous query, it is appropriate to display the animal type, because the type in one row in a group must be the same as the type in any other row in the group. It is appropriate to display the sum of the Costs because they are statistics calculated for the group. It would not be appropriate to display a treatment, however, because the treatment varies on the rows in a group; the animal type is associated with many accounts. SQL would not be able to determine which treatment to display for the group. SQL will display an error message if you attempt to display a field that is not appropriate, such as the treatment.

To Restrict the Groups That Appear

In some cases, CMF Vets might want to display only certain groups. For example, management may want to display only the animal type for which the sum of the current due amounts are less than $200. This restriction does not apply to individual rows, but instead to groups. You cannot use a WHERE clause to accomplish this restriction. *Why? WHERE applies only to rows, not groups.*

Fortunately, SQL provides the **HAVING clause**, which functions with groups similarly to the way WHERE functions with rows. The HAVING clause consists of the word HAVING followed by a criterion. It is used in the following steps, which restrict the groups to be included to those for which the sum of the cost is less than $200.

- Return to SQL view.
- Click the end of the third line (GROUP BY [Animal Type]) and press the ENTER key to insert a new blank line.
- Click the beginning of the new blank line, and then type **`HAVING SUM([Cost]) <200`** as the new fourth line. See Figure 10–24a.

Q&A

What is the purpose of the HAVING clause?

The HAVING clause restricts the groups that will be included to only those satisfying the indicated criteria.

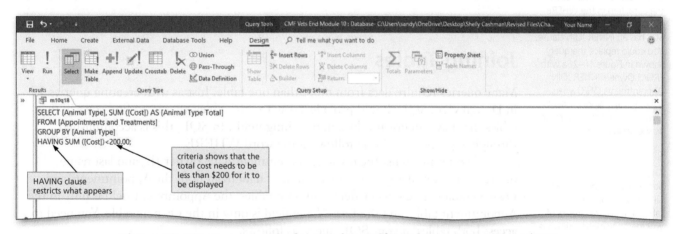

Figure 10–24a Query to Display Total Cost if Total Cost is Less Than $200

- View the results (Figure 10–24b).

Figure 10–24b Results

- Save the query as m10q19.

How do you determine grouping when creating a query?

Examine the question or request to determine whether records should be organized by some common characteristic.

- **Determine whether data is to be grouped in some fashion.** Examine the requirements for the query to see if they contain individual rows or information about groups of rows.

- **Determine the field or fields on which grouping is to take place.** By which field is the data to be grouped? Look to see if the requirements indicate a field along with several group calculations.

- **Determine which fields or calculations are appropriate to display.** When rows are grouped, one line of output is produced for each group. The only output that can appear are statistics that are calculated for the group or fields whose values are the same for all rows in a group. For example, it would make sense to display the manager number, because all the accounts in the group have the same manager number. It would not make sense to display the account number, because the account number will vary from one row in a group to another. SQL could not determine which account number to display for the group.

BTW

Inner Joins

A join that compares the tables in the FROM clause and lists only those rows that satisfy the condition in the WHERE clause is called an inner join. SQL has an INNER JOIN clause. You could replace the query shown in Figure 10–26a with FROM Owners INNER JOIN Appointments ON Owners. [Owner ID] = Appointments. Owner to get the same results as shown in Figure 10–26b.

BTW

Outer Joins

Sometimes you need to list all the rows from one of the tables in a join, regardless of whether they match any rows in the other table. For example, you can perform a join on the Owners and Appointments tables but display all records in Appointments—but display only those records from Owners where the joined fields are equal. This type of join is called an outer join. In a left outer join, all rows from the table on the left (the table listed first in the query) will be included regardless of whether they match rows from the table on the right (the table listed second in the query). Rows from the right will be included only if they match. In a right outer join, all rows from the table on the right will be included regardless of whether they match rows from the table on the left. The SQL clause for a left outer join is LEFT JOIN and the SQL clause for a right outer join is RIGHT JOIN.

Break Point: If you wish to stop working through the module at this point, you can close Access now. You can resume the project later by starting Access, opening the database called CMF Vets, creating a new query in SQL view, and continuing to follow the steps from this location forward.

Joining Tables

Many queries require data from more than one table. Just as with creating queries in Design view, SQL should provide a way to **join** tables, that is, to find rows in two tables that have identical values in matching fields. In SQL, this is accomplished through appropriate criteria following the word WHERE.

If you want to list the owners, appointment date, owner ID, and last name of the owner for all appointments, you need data from both the Appointments and Owners tables. The Owner field is in both tables, the Appointment field is only in the Appointment table, and the Last Name field is only in the Owners table. You need to access both tables in your SQL query, as follows:

1. In the SELECT clause, you indicate all fields you want to appear.
2. In the FROM clause, you list all tables involved in the query.
3. In the WHERE clause, you give the criterion that will restrict the data to be retrieved to only those rows included in both of the two tables, that is, to the rows that have common values in matching fields.

Qualifying Fields

If there is a problem with matching fields, such as a field named Owners that exists in both tables, it is necessary to **qualify** Owners, that is, to specify to which field in which table you are referring. You do this by preceding the name of the field with the name of the table, followed by a period. The Owner ID field in the Owners table, for example, is [Owners].[Owner ID]. And, the owner field in the Appointments table would then be indicated as Appointments.[Owner]. In this case given the fact that one field name is Owner and the other field name is Owner ID, it is not necessary to qualify the fields, however, it is also permissible to qualify fields, even if there is no confusion. For example, instead of [Owner Last Name], you could type [Owners].[Owner Last Name] to indicate the Last Name field in the Owners table. Some people prefer to qualify all fields, and this is not a bad approach. In this text, you will only qualify fields when it is necessary to do so and for learning purposes.

To Join Tables

CMF Vets wants to list the appointment dates, owner, owner ID, and last name of the owner for all appointments. The following steps create a query to join the tables using an INNER JOIN. *Why? The data comes from two tables.* The steps also order the results by appointment date.

- Return to SQL view and delete the previous query.

- Type **SELECT Appointments.[Owner], Appointments.[Appointment Date], Owners. [Owner ID], Owners.[Owner Last Name]** as the first line of the command (be sure to type two spaces between Owner and ID).

- Type **FROM Appointments INNER JOIN Owners ON Appointments.Owner = Owners.[Owner ID]** as the second line (include two spaces between Owner and ID).

Q&A Why does the FROM clause contain more than one table?
The query involves fields from both tables.

- Type **ORDER BY Appointments.[Appointment Date]** as the third line, and then type a semicolon on the fourth line (Figure 10–25a).

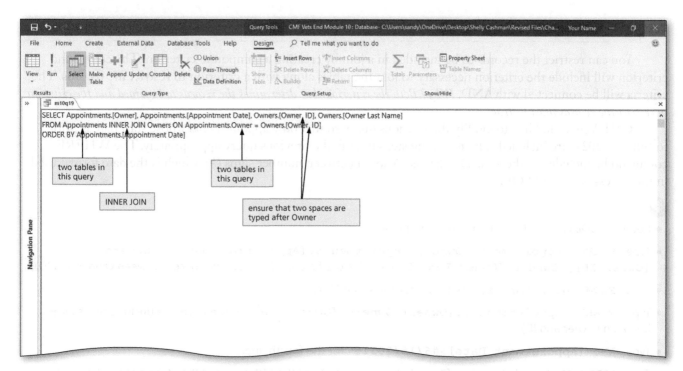

Figure 10–25a Query to Join Tables and Order by Appointment Date

- View the results (Figure 10–25b).

Figure 10–25b Results

- Save the query as m10q20.

To Restrict the Records in a Join

You can restrict the records to be included in a join by creating a compound criterion. The compound criterion will include the criterion necessary to join the tables along with a criterion to restrict the records. The criteria will be connected with AND. *Why? Both the criterion that determines the records to be joined and the criterion to restrict the records must be true.*

CMF Vets would like to modify the previous query so that only appointments whose start date is prior to June 15, 2021, are included. The following steps modify the previous query appropriately. The WHERE command be included as the join. The date is enclosed between number signs (#), which is the date format used in the Access version of SQL.

- Return to SQL view and delete the previous query.
- Type `SELECT Appointments.Owner, Appointments.[Appointment Date], Owners.[Owner ID], Owners.[Owner Last Name]` for the first line (include two spaces between Owner and ID).
- Type `FROM Appointments, Owners` for the second line.
- Type `WHERE [Appointments].[Owner]=Owners.[Owner  ID]` as the third line (include two spaces between Owner and ID).
- Type `AND [Appointment Date]>#6/15/2021#` for the fourth line.
- Type `ORDER BY Appointments.[Appointment Date]` as the fifth line, and then type a semicolon on the sixth line (Figure 10–26a).

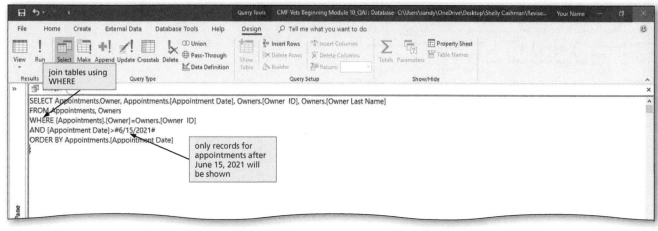

Figure 10–26a Query to Display Appointments After June 15, 2021

Q&A   Could I use other formats for the date in the criterion?
Yes. You could type #June 15, 2021# or #15-June-2021#.

• View the results (Figure 10–26b).

Figure 10–26b Results

• Save the query as m10q21.

Aliases

When tables appear in the FROM clause, you can give each table an **alias**, or an alternative name, that you can use in the rest of the statement. You create an alias by typing the name of the table, pressing the spacebar and then typing the name of the alias. No commas or periods are necessary to separate the two names.

You can use an alias for two basic reasons: for simplicity or to join a table to itself. Figures 10–27 and 10–28 show the same query, but Figure 10–28 assigns the letter A as an alias for the Appointment table and the letter O is assigned as an alias for the Owners table. The query in Figure 10–28 is less complex. Whenever you need to qualify a field name, you can use the alias. Thus, you only need to type A.[Owner] rather than Appointments.Owner.

BTW
Qualifying Fields
There is no space on either side of the period that is used to separate the table name from the field name. Adding a space will result in an error message.

Figure 10–27

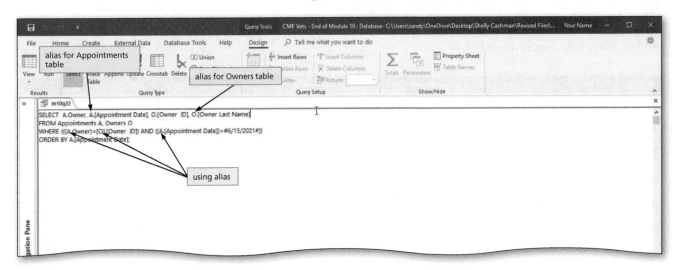

Figure 10–28

To Join a Table to Itself

The other use of aliases is in joining a table to itself. An example of this type of join would enable CMF Vets to find vendor ID numbers and names for every vendor located in the same city. One such pair, for example, would be vendor ID 1 (Duncan Veterinary Supply) and vendor ID 3 (Mayes Supply LLC) because both accounts are located in the same city (Dolores). Because there are two vendors in Dolores, you will see the vendors for Dolores appear on more than one line in the results.

Another example of a pair would be vendor ID 4 (Rodriquez Vet Supplies) and vendor ID 2 (Gaines Pet Supplies) because both accounts are also located in the same city (Blanding). If there were two Veterinary Vendors tables in the database, CMF Vets could obtain the results they want by simply joining the two Veterinary Vendors tables and looking for rows where the cities were the same. Even though there is only one Veterinary Vendors table, you can actually treat the Veterinary Vendors table as two tables in the query by creating two aliases. You would change the FROM clause to:

```
FROM [Veterinary Vendors] D, [Veterinary Vendors] B
```

SQL treats this clause as a query of two tables. The clause assigns the first Veterinary Vendors table the letter, D, as an alias. It also assigns the letter, B, as an alias for the Veterinary Vendors table. The fact that both tables are really the single Veterinary Vendors table is not a problem. The following steps assign two aliases (D and B) to the Veterinary Vendors table and list the vendor ID number and vendor name of both accounts as well as the city in which both are located. The steps also include a criterion to ensure D.[ID Number] < B.[ID Number].

Why? *If you did not include this criterion, the query would contain four times as many results. On the first row in the results, for example, the first vendor ID number is 1 and the second is 3. Without this criterion, there would be a row on which both the first and second vendor ID numbers are 1, a row on which both are 3, and a row on which the first is 1 and the second is 3. This criterion only selects the one row on which the first vendor ID number (1) is less than the second vendor number (3).*

- Return to SQL view and delete the previous query.
- Type `SELECT D.ID, D.[Vendor Name], B.ID, B.[Vendor Name], D.City` as the first line of the command to select the fields to display in the query result.
- Type `FROM [Veterinary Vendors]AS D, [Veterinary Vendors]AS B` as the second line to create the aliases for the first and second Veterinary Vendor tables.
- Type `WHERE D.[City]=B.[City]` as the third line to indicate that the cities in each table must match.
- Type `AND D.[ID]<B.[ID]` as the fourth line to indicate that the account number from the first table must be less than the account number from the second table.
- Type `ORDER BY D.[ID], B.[ID]` as the fifth line to ensure that the results are sorted by the account number from the first table and further sorted by the account number from the second table.
- Type a semicolon on the sixth line (Figure 10–29a).

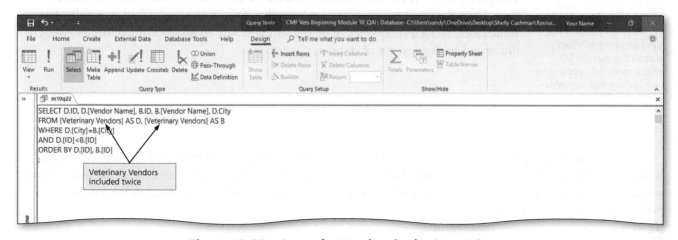

Figure 10–29a Query for Vendors in the Same City

- View the results (Figure 10–29).

Figure 10–29b Results

- Save the query as m10q22.

How do you determine criteria when creating a query?

Examine the query or request to determine any restrictions or conditions that records must satisfy to be included in the results.

- **Determine the fields involved in the criteria.** For any criterion, determine the fields that are included. Determine the data types for these fields. If the criterion uses a value that corresponds to a Text field, enclose the value in single quotation marks. If the criterion uses a date, enclose the value between number signs (for example, #6/15/2021#).

- **Determine comparison operators.** When fields are being compared to other fields or to specific values, determine the appropriate comparison operator (equals, less than, greater than, and so on). If a wildcard is involved, then the query will use the LIKE operator.

- **Determine join criteria.** If tables are being joined, determine the fields that must match.

- **Determine compound criteria.** If more than one criterion is involved, determine whether all individual criteria are to be true, in which case you will use the AND operator, or whether only one individual criterion needs to be true, in which case you will use the OR operator.

BTW
SELECT clause
When you enter field names in a SELECT clause, you do not need to enter a space after the comma. Access inserts a space after the comma when you save the query and close it. When you re-open the query in SQL view, a space will appear after each comma that separates fields in the SELECT clause.

Subqueries

It is possible to place one query inside another. You will place the query shown in Figure 10–30 inside another query. When you have done so, it will be called a **subquery**, which is an inner query, contained within parentheses, that is evaluated first. Then the outer query can use the results of the subquery to find its results. In some cases, using a subquery can be the simplest way to produce the desired results, as illustrated in the next set of steps.

To Use a Subquery

The following steps use the query shown in Figure 10–30 as a subquery. *Why? CMF Vets can use this query to select veterinarians who have at least one office located in Blanding.* After the subquery is evaluated, the outer query will select the vendor ID, first name, and last name for those veterinarians whose veterinarian ID number is in the list produced by the subquery.

 1

- Return to SQL view and delete the previous query.

- Type `SELECT [Veterinarian ID], [First Name], [Last Name],[City]` as the first line of the command.

- Type `FROM [Veterinarians]` as the second line.

- Type `WHERE [City]='Blanding'` as the third line and type a semicolon on the fourth line.

Figure 10–30a Query for Veterinarians in the Same City

- View the results (Figure 10–30b).

Figure 10–30b Results

2

- Return to SQL view and delete the previous query.

- Type **SELECT [Veterinarian ID],[First Name],
  [Last Name]** as the first line of the command.

- Type **FROM [Veterinarians]** as the second line.

- Type **WHERE [Veterinarian ID] IN** as the third line.

- Type **(SELECT [Veterinarian ID]** as the fourth line.

- Type **FROM [Veterinarians]** as the fifth line.

- Type **WHERE [City]='Blanding')** as the sixth line and type a semicolon on the seventh line.

BTW

SQL Standards
The International Standards Organization (ISO)
and the American National Standards Institute
(ANSI) recognize SQL as a standardized
language. Different relational database
management systems may support the entire
set of standardized SQL commands or only a
subset.

Figure 10–31a Query for Veterinarians in the Same City

• View the results (Figure 10–31).

Figure 10–31b Results

• Save the query as m10q23.

BTW
BETWEEN Operator
The BETWEEN operator
allows you to search for a
range of values in one field.
For example, to find all
veterinarian vendors whose
cost is between $10 and $20,
the WHERE clause would
be WHERE [Amount Paid]
BETWEEN 10 AND 20.

BTW
**Union, Pass-Through,
and Data Definition
Queries**
There are three queries that
cannot be created in Design
view. When you click the
button on the ribbon for
any of these three queries in
Design view, the SQL view
window opens. The Union
query combines fields from
more than one table into
one query result set. The
Pass-Through query enables
you to send SQL commands
directly to ODBC (Open
Database Connectivity)
databases using the ODBC
database's SQL syntax.
The Data Definition query
allows you to create or alter
database tables or create
indexes in Access directly.

Using an IN Clause

The query in Figure 10–31 uses an IN clause with a subquery. You can also use an IN clause with a list as an alternative to an OR criterion when the OR criterion involves a single field. For example, to find accounts whose city is Blanding, Dolores, Centerville, or Cortez, the criterion using IN would be City IN ('Blanding', 'Dolores', 'Centerville', 'Cortez'). The corresponding OR criterion would be City='Blanding' OR City= 'Centerville' OR City= 'Cortez' OR City= 'Dolores'. The choice of which one to use is a matter of personal preference.

You can also use this type of IN clause when creating queries in Design view. To use the criterion in the previous paragraph, for example, include the Cost field in the design grid and enter the criterion in the Criteria row.

Comparison with Access-Generated SQL

When you create a query in Design view, Access automatically creates a corresponding SQL query that is similar to the queries you have created in this module. The Access query shown in Figure 10–32, for example, was created in Design view and includes the Veterinarian ID, Veterinarian First Name, and Veterinarian Last Name fields. The City field has a criterion (Blanding).

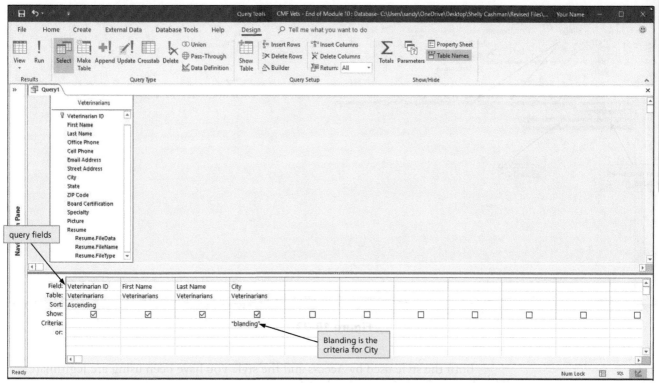

Figure 10–32a Query to List the Veterinarian ID Number, First Name, and Last Name for Vendors in Blanding

Figure 10–32b Results

The SQL query that Access generates in correspondence to the Design view query is shown in Figure 10–33. The query is very similar to the queries you have entered, but there are three slight differences. First, the Veterinarian. [Vendor ID] Veterinarian. [First Name] and Veterinarian. [Last Name] fields are qualified, even though they do not need to be; only one table is involved in the query, so no qualification is necessary. Second, the City field is not enclosed in square brackets. The field is legitimately not enclosed in square brackets because there are no spaces or other special characters in the field name. Finally, there are extra parentheses in the criteria.

Figure 10–33

Both the style used by Access and the style you have been using are legitimate. The choice of style is a personal preference.

BTW
Action Queries
When you use the INSERT, UPDATE, or DELETE commands in SQL, you are creating action queries. The query is making a change to the database. To effect this change, you must click the Run button in the Results group.

Updating Data Using SQL

Although SQL is often regarded as a language for querying databases, it also contains commands to update databases. You can add new records, update existing records, and delete records. To make the change indicated in the command, you will click the Run button.

To Use an INSERT Command

You can add records to a table using the SQL INSERT command. The command consists of the words INSERT INTO followed by the name of the table into which the record is to be inserted. Next is the word VALUE, followed by the values for the fields in the record. Values for text fields must be enclosed within quotation marks. *Why? Just as you needed to type the quotation marks when you used text data in a criterion, you need to do the same when you use text values in an INSERT INTO command.* The following steps add a record that CMF Vets wants to add to the Workshop Offerings table. The record is for owner ID O-4 and Workshop W01 and indicates that the workshop will be offered for a total of 04 hours, of which 0 hours have already been spent.

- If necessary, return to SQL view and delete the existing query.

- Type **INSERT INTO [Workshop Offerings]** as the first line of the command.

- Type **VALUES ('O-4', 'W01',04,0)** as the second line.

- Type a semicolon on the third line (Figure 10–34).

Figure 10–34

Q&A

What is the purpose of the INSERT INTO clause?
The clause indicates the table into which data is to be inserted.

What is the purpose of the VALUES clause?
The VALUES clause, which typically extends over two lines, indicates the values that are to be inserted into a new record in the table. For readability, it is common to place the word VALUES on one line and the actual values on a separate line.

- Run the query by clicking the Run button (Query Tools Design tab | Results group).
- When Access displays a message indicating the number of records to be inserted (appended), click the Yes button to insert the records.

Q&A

I clicked the View button and did not get the message. Do I need to click the Run button?
Yes. You are making a change to the database, so you must click the Run button, or the change will not be made.

How can I see if the record was actually inserted?
Use a SELECT query to view the records in the Workshop Offerings table or you can just open the table and view the records.

- Save the query as INSERT Query m10q24.

To Use an UPDATE Command

You can update records in SQL by using the UPDATE command. The command consists of UPDATE, followed by the name of the table in which records are to be updated. Next, the command contains one or more SET clauses, which consist of the word SET, followed by a field to be updated, an equal sign, and the new value. The SET clause indicates the change to be made. Finally, the query includes a WHERE clause. *Why? When you execute the command, all records in the indicated table that satisfy the criterion will be updated.* The following steps use the SQL UPDATE command to perform an update requested by CMF Vets. Specifically, they change the Hours Spent to 4 on all records in the Workshop Offerings table on which the account number is O-4 and the workshop code is W01. Because the combination of the Account Number and Workshop Code fields is the primary key, only one record will be updated.

1

- Delete the existing query.

- Type **UPDATE [Workshop Offerings]** as the first line of the command.

Q&A What is the purpose of the UPDATE clause?
The UPDATE clause indicates the table to be updated. This clause indicates that the update is to the Workshop Offerings table.

- Type **SET [Hours Spent]=4** as the second line.

Q&A What is the purpose of the SET clause?
The SET clause indicates the field to be changed as well as the new value. This SET clause indicates that the hours spent is to be set to 4.

- Type **WHERE [Owner ID]='O-4'** as the third line.

- Type **AND [Workshop Code]= 'W01'** as the fourth line and type a semicolon on the fifth line (Figure 10–35).

Figure 10–35

Q&A Do I need to change a field to a specific value such as 4?
No. You could use an expression. For example, to add $100 to the Current Due amount, the SET clause would be SET [Current Due]=[Current Due]+100.

2

- Run the query.

- When Access displays a message indicating the number of records to be updated, click the Yes button to update the records.

Q&A How can I see if the update actually occurred?
Use a SELECT query to view the records in the Workshop Offerings table or open the table and view the results.

3

- Save the query as m10q25.

To Use a DELETE Command

You can delete records in SQL using the DELETE command. The command consists of DELETE FROM, followed by the name of the table from which records are to be deleted. Finally, you include a WHERE clause to specify the criteria. **Why?** *When you execute the command, all records in the indicated table that satisfy the criterion will be deleted.* The following steps use the SQL DELETE command to delete all records in the Workshop Offerings table on which the Owner ID is O-4 and the workshop code is W01, as CMF Vets has requested. Because the combination of the Account Number and Workshop Code fields is the primary key, only one record will be deleted.

- Delete the existing query.

- Type **DELETE FROM [Workshop Offerings]**   as the first line of the command.

Q&A   What is the purpose of the DELETE clause?
The DELETE clause indicates the table from which records will be deleted. This DELETE clause indicates that records will be deleted from the Workshop Offerings table.

- Type **WHERE [Owner ID]='O-4'**   as the second line.

- Type **AND [Workshop Code]='W01'**   as the third line and type a semicolon on the fourth line (Figure 10–36).

Figure 10–36

- Run the query.

- When Access displays a message indicating the number of records to be deleted, click the Yes button to delete the records.

Q&A   How can I see if the deletion actually occurred?
Use a SELECT query to view the records in the Workshop Offerings table.

- Save the query as m10q26.

- Close the query.

How do you determine any update operations to be performed?
Examine the database to determine if records must be added, updated, and/or deleted.

- **Determine INSERT operations.** Determine whether new records need to be added. Determine to which table they should be added.

- **Determine UPDATE operations.** Determine changes that need to be made to existing records. Which fields need to be changed? Which tables contain these fields? What criteria identify the rows that need to be changed?

- **Determine DELETE operations.** Determine which tables contain records that are to be deleted. What criteria identify the rows that need to be deleted?

Linking a Table to an Another File

Linking an Access database to data in other programs, such as an Excel worksheet, lets you work with this data in Access without having to maintain a copy of the Excel data in the database. When linking to an Excel workbook, or a named range in Excel, Access creates a new table in the database that is linked to the source cells. New records can be added, records edited, and records deleted in the Excel file, but only in Excel. You cannot make changes to the Excel data in the linked Access table.

To Link a Table to an Outside Data Source

CMF Vets created a file containing information about rescue groups, allowing the practice to contact a rescue group in case an animal is left outside one of CMF Vets offices with no information about the pet, or if a client indicated that they could no longer care for their pet. You will link to the Excel file and then add a record to the file in Excel. *Why? Linking to an external file allows you to store and access information in other file formats.* When you link an Excel file in the database, an Excel icon appears next to the table name. The following steps create a link to the CMF Vets Rescue Groups file.

1

- With the CMF Vets database open, click the External Data tab.

- Click the New Data Source button arrow and point to From File, and then click Excel (Figure 10–37).

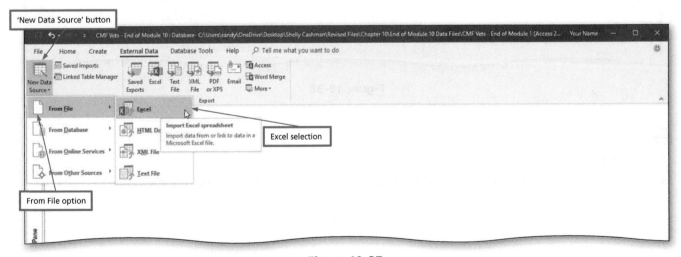

Figure 10–37

2

- Click the Browse button in the Get External Data—Excel Spreadsheet dialog box, navigate to the CMF Vets Rescue Groups Excel file, click to select it, and then click Open.

- Click the 'Link to the data source by creating a linked table.' option button (Figure 10–38).

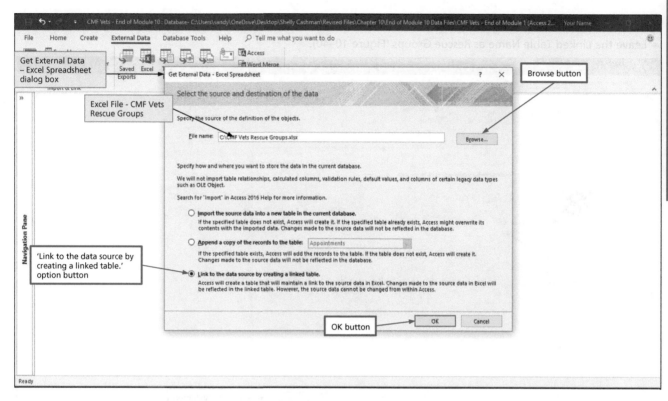

Figure 10–38

③

- Click OK.
- Check the First Row Contains Column Headings check box to select it and then click Next (Figure 10–39).

Figure 10–39

- Leave the Linked Table Name as Rescue Groups (Figure 10–40).

Figure 10–40

- Click Finish.
- Click OK in the Link Spreadsheet Wizard dialog box.
- View the database tables to see the new linked Rescue Groups table (Figure 10–41).

Figure 10–41

● Open the table to view the four records (Figure 10–42).

Figure 10–42

● Click in a cell with no data and try to add a record. Notice that Access prohibits you from entering data.

● Click the Rescue Groups table Close button to close the table in Access.

● Open Excel, navigate to the Data Files, open the CMF Vets Rescue Groups spreadsheet, and add the following record to the worksheet as the fifth row:

Kittens – less than one-year   Tall Tails Rescue   888-553-2713

● Save the Excel file and exit Excel.

8

● Open the Rescue Groups table and view the revised file in Access (Figure 10–43).

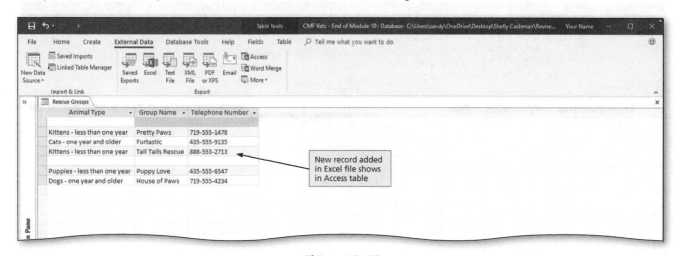

Figure 10–43

To Change Tab Order in a Form

A form created with a form tool or the Form Wizard places the fields in the order they appear in the table design. In many cases, this field order is sufficient. However, if the fields are rearranged for a more logical data entry, the form needs modification to arrange the order of movement through the fields in the form. This order is called the tab order. The following steps change the order of the tab stops in the Veterinarians form. *Why? CMF Vets wants users to tab to the Cell Phone field before the Office Phone field.*

• Open the Veterinarians form in Design view.

• Display the Design tab and in the Tools group, click the Tab Order button to display the dialog box (Figure 10–44).

Figure 10–44

• Click the gray box to the left of Cell Phone to select the Cell Phone field.

• Drag the Cell Phone field by pointing to the gray box to the left of the field name and dragging it below the Last Name field (Figure 10–45).

Figure 10–45

• Click OK to close the Tab Order dialog box.

• Save the changes to the Veterinarians form.

• Switch to Design view to test the results by clicking in the first field and pressing Tab to move to the other fields. If necessary, use the procedure described in the previous step to modify the tab order.

To Restore the Font Size

Earlier you changed the font size from its default setting of 10 to 11 so the SQL queries would be easier to read. Unless you prefer to retain this new setting, you should change the setting back to the default. The following steps restore the font size to its default setting.

1 Click File on the ribbon to open the Backstage view.

2 Click Options to display the Access Options dialog box.

3 If necessary, click Object Designers to display the Object Designer options.

4 In the Query design area, click the Size box arrow, and then click 10 in the list that appears to change the size back to 10.

5 Click the OK button to close the Access Options dialog box.

6 If desired, sign out of your Microsoft account.

7 **sam**⬆ Exit Access.

BTW

Datasheet Font Size

You also can use the Access Options dialog box to change the default font and font size for datasheets. To do so, click Datasheet in the Access Options dialog box and make the desired changes in the Default font area.

Summary

In this module you have learned to create SQL queries, include fields in a query, use criteria involving both numeric and text fields as well as use compound criteria, use computed fields and rename the computation, sort the results of a query, use the built-in functions, group records in a query and also restrict the groups that appear in the results, join tables and restrict the records in a join, and use subqueries. You looked at a SQL query that was generated automatically by Access. Then, you used the INSERT, UPDATE, and DELETE commands to update data. You learned how to create a table in Access that is linked to an Excel spreadsheet. Finally, you learned to change the Tab Order in a form.

CONSIDER THIS: PLAN AHEAD

What decisions will you need to make when creating your own SQL queries?
Use these guidelines as you complete the assignments in this module and create your own queries outside of this class.

1. Select the fields for the query.

a. Examine the requirements for the query you are constructing to determine which fields are to be included.

2. Determine which table or tables contain these fields.

a. For each field, determine the table in which it is located.

3. Determine criteria.

a. Determine any criteria that data must satisfy to be included in the results.

b. If there are more than two tables in the query, determine the criteria to be used to ensure the data matches correctly.

4. Determine sort order.

a. Is the data to be sorted in some way?

b. If so, by what field or fields is it to be sorted?

5. Determine grouping.

a. Is the data to be grouped in some way?

b. If so, by what field is it to be grouped?

c. Identify any calculations to be made for the group.

6. Determine any update operations to be performed.

a. Determine whether rows need to be inserted, changed, or deleted.

b. Determine the tables involved.

How should you submit solutions to questions in the assignments identified with a symbol?
Every assignment in this book contains one or more questions identified with a symbol. These questions require you to think beyond the assigned database. Present your solutions to the questions in the format required by your instructor. Possible formats may include one or more of these options: write the answer; create a document that contains the answer; present your answer to the class; discuss your answer in a group; record the answer as audio or video using a webcam, smartphone, or portable media player; or post answers on a blog, wiki, or website.

Apply Your Knowledge

Reinforce the skills and apply the concepts you learned in this module.

Using Criteria, Joining Tables, and Sorting in SQL Queries in the Financial Services Database

Note: To complete this assignment, you will be required to use the Data Files. Please contact your instructor for information about accessing the Data Files.

Instructions: Start Access and then open the Support_AC_Financial Services database. (If you do not have the database, see your instructor for a copy of the modified database.) Use SQL to query the Financial Services database.

Perform the following tasks:
1. Find all clients whose client type is RET. Display all fields in the query result. Save the query as AYK Step 1 Query.
2. Find all clients whose amount paid or current due is $0.00. Display the Client Number, Client Name, Amount Paid, and Current Due fields in the query result. Save the query as AYK Step 2 Query.
3. Find all clients in the Client table who are not located in Carlton. Display the Client Number, Client Name, and City in the query results. Save the query as AYK Step 3 Query.
4. Display the Client Number, Client Name, Advisor Number, First Name, and Last Name for all clients. Sort the records in ascending order by advisor number and client number. Save the query as AYK Step 4 Query.
5. Display the Advisor Number, First Name, Last Name, and Other Skills for all advisors who are CFA certified. Save the query as AYK Step 5 Query.
6. If requested to do so by your instructor, rename the AYK Step 5 Query as Last Name Query where Last Name is your last name.
7. Submit the revised database in the format specified by your instructor.
8. ✳ What WHERE clause would you use if you wanted to find all clients located in cities beginning with the letter K?

Extend Your Knowledge

Extend the skills you learned in this module and experiment with new skills. You may need to use Help to complete the assignment.

Creating Queries to Find Specific Criteria

Note: To complete this assignment, you will be required to use the Data Files. Please contact your instructor for information about accessing the Data Files.

Start Access and then open the Support_AC_Healthy Pets database. (If you do not have the database, see your instructor for a copy of the modified database.)

Instructions: CMF Vets would like more information about some of the clients of the Healthy Pets practice. Use SQL queries to find specific information.

Perform the following tasks:

1. Find all clients where the client's first name is either Saul or Ira. Display the Client Number, First Name, Last Name, and Address fields in the query result. Save the query as EYK Step 1 Query.

2. Find all clients who live in Cortez. Use the IN operator. Display the Client Number, First Name, Last Name, and City field in the query result. Save the query as EYK Step 2 Query.

3. Find all clients whose amount paid is greater than or equal to $500.00 and less than or equal to $600.00. Use the BETWEEN operator. Display the Client Number, First Name, Last Name, and Amount Paid fields in the query result. Save the query as EYK Step 3 Query.

4. Use an INNER JOIN in a query to find all technicians who are located in Cortez with clients that are also located in Cortez. Display the Client Name, Technician Number, First Name, Last Name, and City fields in the query result. Save the query as EYK Step 4 Query.

5. If requested to do so by your instructor, rename the EYK Step 4 Query as First Name City Query where First Name is your first name and City is the city where you currently reside.

6. Submit the revised database in the format specified by your instructor.

7. ⊛ What WHERE clause would you use to find the answer to Step 2 without using the IN operator?

Expand Your World

Create a solution, which uses cloud and web technologies, by learning and investigating on your own from general guidance.

Problem: Many SQL tutorials are available on the web. One site, www.w3schools.com/sql, has an online SQL editor that allows you to edit SQL commands and then run commands. You will use this editor to create and run queries in the following steps.

Perform the following tasks:

1. Create a blog, Google document, or Word document on OneDrive on which to store your SQL statements and the number of results obtained from the query. Include your name and the current date at the beginning of the blog or document.

2. Access the www.w3schools.com/sql website and spend some time becoming familiar with the tutorial and how it works.

3. Using the website, explain how you would create a query to find records in a table where the Customer name in the table begins with the letter P. Note which section of this website where you located the answer.

4. Submit the document containing your statements and results in the format specified by your instructor.

5. ⊛ Based on your research would you use online SQL research? Why?

In the Labs

Design, create, modify, and/or use a database following the guidelines, concepts, and skills presented in this module.

Lab: **Using SQL in the Lancaster College Database**

Instructions: Open the Support_AC_Lancaster College database. (If you do not have the database, see your instructor for a copy of the modified database.)

Part 1:   The administration at Lancaster College has asked you to perform a number of tasks. Use the concepts and techniques presented in this module to perform each of the following tasks.

a. Create queries using SQL. Find all the Orders where the quantity ordered was less than 75. Show all fields in the results and save the query as ITL Step 1 Query.

b. Create a query using the WHERE command to identify the Coaches with offices in the SM building. Save the query as ITL Step 2 Query.

c. Use the AND command to identify all the students who have waivers and are qualified academically for sports. Show the Student ID field in the query. Save the query as ITL Step 3 Query.

d. Using the NOT command, find all coaches that do not have offices in the JK building. Show the Coach ID field in the query. Save the query as ITL Step 4 Query.

e. Using the ORDER BY command, sort the students that are participating in sports by their student ID and then by the name of the sport they are participating in. Sort both in ascending order. Save the query as ITL Step 5 Query.

f. Use the AND command to find the football fields that are available in the Fall and sort the results in descending order by FieldID. Save the query as ITL Step 6 Query.

g. Group the Orders by Equipment ID and Count the number of orders with quantity ordered of greater than 30. Save the query as ITL Step 7 Query.

h. Close the database.

Submit your assignment in the format specified by your instructor.

Part 2:   You made several decisions while creating these queries, including the decision of which fields to include in the results. What was the rationale behind your decisions? What other queries would you create that you that you think would be relevant?

11 | Database Design

Objectives

You will have mastered the material in this module when you can:

- Understand the terms entity, attribute, and relationship

- Understand the terms relation and relational database

- Understand functional dependence and identify when one column is functionally dependent on another

- Understand the term primary key and identify primary keys in tables

- Design a database to satisfy a set of requirements

- Convert an unnormalized relation to first normal form

- Convert tables from first normal form to second normal form

- Convert tables from second normal form to third normal form

- Understand how to represent the design of a database using diagrams

Introduction

This module presents a method for determining the tables and fields necessary to satisfy a set of requirements. **Database design** is the process of determining the particular tables and fields that will comprise a database. In designing a database, you must identify the tables in the database, the fields in the tables, the primary keys of the tables, and the relationships between the tables.

The module begins by examining some important concepts concerning relational databases and then presents the design method. To illustrate the process, the module presents the requirements for the CMF Vets database. It then applies the design method to those requirements to produce the database design. The module applies the design method to a second set of requirements, which are requirements for a company called Car First Insurers. It next examines normalization, which is a process that you can use to identify and fix potential problems in database designs. The module concludes by explaining how to use a company's policies and objectives — which are typically addressed in existing documentation — to plan and design a database. Finally, you will learn how to represent a database design with a diagram.

Project — Design a Database

This module expands on the database design guidelines presented earlier. Without a good understanding of database design, you cannot use a database management system such as Access effectively. In this module, you will learn how to design two databases by using the database design process shown in Figure 11–1.

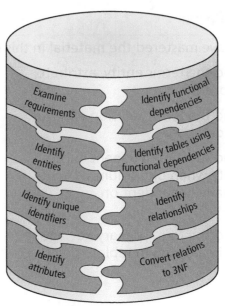

Database Design Process

Figure 11–1

You will design a database for CMF Vets that is similar to the database you have used in the previous modules. You will also design a database for Car First Insurers, a car insurance company.

Entities, Attributes, and Relationships

Working in the database environment requires that you be familiar with some specific terms and concepts. The terms *entity*, *attribute*, and *relationship* are fundamental when discussing databases. An **entity** is like a noun: it is a person, place, thing, or event. The entities of interest to CMF Vets, for example, are such things as owners, patients, veterinarians, and appointments. The entities that are of interest to a college include students, faculty, and classes; a real estate agency is interested in buyers, sellers, properties, and agents; and an automobile dealer is interested in vehicles, accounts, salespeople, and manufacturers. When creating a database, an entity is represented as a table.

An **attribute** is a property of an entity. The term is used here exactly as it is used in everyday English. For the entity *person*, for example, the list of attributes might include such things as eye color and height. For CMF Vets, the attributes of interest for the entity *patient* are such things as name, animal type, breed, and so on. For the entity *faculty* at a school, the attributes would be such things as faculty number, name, office number, phone, department, and so on. For the entity *vehicle* at an automobile dealership, the attributes are such things as the vehicle identification number, model, price, year, and so on. In databases, attributes are represented as the fields in a table or tables.

A **relationship** is an association between entities. There is an association between patients and appointments, for example, at CMF Vets. A patient is associated with all of its appointments, and an appointment is associated with the one patient to whom the appointment is assigned. Technically, you say that a patient is *related* to all of its appointments, and an appointment is *related* to a specific patient.

The relationship between patients and appointments is an example of a one-to-many relationship because one patient is associated with many appointments, but each appointment is associated with only one patient. In a **one-to-many relationship**, a table's record can be related to many records in another table. The other table's records are only related to one record in the first table. In this type of relationship, the word *many* is used in a way that is different from everyday English; it might not always mean a large number. In this context, for example, the term *many* means that a patient might be associated with *any* number of appointments. That is, one patient can be associated with zero, one, or more appointments.

There is also a relationship between veterinarians and patients. Each veterinarian sees many patients, and each patient can be seen by many different veterinarians. This is an example of a **many-to-many relationship**.

How does a relational database handle entities, attributes of entities, and relationships between entities? Entities and attributes are fairly simple. Each entity has its own table; in the CMF database, there is one table for patients, one table for appointments, and so on. The attributes of an entity become the columns in the table. In the table for patients, for example, there is a column for the patient ID, a column for the patient name, and so on.

What about relationships? Relationships are implemented through matching fields. One-to-many relationships, for example, are implemented by including matching fields in the related tables. Patients and appointments are related, for example, by including the Patient ID field in both the Patients table and the Appointments table.

Many-to-many relationships are implemented through an additional table that contains matching fields for both of the related tables. Patients and veterinarians are related, for example, through the Appointments table. The appointments table contains the veterinarian and the patient ID. This table links the two tables, patients and veterinarians, together in the many-to-many relationship.

BTW

Relationships
One-to-one relationships also can occur but they are not common. To implement a one-to-one relationship, treat it as a one-to-many relationship. You must determine which table will be the one table and which table will be the many table. To do so, consider what may happen in the future. In the case of one project that has one employee assigned to it, more employees could be added. Therefore, the project table would be the one table and the employee table would be the many table.

Relational Databases

A relational database is a collection of tables similar to the tables for CMF Vets that appear in Figure 11–2. In the CMF Vets database, the Appointments table contains information about the daily appointments that owners have booked (Figure 11–2a).

Appointments						
Appointment ID	Patient ID	Appointment Date	Appointment Time	Veterinarian	Owner	Treatment Number
1	P-3	6/30/2021	10:00:00 AM	B01	O-6	T-3
2	P-7	10/25/2021	9:00:00 AM	B01	O-8	T-4
3	P-2	1/10/2021	10:00:00 AM	B01	O-5	T-2
4	P-4	6/30/2021	10:00:00 AM	B01	O-1	T-1
5	P-5	8/23/2021	10:00:00 AM	G01	O-4	T-4
7	P-3	6/15/2021	10:00:00 AM	S01	O-6	T-5

Figure 11–2a Appointments Table

CMF Vets assigns each appointment to a specific patient. The Patients table contains information about the patients to whom these appointments are assigned (Figure 11–2b).

Patients				
Patient ID	Patient Name	Animal Type	Breed	Owner ID
P-1	Pepper	Canine	Weimaraner	O-2
P-10	Paws	Feline	Calico	O-2
P-11	Ranger	Canine	Labrador	O-1
P-12	Fluffy	Feline	Tabby	O-1
P-2	Hooper	Canine	Terrier	O-6
P-3	Oliver	Feline	Tabby	O-6
P-4	Chloe	Feline	Calico	O-1
P-5	Max	Feline	Mixed	O-4
P-6	Elvis	Feline	Siamese	O-3
P-7	Milo	Canine	Beagle	O-8
P-8	Millie	Canine	Mixed	O-5
P-9	Skippy	Feline	Mixed	O-1

Figure 11–2b Patients Table

The formal term for a table is relation. If you study the tables shown in Figure 11–2, you might see that there are certain restrictions you should place on relations. Each column in a table should have a unique name, and entries in each column should match this column name. For example, in the Appointment Date column, all entries should in fact *be* appointment dates. In addition, each row should be unique. After all, if two rows in a table contain identical data, the second row does not provide any information that you do not already have. In addition, for maximum flexibility, the order in which columns and rows appear in a table should be immaterial. Finally, a table's design is less complex if you restrict each position in the table to a single entry, that is, you do not permit multiple entries, often called **repeating groups**, in the table. These restrictions lead to the following definition:

A **relation** is a two-dimensional table in which:

1. The entries in the table are single-valued; that is, each location in the table contains a single entry.

2. Each column has a distinct name, technically called the *attribute name*.

3. All values in a column are values of the same attribute; that is, all entries must correspond to the column name.

4. Each row is distinct; that is, no two rows are identical.

Figure 11–3a shows a table with repeating groups, which violates Rule 1. Figure 11–3b shows a table in which two columns have the same name, which violates Rule 2. Figure 11–3c shows a table in which one of the entries in the Appointment Date column is not a date, which violates Rule 3. Figure 11–3d shows a table with two identical rows, which violates Rule 4.

repeating group (more than one entry in a single table location)

Appointments

Appointment ID	Patient ID	Appointment Date	Appointment Time	Veterinarian	Owner	Treatment Number
1	P-3	6/30/2021 7/15/2021 8/14/2021	10:00:00 AM 8:30:00 AM 2:00:00 PM	B01 G01 B01	O-6	T-3 T-5 T-8
2	P-7	10/25/2021	9:00:00 AM	B01	O-8	T-4
3	P-2	1/10/2021	10:00:00 AM	B01	O-5	T-2
4	P-4	6/30/2021	10:00:00 AM	B01	O-1	T-1
5	P-5	8/23/2021	10:00:00 AM	G01	O-4	T-4
7	P-3	6/15/2021	10:00:00 AM	S01	O-6	T-5

Figure 11–3a Appointments Table Violation of Rule 1 — Table Contains Repeating Groups

two columns with the same name

Patients

Patient ID	Patient Name	Animal Type	Animal Type	Owner ID
P-1	Pepper	Canine	Weimaraner	O-2
P-10	Paws	Feline	Calico	O-2
P-11	Ranger	Canine	Labrador	O-1
P-12	Fluffy	Feline	Tabby	O-1
P-2	Hooper	Canine	Terrier	O-6
P-3	Oliver	Feline	Tabby	O-6
P-4	Chloe	Feline	Calico	O-1
P-5	Max	Feline	Mixed	O-4
P-6	Elvis	Feline	Siamese	O-3
P-7	Milo	Canine	Beagle	O-8
P-8	Millie	Canine	Mixed	O-5
P-9	Skippy	Feline	Mixed	O-1

Figure 11–3b Patients Table Violation of Rule 2 — Each Column Should have a Distinct Name

Appointments						
Appointment ID	Patient ID	Appointment Date	Appointment Time	Veterinarian	Owner	Treatment Number
1	P-3	6/30/2021	10:00:00 AM	B01	O-6	T-3
2	P-7	Monday AM	9:00:00 AM	B01	O-8	T-4
3	P-2	1/10/2021	10:00:00 AM	B01	O-5	T-2
4	P-4	6/30/2021	10:00:00 AM	B01	O-1	T-1
5	P-5	8/23/2021	10:00:00 AM	G01	O-4	T-4
7	P-3	6/15/2021	10:00:00 AM	S01	O-6	T-5

value does not correspond to column name: that is, it is not an Appointment Date

Figure 11–3c Appointments Table Violation of Rule 3 — All Entries in a Column Must Correspond to the Column Name

Patients				
Patient ID	Patient Name	Animal Type	Breed	Owner ID
P-1	Pepper	Canine	Weimaraner	O-2
P-10	Paws	Feline	Calico	O-2
P-11	Ranger	Canine	Labrador	O-1
P-12	Fluffy	Feline	Tabby	O-1
P-2	Hooper	Canine	Terrier	O-6
P-2	Hooper	Canine	Terrier	O-6
P-3	Oliver	Feline	Tabby	O-6
P-4	Chloe	Feline	Calico	O-1
P-5	Max	Feline	Mixed	O-4
P-6	Elvis	Feline	Siamese	O-3
P-7	Milo	Canine	Beagle	O-8
P-8	Millie	Canine	Mixed	O-5
P-9	Skippy	Feline	Mixed	O-1

identical rows

Figure 11–3d Patients Table Violation of Rule 4 — Each Row Should be Distinct

In addition, in a relation, the order of columns is immaterial. The order of rows is also immaterial. You can view the columns or rows in any order you want.

A **relational database** is a collection of relations. Rows in a table (relation) are often called **records** or **tuples**. Columns in a table (relation) are often called **fields** or **attributes**. Typically, the terms *record* and *field* are used in Access.

To depict the structure of a relational database, you can use a commonly accepted shorthand representation: you write the name of the table and then within parentheses list all of the fields in the table. Each table should begin on a new line. If the entries in the table occupy more than one line, the entries that appear on the next line should be indented so it is clear that they do not constitute another table. Using this method, you would represent the CMF Vets database as shown in Figure 11–4.

Appointments (Appointment ID, Patient ID, Appointment Date, Appointment Time, Veterinarian, Owner, Treatment Number)
Patients (Patient ID, Patient Name, Animal Type, Breed, Owner ID)

Figure 11–4

The CMF Vets database contains some duplicate field names. For example, the Street Address field appears in *both* the Veterinarians table *and* the Veterinary Vendors table. This duplication of names can lead to possible confusion. If you write Street Address, it is not clear to which Street Address field you are referring.

When duplicate field names exist in a database, you need to indicate the field to which you are referring. You do so by writing both the table name and the field name, separated by a period. You would write the Street Address field in the Veterinarians table as Veterinarians.Street Address and the Street Address field in the Veterinary Vendors table as Veterinary Vendors.Street Address. As you learned previously, when you combine a field name with a table name, you say that you **qualify** the field names. It is *always* acceptable to qualify field names, even if there is no possibility of confusion. If confusion might arise, however, it is *essential* to qualify field names.

Functional Dependence

In the CMF Vets database (Figure 11–2), a given patient ID in the database will correspond to a single patient because patient ID numbers are unique. Thus, if you are given patient ID in the database, you could find a patient name that corresponds to it. No ambiguity exists. The database terminology for this relationship between patient ID numbers and patient names is that Patient ID determines Patient Name, or, equivalently, that Patient Name is functionally dependent on Patient ID. Specifically, if you know that whenever you are given a value for one field, you will be able to determine a single value for a second field, the first field is said to **determine** the second field. In addition, the second field is said to be **functionally dependent** on the first.

There is a shorthand notation that represents functional dependencies using an arrow. To indicate that Patient ID determines Patient Name, or, equivalently, that Patient Name is functionally dependent on Patient ID, you would write Patient ID → Patient Name. The field that precedes the arrow determines the field that follows the arrow.

If you were given a breed and asked to find a patient's name, you could not do it. Given tabby as the breed, for example, you would find two patient names, Fluffy and Oliver (Figure 11–5). Formally, you would say the breed does *not* determine Patient Name, or that Patient Name is *not* functionally dependent on breed.

BTW
Functional Dependence
To help identify functional dependencies, ask yourself the following question. If you know a unique value for an attribute, do you know the unique values for another attribute? For example, when you have three attributes — Patient ID, Patient Name, and Breed — and you know a unique value for Patient ID, do you also know a unique value for Animal Type and Owner? If so, then Animal Type and Owner are functionally dependent on Patient ID.

In the Patients table, is Owner ID functionally dependent on Patient ID?
Yes. If you are given a value for Patient ID, for example P-3, you will always find a *single* Owner ID, in this case O-6, associated with it.

In the Appointments table, is Veterinarian functionally dependent on Patient ID?
No. A given Veterinarian occurs on multiple rows. Veterinarian B01, for example, occurs on many rows and treats patients P-3, P-7, P-2, and P-4. Veterinarian S01 also treats P-3. Thus, veterinarians are associated with more than one appointment.

CONSIDER THIS

Patients				
Patient ID	Patient Name	Animal Type	Breed	Owner ID
P-1	Pepper	Canine	Weimaraner	O-2
P-10	Paws	Feline	Calico	O-2
P-11	Ranger	Canine	Labrador	O-1
P-12	Fluffy	Feline	Tabby	O-1
P-2	Hooper	Canine	Terrier	O-6
P-3	Oliver	Feline	Tabby	O-6
P-4	Chloe	Feline	Calico	O-1
P-5	Max	Feline	Mixed	O-4
P-6	Elvis	Feline	Siamese	O-3
P-7	Milo	Canine	Beagle	O-8
P-8	Millie		Mixed	O-5
P-9	Skippy		Mixed	O-1

(callout: breed is Tabby; name is Fluffy)

(callout: breed is also Tabby, but name is Oliver (same breed but different name))

Figure 11–5

In the Appointments table, is Treatment Number functionally dependent on Patient ID?
No. There is a row, for example, in which the Patient ID is P-7 and the Treatment Number is T-4. There is another row in which the Patient ID is P-5 and the Treatment Number is T-4.

In the Appointments table, is the Veterinarian functionally dependent on the Patient ID?
No. There is a row, for example, in which the Patient ID P-3 is seen by Veterinarian B01 and another row in which the Patient ID P-3 is seen by Veterinarian S01.

On which fields is Treatment Number functionally dependent?
To determine the Treatment Number, you need the Appointment ID.

On which field is Veterinarian functionally dependent?
To determine the Veterinarian, you need the Appointment ID.

Primary Key

The **primary key** of a table is the field or minimum collection of fields — the fewest number of fields possible — that uniquely identifies a given row in that table. In the Appointments table, the Appointment ID uniquely identifies a given row. Any appointment ID appears on only one row of the table. Thus, Appointment ID is the primary key. Similarly, Patient ID is the primary key of the Patients table.

Is the Patient Name another possibility for the key field in the Patients table?
No, because there may be two patients with the same name. A key field must be unique for each row.

Could the combination of the Patient ID and the Appointment Date fields be the primary key for the Appointments table?
Yes, the combination of the two fields, Patient ID and Appointment Date, make each row unique. This would be an alternative to using the current key field, Appointment ID, assuming that each patient had only one appointment each day.

What if some patients had more than one appointment in any day?
In this case, you would need to use three fields, Patient ID, Appointment Date, and Appointment Time, to be key fields. Those three fields are a unique combination for each row.

The primary key provides an important way of distinguishing one row in a table from another. In the shorthand representation, you underline the field or collection of fields that comprise the primary key for each table in the database. Thus, the complete shorthand representation for the CMF Vets database is shown in Figure 11–6.

Appointments (<u>Appointment ID</u>, Patient ID, Appointment Date, Appointment Time, Veterinarian, Owner, Treatment Number)

Patients (<u>Patient ID</u>, Patient Name, Animal Type, Breed, Owner ID)

Figure 11–6

Occasionally, but not often, there might be more than one possibility for the primary key. For example, if the CMF Vets database included the veterinarian's Social Security number in the Veterinarians table, either the Veterinarian ID or the Social Security number could serve as the primary key. In this case, both fields are referred to as candidate keys. Similar to a primary key, a **candidate key** is a field or combination of fields on which all fields in the table are functionally dependent. Thus, the definition for primary key really defines candidate key as well. There can be many candidate keys, although having more than one is very rare. By contrast, there is only one primary key. The remaining candidate keys are called **alternate keys**.

BTW
Candidate Keys
According to the definition of a candidate key, a Social Security number is a legitimate primary key. Many databases use a person's Social Security number as a primary key. However, many institutions and organizations are moving away from using Social Security numbers because of privacy issues. Instead, many institutions and organizations use unique student numbers or employee numbers as primary keys.

Database Design

This section presents a specific database design method, based on a set of requirements that the database must support. The section then presents a sample of such requirements and illustrates the design method by designing a database to satisfy these requirements.

Design Process

The following is a method for designing a database for a set of requirements.

1. Examine the requirements and identify the entities, or objects, involved. Assign names to the entities. The entities will become tables. If, for example, the design involves the entities departments and employees, you could assign the names, Department and Employee. If the design involves the entities accounts, orders, and parts, you could assign the names, Account, Orders, and Part.

NOTE: The word, Order, has special meaning in SQL. If you use it for the name of a table, you will not be able to use SQL to query that table. A common approach to avoid this problem is to make the name plural. That is the reason for choosing Orders rather than Order as the name of the table.

2. Assign a unique identifier to each entity. For example, if one of the entities were "item," you would determine what it takes to uniquely identify each individual item. In other words, what enables the organization to distinguish one item from another? For an item entity, it might be Item Number. For an account entity, it might be Account Number. If there is no such unique identifier, it is a good idea

to add one. Perhaps the previous system was a manual one where accounts were not assigned numbers, in which case this would be a good time to add Account Numbers to the system. If there is no natural candidate for a primary key, you can add an AutoNumber field, which is similar to the ID field that Access adds automatically when you create a new table.

3. Identify the attributes for all the entities. These attributes will become the fields in the tables. It is possible that more than one entity has the same attribute. At CMF Vets, for example, veterinarians and veterinary vendors both have the attributes of street address, city, state, and zip code. To address this duplication, you can follow the name of the attribute with the corresponding entity in parentheses. Thus, Street (Veterinarians) would be the street address of a veterinarian, whereas Street (Veterinary Vendors) would be the street address of an veterinary vendor.

4. Identify the functional dependencies that exist among the attributes.

5. Use the functional dependencies to identify the tables. You do this by placing each attribute with the attribute or minimum combination of attributes on which it is functionally dependent. The attribute or attributes on which all other attributes in the table are dependent will be the primary key of the table. The remaining attributes will be the other fields in the table. Once you have determined all the fields in the table, you can assign an appropriate name to the table.

6. Determine and implement relationships among the entities. The basic relationships are one-to-many and many-to-many.

   One-to-many. You implement a one-to-many relationship by including the primary key of the "one" table as a foreign key in the "many" table. A **foreign key** is a field in one table whose values are required to match the *primary key* of another table. In the one-to-many relationship between appointments and patients, for example, you include the primary key of the Patients Table, which is Patient ID, as a foreign key in the Appointments table. You might have already included this field in the earlier steps. If so, you would simply designate it as a foreign key. If you had not already added it, you would need to add it at this point, designating it as a foreign key.

   Many-to-many. A many-to-many relationship is implemented by creating a new table whose primary key is the combination of the keys of the original tables.

You may have already identified such a table in the earlier steps, in which case, all you need to do is to be sure you have designated each portion of the primary key as a foreign key that is required to match the primary key of the appropriate table. If you have not, you would add the table at this point. The primary key will consist of the primary keys from each of the tables to be related. If there are any attributes that depend on the combination of fields that make up the primary key, you need to include them in this table. (*Note:* There may not be any other fields that are dependent on this combination. In that case, there will be no fields besides the fields that make up the primary key.)

The following sections illustrate the design process by designing the database for CMF Vets. The next section gives the requirements that this database must support, and the last section creates a database design based on those requirements.

Requirements for the CMF Vets Database

Systems analysts have examined the needs and organizational policies at CMF Vets and have determined that the CMF Vets database must support the following requirements:

1. For a patient, CMF Vets needs to maintain the patient's name, type of animal and breed, and the owner of the patient.

2. For an owner, the CMF Vets needs the owner's full name and address, both home and mobile phone numbers, and the owner's email address.

3. For veterinarians, similar information as for the owners needs to be recorded along with board certification and specialty of the vet.

4. Each appointment must be recorded as well. Information for appointments indicates when the appointment is scheduled, the procedure, the patients, and the vet who is handling the appointment.

5. Any given patient can have many appointments, and any vet can also have many appointments.

Design of the CMF Vets Database

The following represents the application of the design method for the CMF Vets requirements.

1. There appear to be four entities: owners, patients, veterinarians, and appointments. Reasonable names for the corresponding tables are Owners, Patients, Veterinarians, and Appointments.

2. The unique identifier for owners is the owner ID. The unique identifier for patients is the patient ID. The unique identifier for veterinarians is veterinarian ID. The unique identifier of appointments is appointment ID. Reasonable names for the unique identifiers are Owner ID, Patient ID, Veterinarian ID, and Appointment ID, respectively.

3. The attributes are:

>**Owner ID**
>
>**First Name (Owners)**
>
>**Last Name (Owners)**
>
>**Street Address (Owners)**
>
>**City (Owners)**
>
>**State (Owners)**
>
>**Postal Code (Owners)**
>
>**Home Phone**
>
>**Mobile Phone (Owners)**
>
>**Email Address (Owners)**
>
>**Patient ID**
>
>**Patient Name**
>
>**Animal Type**
>
>**Breed**

Owner ID

Veterinarian ID

First Name (Veterinarians)

Last Name (Veterinarians)

Street Address (Veterinarians)

City (Veterinarians)

State (Veterinarians)

Zip Code (Veterinarians)

Office Phone

Mobile Phone (Veterinarians)

Email Address (Veterinarians)

Board Certified

Specialty

Appointment ID

Patient ID

Appointment Date

Appointment Time

Veterinarian

Treatment Number

Remember that parentheses after an attribute indicate the entity to which the attribute corresponds. Thus, Street Address (Owners) represents the street address of an owner in a way that distinguishes it from Street Address (Veterinarians), which represents the street address of a veterinarian.

4. The functional dependencies among the attributes are:

> **Owner ID → First Name (Owners), Last Name (Owners), Street Address (Owners), City (Owners), State (Owner), Postal Code (Owners), Home Phone, Mobile Phone (Owners), Email Address (Owners)**
>
> **Patient ID → Patient Name, Animal Type, Breed, Owner ID**
>
> **Veterinarian ID → First Name (Veterinarians), Last Name (Veterinarians), Street Address (Veterinarians), City (Veterinarians), State (Veterinarians), Postal Code (Veterinarians), Work Phone, Mobile Phone (Veterinarians), Email Address (Veterinarians), Board Certified, Specialty**
>
> **Appointment ID → Patient ID, Appointment Date, Appointment Time, Veterinarian, Treatment Number**

The patient ID, appointment date, appointment time, and treatment number are dependent only on appointment ID. Because an appointment has a single veterinarian, the veterinarian is dependent on appointment ID as well. The patient's name, animal type, breed, and owner ID are dependent only on the patient ID. The owner's name, address, phone numbers, and email are dependent only on the owner ID. Similarly, the veterinarian's name, address, phone numbers, email, and other attributes are dependent only on the veterinarian ID. The shorthand representation for the tables is shown in Figure 11–7.

Appointments (<u>Appointment ID</u>, Patient ID, Appointment Date, Appointment Time, Veterinarian, Owner, Treatment Number)

Patients (<u>Patient ID</u>, Patient Name, Animal Type, Breed, Owner ID)

Owners (<u>Owner ID</u>, Last Name, First Name, Street Address, City, State, Postal Code, Home Phone, Mobile Phone, Email Address)

Veterinarians (<u>Veterinarian ID</u>, Last Name, First Name, Street Address, City, State, Postal Code, Work Phone, Mobile Phone, Email Address, Board Certified, Specialty)

Figure 11–7

5. The following are the relationships between the tables:

   a. The Owners and Patients tables are related using the Owner ID fields, which is the primary key of the Owners table. The Owner ID field in the Patients table is a foreign key.

   b. The Appointments, Patients, and Veterinarians tables are related using the Patient ID field, which is the primary key of the Patients table and the Veterinarian ID field, which is the primary key of the Veterinarians table. The Patient ID and Veterinarian ID fields in the Appointments table are both foreign keys.

Does a many-to-many relationship exist between patients and veterinarians?
Yes. The Appointments table is the link between this many-to-many relationship.

CONSIDER THIS

NOTE: In the shorthand representation for a table containing a foreign key, you would represent the foreign key by using the letters FK, followed by an arrow, followed by the name of the table in which that field is the primary key. For example, to indicate that the Patient ID in the Appointments table is a foreign key that must match the primary key of the Patients table, you would write FK Patient ID → Patients.

The shorthand representation for the tables and foreign keys is shown in Figure 11–8. It is common to list a table containing a foreign key after the table that contains the corresponding primary key, when possible. Thus, in the figure, the Appointments table comes after the other tables because it contains foreign keys from the tables listed above.

Owners (<u>Owner ID</u>, Last Name, First Name, Street Address, City, State, Postal Code, Home Phone, Mobile Phone, Email Address)

Patients (<u>Patient ID</u>, Patient Name, Animal Type, Breed, Owner ID)

FK Owner ID Owners

Veterinarians (<u>Veterinarian ID</u>, Last Name, First Name, Street Address, City, State, Postal Code, Work Phone, Mobile Phone, Email Address, Board Certified, Specialty)

Appointments (<u>Appointment ID</u>, Patient ID, Appointment Date, Appointment Time, Veterinarian, Owner, Treatment Number)

FK Patient ID Patient

FK Veterinarian ID Veterinarians

Figure 11–8

Car First Insurers

The management of Car First Insurers, a budget car insurance company, has determined that the company's rapid growth requires a database to maintain policy holders, drivers, and vehicles. With the data stored in a database, management will be able to ensure that the data is current and more accurate. In addition, managers will be able to obtain answers to their questions concerning the data in the database quickly and easily, with the option of producing a variety of reports. Note that the cost of the policies and the payments to the Car First Insurers are handled by a third party and are not requirements of this database design.

Requirements for the Car First Insurers Database

A system analyst has interviewed users and examined documents at Car First Insurers and has determined that the company needs a database that will support the following requirements:

1. For a customer, store the customer's first name, last name, street address, city, state, postal code, telephone number, and email address.

2. For a driver, store the driver's number, first name, last name, street address, city, state, postal code, telephone number, and email address. (Note that there might be many drivers under one customer. For example, a parent could have three teenage drivers.)

3. For an insured vehicle, store the vehicle identification number, make, model, and year. The database also should store the policy number under which each vehicle is registered.

4. The driver and vehicle must be associated; the database must include a table that links these two entities.

5. The analyst also obtained the following information concerning insurance:

    a. A customer could hold more than one policy.

    b. There could be multiple drivers associated with one policy.

    c. A driver can drive multiple cars.

Design of the Car First Insurers Database

BTW

Line Items
A line item is a unit of information that appears on its own line. For example, when you purchase groceries, each grocery item appears on its own line. Line items also can be referred to as order line items or item detail lines.

The following steps apply the design process to the requirements for Car First Insurers to produce the appropriate database design:

1. Assign entity names. There appear to be four entities: customers, drivers, policies, and vehicles. The names assigned to these entities are Customers, Drivers, Policies, and Vehicles, respectively.

2. Determine unique identifiers. From the collection of entities, review the data and determine the unique identifier for each entity. For the Customers, Drivers, and Policies entities, the unique identifiers are the customer ID, driver ID, and policy number, respectively. These unique identifiers are named Customer ID, Driver ID, and Policy Number, respectively. For the Vehicles, the unique identifier is the vehicle identification number, known as VIN, which is unique for each vehicle worldwide.

3. Assign attribute names. The attributes mentioned in the first requirement all refer to customers. The specific attributes mentioned in the requirement are the customer ID, first name, last name, street address, city, state, postal code,

telephone number, and email address. Assigning appropriate names to these attributes produces the following list:

Customer ID

First Name

Last Name

Street

City

State

Postal Code

Telephone

Email Address

The attributes mentioned in the second requirement refer to drivers. The specific attributes are the driver ID, name, street address, city, state, postal code, telephone number, and email address. Assigning appropriate names to these attributes produces the following list:

Driver ID

First Name

Last Name

Street

City

State

Postal Code

Telephone

Email Address

Do you need to include the policy associated with the driver in the list of attributes for the second requirement?

There is no need to include them in this list, because that information will be determined with linkages between tables later on.

CONSIDER THIS

There are attributes named Street, City, State, and Postal Code for customers as well as attributes named Street, City, State, and Postal Code for drivers. To distinguish these attributes in the final collection, the name of the attribute is followed by the name of the corresponding entity. For example, the street for a customer is Street (Customer) and the street for a driver is Street (Driver).

The attributes mentioned in the third requirement refer to the policy. The specific attributes are the policy number, effective date, expire date, and customer, who is the policy holder. Assigning appropriate names to these attributes produces the following list:

Policy Number

Effective Date

Expire Date

Customer ID

The attributes mentioned in the fourth requirement refer to vehicles. The specific attributes include the vehicle identification number, make, model, year, and policy number associated with the vehicle. Assigning appropriate names to these attributes produces the following list:

VIN

Make

Model

Year

Policy Number

The statement concerning the linkage of driver to vehicle indicates that there are specific attributes to be stored for each vehicle. These attributes are the vehicle and driver. Assigning appropriate names to these attributes produces the following list:

VIN

Driver ID

The complete list grouped by entity is as follows:

Customer

> **Customer ID**
>
> **First Name**
>
> **Last Name**
>
> **Street**
>
> **City**
>
> **State**
>
> **Postal Code**
>
> **Telephone**
>
> **Email Address**

Driver

> **Driver ID**
>
> **First Name**
>
> **Last Name**
>
> **Street**
>
> **City**
>
> **State**
>
> **Postal Code**
>
> **Telephone**
>
> **Email Address**

Policy

> **Policy Number**
>
> **Effective Date**
>
> **Expire Date**
>
> **Customer ID**

Vehicle

> **VIN**
>
> **Make**
>
> **Model**
>
> **Year**
>
> **Policy Number**

For drivers of vehicles:

> **VIN**
>
> **Driver ID**

4. Identify functional dependencies. The fact that the unique identifier for customers is Customer ID gives the following functional dependencies:

> **Customer ID → First Name (Customer), Last Name (Customer), Street (Customer), City (Customer), State (Customer), Postal Code (Customer), Telephone (Customer), Email Address (Customer)**

The fact that the unique identifier for drivers is Driver ID gives the following preliminary list of functional dependencies:

> **Driver ID → First Name (Driver), Last Name (Driver), Street (Driver), City (Driver), State (Driver), Postal Code (Driver), Telephone (Driver), Email Address (Driver)**

The fact that the unique identifier for policies is Policy Number gives the following functional dependencies:

> **Policy Number → Effective Date, Expire Date, Customer ID**

The fact that the unique identifier for vehicles is VIN gives the following functional dependencies:

> **VIN → Make, Model, Year, Policy Number**

Do you need to include the name of a customer in the list of attributes determined by the policy number?

There is no need to include the customer name in this list because you can determine them from the customer ID, and they are already included in the list of attributes determined by customer ID.

The final attributes to be examined are those associated with the drivers and vehicles: VIN, Driver ID.

Why is Driver ID not included in the Vehicle table?

There could be multiple drivers for each vehicle, so this requires an additional table.

CONSIDER THIS

CONSIDER THIS

The following shorthand representation indicates that the combination of VIN and Driver ID. There are no functionally dependent fields in this table.

VIN, Driver ID →

The complete list of functional dependencies with appropriate revisions is as follows:

Customer ID → First Name (Customer), Last Name (Customer), Street (Customer), City (Customer), State (Customer), Postal Code (Customer), Telephone (Customer), Email Address (Customer)

Driver ID → First Name (Driver), Last Name (Driver), Street (Driver), City (Driver), State (Driver), Postal Code (Driver), Telephone (Driver), Email Address (Driver)

Policy Number → Effective Date, Expire Date, Customer ID

VIN → Make, Model, Year, Policy Number

VIN, Driver ID →

5. Create the tables. Using the functional dependencies, you can create tables with the attribute(s) to the left of the arrow being the primary key and the items to the right of the arrow being the other fields. For tables corresponding to those entities identified in Step 1, you can simply use the name you already determined. Because you did not identify any entity that had a unique identifier that was the combination of VIN and Driver ID, you need to assign a name to the table whose primary key consists of these two fields. Because this table represents the individual drivers within one vehicle, the name Vehicle Driver is a good choice. The final collection of tables for Car First Insurers is shown in Figure 11–9.

Customer (<u>Customer ID</u>, First Name, Last Name, Address, City, State, Postal Code, Telephone, Email Address)

Driver (<u>Driver ID</u>, First Name, Last Name, Address, City, State, Postal Code, <u>Telephone</u>, Email Address)

Policies (<u>Policy Number</u>, Effective Date, Expire Date, Customer ID)

Vehicle (<u>VIN</u>, Make, Model, Year, Policy Number)

Vehicle Driver (<u>VIN, Driver ID</u>)

Figure 11–9

6. Identify relationships.

   a. The Customer and Policy tables are related using the Customer ID fields. The Customer ID field in the Customer table is the primary key. The Customer ID field in the Policy table is a foreign key.

   b. The Policy and Vehicle tables are related using the Policy Number fields. The Policy Number field in the Policy table is the primary key. The Policy Number field in the Vehicle table is a foreign key.

   c. The Vehicle and Driver tables are related using the VIN and Driver ID fields. Both the VIN and the Driver ID are key fields together.

CONSIDER THIS

Does a many-to-many relationship exist between vehicles and drivers?
Yes. The Vehicle Driver table will implement a many-to-many relationship between vehicles and drivers. You identified this table as Vehicle Driver in the database design process.

In the Vehicle Driver table, the primary key consists of two fields, VN and Driver ID. Do you need both fields to be key fields?
Yes, because this table implements the many-to-many relationship between vehicles and drivers. It is perfectly legitimate for the table that implements a many-to-many relationship to contain only the two columns that constitute the primary key.

The shorthand representation for the tables and foreign keys is shown in Figure 11–10.

Customer (<u>Customer ID</u>, First Name, Last Name, Address, City, State, Postal Code,
  Telephone, Email Address)
Driver (<u>Driver ID</u>, First Name, Last Name, Address, City, State, Postal Code, Telephone,
  Email Address)
Policy (<u>Policy Number</u>, Effective Date, Expire Date, Customer ID)
FK Customer ID → Customer
Vehicle (<u>VIN</u>, Make, Model, Year, Policy Number)
FK Policy → Number Policy
Vehicle Driver (<u>VIN, Driver ID</u>)
FK VIN → Vehicles
FK Driver ID → Driver

Figure 11–10

Sample data for the Car First Insurers database is shown in Figure 11–11.

Customer

Customer ID	Customer First Name	Customer Last Name	Customer Street Address	Customer City	Customer State	Customer Postal Code	Customer Phone	Email Address
M9835	Tricia	Morris	460 West Longberg Road	Gainesville	FL	32603	352-231-4411	tmorris@cengage.com
N7453	Susan	Niack	9874 South Main Street	Gainesville	FL	32605	352-991-5670	sniack@cengage.com

Driver

Driver ID	Driver First Name	Driver Last Name	Driver Street Address	Driver City	Driver State	Driver Postal Code	Driver Phone	Email Address
C010	Steve	Chen	3 Hanover Park	Newberry	FL	32618	352-555-4234	schen@cengage.com
D340	Tiffanie	D'Vivo	14435 Keller Way	Gainesville	FL	32602	352-555-9135	tdvivo@cengage.com
K009	Cyrus	Killigan	784 Hilltop Circle	Gainesville	FL	32602	352-555-6547	ckilligan@cengage.com
K324	Ryan	Kraut	334 Old Farms Road	Gainesville	FL	32604	352-555-1478	rkraut@cengage.com
O543	Liz	O'Leary	13 Griffiths Drive	Gainesville	FL	32602	352-555-6968	loleary@cengage.com
P543	Sana	Patel	76 Jenkins Way	Live Oak	FL	32064	352-555-9865	spatel@cengage.com

Figure 11–11 (Continued)

Policy			
Policy Number	Effective Date	Expire Date	Customer ID
123	2/13/2021	2/13/2022	M9835
124	4/1/2021	4/1/2022	N7453

Vehicle				
VIN	Make	Model	Year	Policy Number
1ALLDVAF7HA470011	Ford	F150	2021	124
1ALSK2D47DA761712	Chevrolet	Cruze	2017	123
JM1BL1H64A1138112	Mazda	3	2016	123

Vehicle Driver	
VIN	Driver ID
1ALLDVAF7HA470011	O543
1ALSK2D47DA761712	C010
JM1BL1H64A1138112	D340
JM1BL1H64A1138112	K009
1ALSK2D47DA761712	K324
1ALLDVAF7HA470011	P543

Figure 11–11

Normalization

After you create your database design, you should analyze it using a process called **normalization** to make sure the design is free of potential update, redundancy, and consistency problems. This process also supplies methods for correcting these problems.

The normalization process involves converting tables into various types of **normal forms**. A table in a particular normal form possesses a certain desirable set of properties. Several normal forms exist, the most common being first normal form (1NF), second normal form (2NF), and third normal form (3NF). The forms create a progression in which a table that is in 1NF is better than a table that is not in 1NF, a table that is in 2NF is better than one that is in 1NF, and so on. The goal of normalization is to take a table or collection of tables and produce a new collection of tables that represents the same information but is free of problems.

First Normal Form

A table that contains a **repeating group**, or multiple entries for a single row, is called an **unnormalized table**. Recall from the definition of relation that an unnormalized table actually violates the definition of relation.

Removal of repeating groups is the starting point in the goal of having tables that are as free of problems as possible. In fact, in most database management systems, tables cannot contain repeating groups. A table (relation) is in **first normal form (1NF)** if it does not contain repeating groups.

In designing a database, you may have created a table with a repeating group. For example, you might have created an Hours Worked table in which the primary key is the Veterinarian ID and there is a repeating group consisting of Treatment Number and Total Hours. In the example, each veterinarian appears on a single row and Treatment Number and Total Hours are repeated as many times as necessary for each account (Figure 11–12).

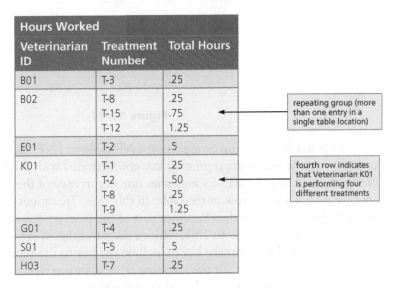

Figure 11–12

In the shorthand representation, you represent a repeating group by enclosing the repeating group within parentheses. The shorthand representation for the Hours Worked table from Figure 11–12 is shown in Figure 11–13.

Hours Worked (<u>Veterinarian ID</u>, Treatment Number, Total Hours)

Figure 11–13

Conversion to First Normal Form

Figure 11–14 shows the normalized version of the table. Note that the second row of the unnormalized table (Figure 11–12) indicates that veterinarian B02 is currently performing treatments T-8, T-15, and T-12. In the normalized table, this information is represented by *three* rows: the second, third, and fourth. The primary key for the unnormalized Hours Worked table was the Veterinarian ID only. The primary key for the normalized table is now the combination of Veterinarian ID and Treatment Number

Hours Worked		
Veterinarian ID	**Treatment Number**	**Total Hours**
B01	T-3	.25
B02	T-8	.25
B02	T-15	.75
B02	T-12	1.25
E01	T-2	.50
K01	T-1	.25
K01	T-2	.50
K01	T-8	.25
K01	T-9	1.25
G01	T-4	.25
S01	T-5	.5
H03	T-7	.25

second, third, and fourth rows indicate Veterinarian B02 is performing treatments T-8, T-15, and T-12

Figure 11–14

In general, when converting a non-1NF table to 1NF, the primary key will typically include the original primary key concatenated with the key of the repeating group, that is, the field that distinguishes one occurrence of the repeating group from another within a given row in the table. In this case, Treatment Number is the key to the repeating group and thus becomes part of the primary key of the 1NF table.

To convert the table to 1NF, remove the parentheses enclosing the repeating group and expand the primary key to include the key to the repeating group. The shorthand representation for the resulting table is shown in Figure 11–15. Notice that the primary key is now the combination of the Veterinarian ID field and the Treatment Number field.

Hours Worked (<u>Veterinarian ID</u>, <u>Treatment Number</u>, Total Hours)

Figure 11–15

Second Normal Form

Even though the following table is in 1NF, problems may exist that will cause you to want to restructure the table. In the database design process, for example, you might have created the Hours Worked table shown in Figure 11–16.

Hours Worked (<u>Veterinarian ID</u>, Veterinarian Last Name, <u>Treatment Number</u>, Treatment Name, Total Hours)

Figure 11–16

This table contains the following functional dependencies:

Veterinarian ID → Veterinarian Last Name

Treatment Number → Treatment Name
Veterinarian ID, Treatment Number → Total Hours

This notation indicates that Veterinarian ID alone determines Veterinarian Last Name, and Treatment Number alone determines Treatment Name, but it requires *both* a Veterinarian ID *and* a Treatment Number to determine Total Hours. Figure 11–17 shows a sample of this table.

| Hours Worked | | | | |
Veterinarian ID	Veterinarian Last Name	Treatment Number	Treatment Name	Total Hours
	Black	T-3	Feline Wellness Exam	.25
B02	Black	T-8	Feline Heartworm	.25
B02	Black	T-15	Recheck	.75
B02	Black	T-12	Canine Neuter	1.25
E01	Edwards	T-2	Canine Wellness Exam	.50
K01	Konig	T-1	Feline Rabies Shot	.25
K01	Konig	T-2	Canine Wellness Exam	.50
K01	Konig	T-8	Feline Heartworm	.25
K01	Konig	T-9	Feline Spay	1.25
G01	Gomez	T-4	Canine Rabies Shot	.25
S01	Schwartz	T-5	Feline Vaccinations	.5
H03	Heller	T-7	Canine Heartworm	.25

name of Veterinarian appears more than once

treatment name appears more than once

Figure 11–17

The name of a specific veterinarian, B02 for example, occurs multiple times in the table, as does the description of a treatment. This redundancy causes several problems. It is certainly wasteful of space, but that is not nearly as serious as some of the other problems. These other problems are called **update anomalies**, and they fall into four categories:

1. **Update.** A change to the name of veterinarian B02 requires not one change to the table, but several: you must change each row in which B02 appears. This certainly makes the update process much more cumbersome; it is logically more complicated and takes longer to update.

2. **Inconsistent data.** There is nothing about the design that would prohibit account B02 from having two or more different names in the database. The first row, for example, might have Black as the name, whereas the second row might have Blacks, a typo.

3. **Additions.** There is a real problem when you try to add a new treatment ID and its name to the database. Because the primary key for the table consists of both Veterinarian ID and Treatment Number, you need values for both of these to add a new row. If you have a new treatment to add (new offerings at the vet clinic to attract new patients) but there are so far no veterinarians scheduled for it, what do you use for a Treatment Number? The only solution would be to make up a placeholder Treatment Number and then replace it with a real Treatment Number once the account requests a workshop. This is certainly not an acceptable solution.

4. **Deletions.** In Figure 11–17, if you delete Treatment Number T-7 from the database, you would need to delete all rows on which the Treatment is T-7. In the process, you will delete the only row on which treatment T-7 appears, so you would also *lose* all the information about treatment T-7. You would no longer know that the last name of the veterinarian H03 is Heller.

These problems occur because there is a field, Veterinarian Last Name, that is dependent only on Veterinarian ID, which is just a portion of the primary key. There is a similar problem with Treatment Name, which depends only on the Treatment Number, not the complete primary key. This leads to the definition of second normal form. Second normal form represents an improvement over first normal form because it eliminates update anomalies in these situations. In order to understand second normal form, you need to understand the term, nonkey field.

A field is a **nonkey field**, also called a **nonkey attribute**, if it is not a part of the primary key. A table (relation) is in **second normal form (2NF)** if it is in first normal form and no nonkey field is dependent on only a portion of the primary key.

Note that if the primary key of a table contains only a single field, the table is automatically in second normal form. In that case, there could not be any field dependent on only a portion of the primary key.

Conversion to Second Normal Form

To correct the problems, convert the table to a collection of tables in second normal form, and then name the new tables. The following is a method for performing this conversion.

1. Take each subset of the set of fields that make up the primary key and begin a new table with this subset as its primary key. The result of applying this step to the Hours Worked table is shown in Figure 11–18.

(Veterinarian ID,

(Treatment Number,

(Veterinarian ID, Treatment Number,

Figure 11–18

2. Place each of the other fields with the appropriate primary key; that is, place each one with the minimal collection of fields on which it depends. The result of applying this step to the Hours Worked table is shown in Figure 11–19.

(Veterinarian ID, Veterinarian Last Name)

(Treatment Number, Treatment Name)

(Veterinarian ID, Treatment Number, Total Hours)

Figure 11–19

3. Give each of these new tables a name that is descriptive of the meaning of the table, such as Veterinarians, Treatments, and Hours Worked.

Veterinarian	
Veterinarian ID	**Veterinarian Last Name**
B01	Black
E01	Edwards
K01	Konig ← veterinarian name appears only once
G01	Gomez
S01	Schwartz
H03	Heller

Figure 11–20 (Continued)

Treatments	
Treatment Number	**Treatment Name**
T-3	Feline Wellness Exam
T-8	Feline Heartworm
T-15	Recheck
T-12	Canine Neuter
T-2	Canine Wellness Exam
T-1	Feline Rabies Shot
T-9	Feline Spay
T-4	Canine Rabies Shot
T-5	Feline Vaccinations
T-7	Canine Heartworm

treatment name appears only once

Hours Worked		
Veterinarian ID	**Treatment Number**	**Total Hours**
B01	T-3	.25
B02	T-8	.25
B02	T-15	.75
B02	T-12	1.25
E01	T-2	.50
K01	T-1	.25
K01	T-2	.50
K01	T-8	.25
K01	T-9	1.25
G01	T-4	.25
S01	T-5	.5
H03	T-7	.25

Figure 11–20

The new design eliminates the update anomalies. A veterinarian last name occurs only once for each veterinarian ID, so you do not have the redundancy that occurred in the earlier design. Changing the name of veterinarian is now a simple process involving a single change. Because the name of veterinarian occurs in a single place, it is not possible to have multiple names for the same account in the database at the same time.

To add a new veterinarian, you create a new row in the Veterinarians table, and thus there is no need to have a treatment already scheduled for that veterinarian. In addition, deleting treatment T-7 has nothing to do with the Veterinarians table and, consequently, does not cause account H01 to be deleted. Thus, you still have her last name, Heller, in the database. Finally, you have not lost any information in the process.

Third Normal Form

Problems can still exist with tables that are in 2NF, as illustrated in the Patients table whose shorthand representation is shown in Figure 11–21.

Patients (<u>Patient ID</u>, Patient Name, Animal Type, Breed, Owner ID, Owner First Name, Owner Last Name)

Figure 11–21

BTW
3NF
The definition given for third normal form is not the original definition. This more recent definition, which is preferable to the original, is often referred to as Boyce-Codd normal form (BCNF) when it is important to make a distinction between this definition and the original definition. This text does not make such a distinction but will take this to be the definition of third normal form.

The functional dependencies in this table are:

Patient ID → Patient Name, Animal Type, Breed, Owner ID, Owner First Name, Owner Last Name
Owner ID → Owner First Name, Owner Last Name

As these dependencies indicate, Patient ID determines all the other fields. In addition, Owner ID determines Owner First Name and Owner Last Name.

Because the primary key of the table is a single field, the table is automatically in second normal form. As the sample of the table shown in Figure 11–22 demonstrates, however, this table has problems similar to those encountered earlier, even though it is in 2NF. In this case, it is the first name and last name of an owner that can occur many times in the table; see owner O-1, Ted Sabus, for example.

Patients						
Patient ID	Patient Name	Animal Type	Breed	Owner ID	Owner First Name	Owner Last Name
P-11	Ranger	Canine	Labrador	O-1	Ted	Sabus
P-12	Fluffy	Feline	Tabby	O-1	Ted	Sabus
P-4	Chloe	Feline	Calico	O-1	Ted	Sabus
P-9	Skippy	Feline	Mixed	O-1	Ted	Sabus
P-1	Pepper	Canine	Weimaraner	O-2	Steven	Nguyen
P-10	Paws	Feline	Calico	O-2	Steven	Nguyen
P-6	Elvis	Feline	Siamese	O-3	Liz	O'Brien
P-5	Max	Feline	Mixed	O-4	Samira	Patel
P-8	Millie	Canine	Mixed	O-5	Ryan	Kraus
P-2	Hooper	Canine	Terrier	O-6	Tiffanie	DiFranco
P-3	Oliver	Feline	Tabby	O-6	Tiffanie	DiFranco
P-7	Milo	Canine	Beagle	O-8	Ian	Kaufman

owner Sabus appears more than once

Figure 11–22

This redundancy results in the same set of problems described previously with the Hours Worked table. In addition to the problem of wasted space, you have similar update anomalies, as follows:

1. **Updates.** A change to the name of an owner requires not one change to the table, but several changes. Again, the update process becomes very cumbersome.

2. **Inconsistent data.** There is nothing about the design that would prohibit an owner from having two different names in the database. On the first row, for example, the name for owner O-1 might read Ted Sabus, whereas on the second row (another row on which the owner is O-1), the name might be Theodore Sabus.

3. **Additions.** In order to add a new owner to the database, she must have at least one pet (which most likely would be the case). For example, consider the situation in which Maryanne Webb, who is not currently an owner, would like to register with the veterinary clinic now because she is about to adopt a dog, but you could not input her owner information without the patient

information. Perhaps you could create a fictitious pet for her to represent while she waits for her adoption. Again, this is not a desirable solution to the problem.

4. **Deletions.** If a pet such as Elvis, P-6, dies, you might delete all the accounts of owner O-3 from the database, then you would also lose all information concerning owner O-3. This could be problematic if she owns another pet in the future.

These update anomalies are due to the fact that Owner ID determines First Name and Last Name, but Owner ID is not the primary key. As a result, the same Owner ID and consequently the same First Name and Last Name can appear on many different rows.

You have seen that 2NF is an improvement over 1NF, but to eliminate 2NF problems, you need an even better strategy for creating tables in the database. Third normal form provides that strategy.

Before looking at third normal form, you need to become familiar with the special name that is given to any field that determines another field, like Owner ID in the Patients table. Any field or collection of fields that determines another field is called a **determinant**. Certainly the primary key in a table is a determinant. Any candidate key is a determinant as well. (Remember that a candidate key is a field or collection of fields that could function as the primary key.) In this case, Owner ID is a determinant, but because several rows in the Patients table could have the same Owner ID, that field is not a candidate key for the Account table shown in Figure 11–22, and that is the problem.

A table is in **third normal form** (3NF) if it is in second normal form and if the only determinants it contains are candidate keys.

Conversion to Third Normal Form

You have now identified the problem with the Patients table: it is not in 3NF. You need a way to correct the deficiency in the Patients table and in all tables having similar deficiencies. Such a method follows.

First, for each determinant that is not a candidate key, remove from the table the fields that depend on this determinant, but do not remove the determinant. Next, create a new table containing all the fields from the original table that depend on this determinant. Finally, make the determinant the primary key of this new table.

In the Patients table, for example, First Name and Last Name are removed because they depend on the determinant Owner ID, which is not a candidate key. A new table is formed, consisting of Owner ID as the primary key, First Name, and Last Name. Specifically, you would replace the Patients table in Figure 11–22 with the two tables shown in Figure 11–23.

Patients (<u>Patient ID</u>, Patient Name, Animal Type, Breed, Owner ID)
Owners (<u>Owner ID</u>, Owner First Name, Owner Last Name)

Figure 11–23

Figure 11–24 shows samples of the tables.

Patients				
Patient ID	**Patient Name**	**Animal Type**	**Breed**	**Owner ID**
P-11	Ranger	Canine	Labrador	O-1
P-12	Fluffy	Feline	Tabby	O-1
P-4	Chloe	Feline	Calico	O-1
P-9	Skippy	Feline	Mixed	O-1
P-1	Pepper	Canine	Weimaraner	O-2
P-10	Paws	Feline	Calico	O-2
P-6	Elvis	Feline	Siamese	O-3
P-5	Max	Feline	Mixed	O-4
P-8	Millie	Canine	Mixed	O-5
P-2	Hooper	Canine	Terrier	O-6
P-3	Oliver	Feline	Tabby	O-6
P-7	Milo	Canine	Beagle	O-8

Owners		
Owner ID	**Owner First Name**	**Owner Last Name**
O-1	Ted	Sabus ← owner Sabus appears only once
O-2	Steven	Nguyen
O-3	Liz	O'Brien
O-4	Samira	Patel
O-5	Ryan	Kraus
O-6	Tiffanie	DiFranco
O-8	Ian	Kaufman

Figure 11–24

This design corrects the previously identified problems. An owner's name appears only once, thus avoiding redundancy and making the process of changing an owner's name a very simple one. With this design, it is not possible for an owner to have two different names in the database. To add a new owner to the database, you add a row in the Owners table; it is not necessary to have a preexisting patient for the owner. Finally, deleting all the patients of a given owner will not remove the owner's record from the Owners table, so you retain the owner's name; all the data in the original table can be reconstructed from the data in the new collection of tables. All previously mentioned problems have indeed been solved.

Special Topics

BTW
Existing Documents
Other examples of existing documents would be purchase orders, procedure manuals, organizational policy manuals, inventory lists, and so on.

In addition to knowing how to design a database and how to normalize tables, there are two other topics with which you should be familiar. First, you may be given a requirement for a database in the form of a document that the database must be capable of producing; for example, an insurance policy. In addition, you should know how to represent your design with a diagram.

Obtaining Information from Existing Documents

Existing documents can often furnish helpful information concerning the database design. You need to know how to obtain information from the document that you will then use in the design process. An existing document, like the car insurance card for the company named Car First Insurers shown in Figure 11–25, will often provide the details that determine the tables and fields required to produce the document.

The first step in obtaining information from an existing document is to identify and list all fields and give them appropriate names. You also need to understand the business policies of the organization. For example, in the order shown in Figure 11–25, the information on Car First Insurers is preprinted on the form, and it is not necessary to describe the company. The following is a list of the fields you can determine from the document shown in Figure 11–25.

Policy Number
Policy Effective Date
Policy Expire Date
Customer Name
Street (Customer)
City (Customer)
State (Customer)
Postal Code (Customer)
Car Insured VIN
Car Make
Car Model
Car Year

Car First Insurance   **INVOICE**

2099 East Boulevard   Policy Number: P59-7628749274950
Gainesville, FL 32601
1-800-999-9999

Insured:
Carmen Delgado
523 Main Street
Gainesville, FL 32601

Policy Period:
        12/31/2021-12/31/2022 12:01 a.m. standard time at the address of the Named Insured 12/31/2021

Vehicle Insured:

VIN	MAKE	MODEL	YEAR
1ALSK2D47DA761712	Chevrolet	Cruze	2017

Figure 11–25

Next, you need to identify functional dependencies. If the document you are examining is unfamiliar to you, you might have difficulty determining the dependencies and might need to get all the information directly from the user. On the other hand, you can often make intelligent guesses based on your general knowledge of the type of document you are studying. You might make mistakes, of course, and these should be corrected when you interact with the user. After initially determining the functional dependencies, you may discover additional information. The following are possible initial functional dependencies:

Customer ID → First Name (Customer), Last Name (Customer), Street (Customer), City (Customer), State (Customer), Postal Code (Customer)

Policy Number → Effective Date, Expire Date, Customer ID
VIN → Make, Model, Year, Policy Number

You might realize that other attributes of the Customer may be required. For example, you may want to include the customer's telephone number and email address. If that is the case, then telephone number and email address are functionally dependent on the customer.

You might also realize that the insurance card does not include any information about approved drivers. For example, the insured shown in Figure 11–25 could have a husband and two teenage dependents who are allowed to drive the vehicle. In that case, you will need to add all information about the driver entity, and then also have an entity that combines the vehicle (VIN) with the drivers that are allowed to operate that specific vehicle.

Given these corrections, a revised list of functional dependencies might look like the following:

Customer ID → First Name (Customer), Last Name (Customer), Street (Customer), City (Customer), State (Customer), Postal Code (Customer), Telephone (Customer), Email Address (Customer)

Driver ID → First Name (Driver), Last Name (Driver), Street (Driver), City (Driver), State (Driver), Postal Code (Driver), Telephone (Driver), Email Address (Driver)

Policy Number → Effective Date, Expire Date, Customer ID
VIN → Make, Model, Year, Policy Number

VIN, Driver ID →

After you have determined the preliminary functional dependencies, you can begin determining the tables and assigning fields. You could create tables with the determinant—the field or fields to the left of the arrow — as the primary key and with the fields to the right of the arrow as the remaining fields. This would lead to the following initial collection of tables shown in Figure 11–26.

Customer (<u>Customer ID</u>, First Name, Last Name, Address, City, State, Postal Code, Telephone, Email Address)

Driver (<u>Driver ID</u>, First Name, Last Name, Address, City, State, Postal Code, Telephone, Email Address)

Policies (<u>Policy Number</u>, Effective Date, Expire Date, Customer ID)

Vehicle (<u>VIN</u>, Make, Model, Year, Policy Number)

Vehicle Driver (<u>VIN, Driver ID</u>)

Figure 11–26

Adding the foreign key information produces the shorthand representation shown in Figure 11–27.

Customer (<u>Customer ID</u>, First Name, Last Name, Address, City, State, Postal Code, Telephone, Email Address)

Driver (<u>Driver ID</u>, First Name, Last Name, Address, City, State, Postal Code, Telephone, Email Address)

Policy (<u>Policy Number</u>, Effective Date, Expire Date, Customer ID)

FK Customer ID → Customer

Vehicle (<u>VIN</u>, Make, Model, Year, Policy Number)

FK Policy → Number Policy

Vehicle Driver (<u>VIN, Driver ID</u>)

FK VIN → Vehicles

FK Driver ID → Driver

Figure 11–27

At this point, you would need to verify that all the tables are in third normal form. If any are not in 3NF, you need to convert them. If you had not determined the functional dependency of Effective Date and Expire Date on Policy Number earlier, for example, you would have had Effective Date and Expire Date as fields in the Customer table. These fields are dependent on Policy Number, making Policy Number a determinant that is not a primary key, which would violate third normal form. Once you converted that table to 3NF, you would have the tables shown in Figure 11–27.

You may have already created some tables in your database design. For example, you may have obtained financial data on customers from the Accounting department concerning the credit card that is used to renew the car insurance policy each year. If so, you would need to merge the tables in Figure 11–27 with those tables you already created. To merge tables, you combine tables that have the same primary key. The new table contains all the fields in either individual table and does not repeat fields that are present in both tables. Figure 11–28, for example, illustrates the merging of two tables that both have the Customer Number field as the primary key. In addition to the primary key, the result contains the Customer Name and credit card information fields, which are included in both of the original tables; the Street, City, State, and Postal Code, Telephone, Email Address fields which are only in the first table; and the Credit Card Number, Expiration Date, and CVV fields, which are only in the second table. The order in which you decide to list the fields is immaterial.

Merging

Customer (<u>Customer ID</u>, First Name, Last Name, Address, City, State, Postal Code, Telephone, Email Address)

And

Customer (<u>Customer ID</u>, credit card number, expiration date, CVV code)

Gives

Customer (<u>Customer ID</u>, First Name, Last Name, Address, City, State, Postal Code, Telephone, Email Address, credit card number, expiration date, CVV code)

Figure 11–28

BTW
Merging Entities
When you merge entities, do not assume that the merged entities will be in 3NF. Apply normalization techniques to convert all entities to 3NF.

Diagrams for Database Design

You have now seen how to represent a database design as a list of tables, fields, primary keys, and foreign keys. It is often helpful to also be able to represent a database design with a diagram. If you have already created the database and relationships in Access, the Relationships window and Relationships report provide a helpful diagram of the design. Figure 11–29 shows the Access Relationship diagram and report for the CMF Vets database. In these diagrams, rectangles represent tables. The fields in the table are listed in the corresponding rectangle with a key symbol appearing in front of the primary key. Relationships are represented by lines with the "one" end of the relationship represented by the number, 1, and the "many" end represented by the infinity symbol (∞).

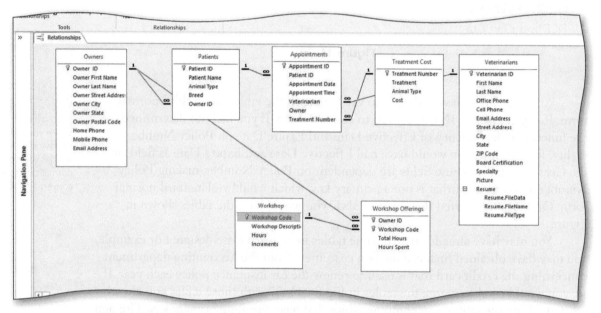

Figure 11–29a Access Relationship Diagram for CMF Vets Database

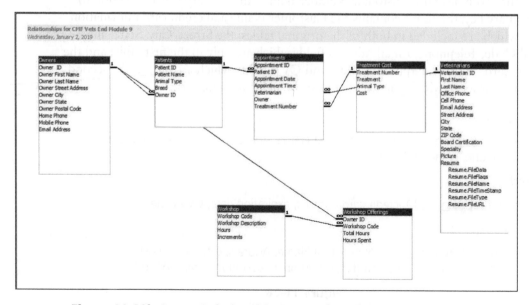

Figure 11–29b Access Relationship Report for CMF Vets Database

Figure 11–30 shows the Access Relationship diagram and report for the Car First Insurers database.

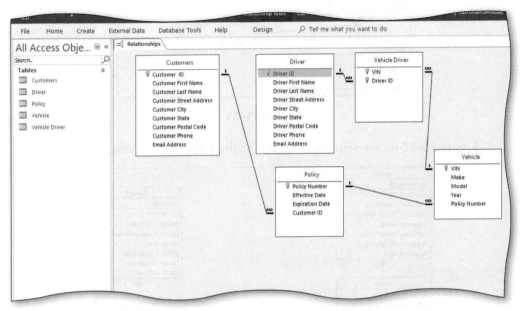

Figure 11–30a Access Relationship Diagram for Car First Insurers Database

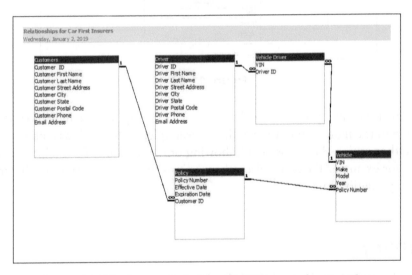

Figure 11–30b Access Relationship Diagram for Car First Insurers Database

Another popular option for diagramming a database design is the **entity-relationship diagram (ERD)**. Figure 11–31 shows a sample ERD for a portion of the CMF Vets database. In this type of diagram, rectangles represent the tables. The primary key is listed within the table above a line. Below the line are the other fields in the table. The arrow goes from the rectangle that represents the many part of the relationship to the one part of the relationship.

Figure 11–31

Figure 11–32 shows a similar diagram for the full Car First Insurers database.

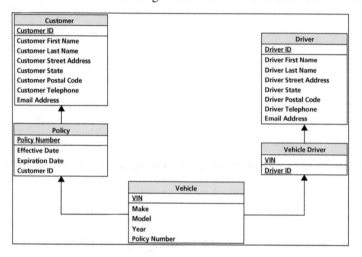

Figure 11–32

There are many options for such diagrams. Some options include more detail than shown in the figure. You can include, for example, such details as data types and indexes. Other options have less detail, showing only the name of the table in the rectangle, for example. There are also other options for the appearance of the lines representing relationships.

Summary

In this module, you have learned the following concepts.

1. An entity is a person, place, thing, or event. An attribute is a property of an entity. A relationship is an association between entities.

2. A relation is a two-dimensional table in which the entries in the table are single-valued, each column has a distinct name, all values in a column are values of the same attribute (that is, all entries must correspond to the column name), and each row is distinct.

3. In a relation, the order of columns is immaterial. You can view the columns in any order you want. The order of rows is also immaterial. You can view the rows in any order you want.

4. A relational database is a collection of relations.

5. Rows in a table (relation) are often called records or tuples. Columns in a table (relation) are often called fields or attributes. Typically, the terms *record* and *field* are used in Access.

6. If you know that whenever you are given a value for one field, you will be able to determine a single value for a second field, then the first field is said to determine the second field. In addition, the second field is said to be functionally dependent on the first.

7. The primary key of a table is the field or minimum collection of fields that uniquely identifies a given row in that table.

8. The following is a method for designing a database for a set of requirements.

   a. Examine the requirements and identify the entities (objects) involved. Assign names to the entities.

   b. Identify a unique identifier for each entity.

   c. Identify the attributes for all the entities. These attributes will become the fields in the tables.

   d. Identify the functional dependencies that exist among the attributes.

   e. Use the functional dependencies to identify the tables.

   f. Identify any relationships between tables by looking for matching fields where one of the fields is a primary key. The other field will then be a foreign key. In the shorthand representation for the table containing the primary key, represent the foreign key by using the letters FK, followed by an arrow, followed by the name of the table containing the primary key.

9. A table (relation) is in first normal form (1NF) if it does not contain repeating groups.

10. To convert a table to 1NF, remove the parentheses enclosing the repeating group and expand the primary key to include the key to the repeating group.

11. A field is a nonkey field (also called a nonkey attribute) if it is not a part of the primary key. A table (relation) is in second normal form (2NF) if it is in first normal form and no nonkey field is dependent on only a portion of the primary key.

12. To convert a table to 2NF, take each subset of the set of fields that make up the primary key and begin a new table with this subset as its primary key. Place each of the other fields with the appropriate primary key; that is, place each one with the minimal collection of fields on which it depends. Give each of these new tables a name that is descriptive of the meaning of the table.

13. Any field (or collection of fields) that determines another field is called a determinant. A table is in third normal form (3NF) if it is in second normal form and if the only determinants it contains are candidate keys.

14. To convert a table to 3NF, for each determinant that is not a candidate key, remove from the table the fields that depend on this determinant, but do not remove the determinant. Create a new table containing all the fields from the original table that depend on this determinant and make the determinant the primary key of this new table.

15. An entity-relationship diagram (ERD) is a diagram used to represent database designs. In ERDs, rectangles represent tables and lines between rectangles represent one-to-many relationships between the corresponding tables. You can also diagram a database design by using the Access relationship window.

How should you submit solutions to questions in the assignments identified with a symbol?

Every assignment in this book contains one or more questions identified with a ✹ symbol. These questions require you to think beyond the assigned database. Present your solutions to the questions in the format required by your instructor. Possible formats may include one or more of these options: write the answer; create a document that contains the answer; present your answer to the class; discuss your answer in a group; record the answer as audio or video using a webcam, smartphone, or portable media player; or post answers on a blog, wiki, or website.

Apply Your Knowledge

Reinforce the skills and apply the concepts you learned in this module.

Understanding Keys and Normalization

Instructions: Answer the following questions in the format specified by your instructor.

1. Figure 11–33 contains sample data for a Student table that could have been used for a college. Use this figure to answer the following:

   a.   Is the table in first normal form (1NF)? Why or why not?

   b.   Is the table in second normal form (2NF)? Why or why not?

   c.   Is the table in third normal form (3NF)? Why or why not?

   d.   Identify candidate keys for the table.

Student				
SID	**FirstName**	**LastName**	**Team ID**	**SportName**
23483	Corey	Gomez	BASK-1	Basketball
23423	Michael	Black	SOC-1	Soccer
23480	Kathy	Reid	SOF-1	Softball
23468	Matthew	Stone	TEN-1	Tennis

Figure 11–33

2. Figure 11–34 contains sample data for pet sitters and customers who hire those sitters. In discussing the data with users, you find that customer IDs — but not customer names — uniquely identify customers and their offered pay rate, and that sitter numbers uniquely identify pet sitters. Multiple customers can use the same sitter and customers can use more than one sitter. For example, Carl Rogers pet sits for Eileen Anderson and Anne Carlson.

   a.   Convert the data in Figure 11–34 into a relation in first normal form (1NF) using the shorthand representation used in this module.

   b.   Identify all functional dependencies using the notation demonstrated in the module.

Pet Sitters				
Sitter Number	**FirstName**	**LastName**	**Customer Name**	**Amount Paid Per Hour**
21	Arnold	Kripsen	Anne Carlson	$20
			Eileen Anderson	$21
			Fabio Lopez	$19
24	Carl	Rogers	Eileen Anderson	$21
			Anne Carlson	$20
27	Jaime	Fernandez	Barb Lenton	$15
34	Jose	Lorenz	Fabio Lopez	$19

Figure 11–34

3. ✸ Using only the data in Figure 11–33, how could you identify the entities and attributes that would be the starting point for a database design?

Extend Your Knowledge

Extend the skills you learned in this module and experiment with new skills. You may need to use Help to complete the assignment.

Modifying a Database Design and Understanding Diagrams

Instructions: Answer the following questions in the format specified by your instructor.

1. Using the shorthand representation illustrated in this module, indicate the changes you would need to make to the CMF Vets database design shown in Figure 11–8 in order to support the following requirements:

   a.   A given appointment may be assigned to more than one veterinarian.
   b.   However, only one treatment is given by one veterinarian at a time.

2. Using the shorthand representation illustrated in this module, indicate the changes you would need to make to the Car First Insurers data design shown in Figure 11–10 to support the following requirements:

   a.   Car First Insurers is expanding its business to insure recreational vehicles (RVs).
   b.   In this expansion, the class of RV must be recorded along with any indication of ownership, loan, or rental.

3. Use the Access Relationships Report for the Financial Services database shown in Figure 11–35 to answer the following:

   a.   Identify the foreign keys in the Client table.
   b.   What is the purpose of the Services table?
   c.   What are the primary keys of the Services table?

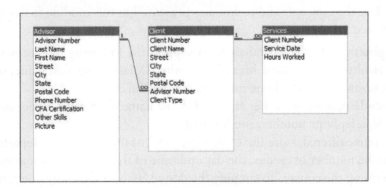

Figure 11–35

4. ✸ Financial Services has decided to add two tax advisors to the database. One tax advisor can service many clients and clients may use different tax advisors during the year, depending on their needs. What changes would you need to make to the database design for Financial Services?

Expand Your World

Create a solution which uses cloud and web technologies, by learning and investigating on your own from general guidance.

Instructions: There are several websites that provide examples of database models, such as www.databaseanswers.org/data_models/index.htm. These models provide a good starting point for creating your own database design.

1. Create a blog, a Google document, or a Word document on OneDrive on which to store your assignment. Include your name and the current date at the beginning of the blog or document.

2. Access the www.databaseanswers.org/data_models/index.htm website or another website of your choice that provides data models.

3. Browse the different database models and select one in which you have an interest.

4. In your own words, create a scenario for which the database model would work. Study the model to see if you need to modify it to make it applicable to your scenario. If changes are necessary, document the required modifications.

5. ✹ Why did you select the model that you did? How easy was it to understand the entities, attributes, and relationships? Were the relations in 3NF?

In the Labs

Design, create, modify, and/or use a database following the guidelines, concepts, and skills presented in this module.

Lab: Designing a Database for Longborough Community College

Instructions: Longborough Community College is a new educational institution in the Midwest. You have been asked to create a database to keep track of the students, faculty, course offerings, and class registration. Use the concepts and techniques presented in this module to design a database to meet the following requirements:

Part 1: The Longborough College database must support the following requirements:

a. For each faculty member, store his or her faculty ID, last name, first name, street address, city, state, postal code, telephone number, and date hired.

b. For each student, store his or her student ID, last name, first name, street address, city, state, postal code, telephone number, and birthdate.

c. For each course offered, store the course ID, name of the course, the department the course resides in, the number of credits, the day and time of the week the course meets and the faculty teaching the course. To simplify the design, assume that only one section of each course is run, as this is a startup college.

d. For each course registration, store student ID and the course ID.

Based on these requirements:

a. Identify and list the entities and attributes of those entities.

b. Identify and list the functional dependencies.

c. Create a set of third normal form (3NF) relations using the shorthand notation given in this module. Be sure to identify all primary keys and foreign keys appropriately.

Submit your database design in the format specified by your instructor.

Part 2: ✹ You made several decisions while designing this database. What was the rationale behind these decisions? Are there other requirements that would have been helpful to you in the design process?

Index